Handbook of
Sexual Assault

*Issues, Theories, and
Treatment of the Offender*

APPLIED CLINICAL PSYCHOLOGY

Series Editors:
Alan S. Bellack, *Medical College of Pennsylvania at EPPI, Philadelphia, Pennsylvania,*
and Michel Hersen, *University of Pittsburgh, Pittsburgh, Pennsylvania*

A Continuation Order Plan is available for this series. A continuation order will bring delivery of each new volume immediately upon publication. Volumes are billed only upon actual shipment. For further information please contact the publisher.

Handbook of
Sexual Assault

Issues, Theories, and
Treatment of the Offender

Edited by

W. L. MARSHALL
Queen's University
Kingston, Ontario, Canada

D. R. LAWS
University of South Florida
Tampa, Florida

and

H. E. BARBAREE
Queen's University
Kingston, Ontario, Canada

PLENUM PRESS • NEW YORK AND LONDON

Library of Congress Cataloging-in-Publication Data

Handbook of sexual assault : issues, theories, and treatment of the
  offender / edited by W.L. Marshall, D.R. Laws, and H.E. Barbaree.
      p.   cm. -- (Applied clinical psychology)
  Includes bibliographical references.
  ISBN 0-306-43272-2
  1. Sex offenders--Mental health. 2. Sex offenders--Psychology.
3. Psychotherapy.   I. Marshall, W. L.   II. Laws, D. Richard.
III. Barbaree, H. E.   IV. Series.
  [DNLM: 1. Paraphilias--therapy. 2. Sex Offenses.   WM 610 H236]
RC560.S47H36 1989
616.85'83--dc20
DNLM/DLC
for Library of Congress   89-23174
                                                               CIP

© 1990 Plenum Press, New York
A Division of Plenum Publishing Corporation
233 Spring Street, New York, N.Y. 10013

Printed in the United States of America

Contributors

Gene G. Abel
  Behavioral Medicine Institute, Atlanta, Georgia 30327-4101

J. Bain
  Department of Endocrinology, Mount Sinai Hospital, Toronto, Ontario M5G 1X5, Canada

H. E. Barbaree
  Department of Psychology, Queen's University, Kingston, Ontario K7L 3N6, Canada

J. M. W. Bradford
  The Royal Ottawa Hospital and the University of Ottawa, Ottawa, Ontario K1Z 7K4, Canada

Juliet L. Darke
  Correctional Service Canada, Prison for Women, Kingston, Ontario K7L 4W7, Canada

Christopher M. Earls
  Department of Psychology, University of Montreal, Montreal, Quebec H3C 3J7, Canada

David Finkelhor
  Family Research Laboratory, University of New Hampshire, Durham, New Hampshire 03824

Kurt Freund
  Department of Psychiatry, University of Toronto, and Department of Behavioral Sexology, Clarke Institute of Psychiatry, Toronto, Ontario M5T 1R8, Canada

Roy Gillis
  Metropolitan Toronto Forensic Service, Toronto, Ontario M6J 1H4, Canada

Judith Lewis Herman
Department of Psychiatry, Harvard Medical School, Cambridge, Massachusetts 02139; and Women's Mental Health Collective, Somerville, Massachusetts 02143

S. J. Hucker
Forensic Division, Clarke Institute of Psychiatry, Toronto, Ontario M5T 1R8, Canada

Raymond A. Knight
Department of Psychology, Brandeis University, Waltham, Massachusetts 02254-9110; and Research Department, Massachusetts Treatment Center, Bridgewater, Massachusetts 02324

Ron Langevin
Clarke Institute of Psychiatry, Toronto, Ontario M5T 1R8, Canada

D. R. Laws
Department of Law and Mental Health, Florida Mental Health Institute, University of South Florida, Tampa, Florida 33612-3899

W. L. Marshall
Department of Psychology, Queen's University, Kingston, Ontario K7L 3N6, Canada

Richard M. McFall
Department of Psychology, Indiana University, Bloomington, Indiana 47405

William D. Murphy
Department of Psychiatry, University of Tennessee, Memphis, Tennessee 38105

Mary R. Murrin
Department of Law and Mental Health, Florida Mental Health Institute, University of South Florida, Tampa, Florida 33612-3899

William D. Pithers
Vermont Center for the Prevention and Treatment of Sexual Abuse, Vermont Department of Corrections, Waterbury, Vermont 05676

Robert A. Prentky
Department of Psychology, Brandeis University, Waltham, Massachusetts 02254-9110; and Research Department, The Massachusetts Treatment Center, Bridgewater, Massachusetts 02324

Vernon L. Quinsey
    Department of Psychology, Queen's University, Kingston, Ontario K7L
    3N6, Canada

Joanne-L. Rouleau
    Behavioral Medicine Institute, Atlanta, Georgia 30327-4101

Zindel V. Segal
    Cognitive Behavior Therapies Section, Clarke Institute of Psychiatry, University of Toronto, Toronto, Ontario M5T 1R8, Canada

Lana E. Stermac
    Forensic Division, Clarke Institute of Psychiatry, University of Toronto, Toronto, Ontario M5T 1R8, Canada

Linda Meyer Williams
    Family Research Laboratory, University of New Hampshire, Durham, New Hampshire 03824

Preface

At the close of the annual meeting of the International Academy of Sex Research held in Amsterdam in September 1986, we were sitting in an outdoor cafe considering what we had learned. In this beautiful city where it is possible to indulge a wide variety of intellectual and sensual appetites, and after having attended one of the most prestigious and information-filled conferences in our field of clinical and research endeavor, dissatisfaction was not what we wished to admit; but the sense that something was missing pervaded our discussions. While some of the topics considered at the conference were relevant to the issues of sex offenders, we were left feeling that a concentrated focus was absent. Indeed, it has largely been through the persistent efforts of the small North American group that has come to be known as the Association for the Behavioral Treatment of Sexual Abusers that research and clinical efforts dealing with sex offenders have blossomed on this continent; there is apparently no similar group on the other continents despite the widespread (albeit recent) acknowledgment by governments that the sexual assault of women and children is an extensive and serious social concern.

While a careful search of the historical literature reveals the efforts of a limited few individuals, prior to the early 1970s very little was known about sex offenders, at least partly because public and scientific awareness of the problem was minimal. Since that time a considerable body of knowledge has been generated on the assessment and treatment of sexual offenders. However, most of this information is scattered throughout a wide range of academic journals; those books which have appeared have, for the most part, reflected the views and described the work of their authors. Certainly these books have been—and continue to be—very valuable, but it seemed to us that what was needed, to facilitate continuing efforts to learn more about this baffling problem, was a book that would bring readers up to date on current knowledge and thinking in the area. There was no such book presently available, and so we resolved, in a moment of bravado, to fill this gap. We could have chosen to write a book ourselves, but we recognized that it might be difficult to coordinate the views of three authors and that, in any case, the likely result would again reflect a narrow viewpoint. Accordingly, we decided that an edited book covering the various issues, with each chapter written by an acknowledged authority on the specific topic, would best meet our goal. With an optimism that was not justified by our editorial experience, we began the task, and, with the help of a number of people, the book has finally come to fruition.

Covering, as it does, the important features involved in the assessment and treatment of sexual aggressors, as well as theories concerning the development and maintenance of such offending, this book summarizes, in the words of experts in each area, current understanding of this pervasive and socially destructive problem.

It is our hope that this book will prove to be valuable to researchers who are concerned with expanding our present understanding of sexual aggressors by encouraging present researchers not only to continue their valuable work, but also to recognize the broader context of their contributions. We also hope the book will spark the investigative interest of those clinicians who presently think that doing research is an impossible task given their workload; almost all the authors of our book are active clinicians as well as outstanding researchers, and their work provides a model of how valuable and manageable it is to combine these two activities. Similarly, clinicians and counsellors who deal with either the sexual aggressors or their victims should find this book to be a source of information which might otherwise be difficult to access. It will, we hope, also encourage them to see the value of their own work in a broader context and perhaps persuade them to expand their range of strategies in treatment. Students who are training in the various disciplines (e.g., psychiatry, psychology, social work, sociology, law, criminology) relevant to the scientific, clinical, and social response to sexual aggression will have available in this book a comprehensive summary of present research findings. Finally, governmental agencies responsible for dealing with sexual offenders and their victims might consider this book as a resource.

We wish to thank all of those researchers, colleagues, and students, past and present, who have encouraged us, given us guidance and advice, and offered their support when needed. Many of them have contributed chapters to this book. In addition, our friends and families gave us their support throughout our careers and during the preparation of this book. We also owe a debt of gratitude to those at Plenum who made our task easier, particularly Eliot Werner, Alyce Hager, and Peter Strupp. Finally, we are grateful to our friend Michel Hersen for his early encouragement and direction.

W. L. Marshall
D. R. Laws
H. E. Barbaree

Kingston, Ontario, and Tampa

Contents

PART I: INTRODUCTION

PART II: FACTORS INFLUENCING SEXUAL ASSAULT

PART III: THEORIES OF SEXUAL ASSAULT

PART IV: TREATMENT OF THE OFFENDER

PART V: CONCLUSION

I
Introduction

Issues in Sexual Assault

W. L. Marshall, D. R. Laws, and H. E. Barbaree

Introduction

The sexual assault of women and children represents a very serious problem in North American society. It is a frequent occurrence, and the effects on its victims are severe and long lasting. While such offenses have been acknowledged for many years, the emergence of the feminist movement forced an awakening of interest in the problem, and finally the full extent of these crimes has been appreciated. Increased public awareness has stimulated discussion of the steps we might take as a society to prevent these crimes. Until recently, the criminal justice system, which has control of apprehending, charging, convicting, and punishing a small minority of offenders, was society's only response to the crime. Even now, although more rational and innovative approaches have been suggested and tried, we cannot say that we have taken more than the initial steps toward adequately addressing the problem. This book is a description of some of those initial steps.

It is generally recognized that progress toward dealing with sexual assault must proceed along three fronts: (1) prevention, (2) treatment of victims, and (3) evaluation and treatment of the perpetrators. The content of this book is confined to the latter, but our choice in setting this boundary does not imply a belief that treatment of the offender is the most important. All three aspects of the approach to the problem are crucial and, indeed, we believe that research in each area contributes significantly to the others as well as to the attempt to achieve an overall reduction in sexual offenses. Our choice in focusing on the assessment and treatment of offenders derives primarily from an appreciation of our own areas of expertise and, not least, our own limits. The research and clinical experience of each of us is restricted to work with offenders, and the same is true of most, but not all, of our contributors.

W. L. Marshall • Department of Psychology, Queen's University, Kingston, Ontario K7L 3N6, Canada.   D. R. Laws • Department of Law and Mental Health, Florida Mental Health Institute, University of South Florida, Tampa, Florida 33612-3899.   H. E. Barbaree • Department of Psychology, Queen's University, Kingston, Ontario K7L 3N6, Canada.

SCOPE OF THE WORK

As the book will reveal, the knowledge and understanding of sexual offenders currently available is quite limited; the information presented here represents only the beginning of systematic research. What we do know, however, stands as a solid foundation for future research. Some of these issues and their limitations are considered in the following pages.

Origins of Sexual Assault

An explanation of sexual assault remains obscure, although the often neglected but rather obvious fact that almost all apprehended offenders are male should provide a focus for investigation. In attempting to provide a perspective on the nature of these men, some writers have focused on biological predispositions, others have limited their consideration to conditioning and social learning experiences, and still others have examined the sociocultural contexts in which the offenses occur. While some authors have considered etiology, others have turned their attention to the factors which maintain assaultive tendencies once they have become well established. These various points of view attest to the diversity of factors which play a part in the etiology and maintenance of sexually assaultive behavior. In the theory section of this book we have tried to represent these diverse approaches to understanding sexual abuse.

Factors Influencing Sexual Assault

Factors influencing sexual assault include a mixture of etiological and maintaining processes. Our goal was to have our authors examine the functional relationship between apparent motives or observed deficiencies in sexual offenders and their actual offensive behavior. Accordingly, these chapters have reviewed a large body of empirical literature which documents the biological, behavioral, cognitive, and historical features that distinguish sexual offenders from nonoffenders.

These chapters also make clear that some factors which do not necessarily distinguish offenders from others may have a strong influence on sexual assault. To take a single example, many sexual offenders drink alcohol to excess, but in this they do not differ from many nonoffenders. This observation, however, does not alter the obvious fact that alcohol abuse is clearly implicated in sexual offending. We are primarily interested in the functional link between relevant factors and the commission of sexual offenses, irrespective of whether or not sexual offenders as a group differ on particular factors from other groups of men.

The Cognition Gap

While it is evident from the extensive body of research considered here that we have made important progress in the past 15 years, it is equally evident that we have a long way to go. This deficit is particularly evident when it comes to understanding the cognitive processes that sex offenders exhibit. It is widely accepted that the offender's attitudes and beliefs are important components of the psychological processes leading to a sexual assault, as well as of the man's apparent inability (or unwillingness) to refrain from repeated offending. Changing the attitudes and beliefs which foster and maintain an assaultive disposition is accepted by all workers as a necessary, but not sufficient, step in treatment. Sadly, in an empirical sense we know little about how deviant sexual cognitions are initiated, how they are shaped and maintained, how they develop into fixed cognitive structures, or how they are used to form imaginary scenarios for current and future offenses. Clearly, this is strategically important both for treatment and for a better understanding of the nature of sexual assault. It has only been in recent years that research attention has begun to focus on this very serious deficiency.

Looking Where the Light Is

There is a story told of a policeman who comes upon a man one very dark night. The man is on his hands and knees under a bright street lamp, apparently searching for something. In response to the policeman's inquiry, the man says he is looking for his key which he dropped as he attempted to put it in the keyhole of his front door. The policeman points out that the door is several meters away from where the man is searching on the sidewalk. "Yes," the man replies, "but the light is over here."

Throughout the development of assessments and treatments for sexual offenders, some of the serious questions have been: On what shall we focus first? What is most important? What can we do right now? What can we afford? We have always spoken of priorities as if it was completely in our power to set them. It did not work out that way; we simply did what we could do. But in doing so, we behaved very much like the unfortunate fellow in the story.

For example, we have for many years had quite sophisticated procedures for investigating sexual interests and preferences, and, consequently, they were evaluated very thoroughly to the relative neglect of other factors. Indeed, the very existence of this technology led many of us to resist for too long the growing evidence that assessing and changing sexual preferences need not (and perhaps should not) be the primary focus of treatment. Similarly, and possibly even more damaging, biological processes offer an apparent concreteness, a definite aura of hard science, that social, cultural, and cognitive factors, at least superficially, appear to lack. In both instances, we may have been looking where the light is rather than where the problem lies.

None of this, of course, is meant to imply that sexual preferences and biological factors are less relevant to an understanding of sexual assault. Indeed, we believe that they are of considerable importance, and the analogy of searching under the light is perhaps not entirely fair. However, it does illustrate that researchers tend to investigate those areas where measurement is most refined and where the issues have been most clearly defined. We are reminded of the physicist Robert Oppenheimer's remark that "It is a profound and necessary truth that the deep things in science are not found because they are useful; they are found because it was possible to find them." Researchers in this area did what they could do. When we looked where the light was, we found something; what we have perhaps failed to do is to loosen our grasp upon those findings and permit ourselves to look beyond them.

A Limited Hierarchy of Knowledge

Following from the preceding, if we were to rank order the extensiveness of our knowledge in the topic areas of this book, certainly sexual preferences and biological processes would be given top ranking. However, as specific chapters reveal, we are still far from understanding even these factors. Cognitive factors would be given the lowest ranking since our knowledge is markedly limited in terms of which attitudes, beliefs, and perceptions are most salient in understanding these offenders. However, due in large part to the impact of feminist writers and other scientists who focus on broad sociocultural issues, these factors have come to be seen by most contemporary researchers and clinicians as critical in understanding and treating sexual offenders. Some readers may see in this a serious defect in the history of the scientific analysis of these men. Indeed, it may be a fair criticism of research in this field that too many investigators (including ourselves) ignored for far too long the claims that sociocultural and cognitive factors are crucial to the understanding and treatment of sexual offenders.

Of course it is the nature of science, specifically, the principle of parsimony (a.k.a. Occam's razor), to start with the simplest analysis and proceed toward more complex conceptualizations only when simple accounts have been exhausted or shown to be limiting. This principle is consistent with a tendency in all of us, scientists and laypersons alike, to seek concrete and simple explanations. That is at least part of the appeal of biological accounts of human behavior and seems to be the basis for views which hold that one factor, or a very limited set of factors, is responsible for causing and maintaining sexual offending. It is our belief that all human behavior is multiply determined by a complex of many interacting variables. Numerous factors contribute to the etiology of any particular behavioral tendency, and various rewards are derived from enactment of that behavior. The section of the book dealing with theoretical views of sexual offenders reflects this belief in multiple causation as do the chapters on classification.

The Bottom Line

Sexual assaults have devastating effects on innocent victims, so that any reduction in the rate of offending should be viewed as beneficial. In fact, an often neglected aspect of offering treatment to offenders is the real reduction in suffering that occurs when even a few of these men are prevented from reoffending. The rate of reoffense among sexual offenders is known to be very high; it is known that in some subgroups the majority of offenders eventually reoffend. Whenever treatment, no matter how unsophisticated, reduces reoffending by *any* degree, it saves innocent victims much suffering.

Since most recidivists offend against more than one victim, success with just 1 offender for every 50 treated can be counted as socially valuable and, in a rather curious calculus, cost beneficial. As Prentky and Burgess (1988) have shown, the costs involved in dealing with a single reoffender (e.g., apprehension, investigation, prosecution, and incarceration, plus assessment and treatment of the victim), balanced against the cost of offering treatment to 50 persons per year, justify, in financial terms alone, the provision of treatment.

As you will see in the relevant section of the book, most treatment programs are far more effective than this minimum criterion. Therefore, even if the reader remains skeptical of the ability of treatment programs to help most of these offenders, an argument can be made for the provision of treatment based on both humanitarian and economic grounds.

Purpose of This Project

We intend that the contents of this book be used in a proactive way, to foster the development and use of effective means to contain the problem which sexual offenders present to society. Optimistically, we can now see that we have the capacity, albeit limited, to reduce the severity of the problem through assessment and treatment of the offender. Clinical evaluation of the cognitive, behavioral, biological, and sociocultural features of the individual offers assistance to the criminal justice system in its management of these men. Treatment of the offender in prison or the community, as well as posttreatment management including long-term follow-up using relapse prevention procedures, will reduce the risk posed to society in at least some offenders. It is our hope and expectation that further research in this area will increase our ability, as a society, to deal with this serious problem.

It is our aim to bring the reader up to date on the latest knowledge available on sexual offenders and encourage optimism for the future reduction of sexual assault. It is also our hope that this book will promote the growth of interest in this field and assist in persuading agencies to fund research and treatment of these offenders. Finally, we hope that society at large, and its governmental representatives, will be persuaded by the observations in this book to more enthusiastically address the serious social problems caused by sexual assault. The voices of women and children who suffer actual or threatened sexual assault must be heard and responded to in more than token gestures. The time is past when we can count child molesters as harmless fondlers and rapists as innocently misunderstanding the victim's intent, or when we can see the victims as willfully neglectful or actively seductive. Such excuses for inaction as a society do not withstand even the most casual scrutiny. Action toward developing preventive strategies, helping victims, and treating offenders, is called for on a far larger scale than is presently offered. We hope this book helps in translating the growing awareness and understanding of the problem into greater action aimed at dealing with the socially destructive reality of sexual assault.

References

Prentky, R., & Burgess, A. W. (1988). *Rehabilitation of child molesters: A cost–benefit analysis.* Unpublished manuscript, Massachusetts Treatment Center, Bridgewater, MA.

2

The Nature and Extent of Sexual Assault

GENE G. ABEL AND JOANNE-L. ROULEAU

INTRODUCTION

In the last decade, the increased access given psychiatrists and psychologists to evaluate sex offenders has improved our understanding of sexual assaults. By developing new methods to assess the sexual assaulter, therapists have begun to clarify potential concerns that need to be evaluated in any sexual offender and to examine the impact of various treatment interventions designed to alter his behavior and thereby reduce sexual assaults. New psychological, behavioral, and physiological assessment methods allow therapists to identify and profile more accurately the various diagnostic categories of sexual assaulters, the true number of an offender's reported victims, the extent of violence during assaults, the age at which an offender develops deviant sexual interest, and the offender's sexual preference pattern.

The nature of the antisocial acts committed by sexual assaulters prohibits a valid random sample of assaulters because of their reluctance to reveal the extent of their actual crimes. Any summary attempting to describe typical sex offenders is thus prejudiced by the population sampled and the nature of the clinical assessment. Realizing the shortcomings of any description of "typical" sexual offenders, we describe in this chapter the controversial findings of an eight-year longitudinal study of 561 male sexual assaulters who sought voluntary assessment and/or treatment for their paraphilic disorders (sexual assaults) at the University of Tennessee Center for the Health Sciences in Memphis, and at the New York State Psychiatric Institute in New York City. At the former site, all categories of paraphiliacs were included, while at the latter site, because of preselection, only subjects whose inappropriate sexual behavior involved children were evaluated.

GENE G. ABEL AND JOANNE-L. ROULEAU • Behavioral Medicine Institute, Atlanta, Georgia 30327-4101.

A number of factors can influence the "who, what, where, and when" of assessing a sample of offenders. However, two factors in particular affect the results of any study: whether the offender was incarcerated (or ran risk of incarceration) and the extent to which the examiner worked toward increasing the validity of the sexual assaulter's self-reports.

Incarceration versus Nonincarceration

Assessment can be invalidated because: (1) Sexual assaulters who can afford competent legal support sometimes avoid incarceration. Therefore, incarcerated assaulters are frequently not representative of the general population of sexual assaulters. Because an average of fewer than 15% of sex crimes lead to incarceration, the majority of sex offenders are not within the prison system but "on the street." (2) New psychophysiological techniques that assess sexual interest and preference are particularly problematic for the offender since prison authorities invariably attempt to obtain the results from such physiological assessments to assist in parole decisions. Knowing this, the incarcerated offender is much more likely to attempt to suppress his psychophysiological sexual arousal in order to conceal from prison authorities the true nature of his past and current sexual interest. (3) When asked to report the sex crimes that he has committed, the prisoner is placed in an intolerable Catch-22. To be forthright and honest about the number of his sex crimes, or the degree to which he used force and violence during his assaults, may severely jeopardize the offender's opportunity to leave prison and might extend his incarceration should he be found guilty of new sex crimes that were revealed during questioning.

Information from outpatient sexual assaulters, therefore, is more representative of the general population of sex offenders.

The Reliability of Self-Report

Therapists evaluating and/or treating sexual assaulters need valid, reliable information from the sex offender. Without this, the therapist is less able to identify the precise treatment needs of the patient, to evaluate precisely the impact of treatment interventions, and to quantify treatment's long-term effects. Since much valuable information is frequently unobservable by the therapist, steps must be taken to insure valid, reliable offender reports. We have found that the skills and experience of the interviewer, the quality of the relationship established during the interview, the duration of the relationship between therapist and offender, and most importantly, protection of confidentiality of the offender's self-report all increase the validity and reliability of the offender's self-reports.

Data supporting the importance of protecting the paraphiliac's confidentiality in order to obtain more valid self-reporting have been collected by Kaplan (Kaplan, 1985). In her study, clinical histories were obtained under two distinct conditions. Offenders on parole were first questioned in their parole office regarding their deviant sexual behavior by a parole officer, who promised them anonymity (as confirmed by a consent form approved by the institutional review board of the local university). After the offenders reported the number of sex crimes they had perpetrated, they were then referred to Kaplan's assessment–treatment program for sex offenders at a completely different setting, outside the criminal justice system and within the mental health system. Here elaborate steps were taken to explain and insure how the confidentiality was obtained (see below). Using a similarly structured interview they were then re-questioned to determine the number of sex crimes they reported perpetrating.

In the criminal justice setting, offenders reported only 5% of the sex crimes they admitted to in the mental health setting. Offenders not only reported greater numbers of paraphilic acts committed but greater numbers of different paraphilias that they had failed to reveal within the criminal justice setting. These results confirm the powerful effect that confidentiality of information can have on the number of sex crimes reported. Since confidentiality is so powerful in influencing such reports, one should use caution when interpreting assessment or treatment studies that omit or leave vague the exact nature of how confidentiality was obtained.

THE PRESENT STUDY

The data reported in this chapter were obtained using a number of steps to insure an offender's confidentiality (Abel *et al.*, 1987; Abel & Rouleau, in press). These steps included:

1. Each patient's personal information was coded under an ID number, which he was asked to memorize. The connection between his name and coded ID number was held by a research collaborator outside the treatment setting. Members of the assessment–treatment team made no attempt to retain the patient's ID number. At each visit to the treatment project, the offender reported his ID number to the receptionist, who obtained his chart for the therapist, who in turn returned the file after treatment or assessment.
2. Results of assessment–treatment were only advanced to the patient. Since the results were in his possession, he had complete opportunity to evaluate them and make his own determination as to the disposition of those results.
3. Whenever evaluation or progress reports were sent (with the offender's permission) to others, such as consulting clinicians, his attorney, or his family, such public information was kept in a separate set of files.
4. The evaluation center was located in a large institute where other categories of patients were concomitantly seeking treatment. In this way, mere entrance into the institute could not be used to identify patients as sex offenders.
5. A Certificate of Confidentiality (Federal Regulation 4110-88-M) prevented members of the staff from revealing information related to an

individual offender's participation (Federal Register, 1975). This regulation superseded city, county, state, or federal regulations and is often obtained in studies working with patients committing crimes (such as drug abusers).

6. Patients were instructed not to disclose the specifics of any particular incident of sexual assault, for such details could be used to associate them with a particular crime.

7. Review boards completely separate from the assessment–treatment program were established to oversee the clinical and ethical conduct of the study. These included the institutional review boards of the respective organizations and the Institutional Review Board of NIMH, which constantly supervised the program before and after its inception, as well as a community board and a patient advocate.

Recruiting Sexual Assaulters

Contrary to popular belief, sexual assaulters can be recruited into programs much as other individuals who commit antisocial acts (e.g., drug abusers, alcoholics, etc.). A total of 561 participants were recruited through informal discussions with mental health care providers, through formal presentations at meetings and conventions of parole, probation, forensic, and criminal justice organizations, as well as through advertising in local media.

Assessment Methods

Subjects underwent a structured clinical interview already described elsewhere (Abel, 1985). Interviews lasted from 1 to 5 hours, depending upon the subject's ability to describe or recall his deviant past history. The interview primarily focused on demographic characteristics of the offender, the number of his victims, and the number and types of paraphilic acts, as well as the onset and frequency of the subject's various deviant interests. In all cases, diagnosis and frequency of crimes were recorded while the subject clearly admitted his deviant interests and behaviors. These diagnostic interviews were completed between 1977 and 1985.

RESULTS AND RECOMMENDATIONS

Demographic Characteristics

The majority of our patients were young, ranging in age from 13 to 76 years, with an average age of 31.5 years. Contrary to stereotypical views, the majority were moderately educated, and 40% had gone through one year of college. Two-thirds were working. They came from all socioeconomic levels and were surprisingly representative of the ethnic subgroups of the general population of each of the cities in which these studies were conducted. Approximately one-half of the participants were presently living with a woman or had been previously married.

These results suggest that evaluation–treatment programs should assume that sexual assaulters, although somewhat younger than the average population, will be cross-representative of the population without overly representing any ethnic or socioeconomic group. Assessment and treatment methods should therefore be adjusted to accommodate this expected population.

Age of Onset of Deviant Sexual Interest

Careful histories were taken to determine the age of onset of an offender's sexual interests, the variety and frequency of his sex offenses, the number of victims, and other characteristics of the offenders. Of 561 male offenders evaluated, 53.6% reported the onset of at least one deviant sexual interest prior to age 18.

Figure 1 shows the cumulative age of onset of the first paraphilia of all 561 adult subjects. Fifty percent (50%) of voyeurs had interest in that deviant behavior prior to age 15; 50% of male nonincest pedophiles by age 16; 50% of frotteurs by age 17; 50% of exhibitionists by age 18. More than 40% of female nonincest pedophiles had acquired that interest by age 18; 40% of male incest pedophiles, 30% of rapists, and 25% of female incest pedophiles had acquired their interests prior to age 18.

Of the 53.6% of adult offenders reporting the onset of deviant sex interest prior to age 18, each reported two different paraphilias and an average commission of 380.2 sex offenses by the time he reached adulthood. Similar information from adolescent sex offenders (younger than 18) revealed that each adolescent offender had 1.9 paraphilias and had committed an average of 6.8 sex offenses, with child molestation or rape represented by 54.1% of his deviant sex acts.

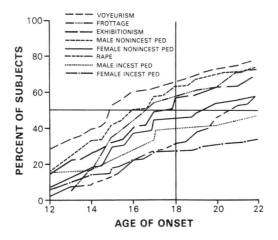

FIGURE 1. Age of onset of first paraphilia.

These data reveal that the majority of sexual assaulters develop deviant sexual interest prior to age 18. Of course, individuals who developed deviant sexual interest early in their lives but stopped their deviant behavior could not be included in the study. Ample evidence, however, confirms that sex offenders with chronic careers do develop that interest at a very early age. Assessment–treatment programs must therefore be established to accommodate these young sex offenders. This is especially true when we see the tremendous number of crimes committed by such adolescent sex offenders by the time they reach adulthood. Considering the severe consequences of sexual assaults upon the numerous victims throughout the offender's life span, a significant reduction in victim injury could be accomplished if effective treatment were provided early in the sex offender's career. Such early intervention is usually fraught with objections for various religious and ethical reasons. These objections, however, must be compared to the objective data that show the consequence to our society of not intervening early.

Deviant Sex Acts by Specific Category of Paraphilia

Histories from offenders clearly indicate that one individual can have multiple paraphilic interests throughout his lifetime. As an initial paraphilia fades, a second paraphilia begins, accelerates in frequency, and may overtake the initial paraphilia as the most common deviant sexual behavior. In this fashion, some sex offenders have as many as 10 categories of paraphilic interest throughout their lifetime. To fully understand this population, we chose to tally all paraphilias that an offender had engaged in during his lifetime, even though some paraphilias were no longer present at the time of the evaluation (Abel *et al.*, 1988).

Table 1 shows the high frequency of deviant sexual acts committed by various paraphiliacs, especially exhibitionists, voyeurs, frotteurs, transvestites, and masochists. Of the four subcategories of child molestation, nonincest paraphiliacs targetting young boys committed the greatest number of crimes.

The total number of rapes of adult females committed by the 126 rapists evaluated was relatively small compared to the number of crimes committed by child molesters, masochists, and frotteurs. Nevertheless, these findings do not minimize the severity and seriousness of rape as a crime.

A number of paraphiliacs are repeatedly involved with the same victim, such as incest pedophiles, sadists, fetishists, and masochists. We also investigated the age of target victims, their gender, assaultive versus nonassaultive behavior, and incestuous versus nonincestuous sexual behavior.

Age of Target Victims

The ages of target victims were divided into three categories: children (under the age of 14), adolescents (14–17 years of age), and adults (over 17 years of age). Of the 561 subjects, 275 (49%) had target victims only in one age group, 176 (31.3%) were involved with two age groups, and 63 (11.2%) were involved in all three age categories. Of our subjects, 47 (8%) were involved in deviant behaviors

TABLE 1. Completed Paraphilic Acts and Victims/Partners by Diagnosis

Paraphilia	Number of subjects seen	Total completed paraphilic acts	% of total completed paraphilic acts	Total victims	% of total victims
1. Pedophilia (nonincest) female target	224	5,197	1.8	4,435	2.3
2. Pedophilia (nonincest) male target	153	43,100	14.8	22,981	11.8
3. Pedophilia (incest) female target	159	12,927	4.4	286	0.2
4. Pedophilia (incest) male target	44	2,741	0.9	75	0.0
5. Rape	126	907	0.3	882	0.5
6. Exhibitionism	142	71,696	24.6	72,974	37.3
7. Voyeurism	62	29,090	10.0	26,648	13.6
8. Frottage	62	52,669	18.1	55,887	28.6
9. Obscene mial	3	3	0.0	3	0.0
10. Transsexualism	29	5,539	1.9	12	0.0
11. Transvestitism	31	20,779	7.1	NA	NA
12. Fetishism	19	6,863	2.4	160	0.1
13. Sadism	28	3,800	1.3	132	0.1
14. Masochism	17	19,366	6.6	37	0.0
15. Homosexuality	24	3,701	1.3	2	0.0
16. Obscene phone calling	19	2,578	0.9	1,955	1.0
17. Public masturbation ·	17	6,423	2.2	6,870	3.5
18. Bestiality	14	3,114	1.1	1,676	0.9
19. Urolagnia	4	409	0.1	385	0.2
20. Coprophilia	4	107	0.0	7	0.0
21. Arousal to odors	2	728	0.3	NA	NA
Total		291,737	100.1	195,407	100.1

Note. From G. G. Abel et al. (1987). "Self-reported sex crimes of nonincarcerated paraphiliacs." *Journal of Interpersonal Violence, 2*(6), 3–25. Reprinted with permission.

which could not be classified according to age of target victim, such as bestiality, fetishism, and the like.

Gender of Victims

Of the 561 subjects, 377 (67.2%) targetted only females, and 67 (11.9%) only targetted males. Finally, 120 (20%) of our subjects participated in deviant behavior irrespective of gender of the victims.

Assaultive versus Nonassaultive Behavior

We were also interested in knowing whether individuals who had committed assaultive crimes (rape, child molestation, frottage) also committed non-assaultive paraphilic behaviors (public masturbation, voyeurism).

In this sample, 331 individuals (59%) participated in assaultive deviant behavior only, while 84 (14.9%) participated in nonassaultive behavior only. However, 146 subjects (26%) used both touching and nontouching behaviors when offending against their victims.

Incestuous versus Nonincestuous Behavior

It is commonly assumed that paraphiliacs involved within their family will not offend against a nonfamily victim. In this sample, 315 men (56.1%) participated in nonincestuous deviant behavior only, and 68 (12%) participated in incestuous behavior only. Nonetheless, 131 individuals (23.3%) offended against both family and nonfamily victims, irrespective of familial relationship.

It must be emphasized that since the sex offenders who participated in this study were preselected, it cannot be assumed that this sample is representative of the general population of sex offenders. To obtain a less biased appraisal of the number of different paraphilias engaged in by offenders, we calculated the percentage of offenders who participated in each of the major 16 paraphilic interests and then averaged across all 16 paraphilic categories. The percentage of individuals in each of the diagnostic categories who had one or more paraphilic diagnoses is shown in Table 2. Other categories, such as obscene mail, bestiality, urolagnia, coprophilia, and attraction to specific odors, were eliminated because fewer than 12 subjects were present in each of these categories, and these numbers were felt to be too small to represent these infrequently seen paraphilias.

The results presented in Table 2 demonstrate that, irrespective of the category of specific paraphilia, members in any one specific category were concurrently involved, or had been involved, in other specific categories of paraphilic behavior. These data contradict the conventional literature that paraphiliacs have one and only one specific category of deviant sexual behavior. These results reflect quite the opposite finding; that individuals with one and only one paraphilia are rather uncommon, and that the majority of paraphiliacs have or have had multiple, specific categories of paraphilic interest.

The conclusions and recommendations for assessment and treatment that can be drawn from these analyses run counter to much of the psychological lore related to sex offenders. Although in some cases the age of the preferred victim remains in a distinctive age range, a large percentage of offenders perpetrate sex crimes against the very young, adolescents, and adults. Furthermore, although a large percentage of offenders perpetrate crimes against one gender, a significant proportion perpetrate crimes against victims irrespective of gender. Although over half of this sample's offenders perpetrated only assaultive sexual behaviors, while a minority perpetrated only nonassaultive sexual behaviors, a surprisingly high percentage perpetrated sex crimes of both types. Examining whether the offender perpetrated only nonincestuous sex crimes, incestuous sex crimes, or both, we found that a significant proportion perpetrated sex crimes both outside and within the family.

Since many offenders assault victims of various ages, various genders, with both assaultive and nonassaultive behavior, and both outside and within their families, one can only conclude that sex offenders have a general deficit that

TABLE 2. Percentage of Paraphiliacs with Multiple Paraphilias

Diagnosis	N	Number of paraphilias									
		1	2	3	4	5	6	7	8	9	10
Pedophilia (nonincest) female target	224	15.2	23.7	19.2	14.7	9.4	4.5	6.7	3.1	1.3	2.2
Pedophilia (nonincest) male target	153	19.0	26.8	19.6	12.4	4.6	3.9	6.5	3.9	0.7	2.6
Pedophilia (incest) female target	159	28.3	25.8	17.0	5.7	8.2	3.8	5.0	1.9	0.6	3.8
Pedophilia (incest) male target	44	4.5	15.9	20.5	18.2	13.6	6.8	9.1	2.3	0.0	9.1
Rape	126	27.0	17.5	19.0	12.7	7.1	3.2	7.9	1.6	1.6	2.4
Exhibitionism	142	7.0	20.4	22.5	15.5	7.0	7.0	9.2	4.9	2.8	3.5
Voyeurism	62	1.6	9.7	27.4	14.5	12.9	8.1	11.3	8.1	3.2	3.2
Frottage	62	21.0	16.1	12.9	16.1	11.3	3.2	12.9	3.2	0.0	3.2
Transsexualism	29	51.7	31.0	13.8	3.4	0.0	0.0	0.0	0.0	0.0	0.0
Transvestitism	31	6.5	29.0	29.0	9.7	0.0	6.5	12.9	0.0	6.5	0.0
Fetishism	19	0.0	15.8	21.1	15.8	26.3	5.3	10.5	0.0	5.3	0.0
Sadism	28	0.0	17.9	28.6	14.3	14.3	3.6	3.6	3.6	7.1	7.1
Masochism	17	0.0	41.2	11.8	5.9	11.8	5.9	5.9	5.9	5.9	5.9
Homosexuality	24	25.0	41.7	25.0	4.2	0.0	0.0	0.0	4.2	0.0	0.0
Obscene phone calling	19	5.3	5.3	21.1	21.1	5.3	10.5	15.8	5.3	5.3	5.3
Public masturbation	17	5.9	17.6	0.0	17.6	17.6	17.6	5.9	5.9	5.9	5.9

Note. From G. G. Abel et al. (1988). "Multiple paraphilic diagnoses among sex offenders." Bulletin of the American Academy of Psychiatry and the Law, 16, 153–168. Reprinted after revision with permission.

leads them to perpetrate these crimes. If specific emotional conflicts produced specific sexual offenses, why would paraphiliacs perpetrate such varied sex crimes? Instead of assuming that many sex offenders have multiple, specific emotional conflicts, one could assume more parsimoniously that a general deficit of control over deviant behavior is at fault in many sex offenders (Abel *et al.*, 1988).

These findings, of course, have far-reaching ramifications for the assessment and treatment of sex offenders. Assessment must take into consideration all of the commonly reported paraphilias and must evaluate any one offender to see which of the many paraphilic interests he might have. To assume that a man charged with molesting young boys has that sole deviant interest runs counter to the available information. Assessment programs must expand their evaluations to include many possible paraphilic interests and accordingly adjust the clinical interview, paper-and-pencil testing, and psychophysiological assessment. Treatment programs must also be adapted to fit all the paraphilic interests of any one sex offender. Treatments must be directed toward helping the offender reduce or eliminate not only his major paraphilic interest but each of his other paraphilic arousal patterns. If treatment only focuses on the paraphilic interest that brought about the individual's arrest or that brought him to the attention of others, it is very likely that treatment directed at that one singular interest may be very effective; but rearrest for "new" sex crimes will result from his perpetrating assaults linked to other paraphilic interests that were not treated. Since the goal of treatment is to eliminate all paraphilic behavior, treatment programs must be adjusted to help the offender deal with each of his deviant interests.

Rape as a Paraphilia

An especially problematic area is whether rape of adults is a true paraphilia. Although the major treatment programs for paraphiliacs in North America have always treated rapists of adults as if they were paraphiliacs, this does not necessarily mean they are best construed as such. Similarly, in specific treatment programs for such offenders, the mere fact that clinical treatment has been made available for some years to rapists does not, by itself, justify consideration of rape as a paraphilia.

Clinical interviews of rapists, however, provide support for the classification of rape as a paraphilia, because many individuals report having recurrent, repetitive, and compulsive urges and fantasies to commit rapes. These offenders attempt to control their urges, but the urges eventually become so strong that they act upon them, commit rapes, and then feel guilty afterwards with a temporary reduction of urges, only to have the cycle repeat again. This cycle of ongoing urges, attempts to control them, breakdown of those attempts, and recurrence of the sex crime is similar to the clinical picture presented by exhibitionists, voyeurs, pedophiles, and other traditionally recognized categories of paraphiliacs.

Further support for rape as a paraphilia comes from the age of onset of interest in rape and rape's association with other common paraphilias. Figure 1 shows that 50% of individuals who rape have the onset of this deviant interest by age 21, which is similar to the early onset of arousal in other paraphilias. Rapists of adults have a high likelihood of having past history or concomitant history of other paraphilias associated with their interest in rape. Of the 126 subjects who had raped an adult female, 44% had also been involved in nonincestuous female pedophilia, 28% had interest in exhibitionism, 24% in female incestuous pedophilia, 18% in voyeurism, 14% in nonincestuous male pedophilia, 11% in frottage, 10% in sadism, and the remainder had been involved, to a lesser degree, in other types of paraphilia (Abel *et al.*, 1988).

The psychophysiological laboratory provides the final source of information regarding this controversy. A major issue is whether rapists are simply variants of sadists, since both perpetrate aggressive crimes against their victims. Psychophysiological assessment in the laboratory demonstrates significant differences between these two categories. Both groups are aroused to depictions of physical assaults upon victims. Rapists, however, are also aroused to depictions of mutually consenting intercourse with adult partners, while sadists are not. Sadists by contrast are particularly aroused to depictions of physical (nonsexual) assaults upon victims, which do not produce arousal for rapists (Abel, Becker, Blanchard, & Flanagan, 1981).

The weight of scientific evidence, therefore, supports rape of adults as a specific category of paraphilia. If the weight of scientific evidence supports rape as being a specific paraphilia, why has rape not been incorporated into the APA's DSM-III-R (American Psychiatric Association, 1987) classification for psychiatric disorders? A number of factors contribute to this omission.

First, psychiatry and psychology have had limited contact with the more aggressive sex offenders, and as a consequence, less information has been available regarding sexual aggressives as compared to the less aggressive paraphiliacs, such as voyeurs, exhibitionists, and the like.

Second, the scientific evidence must be balanced with society's acceptance of such a categorization. The less aggressive but equally peculiar arousal patterns, such as frottage, are accepted as psychiatric disorders because the assumed consequences to the victim are less severe; therefore, by society's standards, punishment to the offending individual is seen as less necessary, and treatment through psychological and psychiatric channels is more accepted. As the ability of the victim to ward off a sex offense decreases (such as in pedophilia) or the degree of force increases during the perpetration of the crime (such as in sadism and rape), our culture is less accepting of psychiatric justification for such crimes and is more in favor of punishment through the criminal justice system.

Society in the past has traditionally neglected the needs of sexual assault victims and has attempted to ignore the severe ramifications of victims of rape and child molestation. In recent years, this trend has been reversed predominantly by the women's movement, spearheaded by the National Organization for Women, which has identified the needs of sexual assault victims as a high priority for our culture. Many believe that accepting rape as a paraphilia will reverse the excellent work done by the women's movement because individuals who would otherwise be less likely to escape punishment for their sexual assaults may use a diagnosis of paraphilic rape as a means to escape the criminal justice system. In practice, this has not been the case. To be identified as a paraphiliac, a rapist must have a recurrent, compulsive urge and need to re- petitively carry out psychologically driven rape. These features permit rape's incorporation into the category paraphilia. Such a categorization raises the issue of the offender's need for psychiatric and psychological treatment before he can gain control over his sexual assaultiveness. In our culture, this has meant that not only must the individual so categorized serve his time for his illegal act of sexual assault, but he must also serve time receiving psychiatric and psychologi- cal treatment for his paraphilia. A nonparaphilic rapist anxious to serve as little time as possible would be wise to avoid the categorization of his rape as a paraphilia, since by definition he will also increase the likelihood of his pro- longed incarceration, not only for the legal crime, but for treatment of his para- philic interests.

The resolution of this issue probably necessitates increased education of our culture regarding the scientific evidence that justifies rape as a paraphilia and a greater appreciation of the incarceration consequences for an individual diag- nosed as being a paraphilic rapist.

CONCLUSIONS

These results, as is the case with all scientific data, are not representative of a total population of paraphiliacs, are tentative until corroborated by others, and should only be used to guide researchers in new directions to better understand the paraphiliac. A greater understanding of the sexual assaulter is more than an interesting investigation of a subpopulation of our society. For the men and women who conduct this research, the ultimate objective is the prevention of paraphilic behavior. For too long, our culture has sought the quick fix for the problem of sexual violence, hoping that increased services for the victims would resolve the problem of sexual violence. Nothing could be further from the truth.

There has never been a public health problem successfully reduced by treat- ing individuals after they have developed the problem, and we can expect that sexual assaults in our culture will not significantly decrease by treating the victimized. Ultimately, we must aim our scientific investigations at the primary, secondary, and tertiary prevention of the development of these paraphilic in- terests and paraphilic behaviors. It is hoped that these data will help steer future researchers toward prevention so that there will be no victims to treat or chronic offenders to rehabilitate.

REFERENCES

Abel, G. G. (1985). A clinical evaluation of possible sex offenders. In *The incest offender, the victim, the family: New treatment approaches* (pp. 1–8). White Plains, NY: The Mental Health Association of Westchester County.

Abel, G. G., & Rouleau, J.-L. (in press). Outpatient treatment of sex offenders. In M. E. Thase, M. A. Edelstein, & M. Hersen (Eds), *Handbook of outpatient treatment of adults*. New York: Plenum.

Abel, G. G., Becker, J. V., Blanchard, E. B., & Flanagan, B. (1981). The behavioral assessment of rapists. In J. Hays, T. Roberts, & K. Solway (Eds.), *Violence and the violent individual* (pp. 211–230). Holliswood, NY: Spectrum Publications.

Abel, G. G., Becker, J. V., Mittelman, M. S., Cunningham-Rathner, J., Rouleau, J.-L., & Murphy, W. D. (1987). Self-reported sex crimes of nonincarcerated paraphiliacs. *Journal of Interpersonal Violence, 2*(6), 3–25.

Abel, G. G., Becker, J. V., Cunningham-Rathner, J., Mittelman, M. S., & Rouleau, J.-L. (1988). Multiple paraphilic diagnoses among sex offenders. *Bulletin of the American Academy of Psychiatry and the Law, 16*, 153–168.

American Psychiatric Association (1987). *Diagnostic and statistical manual of mental disorders* (3rd ed., revised). Washington, DC: Author.

Federal Register (1975, December 5). *Protection of identity: Research subjects* (Vol. 40, No. 234). Washington, DC: U.S. Government Printing Office.

Kaplan, M. S. (1985). *The impact of parolees' perceptions of confidentiality on the reporting of their urges to interact sexually with children*. Unpublished doctoral dissertation, New York University.

3

Classifying Sexual Offenders

The Development and Corroboration of Taxonomic Models

RAYMOND A. KNIGHT AND ROBERT A. PRENTKY

Classification is a fundamental cognitive operation. From the first perceptual contact with stimuli (Pomerantz, 1986; Treisman, 1986) through the ultimate integration and storage of information in long-term memory (Rosch & Lloyd, 1978), the identification, organization, and integration of elements that share common characteristics has been shown to be an essential component of perception and cognition. The critical function of classification in scientific investigation mirrors its central role in general cognition. Phenomenalists, realists, and conceptualists, despite their diverse metaphysical perspectives, all recognize the vital role of classification in science (Ghiselin, 1981). It stands as a necessary precursor and pervasive sustainer of all scientific progress (Hempel, 1965).

In the scientific study of anomalous behavior, the indispensable role of classification is well established. Understanding the taxonomic structure of a deviant population is the keystone of theory building and the cornerstone of intervention. It provides a pivotal underpinning for research on a population and is an essential prerequisite for determining the optimum response of society to deviance. Whether the goal is making decisions about intervention, treatment, and disposition, tracking down the developmental roots of a deviant behavioral pattern, or following the life course of this pattern, failure to take the taxonomic structure of a population into account can lead to serious practical, methodological, and theoretical errors.

RAYMOND A. KNIGHT AND ROBERT A. PRENTKY • Department of Psychology, Brandeis University, Waltham, Massachusetts 02254-9110; and Research Department, Massachusetts Treatment Center, Bridgewater, Massachusetts 02324.

In the study of sexual aggression the importance of taxonomic issues has been widely acknowledged in the clinical literature (see Knight, Rosenberg, & Schneider, 1985). Clinical investigators, working with rapists and child molesters, have responded both to the apparent heterogeneity of these offenders and to the demands placed on clinicians to make discrete decisions about treatment and disposition. They have described the consistencies they have observed among these offenders and have proposed typologies that were intended to increase group homogeneity and to inform clinical judgments (e.g., Fitch, 1962; Gebhard, Gagnon, Pomeroy, & Christenson, 1965; Groth & Birnbaum, 1979; McCaghy, 1967; Seghorn & Cohen, 1980). Although there are some basic similarities in the most salient types identified in the various proposed systems (see Knight *et al.*, 1985) and the most widely used subtype-defining dimensions appear to have reasonable discriminatory power (Knight *et al.*, 1985), these systems have remained only speculative models with little or no evidence of reliability or validity. Their potential for enhancing the efficacy of clinical decisions about treatment, management, and disposition has not been tested; and they have provided little guidance to the investigation of etiology, recidivism, or the life-span adaptation of sexual offenders.

Agreement about the level at which taxonomic differentiation among sexual offenders should occur has not been universal. For instance, some have challenged the attempt to subdivide rapists, arguing that the supposed heterogeneity of rapists is simply random variation at the extreme end of a normal distribution of all males (e.g., Brownmiller, 1975; Scully & Marolla, 1985). The *Diagnostic and Statistical Manual of Mental Disorders* (DSM-III-R; American Psychiatric Association, 1987) does not include a diagnostic category for rapists—although the advisory committee on the paraphilias recommended one—and only contains the global category of pedophilia for child molesters. Thus, not only is there little evidence about what types of sexual offenders may exist, there does not even seem to be a consensus about where group differentiation should be attempted. Clearly, the critical issue of whether there are useful subtypes of rapists and child molesters is an empirical question. One can rely on neither the clinical intuitions that have inspired sexual offender typologies nor the unsubstantiated conjectures that have rejected such systems. The difficulties encountered when depending exclusively on such intuitions and conjectures have been amply demonstrated (e.g., Knight & Roff, 1985; Meehl, 1957, 1959; Monahan, 1981).

Fortunately, a powerful methodology for generating and testing tyological schemes in deviant populations has been clearly delineated (e.g., Blashfield, 1980; Meehl, 1979; Skinner, 1981, 1986), and a detailed description of how these techniques can be applied to the study of sexual offenders has been provided (Knight *et al.*, 1985). One of the major goals of our research program at the Massachusetts Treatment Center during the 1980s has been addressing these critical taxonomic problems by systematically applying this approach to the study of sexual offenders. It is the intent of this chapter to give an overview of this programmatic approach and to summarize some of the taxonomic structures that have emerged from our research.

CLASSIFICATION RESEARCH PROGRAM

Figure 1 depicts a flow chart of the plan of our research program. A more detailed description of how this program was applied has been presented elsewhere (Knight *et al.*, 1985; Knight, 1988). We will simply summarize the essential aspects of the process here.

As can be seen in the diagram, in our attempts to determine whether reliable and valid typologies could be created for rapists and child molesters, we have employed both deductive–rational and inductive–empirical research strategies simultaneously. As is evident in the chart, these two strategies differ in how initial typological models are generated, but they are not completely independent. They interface at several critical junctures and should ultimately converge on similar structures. In the flow diagram, rectangular shapes designate operations that occur within a particular strategy, and the oval shapes indicate points of intersection between the two strategies.

Stage I: Theory Formulation

The aim of the deductive approach is to put the most promising theoretical system at severe risk for disconfirmation (Popper, 1972). Identification of a preliminary target for such a critical assessment required a thorough evaluation of the current status of the theory and research on sexual offenders. In a relatively undeveloped area like the study of sexual aggression, where data on the validation of typological systems were virtually nonexistent, we had to use other factors to guide our choice of a preliminary model. We compared the available typologies of sexual offenders to determine whether specific types of offenders were described across a number of systems (see Knight *et al.*, 1985). We reasoned that if such types could be identified, they would represent a consensus among clinicians of the most salient subtypes of sexual offenders and thus would provide the best available guesses about taxonomic structure. As preliminary models for our deductive strategy, we chose the two typologies described by Cohen and his colleagues (Massachusetts Treatment Center: Child Molester Typology 1 [MTC:CM1] and Massachusetts Treatment Center: Rapist Typology 1 [MTC:R1]; see Cohen, Garofalo, Boucher, & Seghorn, 1971; Cohen, Seghorn, & Calmas, 1969; Seghorn, 1971), because these systems included representatives of the types that were most frequently described in the clinical literature (see Knight *et al.*, 1985).

Although there was no evidence on the reliability of raters' classifications of offenders to these types, there was at least one study demonstrating that the two systems had some validity (Cohen *et al.*, 1969). Another source of evidence for the validity of these types was also assessed. From the prototypic descriptions of these types in the literature we abstracted the major, defining variables that apparently differentiated among types. Then, we reviewed the empirical literature to assess the discriminatory power of these dimensions among sexual offenders (see Knight *et al.*, 1985). The confirmation in this literature that the type-defining dimensions (e.g., amount and nature of aggression, lifestyle im-

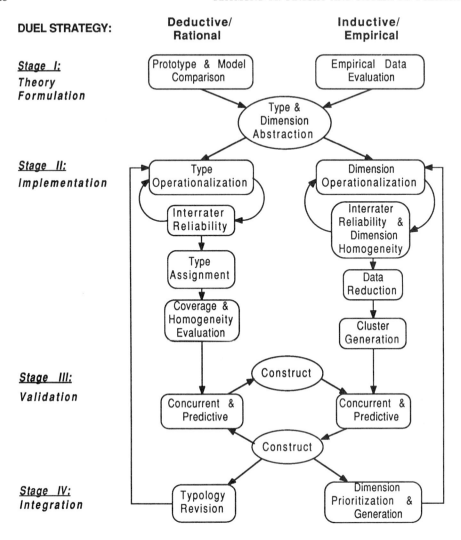

FIGURE 1. A flow diagram of the classification research program at the Massachusetts Treatment Center.

pulsivity, etc.) differentiated among sexual offenders provided some indirect evidence for the validity of a system that incorporated these dimensions (Knight *et al.*, 1985), and it suggested in the absence of other evidence that the proposed types constituted a reasonable point of departure for our deductive strategy. In the flow chart this process, which we called Type Abstraction, is represented by an oval, because it was informed by inputs both from the deductive–rational and the inductive–empirical sides. Type abstraction and selection depended both on the theoretical speculations about taxonomic structures and on the degree of validation evident for these structures in the empirical literature.

The inductive approach concentrates on the manipulation of critical empirical data. It focuses on the acquisition of reliable, unbiased data, and it attempts through cluster analyses to find naturally occurring homogeneous groups on the basis of offenders' similarities and differences on a specific set of attributes. Because the selection of initial input variables is not a random process, the inductive approach must also be guided by some theoretical notions (Popper, 1972), and it is likely to fail without the benefit of such direction (Blashfield, 1980; Meehl, 1979). The difference between the role of theory in the deductive and inductive strategies is that in the latter it can be less structured and elaborated. When applying the inductive approach, one hopes that by analyzing hypothetically important variables with methods that are reasonable and consistent, valid organizing structures will emerge.

In selecting variables for our cluster analyses, we sought to include the most relevant variables available for differentiating among sexual offenders. We focused both on those dimensions we had identified as important for discriminating among the most commonly proposed types of offenders and on those variables that had been shown to have some discriminating potential in the empirical studies of sexual offenders (see Knight *et al.*, 1985). Thus, consistent with its oval designation in the flow chart, the process of Dimension Abstraction had both theory-generated and empirically driven components, involving inputs from both the deductive–rational and inductive–empirical approaches.

Stage II: Implementation

Having distinguished initial types and critical dimensions, we moved to the second stage in Figure 1, Implementation. The types and dimensions had to be operationalized, and the reliability of type classification or dimension rating had to be assessed. The curved arrows between operationalization and interrater reliability within both strategies indicate the cycling between revising and testing of type-defining criteria and dimensions that was necessary until adequate reliabilities were attained.

In implementing the deductive strategy, once we judged that a typological system was adequately defined so that acceptable reliability was likely, we classified offenders into types, assessed the attained level of interrater classification agreement, checked the system for coverage (i.e., the proportion of the sample that can be classified) and homogeneity of the types (i.e., how tight, compact, and cohesive types are), and moved to the next stage, Validation. As we will see in our discussion of the child molester typology below, because our first revision of the system (MTC:CMZ) failed to attain adequate reliability and coverage, we were forced to cycle back to and repeat the operationalization process after we had assigned types to this first revision, but before validation. Thus, the theoretically driven child molester typology was revised twice before it was validated as MTC:CM3. Our first attempt to revise and operationalize the rapist typology (MTC:R2) yielded acceptable reliability (Prentky, Cohen, & Seghorn,

1985). Although coverage and homogeneity of these rapist types were not ideal, we decided to proceed with testing the validity of this system, anticipating that these analyses would help us to revise this system again.

The implementation of the inductive strategy paralleled that of the deductive strategy. After the interrater reliabilities and homogeneities of the selected dimensions had been established, an important process, data reduction, ensued. Reducing the large number of variables we had measured into a smaller number of homogeneous scales was essential for ensuring that only the most reliable and relevant variables were used in our cluster analyses (Meehl, 1979; Skinner, 1981) and for facilitating interpretation of the clusters that were generated. We employed principal components analysis with Varimax rotation as our data reduction technique, thereby maximizing the orthogonality among our dimensions and reducing the potential for overweighting any single factor in the cluster analyses (Friedman & Rubin, 1968). Cluster analyses, a set of statistical procedures for sorting individuals into groups on the basis of their similarities on input dimensions, were calculated on the resultant dimensions (see Rosenberg & Knight, 1988).

Stage III: Validation

No matter how elegantly structured, intuitively sensible, and reliable a theoretically or empirically generated typology may be, it is useless if it is not valid. It must be able to advance our knowledge about etiology, provide a basis for more diversified and effective therapeutic interventions, or improve our dispositional decisions by enhancing our ability to predict. Thus, in Stage III of our program (see Figure 1) we have been assessing the external validity of our classification systems. We have tested the validity of the third version of our child molester typology (MTC:CM3), the second version of our rationally derived rapist typology (MTC:R2), and our various cluster typologies. Because the primary emphasis of our taxonomic studies has been understanding the nature and source of the many varieties of sexual aggression, our first assessments of the validity of our systems focused on family and developmental pathology, childhood and juvenile behavior, and adult adaptation (Knight & Prentky, 1987; Prentky & Knight, 1986; Prentky, Knight, & Rosenberg, 1988; Prentky, Knight, Rosenberg, & Lee, 1989; Rosenberg & Knight, 1988; Rosenberg, Knight, Prentky, & Lee, 1988). We reasoned that if the various types could be shown to have distinctive, theoretically coherent developmental roots, this would strongly support their validity.

Assessment of the concurrent and predictive validity of each of the typologies generated by our deductive and inductive strategies constitutes only the first step in the Validation stage. These analyses provide essential groundwork for construct validation (Campbell & Fish, 1959; Cronbach & Meehl, 1955; Skinner, 1986), in which the converging lines of evidence both within and across systems and strategies are examined. This cross-strategy fertilization is indicated in the flow diagram by the oval that encloses construct validity.

Stage IV: Integration

The analyses of construct validity in Stage III inevitably give way to the Typology Revision and Dimension Prioritization and Generation of Stage IV. As we shall see in our program, cluster analyses can uncover or corroborate previously neglected types and can provide new insights into the organizational structures of existing typologies. Analyses of typologies that have been assessed by the deductive strategy can suggest new dimensions for cluster analyses or indicate differential weighting for existing dimensions. Because such integrations and changes both within and across strategies resulted from the corroborations and disconfirmations of numerous analyses of the available data, they are compelling. They require, however, cross validation. The process of comparing numerous types on multiple dimensions and of assessing the interrelations and discriminations of numerous attributes allows ample opportunity for chance findings to reach significance. Thus, such integrative notions must be tested. This is indicated in Figure 1 by the arrows from Stage IV pointing back to the implementation process.

Although the same basic programmatic method was applied to both child molesters and rapists, the specific problems we encountered in each application, and the structures we uncovered, forced us to rely on different kinds of analyses and yielded radically different types of solutions for each population. We have already described some of the details of the generation of our child molester typology (Knight, 1988). We will simply highlight the critical aspects of this process here, and we will provide greater detail on the solution to the rapist typology.

CHILD MOLESTER TYPOLOGY

The application of this program to child molesters offers a good example of the importance of combining both deductive and inductive strategies in typology construction. After we had compared the extant clinical systems to ascertain the most salient types and to extract the most widely used discriminating typological dimensions (see Knight *et al.*, 1985), and after we had combed the empirical literature to determine the status of these types and dimensions and to identify other variables with discriminatory potential (Knight *et al.*, 1985), we proceeded to operationalize both a preliminary rational system and the relevant dimensions.

We chose as our point of departure a rationally derived system that contained versions of the most salient child molester types (MTC:CM1; Cohen *et al.*, 1969). We attempted to operationalize the four types described in this system and to assign child molesters to these types, but we were not able to attain adequate interrater reliability for these types. This led to our first revision of the system (MTC:CM2), a compromise system that extended and clarified, but did not change, the theoretical underpinnings of the original system (Knight, 1988). The major revision involved a reconceptualization of two critical constructs:

fixation and regression. In the original system these two constructs defined separate types. A number of critical notions were confounded in differentiating these types, including the child molester's style of offending, his interpersonal relationship with his victims, the intensity of the offender's pedophilic interest, and the level of social competence he had achieved prior to his sexual assaults. On the basis of a case-by-case analysis of classification discrepancies, we decided to separate both the offender's style and his relationship with his victims from both the intensity of his pedophilic interest and his achieved social competence. The style and relationship constructs were joined with additional characteristics to differentiate object-related from exploitative offense styles. Intensity of pedophilic interest and social competence were employed to define a fixation–regression dichotomization (high intensity, low social competence versus low intensity, high social competence). These offense-style and fixation–regression bifurcations were crossed with each other and with an instrumental–expressive aggression distinction to yield an eight group typology (see Knight, 1988; Knight *et al.*, 1985).

When we assigned 68 child molesters to this revised system, several problems became apparent. First, the interrater reliabilities of classification were still unacceptably low. Second, certain types (e.g., the Instrumental–Exploitative–Fixated type) were extremely heterogeneous. Third, during the classification process we encountered child molesters who seemed to fall between the types that were defined by the system (e.g., offenders with both high fixation on children and high social competence). Thus, data on the reliability, homogeneity, and coverage of this revised typology clearly indicated that it required additional restructuring.

The process of the second revision (MTC:CM3) had three major advantages over that of the first revision (MTC:CM2). First, we had a sufficiently large sample of child molesters assigned to MTC:CM2 that we could statistically analyze the cases on which there were classification discrepancies. We compared on critical variables those cases on which raters disagreed to the agreed cases in the types assigned by each of the disagreeing raters. This provided feedback both about the variables that might be creating classification difficulties between specific types and about the possible characteristics of mixed types. Second, we had completed several cluster analyses of the entire sex offender population at MTC (see Rosenberg & Knight, 1988), and the results of these analyses provided some solid empirical boundaries that guided our attempts to revise the system (Knight, 1988). Third, we now had a computerized data base on a large number of sexual offenders. Thus, when problems arose during the revision process about the coexistence of particular characteristics in offenders or about the consequences of making certain typological distinctions, we were able to resolve these difficulties empirically.

The integration of the results of our discrepancy analyses of rater disagreements, our cluster analyses, and numerous analyses directed at specific questions (Knight, 1988) yielded the hierarchical, two-axis typology depicted in Figure 2. Three structural innovations distinguish this system both from earlier versions of this typology and from other proposed typologies:

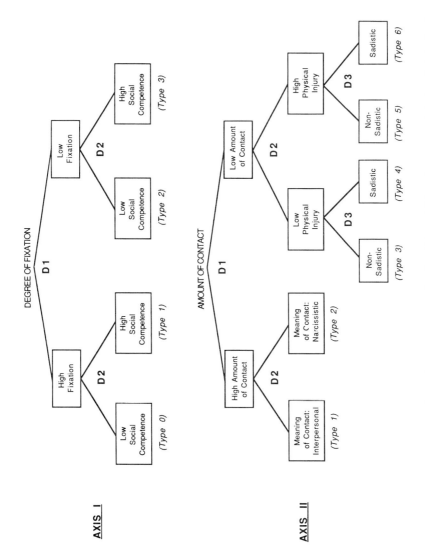

FIGURE 2. A flow diagram of the decision process for classifying child molesters on Axis I and Axis II of MTC:CM3. D1, Decision 1; D2, Decision 2; and D3, Decision 3.

1. The fixated–regressed distinction of MTC:CM2 has been partitioned into two separate, independent factors—the degree of fixation on children (i.e., the intensity of pedophilic interest) and the level of social competence. These two judgments have been placed together on a separate axis from the rest of the system.
2. A new type, the "Narcissistic," has been incorporated into the system to resolve the problems of differentiating between Object-Related and Exploitative types and to represent a type that emerged in our cluster analyses. The integration of this type required a restructuring of the typology and the introduction of the offender's contact with children as an initial, preemptive discriminator on Axis II.
3. The violence in the sexual offense has been differentiated into independent physical injury and sadistic components.

A full exposition of both the criteria for assigning offenders to the types in MTC:CM3 and the interrater reliabilities for all classifications in this typology can be found elsewhere (Knight, Carter, & Prentky, 1989a). We will only summarize the most prominent aspects of the system here.

As can be seen in Figure 2, Axis I in MTC:CM3 consists of dichotomous, crossed decisions on two independent constructs—fixation and social competence—yielding the four types depicted. Fixation (Decision 1 on Axis I) assesses the strength of an individual's pedophilic interest, that is, the extent to which children are a major focus of the individual's cognitions and fantasies. It is measured either directly by an offender's report of the degree to which children constitute a focus of his attention or indirectly by behaviors that indicate the duration of the offender's sexual and/or interpersonal involvement with children. Social competence (Decision 2 on Axis I) assesses the offender's success in employment and adult relationships and social responsibilities.

Analyses of the classification of 177 child molesters to these Axis I types confirmed our hypothesis that these two constructs were statistically independent, and thus corroborated our decision to consider each as a separate dimension in the typology (Knight, 1989). The unconfounding of these dimensions also solved the classification problems that we had encountered in our analyses of the discrepant cases in the earlier version of the typology (MTC:CM2). The fixation judgment had "good" interrater reliability ($\kappa = .67$), and the social competence decision had "excellent" reliability ($\kappa = .84$), according to Cicchetti and Sparrow's (1981) interpretive guidelines for kappa coefficients. Furthermore, subsequent analyses of the developmental antecedents of these fixation and social competence components (see Prentky *et al.*, 1989) have revealed that each is preceded by unique life experiences and adaptations, suggesting that each has traitlike temporal stability and specific developmental roots.

Axis II consists of a hierarchical series of decisions, beginning with the amount of contact with children (see Decision 1 on Axis II in Figure 2). This distinction focuses on the amount of time that an offender spends in close proximity with children. An individual is coded as high in contact if there is clear evidence that he spends time with children in multiple contexts, both sexual and nonsexual. Although spending a large amount of time in close proximity to children is often linked to high fixation on children, low contact with children can be coupled either with high or low fixation.

If an offender is coded as high in contact, a second-level decision (see Decision 2 among high-contact offenders on Axis II in Figure 2) is made between Type 1 (Interpersonal) and Type 2 (Narcissistic). This distinction is based on two criteria. First, it is determined whether there is evidence that the offender has attempted to establish interpersonal (not exclusively sexual) relationships with children. Type 1 offenders have such relationships and Type 2 lack them. Second, the sexual offenses are rated as having either a nonorgasmic aim (Type 1) or a phallic, orgasmic aim (Type 2).

For all offenders judged to be low in their contact with children, two additional distinctions are made. First, these offenders are divided into low (Types 3 and 4) and high (Types 5 and 6) physical injury groups (see Decision 2 among low-contact offenders on Axis II in Figure 2) on the basis of the evidence of the physical injury inflicted on the victim. Whereas in high physical injury cases the victim shows clear physical signs of the assault, in low-injury cases the offense is characterized either by an absence of physical injury or the presence of only such acts as pushing, slapping, holding, and threats.

Second, each of the two physical injury groups is subdivided according to the presence or absence of sadistic fantasies and/or behaviors (Decision 3 on Axis II in Figure 2). Within the low-injury group a distinction between Type 3 (Exploitative, Nonsadistic) and Type 4 (Muted Sadistic) is made on the basis of either the offender's description of his sexual fantasies or behaviors that suggest the offense is being motivated in part by sadistic fantasies (e.g., bondage, urination, spanking, or peculiar acts, etc.). Within the high-injury group the sadism distinction is made on the basis of evidence that the aggression is eroticized. For example, the presence of violent sexualized fantasies, ritualized behavior, bizarre or peculiar sexual acts, or indications that the offender was aroused by seeing that the victim was in fear or pain would all lead to a Type 6, Sadist, assignment. The absence of such evidence results in a Type 5, Nonsadistic, Aggressive, decision.

The overall reliability of classification to Axis II types ($\kappa = .56$; see Knight *et al.*, 1989) is "fair" (see Cicchetti & Sparrow, 1981), with kappas ranging from "excellent"—the amount of injury ($\kappa = .76$)—to minimally adequate—the presence of sadism for high-injury cases ($\kappa = .41$). Although the judgment of sadism among high-injury cases obviously requires some refinement, the overall reliability of Axis II represents a distinct improvement in reliability over the system's predecessor (MTC:CM2). This new system has reached a sufficient level of reliability to serve as a disconfirmable typology for child molesters.

The structural innovations introduced into Axis II have been supported both by the enhanced reliability of type assignment that has resulted and by our preliminary validity analyses of the discriminations on this axis. Our decision to make the amount of contact with children a primary, preemptive discriminator on Axis II has been supported both by the high reliability of this judgment ($\kappa = .70$) and by the theoretically meaningful differences in life-span adaptation that have been found to characterize low- and high-contact offenders (Prentky *et al.*, 1989). The differentiation of aggression into separate physical injury and sadistic components has been supported by the improved reliability this distinction has yielded (Knight *et al.*, 1989a), by the evidence that these components are statistically independent (Knight, 1989), by the fact that each has a different relation with the fixation and social competence components of Axis I (Knight, 1989), and by evidence that they each have somewhat different developmental roots (Prentky *et al.*, 1989).

In the present system each offender is assigned a separate Axis I and Axis II type. Crossing the four types of Axis I with the six types of Axis II yields 24 possible two axes combinations, which seems an excessive number of types. The complex interactions among Axis I and Axis II components (Knight, 1989) indicates, however, that our decision to set them up as separate axes was judicious. The only viable alternative, a complex nesting of some factors within others, would have required a certainty about the interrelations among Axis I and Axis II variables that we had not attained at the time the typology was revised. The precise form of the possible interrelations was either only hypothetical (e.g., the proposed independence of fixation and social competence and the interaction of fixation with the amount of contact with children) or not known (e.g., the interaction of the Axis I variables with the sadistic and injury distinctions). Thus, the only safe *a priori* stance was to create separate axes, to assign offenders independently to each, and to let our empirical studies provide feedback about which of the combination types were viable. Thus far, distribution analyses of the crossing of these axes have indicated that 11 of the 24 possible cells have been either empty or so low in frequency that for practical purposes they should be considered empty (Knight, 1989). The final decision to drop cells from the Axis I–Axis II matrix must, however, await further studies. Generalization studies may show that cells absent in the inpatient sample that we analyzed may be found in other samples (e.g., outpatient child molesters). If these cells remain empty in generalization studies, this would provide a clear, empirically based criterion for streamlining the system.

RAPIST TYPOLOGY

Although the same taxonomic program was applied to study rapists, different analyses proved to be critical for generating a new typological structure, and a distinctly different kind of organizational scheme ultimately emerged. This illustrates one of the major advantages of the programmatic approach we employed. Every emergent taxonomic structure is critically scrutinized and tested empirically. Its viability is determined by its ability to survive disconfirmation. Such an emphasis on empirical validation provides a safeguard against being blinded by theoretical biases and increases sensitivity to the structures apparent in the data.

Initially, the program for studying rapists closely paralleled that of the child molesters. As in our investigation of child molesters, we chose a preliminary rationally derived system that included those types that had been most consistently described in the clinical literature (Cohen *et al.*, 1969; see Knight *et al.*, 1985). This typology proposed four types—the Compensatory, the Impulse, the Displaced-Aggression, and the Sex-Aggression Defusion—that could hypothetically be differentiated on the basis of dichotomous judgments of the presence and absence of two motivations for rape, sex, and aggression. The Compensatory and Impulse types were hypothesized to show relatively lower aggression than the other two types, and the Impulse and Displaced-Aggression types were characterized as lower in sexual motivation.

Analyses of the interrater agreement in assigning rapists to these four types yielded unsatisfactory results, with the majority of disagreements confined to distinguishing between the Compensatory and Impulse types. A case-by-case analysis of these discrepant assignments suggested that a mixed presentation group might constitute a distinct, cohesive type. Attempts to distinguish this hybrid type led us to introduce life-style impulsivity into the system as a typological criterion and to reconceptualize the basic organization of the typology. A hierarchical, three-step decision tree structure evolved that required sequentially applied dichotomous discriminations on the meaning of the aggression employed in the offense (instrumental versus expressive; Decision 1 in Figure 3), the nature of the motivation for the sexual assaults (sexual versus either exploitative or angry; Decision 2 in Figure 3), and the relative amount and quality of impulse control in the life history of the offender (high- or low-impulsivity lifestyle; Decision 3 in Figure 3; also see Knight *et al.*, 1985; Prentky *et al.*, 1985).

Since the adoption of this revised system in 1980, we have used it to classify 201 rapists, and we have examined the reliability and validity of its types in a series of studies. In general, these studies demonstrated that this revision had adequate, but clearly not optimal, reliability, with some judgments, like the differentiation between Compensatory and Exploitative types, showing poor reliability (Prentky *et al.*, 1985). Although the validity analyses yielded some results that supported the explanatory power of aspects of this revised system (Knight & Prentky, 1987; Prentky, Burgess, & Carter, 1986; Prentky & Knight, 1986; Rosenberg *et al.*, 1988), it also revealed multiple structural and definitional deficiencies at each decision level that had to be rectified. The data clearly indicated that a second revision was needed. We will first describe the problems with this system and then summarize the process that led to an improved revision of its structure.

Problems of the Revised Rapist Typology (MTC:R2)

First Decision

The first decision of the revised system (see Figure 3) divided offenders into those who used only the amount of aggression necessary to attain victim compliance (instrumental) and those whose aggression clearly exceeded what was necessary to force compliance (expressive). Although this distinction showed a good degree of interrater reliability ($\kappa = .63$; Prentky *et al.*, 1985), it proved to be

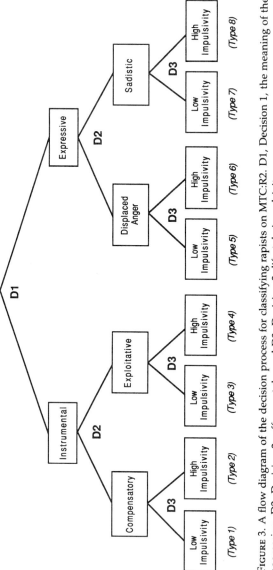

FIGURE 3. A flow diagram of the decision process for classifying rapists on MTC:R2. D1, Decision 1, the meaning of the aggression; D2, Decision 2, offense style; and D3, Decision 3, lifestyle impulsivity.

too elusive to serve the important role afforded it. In this system it functioned as a preemptive channeler of offenders into supposedly independent groups that were subsequently subdivided on the basis of subgroup-specific criteria. Because it required that clinical inferences about an internal motivational states be made on the basis of sometimes ambiguous behavioral data, it failed to attain the high level of reliability necessary for the role it was assigned. In addition, it became apparent in applying the distinction that the assumed simple dichotomization of offenders was not sufficient. For instance, we encountered offenders who did not inflict severe physical damage on their victims, but nonetheless their sexual assaults appeared to be motivated by sadistic or angry fantasies. Moreover, when victims resisted, it was difficult to determine whether any increased violence was limited to gaining compliance and lacked an expressive component (Prentky *et al.*, 1986).

The more serious problem with the instrumental–expressive distinction was, however, its validity. In a path-analytic study of its life-span correlates, the *only* component that was found related to it was alcohol abuse, which was more frequently found in expressive offenders (Rosenberg *et al.*, 1988). In six separate survival analyses looking at subsequent charges of a particular type of crime, instrumental and expressive offenders were not found to differ in their reoffense rates. Only a subgroup of expressively aggressive offenders, the Sadistic type, showed a significantly more rapid reoffense rate than other types. Because this distinction is not sufficiently reliable to function as a preemptive, primary taxonomic discriminator and does not appear to be related to important developmental antecedents and adult characteristics, its role in any new system had to be reconsidered.

Second Decision

At the second decision level (see Figure 3) instrumental offenders were subdivided into Compensatory and Exploitative types by determining whether their sexual assaults were primarily sexually or opportunistically motivated. Likewise, expressive offenders were subdivided into Displaced Anger and Sadistic types by differentiating angry and sadistic motivation. Although some theoretically appropriate discriminations among these second-level types were evident (Knight & Prentky, 1987; Rosenberg *et al.*, 1988), significant definition and discrimination problems plagued these distinctions, and there were some major disconfirmations of the characteristics that have been attributed to the types at this level in the clinical literature (e.g., Knight & Prentky, 1987; Prentky *et al.*, 1988). We will discuss those difficulties that were most critical for renovating the system.

Social competence, a neglected construct in MTC:R2, emerged in various cluster analyses as a formidable group delimiter that had to be integrated into a new system. It appeared to identify distinguishable subtypes in the Compensatory (Rosenberg & Knight, 1988), the Exploitative (Prentky *et al.*, 1988), and the Displaced Anger groups. The importance of this component should not be surprising, given its role as a critical component of treatment programs for sexual offenders (Becker, Abel, Blanchard, Murphy, & Coleman, 1978; Marshall, Earls, Segal, & Darke, 1983; Whitman & Quinsey, 1981), its contribution to the establishment and maintainance of sexual relationships (Skinner & Becker, 1985), and the discriminatory and predictive power it has shown in other areas of psychopathology (Harrow & Westermeyer, 1987; Knight, Roff, Barrnett, & Moss, 1979; Prentky, Lewine, Watt, & Fryer, 1980). It is noteworthy, however, that previous speculations about the social competence levels of various types at this level proved to be wrong (see Prentky *et al.*, 1985). In our comparative analyses we found that, contrary to hypothesis, the Compensatory offenders, and not the Displaced Anger offenders, showed the highest level of social competence as adults (Knight & Prentky, 1987).

Another deficiency at this level was that the Exploitative type failed to cohere as hypothetically predicted. Offenders assigned to this type splintered into multiple clusters (Rosenberg & Knight, 1988). A separate cluster analysis of Exploitative offenders identified three interpretable subgroups and suggested that social competence and offense impulsivity may be important for isolating more homogeneous subgroups of Exploitative offenders (Prentky *et al.*, 1988). The assignment process itself might have accounted for the heterogeneity of this type. Often offenders were assigned to the Exploitative type by default rather than by any clear match to the hypothesized motivational pattern of this type. These cases simply showed little (or questionable) evidence of expressive motivation (Decision 1) and lacked obvious sexual meaning in their offenses (Decision 2). If a new system were going to address this problem successfully, a set of clearly defined criteria would have to determine whether an offender was assigned to this type, and the default problem would have to be eliminated.

Consistent with its heterogeneity and its tendency to serve at times as a default category, the Exploitative type also had serious reliability problems. Difficulties arose in differentiating its from all other types at this level, but especially from the Compensatory type (Prentky *et al.*, 1985). Thus, the introduction of life-style impulsivity, which was intended specifically to solve the problem of discriminating Compensatory and Exploitative types (see Knight *et al.*, 1985), had failed to attain its achieved purpose.

Many of the clinical speculations about the characteristics thought to differentiate the Displaced Anger and Sadistic types were not corroborated. Only a higher propensity for acting out impulsively as adults and a faster reoffending rate significantly differentiated Sadistic from Displaced Anger types (Prentky *et al.*, 1988). Part of the poor discrimination was most likely due to the problem of reliably differentiating the two types ($\kappa = .44$; Prentky *et al.*, 1985). One factor that reduced agreement was a previously unspecified type of expressively aggressive offenders, who exhibited neither the exclusively misogynic anger of the Displaced Anger type nor the sex-aggression fusion of the Sadistic type. They seemed indiscriminately angry at everyone and inflicted considerable damage on their victims but could not be reliably placed in either expressive type. In our cluster analysis of the entire resident population at MTC, this type emerged as a cohesive cluster (Cluster 4; Rosenberg & Knight, 1988). It reappeared both in our cluster analyses of all the rapists in the resident and released samples from MTC and again in a cluster analysis of only expressively aggressive rapists. Because this type has good cohesion and its inclusion could possibly help to improve the reliability of classifying expressively aggressive offenders, it had to be considered in any revision of the typology.

Third Decision

The lifestyle impulsivity judgment, which essentially assessed the presence of a pervasive and enduring pattern of poor impulse control and irresponsible behavior, concentrated on preadolescent behaviors indicative of poor impulse control that developed into varied styles of acting out as adults (see Prentky *et al.*, 1985). It was introduced to address the problem of reliably distinguishing Exploitative and Compensatory types (see Knight *et al.*, 1985). It was crossed with the four offense styles created by the decisions at the second level, introducing high- and low-impulsivity variants of each (see Decision 3 in Figure 3).

This decision evidenced both strengths and weaknesses. Its relation to measures of antisocial behavior and criminality indicated that it tapped a valid construct. The judgment correlated with independently assessed patterns of antisocial acting out in adolescence and adulthood and was related to a higher number of rapes in adulthood (Prentky & Knight, 1986; Rosenberg *et al.*, 1988). Moreover, in a series of analyses examining the proportional probabilities of reoffense in six different crime categories for high- versus low-impulse offenders, rapists classified as high in lifestyle impulsivity reoffended earlier in three categories (Prentky, Knight, & Lee, 1989).

On the negative side, the judgment suffered from reliability problems, especially among the instrumental offender types (Prentky *et al.*, 1985). In addition, it identified as high in impulsivity too great a proportion of rapists (approximately 75%; Prentky *et al.*, 1985). Other, more conservative measures, like the DSM-III (American Psychiatric Association, 1980) Axis II Antisocial Personality Disorder and Hare's Checklist for Psychopathy (Hare, 1980), categorized fewer rapists as high in impulsivity (approximately 41%; see Knight, Fleming, Ames, Straus, & Prentky, 1989b). Most importantly, in cluster analyses this dichotomization did not prove to be an effective group delimiter (Rosenberg & Knight, 1988). Thus, lifestyle impulsivity was capturing meaningful variance, but it was not defined with sufficient stringency and clarity to attain optimal reliability and discrimination.

Additional Problems

As can be seen in Figure 3, the three dichotomous decisions of MTC:R2 yielded eight types. The sequential application of these three decisions in the order depicted also produced the relative positioning of the types that is shown at the bottom of the figure. Ideally, because these decisions supposedly tapped critical discriminating characteristics and were applied in the order of their hypothesized importance, the final positioning of types should reflect their relative similarity on a set of factors designed to capture the important dimensions of the typology (Rosenberg & Knight, 1988). That is, adjacent types should share more commonalities on these dimensions than more distant types. This, unfortunately, was not the case. Juxtaposed types often bore less resemblance to each other on these dimensions than they did to types that were relatively farther away. This additional inelegance of MTC:R2 suggested that the system was not optimally structured. In creating a new structure, we sought to remedy this problem.

The Process of Revising MTC:R2

As we indicated in the last section, our analyses of interrater discrepancies on MTC:R2, the various validity analyses we carried out on this typology, and the cluster analyses we did on our entire sample of sexual offenders suggested problems in MTC:R2 that had to be addressed if reliability and utility were to be maximized. Although some of the problems we had identified required only an increased concretization and specification of discriminating criteria, others could be implemented only with some basic structural renovations of the system.

In contrast with the child molester typology, where the analyses of discrepant cases had provided some guidance for generating efficient structural solutions (Knight, 1988), the discrepancy analyses of the rapist typology revealed problems without yielding hints about structural solutions. In retrospect, the reason for this failure appears clear. Discrepancy analyses depend on the agreed cases to provide a core of homogeneity against which the disagreed cases can be compared. The types in MTC:R2 were too heterogeneous to profit from discrepancy analyses for several reasons. First, the system failed to include important discriminators like social competence. Second, its criteria were too loosely defined. Third, two group assignments could be based primarily on the absence of a characteristic, that is, they could be made by default. Such default assignments can reduce the homogeneity of even the agreed cases in a particular type, and thus, they dilute the analyses based on these agreements. As we indicated earlier, the Exploitative type was most seriously affected by default assignments. The Sadistic–Displaced Anger distinction was also vulnerable to this default problem. The presence of obvious expressive aggression without clear evidence for sadism could yield agreement on a Displaced Anger assignment without the case being a good match to the description of the Displaced Anger type.

Although the problems with the old typology were now obvious, we lacked a model whose structure provided some guidance for incorporating the required changes and whose flexibility allowed efficient implementation of such modifications. Initially, we attempted to maintain the balanced monothetic structure of the old system. When either new discriminators or new types were incorporated into this system, however, additional types had to be introduced to retain the basic bifurcated classification structure of the system. Even the attempt to nest progressive splits within certain branches of the hierarchical structure—a solution that was successful in revising the child molester typology—did not work. Although the target problem would improve when an appropriate new dimension or type was introduced, the types added to maintain the balanced structure appeared to have little empirical or clinical reality. It became obvious that in this instance the advantages that a monothetic model provided for simplifying and clarifying class definitions, communicating the system, guiding case assignment, and testing the validity of the type discriminators were greatly outweighed by the structural burdens it imposed. The complexity of the relations among variables and among types led us to incorporate the more flexible procedures of a polythetic structure in which the overall similarity among members is assessed simultaneously on critical discriminating variables. Thus, each type is defined by a series of specific criteria, rather than by the sequential application of a few hierarchically embedded general discriminations.

Like the prototype approach of natural categorization (e.g., Cantor & Genero, 1986), the polythetic approach focuses on the identification of core types with high internal cohesion and similarity. In contrast to the monothetic approach, it emphasizes a bottom-up rather than a top-down strategy for seeking taxonomic structure (Brennan, 1987). Consequently, it introduced a major change in our perspective and led us to explore whether a better organizational structure could be generated from such a bottom-up strategy. In general, we implemented this bottom-up approach by identifying stable prototypes that emerged repeatedly in varying types of analyses, by assessing the similarities among these stable types on profiles of critical variables, and by generating and testing models that were based on the juxtaposition of similar types.

More specifically, we computed three additional cluster analyses, so that with our previous solution we had four cluster solutions. These all employed Ward's (1963) "minimum-variance" cluster method, an algorithm that has performed well in Monte Carlo studies that tested its ability to recover known structures (Edelbrock, 1979; Milligan, 1980) and has been successfully applied to another criminal population (Megargee & Bohn, 1979). More importantly, it appeared to yield meaningful clusters in our earlier study of the entire sample of sexual offenders who resided at MTC in 1981, which also included child molesters (see Rosenberg & Knight, 1988). The samples in these three additional analyses were (1) all rapists committed to MTC between 1958 and 1981, (2) a subsample of only rapists judged instrumentally aggressive by the MTC:R2 subtypers, and (3) another subsample of only rapists judged expressively aggressive. We identified those profile types that emerged in more than one of the four cluster solutions we now had. Our assumption here was that those types that had sufficient cohesion to yield clusters in multiple analyses with different subjects warranted closer scrutiny. We discerned the core characteristics of these replicable clusters by studying their cluster profiles, determining what MTC:R2 types were most frequently found in each of these clusters, examining the differences among these clusters on variables that had not been used in the cluster analyses, and rereading detailed abstracts of the criminal histories and life-span adaptations of exemplary cases of these types.

When we had isolated the stable cluster types that made empirical and clinical sense, we determined which types most closely resembled other types by examining several estimates of type similarity. First, we carefully analyzed the "dendrogram" structures of the cluster analyses. These hierarchical tree structures graphically depict the similarity levels at which all linkages among individuals and groups occur, visually representing one estimate of type similarity. Second, we compared the cluster profiles of each of the apparently stable types. Because our validity analyses had suggested that some variables might be more important than others for differentiating certain groups, we examined type differences in light of the relative importance of certain variables across types. Third, we compared the target types on variables that had not been used in the cluster analyses, so that we could determine other domains of similarity and difference among the types. By juxtaposing types that evidenced the greatest similarity across these various analyses, we generated an ordering of these types. This yielded a preliminary, testable structural model.

Next, we critically scrutinized this preliminary model and attempted to address a series of problems that originated from two sources. First, several potential difficulties about the relative similarity of certain types and the importance of particular variables in differentiating specific types had arisen during the revision process, but they had not been adequately resolved. To address these remaining questions we used the multiple group assignments of subjects and their scores on relevant variables in our data base to identify small samples of subjects who were likely to suggest tentative solutions. Second, we had examined the type assignments of offenders across MTC:R2 and the various cluster solutions in which they had been involved. Some discrepant classifications across these typologies posed apparent predicaments for the new model. For example, three of our cluster analyses (those involving all currently committed sexual offenders, all rapists ever committed to MTC, and only expressively aggressive rapists) yielded clusters that we had identified as a Pervasively Angry type. However, in examining the two cluster solutions that had a substantial overlap in subjects (the expressively aggressive rapist and the all-rapist solutions), we found that a number of rapists who were assigned to the Pervasively Angry cluster in the analysis of the expressively aggressive rapists migrated to a new, separate cluster in the all-rapist solution. This new split-off cluster differed from the profile of the Pervasively Angry clusters only in its lower level of life management. In the all-rapist analysis it was very close in its cluster similarity index to the Overt Sadistic cluster, differing from the sadists only in its greater impulsivity in sexual assaults. Thus, these data posed the problem of whether this new cluster was low life management skills, a Pervasively Angry cluster, or a Sadistic cluster with high Offense Impulsivity. Resolving such a problem was critical to determining the criteria for inclusion in the Pervasively Angry and Overt Sadistic types.

These two sources of problems yielded 10 focused questions similar to the example just described. To answer these questions we identified through our data base 60 cases whose scores on critical variables and assignments in multiple typological solutions indicated they were central to particular questions. Clinicians who had previously been trained to apply MTC:R2 typing criteria then read the clinical files of these selected cases. They were given specific questions to answer about each of the cases they read, but they were unaware of how these cases had been typed previously, into what groups these offenders had been clustered, or how their answers to the specific questions would impact on the new system. The answers provided to these questions were then combined with both the individual profiles of these selected offenders and information about all their group classifications and were used as the basis for solving the critical problems. The model was then adjusted slightly to reflect these resolutions. Finally, offenders who would hypothetically be core members of the types in the new system were identified as aids in concretizing the criteria for group assignments.

The structure of the new system is depicted in Figure 4. Space limitations prohibit a full explication of this new system, but we will summarize its structure and the types it comprises, illustrate how particular aspects of the generation process contributed to a couple of its prominent structural components, and describe briefly how this revision has incorporated solutions to the problems of MTC:R2 that we enumerated earlier.

MTC:R3—The Revised Rapist Typology

As can be seen in Figure 4, MTC:R3 includes nine types. They are arranged in this chart so that each type juxtaposes the types that are most similar to it in profiles on critical variables (unsocial behavior, sexualized aggression, offense impulsivity, and substance abuse). In all instances except the opportunistically motivated types, high and low social competence variants of a type naturally fell out of the various analyses in close proximity, and thus they were juxtaposed. Each of the Opportunistic types was closely linked in the dendrogram of the all-rapist cluster analysis with one of the two social competence variants of the Pervasively Angry type that we discussed earlier. Because we found that life management (i.e., employment and interpersonal competence) differences among Pervasively Angry offenders simply reflected how early their anger got them incarcerated, and did not indicate basic typological differences, we amalga-

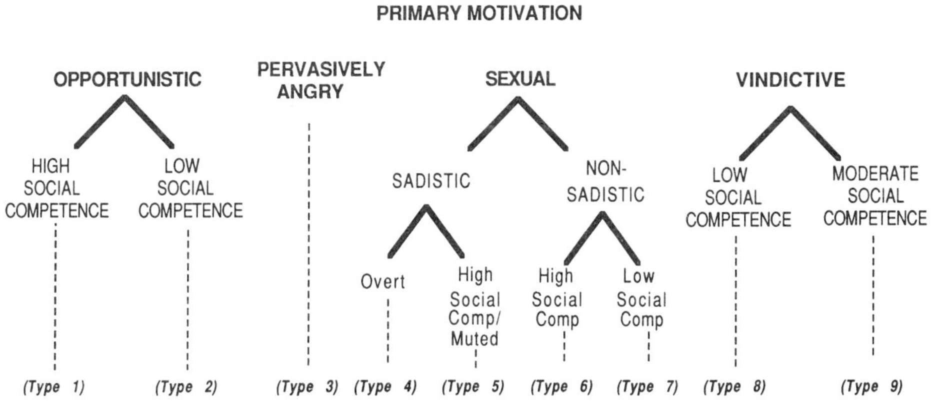

FIGURE 4. Relative similarity positioning and hierarchical organization of the polythetic rapist types in MTC:R3.

mated the high and low social competence variants of this type. Consequently, the High and Low Social Competence Opportunistic types fit best in the model in the locations they currently occupy, because they both juxtapose the Pervasively Angry type they most closely resemble.

The four descriptive summary categories that appear at the top of the system identify some of the more salient features that are shared by groups of adjacent types. These categories describe four motivations for rape—opportunity, pervasive anger, sexual gratification, and vindictiveness. In this system each motivation is distinctively more characteristic of the types subsumed in that category than it is of the types in the other categories. These four differentiating motivational components appear to be related to enduring behavioral patterns that distinguish particular groups of offenders. Because they are discriminating characteristics, each motivational component is represented in the diagnostic criteria that define the types. Their prominence as summary components is not meant to imply, however, that they serve as preliminary distinctions in a series of contingent, hierarchically embedded decisions. Rather, assignment of a case to a type is determined by judging individual offenders on the sets of specific criteria that define each type.

For the Opportunistic types the sexual assault appears to be an impulsive, typically unplanned, predatory act, controlled more by contextual and immediately antecedent factors than by any obvious protracted or stylized sexual fantasy. The sexual assault for these individuals appears to be simply one among many instances of poor impulse control, as evidenced by their extensive history of unsocialized behavior in multiple domains. In their assaults they show no evidence of gratuitous force or aggression and exhibit little anger except in response to victim resistance. Their behavior suggests that they are seeking immediate sexual gratification and are willing to use whatever force is necessary to achieve their goal. They seem to be indifferent to the welfare and comfort of the victim. When they happen to know their victims, which appears from the preliminary analysis of cases we described earlier to be more common in the High Social Competence type, they use the relationship to gratify their immediate needs, with little concern about how this will affect the woman.

The primary motivation in the assaults of Pervasively Angry offenders appears to be undifferentiated anger. Their aggression is gratuitous and occurs in the absence of victim resistance, but it might also be exacerbated by such resistance. They often inflict serious physical injury on their victims, up to and including death. Although they sexually assault their female victims, their rage does not appear to be sexualized, and there is no evidence that their assaults are driven by preexisting fantasies. Moreover, their anger is also not limited to women. It is directed toward men with equal vehemence. An extreme problem controlling aggression is only one area in which this type of offender manifests impulsivity difficulties. From childhood and adolescence through adulthood these rapists' histories are marked with difficulties controlling their impulses in many domains of their adaptation.

The four rapist types whose motivation is characterized as "sexual" have in common the presence of either protracted sexual or sadistic fantasies or preoccupations that motivate their sexual assaults and influence the way in which their offenses are executed. Thus, for all these types some form of enduring sexual preoccupation, however distorted by fusion with aggression, dominance needs, coercion, and felt inadequacies, is a cardinal feature of their sexual assaults. As can be seen in Figure 4, within the Sexual types, two major subgroups can be distinguished on the basis of the presence or absence of sadistic fantasies or behaviors—the Sadistic and Nonsadistic groups. The former group comprises Overt and Muted Sadistic types, and the latter group includes High and Low Social Competence types.

Both of the Sadistic types show evidence of poor differentiation between sexual and aggressive drives and a frequent occurrence of erotic and destructive thoughts and fantasies. For the Overt Sadistic type the aggression is manifested directly in physically damaging behavior in their sexual assaults. For the Muted Sadistic type the aggression is expressed either symbolically or through covert fantasy that is not acted out behaviorally. Thus far in our preliminary analyses of our sample, this overt–muted distinction has correlated highly with social competence, the former type being low and the latter high. Because sadism is such an important construct in sexual aggression, we have decided not to use social competence as a diagnostic criterion to distinguish these types. Rather, we have defined these types solely on the basis of their sexual and aggressive behavior, allowing empirical analyses to corroborate what appear to be strong correlates with associated features. The Overt Sadistic offenders appear to be angry, belligerent rapists, who, except for their sadism and the greater planning of their sexual assaults, look very similar to the Pervasively Angry types. The Muted Sadistic types, except for their sadistic fantasies and their slightly higher lifestyle impulsivity, resemble the High Social Competence, Nonsadistic types, who are located alongside them in Figure 4.

For the Nonsadistic Sexual types, the sexual fantasies that are associated with their sexual assaults are devoid of the synergistic relation of sex and aggression that characterizes the Sadistic types. Indeed, the two offender types that are subsumed in this group are hypothesized to manifest *less* interpersonal aggression in *both* sexual and nonsexual contexts than any of the other rapist types. If confronted with victim resistance, these offenders may flee rather than fight. Their fantasies and assault behaviors are hypothesized to reflect an amalgam of sexual arousal, distorted "male" cognitions about women and sex, and feelings of inadequacy about their sexuality and masculine self-image.

The final motivational grouping, the Vindictive types, manifest a behavioral pattern that suggests that women are a central and exclusive focus of their anger. Their sexual assaults are marked by behaviors that are physically harming and appear to be intended to degrade and humiliate their victims. The rage evident in these assaults runs the gamut from verbal abuse to brutal murder. Yet, unlike the Pervasively Angry types, they show little or no evidence of undifferentiated anger (e.g., instigating fights with or assaulting men). Although there is a sexual component in their assaults, there is no evidence that their aggression is eroticized, as it is for the Sadistic types, and no evidence that they are preoccupied with sadistic fantasies. Moreover, like the Nonsadistic

Sexual types, they differ from both the Pervasively Angry and Overt Sadistic types in their relatively lower level of lifestyle impulsivity.

MTC:R3—The Generation of Prominent Structural Features

The current rapist typology is the product of a complex interplay of deductive and inductive strategies of typology construction. Theoretical notions infused and guided to a greater or lesser extent the implementation of both strategies and were obviously influential in our attempts to integrate the results of both strategies. The cornerstone of the program has been, however, its responsiveness to empirical feedback. In the case of the rapist typology, the data indicated the significant structural and definitional problems of the earlier rapist systems. Moreover, when our attempts to generate top-down solutions to these problems failed, more data-driven inductive manipulations suggested a taxonomic structure that allowed efficient solutions to the difficulties of the previous system. A brief summary of some of the results of our empirical analyses illustrates how some critical anchors of the present system evolved.

As we indicated earlier, a major source for developing the new taxonomic structure was the dendrogram depictions of our cluster analyses. For instance, these analyses clearly showed the close similarity between the Nonsadistic Sexual and Vindictive types (Types 6 to 9 in Figure 4). Indeed, in the all-rapist cluster analysis the Low Social Competence variants of these two groups were not distinguished. Their cluster profiles differed only in the amount of aggression in their assaults. Both of these types are low substance abusing, low lifestyle impulsivity, socially isolated, inadequate males. The Sexual type appears to be preoccupied with sexual difficulties, and his rapes are hypothesized to constitute a distorted attempt to establish the sexual relationship he desires but is unable to attain. The Low Social Competence Vindictive type apparently responds to similar circumstances by becoming angry and punitive toward women and expressing his rage in his sexual assault.

The dendrograms and profile analyses also showed the close proximity of the Pervasively Angry and Overt Sadistic types to each other and the greater similarity of these two types to the Opportunistic than to the Vindictive types. Thus, the high lifestyle impulsivity, high unsocialized aggression, more antisocial types (Types 1 to 4 in Figure 4) naturally fell together, and those lacking these features (Types 6 to 9 in Figure 4) also clustered together. The Muted Sadistic type, which had the highest variance of all types on unsocial aggression, fell in between the Sadistic and the High Social Competence Nonsadistic types, sharing features of each.

These empirical anchors indicate how the structure of the MTC:R3 emerged. Integrating these and other results yielded a similarity-based ordering of replicable types. The types within this ordered set could then easily be grouped into the motivational groups depicted in Figure 4. It is noteworthy that although this system was generated from a bottom-up structuring of similar types, a hierarchical organization of types in terms of motivational components naturally emerged. The structure is not only data driven, but it also makes theoretical sense. Moreover, it incorporates, albeit in a somewhat transformed and more narrowly defined state, versions of the types frequently observed and described by clinicians. Finally, the structure suggests multiple, theoretically meaningful ways of collapsing types for validity analyses (e.g., by motivational groupings, by social competence level, by lifestyle impulsivity; Types 1 to 4 *vs.* Types 6 to 9 in Figure 4).

MTC:R3—Solving the Problems of MTC:R2

The structure of the revised typology not only corrected the inelegance of the relative positioning of the types in MTC:R2, it also provided a flexible framework that either solved or could efficiently accept solutions to the major difficulties we had identified in our analyses of MTC:R2. Consequently, this new system addressed all the major difficulties of its predecessor. First, the instrumental–expressive aggression distinction is no longer a preemptory, preliminary discriminator. It has been more precisely and concretely operationalized and has been assigned the more appropriate function of serving as one among many specific diagnostic criteria for individual types. Second, social competence has been afforded a major role as a typological definer in accord with the results of our cluster analyses. It has been operationalized with concrete criteria that were generated on a sample of rapists. Third, the heterogeneous Exploitative types have been replaced by two more tightly defined Opportunistic types. Assignment to these two new types cannot occur by default, as frequently was the case with the Exploitative types. Rather, the offender must now reach a set of clearly defined behavioral criteria to be classified Opportunistic. Fourth, the problems of reliably differentiating Displaced Anger from Sadistic types have been addressed by three changes: (1) we introduced two new types (the Pervasively Angry and the Muted Sadistic) to accommodate expressively aggressive offenders who did not match the characteristics of either the Displaced Anger or Sadistic and thus created assignment inconsistencies; (2) we more clearly delineated the criteria for sadism; and (3) we replaced the Displaced Anger types with more tightly and narrowly defined Vindictive types, that include only offenders with low lifestyle impulsivity and no longer require the inherently problematic diagnostic criterion of "displacement." Fifth, lifestyle impulsivity has been divided into adolescent and adult components, more stringently defined by concrete behaviors, and is now applied only to differentiating specific types.

Thus, the major problems that we encountered in our discrepancy and validity analyses of MTC:R2 have been solved without proliferating empty types or creating an unwieldy system. The polythetic format of the present system has provided a more flexible structure that permits greater specificity and individualization of criteria. Consequently, the criteria for case assignment in the revised system are far better anchored than those of its predecessor, and thus this typology should yield higher reliability. In addition, the introduction of the High Social Competence variants of the Opportunistic, Muted Sadistic, and Nonsadistic Sexual types may provide a practical and theoretical bridge for applying the system to noninstitutionalized rapist samples.

Conclusions

Our application of a programmatic approach to typology construction and validation has produced taxonomic systems for both child molesters and rapists. The former has already demonstrated reasonable reliability and consistent ties to distinctive developmental antecedents. In addition, preliminary results of a 25-year recidivism study of child molesters that we are just completing indicate that aspects of the model have important prognostic implications. In contrast, our recently refined typological model for rapists remains untested. It was fashioned in a data-driven manner, aimed both at retaining its predecessor's empirically validated pockets of strength and at remedying the earlier system's reliability, homogeneity, and validity problems. To the degree that it has achieved these goals, it should prove to be a useful and reliable system for classifying rapists.

The typological structures that our program has thus far produced provide a clear answer to the query posed earlier in this chapter about what should be the appropriate level of taxonomic abstraction for sexual offenders. The data we have presented on the child molester typology strongly support the subdivision of these offenders and indicate that considerable explanatory power (and it appears from our ongoing analyses—predictive power) will be sacrificed if child molesters are considered a homogeneous group. For rapists further subdivision also appears warranted. Although MTC:R2 does not appear to have cut this population at its hinges, its groups still managed to capture sufficient taxonomic invariance to suggest that a more cohesive structuring of these offenders was possible. We hope that our revised typology has adequately incorporated the consistencies we have observed among rapist subgroups and will prove more efficacious than its predecessor, but this system requires validation. Thus, although it appears that subdividing rapists will ultimately be fruitful, a definite answer to the level of taxonomic abstraction question awaits further data.

Our attempts at uncovering taxonomic structures for sexual offenders is an example of a general move in taxonomic research on criminals toward creating more particularized systems within relatively circumscribed behavioral domains (Brennan, 1987). Because of the greater precision and homogeneity that can be achieved within narrower populations, the potential for success is increased. The disadvantages of such an approach are that types that cohere across behavioral domains might be missed, and interrelating various systems that have been created within limited domains may prove difficult. This is, of course, another side of the problem of determining at what level of abstraction taxonomic distinctions should be made. To overcome the parochialism that might result from a narrowness of focus, we have begun to relate our typologies to other extant systems appropriate for sexual offenders. Such a broadening of scope is most profitably undertaken only after some clarity of taxonomic structure has emerged at the narrower level.

The data that we have presented illustrate the importance of applying both deductive and inductive strategies simultaneously. Each approach has its inherent strengths and weaknesses (Brennan, 1987; Meehl, 1979; Skinner & Blashfield, 1982). When applied concurrently, the two approaches provide complementary methods with reciprocal benefits. The results of each can enrich the interpretation of the other and generate new research questions. Differences in structures, when they arise, can often lead to important advances in understanding, and convergences across methods help to highlight prepotent structures. Indeed, the comparison of multiple solutions generated from different sources enhances falsifiability. The failure of a particular model to work in an area where another is successful makes us more likely to discard the unsuccessful model. If we know only that one model has not worked, we are likely to attribute its poor showing to auxiliary theory problems or experimental particular, especially if our theoretical biases have been disconfirmed (Meehl, 1978). Because different systems often share auxiliary theories, the presence of a successful structure undercuts the saving explanations for the failure of the alternative structure and thereby increases falsifiability, which is, of course, the lifeblood of science (Popper, 1972).

Although the same programmatic approach was applied to both the child molesters and rapists, very different kinds of analyses were ultimately critical in revealing important structures. For the child molesters the statistical analyses of discrepant case assignments not only helped us to identify the source of reliability problems, but they also suggested structural changes that assisted in revising the system. For the rapists the discrepancy analyses highlighted problems, but a complex comparison of multiple typological solutions was necessary to generate a structure that could accommodate the required changes. Thus, in such a bootstrapping operation it is important to keep in mind that there are no set paths to solutions. One has to generate and test multiple structural variations and keep a constant eye on the empirical feedback for emergent, consistent patterns.

ACKNOWLEDGMENTS. Preparation of this chapter was supported by the National Institute of Mental Health (MH 32309), the National Institute of Justice (82-IJ-CX-0058), and the Commonwealth of Massachusetts. We wish to thank Ruth Rosenberg and Judith Sims-Knight for their helpful comments on an earlier version of this chapter.

REFERENCES

American Psychiatric Association. (1980). *Diagnostic and statistical manual of mental disorders* (3rd ed.). Washington, DC: Author.

American Psychiatric Association. (1987). *Diagnostic and statistical manual of mental disorders* (3rd ed., revised). Washington, DC: Author.

Becker, J. V., Abel, G. G., Blanchard, E. B., Murphy, W. D., & Coleman, E. (1978). Evaluating social skills of sexual aggressives. *Criminal Justice and Behavior, 5,* 357–367.

Blashfield, R. K. (1980). Propositions regarding the use of cluster analysis in clinical research. *Journal of Consulting and Clinical Psychology, 48,* 456–459.

Brennan, T. (1987). Classification: An overview of selected methodological issues. In D. M. Gottfredson & M. Tonry (Eds.). *Prediction and classification: Criminal justice decision making* (pp. 201–248). Chicago: The University of Chicago Press.

Brownmiller, S. (1975). *Against our will.* New York: Bantam Books.

Campbell, D. T., & Fiske, D. W. (1959). Convergent and discriminate validation by the multitrait–multimethod matrix. *Psychological Bulletin, 56,* 81–105.

Cantor, N., & Genero, N. (1986). Psychiatric diagnosis and natural categorization: A close analogy. In T. Millon & G. L. Klerman (Eds.), *Contemporary directions in psychopathology: Toward the DSM-IV* (pp. 233–256). New York: The Guilford Press.

Cicchetti, D. V., & Sparrow, S. S. (1981). Developing criteria for establishing interrater reliability of specific items: Applications of assessment of adaptive behavior. *American Journal of Mental Deficiency, 86,* 127–137.

Cohen, M. L., Seghorn, T., & Calmas, W. (1969). Sociometric study of sex offenders. *Journal of Abnormal Psychology, 74,* 249–255.

Cohen, M. L., Garofalo, R. F., Boucher, R., & Seghorn, T. (1971). The psychology of rapists. *Seminars in Psychiatry, 3,* 307–327.

Cronbach, L. J., & Meehl, P. E. (1955). Construct validity in psychological tests. *Psychological Bulletin, 52,* 281–302.

Edelbrock, C. (1979). Mixture model tests of hierarchical clustering: The problem of classifying everybody. *Multivariate Behavior Research, 14,* 367–384.

Fitch, J. H. (1962). Men convicted of sexual offenses against children: A descriptive follow-up study. *British Journal of Criminology, 3*(1), 18–37.

Friedman, H. P., & Rubin, J. (1968). Logic of statistical procedures. In R. R. Grinker (Ed.), *The borderline syndrome* (pp. 53–72). New York: Basic Books.

Gebhard, P. H., Gagnon, J. H., Pomeroy, W. B., & Christenson, C. V. (1965). *Sex offenders: An analysis of types.* New York: Harper & Row.

Ghiselin, M. T. (1981). Categories, life, and thinking. *The Behavioral and Brain Sciences, 4,* 269–313.

Groth, A. N., & Birnbaum, H. J. (1979). *Men who rape.* New York: Plenum.

Hare, R. D. (1980). A research scale for the assessment of psychopathy in criminal populations. *Personality and Individual Differences, 1,* 111–119.

Harrow, M., & Westermeyer, J. F. (1987). Process-reactive dimension and outcome for narrow concepts of schizophrenia. *Schizophrenia Bulletin, 13,* 361–368.

Hempel, C. G. (1965). *Aspects of scientific explanation.* New York: Free Press.

Knight, R. A. (1988). A taxonomic analysis of child molesters. In R. A. Prentky & V. Quinsey (Eds.), *Human sexual aggression: Current perspectives* (Vol. 528, 2–20). New York: New York Academy of Sciences.

Knight, R. A. (1989). An assessment of the concurrent validity of a child molester typology. *Journal of Interpersonal Violence, 4,* 131–150.

Knight, R. A., & Prentky, R. A. (1987). The developmental antecedents and adult adaptations of rapist subtypes. *Criminal Justice and Behavior, 14,* 403–426.

Knight, R. A., & Roff, J. D. (1985). Affectivity in schizophrenia. In M. Alpert (Ed.), *Controversies in schizophrenia* (pp. 280–316). New York: The Guilford Press.

Knight, R. A., Roff, J. D., Barrnett, J., & Moss, J. (1979). The concurrent and predictive validity of thought disorder and affectivity: A 22-year follow-up of acute schizophrenics. *Journal of Abnormal Psychology, 88,* 1–12.

Knight, R. A., Rosenberg, R., & Schneider, B. (1985). Classification of sexual offenders: Perspectives, methods and validation. IN A. Burgess (Ed.), *Rape and sexual assault: A research handbook.* (pp. 222–293). New York: Garland Publishing.

Knight, R. A., Carter, D. L., & Prentky, R. A. (1989a). A system for the classification of child molesters. Reliability and application. *Journal of Interpersonal Violence, 4,* 3–23.

Knight, R. A., Fleming, R., Ames, A., Straus, H., & Prentky, R. A. (1989b). *Antisocial personality disorder and Hare assessments of psychopathy among sexual offenders.* Manuscript in preparation.

Marshall, W. L., Earls, C. M., Segal, Z., & Darke, J. (1983). A behavioral program for the assessment and treatment of sexual aggressors. In K. Craig & R. McMahon (Eds.), *Advances in clinical behavior therapy* (pp. 148–174). New York: Brunner/Mazel.

McCaghy, C. H. (1967). *Child molesters: A study of their careers as deviants.* New York: Holt, Rinehart & Winston.

Meehl, P. E. (1957). When shall we use our heads instead of the formula? *Journal of Counseling Psychology, 4,* 268–273.

Meehl, P. E. (1959). Some ruminations on the validation of clinical procedures. *Canadian Journal of Psychology*, 13, 102–128.
Meehl, P. E. (1978). Theoretical risks and asterisks: Sir Karl, Sir Ronald, and the slow progress of psychology. *Journal of Consulting and Clinical Psychology*, 46, 806–834.
Meehl, P. E. (1979). A funny thing happened on the way to the latent entities. *Journal of Personality Assessment*, 43, 564–581.
Megargee, E. I., & Bohn, M. J. (1979). *Classifying criminal offenders*. Beverly Hills, CA: Sage Publications.
Milligan, G. W. (1980). An examination of the effect of six types of error peturbation on fifteen clustering alogorithms. *Psychometrika*, 45, 325–341.
Monahan, J. (1981). *The clinical prediction of violent behavior*, Rockville, MD: National Institute of Mental Health.
Pomerantz, J. R. (1986). Visual form perception: An overview. In E. Schab & H. Nusbaum (Eds.), *Pattern recognition by humans and machines: Visual perception (Vol. 2)* (pp. 1–30). New York: Academic Press.
Popper, K. R. (1972). *The logic of scientific discovery*. London: Hutchinson.
Prentky, R. A., & Knight, R. A. (1986). Impulsivity in the lifestyle and criminal behavior of sexual offenders. *Criminal Justice and Behavior*, 13, 141–164.
Prentky, R. A., Lewine, R. R. J., Watt, N. F., & Fryer, J. H. (1980). A longitudinal study of psychiatric outcome, developmental variables vs. psychiatric symptoms. *Schizophrenia Bulletin*, 6, 139–147.
Prentky, R. A., Cohen, M. L., & Seghorn, T. K. (1985). Development of a rational taxonomy for the classification of sexual offenders: Rapists. *Bulletin of the American Academy of Psychiatry and the Law*, 13, 39–70.
Prentky, R. A., Burgess, A. W., & Carter, D. L. (1986). Victim responses by rapist type: An empirical and clinical analysis. *Journal of Interpersonal Violence*, 1, 73–98.
Prentky, R. A., Knight, R. A., & Rosenberg, R. (1988). Validation analyses on the MTC Taxonomy for Rapists: Disconfirmation and reconceptualization. In R. A. Prentky & V. Quinsey (Eds.), *Human sexual aggression: Current perspectives* (Vol. 528, pp. 21–40). New York: The New York Academy of Sciences.
Prentky, R. A., Knight, R. A., Rosenberg, R., & Lee, A. (1989). A path analytic approach to the validation of a taxonomic system for classifying child molesters. *Journal of Quantitative Criminology* 5, 231–257.
Prentky, R. A., Knight, R. A., & Lee, A. (1989). *A twenty-five follow-up of sex offenders discharged from the Massachusetts Treatment Center*. Manuscript in preparation.
Rosch, E., & Lloyd, B. B. (1978). *Cognition and categorization*. New York: John Wiley & Sons.
Rosenberg, R., & Knight, R. A. (1988). Determining male sexual offender subtypes using cluster analysis. *Journal of Quantitative Criminology*, 4, 383–410.
Rosenberg, R., Knight, R. A., Prentky, R. A., & Lee, A. (1988). Validating the components of a taxonomic system for rapists: A path analytic approach. *Bulletin of the American Academy of Psychiatry and the Law*, 16, 169–185.
Scully, D., & Marolla, J. (1985). Rape and vocabularies of motives: Alternative perspectives. In A. Burgess (Ed.), *Rape and sexual assault: A research handbook* (pp. 294–312). New York: Garland Publishing.
Seghorn, T. K. (1971). Adequacy of ego functioning in rapists and pedophiles (Doctoral dissertation, Boston University Graduate School, 1970). *Dissertation Abstracts International*, 31, 7613A–7614A. (University Microfilms No. 70-22, 413).
Seghorn, T., & Cohen, M. (1980). The psychology of the rape assailant. In W. Cerran, A. L. McGarry, & C. Petty (Eds.), *Modern legal medicine, psychiatry, and forensic science* (pp. 533–551). Philadelphia: F. A. Davis.
Skinner, H. A. (1981). Toward the integration of classification theory and methods. *Journal of Abnormal Psychology*, 90, 68–87.
Skinner, H. A. (1986). Construct validation approach to psychiatric classification. In T. Millon & G. L. Klerman (Eds.). *Contemporary directions in psychopathology: Toward the DSM-IV* (pp. 307–330). New York: The Guilford Press.

Skinner, H. A., & Blashfield, R. K. (1982). Increasing the impact of cluster analysis research: The case of psychiatric classification. *Journal of Consulting and Clinical Psychology, 50,* 727–735.

Skinner, L. J., & Becker, J. V. (1985). Sexual dysfunction and deviations. In M. Hersen & S. M. Turner (Eds.), *Diagnostic Interviews* (pp. 205–242). New York: Plenum.

Treisman, A. (1986). Features and objects in visual processing. *Scientific American, 255,* 114b–125.

Ward, J. H. (1963). Hierarchical grouping to optimize an objective function. *Journal of the American Statistical Association, 58,* 236–244.

Whitman, W. P., & Quinsey, V. L. (1981). Heterosocial skill training for institutionalized rapists and child molesters. *Canadian Journal of Behavioral Science, 13,* 105–114.

II

Factors Influencing Sexual Assault

4

Sexual Aggression
Achieving Power through Humiliation

JULIET L. DARKE

In recent years a shift in the focus of both theoretical and research issues concerning sexual violence has been observed in the scientific community. This changed emphasis can be linked to the resurgence of the feminist movement and to the early writings of women such as Brownmiller (1975) who forced us to view rape in cultural, political, and historical contexts. With the benefit of a sociopolitical framework, a growing awareness of the nonsexual needs served by sexual assault and a redefinition of sexual assault as an assaultive act with sexual components have been evident.

Although previously considered essentially sexual in nature, sexually violent behavior is presently thought to be primarily motivated by the desire for power and control (Brownmiller, 1975; Clark & Lewis, 1977; Groth & Burgess, 1977a). This view is reflected in the literature dealing with both offender (Groth, 1979) and control populations (Donnerstein, 1980; Malamuth, Haber, & Feshbach, 1980). In addition, feminist scholars have emphasized the commonalities among various forms of sexual aggression, previously viewed as distinct phenomena and have immutably linked the sexual abuse of children with the sexual abuse of women (e.g., Dworkin, 1979; Rush, 1980; Russell, 1984; Stanko, 1985). The following examination of power and humiliation in sexual aggression will primarily focus on sexual aggression against women. Although the discussion is applicable to the sexual abuse of children, space considerations will limit my comments on men who sexually aggress against children.

SEXUAL GRATIFICATION AS A PRIMARY MOTIVATION

It is not surprising that initial controlled investigations of sexually aggressive behavior emphasized the sexual elements of those acts. This emphasis

JULIET L. DARKE • Correctional Service Canada, Prison for Women, Kingston, Ontario K7L 4W7, Canada.

has relevance for the assessment and treatment of offenders; however, the limitations of this direction are becoming clear, and the theoretical significance of deviant arousal warrants close scrutiny. Although identified aggressors have been distinguished from control subjects on the basis of their sexual arousal profiles (Abel, Barlow, Blanchard, & Guild, 1977; Barbaree, Marshall, & Lanthier, 1979; Earls & Proulx, 1987; Quinsey & Chaplin, 1984; Quinsey, Chaplin, & Varney, 1981), differentiation is sometimes achieved with difficulty, or not at all. A high degree of variability characterizes both offender and control data, and deviant arousal is neither inevitable in, nor limited to, incarcerated rapists. Evidence of equivalent arousal by control subjects to rape and nonrape depictions (Seidman, 1985) and lower arousal to rape than to consenting sex stimuli by rapist samples are available (Baxter, Marshall, Barbaree, Davidson, & Malcolm, 1984; Baxter, Barbaree, & Marshall, 1986). Some control subjects in most experiments are equally aroused by rape and consenting sex stimuli (Abel, Blanchard, Becker, & Djenderedjian, 1978; Baxter et al., 1986; Blader, 1983; Christie, 1985); and the absolute levels of arousal to rape produced by control subjects are quite high in some studies, even if lower than arousal to consenting themes (e.g., Malamuth, 1981; Murphy, Haynes, Coleman, & Flanagan, 1985). Careful stimulus construction is often required to obtain differential responding by rapist and control subjects. Quinsey, Chaplin and Upfold (1984), for example, suggest that even some nonconsenting bondage scenarios are "simply not cruel enough" to produce differentiation (p. 657). Overall, these reports suggest that a large proportion of incarcerated rapists and a considerable segment of the general male population are aroused to both rape and nonrape pornography.

It is also significant that the erectile responses of college males are easily disinhibited in the laboratory; that is, "normal" heterosexual males produce deviant arousal profiles when they have ingested alcohol (Barbaree, Marshall, Yates, & Lightfoot, 1983), when they believe that they have ingested alcohol (Briddell, Rimm, Caddy, Kravitz, Sholis, & Wunderlin, 1978), when given permissive instructions (Quinsey et al., 1981), or when angered prior to physiological assessment (Yates, Barbaree, & Marshall, 1984). Rape descriptions which portray the victim as becoming sexually aroused by the assault also disinhibit college males' sexual arousal (Darke, 1986; Malamuth & Check, 1980a,b; Malamuth, Heim, & Feshbach, 1980).

It appears, then, that aggressive cues do not always enhance the sexual arousal of rapists; yet neither do they always inhibit the sexual arousal of normal males under a variety of conditions. In fact, it is becoming increasingly difficult to identify the factors which readily differentiate men who rape from those who do not.

Methodological considerations also raise questions concerning the utility of an approach which emphasizes sexual arousal. Although genital measures of sexual arousal are less susceptible to voluntary distortion than are verbal reports, penile tumescence is not simply a reflexive response. In control subjects and a variety of sex offenders, erectile increases and decreases to sexual stimuli have been produced in accordance with experimenter instructions to inhibit or enhance sexual arousal (Abel, Barlow, Blanchard, & Mavissakalian, 1975; Henson & Rubin, 1971; Laws & Rubin, 1969; Quinsey & Bergersen, 1976; Quinsey &

Carrigan, 1978; Wydra, Marshall, Earls, & Barbaree, 1983). Thus, concern with faking erectile responses is justified, particularly since incarcerated rapists are able to recognize those behaviors which are socially inappropriate, and which define sexual assault, just as ably as are control subjects (Wydra *et al.*, 1983).

In summary, sexual arousal to aggressive sexual stimuli does not appear to be an exclusive, or essential, characteristic of identified sexual aggressors. Neither does lack of access to a consenting sexual partner appear to be a relevant factor in sexual aggression, as the majority of convicted offenders are involved in consenting sexual relationships at the time of their assaults (Groth & Burgess, 1977a). Although earlier reports implicated social skills deficits in sexual aggression (e.g., Abel, Blanchard, & Becker, 1978), more recent research reveals that neither generalized social nor heterosocial skills deficits characterize identified rapists, although findings are more equivocal for men who sexually abuse children (Segal & Marshall, 1985; Stermac & Quinsey, 1986). These variables are closely linked to socioeconomic factors but not to the nature of criminal charges. Offenders evidence a surprisingly high incidence of sexual dysfunction during their assaults (Clark & Lewis, 1977; Groth & Burgess, 1977b), and sexual satisfaction derived from rape is typically reported by only a small percentage of offenders, who are usually described as sadistic rapists (Groth, 1979).

While the use of force in excess of that required to subdue a victim has been noted by a variety of researchers (Amir, 1971; Christie, Marshall, & Lanthier, 1979; Groth & Burgess, 1977a; Quinsey *et al.*, 1981), such aggression does not necessarily serve to increase the sexual arousal of rapists (Quinsey *et al.*, 1981). However, the failure to obtain sexual arousal to depictions of nonsexual assault does not, as implied by Quinsey *et al.*, invalidate the roles which anger, control, and domination may serve in rape. Instead it suggests that violence is not perpetrated for the purpose of increasing sexual arousal. This finding is consistent with earlier data indicating that aggressive cues do not increase arousal; rather, aggression fails to inhibit arousal in those rapists with deviant arousal profiles (Barbaree *et al.*, 1979).

Nevertheless, with rapist samples for which deviant arousal was evident, the degree of deviant arousal was demonstrated to be a function of the frequency of offenses and the amount of violence used in the commission of offenses (Abel *et al.*, 1977; Abel, Blanchard, Becker, & Djenderedjian, 1978). These data suggest that deviant arousal may characterize the most habitual and violent rapists. However, when deviant arousal was not evident (i.e., when responses to consenting sex were greater than responses to rape), a significant correlation was not obtained between arousal to rape and either chronicity or the degree of violence used in offenses (Baxter *et al.*, 1986), although chronicity was associated with the degree of violence in the most recent assault. Therefore, some relationship between laboratory-assessed arousal to sexual violence and the perpetration of sexual assault does appear to exist in some identified offenders; although, as a whole, the data strongly suggest that sexual motivation is not primary in sexual aggression.

If, however, sexuality is viewed as the means through which alternate aims are achieved (e.g., exercising power and control), then the mixed reports from laboratory assessments are understandable. Such a perspective is not incompatible with sexual arousal assessments in the evaluation and treatment of offenders, or with sexual arousal research which may elucidate the mechanisms operating in the erotization of cues associated with more primary motivations.

POWER AND HUMILIATION

A number of researchers have been readdressing the issues of power, domination, and hostility in rape. For example, Groth (1979) suggests that sexual assault serves to fulfill the need for power and the expression of anger in up to 95% of sexual aggressors. Similar sentiments have been expressed by others in relation to subsamples of rapists and men who aggress against children (Amir, 1971; Cohen, Garofalo, Boucher, & Seghorn, 1977; Howells, 1981).

It is proposed here, however, that *all* sexual assaults are perpetrated to satisfy the aggressor's desire for, and to enhance feelings of, power. Although power has been defined as both an ability and a feeling, inherent in all definitions is the notion of creating an impact on the environment (Lips, 1981). Lips views the control of others as a reflection of the successful use of power; however, it is difficult to disentangle the two concepts. For the purpose of this chapter, power will be considered both the ability to control and the feeling of power resulting from control.

A sexual assault represents a blatant attempt to physically and emotionally control another person. However, why men target females for abuse and why a sexual as opposed to a nonsexual assault is enacted are difficult to address outside a cultural context. From a sociopolitical perspective, females are characterized by a lack of power, relative to males, in political, economic, and social spheres. Most positions of power that shape and maintain legal, financial, and social institutions are occupied by males, and high value is placed on male modes of thought and behavior (Canadian Advisory Council, 1980; Lipman-Blumen, 1984). Identifiable consequences of a patriarchal system are apparent in the socialization of males and females. Characteristics developed in and ascribed to females, such as dependency, emotionality, weakness, and passivity, are considered less desirable than those attributed to males, such as strength, logic, aggressiveness, and independence (e.g., Unger, 1979). Female socialization, which entails the suppression of overt manifestations of qualities such as intelligence, strength, physical prowess, achievement orientation, and competence (Kaplan & Bean, 1976; Unger, 1979), can be seen as training in the abdication of personal and social power. Implicit in the concept of masculinity is the notion of sexual dominance; that is, males are encouraged to exercise leadership and control, particularly over women. Conversely, femininity implies submission, particularly toward males, with its concomitant displays of patience, caution and restraint (Lips, 1981). This cultural reality both reflects and maintains the power imbalance between women and men.

Thus males, by virtue of this power differential, possess the means or the ability to control females. Indeed, we have a long history of men controlling women through physical aggression. The corporal punishment of women and children has, until fairly recently, been an expected and acceptable responsibility of the male head of household (Dobash & Dobash, 1979). Although currently considered less acceptable, domestic violence against women and children continues to occur with great frequency (Dobash & Dobash, 1979; MacLeod, 1987).

Thus a man in crisis, seeking a victim for abuse, will find a female to be a considerably safer target than another male. However, the need for the assault to contain sexual elements is not readily apparent without recognition of the social construction of heterosexual sexuality and relationships. Historically, the ownership of women clearly, and perhaps primarily, encompassed female sexuality and reproductive abilities. As a crime against property in Anglo-Saxon law, rape violated a husband's exclusive access to his sexual property, thus confounding patrilineage (see Brownmiller, 1975; Clark & Lewis, 1977). A woman's value was, and continues to be to a large extent, based in her ability to attract men and provide sexual and reproductive services (Lips, 1981; Unger, 1979). In fact, the concept of sex has been inextricably linked to that of female. Referent power, frequently identified as sexual, has been cited as one of the few sources of power available to women (e.g., Lips, 1981). In the eyes of the aggressor, to control a woman sexually, or in a sexual context, may represent the denigration or destruction of her most fundamental value.

A sexual assault represents a gross personal invasion and an extreme violation of bodily integrity. Although the victim of a nonsexual assault may experience intense feelings of powerlessness, a sexual assault involves a degree of victim vulnerability and intrusion rarely found with physical assault. It is proposed here that men sexually assault in order to control, dominate, and *humiliate* their victims. Humiliation is accomplished from a position of power; therefore, control and domination can be seen as necessary prerequisites, with forced sex providing the vehicle for humiliation.

If sexual assault symbolizes the control and denigration of a woman's most valuable asset, then any forced sexual act may be considered degrading. In addition, Marshall, Christie and Lanthier (1979) report data indicating that incarcerated offenders typically hold traditional attitudes about sex in general, and they consider all but the most conservative sexual practices to be deviant. Thus, for identified aggressors, participation in sexual acts other than the most conservative ones may be considered particularly humiliating. To perpetrate or forcibly elicit sexual activities against another's will must represent the ultimate in power and control. To be powerless to stop such abuse must represent the ultimate humiliation.

Although sexual gratification appears to be neither the primary aim of sexual assault nor the primary outcome (Clark & Lewis, 1977; Groth & Burgess, 1977a), it is not difficult to envision the conditioning process which may result in the erotization of behaviors used in sexual assaults (see Laws & Marshall, Chapter 13, this volume). Similarly, victim reactions to the offender's control and humiliation of them may come to elicit sexual arousal. For example, as cues associated with feelings of power (e.g., restraining the victim, expressions by the victim of fear or shame) are paired with sexual cues and behaviors (e.g., penile stimulation), we would expect the aggressive behaviors and the victim reactions to eventually elicit increasing levels of sexual arousal. For men who sexually aggress against children, additional reflections of powerlessness or vulnerability reside in the very nature of the victim chosen (i.e., a child). The victim *per se*, as well as cues previously mentioned, may become eroticized. Hence sexual arousal to sexually aggressive images is explicable for those who perpetrate sexual violence and for those who view sexual aggression as a method for increasing personal power.

Although a number of writers have made references to power and humiliation within rape, they have yet to be examined in a controlled or organized fashion. Our (Darke, Marshall, & Earls, 1982) initial investigations on humiliation and sexual assault reported here include an examination of the perceptions of victims and offenders and an evaluation of the behavior of sexually aggressive men. Since this project was a preliminary investigation, the data are limited in range and nature; nevertheless, what data are available are persuasive and warrant serious examination. Following is a description of these, albeit limited, data and a discussion of the general issues relevant to research which may elucidate the role of power and humiliation in sexual aggression. Although new research findings on the role of power in sexual aggression are not presented, suggestions for future research are made, as current laboratory work does not directly address theoretical assumptions concerning power and sexual violence.

Victim Reports

Victims of sexual assault perceive their assaults as humiliating (Kilpatrick, Veronen, & Resick, 1982), as shown by the following sentiments, which are repeatedly heard by those who work with survivors of sexual violence:

> I felt dirty and degraded. (Levine & Koenig, 1980, p. 126)
>
> It was the most humiliating, terrible feeling. (Griffin, 1977, p. 65)
>
> They knew I'd been beaten up on, but I couldn't bring myself to say that he had actually ejaculated inside my vagina. It was too terrible to say. (Connell & Wilson, 1974, p. 23)
>
> I felt so dirty-filthy. I took a shower and let the hot water hit me, but I couldn't touch myself. My own body was revolting, disgusting. I just stood there crying, holding a washcloth in my hand, but I couldn't touch myself. God how I wanted to go down the drain with the rest of the water. (Horos, 1974, p. 79)

The embarrassment and shame consistently reported by victims are, in part, a function of attitudes which encourage victims to feel responsible for their assaults. However, given the very nature of sexual assault, combined with a variety of verbal and behavioral abuses, feelings of humiliation seem inevitable and may well be the intention of the assailant.

Further victim research is required, as it has been suggested that the frequency and range of sexual acts involved in sexual assaults may be even greater than those reported in the literature. For example, Holmstrom and Burgess (1980) have observed that a woman's credibility may be questioned if she reports acts that do not fit with preconceived notions of the nature of rape. It is also likely that many interviewers do not explicitly seek out such details and that victims feel uncomfortable and, therefore, reluctant to offer descriptions which are in most cases not relevant to legal proceedings. Thus, careful interviewing of victims concerning specific verbal and nonverbal assailant behavior may offer further insight into offender motivations and result in a more realistic conception of sexual assault. The potential psychological stress to victims interviewed must be carefully considered, and precautions designed to minimize distress need to be introduced. However, it has been found that disclosure of the details of a sexual assault in a nonjudgmental, supportive context, in fact, speeds resolution for sexual assault survivors rather than creating further trauma (Burgess & Holmstrom, 1979). It is hoped that investigations concerning the construct of humiliation will yield information of use to those who work with survivors of sexual violence.

Offender Reports

Considerable caution is required when examining offenders' self-reported motivation, but analyses of transcripts of interviews with 10 incarcerated rapists reported by Levine and Koenig (1980) revealed relevant material (Marshall & Darke, 1982). We approached these transcripts with skepticism, as preselection of the subjects, their participation in a prison treatment program, and the pressures bearing on offenders to present a rehabilitated image represented limitations additional to those usually ascribed to self-reports. A brief summary of our observations will be provided, as the frequent mention of power, hostility, and humiliation by these offenders was startling. Although the interviewer's questions appeared to be based on a traditional understanding of sexual assault, the offenders themselves described their motivations as being primarily nonsexual. It is of interest that this material was virtually ignored by Levine and Koenig in their overview, suggesting that they were neither expecting nor seeking information relevant to a nonsexual orientation to rape.

Nine of the ten men interviewed stated that the sexual elements were of secondary importance to them during their assaults, in spite of the fact that they spent considerable time discussing their sexually "repressed" upbringings and heterosocial anxieties. These nine offenders explicitly stated that either anger or the need to dominate were the most important factors operating in their assaults. Of these nine, five made specific reference to their intent to humiliate or degrade their victims. Some particularly salient remarks made by these offenders are as follows (Levine & Koenig, 1980):

It's mostly humiliating the victim, but not hurting or any heavy violence. (p. 25)

When I was becoming angry . . . I felt that I had to have sex at any cost as a reversal of caring. To go as far as I could away from that caring, to cheapen that person. (p. 46)

I made hate to her. (p. 51)

I know that I purposely degraded them. (p. 59)

I fantasized about stabbing her with a knife in the anus—of all places. Just a degrading thought. Put her down and put her in her place for challenging me. (p. 66)

I think the reason we used to do this (gang rape) was because I like to lower the chicks to me, that's the way I used to think, that I was lowering them and making them look

> cheap . . . and making them look like dirty tramps. (p. 71) . . . she (the victim) was really humiliated; she was really put down. (p. 75)

And finally, a date rapist stated:

> I'd become rather arrogant and I'd talk down to them afterwards. "You bitch!" you know, things like that. I'd become quite disgusted. I'd show my disgust with them, really; and I think the disgust really is probably more directed at myself, but I take it out on them. (p. 84)

woman

These statements clearly reflect a great deal of hostility toward, and a desire to humiliate, the victim. Again it is important to note that the interviewers did not appear to recognize the relevance of these remarks; thus it is unlikely that their questions directly elicited such statements.

Offender Behavior

In addition to offender reports, offender behavior during assaults also suggests an intent to humiliate. Although forced sex, of any form, may be perpetrated with the purpose of degrading the victim, a range of sexual acts in assaults appears to be more common than is generally believed. Amir (1971) reported that more than 25% of the cases he studied contained instances of what he termed "sexual humiliation." Amir's definition refers specifically to acts of forced oral and anal penetration, cunnilingus, and repeated penile–vaginal intercourse. Amir appears to have arbitrarily defined these acts as humiliating, and although we question his labeling of these acts, in and of themselves, we consider some of these behaviors, within a particular context, to be intentionally humiliating.

Other researchers have examined a range of acts accompanying penile–vaginal rape which broaden Amir's definition of sexual humiliation. Holmstrom and Burgess (1980), for example, report the frequency of excretory, sadistic, and sexual acts, noting the wide variety of behaviors to which victims are subjected. Although their data presentation does not permit a determination of the total number of assaults in which this variety of abusive behaviors occurred, fellatio was the most frequent sexual act (22%) following penile–vaginal penetration. In Clark and Lewis' (1977) sample, 23.3% of the assaults involved one or more of the following acts: oral or anal penetration, cunnilingus, victim stimulation of the offender, or offender masturbation. Again, fellatio was the most common act (47.8% of the cases) accompanying vaginal penetration.

Amir's definition of humiliating behaviors has been supported by others, but while we agree that many of these sexual acts appear to be intended to degrade the victim, the norms for acceptable sexual practices and additional information concerning the assault must be considered. For example we are, at the present time, unwilling to label fellatio, *per se,* as a more intentionally humiliating act than, say, vaginal penetration. Future examinations of rapist's and control subject's attitudes concerning specific sexual practices within consenting relationships may help us to differentiate levels of intended humiliation in various sexual behaviors. However, if the data collected by Marshall *et al.* (1979)

indicating that incarcerated offenders are typically conservative about sex are substantiated, then to force a woman to engage in acts other than intercourse might, indeed, be initiated with the intention of humiliating her.

To examine the issue of offender behavior further, 43 police files of incarcerated sex offenders were inspected (Darke *et al.*, 1982). Of these 43 files, 36 provided relevant material on 68 sexually assaultive incidents. Eight of these offenders (accounting for 20 incidents) aggressed against children. Because initial examination revealed no differences, other than age of victim, between the assaults against children and those against women, the two groups of offenders were combined.

Police records are often sketchy, and the types of information obtained and recorded varies among police departments and with the nature of the specific charge. Nevertheless, behaviors which we designated as intentionally humiliating were extracted from reports by victims, witnesses, and offenders. At this point we do not have an operational definition of humiliation, and our working definition is rather vague and intuitive. Concepts of power, hostility, and control are closely tied to the notion of humiliation; however, the behaviors under consideration did not seem to fall clearly into those categories. For ease of conceptualization and analysis, nonverbal and verbal behaviors were examined separately.

The *nonverbal* behaviors that were identified as humiliating tended to fall into two broad categories: sexual behaviors which are traditionally considered unacceptable (such as anal penetration) and blatant acts of abuse which are not necessarily physically injurious (such as ejaculation on the victim's face). Similarly, *verbal* humiliation appeared to include: abusive statements, comments, or questions of a sexual nature ("I know 13 other guys who want to screw you"; "Have you ever fucked before?") and nonsexual verbal abuse ("You're not worth a shit"). Each of these categories, for both verbal and nonverbal behaviors, appears to vary within two dimensions: (1) the acceptability of the behavior itself and (2) the context in which the behavior is enacted, beyond the context of a rape. Therefore, judgments concerning the degree of intended humiliation are a function of both the behavior itself and the context within which that behavior occurs. Some behaviors are unequivocally intended to humiliate, such as ejaculating or urinating on the victim's face, or statements like, "You've probably fucked every man in town, you whore." Others are judged to be so on the basis of additional factors. For example, manual stimulation of the penis is an acceptable practice in consenting relationships, but in an assaultive situation— particularly when accompanied by statements such as, "I know you like to do this, bitch"—it is difficult to imagine an intent other than humiliation (assuming that the offender was not having erectile difficulties, in which case the verbal statement would be judged as humiliating, but the forced behavior itself might not).

Of the 68 cases in which sufficient details of the assault were available, 43 cases (63%) were identified in which one or more of these humiliating behaviors was reported. Although several humiliating behaviors may have been evident in a particular assault, that case was counted as one incident. This was done in an attempt to provide a more conservative estimate of the frequency of humiliation, given the lack of a precise working definition and the absence of reliability checks. Because the status of fellatio in sexual assault is not as clear to us as are other behaviors, it was also excluded from our tally. However, when non-overlapping instances of fellatio are added to the 43 cases mentioned, the percentage of cases involving humiliation rises to 82.4%. When incidents of forced fellatio are excluded, an equal number of verbal and nonverbal humiliating behaviors was observed.

Examples of the nonverbal acts tentatively labeled as humiliating include: shaving the victim's pubic hair, taking photos of the victim's genitalia, ejaculating on the victim's face, and pouring beer into the victim's vagina.

Some of the verbal statements are difficult to classify without contextual cues. The following are examples of those identified in context as humiliating:

> A lone assailant threatened his victim with a knife. During the assault he stated "Me and a friend want to fuck you while seven other men watch."

> The assailant used physical violence to subdue his victim. During the assault he said, "Thirteen other guys want to screw you." He also indicated that he was raping her because he couldn't go to a "whorehouse."

> The assailant referred to his victim as his "white squaw" and his "slave."

> Following physical and sexual assault, the assailant told his victim that she wasn't "worth a shit."

> Using physical violence to subdue his 15-year-old victim the assailant then said, "Look at the mess you've gotten yourself into. It was dumb to take a ride from someone you don't know. . . . Have you ever been fucked before?" The victim responded "yes" and the assailant stated, "You should have said no. Are you going to let this happen? Don't you have any respect for yourself?"

> The assailant bound the victim's hands and forced her, nude, into a "mounting" position. He held his buck knife against her anus, made a small cut and said, "You've got a nice ass." During fellatio he slapped the victim on the head and said, "Bitch, make it feel good!"

> The victim was offered a ride while waiting at a bus stop and then threatened with a knife. When she stated where she wanted to go the offender said, "No you're going to suck my dick first." He ejaculated in her mouth and after again threatening her with his knife he engaged in penile–vaginal intercourse. During this he asked, "Do you like it?" She replied no, and he responded "Good!"

The validity of both the humiliation hypothesis and the high percentage of humiliating behaviors is dependent on the accuracy of our labeling of these behaviors as intentionally humiliating. However, in this preliminary investigation, there emerged a surprisingly high frequency of acts that were not easily classified as primarily contributing to subduing the victim, serving sexual needs, or simply venting anger. For future research, in addition to structured interviews with identified rapists, access to a second sample of offender files would allow a comparison of the content and frequency of humiliating acts with those of the original sample. Ratings by independent judges of a sample of the behaviors from the files would establish the extent to which they are considered to be intentionally humiliating or degrading, as opposed to simply aggressive. In addition, the contexts in which the behaviors are described as occurring require manipulation in order to assess the nature of those factors which define or contribute to humiliation. It should be noted that written transcripts of offender behavior may well result in underestimates of the intent to humiliate. Visual observation may facilitate recognition of intentionally humiliating behaviour.

FUTURE RESEARCH DIRECTIONS

Attitude Research

An issue of particular relevance is the relationship of humiliation to attitudes toward women, sexual activity, sexual assault, and interpersonal violence. The offender comments which we examined frequently implied that the victim was, or deserved to be treated as if she were, a prostitute. Given the social status of prostitutes, such treatment is strongly suggestive of a desire to humiliate. It has been suggested that the ubiquitous pornographic images of women in advertising, as well as in pornography, both shape and perpetuate the widely held, unspoken belief that women are carnal beings, who crave sexual fulfillment at almost any cost and with any man (Courtney & Whipple, 1978; Dworkin, 1974, 1979; Fraser Commission, 1985; Griffin, 1981; McConahay & McConahay, 1973; Tieger & Aronstam, 1981). This generalized belief can be seen as generating and feeding rape myths which reflect an appalling lack of concern, if not contempt, for victims of sexual assault (Burt, 1980; Feild, 1978). Belief in these myths have been found to be associated with self-reported sexual aggression in groups of undetected sexual aggressors (Koss, Leonard, Beezley, & Oros, 1985; Mosher & Anderson, 1986; Rapaport & Burkhart, 1984) and with the self-reported likelihood of sexually assaulting a woman (Briere & Malamuth, 1983; Malamuth & Check, 1983; Malamuth, Haber, & Feshbach, 1980; Tieger, 1981).

Of relevance here are studies demonstrating that college males are significantly more aroused to rape depictions when the victim is portrayed as becoming involuntarily sexually aroused by the assault (Darke, 1986; Malamuth & Check, 1980a, 1980b; Malamuth, Heim, & Feshbach, 1980). These depictions not only suggest that the offender is able to dominate and control his victim, but that he is also endowed with sexual prowess or power. It is not unreasonable to assume that sexually arousing a woman, against her will, would be considered degrading by most objective viewers.

It is suggested that the relationships among the power motive and attitudes reflecting hostility toward women, rape myth acceptance, and sex-role stereotyping be explored. Building on the early work of Winter and Stewart (1978), projective techniques may be employed; however, behavioral measures of a desire to control can be developed for use as dependent variables.

In addition, attitude test items that are not simply sexist, but blatantly contemptuous of women, can be developed or partialed out of attitude scales currently in use. For example, the myth that women are aroused by, or in spite of, pain elicits not only images of control but of derision for the victim who is aroused against her will. The relationships among endorsement of such items and the power motive, self-reported likelihood to rape, sexual arousal to standardized sexually aggressive stimuli, and nonsexual aggression in the laboratory can be examined in offender and control subject populations.

Sexual Arousal Studies

A final research strategy that may help clarify the role of humiliation in sexual assault involves assessing the effects on sexual arousal of the addition of degrading acts to descriptions of forced and consenting sex. If descriptions of humiliation do not enhance sexual arousal, particularly in offenders who characteristically employ such tactics, then we can conclude that such acts do not serve a sexual end. Similarly, if these descriptions fail, as aggression does, to inhibit sexual arousal in rapists, then presumably, as is the case with violence, degrading acts serve some nonsexual purpose. If arousal is augmented by descriptions of degradation, we can conclude that humiliating acts contribute to sexual excitement, and we can then proceed to identify the factors contributing to the erotization of these acts. In the unlikely event that humiliation inhibits sexual arousal, then clearly nonsexual needs are being served, but the role of these acts in sexual assaults will be more difficult to comprehend. However, some rapists also display inhibition of arousal to cues of violence (Baxter *et al.*, 1984), suggesting that the role of sexual arousal in sexual assault is idiosyncratically determined. Thus, we may observe enhancement, inhibition, or maintenance of arousal levels in offenders in response to cues of humiliation.

Similarly, conditions which reflect varying degrees of power imbalances, beyond gender, can be manipulated in experimental stimuli in order to examine the role of power and its erotization in sexual aggression. For example, the age, social status, assertiveness, and physical stature of the female can be varied, and the effects on sexual responsivity observed. Females characterized by considerable power, and those associated with little power, can be depicted in sexually aggressive and nonaggressive stimuli. If power-related motives are central to the commission of, or arousal to, sexual aggression, then evidence of disinhibition would be predicted under conditions of high-male versus low-female power. In addition, given that women continue to be seen as illegitimate possessors of many forms of power traditionally associated with men, a condition of very high-female power would be expected to engender hostility in many males thus facilitating disinhibition. The potential hostility elicited by conditions of high-female power, when contrasted in offender and control populations, may offer some interesting insights into the role of power, hostility toward women, and humiliation in sexual aggression.

TREATMENT AND PREVENTION

Given the paucity of data relevant to humiliation and sexual assault, specific treatment recommendations cannot be offered as yet. However, it is expected that, within the multifaceted treatment programs available (Abel, Blanchard, &

Becker, 1978; Marshall, Earls, Segal, & Darke, 1983), considerably greater focus on attitudinal variables will be required. Goals may include a comprehensive understanding of the social context of male violence, as well as changes regarding specific attitudes about women, sexuality, and male identity. Similarly, greater emphasis on redefining personal and social power may prove efficacious. In addition to anger control and assertion training components, a reconceptualization of power as the ability to control one's own life (as opposed to the lives of others) may be creatively integrated into additional treatment facets. Controlled outcome studies will, of course, determine the utility of this changed focus.

A particular act of rape is probably multidetermined, and individual offenders may require individualized treatment to identify triggers and overcome idiosyncratic behavioral difficulties (such as anger control, substance abuse, or social skills deficits). However, it is unlikely that conditions determining the target for abuse (i.e., a female) are idiosyncratically determined. Hostility toward women has long been recognized as a feature in sexual assault; however, in the past, writers acknowledging this expression of misogyny have tended to view it as an individual problem. Accordingly, instances of real or perceived abuse by women significant in rapists' lives were sought. An example of this approach is to be found in the oft-cited discussion by Abrahamsen (1960), in which the personality profiles of the wives of rapists are used to explain the behavior of these offenders. The search for individual sources of woman hatred has not been particularly productive, and current knowledge suggests that it is misguided. Similarly, biological and sociobiological theories have produced scant data (Spinner, 1985), and cultural factors appear to override potential biological propensities (Sanday, 1981; Schwendinger & Schwendinger, 1983).

It is estimated that in Canada up to 50% of females under the age of 18 are sexually abused (Badgley Report, 1984) and 20% of adult women are sexually assaulted (Canadian Advisory Council, 1985). Sexual aggression is perpetrated at high rates; indeed, Russell found that 92.3% of a large community sample of women had been subject to some form of male sexual aggression (compiled for MacKinnon, 1985). The majority of sexual assaults are not reported, and conviction rates for reported rapes are well below 10% (Brownmiller, 1975; DiVasto *et al.*, 1984; FBI Uniform Crime Reports, 1980; Russell, 1982, 1984). This reality has far-reaching implications for sexual aggression research, particularly that which targets incarcerated offenders, who are not representative of the population of sexual aggressors (Russell, 1984; Smithyman, 1978). Yet research proceeds as if a relatively small group of deviant men is responsible, and a dichotomized conceptualization of sexual aggression (rape *vs.* nonrape) forms the foundation of most research.

The sexual abuse of women and girls has emerged as a cultural, not an individual, problem. Sexual violence against women presents as a logical and inevitable extension of attitudes and practices surrounding male–female relationships in a male-dominated culture (Brownmiller, 1975; Clark & Lewis, 1977; Gager & Schurr, 1976). When over 50% of a male college sample acknowledge that they might rape if they could be assured that they would not be caught

(Malamuth, Haber, & Feshbach, 1980), and the majority of a male high school sample reports that date rape is acceptable under a variety of circumstances (Goodchilds & Zellman, 1984), it is difficult to view the sexual abuse of women as other than a culturally acceptable practice. Long-term prevention, therefore, necessitates changing the societal conditions which encourage and sanction a generalized hostility toward women and the consequent sexual abuse of them. A detailed description or analysis of the varied aspects of our daily lives which reflect misogynist attitudes and practice is beyond the scope of this chapter; however, the most blatant practices are those which objectify women and portray them as commodities for male use. Such representations are pervasive in advertising and pornography, and they set up females as ready targets for abuse. Similarly, attitudes which trivialize or erase the damage done to women and girls protect aggressors and create a climate that is hostile to females. The conditions that render pornography acceptable, and rape myths believable, ultimately breed sexual violence. Although the existence of gender inequities is no longer disputed, the cultural insistence on perpetuating these disparities and, therefore, male dominance is rarely acknowledged. Cultural institutions are designed to maintain the status quo, including sexual violence against women and girls. To this end, we socialize males to be aggressive, to devalue women, and to relate to others in minimally empathic ways. It has been suggested that sexual violence is a powerful tool used to control women as a group (Brownmiller, 1975) and an outgrowth of structural inequalities (Clark & Lewis, 1977). Either way, sexual violence will end when men no longer have the "power to define what and who the problem is" (Russell, 1984, p. 289).

ACKNOWLEDGMENTS. The author wishes to acknowledge the valuable contributions made by Dr. W. L. Marshall and Dr. Christopher M. Earls; and the assistance of Dr. Richard Laws and Ms. Beverly Turner.

REFERENCES

Abel, G. G., Blanchard, E. B., Barlow, D. H., & Mavissakalian, M. (1975). Identifying specific erotic cues in sexual deviants by audiotaped descriptions. *Journal of Applied Behavior Analysis, 8,* 247–260.

Abel, G. G., Barlow, D. H., Blanchard, E. B., & Guild D. (1977). The components of rapists' sexual arousal. *Archives of General Psychiatry, 34,* 895–903.

Abel, G. G., Blanchard, E. B., & Becker, J. V. (1978). An integrated treatment program for rapists. In R. Rada (Ed.), *Clinical aspects of the rapist* (pp. 161–214). New York: Grune & Stratton.

Abel, G. G., Blanchard, E. B., Becker, J. V., & Djenderedjian, A. (1978). Differentiating sexual aggressives with penile measures. *Criminal Justice and Behavior, 5,* 315–332.

Abrahamsen, D. (1960). *The psychology of crime.* New York: Columbia University Press.

Amir, M. (1971). *Patterns in forcible rape.* Chicago: University of Chicago Press.

Badgley Report. (1984). *The report of the committee on sexual offenses against children and youths.* Ottawa: Supply & Services Canada.

Barbaree, H. E., Marshall, W. L., & Lanthier, R. D. (1979). Deviant sexual arousal in rapists. *Behavior Research and Therapy, 17,* 215–222.

Barbaree, H. E., Marshall, W. L., Yates, E. P., & Lightfoot, L. O. (1983). Alcohol intoxication and deviant sexual arousal in male social drinkers. *Behavior Research and Therapy, 21*, 365–373.

Baxter, D. J., Marshall, W. L., Barbaree, H. E., Davidson, P. R., & Malcolm, B. P. (1984). Deviant sexual behaviour: Differentiation of sex offenders by criminal and personal history, psychometric assessment, and sexual response. *Criminal Justice and Behavior, 11*, 477–501.

Baxter, D. J., Barbaree, H. E., & Marshall, W. L. (1986). Sexual responses to consenting and forced sex in a large sample of rapists and non-rapists. *Behavior Research and Therapy, 24*, 513–520.

Blader, J. C. (1983). *The relationship between subjective and objective measures of sexual arousal in males as a function of stimulus inappropriateness.* Unpublished master's thesis, Queen's University, Kingston, Ontario.

Briddell, D., Rimm, D., Caddy, G., Kravitz, G., Sholis, D., & Wunderlin, R. (1978). Effects of alcohol and cognitive set on sexual arousal to deviant stimuli. *Journal of Abnormal Psychology, 87*, 418–430.

Briere, J., & Malamuth, N. M. (1983). Self-reported likelihood of sexually aggressive behavior: Attitudinal versus sexual explanations. *Journal of Research in Personality, 17*, 315–323.

Brownmiller, S. (1975). *Against our will: Men, women, and rape.* New York: Bantam Books.

Burgess, A. W., & Holmstrom, L. L. (1979). *Rape: Crisis and recovery.* Bowie, MD: Robert J. Brady Co.

Burt, M. R. (1980). Cultural myths and supports for rape. *Journal of Personality and Social Psychology, 38*, 217–230.

Canadian Advisory Council (1980). *Women in the public service: Overlooked and undervalued.* Ottawa: Canadian Advisory Council on the Status of Women.

Canadian Advisory Council (1985). *Sexual assault.* Ottawa: Canadian Advisory Council on the Status of Women.

Christie, M. M. (1985). *The disinhibiting effects of alcohol, expectancies and instructional set on patterns of male sexual arousal.* Unpublished doctoral dissertation, Queen's University, Kingston, Ontario.

Christie, M. M., Marshall, W. L., & Lanthier, R. D. (1979). *A descriptive study of incarcerated rapists and pedophiles.* Report to the Solicitor General, Government of Canada, Ottawa.

Clark, L., & Lewis, D. (1977). *Rape: The price of coercive sexuality.* Toronto: Women's Educational Press.

Cohen, M. L., Garofalo, R., Boucher, R. B., & Seghorn, T. (1977). The psychology of rapists. In D. Chappell, R. Geis, & G. Geis (Eds.), *Forcible rape: The crime, the victim and the offender* (pp. 291–314). New York: Columbia University Press.

Connell, N., & Wilson, C. (Eds.). (1974). *Rape: The first source-book for women.* New York: Plume.

Courtney, A. E., & Whipple, T. W. (1978). *Canadian perspectives on sex stereotyping in advertising.* Ottawa: Canadian Advisory Council on the Status of Women.

Darke, J. L. (1986). *The role of aggression and consent in the deviant sexual arousal of university males.* Unpublished doctoral dissertation, Queens's University, Kingston, Ontario.

Darke, J. L., Marshall, W. L., & Earls, C. M. (1982, April). *Humiliation and rape: A preliminary inquiry.* Fourth National Conference on the Evaluation & Treatment of Sexual Aggressors, Denver, Colorado.

DiVasto, P. V., Kaufman, A., Rosner, L., Jackson, R., Christy, J., Pearson, S., & Burgett, T. (1984). The prevalence of sexually stressful events among females in the general population. *Archives of Sexual Behavior, 13*, 59–67.

Dobash, R. E., & Dobash, R. (1979). *Violence against wives: A case against the patriarchy.* New York: The Free Press.

Donnerstein, E. (1980). Aggressive erotica and violence against women. *Journal of Personality and Social Psychology, 39*, 269–277.

Dworkin, A. (1974). *Woman hating.* New York: Dutton.

Dworkin, A. (1979). *Pornography: Men possessing women.* New York: Perigee.

Earls, C. M., & Proulx, J. (1987). The differentiation of francophone rapists and nonrapists using penile circumferential measures. *Journal of Criminal Justice and Behavior, 13*, 419–429.

Federal Bureau of Investigation (FBI). (1980). *Uniform crime reports—1979.* Washington, DC: U.S. Government Printing Office.

Feild, H. S. (1978). Attitudes toward rape: A comparative analysis of police, rapists, crisis counselors and citizens. *Journal of Personality and Social Psychology, 36,* 156–179.

Fraser Commission. (1985). *Report of the special committee on pornography and prostitution.* Ottawa, Ontario: Canadian Government Publishing Centre, Supply & Services Canada.

Gager, N., & Schurr, C. (1976). *Sexual assault: Confronting rape in America.* New York: Grosset & Dunlap.

Gebhard, P., Gagnon, J., Pomeroy, W., & Christenson, C. (1965). *Sex offenders.* New York: Harper & Row.

Goodchilds, J. D., & Zellman, G. (1984). Sexual signalling and sexual aggression in adolescent relationships. In N. M. Malamuth & E. Donnerstein (Eds.), *Pornography and sexual aggression* (pp. 233–243). New York: Academic Press.

Griffin, S. (1977). Rape: The all-American crime. In D. Chappell, R. Geis, & G. Geis (Eds.), *Forcible rape: The crime, the victim and the offender* (pp. 47–66). New York: Columbia University Press.

Griffin, S. (1981). *Pornography and silence: Culture's revenge against nature.* New York: Harper & Row.

Groth, N. A. (1979). *Men who rape: The psychology of the offender.* New York: Plenum.

Groth, N. A., & Burgess, A. W. (1977a). Rape: A sexual deviation. *American Journal of Orthopsychiatry, 47*(3), 400–406.

Groth, N. A., & Burgess, A. W. (1977b). Sexual dysfunction during rape. *The New England Journal of Medicine, 297,* 764–767.

Henson, D. E., & Rubin, H. B. (1971). Voluntary control of eroticism. *Journal of Applied Behavior Analysis, 4,* 37–44.

Holmstrom, L. L., & Burgess, A. W. (1980). Sexual behavior of assailants during reported rapes. *Archives of Sexual Behavior, 9,* 427–440.

Horos, C. V. (1974). *Rape.* New Canaan, CT: Tobey Publishing.

Howells, K. (1981). Adult sexual interest in children: Considerations relevant to theories of aetiology. In M. Cook & K. Howells (Eds.), *Adult sexual interest in children* (pp. 55–94). New York: Academic Press.

Kaplan, A. G., & Bean, J. P. (Eds.). (1976). *Beyond sex-role stereotypes: Readings toward a psychology of androgyny.* Toronto: Little, Brown.

Kilpatrick, D. G., Veronen, L. J., & Resick, P. A. (1982). Psychological sequilae to rape: Assessment and treatment strategies. In D. M. Doleys, R. L. Meredith, & A. R. Ciminero (Eds.), *Behavioral medicine: Assessment and treatment strategies* (pp. 473–497). New York: Plenum.

Koss, M. P., Leonard, K. E., Beezley, D. A., & Oros, C. J. (1985). Nonstranger sexual aggression: A discriminant analysis of psychological dimensions. *Sex Roles, 12,* 981–992.

Laws, D. R., & Rubin, H. B. (1969). Instructional control of an autonomic response. *Journal of Applied Behavior Analysis, 2,* 93–99.

Levine, S., & Koenig, J. (Eds.). (1980). *Why men rape: Interviews with convicted rapists.* Toronto: Macmillan.

Lipman-Blumen, J. (1984). *Gender roles and power.* Englewood Cliffs, NJ: Prentice-Hall.

Lips, H. M. (1981). *Women, men, and the psychology of power.* Englewood Cliffs, NJ: Prentice-Hall.

MacKinnon, C. A. (1985). Pornography, civil rights and speech. *Harvard Civil Rights-Civil Liberties Law Review, 20,* 1–70.

MacLeod, L. (1987). *Battered but not beaten: Preventing wife battering in Canada.* Ottawa: Canadian Advisory Council on the Status of Women.

Malamuth, N. M. (1981). Rape proclivity among males. *Journal of Social Issues, 37,* 138–157.

Malamuth, N. M., & Check, J. V. P. (1980a). Penile tumescence and perceptual responses to rape as a function of victim's perceived reactions. *Journal of Applied Social Psychology, 10,* 528–547.

Malamuth, N. M., & Check, J. V. P. (1980b). Sexual arousal to rape and consenting depictions: The importance of the woman's arousal. *Journal of Abnormal Psychology, 89,* 763–766.

Malamuth, N. M., & Check, M. V. P. (1983). Sexual arousal to rape depictions: Individual differences. *Journal of Abnormal Psychology, 92,* 55–67.

Malamuth, N. M., Haber, S., & Feshbach, S. (1980). Testing hypotheses regarding rape: Exposure to sexual violence, sex differences, and the "normality" of rapists. *Journal of Research in Personality, 14*, 121–137.

Malamuth, N. M., Heim, M., & Feshbach, S. (1980). Sexual responsiveness of college students to rape depictions: Inhibitory and disinhibitory effects. *Journal of Personality and Social Psychology, 38*, 399–408.

Marshall, W. L., & Darke, J. L. (1982). Why men rape (Levine & Koenig): A review. *Queen's Quarterly, 89* 434–436.

Marshall, W. L., Christie, M. M., & Lanthier, R. D. (1979). *Social competence, sexual experience and attitudes to sex in incarcerated rapists and pedophiles.* Report to the Solicitor General, Government of Canada, Ottawa.

Marshall, W. L., Earls, C. M., Segal, Z., & Darke, J. L. (1983). A behavioural program for the assessment and treatment of sexual aggressors. In K. D. Craig & R. McMahon (Eds.), *Advances in clinical behavior therapy* (pp. 148–174). New York: Bruner/Mazel.

McConahay, S. A., & McConahay, J. B. (1973). *Explorations in sex and violence.* Unpublished manuscript. Yale University.

Millet, K. (1969). *Sexual politics.* New York: Ballentine.

Mosher, D. L., & Anderson, R. D. (1986). Macho personality, sexual aggression, and reaction to guided imagery of realistic rape. *Journal of Research in Personality, 20*, 77–84.

Murphy, W. D., Haynes, M. R., Coleman, E. M., & Flanagan, B. (1985). Sexual responding of "nonrapists" to aggressive sexual themes: Normative data. *Journal of Psychopathology and Behavioral Assessment, 7*, 37–47.

Quinsey, V. L., & Bergersen, S. G. (1976). Instructional control of penile circumference in assessments of sexual preferences. *Behavior Therapy, 7*, 489–493.

Quinsey, V. L., & Carrigan, W. F. (1978). Penile responses to visual stimuli. *Criminal Justice and Behavior, 5*, 333–342.

Quinsey, V. L., & Chaplin, T. C. (1984). Stimulus control of rapists' and non-sex offenders' sexual arousal. *Behavioral Assessment, 6*, 169–176.

Quinsey, V. L., Chaplin, T. C., & Varney, G. (1981). A comparison of rapists' and non-sex offenders' sexual preferences for mutually consenting sex, rape, and physical abuse of women. *Behavioral Assessment, 3*, 127–135.

Quinsey, V. L., Chaplin, T. C., & Upfold, D. (1984). Sexual arousal to nonsexual violence and sadomasochistic themes among rapist and non-sex offenders. *Journal of Consulting and Clinical Psychology, 52*, 651–657.

Rapaport, K., & Burkhart, B. R. (1984). Personality and attitudinal characteristics of sexually coercive college males. *Journal of Abnormal Psychology, 93*, 216–221.

Rush, F. (1980). *The best kept secret: Sexual abuse of children.* New York: McGraw-Hill.

Russell, D. E. H. (1982). *Rape in marriage.* New York: MacMillan.

Russell, D. E. H. (1984). *Sexual exploitation: Rape, child sexual abuse and workplace harassment.* Beverly Hills, CA: Sage Publications.

Sanday, P. R. (1981). *Female power and male dominance.* London: Cambridge University Press.

Schwendinger, J. R., & Schwendinger, H. (1983). *Rape and inequality.* Beverly Hills, CA: Sage Publications.

Segal, Z. V., & Marshall, W. L. (1985). Heterosexual social skills in a population of rapists and child molesters. *Journal of Consulting and Clinical Psychology, 53*, 55–63.

Seidman, B. T. (1985). *Male sexual arousal to rape depictions following exposure to forced and consenting sexual stimuli.* Unpublished master's thesis, Queen's University, Kingston, Ontario.

Smithyman, S. D. (1978). *The undetected rapist.* Unpublished doctoral dissertation, Claremont Graduate School.

Spinner, B. (1985). A comparison of evolutionary and environmental theories of erotic response— Parts I & II. *Journal of Sex Research, 21*, 229–374.

Stanko, E. A. (1985). *Intimate intrusions: Women's experience of male violence.* London: Routledge & Kegan Paul.

Stermac, L. E., & Quinsey, V. L. (1986). Social competence among rapists. *Behavioral Assessment, 8*, 171–185.

Tieger, T. (1981). Self-reported likelihood of raping and the social perception of rape. *Journal of Research in Personality, 15*, 147–158.

Tieger, T., & Aronstam, J. (1981, August). *"Brutality chic" images and endorsement of rape myths.* Paper presented at the annual convention of the American Psychological Association, Los Angeles.

Unger, R. K. (1979). *Female and male: Psychological perspectives.* New York: Harper & Row.

Winter, D. G., & Stewart, A. J. (1978). The power motive. In H. London & J. E. Exner, Jr. (Eds.), *Dimensions of personality* (pp. 391–449). New York: John Wiley.

Wydra, A., Marshall, W. L., Earls, C. M., & Barbaree, H. E. (1983). Identification of cues and control of sexual arousal by rapists. *Behavior Research and Therapy, 21*, 469–476.

Yates, E. P., Barbaree, H. E., & Marshall, W. L. (1984). Anger and deviant sexual arousal. *Behavior Therapy, 15*, 287–294.

5

The Influence of Pornography on Sexual Crimes

MARY R. MURRIN AND D. R. LAWS

There are several approaches to the study of the role of pornography in the etiology and maintenance of sexual crimes. One may (1) study the correlation between pornography consumption in the general population and the incidence of sexual crimes, (2) examine this relationship cross-culturally, (3) examine the effect of these materials on normals in the laboratory, (4) examine the effects of these materials on sex offenders, or (5) attempt a synthesis of this research through a comparative study of the similarities and differences between sex offenders and other males. The simple approach is to draw a sample of sex offenders and ask them about their pornography consumption. All of these approaches have basic flaws, but each contributes to the complete picture.

These approaches are attempts to gain some insight into the role that pornography consumption plays in contributing to sexual crimes. The most frequently asked research questions are: Does exposure to pornography predispose persons to become sexually deviant? Does exposure to pornography cause those who are sexually deviant to commit sexual crimes? Or conversely, does exposure to pornography suppress the urges of those sexual deviants who are likely to otherwise commit sexual crimes? Is pornography consumption simply part of a deviant lifestyle, or does pornography consumption act to validate the beliefs supporting that lifestyle? Is there any difference in pornography consumption between those who commit sexual crimes and those who do not? None of these questions are likely to be definitely answered in the near future, but we can integrate the available evidence in an attempt to arrive at some reasonably plausible conclusions.

MARY R. MURRIN AND D. R. LAWS • Department of Law and Mental Health, Florida Mental Health Institute, University of South Florida, Tampa, Florida 33612-3899.

Availability of Pornography and the Incidence of Sexual Crimes

Two of the earliest studies on the relationship between the incidence of sexual crimes and the availability of pornography were Danish studies commissioned by the 1970 President's Commission on Obscenity and Pornography (Ben-Veniste, 1971; Kutchinsky, 1971). These reports stressed the tentative nature of the results, and both cast some doubt on the assertion that the decrease in sexual crime rates was due simply to a reduced tendency to men to commit sexual crimes. However, the commission interpreted these studies to mean that the reduction in the reported incidence of sexual offenses in Denmark was due to the liberalization of the pornography law (Cline, 1974; Court, 1984).

Ben-Veniste (1971) reported that the increased pornography use in Denmark had not led to an increase in sexual crimes. However, he also reported that Denmark at that time had very little sexually violent pornography, that this variety of pornography was becoming increasingly available, and that future study was needed to determine if this change would lead to an increased crime rate. Kutchinsky (1971) interviewed a representative sample ($N=398$) of the Danish population regarding four different sexual crimes: (1) exhibitionism, (2) peeping, (3) "physical indecency" toward women, and (4) "physical indecency" toward girls (child molestation). Subjects were asked to report their reactions if they or a member of their family were to become a victim of one of these offenses. Kutchinsky (1971, 1973) concluded that much of the reported decrease in exhibitionism and in physical indecency toward women could be explained by the decreased likelihood of the victim to report the crime. The decrease in reported rates of peeping and child molestation, however, could not be explained by a decreased likelihood to report. Changing police attitudes toward the seriousness of the crime was suggested as a possible factor in the case of peeping, but not for child molestation. Therefore, the decrease in the reported rate of female child molestation could not be explained either by a reduced tendency for adults to report or by a failure of the police to act on those reports.

Neither study separated the effects of changing incidence rates of violent sexual crimes from the effects of changing incidences of relatively nonviolent sex crimes such as peeping (Court, 1984). An examination of the reported incidence of sexually violent crimes in Denmark in the same period reveals a quite different picture. The change in the Danish pornography law occurred in 1965, and while the overall incidence of violent sex crime from 1966–1970 in Denmark showed an 8% decrease from that reported in 1960–1964 (Cline, 1974), the reported incidence of rape increased by 22% in Copenhagen.

Court (1984) attempted to relate the longitudinal changes in rape rates to changes in government policy concerning censorship of pornography. For example, he showed that the rape rates from the years 1964–1974 increased dramatically (Range = 84–160%) in five areas where pornography laws were liberalized (United States, England, Copenhagen, Australia, and New Zealand) but did not increase as much (< 60%) in areas where pornography laws were not liberalized (South Africa, among whites only, and Singapore). Somewhat more convincingly, he showed that two states in Australia with almost identical rape statistics prior to 1970 diverged dramatically after 1970, when South Australia implemented liberal pornography laws while Queensland retained the more conservative standards. Queensland's rape statistics remained quite low, but South Australia's statistics jumped sharply after 1972 and continued to increase sharply until the end of the study in 1977. Also persuasive were longitudinal studies conducted in New Zealand and Hawaii showing dramatic increases in rape rates after liberalization of pornography laws; these trends were reversed after more conservative laws were reinstated.

All of these studies have serious methodological flaws, including (1) direct comparisons being made among nonequivalent countries or regions; (2) failure to take account of additional possibly influential variables, such as the widely differing cultural, geographical, and historical backgrounds of the various societies; and (3) failure to measure whether the liberalization of pornography laws had any effect upon either pornography consumption, the content of pornography, or the frequency with which sexual crimes were reported. Additionally, Court apparently did not randomly select countries for his analysis (Donnerstein, Linz, & Penrod, 1987).

Baron and Straus (1984) also reported a significant correlation between the consumption of pornography (in this case soft-core) and the incidence of reported rape using the 50 U.S. states as cases. This well-controlled study took many extraneous variables into account and extensively tested the reliability of the data by using other rape indices and cross-matching techniques. The author's measure of pornography was derived by tabulating the consumption of eight soft-core magazines, adjusting for population in a state, and taking a single factor score that accounted for 75% of the variance in consumption scores between magazines. They controlled for four population characteristics shown to be highly correlated with rape statistics: (1) percentage of the population living in urban areas, (2) percentage of the population which was black, (3) percentage of the population living below the poverty level, and (4) the per capita male population aged 18–24 years. In a multiple regression analysis, which included not only the highly correlated control measures but additional control variables, such as the rate of other violent crimes, the rate of nonviolent crime, and the status of women, the magazine index was the most highly weighted of all the variables. This index had a regression coefficient of 6.99, indicating that for every increase in pornographic magazine consumption of approximately 1 standard deviation, the reported incidence of rape increased by 7 per 100,000 population.

In subsequent analyses of this data set, using per capita police expenditures, number of rate crisis centers, National Organization of Women (NOW) membership, *Ms. Magazine* circulation, number of battered women's shelters, and average temperature as control variables, Baron and Straus (1985) found that six factors accounted for 83% of the variation in the rape rate. These six factors were the above-mentioned sex magazine index, indices of sexual inequality, economic inequality, social disorganization, level of urbanization, and unemployment. Jaffe and Straus (cited in Attorney General's Commission on Pornography, 1986, p. 947) found the same relationship between the sex magazine index and rape rate, this time ruling out the possibility that sexual liberalism played a major role in explaining the simultaneous variation in sex magazine circulation and rape rate.

Similar analyses on this same data set do not indicate that pornography consumption and rape rate relate to one another in ways that would be expected if pornography consumption was a causal factor. For example, Scott and Schwalm (cited in Attorney General's Commission on Pornography, 1986, p. 947) found that circulation for magazines such as *Playboy, Penthouse,* and *Oui* was significantly related to the rape rate, but circulation of *Hustler* was not. Since *Hustler* is often considered to be semi-hard-core pornography and the others relatively soft-core, this relationship does not make sense if pornography was influencing rape rate fluctuations. Likewise, Scott (1985) found that other indices of hard-core pornography consumption, such as number of adult theaters or number of adult bookstores, was not significantly related to the rape rate, while circulation of outdoor magazines such as *Field and Stream* were.

While Court's (1984) data suggest that liberalizing pornography laws influences rape rates, studies using the Baron and Straus (1984) methodology suggest that *if* pornography influences the rape rate, it is the general consumption of pornography rather than the use of any particular form that influences offending. On a commonsense basis, it would seem that if any type of pornography use directly influences rape rates, it ought to be the use of sexually violent materials.

Of course, the correlation between the general availability or pornography and rape rates might be due to a third underlying variable responsible for both. Baron and Straus (1984), for example, suggested that a "hypermasculine" cultural pattern, characterized by social norms and values supporting male dominance and male interests, might encourage beliefs in rape myths and the use of women as sexual objects, as well as encourage the acceptance of interpersonal violence. To test this hypothesis, Baron and Straus (1986) devised an index derived from 14 items from the General Social Survey (Davis & Smith, 1982) which they called the "Violence Approval Index." This index was intended to reflect values and beliefs which were characteristic of a hypermasculine cultural pattern. When this new measure was entered into the regression analysis on the 40 states for which a Violence Approval Index could be derived, the relationship between rape rates and sex magazine circulation rates become statistically insignificant.

Another puzzling finding in this type of research is the lack of rape in some cultures where violent sexual imagery is extremely popular. For example, Abramson and Hayashi (1984) reported that although sexually violent pornography is currently very popular among male audiences in Japan, the reported incidence of rape is substantially lower than in Western nations. They report that although the pornography in Japan is less sexually explicit than that of Western nations, the best way to guarantee the success of a Japanese adult film is to include bondage and rape scenes. The juxtaposition of sex and violence is also reported to be very popular in Japanese novels, sex cartoons, and sexological museums.

While Abramson and Hayashi's conclusions are speculative, there are noticeable differences in the way stimuli which Westerners would regard as pornographic are dealt with in Japan as compared to Western cultures. Japan has less compartmentalization of sexual themes than is the case in Western nations. While sexually explicit themes are restricted to pornography in the West, in Japan mild degrees of nudity are present in general interest magazines and on public television. Japan also has strong social sanctions against rape, which Abramson and Hayashi believe prevent rape due to the "shame" associated with being caught.

The Attorney General's commissioners argued that the rape rate in Japan is grossly underestimated from official records. They cited Goldstein and Ibaraki (Attorney General's Commission on Pornography, 1986, p. 942), who found in an informal survey that 90% of the Japanese women interviewed declared they would not report being raped. However, that is not very different from the case in Western countries. Estimates of the likelihood that American women would report a rape range from 10–40% (Clark & Lewis, 1977).

Whatever the case, there does seem to be some evidence that free availability of pornography, even violent pornography, does not lead inevitably to higher rates of sexually violent crime. The coincidence of pornography consumption and reported incidence of rape within Western society does indicate that there is sufficient cause for concern. However, the mere fact that increases in rape and increases in consumption of pornography appear coincidentally does not necessarily indicate they are causally related. This relationship may indicate that other changing societal values and pressures producing these periodic fluctuations may equally and simultaneously affect pornography consumption, legislation concerning pornographic regulation, and the incidence of sexually violent crimes.

CULTURAL VALUES AND PREVALENT PORNOGRAPHY THEMES

If changing societal values do tend to concomitantly affect these three factors, then it should be possible to find particular cultural values which are related to the incidence of sexually violent crime. Sanday (1981) presented evidence tending to support this conclusion. She investigated the incidence of rape as reported from accumulated anthropological research examining 156 tribal societies in existence from 1750 B.C. until the late 1960s. She defined a society as rape-prone when the incidence of intrasocietal rape was high, when rape was allowed as a ceremonial act, or when rape was used to threaten or punish women. A society was described as rape-free when rape was infrequent or did not occur at all. In her analysis, 47% of these societies were defined as rape-free, 18% were defined as rape-prone, and the rest were placed in an intermediate category. Sixteen variables were examined for possible relationships with her rape categorizations of the society. Among these were indices of sexual repression, interpersonal violence, child-rearing, and the ideology of male dominance. Of these, all indices of intergroup and interpersonal violence were associated with rape-proneness, as were all indices of male dominance. No relationship was found between indices of sexual repression and rape-proneness, and there was no relationship between the distance in mother–son relationships and rape-proneness. This analysis suggests that those societies which are accepting of interpersonal violence and promote male dominance tend to be more accepting of rape and/or produce more rapists. These are the same values and norms which fit Baron and Straus's hypermasculinity factor.

If rape-prone cultural values are increasingly evident in Western pornography, then we might expect the relationship between pornography consumption and sex crimes to be stronger in recent years than it was at the time the President's Commission on Obscenity and Pornography (1970) conducted it's research. Since 1970 the volume of pornography has increased dramatically, partially due to the liberalization of pornography laws (Court, 1984). Empirical studies examining the content of pornography have shown an increase in the percentage of sexually violent and male domination themes in over-the-counter pornography during the same period (Malamuth & Spinner, 1980; Smith, 1976). Dietz and Evans (1982) found that 89.3% of the covers included in their survey of readily available pornography magazines belonged to categories that were either unavailable in 1970 or were previously sold only under the counter.

On the other hand, such changes are not limited to pornographic materials. Palys (1986) sampled home videos in Vancouver, Canada. He found that in a comparison of Canadian "adult" home videos, which are sexually suggestive, but not explicit (equivalent to an "R" rating in the United States), and Canadian "triple-X" home videos, which are sexually explicit, the triple-X videos displayed more egalitarian sex roles between men and women and were much less violent than the adult videos. Over the years 1979–1983, Palys (1986) reported that the difference between these two types of videos may be widening, due mainly to the triple-X video becoming less violent over time. On the average, the adult films had 45 scenes involving aggression per video, compared to only 1.6 aggressive scenes for triple-X movies.

Another comparison worth noting is the prevalence of bondage–discipline themes in pornographic versus nonpornographic literature. Dietz and Evans (1982) found that 17.2% of the covers of magazines in adult bookstores depicted bondage or domination themes, while Winick (1985) found such themes comprised 4.9% of the content of magazines in these bookstores. By comparison, Dietz, Harry, and Hazelwood (1986) found that 38% of the covers of detective magazines, not generally considered to be pornographic, depicted bondage themes, and 76% of the covers depicted domination. Thus, it would appear that aggressive and sexual domination themes are not limited to pornography and probably reflect the popularity of these themes in our present culture.

These data suggest that the worldwide liberalization of pornography laws in the late 1960s and early 1970s created two effects: (1) an increased volume of sexually explicit materials on the market and (2) a proliferation of sexually violent or degrading pornography that was not easily obtainable prior to the liberalization laws. It appears that as pornography becomes more widely available, the content changes and increasingly endorses those attitudes found to be corre- lated with rape-proneness in Sanday's analysis: the acceptance of interpersonal violence (with pornography expressly focusing that violence on women) and the ideology of male dominance. Although there is some suggestion that this trend appears to be reversing for pornographic imagery, probably due mainly to in- creased public concern over violent pornography (Donnerstein *et al.*, 1987; Palys, 1986), those forms of media which are not as vigilantly monitored as hard- core pornography appear to retain violence as a major theme. If it is the depic- tion of violence rather than the depiction of explicit sex, then perhaps public concern should be shifted toward more popular and available media forms.

The question of the relationship between sexual crimes and pornography then becomes a decision among several plausible causal models. One possibility, the pornography–rape model, suggests that as pornography becomes more widely available, mildly sexually explicit stimuli become boring. This results in an increased tendency to incorporate themes in the material that the buyer will find attractive, such as depicting the male as strong and powerful. Violence and male domination over women, then, is incorporated as a way to ensure the continued sales of pornography by making it more ego-gratifying to the con- sumer. As the prevalence of these types of images increases, the attitudes of the pornography-consuming public change in the direction of attitudes reflective of those of a rape-prone society, and it is by this route that pornography increases (if indeed it does) the incidence of violent sexual crime. Other forms of media may then take on some of these features of pornography and, as a result, desensitize a large percentage of the population to violent sex.

An alternative model, the culture–rape model, postulates that as societal values change toward those of a rape-prone culture, acceptance of pornography increases, resulting in the liberalization of pornography laws. The relaxing of these laws results in increased consumption of pornography. The changing content of pornography and other forms of media and the increase in the rape rates can then all be seen as a by-product of a progressive change in societal values.

The pornography–rape model declares that the consumption of pornogra- phy plays a major role in the creation of deviant sexual interests and thus increases the incidence of sexual offending. The culture–rape model suggests that the prevailing attitudes of the culture influence both the incidence of sexual crimes and pornography consumption. In order to correctly differentiate be- tween these two models, we must first examine the literature on reactions of normal human males to pornographic imagery. The non-sex-offender male can be considered as a model to study some of the processes which may occur in sex- offender males in reaction to pornography.

EFFECTS OF PORNOGRAPHY ON NONOFFENDER MALES

The first assumption underlying the pornography–rape model is the idea that pornography becomes boring with continued use. There is a substantial body of literature suggesting that normal males lose their sexual interest in pornography after repeated exposure to it (Kutchinsky, 1971; Reifler, Howard, Lipton, Liptzin & Widmann, 1971; Schaefer & Colgan, 1977; Schmidt, 1975). Most of these studies required subjects to simply watch pornographic films, whereas Schaefer and Colgan (1977) required some of their subjects to masturbate immediately after exposure to erotic stimuli. Those subjects required to masturbate showed enhanced arousal to erotic stimuli compared to control subjects, who showed reduced arousal with continued exposure. To the extent that masturbation to erotic stimuli is part of the usual behavioral repertoire of pornography consumers, then pornography may not typically become boring with continued use.

However, the supposition that the tendency to progress toward more violent pornographic images as a result of boredom, and that such exposure will lead a person to become more violence oriented, is certainly not supported by data which show that violent pornography becomes boring with repeated use, even amongst force-oriented males (Ceniti & Malamuth, 1984). Boredom may not be the most critical element in explaining the changing content of pornography over time. Laws and Marshall (Chapter 13, this volume) suggest that via conditioning processes, fantasies become progressively refined as the individual attends to those elements in the fantasy that are appealing. Thus, it might be that pornography changes over time to incorporate those themes that are attractive to the male ego.

The third component of the pornography–rape model suggests that violent and male domination themes in pornography produce attitudinal changes in the consumer similar to those of individuals in rape-prone cultures. Support for this view comes from a series of experiments which dramatically indicate that pornography consumption results in increased sexual "callousness," negative attitudes toward women, and acceptance of rape and other forms of interpersonal violence against women (Malamuth & Check, 1980, 1981; Malamuth, Haber, & Feshbach, 1980; Zillman & Bryant, 1984). In particular, Zillman and Bryant (1984) found such changes despite decreased autonomic arousal to pornographic images after massive exposure to nonviolent sexual themes which degraded women.

Donnerstein *et al.* (1987) report two unpublished doctoral dissertations (Krafka, 1985; Linz, 1985) both of which failed to replicate the finding that massive exposure to dehumanizing but nonviolent pornography led to increased callousness toward women and acceptance of rape. Krafka and Linz, however, used feature-length films containing only brief segments of the relevant themes, whereas Zillman and Bryant used excerpts which exclusively depicted degrading activities. Donnerstein *et al.* (1987) suggest that a low ratio of dehumanizing scenes to neutral scenes may modify the immediate impact that is seen when only the dehumanizing scenes are presented. Donnerstein *et al.* (1987) suggest that a more concentrated dosage of sexually degrading themes or a longer term of exposure may be needed for these effects to occur.

If we accept Donnerstein's explanation, the next step is to show that the accumulated effects of currently available pornography over time result in an increased callousness toward women or an increased acceptance of rape. Such a study would be unfeasible in the laboratory but might be possible via retrospective methods. Garcia (1986) presented male college students with three questionnaires: the Attitudes Towards Women Scale (Spence & Helmreich, 1972), the Attitudes Toward Rape Scale (Feild, 1978), and a questionnaire asking about the type and frequency of pornography use. Scores on the two attitude scales were not correlated with the frequency of using nonviolent pornography, but many of the correlations of the subscales of these questionnaires were correlated in the expected direction with the frequency of using pornography with violent themes. These correlations were of extremely low magnitude, and there is no evidence that pornography use preceded the self-reported attitudes. However, the findings do suggest that high-frequency use of violent pornography and strong negative attitudes toward women tend to coincide.

Another negative effect of viewing pornography postulated by the pornography–rape model is an increase in aggressive tendencies. From the standpoint of this chapter, the most useful data come from studies examining aggression by males against a female victim. Studies of this type require subjects to deliver "shocks" or other punishment in an experimental task, where the subject to be shocked is actually a confederate of the experimenter.

In his review of these studies, Donnerstein (1984) concluded that investigations which showed increases in aggression against female confederates after viewing nonaggressive pornography usually employed highly arousing stimuli and required the use of a procedure which reduced the inhibitions to aggress against a woman. For example, in one paradigm the subject is made angry before or immediately after a pornographic stimulus presentation (Donnerstein & Barrett, 1978). In another, the subject is provided with several opportunities to aggress (Donnerstein & Hallam, 1978).

While it may be necessary to associate anti-inhibition procedures with the nonaggressive sexual stimuli in these paradigms, pornography which combines aggressive and sexual themes is capable of increasing aggression against female confederates without any additional procedure. In fact, after exposure to violent pornography, the intensity of shock given to female confederates is generally greater than that given to male confederates (Donnerstein, 1980; Donnerstein & Hallam, 1978). Similar results have been obtained with so-called nonpornographic films which combine sexual and aggressive themes (Donnerstein, 1983). Inhibition-releasing factors appear to be necessary to facilitate subsequent aggression only when the violent pornographic film depicts the female as being an unwilling participant (Donnerstein & Berkowitz, 1981). When the female is perceived as being willing, aggression is released with no inhibition-releasing pretreatment (Donnerstein & Berkowitz, 1981). This suggests that portrayal of a woman's willingness to accept violence, itself, acts as a releaser to aggression against women in general. Such depictions are common in rape pornography.

The culture–rape model (the hypothesis that the correlation between pornography consumption and sexual crime is due to the fact that both are caused by societal values and attitudes) presents some problems of experimental evaluation. The correlations reported by Garcia (1986) showing a relationship between negative attitudes toward women, as well as callous attitudes toward rape, and the frequency of violent pornography use can be as readily explained by this model as they can by the pornography–rape model. However, there is evidence suggesting that exposure to pornography and societal attitudes conducive to rape may mutually contribute to rape-proneness. First, there are data indicating that exposure to violent or degrading pornography may have detrimental effects, such as enhancing negative attitudes toward women and increasing the acceptance of rape myths (Malamuth & Check, 1981), lower inhibitions to aggress against women (Donnerstein, 1980; Donnerstein & Berkowitz, 1981), and producing subsequent violent sexual fantasies in the viewer (Malamuth, 1981). Conversely, such variables as preexisting pro-rape attitudes, negative attitudes toward women, and self-reported likelihood of raping have been found to be correlated with both physiological and subjective arousal to rape depictions (Malamuth & Check, 1980, 1983; Malamuth, Check, & Briere, 1986). Malamuth (1986) found that physiological and subjective arousal to rape, negative attitudes toward women, power as a motive for sexual acts, and acceptance of violence toward women all interactively predicted self-reported aggression against women. The upshot of all of this research is that neither a pornography–rape model nor a culture–rape model is completely adequate in and of itself. It is probably most beneficial to consider both models as mutually interactive.

One factor to consider in evaluating these studies is the individual differences existing prior to laboratory exposure to erotic stimuli, particularly rape stimuli. Males who report a low tendency to react aggressively toward women in sexual situations do not show a great deal of arousal to rape depictions, especially if the woman is portrayed as suffering from the experience (Malamuth & Check, 1983). The depicted victim pain, suffering, and abhorrence of the act tend to reduce the arousal of males who report a likelihood of raping, but these men still show considerable arousal to those rape depictions which reinforce both the idea that women enjoy rape and the notion of male domination (Malamuth & Check, 1983; Malamuth et al., 1986). Similarly, convicted rapists show considerable arousal to rape depictions, even if the victim is described as suffering (Quinsey & Chaplin, 1984). Not surprisingly, men who report a high likelihood of raping are similar to rapists in that both hold callous attitudes towards rape and are likely to endorse rape myths (Malamuth, 1981).

The data suggest that the male population is distributed along a continuum of proneness to sexual aggression (Malamuth, 1984), with men having no tendency to aggress sexually at one end and violent rapists at the other. The position occupied by a person along this continuum appears to moderate the effect pornography may have on his sexual arousal and attitudinal changes due to exposure. The power of pornography to change the location of an individual along this continuum has not yet been examined.

The similarity among the cultural views associated with a society classified as rape-prone, the prevalent themes in pornographic literature, and the beliefs which characterize sexually force-oriented males leads to the tentative conclusion that rapists have been excessively exposed to societal attitudes that contribute to sexual violence. These beliefs or attitudes may have arisen due to pornography consumption, or pornography simply may have served to reflect and perpetuate deviant beliefs preexisting in the sex offender prior to exposure. A third possibility is that pornography plays no role whatever in the life of the sex offender.

PORNOGRAPHY IN THE LIFE OF THE SEX OFFENDER

One way of ascertaining the possible role of pornography in the etiology of sex offenses is to examine patterns of pornography use among known sex offenders and among the noncriminal population. Conceivably, pornography use may have differential effects at various stages of life. To examine pornography use at different ages, the researcher might interview adults who have and have not been convicted of a sex offense and question them about the history of their pornography use. This approach is not ideal due to various inevitable problems (e.g., retrospective report, selective memory, desire to justify actions, covering up due to guilt, etc.). Also, since pornography availability varies across time, experiences among populations differing in age may differ in terms of the type of pornography to which they were exposed at different periods.

Goldstein, Kant, and Hartman (1974) extensively investigated the history of pornography use among three groups of sex offenders: rapists, heterosexual pedophiles, and homosexual pedophiles. They compared the histories of these men to those obtained from a group of semimatched normal controls. Superficially, there was very little difference between the use reported by the sex offender and that reported by the control groups. No differences between groups were evident in the percentages exposed to pornography prior to age 12 years. Approximately two-thirds of each group reported exposure before age 12, with 22% having their first exposure prior to age 9 and 45% having their first exposure between 9 and 12 years. While most of the members of all groups reported having some exposure to pornography during adolescence, all sex offenders reported less variety in the types of pornographic media to which they had been exposed than did the controls.

Similar findings regarding the use of pornography in general were reported in another study sponsored by the President's Commission on Obscenity and Pornography (Cook, Fosen, & Pacht, 1971). Cook et al. (1971) interviewed two groups drawn from a prison population: sex offenders and criminal code violators. Only 28% of the sex offenders compared to 51% of the criminal code violators reported being exposed to pornography prior to age 10. The sex offenders reported less exposure to pornography during adolescence and claimed they used milder forms of pornography than those reported by the criminal code violators. Despite the fact that these groups were not matched on demographic variables or in the degree of violence employed in their offense, Cook et al. (1971) concluded that sex offenders were more "sexually repressed" than other types of prison offenders.

Since Goldstein et al. (1974) reported that 22% of their sample of sex offenders reported using pornography prior to age 9 years, while Cook et al. (1971)

found that 28% of their sex offenders reported using pornography prior to age 10 years, the percentages obtained probably are representative of the preadolescent exposure to pornography among imprisoned sex offenders. These percentages are not that different from those obtained from other adult men with similar socioeconomic and educational backgrounds (Goldstein *et al.*, 1974), but they are much lower than that obtained from other members of the prison population (51%; Cook *et al.*, 1971). One possible explanation is that the criminal offender population came from cultural backgrounds in which exposure to pornography was more common at a young age.

While Goldstein *et al.* (1974) did not find differences between the sex offenders and the control subjects in overall exposure to pornography, they did find differences in the histories of pornography use between the rapist and control groups. These two groups differed in the explicitness of the pornography used as young children. Thirty percent of the rapists compared to 2% of the controls had experience with stimuli depicting explicit sexual acts rather than simple nude photographs. The groups also differed in parental supervision and parental reaction to pornography use; only 18% of the parents of future rapists discovered that their children were using pornography compared to 37% of the parents of the controls. However, all of the rapists who were caught reported being punished, whereas only 7% of the controls were punished. Many of the controls reported that their parents had taken the time to explain what they were seeing; none of the rapists reported this positive parental response.

During adolescence the picture is much the same. Goldstein *et al.* (1974) reported very few statistically significant differences between the sex-offender groups and the normal controls on the types of pornography they were exposed to as adolescents or in the frequency with which these materials were used. Cook *et al.* (1971) found that during adolescence, sex offenders were exposed to pornography less frequently and used less explicit forms than did criminal code offenders.

More recently, Marshall (1988) interviewed a sample of outpatient sex offenders admitted to his clinic over a 6-year period and compared their reports to those obtained from a matched sample of nonoffenders who had volunteered to participate in other research. Around the time of pubescence, 33% of heterosexual pedophiles, 39% of homosexual pedophiles, 33% of rapists, and 21% of normals reported contact with hard-core pornography, but incest offenders reported no contact. The groups differed in the method by which they obtained these materials. Most subjects reported discovering such materials by accident at home or at a friend's house. Very few reported actively seeking out such materials, but all who did (8/11 heterosexual pedophiles, 1/7 homosexual pedophiles, 2/8 rapists and 0/5 nonoffenders who reported any exposure at this age) were members of one of the sex-offender groups.

Although not dealing directly with sex offenders, Davis and Braucht (1973) examined the role that adolescent use of pornography, family deviance, and neighborhood deviance may have played in the criterion variables of character development and self-reported sexual deviance. They collected data from 365 subjects in seven different populations ranging from jail inmates to Catholic seminary students. Series of simple correlations between the predictor variables and the criterion variables were compared. The total sample was divided into three parts: those having experience with pornography before age 13 years, those with first exposure between ages 13–17, and those exposed to pornography after age 17 years.

Davis and Braucht found that "moral character" (a composite score based on subject's answers to situation-based alternative moral–less-moral choices, their score on Kohlberg's (1969) moral reasoning task, and ratings of moral character by significant others) was negatively correlated with exposure to pornography only for those subjects whose first exposure was after age 17 years. The investigators failed to report whether or not membership in the various subgroups (i.e., inmates, seminary students, etc.) was evenly distributed across all initial age of exposure subgroups. It might well be that certain subgroups scoring high on moral character indices (such as the seminary students) might not be exposed to pornography at all or not until quite late in life; such subjects would thus be disproportionately represented in the late age of exposure group.

For all groups, both deviance in the family and neighborhood deviance was negatively correlated with character development. All three predictor variables were significantly correlated with the measure of self-reported sexual deviance. Davis and Braucht (1973) did not consider this pattern of results to be evidence ruling out a possible causal relationship between sexual deviance and pornography. However, they did emphasize that the existing data suggested that pornography use was a part of a generally deviant life-style. This may help to explain the Cook *et al.* (1971) data which showed criminal code violators to be more likely than sex offenders to use pornography as children.

While the differences between sex-offender groups and control groups in childhood use of pornography appear to be very subtle, there are marked differences between the groups in their pornographic use as adults. For example, Goldstein *et al.* (1974) found that 46% of rapists, 59% of homosexual pedophiles, and 50% of heterosexual pedophiles reported that they would like to own some pornography, while only 29% of the normal controls reported this desire. Of those men reporting a desire to own pornography, 100% of the rapists, 80% of the homosexual pedophiles, and 83% of the heterosexual pedophiles actually owned some type of pornographic material. Only 50% of the normal controls who reported a desire to own pornography actually did so. Therefore, the men in the sex-offender groups were about three times more likely to own pornography as adults than normal controls.

These investigators also reported that while the vast majority of subjects in both rapist and non-sex-offender groups masturbated to erotica during adolescence, by adulthood the majority of rapists still used pornography for masturbatory purposes, but few of the non-sex-offenders did. Cook *et al.* (1971) reported that as adults, sex offenders also responded differently to pornography than did the criminal code offenders. Sex offenders were more likely to masturbate after viewing pornography, while criminal code offenders were more likely to engage in sexual intercourse.

Marshall (1988) also investigated this issue. About half of his sample of child molesters and rapists reported that they always or usually incorporated deviant fantasy material into their masturbatory activities, while none of the incest or nonoffenders admitted to more than occasional use of deviant themes. Approximately two-thirds of the rapists and child molesters reported that they also engaged in deviant fantasies independent of masturbation. Of most interest is the finding that the majority of sex offenders who reported high-frequency rates of masturbation were more likely to be current users of pornography.

Carter, Prentky, Knight, Vanderveer, and Boucher (1986) compared groups of incarcerated pedophiles and rapists. Pedophiles were more likely to report exposure to pornography as adults and to report that pornography had a greater overall influence on their lives than the rapist group. Only 6.6% of the pedophiles reported that pornography had little or no influence on their lives, but 38.7% of the rapists reported little or no influence.

Even if it could be established that sex offenders use pornography more than other groups, this would not indicate that pornography use tends to increase the risk of sex offenses. Goldstein *et al.*'s (1974) sex offenders denied that the use of pornography played a significant role in the commission of their offenses. However, Carter *et al.* (1986) reported that child molesters were twice as likely as rapists to report having used pornography prior to the offense, during an offense, or to relieve the urge to commit an offense. Marshall (1988) found that more than one-third of his sample of rapists and child molesters had been incited by the use of hard-core sexual stimuli to commit an offense. In addition, 53% of the child molesters and 33% of the rapists who admitted that pornography use incited their offense deliberately used such material as part of their pre-offense preparation. Marshall found that the subgroup of sex offenders who were higher-frequency masturbators (more than twice a week; 42%) were more likely to report pornography use as an instigator of their offense than the low-frequency masturbators.

In our outpatient clinic (Laws, 1988), we routinely ask pedophiles questions about their pornography use on a pencil-and-paper intake questionnaire. One might expect a tendency to underreport pornography use on such a questionnaire, especially since trust between therapist and client is not clearly established at the time of reporting. Despite these reservations, almost all the pedophiles have admitted to being exposed to adult erotica at least once in their lives (52 out of 55, or 95%), but relatively few admit ever having been exposed to any type of child pornography (5 out of 55, or 9.1%). Eight of the pedophiles admitted to taking pictures of their victims (14.5%) for their own personal use, and yet six of these eight reported that they had never viewed any other child erotica. If we include those offenders who report taking pictures of their victims, then the total who admit exposure to child erotica is 8 (20%). This 8 does not include three pedophiles who took only clothed pictures of the victims and did not report any other exposure to child erotica. The data on picture production is also evidence suggesting that pornography use plays a role in the commission of a small percentage of child molestation offenses.

Yet another view of the use of pornography use by sex offenders comes from their victims. Silbert and Pines (1984) interviewed 200 female prostitutes working in the San Francisco Bay area, of whom the majority (60%) were under age 16 years. These subjects were asked about rape experiences and early childhood sexual victimization (independent of their prostitution). The investigators made no attempt to question their subjects on the involvement of pornography in the perpetration of sexual crimes against them, but many of the subjects volunteered such information.

Of these 200 females, 193 reported rape victimization, and 24% said that the rapist referred to specific pornographic materials he had seen. The comments in these cases followed a particular pattern. The rapist first referred to the materials he had seen, then insisted that the victim was actually enjoying the rape, including the violence. In 19% of the rapes the victim revealed that she was a prostitute, hoping to prevent some of the violence. Instead, the rapist escalated the violence. In 12% of the 193 cases, the knowledge that the victim was a prostitute also elicited comments from the rapist about pornography. Most of these comments referred to specific literature the rapist had seen in which prostitutes preferred excessive violence.

A similar pattern was found in the unsolicited comments from the 178 cases of reported juvenile sexual abuse prior to becoming a prostitute. Of these subjects, 22% mentioned varied use of pornography by the offender prior to the act. Some abusers used sexual materials to try to entice the victims, others used sexual materials to justify their actions, while still others used them in the presence of the victim prior to the offense in order to arouse themselves sexually.

While the data from childhood use of pornography does not lead to the inevitable conclusion that early use of pornography leads to a career of sexual deviance, some evidence suggests that adult patterns of pornography use differ not only between normal controls and sex offenders but also between selected types of sex offenders (Carter et al., 1986; Goldstein et al., 1974; Marshall, 1988). Early studies using interviews with sex offenders led to the conclusion that pornography did not play an important role in the commission of sexual offenses (Goldstein et al., 1974). But more recent studies, which have employed means of assuring client confidentiality, reveal that at least a proportion of offenders use pornography prior to or during an actual offense (Carter et al., 1986; Marshall, 1988). In addition, the indirect evidence obtained in the Silbert and Pines' (1984) study suggests that in a large proportion of the cases, the sex offender's deviant actions were justified, at least in his own mind, by the pornography he consumed. Since these comments were unsolicited, the true proportions of such statements during the commission of their acts may be much larger. Indeed, the Attorney General's Commission on Pornography (1986) published excerpts from victim testimony clearly showing that many of them had reason to believe that pornography played a role in the offender's preoffense preparation or was used in the actual offense.

Based on the data presented here, it seems that pornography use is a factor in the lives of sex offenders, and it appears to play a role in inciting at least some of these offenders to commit an offense. However, the evidence does not support the claim that pornography plays a causal role in the etiology of a deviant sexual orientation. First, in order to find early patterns of pornography use which differentiate sex offenders from normals, one must examine patterns of pornography use before the age of 8 or 9 years. The only research examining pornography use at this age suggests that the home life of the sex offender is significantly different from that of the nonoffender (Goldstein *et al.*, 1974). Future rapists are more likely to find hard-core pornography in the home and are more likely to be punished for using such material than are the future nonoffenders.

Adolescent use patterns are remarkably consistent across all studies, indicating that on most measures sex offenders report patterns of use similar to those of nonoffenders. The sole discrepancy is Marshall's (1988) finding that sex offenders report a greater willingness to procure pornographic material for themselves in adolescence than the nonoffender comparison group.

By the time they are adults, the self-reported data of sex offenders indicate the important role pornography has come to play in their lives. While both nonoffenders and sex offenders report masturbating to pornography in adolescence, adult masturbatory activity in reaction to pornography is more common in sex offenders than in nonoffenders. Sex offenders show a greater desire to own pornography and report owning more pornography than do normals. Sex offenders also report that pornography use plays an important role in inciting them to offend, and this may be more often true for those offenders for whom masturbatory activity is an important sexual outlet.

CONCLUSIONS

Most of the studies on which this review is based have focused on the role pornography plays in the commission of rape. Rape statistics are frequently used to gauge sex crime frequencies in cross-cultural studies. Also, most of the research looking at the effects of erotic stimulation on normals has concentrated on the role pornography may play in the etiology of a deviant interest in rape. Therefore, in arriving at any conclusions, it is simplest to consider the rapist population.

Cultures which are rape-prone tend to overemphasize male dominance and separation of the sexes, and they tend to accept violence against women (Sanday, 1981). On an individual level, Malamuth (1986) found that male college students' sexual aggression against women could be predicted by a number of variables, including belief in male dominance, acceptance of interpersonal violence, and sexual arousal to rape. Examination of the available studies of the reactions of rape-prone college students to various types of sexually aggressive depictions and those of rapists to similar materials leads to one noticeable difference. Rapists are more likely to be aroused by rape scripts which show considerable abuse of the victim, whereas male college students are not. In other words, rapists become sexually aroused by stimuli which show the male achieving more dominance over the woman, and these men are more accepting of interpersonal violence than are force-oriented male college students. Content analyses of pornography show that the prevalent themes depict men achieving their sexual aims by dominating women who enjoy being humiliated. In addition, the very tolerance of violence in these materials implies an acceptance of violence. In other words, pornography reinforces the views that sexually aggressive men already hold.

Studies of sex offenders find that pornography plays a much more important role in the life of the pedophile than in the life of the rapist. In Marshall's (1988) study, more pedophiles were high-frequency masturbators, and this particular behavior pattern predicted general pornography use and the use of pornography in the commission of the offense. Existing research in nonoffender populations has concentrated on themes that may shed some light on rapist populations, but as yet there is very little knowledge concerning why pornography comes to play such an important role in the life of some pedophiles.

However, comparison studies of the life histories of sex offenders and nonoffenders do tend to suggest that the early home environment of the sex offender differs in important ways from that of the nonoffender, particularly regarding the general availability of pornography and parental reaction to pornography use. Sex offenders also differ from normals in the developmental characteristics of pornography use. Nonoffenders tend to outgrow pornography in adolescence, whereas pornography becomes increasingly important to many sex offenders after they grow into adulthood. Even in nonoffender populations, the preexisting sociocultural attitudes of the subject has an important influence on the effect of exposure to pornography.

All this tends to suggest that it is not exposure to pornography *per se* that has an influence upon the incidence of sexual crime, but rather the nature of the person being exposed and the existing cultural milieu in which that exposure occurs. In a cultural environment where people are not considered to be sexual objects, pornography use probably would have little effect on sexual crime. Ironically, in such a culture, pornography itself would most likely not exist.

REFERENCES

Abramson, P., & Hayashi, H. (1984). Pornography in Japan: Cross-cultural and theoretical considerations. In N. M. Malamuth & E. Donnerstein (Eds.), *Pornography and sexual aggression* (pp. 173–183). Orlando, FL: Academic Press.

Attorney General's Commission on Pornography. (1986, July). *Final Report*. Washington, DC: U.S. Department of Justice.

Baron, L., & Straus, M. (1984). Sexual stratification, pornography and rape in the United States. In N. M. Malamuth & E. Donnerstein (Eds.), *Pornography and sexual aggression* (pp. 185–209). Orlando, FL: Academic Press.

Baron, L., & Straus, M. (1985). *Legitimate violence, pornography, and sexual inequality as explanations for state and regional differences in rape.* Unpublished manuscript, Yale University, New Haven, CT.

Baron, L., & Straus, M. (1986). *Rape and its relation to social disorganization, pornography, and sexual inequality in the United States.* Unpublished manuscript, Yale University, New Haven, CT.

Ben-Veniste R. (1971). Pornography and sex crime: The Danish experience. Technical report of the commission on obscenity and pornography: Erotica and behavior, Vol. 8. Washington, DC: U.S. Government Printing Office.

Carter, D. L., Prentky, R., Knight, R. A., Vanderveer, P., & Boucher, R. (1986). *Use of pornography in the criminal and developmental histories of sexual offenders.* Unpublished manuscript, Massachusetts Treatment Center, Research Department, Bridgewater, MA.

Ceniti, J., & Malamuth, N. M. (1984). Effects of repeated exposure to sexually violent or non-violent stimuli on sexual arousal to rape and nonrape depictions. *Behaviour Research and Therapy, 22,* 535–548.

Clark, L., & Lewis, D. (1977). *Rape: The price of coercive sexuality.* Toronto: The Women's Press.

Cline, V. B. (1974). *Where do you draw the line?* Provo, UT: Brigham Young University Press.

Cook, R., Fosen, R. H., & Pacht, A. (1971). Pornography and the sex offender: Patterns of exposure and immediate arousal of effects of pornographic stimuli. *Journal of Applied Psychology, 55*(6), 503–511.

Court, J. H. (1984). Sex and violence: A ripple effect. In N. M. Malamuth & E. Donnerstein (Eds.), *Pornography and sexual aggression* (pp. 143–172). Orlando, FL: Academic Press.

Davis, K. E., & Braucht, G. N. (1973). Exposure to pornography, character, and sexual deviance: A retrospective survey. *Journal of Social Issues, 29,* 183–196.

Davis, J., & Smith, T. (1982). *General social surveys, 1972–1982: Cumulative codebook.* Chicago: University of Chicago Press.

Dietz, P. E., & Evans, B. (1982). Pornographic imagery and prevalence of paraphilia. *American Journal of Psychiatry, 139,* 1493–1495.

Dietz, P. E., Harry, B., & Hazelwood, R. R. (1986). Detective magazines: Pornography for the sexual sadist? *Journal of Forensic Sciences, 31,* 197–211.

Donnerstein, E. (1980). Aggressive erotica and violence against women. *Journal of Personality and Social Psychology, 39,* 269–277.

Donnerstein, E. (1983). Erotica and human aggression. In R. Geen & E. Donnerstein (Eds.), *Aggression: Theoretical and empirical reviews* (Vol. 2, pp. 127–154). New York: Academic Press.

Donnerstein, E. (1984). Pornography: Its effect on violence against women. In N. M. Malamuth & E. Donnerstein (Eds.), *Pornography and sexual aggression* (pp. 53–81). Orlando, FL: Academic Press.

Donnerstein, E., & Barrett, G. (1978). The effects of erotic stimuli on male aggression toward females. *Journal of Personality and Social Psychology, 36,* 180–188.

Donnerstein, E., & Berkowitz, L. (1981). Victim reactions in aggressive-erotic films as a factor in violence against women. *Journal of Personality and Social Psychology, 41,* 710–724.

Donnerstein, E., & Hallam, J. (1978). The facilitating effects of erotica on aggression towards females. *Journal of Personality and Social Psychology, 36,* 1270–1277.

Donnerstein, E., Linz, D., & Penrod, S. (1987). *The question of pornography: Research findings and policy implications.* New York: The Free Press.

Feild, H. S. (1978). Attitudes toward rape: A comparative analysis of police, crisis counselors and citizens. *Journal of Personality and Social Psychology, 36,* 156–179.

Garcia, L. T. (1986). Exposure to pornography and attitudes about women and rape: A correlation study. *Journal of Sex Research, 22,* 378–385.

Goldstein, M. J., Kant, H. S., & Hartman, J. J. (1974). *Pornography and sexual deviance.* Berkeley: University of California Press.

Kohlberg, L. (1969). Stage and sequence: The cognitive-development approach to socialization. In D. A. Goslin (Ed.), *Handbook of socialization theory and research* (pp. 347–480). Chicago: Rand-McNally.

Krafka, C. L. (1985). *Sexually explicit, sexually violent, and violent media: Effects of multiple naturalistic exposures and debriefing on female viewers.* Unpublished doctoral dissertation, University of Wisconsin, Madison.

Kutchinsky, B. (1971). Towards an explanation of the decrease in registered sex crimes in Copenhagen. *Technical report of the commission on obscenity and pornography: Erotica and behavior, Vol. 8.* Washington, DC: U.S. Government Printing Office.

Kutchinsky, B. (1973). The effect of easy availability of pornography on the incidence of sex crimes: The Danish experience. *Journal of Social Issues, 29*(3), 163–181.

Laws, D. R. (1988). [Use of pornography by pedophiles]. Unpublished raw data.

Linz, D. (1985). *Sexual violence in mass media: Social psychological implications for society.* Unpublished doctoral dissertation, University of Wisconsin, Madison.

Malamuth, N. M. (1981). Rape fantasies as a function of exposure to violent sexual stimuli. *Archives of Sexual Behavior, 10,* 33–47.

Malamuth, N. M. (1984). Aggression against women: Cultural and individual causes. In N. M. Malamuth & E. Donnerstein (Eds.), *Pornography and sexual aggression* (pp. 19–52). Orlando, FL: Academic Press.

Malamuth, N. M. (1986). Predictors of naturalistic sexual aggression. *Journal of Personality and Social Psychology, 30*, 953–962.

Malamuth, N. M., & Check, J. V. P. (1980). Penile tumescence and perceptual responses to rape as a function of victim's perceived reactions. *Journal of Applied Social Psychology, 10*, 528–547.

Malamuth, N. M., Check, J. V. P. (1981). The effects of mass media exposure on acceptance of violence against women: A field experiment. *Journal of Research in Personality, 15*, 436–446.

Malamuth, N. M., & Check, J. V. P. (1983). Sexual arousal to rape depictions: Individual differences. *Journal of Abnormal Psychology, 92*, 55–67.

Malamuth, N. M., & Spinner, B. (1980). A longitudinal content analysis of sexual violence in the best-selling erotic magazines. *Journal of Sex Research, 16*, 226–237.

Malamuth, N. M., Haber, S., & Feshbach, S. (1980). Testing hypotheses regarding rape: Exposure to sexual violence, sex differences, and the "normality" of rapists. *Journal of Research in Personality, 14*, 121–137.

Malamuth, N. M., Check, J. V. P., & Briere, J. (1986). Sexual arousal in response to aggression: Ideological, aggressive and sexual correlates. *Journal of Personality and Social Psychology, 50*, 330–340.

Marshall, W. L. (1988). The use of explicit sexual stimuli by rapists, child molestors and nonoffender males. *Journal of Sex Research, 25*, 267–288.

Palys, T. S. (1986). Testing the common wisdom: The social content of video pornography. *Canadian Psychology, 27*, 22–35.

Quinsey, V. L., & Chaplin, T. C. (1984). Stimulus control of rapists' and non-sex offenders' sexual arousal. *Behavioral Assessment, 6*, 169–176.

Reifler, C. B., Howard, J., Lipton, M. A., Liptzin, M. B., & Widmann, D. E. (1971). Pornography: An experimental study of effects. *American Journal of Psychiatry, 128*, 575–582.

Sanday, P. R. (1981). The socio-cultural context of rape: A cross-cultural study. *Journal of Social Issues, 37*, 5–27.

Schaefer, H. H., & Colgan, A. H. (1977). The effect of pornography on penile tumescence as a function of reinforcement and novelty. *Behavior Therapy, 8*, 938–946.

Schmidt, G. (1975). Male–female differences in sexual arousal and behavior during and after exposure to sexually explicit stimuli. *Archives of Sexual Behavior, 4*, 353–364.

Scott, J. E. (1985, May). *Violence and erotic material: The relationship between adult entertainment and rape.* Paper presented at the annual meeting for the American Association for the Advancement of Science, Los Angeles, California.

Silbert, M. H., & Pines, A. M. (1984). Pornography and sexual abuse of women. *Sex Roles, 10*, 857–868.

Smith, D. G. (1976). The social content of pornography. *Journal of Communication, 26*, 16–33.

Spence, J., & Helmreich, R. (1972). The attitudes towards women scale: An objective instrument to measure attitudes towards the rights and roles of women in contemporary society. *JSAS Catalog of Selected Documents in Psychology, 2*, 66.

Winick, C. (1985). A content analysis of sexually explicit magazines sold in adult bookstores. *Journal of Sex Research, 21*, 206–210.

Zillman, D., & Bryant, J. (1984). Effects of massive exposure to pornography. In N. M. Malamuth & E. Donnerstein (Eds.), *Pornography and sexual aggression* (pp. 115–141). Orlando, FL: Academic Press.

6

Androgenic Hormones and Sexual Assault

S. J. Hucker and J. Bain

In lower animals, the role of hormones in reproduction is fundamental. In humans, however, sexual behavior appears to be multidetermined, and it involves a complex interaction not only of hormones but of environmental and social learning factors as well. In this chapter, the elementary physiology of sex hormone production in humans will be outlined, followed by a review of the effects of these hormones on normal human sexual development, adult sexual behavior, and aggressiveness. Finally, the evidence for endocrinological abnormalities in individuals who have committed various types of nonsexual as well as sexually motivated assault will be scrutinized.

Basic Physiology of Sex Hormones in the Human Male

The stimulus for synthesis and secretion of androgens originates in the hypothalamus, where gonadotropin-releasing hormone (GnRH) and corticotropin-releasing factor (CRF) are produced (see Figure 1). These hormones are transported by means of a special system of blood vessels called the *hypophyseal portal system* to the anterior lobe of the pituitary, where the biosynthesis of luteinising hormone (LH) and follicle-stimulating hormone (FSH) is stimulated by GnRH, and that of adrenocorticotropic hormone (ACTH) is stimulated by CRF.

Both LH and FSH are released by the pituitary into the circulating blood and travel to their site of action, the testes. There, specific receptors for these hormones are found: those for LH occur only on Leydig (interstitial) cells, whose primary secretion is testosterone; those for FSH are found only on the Sertoli cells of the seminiferous tubules, which produce spermatozoa. In turn, a feed-

S. J. Hucker • Forensic Division, Clarke Institute of Psychiatry, Toronto, Ontario M5T 1R8, Canada.
J. Bain • Department of Endocrinology, Mount Sinai Hospital, Toronto, Ontario M5G 1X5, Canada.

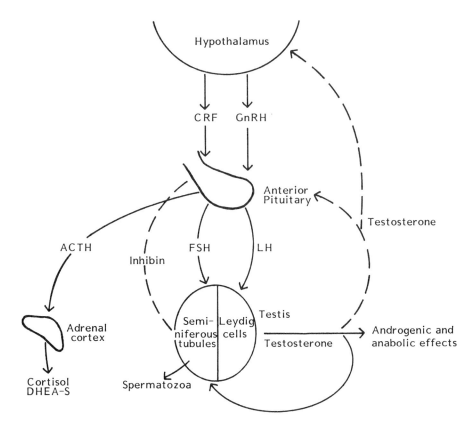

FIGURE 1. The hypothalamic–pituitary–testicular axis. ACTH, adrenocorticotropic hormone; DHEA-S, dehydroepiandrosterone sulphate; CRF, corticotropin-releasing factor; GnRH, gonadotropin-releasing hormone; FSH, follicle-stimulating hormone; LH, luteinising hormone.

back loop from these sites modulates production of these hormones. For example, LH secretion is inhibited by testosterone at both hypothalamic and pituitary levels. Testosterone may also modulate FSH secretion, but inhibin, a hormone also secreted by the Sertoli cells, may be a more important inhibitor (Jeffcoate, 1975).

Production by the adrenal glands of adrenocortical hormones, especially glucocorticoids and androgens, is stimulated by ACTH. The adrenals are a far less important contributor to the body's output of testosterone (about 5%) than the testes, although precursors of testosterone such as dehydroepiandrosterone sulphate (DHEA-S) and androstenedione are also weak androgens (Wand & Ney, 1985).

Testosterone effects its action after conversion to dihydrotestosterone, a more potent androgen. This occurs at several end-organ sites in tissues containing the enzyme 5-α-reductase. Testosterone is also metabolized to estradiol through the enzyme aromatase. These androgens circulate in the blood in two forms: free or unbound (2% of the total) and bound to proteins. It is the un-bound fraction which is biologically active. More than 50% of testosterone is bound to a specific protein (sex hormone binding globulin, SHBG), with the remainder more loosely bound to albumin and a further 2% bound to transcortin, the cortisol-binding protein (Vermeulen, 1977).

Unbound androgens only become metabolically active when they come into contact with target tissues possessing intracellular receptors for testosterone and dihydrotestosterone, and it is this contact which induces the cell to produce androgenic effects. These effects include physical changes such as increases in body hair, enlargement of the penis, increase in muscle mass, and increases in sebum production. As can be seen from the following account, androgens are believed to be related to sexual behavior as well as to physical changes in the body.

HORMONES AND SEX DRIVE IN MALES

Sexual behavior occurs in humans before adolescence. However, when a young boy reaches puberty, sex drive surges dramatically, with more frequent and intense erections, ejaculations, and orgasms, and at the same time the sex organs increase in size. All of these changes are correlated with a major increase in testicular production of testosterone. This observation has led many to conclude that testosterone is the primary biological factor responsible for normal, and perhaps abnormal, sexual behavior. Further support for this conclusion is given by reports that hypogonadal men experience a return of libido and potency when administered exogenous testosterone.

However, while there is obviously some relationship between adequate levels of testosterone in the circulation and sexual arousability, other factors, such as social expectations, may also be important. Udry and coworkers (Udry, Billy, & Morris, 1984) administered questionnaires to 102 ninth- and tenth-grade boys to obtain information about their sexual motivation and behavior. Correlating these with measures of several sex hormones, these researchers found that the closest relationship with behavioral measures was with the free testosterone index (FTI), an indirect measure of unbound testosterone. Those with high FTIs reported the greatest degree of sexual activity, such that, for example, 69.2% of those in the high-FTI quartile had already experienced sexual intercourse compared with only 16% of those in the lowest quartile. Similar relationships were found for a variety of other sexually related behavioral ratings. Udry *et al.* concluded that sexual motivation and behavior operate through a biological mechanism mediated by androgens, and not simply through the changing socialization pattern which accompanies adolescence.

Once puberty is complete and various aspects of sexual activity and interest are established, the relationship between sexual activity and blood hormone levels becomes less clear. Brown, Monti, and Corriveau (1978), for example, interviewed 101 men aged between 20 and 30 years and found no statistically significant relationship between behavioral assessments and sex hormone measures. However, in interpreting studies involving such sex hormone assays, it must be remembered that, like most hormones, testosterone is secreted intermittently with a diurnal and seasonal variation, higher levels being recorded in the mornings and during the fall months. Testosterone rises during REM sleep, and overall levels decline with advancing age (Nieschlag, 1979). Thus, random blood tests to measure testosterone levels may be misleading when blood is taken at different times and under different circumstances.

Nevertheless, much can be learned about hormone–behavior interrelationships by studying the effects of experimental interference with the endocrine system. Three particular disturbances involve hormone responses to erotic stimuli, treatment of hypogonadal men with testosterone, and the effects of castration.

Testosterone-Level Responses to Erotic Stimulation

Ismail and Harkness (1967) found an increase in urinary testosterone in two males following sexual activity. During an extended follow-up study, Fox, Ismail, Love, Kirkham, and Loraine (1972) found that their subject's testosterone level rose after every occasion of sexual intercourse. Pirke, Kockott, and Dittmar (1974) measured plasma testosterone in eight male subjects before, during, and after showing them an erotic film. There was an average increase of 35%, with the peak occurring 60 to 90 minutes after the movie was over. There was no such increase in the controls shown a sexually neutral film. Rubin, Henson, Falvo, and High (1979) used a phallometric procedure in a similar kind of experiment and concluded that sexual arousal and arousability were directly influenced by fluctuations in the levels of endogenous testosterone. In reviewing these and other similar studies, Bancroft (1978) noted that the results of the experiments have tended to be conflicting, although the general implication seems to be that testosterone and LH levels may rise following erotic stimulation.

Treatment of Hypogonadal Men with Testosterone

Hypogonadism may be due to a primary failure of the gonads themselves (as in Klinefelter's syndrome, following castration, etc.) or to a failure of the hypothalamic–pituitary axis to provide appropriate stimulation to the testes (e.g., in pituitary tumors). Whether the disorder is primary or secondary the effect is the same: very low levels of testosterone in the blood. It has proven interesting and valuable to study the sexual behavior of such patients before, during, and after testosterone replacement therapy.

Bancroft and Wu (1983) found that hypogonadal men, in the absence of treatment with testosterone, responded to erotic movies with penile erections to much the same degree as normal controls. Furthermore, the erections of the hypogonadal men were not improved by testosterone therapy, in contrast to other behavioral measures which increased substantially. This suggested that if the stimulus is adequate, erectile mechanisms are not affected by androgen withdrawal. In contrast, erections in response to erotic fantasy were significantly less in the hypogonadal men than in controls, and they were increased significantly by androgen replacement, suggesting that the cognitive process involved in fantasy or the central response to fantasy may be androgen dependent.

In another study of hypogonadal men, Kwan, Greenleaf, Mann, Crapo, and Davidson (1983) noted that all six of their subjects reported low libido, difficulty in achieving an erection, and little or no sexual activity. Every one of these men, even without testosterone replacement therapy, responded with full erections to erotic movies; even fantasy, a less potent stimulus, evoked erections in half the men. Although not essential for erections to occur in the laboratory, testosterone was essential for the occurrence of spontaneous erections whether awake or asleep.

In these studies it appears that testosterone is more important in maintaining than achieving erection to appropriate erotic stimuli.

Behavioral Effects of Castration

Castration, which produces an abrupt and dramatic reduction of circulating testosterone, has been used in some countries as a treatment for sex offenders and for ego-dystonic homosexuality (Bremer, 1959; Sturup, 1960, 1968). An extensive recent review of the effects of and problems with this procedure has been provided by Heim (1981). A group of 39 castrated rapists, pedophiles, and homosexuals was studied. Their mean age was 49.3 years, and the mean age at which castration had been carried out was 42.5 years. All were administered a questionnaire of 46 items relating to sexual functioning before and after the operation. The frequency of intercourse, masturbation, sexual thoughts, and sexual arousability were all reported to be reduced. However, only 41% lost their potency soon after the surgery, and 46% stated that they could still masturbate or have sexual intercourse. Those castrated between the ages of 25 and 44 appeared to maintain a greater degree of sexual activity than those castrated later in their lives.

The effects of abrupt reductions in circulating testosterone by castration is therefore variable. However, testosterone again emerges as a significant factor in sexual arousability and functioning, but obviously it is not the sole contributor, as sexual activity can continue in its absence or, at least, with very low levels.

In this context, mention must be made of the effects of antiandrogenic medications such as cyproterone acetate (Androcur) and medroxyprogesterone acetate (Provera), which reduce serum testosterone levels for as long as they are taken. A number of workers have been impressed by the efficacy of these substances in curbing sexual drive and hope they may be used to reduce recidivism (see Bradford, Chapter 17, this volume).

TESTOSTERONE AND AGGRESSION IN NORMAL MALES

Men are usually considered more physically violent than women. While this may be a result of different social expectations, it is also generally the case that men are physically stronger than women. What is unclear is whether testosterone actually produces aggressiveness or simply causes the increase in muscle bulk and strength which allows aggression to be manifested more effectively.

There have been several investigations of the relationship between testosterone and mood states in normal males. For example, Persky, Smith, and Basu (1971) assessed testosterone levels, production rates, and scores on the Buss–Durkee Hostility Inventory in a group of 18 healthy young men (average age 22 years), 15 healthy older men (average age 45 years), and 6 male psychiatric ("dysphoric") patients (average age 39 years). A highly significant relationship was found between testosterone production rate and "aggressive feelings" in the group of young men. None of the psychometric variables correlated with testosterone in the older men. However, Meyer-Bahlberg, Nat, Boon, Sharma, and Edward (1974) could not replicate these results in a study in which comparisons of testosterone metabolism were made between a group of men rated as "lower aggression" and a group of "high-aggression" men. They concluded that the relationship between aggression, as measured by questionnaires, and androgen production was tenuous.

In an interesting study by Scaramella and Brown (1978), testosterone levels in 14 male college hockey players were compared with coaches' ratings of aggressiveness during games. Items rated included: leadership, competitiveness, offense play, frustration tolerance, body contact, response to threat, and global aggressiveness. While there was only a weak correlation between response to threat and testosterone levels, there was no correlation at all with global aggressiveness.

Olweus, Matteson, Schalling, & Low (1980) investigated the relationship between testosterone levels and scores on an extensive battery of personality inventories in 58 normal adolescent Swedish boys (average age 16). Testosterone levels correlated significantly with self-reports of physical and verbal aggression on the Olweus Aggression Inventory, which reflected responsiveness to provocation and threat. These results are similar to the observations of Scaramella and Brown (1978). The only other variable that related significantly to testosterone levels was lack of frustration tolerance.

As Meyer-Bahlberg *et al.* (1974) noted, questionnaires tend to measure traits of aggressiveness, and these measures usually correlate very poorly, if at all, with measures of overt aggressive behavior or even with state measures of hostility. Other research has therefore been conducted of men who have actually acted out their aggressive feelings.

Testosterone and Aggression in Male Offenders

Kreutz and Rose (1972) found that, while testosterone levels did not differ between low and high levels of fighting among incarcerated offenders, prisoners with histories of more violent crimes in adolescence had significantly higher testosterone levels than those without such histories. There was also no correlation in this study between testosterone levels and scores on the Buss–Durkee

Hostility Inventory. Kreutz and Rose suggested that testosterone levels may predispose men to aggression in the presence of socioeconomic factors.

Ehrenkranz, Bliss, and Sheard (1974) provided further supporting evidence for the suggestion that testosterone may play a role in inducing or facilitating aggression in men conditioned to such behavior by other biological or environmental influences. In their study, plasma testosterone levels were measured in 36 male prisoners, of which 12 were physically aggressive, 12 were socially dominant but not aggressive, and 12 were neither physically aggressive nor socially dominant. In the first two groups, testosterone levels were not significantly different from each other but were from the third, nonaggressive, nondominant group. Also noteworthy was the lack of significant correlations between testosterone levels and self-reports on various questionnaires.

HORMONES AND SEXUAL AGGRESSION

Since sexual assault is an offense which combines both aggression and sexual behavior, studies of male hormone levels in rapists might be expected to yield interesting results. Rada, Laws, and Kellner (1976) measured plasma testosterone levels in 52 rapists and 12 child molesters who also completed the Buss–Durkee Hostility Inventory and other psychometric tests. The rapists were classified according to the degree of violence shown during their offenses. Mean testosterone levels of the rapists and child molesters were within normal limits. However, the group of rapists judged to be the most violent had significantly higher mean testosterone levels than did the normals, child molesters, and other rapists. Mean Buss–Durkee Hostility Inventory scores for all rapists were significantly higher than for controls, but just as other workers had found, there was no correlation between hostility scores and plasma testosterone. The researchers concluded that plasma testosterone levels correlated with a history of violent sexual crimes, but not on self-reported hostility.

However, these workers (Rada, Laws, Kellner, Stiristava, & Peake, 1983) conducted a further study of 18 rapists, 26 child molesters, and 11 controls, in which they examined plasma testosterone, dihydrotestosterone, and LH levels and administered the Buss–Durkee Hostility Inventory, together with Megargee's Overcontrolled Hostility Scale and the Michigan Alcohol Screening Test. This time there were no group differences among the hormones and, in contrast to their earlier study, no evidence that alcoholic rapists had higher testosterone levels than nonalcoholics. A similar lack of correlation between serum testosterone and a high degree of violence in sexual offenders was found by Bradford and Maclean (1984).

Indeed, at least some sexual assaults have been committed by individuals with very low plasma testosterone levels. Raboch, Cerna, and Zemek (1987), for example, reported cases of sexually motivated homicide by two individuals, one of whom suffered from Klinefelter's syndrome, while the other had been previously castrated. Langevin et al. (1985) conducted an extensive hormone profile on sadistic and nonsadistic rapists and found no differences in levels of testosterone, androstenedione, LH, FSH, estradiol, prolactin, and cortisol. In both rapist groups, however, the levels of the adrenal androgen DHEA-S were significantly elevated. This result suggested that any disorder of sex hormones in rapists might lie in the adrenals rather than the testes, although because of the small size of the sample and the fact that the differences were not great, a firm conclusion could not be drawn. On the basis of this finding, however, the same research group extended their investigation to see if this result could be replicated and also to determine whether there was any unusual response to stimulation of the hypothalamic–pituitary–adrenal axis with ACTH. This group (Bain, Langevin, Dickey, Hucker, & Wright, 1988) examined 36 men aged 16 years or older who had carried out sexually aggressive acts against physically mature women. Based on DSM-III criteria, they were divided into sadistic ($N = 20$) and nonsadistic ($N = 14$) offenders and compared with 15 nonviolent non-sex-offender controls. On this occasion there were no statistically significant differences in mean hormone levels between the groups. Neither did alcoholic history and mean values for liver function tests—which might have influenced the metabolism of testosterone and thereby produce spurious results—correlate with hormone levels. Similarly, no differences in hormones were found among the groups following ACTH stimulation, suggesting that a disorder of the hypothalamic–pituitary–adrenal axis is not a significant factor in sexually aggressive behavior.

However, Gaffney and Berlin (1984) did obtain a positive result in their investigation of the hypothalamic–pituitary–gonadal axis in seven pedophiles. In response to the administration of GnRH, mean LH levels in the pedophiles rose much higher than in a normal control group and a group of nonpedophilic, nonviolent paraphiliac men. There was also a greater FSH rise in the pedophiles after administering GnRH, but the result was not statistically significant. Although these authors cautioned that their results were preliminary and tentative, these findings suggest that further research is justified and that experimental interferences with the endocrine systems of sex offenders may be more revealing than determinations of individual plasma hormone levels, which has been the feature of most of the previous work in this area.

Conclusions

Although in men sexual arousability and interest appears to be dependent upon adequate levels of testosterone in the blood, the suggestion that there may be an abnormality of androgen metabolism in individuals who display aberrant sexual behavior is far less well supported by experimental evidence. Studies on hormones, sex, and aggression reviewed in this chapter are characterized often by small groups of subjects and results that are conflicting. Even those which report an association among general aggression, sexual aggression, and androgen levels have either not turned out to be replicable or the differences observed have been of marginal clinical meaning. When evidence of disturbances in early life and family characteristics are well established in individuals who have committed sexual assault, the results of hormone studies do not appear very impressive. Nevertheless, while the possibility remains of some subtle, as yet unexplored, abnormality perhaps of androgen receptors or neurotransmitters, there is need for further research (Bain, 1987). However, even if there is no specific abnormality of androgen metabolism in sexual assaulters, testosterone nevertheless provides the basis for general sexual drive, modified no doubt by social learning factors (Meyer-Bahlberg, 1987).

REFERENCES

Bain, J. (1987). Hormones and sexual aggression in the male. *Integrative Psychiatry*, 5, 182–93.
Bain, J., Langevin, R., Dickey, R., Hucker, S., & Wright, P. (1988). Hormones in sexually aggressive men. I. Baseline values for eight hormones. II. The ACTH test. *Annals of Sex Research*, 1, 63–78.
Bancroft, J. (1978). The relationship between hormones and sexual behavior in humans. In J. Hutchison (Ed.), *The biological determinants of sexual behavior* pp. 493–519. Chichester: Wiley.
Bancroft, J., & Wu, F. C. (1983). Changes in erectile responsiveness during androgen replacement therapy. *Archives of Sexual Behavior*, 12, 59–66.
Bradford, J., & Maclean, D. (1984). Sexual offenders, violence and testosterone: A chemical study. *Canadian Journal of Psychiatry*, 29, 335–343.
Bremer, J. (1959). *Asexualisation: A follow up of 244 Cases*. New York: MacMillan.
Brown, W. A., Monti, P. M., & Corriveau, D. P. (1978). Serum testosterone and sexual activity and interest in men. *Archives of Sexual Behavior*, 7, 97–103.
Ehrenkranz, J., Bliss, E., & Sheard, M. (1974). Plasma testosterone: Correlation with aggressive behavior and social dominance in man. *Psychosomatic Medicine*, 36, 469–475.
Fox, C. A., Ismail, A. A., Love, D. N., Kirkham, J. E., & Loraine, J. A. (1972). Studies in the relationship between plasma testosterone levels and human sexuality. *Journal of Endocrinology*, 52, 51–58.
Gaffney, G. R., & Berlin, F. S. (1984). Is there hypothalamic–pituitary–gonadal dysfunction in pedophiles? *British Journal of Psychiatry*, 145, 657–660.
Heim, H. (1981). Sexual behavior of castrated sex offenders. *Archives of Sexual Behavior*, 10, 11–10.
Ismail, A. A., & Harkness, R. A. (1967). Urinary testosterone excretion in men, in normal and pathological conditions. *Acta Endroncinologia*, 56, 469–480.
Jeffcoate, S. L. (1975). The control of testicular functions in the adult. *Journal of Clinical Endocrinology and Metabolism*, 4, 521–543.
Kreutz, L. E., & Rose, R. M. (1972). Assessment of aggressive behavior and plasma testosterone in a young criminal population. *Psychosomatic Medicine*, 34, 321–332.
Kwan, M., Greenleaf, W. J., Mann, J., Crapo, L., & Davidson, J. M. (1983). The nature of androgen action on male sexuality: A combined laboratory-self-report study on hypogonadal men. *Journal of Clinical Endocrinology and Metabolism*, 57, 557–562.
Langevin, R., Bain, J., Ben-Aron, M., Coulthard, R., Day, D., Handy, L., Heasman, G., Hucker, S. J., Purins, J. E., Roper, V., Russon, A. E., Webster, C. D., & Wortzman, G. (1985). Sexual aggression: constructing a predictive equation. A controlled pilot study. In R. Langevin (Ed.), *Erotic preference, gender identity & aggression in men: New research studies* (pp. 39–72). Hillsdale, NJ: Lawrence Erlbaum.
Meyer-Bahlberg, H. (1987). Commentary on Bain's "Hormones and sexual aggression in the male." *Integrative Psychiatry*, 5, 89–91.
Meyer-Bahlberg, H., Nat, R., Boon, D. A., Sharma, M., & Edward, J. A. (1974). Aggressiveness and testosterone measures in man. *Psychosomatic Medicine*, 36, 269–274.
Nieschlag, E. (1979). In E. J. Sachar (Ed.), *Sex hormones and behavior. Ciba Foundation Symposium No. 62* (pp. 183–208). West Caldwell, NJ: Ciba.
Olweus, D., Matteson, A., Schalling, D., & Low, H. (1980). Testosterone, aggression, physical, and personality dimensions in normal adolescent males. *Psychosomatic Medicine*, 42, 253–269.

Persky, H., Smith, K. D., & Basu, G. K. (1971). Relations of psychologic measures of aggression and hostility to testosterone in man. *Psychosomatic Medicine, 33,* 265–277.

Pirke, K. M., Kockott, G., & Dittmar, F. (1974). Psychosexual stimulation and plasma testosterone in men. *Archives of Sexual Behavior, 3,* 577–584.

Raboch, J., Cerna, H., & Zemek, P. (1987). Sexual aggressivity and androgens. *British Journal of Psychiatry, 151,* 398–400.

Rada, R., Laws, D., & Kellner, R. (1976). Plasma testosterone levels in the rapist. *Psychosomatic Medicine, 38,* 257–268.

Rada, R., Laws, D., Kellner, R., Stiristava, L., & Peake, G. (1983). Plasma androgens in violent and non-violent sex offenders. *Bulletin of the American Academy of Psychiatry and Law, 11,* 149–158.

Rubin, H. B., Henson, D. E., Falvo, R. E., & High, R. W. (1979). The relationship between men's endogenous levels of testosterone and their penile responses to erotic stimuli. *Behavior Research and Therapy, 17,* 305–312.

Scaramella, J. J., & Brown, W. A. (1978). Serum testosterone and aggressiveness in hockey players. *Psychosomatic Medicine, 40,* 262–265.

Sturup, G. (1968). Treatment of sex offenders in Herstedvester, Denmark. *Acta Psychiatrica Scandinavica, 44,* (Suppl. 204), 1–63.

Sturup, G. (1976). Sex offenses: The Scandinavian experience. *Law and Contemporary Problems, 25,* 361–375.

Udry, J. R., Billy, J. O. G., & Morris, N. M. (1984). Serum androgenic hormones motivate sexual behavior in adolescent boys. *Fertility and Sterility, 42,* 683–685.

Vermeulen, A. (1977). Transport and distribution of androgens at different ages. In L. Martini & M. Motta (Eds.), *Androgens and antiandrogens* (pp. 53–65). New York: Raven Press.

Wand, G. S., & Ney, R. L. (1985). Disorders of the hypothalamic–pituitary axis. *Journal of Clinical Endocrinology and Metabolism, 14,* 33–53.

7

Sexual Anomalies and the Brain

Ron Langevin

Brain damage and dysfunction resulting from accidents, surgery, epilepsy, and toxic substances, among other causes, have been associated with changes in personality and behavior. One also sees changes in sexual behavior, including the first appearance of sexually anomalous or sexually deviant behaviors, such as fetishism, exhibitionism, pedophilia, and gender behavior changes (see Cummings, 1985, for a review). These clinical findings raise the hypothesis of an association between sexual anomalies in general and brain anomalies.

Gross damage to the brain may lead to changes in sexual behavior. For example, a 26-year-old male was seen in our clinic after an extremely violent attack on a young woman. He appeared to be in a constant rage and had hacked through a door with an axe to reach the woman. The sexual assault was out of character for the young man. Neurological examination revealed global degenerative brain changes, possibly associated with mercury poisoning. Such findings leave open the question of exactly what specific brain sites may have been associated with his deviant behavior. If a specific area of his brain was instrumental in his aberrant sexual behavior, it remained masked by global changes in the brain.

A more revealing case was a 28-year-old married man with no previous criminal record for sexual offences. After a heavy drinking bout, he stripped from the waist down, entered a house full of people, and attempted to sexually assault a female child. When he was strangled by the child's father, the offender "woke up" and cooperated while the police were called. Phallometric testing of this offender suggested a conventional sexual preference for adult females. A computer tomography (CT) scan showed a large glioma on the left side of the brain, in the frontal and temporal areas. The glioma was large enough that other areas of the brain were affected, but the findings pointed to specific foci possibly associated with sexual behavior. In fact, both numerous case reports on humans and animal studies have suggested that the temporal lobes of the brain are most often linked with sexual behavior.

Ron Langevin • Clarke Institute of Psychiatry, Toronto, Ontario M5T 1R8, Canada.

The Temporal Lobes and Sexual Behavior

Animal Studies

Animal research long has pointed to the temporal lobes of the brain and to their associated limbic structures as sites associated with sexual arousal. The Kluver–Bucy syndrome is noteworthy. Kluver and Bucy (1939) found that removal of the temporal lobes of old world monkeys resulted in sexually indiscriminate behavior, whereby the monkeys would attempt to mate not only with available females from their own species but with animals of others species as well. The monkeys seemed "hypersexual," a feature also seen in some human cases of brain dysfunction (see Cummings, 1985). The monkeys' increased frequency of sexual outlet was considered "aggressive" because they sexually approached larger animals they ordinarily feared.

Work by McLean (1973) is particularly interesting because he showed that stimulation of monkeys' brains in the diencephalic area resulted in erection, whereas stimulation a mere millimeter away resulted in the showing of fangs and aggressive behavior. This finding suggests a reason why sexual and aggressive behaviors are so commonly associated in lower animals. The finding also raises the question of a possible parallel phenomenon in humans.

Human Studies

Epilepsy

A number of studies have shown that the onset of temporal lobe epilepsy may be associated with changes in sexual behavior (Cummings, 1985; Davies & Morgenstern, 1960; Epstein, 1961; Hunter, Logue, & McMenemy, 1963; Taylor, 1969). Most often there is impotence as well as a loss of libido. However, in other cases there is an increase of libido and, for some, the appearance of anomalous sexual behavior. The unusual behavior may take a variety of forms, including bizarre behavior. Mitchell, Falconer, and Hill (1954), for example, reported a case in which an individual was attracted sexually to safety pins. Another male showed gender changes and believed he was Mary Magdalene reincarnated (see Cummings, 1985). Some cases show more common and integrated behaviors, such as homosexuality, pedophilia, or incest (e.g., Regenstein & Reich, 1978). The most common sexual behavior manifested with epilepsy is fetishism, although a wide range of sexual anomalies have been reported (see Purins & Langevin, 1985, for a review).

The systematic work by Kolarsky, Freund, Machek, and Polak (1967) highlighted the importance of the temporal lobes in the genesis of sexual anomalies. In their study, 86 patients from a neurology clinic were examined blind by sexologists for the presence of sexual anomalies. Phallometric testing was employed in some cases. The authors found that there was a significantly greater proportion of sexual anomalies associated with temporal lobe epilepsy as opposed to other brain sites for the seizure focus. The results showed that almost one in five temporal lobe epileptics (TLEs) reported some sexually anomalous behavior. Certainly the temporal lobes are large structures of the brain, which may explain why not all TLE cases showed unusual sexual behavior. The evidence does, however, suggest that the temporal lobes should be explored more carefully in relationship to sexually anomalous behavior in general.

The Brains of Sex Offenders

So far, the brain studies of sex offenders have considered predominantly neurology clinic cases. The cumulative animal research, clinical case evidence, and the systematic study of Kolarsky et al. (1967) suggest that the temporal lobes of the brain are more often implicated when sexual behaviors are concerned. However, this does not mean that sex offenders in general have some neurological problem. The cases seen in neurology clinics may be unusual or self-selected in unknown ways. It would be important to know how many sex offenders in general show brain damage and dysfunction, particularly in the temporal lobes. Several studies have examined sexual aggressives and pedophiles seen in forensic clinics either pretrial or for treatment.

Sexual Aggressives. Abel, Barlow, Blanchard, and Guild (1977) coined the term "sexual aggressive" (SA) to describe men who rape and carry out other forceful sexual acts on women. The term is useful in that it does not restrict sexual aggression to rape, and it includes the variety of aggressive and sometimes bizarre behavior carried out by sexual sadists. The cases considered here involved offenses against adult females.

The brain is complex and may be impaired structurally or functionally. The new imaging technology, such as computer tomography (CT) imaging, is essentially an X ray that presents a relatively fine picture of the brain and other body organs. It is limited in examining only the structure of the brain, whereas magnetic resonance (MR) and positron emission tomography (PT) machines also examine brain function. The MR and PT are not widely available, so brain function is often examined via neuropsychological test batteries.

Scott, Cole, McKay, Golden, and Liggett (1984) used the Luria–Nebraska Neuropsychological Test Battery (LN test) to examine brain function in 36 sex offenders, of whom 22 were SAs. The LN test consists of 12 subtests that examine perception, central processes, and motor output. The subtests are Motor, Rhythm, Tactile, Visual, Perceptive Speech, Expressive Speech, Writing, Reading, Arithmetic, Memory, Intellectual Processes, and Pathognomonic. The LN test is new and interesting, but it is difficult to interpret because of the lack of normative information.

Scott et al. found that 55% of the SAs scored in the brain-damaged range, and an additional 32% showed "borderline performance." Hucker et al. (1988) found that 31 SAs were more impaired on the LN test than were 12 nonviolent, non-sex-offender controls. Both the Scott et al. and Hucker et al. studies reported global impairment of SAs but the LN test lacks specificity in identifying brain sites involved.

The Halstead–Reitan (H–R) Neuropsychological Test Battery (Reitan, 1979) is older and has considerable normative information. The subtests of the H–R battery measure behavior associated with different brain sites. For example, the Categories Test is considered a "frontal lobe" task, since it has been used to identify brain injuries in the frontal cortex. The battery consists of the Wechsler Adult Intelligent Scale (WAIS), Categories Test, Speech Perception Test, Rhythm Test, Tapping, Trails Making A and B, Aphasia Screening Test, and the Tactual Performance Test, among others.

Each test is associated with cerebral impairment in different brain sites, but the overall pattern of results is used by trained neuropsychologists to localize the brain impairment. Moreover, from the H–R normative data, a clear-cut criterion score of .51 provides an index of clinically significant brain impairment.

Langevin *et al.* (1985a) compared 20 SAs with 20 nonviolent, non-sex-offender controls on the H–R Battery as well as on CT scans of the brain administered by neuroradiologists who did not know the nature of the offenders' crimes. The authors found that the incidence of brain dysfunction in general for the SA and control groups was not significantly different as measured by the H–R battery. Nor were there differences in WAIS intelligence quotients. Results for CT scans were also negative. Although 45% of the cases showed some pathology, SAs did not differ from controls. When only damage to the temporal lobes was considered, 30% of the SAs showed some damage in that area, compared to 11% of the controls. However, this result was also not statistically significant, possibly because of the small sample size. The group of SAs examined was unusual because of the large proportion of sadists. Although sadists are believed to be only 2–5% of SAs, 45% of our cases were sadistic. The sadists presented a number of new and surprising findings.

Sadism is a sexual anomaly whereby an individual derives sexual gratification from the power and control over his victim, from their fear, terror, humiliation, and degradation, as well as from their injury and death. In some cases, only part of the anomaly may be seen, for example, power and control or only injuring. Usually sadists are men who are aroused as much by the force and power as by the sexual acts. They may also engage in bizarre ritualistic behavior and, in conjunction with the sexual entrapment of their victims, they may be sexually aroused by the unconscious or dead body.

Prior to carrying out our series of studies at the Clarke Institute of Psychiatry in the 1980s, only a collection of sadistic cases seen by Sir Robert Brittain (1970) had been reported. In the Langevin *et al.* (1985a) study in our clinic, therefore, we took the opportunity to examine the sadists in detail.

The pilot data provided results which were at odds with previous conceptions of sadism, not only in terms of the frequency with which this anomaly was seen, but also in terms of the behavioral patterns. Certainly our sadists had engaged in aggressive sexual acts toward their victims and appeared to prefer this over more conventional sexual outlets. However, they also manifested gender disturbances, as measured by the Freund Gender Identity Scale (Freund, Langevin, Satterberg, & Steiner, 1977). They showed either gender indifference or feminine longings. Since these initial findings, four cases have come to this author's attention in which men who have served time for charges of rape have sought out sex reassignment surgery to change them into women.

The sadist also shows interest in masochism and may engage in these behaviors himself. The linking of masochism and feminine gender identity is not a new idea (see Gebhard, 1965), but the possibility that these three behaviors are merged in the sexual sadist is an important consideration. More often, however, these men are interested in inflicting injuries on others as a source of sexual gratification.

There were other disturbances in the sadist's behavior that are noteworthy (see Langevin et al., 1985a, for details). Retarded ejaculation as well as impotence were common. Impotence may be psychological in nature in that the attraction to an adult female under conventional circumstances may be minimal, and the individual may not be able to achieve arousal and climax, although he is capable of performing sexually. This pattern is not unusual in men who are sexually anomalous (see Langevin, 1983) and attempt to have sexual relationships with adult women. However, it is also possible that the impotence seen in some sadists is a manifestation of a temporal lobe phenomenon since, as noted earlier, temporal lobe epilepsy is often associated with impotence.

The pilot findings on brain dysfunction and damage were different for the sadists and the nonsadistic SAs. The sadists showed more overall impairment on the H–R battery than did nonsadistic SAs or controls. The Speech Perception and Trails Making subtests were significantly poorer in the sadists than in the other groups. Intelligence test scores overall tended to be in the average range for all groups. The pattern of results suggested temporal–parietal lobe dysfunction, but the results were weak, with 33% of sadists versus 8% of nonsadists and 18% of controls showing clinically significant impairment.

The CT scans were interesting because 67% of the small group of sadists versus 36% of nonsadistic SAs showed structural damage or anomalies (compared to 39% of controls). This finding was not statistically significant, but when temporal lobe damage alone was considered, 56% of sadists versus 0% of nonsadistic SAs and 11% of controls showed it, most often as dilatation of the right temporal horn.

These findings were subtle, and the sample size was small, so a replication of results on a large number of cases was undertaken. Because sadism was considered so rare among SAs, and we found so many, a reliability check on diagnosis was made in the replication study. Moreover, the CT findings were subtle, so reliability of neuroradiological diagnosis was also examined. For both DSM-III and neuroradiological diagnoses, agreement was significant and over 90%.

A number of changes were also made to the procedure. CT scans were taken in only one dimension in the pilot study, and in the replication study, the CT scans were reconstructed in all three dimensions. The H–R battery was also replaced by the newer LN test for comparison, with the possible result of detecting more cases of brain pathology. The results were reported by Hucker et al. (1988).

The LN results have already been noted and were not as helpful as we had hoped. Moreover, the CT scans in all three dimensions added no new information. When combined with the data of Langevin *et al.* (1985a), there was a total of 51 SAs—22 sadists, 21 nonsadistic SAs, and 8 uncertain cases—as well as 36 nonviolent, non-sex-offender controls. The sadists showed more CT abnormalities in general (50%) than other SAs (39%) or controls (30%), but the differences were not statistically significant. However, right temporal horn dilatation was significantly more common in sadists (41%) than in other SAs (11%) or in controls (13%), thus extending and replicating the Langevin *et al.* (1985a) pilot results.

The importance of the temporal lobes in at least one sexual anomaly was supported by the two studies in our clinic. However, many questions remained. It was puzzling why only the sadists showed the significant temporal lobe findings. One could argue that their sexual anomaly has its source in an underlying brain abnormality, whereas nonsadistic SAs may be antisocial men "stealing" conventional sex. Alternatively, the nonsadists may show cerebral impairment that went undetected in our studies. At the time the pilot project (Langevin *et al.*, 1985a) was completed, the question also arose whether other sexual anomalies would be associated with brain damage and dysfunction. Pedophiles were studied first.

Pedophilia. Pedophilia is a term often applied to a collection of sexual anomalies which involve children as the sexual partners of adults, usually males. In fact, included in this group are heterosexual pedophiles who interact with female minors, homosexual pedophiles who interact with male minors, and bisexual pedophiles who interact with minors of both sexes. Within the group of pedophiles are men who do not erotically prefer children but engage the child for some surrogate reason. This may be, for example, the exhibitionist who erotically prefers adult women but who, on occasion, exposes to children. One also sees the elderly offender in this group, who may be responding out of loneliness rather than from a long-term sexual preference for children (Hucker & Ben-Aron, 1985). Pedophiles as a group react more erotically to children than they do to adults. However, individual variation in phallometric profiles is substantial and noteworthy.

Popular theories have suggested that the pedophile was socially and perhaps mentally handicapped and, therefore, sought out children as his companions, who were more in keeping with his own emotional and mental development (see Langevin, 1983; Mohr, Turner, & Jerry, 1964, for reviews). This statement from earlier research has generally not been supported, although skewing of pedophiles' intelligence scores to the lower end of the normal range may indicate some learning disability or other brain pathology (Langevin *et al.*, 1985b).

Hucker *et al.* (1986) compared heterosexual, homosexual, and bisexual pedophiles with nonviolent non-sex-offender controls on the H–R and LN test batteries as well as on CT scans. The results were consistent in pointing to the left hemisphere as a problem area in this group of offenders. In particular, the anterior and temporal horns in the left hemisphere of the brain were dilatated on CT scans. This result occurred in 40% of the pedophiles but was not seen in the controls at all. The pedophiles also showed clinically significant impairment on the H–R battery, which was consistent with the findings of the CT scan. Taking either a CT or an H–R battery result as a significant indicator of left-hemispheric pathology, two in three pedophiles showed this pattern compared to none of the controls. The LN test showed pedophiles as more impaired than controls, as it did in Scott *et al's.* (1984) study, but once again interpretation of results was problematic because of the lack of normative information.

The overall results for pedophiles were interesting because they showed temporal lobe damage and dysfunction, but it was distinct from the pattern found in sadists and in controls. Questions about the possible differential etiology of sexual anomalies arose, and other groups currently are being examined.

Other Sexual Anomalies. Very few studies are available which examine brain damage and dysfunction in other sex-offender groups. In two studies, Flor-Henry and his colleagues (Flor-Henry & Lang, 1988; Flor-Henry, Koles, Reddon, & Baker, 1986) examined 50 exhibitionists and 50 community controls matched for age, sex, and handedness. The electroencephalogram (EEG) was used to compare the groups at rest and during verbal and nonverbal spatial tasks. Computerized analysis of EEG frequency bands showed the exhibitionists had significant alteration of frequency patterns, especially during verbal tasks, compared to matched controls. Flor-Henry *et al.* concluded that the exhibitionists showed altered left-hemispheric brain function and disruption of interhemispheric EEG relationships.

Other sex-offender groups are yet to be studied systematically, but the existing results are encouraging in suggesting a relationship between sexual anomalies and brain damage and dysfunction.

Related Issues

Criminal and Community Control Groups

Control groups are used in an attempt to eliminate possible competing explanations for results of experimental studies. When community controls are used in research on sex offenders, many questions can be addressed, but offender controls are often more satisfactory since they are better matched to sex offenders in education, intelligence, and social class, all of which can influence a variety of test results. Moreover, using offenders for comparison also controls for offender status and, in our clinic, for patient status, since our sex offenders and non-sex-offenders alike are referred for psychiatric examination.

The norms for the Halstead-Reitan battery are based on nonoffender cases. It is these norms which were applied in comparisons of sex offenders and non-sex-offenders. Thus, the sex offenders showed neuropsychological deficits in reference to both offender and community controls. Similarly, CT findings have been compared on offender groups, but an examination of the temporal lobe findings indicates that less than 1% of general referrals to our neurological clinic show the pattern of results seen in sadists and pedophiles. Thus, CT findings also appear too pronounced in sex offenders compared to non-sex-offenders and community volunteers to be chance findings.

Two important additional issues have been examined in reference to our findings: substance abuse and general violence.

Substance Abuse

Alcohol abuse is common in the offender population. Approximately two in five sexual aggressives and one in three pedophiles are heavy drinkers or alcoholics (Langevin 1985a; Langevin 1985b; Rada, 1978). Smaller numbers also abuse drugs, which creates additional clinical problems and makes the role of brain damage in sexual behavior *per se* more difficult to evaluate.

Alcohol is the most problematic because it is more readily available and is more commonly abused than are street drugs. Alcohol abuse often results in diffuse or global brain damage, but there may also be specific atrophy such as that localized in the cerebellum, a brain center involved in coordination and balance. When carrying out the pilot project on sexual aggressives (Langevin *et al.*, 1985a), we found that 71% of the sexual aggressives were "alcoholic," based on scores of the Michigan Alcoholism Screening Test (MAST; Selzer, 1971). The MAST is a 25-item self-report inventory of the common signs of alcoholism (e.g., memory loss, blackouts, family fighting over alcohol, etc.). About 25% of these alcoholics in the pilot project and subsequent studies (Hucker *et al.*, 1986, 1988) showed liver enzyme abnormalities usually related to alcohol and drug abuse.

With such a small sample (20 SAs and 20 controls), the contribution of alcohol to brain results loomed large. In the 1985 pilot study, the sadists showed the temporal lobe anomalies, but only 50% were MAST alcoholics compared to 82% of other SAs and 76% of controls. Although temporal horn dilatation seen in the sadists was less likely to be associated with alcohol abuse, it could have been masked by the higher incidence of substance abuse in the nonsadistic SA group.

In the replication and extension study (Hucker *et al.*, 1988), 52% of the 51 SAs were MAST alcoholics and 55% of the 36 controls were. When alcoholics were excluded, CT and LN test results were unchanged. Similarly, alcoholic and nonalcoholic groups did not differ in brain results, likely because the men were young (mean age of 27 years for SAs and 25 years for controls).

Results were similar when pedophiles were examined (Hucker *et al.*, 1986). CT and H–R battery findings were similar when alcoholics were excluded. An additional concern was the significantly older age of pedophiles compared to the control group. The older alcoholic pedophiles possibly could show more brain impairment because of a longer period of substance abuse. However, the brain findings essentially were unchanged when age was covaried or when subgroups of pedophiles and controls were matched for age.

Drug abuse was more difficult to evaluate because of the extensive experimentation in street drugs by criminals in general. Moreover, they may have reported use of marijuana, but it could have been mixed with phencyclidene (PCP) or other substances, unknown to them. Thus, it is difficult to evaluate the role of particular drugs in brain pathology. More cases are required to evaluate the influence of drugs on brain findings in our sex offenders, but initial unpublished results suggest that street drugs, too, cannot account for the temporal lobe findings.

General Violence

Our research has employed nonviolent non-sex-offenders as controls. These "general" offenders control for many confounding variables, such as social class, noted earlier. They were also selected to be "nonviolent" because nonsexually violent individuals may suffer from brain damage and dysfunction (see Goldstein, 1974; Langevin, Ben-Aron, Wortzman, Dickey, & Handy, 1987; Monroe, 1978, for reviews). Possibly, the pattern of brain damage seen in sexually violent men would not be different from that seen in nonsexually violent men. Since SAs share many features with nonsexually violent men (e.g., substance abuse and violent life-style), it is possible that the temporal lobe findings noted above for sadists would be similar in nonsexually violent men.

Langevin *et al.* (1987) examined the incidence of brain damage and dysfunction in non-sex-offenders who were violent. They compared three groups: 18 men who had killed (homicide), 21 common (nonhomicidal) assaulters, and 16 nonviolent, non-sex-offender controls on the H–R and LN tests and CT scans (The homicide group contained some sexually motivated aggressive cases and will not be discussed here). All men were being seen for psychiatric assessment and had criminal records.

Of the nonhomicidal assaulters, 17% had a clinically significant H–R impairment index compared to none of the controls. The differences on the Rhythm, Tapping, Tactual Performance, and Trails Making subtests were statistically significant, and assaulters showed more impairment than controls, except on Tapping. The pattern of results was similar to that seen for sadists in the Langevin *et al.* (1985a) study, with the exception of the presence of significant Tapping results and the absence of Speech Perception deficits noted in sadists. The LN test also showed more dysfunction in violent men (47%) than in controls (25%), but the difference was not statistically significant.

Of the common assaulters, 25% showed some CT brain abnormality compared to 29% of controls. In the temporal lobes, 18.8% of assaulters and 21.4% of controls showed abnormalities. None of the CT findings were statistically significant. Moreover, in this study the assaulters showed a frequency of temporal lobe abnormalities comparable to controls and lower than the rate seen in sadists (41%) in the Langevin *et al.* (1985a) study. The findings here suggest that the temporal lobe deficits are more common in sadists than in generally violent men, but a direct comparison between sexually and nonsexually violent men is needed.

CONCLUSIONS

It appears that the cumulative body of literature, in particular systematic studies of brain pathology in sexually anomalous men, has suggested a link between temporal lobe impairment and sexually anomalous behaviors. This appears to be a link which is independent of criminality in general, is distinct from general learning disabilities, is not a function of alcohol abuse, and may be unrelated to general violence and drug abuse. There is some suggestion that the sadists and pedophiles show differential brain pathology in the temporal lobes, with the former group showing structural anomalies to the right lobe, while the pedophiles appear to have anomalies in the left lobe.

The brain pathology seen in sexually anomalous men was quite subtle and, to some extent, our ability to detect it was dependent on the availability of modern imaging technology. Moreover, the brain can be studied in a variety of ways (e.g., PT and MR scans, EEG, neuropsychological tests, etc.) that may provide new insights into the role of the brain in sexually unusual behavior. Future studies to examine the brain during sexual arousal may be informative in understanding both conventional and anomalous sexual behavior.

REFERENCES

Abel, G. G., Barlow, D. H., Blanchard, E. B., & Guild, D. (1977). The components of rapists' sexual arousal. *Archives of General Psychiatry, 34*, 895–903.

Brittain, R. (1970). The sadistic murderer. *Medicine Science and the Law, 10*, 198–207.

Cummings, J. L. (1985). *Clinical neuropsychiatry*. New York: Grune & Stratton.

Davies, B. M., & Morgenstern, F. S. (1960). A case of cysticercosis, temporal lobe epilepsy, and transvestism. *Journal of Neurology, Neurosurgery & Psychiatry, 23*, 247–249.

Epstein, A. W. (1961). Relationship of fetishism and transvestism to brain and particularly to temporal lobe dysfunction. *Journal of Nervous & Mental Diseases, 133*, 247–253.

Flor-Henry, P., & Lang, R. (1988). Quantitative EEG analysis in genital exhibitionists. *Annals of Sex Research, 1*, 49–62.

Flor-Henry, P., Koles, Z. L., Reddon, J. R. & Baker, L. (1986). Neuropsychological studies (EEG) of exhibitionism. In M. C. Shagrasi, R. C. Josiassen, & R. A. Roemer (Eds.), *Brain electrical potentials and psychopathology* (pp. 279–306). Amsterdam: Elsevier Science Publishing.

Freund, K., Langevin, R., Satterberg, J., & Steiner, B. (1977). Extension of the gender identity scale for males. *Archives of Sexual Behavior, 6*, 507–519.

Gebhard, P. H. (1969). Fetishism and sadomasochism. *Science and Psychoanalysis, 15*, 71–80.

Goldstein, M. (1974). Brain research and violent behavior. *Archives of Neurology, 30*, 1–35.

Hucker, S., & Ben-Aron, M. H. (1985). Elderly sex offenders. In R. Langevin (Ed.), *Erotic preference, gender identity, and aggression in men* (pp. 211–224). Hillside, NJ: Lawrence Erlbaum.

Hucker, S., Langevin, R., Wortzman, G., Bain, J., Handy, L., Chambers, J., & Wright, S. (1986). Neuropsychological impairment in pedophiles. *Canadian Journal of Behavioral Science, 18*, 440–448.

Hucker, S., Langevin, R., Wortzman, G., Dickey, R., Bain, J., Handy, L., Chambers, J., & Wright, S. (1988). Cerebral damage and dysfunction in sexually aggressive men. *Annals of Sex Research, 1,* 33–47.

Hunter, R., Logue, V., & McMenemy, W. H. (1963). Temporal lobe epilepsy supervening on long-standing transvestism and fetishism. *Epilepsia, 4,* 160–165.

Kluver, H., & Bucy, P. E. (1939). Preliminary analysis of functions of the temporal lobes in monkeys. *Archives of Neurology & Psychiatry, 42,* 979–1000.

Kolarsky, A., Freund, K., Machek, J., & Polak, O. (1967). Male sexual deviation: Association with early temporal lobe damage. *Archives of General Psychiatry, 17,* 735–743.

Langevin, R. (1983). Transsexualism and transvestism. In R. Langevin (Ed.), *Sexual strands: Understanding and treating sexual anomalies in men* (pp. 171–242). Hillsdale, NJ: Lawrence Erlbaum.

Langevin, R., Bain, J., Ben-Aron, M., Coulthard, R., Day, D., Handy, L., Heasman, G., Hucker, S. J., Purins, J. E., Roper, V., Russon, A., Webster, C. D., & Wortzman, G. (1985a). Sexual aggression: Constructing a predictive equation. In R. Langevin (Ed.), *Erotic preference, gender identity, and aggression in men* (pp. 39–76). Hillsdale, NJ: Lawrence Erlbaum.

Langevin, R., Hucker, S. J., Handy, L., Hook, H. J., Purins, J. E., & Russon, A. E. (1985b). Erotic preference and aggression in pedophilia: A comparison of heterosexual, homosexual, and bisexual types. In R. Langevin (Ed.), *Erotic preference, gender identity, and aggression in men* (pp. 137–160). Hillsdale, NJ: Lawrence Erlbaum.

Langevin, R., Ben-Aron, M., Wortzman, G., Dickey, R., & Handy, L. (1987). Brain damage, diagnosis, and substance abuse among violent offenders. *Behavioral Science and Law, 5,* 77–94.

MacLean, P. D. (1973). New findings on brain function and sociosexual behavior. In J. Zubin & Money (Eds.), *Contemporary sexual behavior: Critical issues in the 1970s* (pp. 53–74). Baltimore, MD: The Johns Hopkins University Press.

Mitchell, W., Falconer, M. A., & Hill, D. (1954). Epilepsy with fetishism relieved by temporal lobectomy. *Lancet, 2,* 626–630.

Mohr, J., Turner, R. E., & Jerry, M. (1964). *Pedophilia and exhibitionism.* Toronto: University of Toronto Press.

Monroe, R. R. (1978). *Brain dysfunction in aggressive criminals.* Lexington, MA: D.C. Heath.

Purins, J., & Langevin, R. (1985). Brain correlates of penile erection. In R. Langevin (Ed.) *Erotic preference, gender identity, and aggression in men* (pp. 113–133). Hillsdale, NJ: Lawrence Erlbaum.

Rada, R. T. (1978). *Clinical aspects of the rapist.* New York: Grune & Stratton.

Regenstein, Q. R., & Reich, P. (1978). Pedophilia occurring after onset of cognitive impairment. *Journal of Nervous and Mental Diseases, 166,* 794–798.

Reitan, R. M. (1979). *Manual for the administration of the neuro-psychological test battery for adults and children.* Tuscon, AZ: Neuropsychological Laboratory.

Scott, M. L., Cole, J. K., McKay, S. E., Golden, C. J., & Liggett, K. R. (1984). Neuropsychological performance of sexual assaulters and pedophiles. *Journal of Forensic Sciences, 29,* 1114–1118.

Selzer, M. (1971). The Michigan Alcoholism Screening Test: The quest for a new diagnostic instrument. *American Journal of Psychiatry, 127,* 1653–1658.

Taylor, D. (1969). Sexual behavior and temporal lobe epilepsy. *Archives of Neurology, 21,* 510–516.

8

Stimulus Control of Sexual Arousal

Its Role in Sexual Assault

H. E. Barbaree

Introduction

Current thinking concerning sexual assault includes two extreme and opposing views (Malamuth, Check, & Briere, 1986). On the one hand, there is a widely held belief that men who sexually assault women and children are best characterized as sexual deviates. According to a prominent version of this view, these men are motivated by a "sexual preference" for children, as in the case of the pedophile, or for violent or aggressive interactions, as in the case of the rapist (Abel, Barlow, Blanchard, & Guild, 1977; Freund & Blanchard, 1981). On the other hand, feminist writers (Brownmiller, 1975; Burt, 1980; Clark & Lewis, 1977; Russell, 1975, 1988) argue that sexual assault is primarily aggressive in nature and represents a specific instance of a male-centered society's more general hostility toward women and children. While both groups can point to empirical support for their views, it is becoming increasingly apparent that sexual assault is the product of many interacting variables, and no single variable can account for all aspects of the phenomenon (Barbaree & Marshall, 1988; Finklehor, 1986; Malamuth, 1986). It seems clear that sexual and aggressive processes interact in sexual assault, but it is not at all clear what form this interaction takes.

The present chapter will examine this interaction by focusing on stimulus control of sexual arousal. The chapter will make the argument that stimulus control of sexual arousal is important in sexual assault in two ways. First, in child molestation, stimulus control determines "object" choice and provides an important motivation for sexual interactions with children. Second, in coercive sexual interactions, stimulus control of arousal is part of a complex integrated

H. E. Barbaree • Department of Psychology, Queen's University, Kingston, Ontario K7L 3N6, Canada.

115

aggressive response which has cognitive and motor as well as psychophysiological components.

Sexual Preferences

The "sexual preference hypothesis" can be simply stated. If a man is maximally aroused by a deviant stimulus or act, his eventual satisfaction or reward will be greater than that resulting from less strong responses to normalized or socially acceptable stimuli or acts. It is a time-honored psychological principle that organisms perform behaviors which produce greater reward more frequently and vigorously than other less rewarding behaviors. Therefore, the sexual preference hypothesis is a two-stage explanation of deviance. First, deviant sexual cues or behaviors elicit optimal or maximal arousal in the man. Second, the man expresses a preference for these cues or for behaviors motivated by the stronger sexual arousal. The sexual preference hypothesis is not so much a formal hypothesis or theory articulated by a single author or group as much as it is an implied set of working assumptions shared by many clinicians in the field. The concept of a sexual preference forms the basis of the modern clinical assessment of sexual deviates, and some of the most popular classificatory systems (see Knight, Rosenburg, & Schneider, 1985, for a review) are based, at least in part, on the classification of the stimuli which elicit sexual arousal and fantasies in the individual. In the recent revision of the DSM-III-R (American Psychiatric Association, 1987), the paraphilias are characterized by sexual fantasies and arousal in response to sexual objects or behaviors that are not part of normative arousal-activity patterns.

A sexual preference is thought to be a relatively stable individual trait. When a man is identified as a sexual deviate, it would be usual for the clinician to recommend that he seek and receive treatment to normalize his pattern of sexual arousal. Numerous treatment procedures have been developed over the past 20 years (Quinsey & Marshall, 1983), and the modification of sexual preferences is an important component of a number of comprehensive treatment programs (see Barbaree & Marshall, in press).

Laboratory Assessments of Sexual Preferences

Following from this model of sexual deviance, the laboratory assessment of sexual preferences has become an important part of a complete clinical assessment of sexual offenders. The laboratory procedure involves presenting sexual stimuli to men while monitoring their erectile responses (Earls & Marshall, 1983; Laws & Osborne, 1983). Stimuli take the form of still pictures of nude males and females of all ages and audio- or videotaped depictions of sexual interactions, including consenting acts between adult partners and nonconsenting forceful acts. In the assessment, when the man shows significant arousal to deviant cues, it identifies him to the clinician as a sexual deviate. As a consequence, there has been a great deal of interest in the development of these assessment procedures.

Murphy and Barbaree (1988) have written a detailed critical review of the psychometric properties of these assessments and evaluated them using criteria established for psychological tests by the American Psychological Association (1985). The review has concluded that, for the child molester, assessment procedures which compare erectile responses to still pictures of nudes of varying ages have good criterion-related validity (both concurrent and predictive). Criterion groups show different patterns of arousal, and patterns of arousal are related to criminal history and reoffense. In the assessment of the rapist, assessment procedures which compare erectile responses to verbal descriptions of rape and mutually consenting interactions between a man and a woman have not shown consistently good criterion-related validity. In addition, the reliability of the procedures for use with both groups of offenders has not been adequately tested as yet. The establishment of the validity of these tests depends in part on the results of studies which will be reviewed subsequently in this chapter, but the psychometric issues will not be addressed directly. Some offenders are able to suppress erectile responses at will or when instructed to do so (e.g., Abel, Barlow, Blanchard, and Mavissakalian, 1975; Freund, 1963; Wydra, Marshall, Earls, & Barbaree, 1983), and some nonoffenders are able to produce moderate erectile responses to nonpreferred stimuli (e.g., Quinsey & Bergersen, 1976). Presumably then, offenders with these abilities may distort their true sexual responses during assessment. Some offenders have been observed using mechanical methods of control, such as manipulating the strain gage (Laws & Holmen, 1978), and nonerectile responses, like tensing of the pelvic musculature or hyperventilation to influence the strain gage (Quinsey & Bergersen, 1976). These methods of distortion can be easily detected or prevented by monitoring with a video camera, movement detectors, or additional psychophysiological measures. Subjects may control stimulus input by averting their gaze from a slide or video presentation (Laws & Rubin, 1969), but this may be prevented using a video monitoring camera focusing on the subject's face, or by a "detection task" which requires the subject to report a signal which is presented randomly as part of the stimulus display (Laws & Rubin, 1969). The more difficult faking to detect and prevent is the subject's own cognitive control of the stimulus presentation. For example, Geer and Fuhr (1976) have demonstrated that when men are required to engage in a complex secondary task, arousal to an erotic stimulus is suppressed. Subjects attempting to suppress arousal to deviant stimuli might use self-distraction, and, indeed, when subjects have been instructed to fake suppression of response to a preferred erotic stimulus, they reported using such a strategy to minimize arousal (Wydra *et al.*, 1983).

Two studies have attempted to combat faking in the laboratory. In the first, Malcolm, Davidson, and Marshall (1985) switched to various deviant and nondeviant sexual stimuli after subjects had been aroused to different levels (25, 50, and 75% of full erection). At the switch, subjects were instructed to detumesce as quickly as possible, while attending to the switched stimulus. At 50% of full erection, these nonoffender subjects showed the most difficulty detumescing to the nude female, compared with deviant and neutral stimuli. Presumably, if offenders were to show longer latencies in detumescing to the deviant stimulus, a preference for the deviant stimulus would have been determined. In the second study, Quinsey and Chaplin (1988) asked normal subjects to attend to a sexual stimulus under normal instructions, under fake instructions, and under fake instructions with a secondary semantic tracking task. The task required subjects to press one button whenever sexual activity was being described and another button whenever violence occurred. While subjects were able to fake inappropriate sexual preferences without the task, the task interfered with their ability to fake a preference.

Stimulus Control of Sexual Arousal

Sexual Reflexes

A sexual stimulus, defined for the purpose of this chapter, is a stimulus which elicits sexual arousal. Sexual arousal in men is defined as any increase in volume, length, or circumference of the penis (Zuckerman, 1972). A sexual reflex is an erectile response to a stimulus, and its strength can be defined as the magnitude of the erectile response elicited by the stimulus, in terms of increases in millimeters of circumference, increases in cubic centimeters of volume, or increases in millimeters of length. The largest, or peak, response during a stimulus is highly correlated with area under the curve, or a measure of average arousal during the stimulus (Quinsey & Harris, 1976), so researchers have usually analyzed peak response since it is so much easier to record and calculate.

However, there is disagreement concerning how the peak response should be transformed for presentation and analysis. Some authors (e.g., Malamuth *et al.*, 1986) have simply presented the raw scores (e.g., millimeters of circumference change). Since there is large variation in the size of the male penis, both in the flaccid state and in the degree to which there is change during erection (Farkas *et al.*, 1979), many researchers have transformed raw scores in an attempt to correct this inequality. Some authors have expressed the peak response as a percentage of the erectile response at full erection (e.g., Abel *et al.*, 1977; Barbaree, Marshall, & Lanthier, 1979). But, in response to the fact that sometimes subjects fail to achieve a full erection and to present the data in a form which reflects the subject's relative preferences, others have recommended that raw scores also be converted to ipsative z scores (e.g., Freund, Scher, Racansky, Campbell, & Heasman, 1986; Quinsey, Chaplin, & Carrigan, 1979). Earls, Quinsey, and Castonguay (1987) have argued that a greater proportion of response variance could be accounted for by stimulus presentations using the z score transformation. They argued further that use of this transformation would lead to an increase in the power of statistical hypothesis testing and to a decrease in the risk of a Type II error. In contrast, Barbaree and Mewhort (1989) have argued that the z score transformation is undesirable for two reasons. First, it distorts the information contained in the individual subject's raw scores, and over a group of subjects, this distortion serves to increase the relative proportion of actual random error. Second, it increases the risk of a Type II error.

Sexual Stimuli and Stimulus Control

Quinsey (personal communication, January, 1987) has argued that men perceive visual sexual stimuli as a whole, or as a "Gestalt." Much of the current literature is written as if men respond in this way to all manner of sexual stimuli. It is as if, upon being presented with the stimulus, the man labels it as belonging to one or another generic category (e.g., "consenting sex" or "rape"; "adult" or "child"). But stimuli (e.g., verbal descriptions or movies) occur over a period of time, so the label may change from one category to another as more information is received concerning the interactions. Then, on the basis of the label, a generic response is evoked (e.g., "consenting arousal" or "rape arousal"). This chapter espouses an alternative to this assumption and views sexual stimuli as compound stimuli, made up of various discrete elements. According to this view, a man's sexual reflex is a synthesis of the various responses to the different elements in the stimulus. For the purposes of this argument, a sexual element of a compound stimulus will be defined as the smallest "bit" of information in the stimulus which can be shown to increase sexual arousal.

The complexity of sexual stimuli complicates our interpretation of sexual reflexes. To illustrate this, let us take as an example an audiotaped verbal description of a sadomasochistic interaction. If a man were to show a response equal to 40% of a full erection to this description, some clinicians might worry about his potential for sexual aggression. However, if you were to listen carefully to the description and were to find explicit descriptions of foreplay and intercourse, the meaning of the man's arousal becomes ambiguous. It is true that there are elements in the compound that make the stimulus an inappropriate sexual stimulus according to societal values; namely, the pain suffered by the woman and the violence perpetrated by the man. However, there are many elements in the compound that are normative sexual cues and are often associated with arousal, namely, the foreplay and intercourse. The clinician would not know which element(s) in the compound have elicited the arousal. However, when a second stimulus is presented, the meaning of the first can be interpreted. Let us say that in this second stimulus the masochistic elements are omitted and the description includes only explicit details of their foreplay and intercourse, similar to those in the first stimulus. Now, the meaning of the 40% full erection to the first stimulus can be determined by comparison with the response to the second (discounting for the moment any order or time effects). If the man shows a full erection to the second stimulus, then the interpretation of the response to the first description might be that the man was appropriately aroused by the sexual elements, and his response reflected an appropriate inhibition of arousal in response to the sadomasochistic elements. On the other hand, should the man show 20% of full erection to the second stimulus, the response to the first may be interpreted as reflecting a sexual interest in the sadomasochistic elements.

The present argument is not meant necessarily to prejudge the issue of whether men respond to some combination of "bits" of stimuli or to a gestalt. However, a methodological problem which could pose a threat to the internal validity of experiments becomes apparent when the synthetic view (i.e., considering stimuli as compounds) is given careful consideration. The "synthetic" view predicts that response strengths to a particular generic category of stimulus will vary greatly. For example, it should be possible to write verbal descriptions of "consenting" sexual interactions which do not evoke much arousal, by including only a few weak sexual elements or by describing the female as unattractive. Also, it should be possible to write descriptions of deviant sexual episodes which evoke strong responses in normal men by including many powerful sexual elements and infrequent, more benign references to the deviant elements. Variations from study to study in the way in which generic categories of sexual stimuli have been constructed have produced conflicting results in the published literature. A large number of studies have reported that nonrapists exhibit much less arousal to rape cues compared with consenting cues (e.g., Abel *et al.*, 1977; Barbaree *et al.*, 1979). However, other studies have reported that rape cues are as arousing as consenting cues for the nonrapist (Farkas, 1979; Malamuth, 1981a; Malamuth & Check, 1980). This seemingly inconsistent set of results has been explained by Malamuth (1981a), who has noted that when the victim is portrayed as becoming involuntarily aroused during the assault, the rape episode evokes arousal equal in strength to consenting cues (Malamuth & Check, 1980; Malamuth, Heim, & Feshbach, 1980). However, when the rape descriptions portray the woman as abhorring the act throughout, rape arousal is greatly suppressed compared with consenting arousal (Malamuth & Check, 1980; Malamuth, Heim, & Feshbach, 1980). Similar variations in levels of arousal can be obtained within the consenting category of descriptions. When the woman is described to nonrapists as being enthusiastic about the interaction and initiates sexual behavior with the man, greater arousal is evoked than when she is described as being a reluctant partner (Baxter, Barbaree, & Marshall, 1986). Armed with this information, an experimenter could construct stimulus materials for use in a study in which any desired result could be obtained. These observations appear to render meaningless the question as to whether or not generic "rape" arousal is greater than, less than, or equal to generic "consenting" arousal for any population of men.

Therefore, it is important to make a clear distinction between the strength of a sexual reflex, on the one hand, and the strength of stimulus control of sexual arousal, on the other. For an experimenter or clinician to establish stimulus control of arousal, at least two compound stimuli must be presented with one "key" element systematically varied between stimuli. Further, as many extraneous elements as possible must be kept constant from stimulus to stimulus. Then, differential responding to the two stimuli can be attributed to the element that has been systematically varied. Tests of stimulus control of sexual arousal are only informative and useful in a research and clinical sense when they allow the researcher or clinician to attribute control of sexual arousal to the key element in the stimulus compound.

Child Molesters

Studies of the sexual responses of child molesters nicely illustrate this concept of stimulus control. The first of these was the pioneering work of Kurt Freund (1967a, 1967b; 1981). In these studies, still photographs were presented as 35-mm slide transparencies projected on a screen in front of the subject. The target persons depicted in the slides were nude or partially clad males and females. In the series of pictures, the age of the targets was systematically varied, with different targets exhibiting different age-related physical attributes, including size, muscular development, maturity of facial features, and secondary sexual characteristics (e.g., the presence or absence of pubic, facial, and body hair, and variation in breast size, etc.). Of course, included in these sexual stimuli were age-unrelated sexual elements, such as the color of hair, pose, and the attractiveness of the target, and nonsexual elements, such as backdrop, quality of the photography, and so on. For the purpose of these studies, age-unrelated elements and nonsexual elements have been regarded as extraneous variables, and as much as possible, these have been randomly varied over the different age targets. At the very least, experimenters have avoided confounding influences, as would happen if, for example, all children were clothed and all adults nude or all children were photographed in black and white and adults in color.

In some of the studies (e.g., Freund, 1967a, 1967b; 1981; Freund, McKnight, & Langevin, 1972; Quinsey et al., 1979; Quinsey, Steinman, Bergersen, & Holmes, 1975) the researchers have divided the target stimuli into broad categories, such as children, adolescents, and adults, and have compared the strength of sexual arousal to each category. Other studies have divided the stimuli into 1 to 2 year age groupings and have plotted the strength of sexual arousal over the age-of-target continuum, resulting in what is known as an "age-preference profile" (e.g., Baxter, Marshall, Barbaree, Davidson, & Malcolm, 1984; Marshall, Barbaree, & Butt, 1988; Marshall, Barbaree, & Christophe, 1986; Murphy, Haynes, Stalgaitis, & Flanagan, 1986).

The studies have been quite consistent in their findings. As a group, men who have molested nonfamilial female children have shown greater arousal to young girls than did matched nonoffenders, although they also responded quite strongly to adult women. Men who have molested nonfamilial male children have shown greater arousal to young boys than did matched nonoffenders, although again this group has shown at least moderate arousal to adult men and women. Incestuous child molesters, as a group, did not show strong responses to children, but their responses to adults were relatively weak. Nonoffenders have shown strong arousal to adult females and a sharp drop in arousal to adolescent and child targets.

Recognizing that individual men might show idiosyncratic patterns of stimulus control, and that offender groups might be heterogeneous in the shapes of individual age-preference profiles, Barbaree and Marshall (1989) conducted an analysis of profile shapes among female-child molesters, father–daughter incest offenders, and a group of matched nonoffenders. A computer program sorted the profiles among five shape categories as follows: (1) an "adult" profile in which subjects showed strong responses to adult females aged 20 years and older, moderate responses to 16- and 18-year-old targets, and minimal or no responses to targets below age 15; (2) a "teen-adult" profile in which subjects showed strong responses to female targets aged 13 and older, with a decreasing response to younger-aged targets; (3) a "non-discriminating" profile in which subjects showed moderate arousal to targets of all ages; (4) a "child–adult" pattern in which subjects showed strong responses both to targets 18 years and older and to targets 11 years and younger, but showed only weak responses to targets aged from 12–14; and (5) a "child" profile in which subjects showed strong responses to targets 11 years of age and younger, but only minimal responses to targets aged 13 and older. The profiles are presented in Figures 1–3.

Almost 70% of nonoffenders showed profiles categorized as "adult" profiles. The remainder of the nonoffenders were approximately evenly distributed between the teen–adult and nondiscriminating profile categories. Of incest offenders, 40% showed an adult profile, and an equal number showed a nondiscriminating pattern of response. Most of the remaining incest offenders showed a teen–adult profile, with only one incest offender showing a child–adult profile. None of the nonoffenders showed profile shapes that indicated responses to children, and none of the incest offenders showed responses exclusively to children. In contrast, the child molesters showed remarkably heterogeneous patterns of response. The largest subgroup (35%) showed a child profile. The remainder of the child molester group was approximately equally distributed among the other four profile categories. It is clear from this close examination of individual profile shapes that child molesters do not uniformly show sexual preferences for children, and they certainly do not show exclusive sexual responses to children. Responders to children (the child and the child–adult profile groups) were found to have lower than average intelligence and

NONRESPONDERS TO CHILDREN

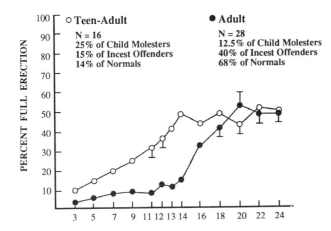

FIGURE 1. Mean age preference profiles for the "adult" and the "teen–adult" profile groups. (From H. E. Barbaree & W. L. Marshall, 1989. "Erectile Responses amongst Heterosexual Child Molesters, Father–Daughter Incest Offenders and Matched Non-Offenders: Five Distinct Age Preference Profiles." *Canadian Journal of Behavioral Sciences, 21,* 70–82.) Copyright 1989, Canadian Psychological Association. Reprinted with permission.

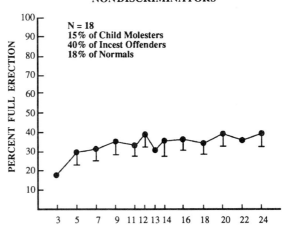

FIGURE 2. Mean age preference profiles for the "nondiscriminator" profile group. (From H. E. Barbaree & W. L. Marshall, 1989. "Erectile Responses amongst Heterosexual Child Molesters, Father–Daughter Incest Offenders and Matched Non-Offenders: Five Distinct Age Preference Profiles." *Canadian Journal of Behavioral Sciences, 21*, 70–82.) Copyright 1989, Canadian Psychological Association. Reprinted with permission.

lower socioeconomic status. Further, the men who exhibited the child profile had used more force in the commission of their offenses and reported having offended against a larger number of victims.

Therefore, when age of target has been systematically varied over a number of stimuli, stimulus control of sexual arousal has been demonstrated, indicating control of the strength of arousal by age of the target as a key element of the compound stimulus. The pattern of stimulus control has varied from man to man, and a profile analysis detected numerous subgroups of men, each sharing a common pattern of stimulus control. Furthermore, and this is especially important for the understanding of sexual deviance, the pattern of stimulus

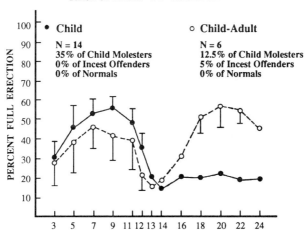

FIGURE 3. Mean age preference profiles for the "child" and the "child–adult" profile groups. (From H. E. Barbaree & W. L. Marshall, 1989. "Erectile Responses amongst Heterosexual Child Molesters, Father–Daughter Incest Offenders and Matched Non-Offenders: Five Distinct Age Preference Profiles." *Canadian Journal of Behavioral Sciences, 21*, 70–82.) Copyright 1989, Canadian Psychological Association. Reprinted with permission.

control differentiated child molesters from nonoffenders and distinguished various important subcategories of offenders.

RAPISTS

Sexual arousal in men to both sexual and nonsexual violence has been a subject of recent theoretical interest and empirical study. These responses have been interpreted by clinical and social scientists as indicating a propensity in an individual man for committing sexual violence (Abel *et al.*, 1977; Malamuth, 1981a) and by feminist writers as being indicative of man's inherent potential for violence against women (Russell, 1988). Despite the importance of this issue, the relevant empirical results have been inconsistent, and the interpretations based on these results have been accepted uncritically. Abel *et al.* (1977) have suggested that rapists are paraphiliacs in the same sense that pedophiles are, except that instead of showing a preference for children as sexual objects, rapists prefer nonconsenting aggressive sexual interactions. These authors conducted the first major examination of deviant sexual arousal in rapists by recording the sexual arousal of these offenders and a group of nonrapist sexual deviates during 2-minute verbal descriptions of mutually consenting sex and rape. Abel *et al.* found that the rapists were more aroused by descriptions of forced sex than were nonrapists, although the rapists did not show a sexual preference for rape. As a group, the rapists were equally aroused by rape and consenting cues, while nonrapists were considerably less aroused by rape than they were by the consenting sexual descriptions.

The findings of Abel *et al.* (1977) were supported by studies reported soon after (Barbaree *et al.*, 1979; Quinsey & Chaplin, 1982, 1984). Later, however, in strong support of the sexual preference hypothesis, Quinsey, Chaplin, and Upfold (1984) reported that rapists showed stronger arousal to rape cues than did nonoffenders and stronger arousal to rape cues than to consenting cues (Quinsey, personal communication, January, 1988). Earls and Proulx (1987) have recently reported similar findings in a Francophone population of rapists, using translations of the Abel, Blanchard, Becker, and Djenderedjian (1978) verbal descriptions of rape, consenting sex, and assault. However, Baxter *et al.* (1986) reported results from 60 rapists and 41 nonrapists which indicated that both groups showed significantly less arousal to rape that to mutually consenting cues. Similarly, Murphy, Krisak, Stalgaitis, and Anderson (1984) and Langevin *et al.* (1985) failed to find significant differences between rapists and nonrapists in their responses to sexual violence.

While a number of other aspects of the research may have to be examined to resolve these inconsistencies, the present chapter will focus on the differences between the studies in the construction of the test stimuli. Abel *et al.* (1977) wrote individual descriptions of actual rapes committed by their subjects. This method presents a number of difficulties in interpretation, including the fact that nonrapists had no direct experience with rape, so no individualized description of rape could be written for them, and the comparison between rapists and nonrapists was thereby confounded. Quinsey and his associates (Quinsey & Chaplin, 1982, 1984; Quinsey *et al.*, 1984) wrote standardized verbal descriptions of numerous rapes and mutually consenting interactions and presented these to both rapists and nonrapists. However, there were numerous differences between the rape and mutually consenting episodes which confounded the comparison between consenting and nonconsenting sexual interactions, including the mood of the man (bored and uneasy vs. a natural feeling of warmth and peace), the relationship between the man and woman (hitchhiker vs. girlfriend), and the environmental context (outskirts of town vs. bedroom). In one of the rape episodes, the subject committed the crime with several of his friends, and in two of the five rape episodes, the man was described as having been drinking before the assault.

The rape episodes used by Abel and Quinsey may be thought to have ecological validity, in the sense that they were representative of crimes committed by convicted or self-confessed rapists, and the differences between the two kinds of episodes may have accurately reflected the differences between these two kinds of experiences in the natural environment. However, these episodes have not lent themselves to an analysis of stimulus control of sexual arousal in rapists, because differences in responding to the two sets of stimuli distinguishing rapists from nonrapists cannot be attributed to a single key element or set of elements in the compound stimulus.

Barbaree *et al.* (1979) took a more systematic stepwise approach to the construction of episodes. For this purpose, what was needed was to break up, or degrade, the rape and consenting stimuli into various elements and to test the effects of each on arousal. A similar problem has been faced in ethology in the study of releasing or "key" stimuli (e.g., Tinbergen, 1951), where ethologists have shown that, in some specific instances, only one crucial part of the stimulus complex was necessary to elicit the behavioral sequence, while other parts had no effect. We (Barbaree *et al.*, 1979) wrote and recorded six different kinds of sexual episodes in which as many elements as possible were kept constant (e.g., the man and woman met at a party, they returned to an apartment, the descriptions of sexual behavior included foreplay and vaginal intercourse). Each specific sexual behavior was located at approximately the same temporal locus in each of the episodes. The episodes varied in two key elements, namely, the degree of consent given by the woman to the proposed and ongoing sexual behavior and the force and violence perpetrated by the male protagonist on the woman victim. We regarded Episode 2 as the benchmark. In it, the woman was passive, neither initiating nor rejecting sexual activities with the subject. Then, on either side of this benchmark, we varied the behavior of the woman. In Episode 1, the woman was described as being aroused, and she initiated most of the sexual behavior. In Episode 3, the woman was at first reluctant but was later seduced by the subject. Constructing the stimuli in this way, we were able to assess the effects of the woman's sexual behavior on the men's sexual arousal. As a group, the three rape episodes described nonconsenting behavior on the part of the woman. She objected to the man's sexual approaches and was described as being highly distressed at his sexual aggression. Among the three rape episodes, the force and violence used by the man were varied as key elements. In Episode 4, the male subject used verbal threats to obtain the woman's compliance with his sexual behaviors. In Episode 5, the subject physically restrained his victim while he raped her. In Episode 6, the subject restrained the woman and physically assaulted her, punching and slapping the woman while he raped her.

In nonrapists, the effects of our stimulus compounds were very clear. In general terms, the woman's consent as an element of the compound stimulus had strong control over arousal. Consenting episodes evoked 50–60% of full erections on average, while nonconsenting or rape episodes evoked weaker or much reduced arousal. The more violent rape episode evoked less arousal than the two less severe rapes. The differences in arousal to the consenting versus the rape cues were most pronounced in the nonrapists during a second session, suggesting a practice effect. In rapists, the results were less clear cut. In the earlier study (Barbaree *et al.*, 1979), rapists showed no significant reduction in arousal to rape cues, although there was a trend in that direction. In our subsequent report (Baxter *et al.*, 1986), with a much larger N, we did find a statistically significant reduction in arousal to rape compared to consenting cues among rapists. However, the reduction was not as large as among nonrapists.

STIMULUS INHIBITION OF SEXUAL AROUSAL

In an attempt to account for our findings, we (Barbaree *et al.*, 1979; Marshall & Barbaree, 1984) offered an inhibition hypothesis of sexual aggression as an alternative to the sexual preference hypothesis. The concept of stimulus inhibition has a long history (Pavlov, 1927), and the application of this concept in accounting for sexual reflexes has been suggested by other authors (Abel *et al.*, 1977; Malamuth *et al.*, 1980). We postulated that a single element of a compound stimulus may have one of two effects on sexual arousal: excitation or inhibition. We proposed that the descriptions of sexual interactions between the man and woman—the foreplay and intercourse—would be excitatory elements and would serve to increase sexual arousal in most men. Similarly, descriptions of the woman, her physical attributes, her sexual arousal, and aspects of her behavior may be excitatory in effect. In contrast, we hypothesized that nonconsent on the part of the woman and her displays of pain, fear, and discomfort, as well as force on the part of the man, would serve to inhibit the sexual arousal of most men to the interactions. We argued that the results we had observed in our study were the product of these two opposing effects. In consenting episodes containing excitatory elements but no inhibitory elements, sexual arousal was greatest. In rape episodes, containing inhibitory elements, the sexual arousal that would otherwise be elicited by the excitatory cues was inhibited at least to some degree. The concept of stimulus inhibition can be applied to help us understand sexual assault in the natural environment. According to the inhibition hypothesis, sexual aggression is more likely when cues of nonconsent and force fail to inhibit a man's arousal and motor behavior, either because the man has failed to acquire this inhibitory process or because the inhibitory process has been somehow disrupted.

Mechanisms of Stimulus Inhibition

As we pointed out in our original paper (Barbaree *et al.*, 1979), the mechanism by which inhibitory cues come to reduce arousal is not known. However, we suggested two possible explanations. Firstly, inhibition might come about through the operation of a complex cognitive-psychophysiological response to the violence and pain depicted in the rape episode. The subject may become emotionally aroused by fear or anxiety in response to the descriptions of a violent and criminal act. Similar emotional responses may be evoked as a result of empathy for the victim. These emotional responses may inhibit sexual arousal through activation of the sympathetic nervous system, which is known to decrease the erectile response. Malamuth and Check (1980, 1983) have provided indirect support of the competing emotion explanation by showing that when the victim is described as being in greater pain and distress—which might be expected to evoke an even stronger emotional response in the subject—sexual arousal to the rape descriptions was reduced. Secondly, inhibition might come about through the subject responding to experimenter demands. Subjects recognize that arousal to the rape descriptions would be regarded by most persons, including the experimenter, as inappropriate, and they may wish to appear "normal." In addition, they may perceive a purpose to the experiment and want to appear as a cooperative subject. Accordingly, they may consciously and deliberately suppress arousal to the rape descriptions and attempt to enhance arousal to the consenting scenes. We have reported on numerous occasions (Barbaree *et al.*, 1979; Barbaree, Marshall, Yates, & Lightfoot, 1983; Baxter *et al.*, 1986) that nonrapists show a more pronounced discrimination between mutually consenting cues and rape cues in a second assessment session, due to both enhanced arousal to consenting cues as well as reduced arousal to rape cues. Presumably, with practice, nonrapists become more proficient in making themselves look appropriate. In a more direct test of the experimenter demand hypothesis, Quinsey, Chaplin, and Varney (1981) instructed a group of nonrapists that arousal to rape cues was common among normal men and found that these instructions increased rape arousal in these subjects. Presumably these instructions served to relieve subjects to some extent from the demands to inhibit arousal to rape.

Following from this account of possible mechanisms, inhibition of sexual arousal to rape cues can be viewed as a prosocial act. The more concern the subject has for the victim in the description, the more positive his attitudes toward women, the more sensitive he is to her pain and suffering, and the stronger will be the emotional response component which produces the inhibition. Also, the more sensitive the subject is to societal restrictions concerning inappropriate sexual behavior, the more likely he will be to expend the effort required to reduce his arousal to rape in the laboratory.

Individual Differences

We (Barbaree *et al.*, 1979) have postulated that, in the general population of men, individuals differ in the strength of their inhibition to rape cues. Other authors have postulated a continuum of individual differences in responses thought to be important in rape in the general population of men. Abel *et al.* (1977), for example, computed a "rape index" (rape arousal/consenting arousal) and showed that the mean index was higher among rapists than nonrapists; this index has been found to be correlated with the rapist's number of previous victims and the likelihood of victim injury (Abel *et al.*, 1978). Presumably, the index quantifies the tendency in the individual to inhibit sexual arousal to cues of nonconsent and force. Similarly, Malamuth and his associates (Malamuth, 1981a, 1983, 1986; Malamuth & Check, 1983) have suggested that a continuum exists of the "likelihood of raping" among the general male population. Malamuth and Check (1983) have reported that when a rape description portrays a woman as abhorring the rape throughout, those men who deny any likelihood of raping show a strong inhibition of arousal to the rape cues, whereas men who admit to some potential for raping if there was no chance of being caught, show weaker inhibition. Furthermore, according to Malamuth, sexual arousal to rape cues is only part of an integrated set of behaviors and cognitions which characterize the rapist. Men who admit a potential for raping also have more callous attitudes toward rape and are more likely to believe in rape myths than are men who deny such a potential (Malamuth, 1981a; Malamuth & Check, 1980; Malamuth, Haber, & Feshbach, 1980). Additionally, men who respond to rape cues with relatively strong erectile responses, and who also express attitudes accepting of sexual violence toward women, are more likely to aggress against women when given the opportunity in the laboratory (Malamuth, 1983). Finally, Malamuth (1986) has reported that a complex of factors together predict sexually aggressive behavior among males in the natural environment, including sexual arousal in response to aggression, the identification of dominance as a motive for sexual acts, hostility toward woman, and attitudes accepting of violence against women.

DISINHIBITION OF RAPE AROUSAL

When a stimulus abruptly loses its inhibitory power due to some disruptive event, the process is known as disinhibition. Like the concept of inhibition, the concept of disinhibition has a long history (Pavlov, 1927) and has been applied to processes associated with the sexual response (Malamuth, Heim, & Feshbach, 1980; Yates, Barbaree, & Marshall, 1984). Circumstantial variables and events surrounding a sexual assault might influence its occurrence through the disruption of stimulus inhibition. The following review describes laboratory experiments in which the disinhibition of rape arousal has been brought about by (1) portraying behavior on the part of the woman in the description which increases the perception of her blame for the assault, (2) inducing anger in the subject, and (3) inducing alcohol intoxication in the tested subject.

Disinhibition by Victim Blame

Sundberg, Barbaree, and Marshall (1989) examined the role of victim blame in disinhibiting arousal to rape cues in three separate studies. In the first study, rape vignettes were rated by 384 university undergraduates, both male and female, on the extent to which the victim was responsible or blameworthy in the assault. The vignettes varied in the clothing worn by the victim and her location when first observed by the rapist. Victims wore revealing or conservative dress and were located in a deserted park or in a library. These two variables were combined factorially to construct four separate vignettes. When the victim wore revealing dress while walking in a deserted park, both male and female raters judged her to be significantly more blameworthy than when the victim wore conservative dress or wore a revealing dress in a library.

In a second experiment, a between-groups experimental design was used to compare erectile responses to vignettes in which victim blame was manipulated by varying the victim's dress and location. All subjects were tested while listening to both mutually consenting and rape cues in the first session. In the second session, some subjects listened to a similar consenting vignette and to a rape vignette in which the woman wore revealing clothing while walking through a deserted park. Other subjects listened in this second session to rape vignettes in which the woman was more conservatively dressed while in a library. For those subjects who listened to the rape of the victim judged earlier to be more blameworthy, the discrimination between rape and consenting cues was markedly reduced. In the third experiment, a within-subject experimental design was used. Twelve male university students listened to low-, medium-, and high-blame vignettes of rape and to descriptions of consenting sex. Once again, the high-blame condition produced smaller differences between consenting and rape arousal.

Disinhibition by Anger

Yates *et al.* (1984) presented, in each of two sessions, six verbal descriptions of sexual interactions (three rape and three consenting) to 24 male university students. Prior to measuring their arousal in Session 2, subjects were told that the purpose of the study was to examine the effects of physical exercise on sexual arousal. The control group was simply tested again as in Session 1. Subjects in the exercise-only group were asked to pedal on a bicycle ergometer as fast as they could for 1 minute, after which they were tested as in Session 1. The third group was also asked to pedal the bicycle ergometer. However, just before they commenced pedaling, a woman dressed in a laboratory coat (actually a confederate of the experimenter) entered the room and asked to borrow a piece of equipment. The experimenter told the woman to wait until she had finished with the subject. At the end of the minute, the subject was told how "far" he had pedaled. In response to hearing this, the female confederate made a disparaging remark. This same provocation had been shown in an earlier pilot study to increase aggression in men toward a woman in the laboratory. The subject was then immediately tested as in Session 1. Both the control group and the exercise-only group showed the usual strong inhibition of arousal to the rape cues. However, the angered group showed equally strong responding to rape cues as to consenting cues, indicating a complete lack of stimulus inhibition.

Disinhibition by Alcohol Intoxication

Offenders will often claim that their sexual assault was committed while they were severely intoxicated. It is estimated that up to 50% of rapists are intoxicated at the time of their offense (Christie, Marshall, & Lanthier, 1979; Gebhard, Gagnon, Pomeroy, & Christenson, 1965). The implication has been that alcohol intoxication causes sexual assault or facilitates processes which cause sexual assault. However, the effects of alcohol intoxication on rape arousal are complex. Early studies in this area suggested that much of the alcohol effects were due to the subject's expectations rather than to direct pharmacological action. For example, Briddell et al. (1978) used an experimental design known as the "balanced-placebo design," in which subjects are divided into two equal groups, with one group being told that they will recieve an alcoholic beverage and the other group being told that they will receive a nonalcoholic beverage. Then, each group is further subdivided into two subgroups, with one subgroup actually receiving alcohol and the other receiving a nonalcoholic beverage. After subjects had ingested their beverages, Briddell et al. presented both consenting and rape cues to men, while monitoring erectile responses. They reported that subjects who thought they had consumed alcohol showed greater arousal to rape cues than men who thought they had drunk no alcohol. Whether their subjects actually drank alcohol or not did not influence sexual arousal to rape.

This study has been criticized on a number of grounds. First, the study did not use properly counterbalanced stimuli (Lansky & Wilson, 1981). Second, as we (Barbaree et al., 1983) pointed out, it is possible to explain the Briddell et al. findings on the basis of increased sexual arousal to all cues due to general increases in arousal caused by alcohol expectancy (Lansky & Wilson, 1981; Wilson & Lawson, 1976). Also, Briddell et al. used a low dose of alcohol, which might account for the absence of an alcohol effect. Finally, the validity of the balanced-placebo design in actually producing an alcohol expectancy has been questioned (Knight, Barbaree, & Boland, 1986).

We (Barbaree et al., 1983) used the balanced-placebo design in a study much like that of Briddell et al. (1978). After being tested in a baseline session, subjects returned to the laboratory and were administered their expectancy instructions and a beverage to consume. The amount of alcohol consumed was calculated to increase their blood alcohol level to 0.07% during arousal assessment, a larger dose than that used by Briddell et al. After drinking their beverages, subjects were again presented with rape and consenting cues while their arousal was monitored. We found effects of alcohol intoxication, but they were not straight-forward. There were no effects of alcohol expectancy. Further, there were no effects of alcohol on overall levels of rape arousal. However, subjects who were intoxicated failed to show the increase in discrimination between consenting and rape cues that we have previously seen in nonoffenders and which we saw in this study in the men who had not drunk alcohol. In this respect, our intoxicated nonoffenders were behaving like rapists we have tested.

It is not clear what implications these results might have for our understanding of sexual assault. If the increase in discrimination in nonintoxicated men results from their responses to experimenter demands, and the failure of this to occur in the intoxicated men indicates less sensitivity to experimenter demands, then alcohol intoxication might facilitate sexual assault by reducing men's sensitivity to societal demands for appropriate behavior. Wydra *et al.* (1983) have begun an examination of this proposition. These authors asked nonoffenders—both sober and intoxicated—and rapists to indicate when during presentation of the rape verbal descriptions the behavior of the man was inappropriate. Intoxicated nonoffenders seemed to indicate inappropriate behavior earlier in the sequence than did either rapists or nonintoxicated nonoffenders. So, if alcohol intoxication interferes with the sensitivity of subjects in responding to experimenter demands, it is not because they are impaired in their ability to identify inappropriate sexual behavior. Therefore, it is likely that alcohol intoxication disrupts normal stimulus control of sexual arousal, but we do not know enough yet to specify clearly the nature of this interaction.

Disinhibition by Preexposure to Aggressive Pornography

It is commonly argued that when men are exposed to pornography, their risk for committing sexual offenses may increase. Malamuth and Check (1981) exposed a group of undergraduate students to a violent, sexually explicit movie and a second group to a control feature-length film. Results indicated that exposure to the sexually violent film increased male students' acceptance of interpersonal violence. In a similar vein, Malamuth and Check (1985) exposed undergraduate students to a verbal description of an aggressive sexual interaction in which the female victim was described as becoming sexually aroused. In subsequent measures of attitudes toward rape, these male students were more likely to endorse the rape myth that views women as enjoying rape encounters. This effect was particularly strong in men who showed a preexisting inclination toward sexual aggression. Further, Malamuth (1981b) has shown that men who have been exposed to a rape version of a slide–audio show generate more violent sexual fantasies than men exposed to a mutually consenting slide–audio show. Finally, Sommers and Check (1987) have found that partners of battered women, who were shown to be sexually aggressive, were more likely to be consumers of pornography than a matched comparison group.

It is possible, that exposure to particular varieties of pornography may change, even momentarily, the nature of stimulus control of arousal in a man, and this disruption in stimulus control may be related to increased risk for offending. This possibility has been examined by Seidman, Marshall, and Barbaree (1989). During "preexposure," male university students were presented with short videotaped sequences depicting either explicit or nonexplicit mutually consenting sex, explicit or nonexplicit rape, or a nonsexual scene. Explicit scenes depicted actors with full frontal nudity and a focus on the genitals during intercourse, and the presentation was in color with an audible sound track. Nonexplicit scenes did not depict nudity nor any display of genitalia, and the presentations were in black and white with no audible sound track. The nonsexual scene involved an aviation theme. Then, subjects were presented with the same audiotaped mutually consenting episodes used by Barbaree *et al.* (1979), while erectile responses were monitored. During this latter test, subjects who had been preexposed to rape scenes showed reduced discrimination between rape and mutually consenting stimuli compared with subjects who had been preexposed to consenting or neutral stimuli. Therefore, this study provides empirical evidence that prior exposure to rape themes disinhibits men's arousal to rape cues.

EXCITATION BY NONSEXUAL VIOLENCE

A number of studies have presented verbal descriptions of nonsexual violence—usually a graphic description of a man physically assaulting a woman—and studied resulting erectile responses of rapists (Abel *et al.*, 1977), rapists and nonrapists (Barbaree *et al.*, 1979; Earls & Proulx, 1987; Quinsey & Chaplin, 1982; Quinsey *et al.*, 1984; Quinsey *et al.*, 1981), and nonrapists (Malamuth *et al.*, 1986). These studies have examined two important aspects of the male's sexual response; (1) the magnitude of the response to nonsexual violence and (2) the difference between offenders and nonoffenders in their responses to nonsexual violence.

These studies indicate that while men do respond significantly to nonsexual violence, the response is very small. Earls and Proulx (1987) have reported that arousal in both rapists and nonrapists to nonsexual violence was significantly greater than to a neutral nonsexual passage read from a newspaper. Quinsey *et al.* (1984) have found that rapists' arousal to a description of nonsexual violence was significantly greater than to a neutral passage describing a nonsexual interaction between a man and a woman, while no such differences were found in nonrapists. However, the absolute magnitudes of these responses have been very small. Only studies which report arousal in terms of percentage of full erection can be used to make this judgment. The mean strength of response to nonsexual violence in the Earls and Proulx study was 25% of full erection. Barbaree *et al.* (1979) reported mean strength of arousal to nonsexual violence to be just over 20% in rapists and approximately 10% of full erection in nonrapists.

In some studies, different criterion groups have responded with different levels of arousal to nonsexual violence. Quinsey and Chaplin (1982) have found that the more violent rapist responds more strongly than less violent rapists to these cues. Quinsey *et al.*, (1984) found that rapists showed greater responses to nonsexual violence than did matched nonoffenders. However, some studies have not found differences between criterion groups. Quinsey *et al.*, (1981) and Earls and Proulx (1987) have reported that rapists did not differ from nonrapists in responses to nonsexual violence.

In summary, then, it may be said that men respond with small but significant arousal to descriptions of nonsexual violence perpetrated by a man on a woman. Further, men may differ in the strength of their arousal to these cues depending on their history of sexual aggression; however, just how these responses are to be interpreted is not clear. While it is true that these episodes do not themselves contain explicit sexual cues, there may be implicit sexual cues and expectations on the part of the subject that sexual cues will follow. These descriptions of nonsexual violence have been presented in a single session among a number of other descriptions which have explicit sexual content and which have elicited strong sexual arousal. Also, the measure taken is a peak measure, and the subject's peak response may have occurred early in the descriptions, before it became clear to the subject just what kind of description it was.

Quinsey et al., (1984) also prevented verbal descriptions of violence perpetrated by a man against another man and found that the sexual responses to these cues were not significantly greater than those to neutral cues. Therefore, it is not the violence cues on their own which cause arousal to the nonsexual violence against women. According to Quinsey et al. (1984), "The finding that rapists respond to nonsexual violence involving female but not male victims suggests that sexual arousal to descriptions of nonsexual violence occurs because the descriptions resemble violence in a sexual context." These authors interpret arousal to nonsexual violence as if it were a response to implied sexual elements.

In summary, stimulus control of sexual arousal to rape cues is best understood as a synthesis of excitatory and inhibitory effects. Stimulus elements in these compound stimuli elicit arousal, and this excitatory effect is counteracted by inhibitory effects of the elements of nonconsent, force, and distress of the victim. Men vary in the strength of their inhibition to rape cues, in accordance with their prosocial attitudes and behavior toward women. It is assumed that the more negative a man's attitudes and behaviors toward women, and the weaker his inhibition to rape cues, the more at risk he is for committing sexual assault. In addition, some circumstances have been identified which disinhibit rape arousal, apparently by momentarily disrupting a man's prosocial behavior toward women. Therefore, stimulus control of sexual arousal in sexual assault can be seen to be a integral part of a complex aggressive response which includes cognitive, behavioral, and physiological components.

The Preferential Rape Pattern in a Single Rapist

While group studies of sexual arousal among rapists show inhibited responding to rape cues, there are a few individual rapists who have been tested who show a pattern of stimulus control which is in strong support of the sexual preference hypothesis, and this pattern has been called the "preferential rape pattern" (Freund et al., 1986). The following is a presentation of selected assessment results from a 27-year-old man serving a 7-year sentence for rape in a Canadian Federal Penitentiary.

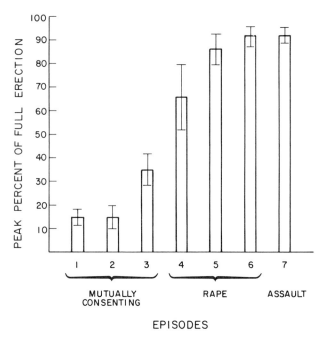

FIGURE 4. Mean peak percentage of full erection to verbal descriptions of mutually consenting intercourse, rape, and nonsexual assault for a single incarcerated rapist.

Figure 4 presents mean erectile responses to the seven episodes used by Barbaree *et al.* (1979), averaged over the first five assessment sessions administered to this man. As can be seen in the figure, this man did not respond very strongly to mutually consenting episodes, but he responded very strongly to rape and assault episodes. Within the mutually consenting episodes, the description of the woman being reluctant evoked the strongest arousal. Within the rape episodes, the more severe rapes evoked the strongest arousal, with the most severe rape and the nonsexual assault eliciting almost maximum arousal in all five sessions. The traditional interpretation of these data would be that force, violence, and nonconsent were sexually arousing for this man and that this sexual arousal was a motivation for his sexually aggressive behavior. Other assessment results, which will be presented here, seem to suggest that the underlying motivation of this man was more complicated than that simply due to a sexual preference.

The first of these results came from unsuccessful attempts to treat the man with aversion therapy. In this electrical aversion therapy procedure, a verbal description of the man's current offense was presented, and a brief, uncomfortable (but not painful) electric shock was delivered to the subject's calf at the end of each sentence which described a deviant behavior. The subject's erectile response was monitored throughout each session, and Figure 5 presents the polygraph output of the penile plythysmograph over the eight sessions. Examination of the figure reveals a tendency for the erectile response to increase over

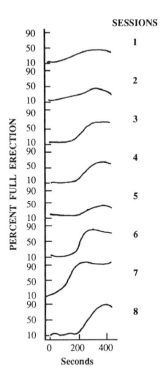

FIGURE 5. Polygraph output of erectile responses in a single subject over eight sessions of aversion therapy.

the sessions rather than to decrease. Of the first five sessions, three do not show increases in erectile response above 50% of a full erection. However, in each of the last 3 sessions, the erectile response increased above 90% of full erection.

Because these results were at once distressing and perplexing, treatment was halted and an explanation of the results was sought. Observation of the subject during the aversion procedure indicated that he was becoming increasingly dysphoric. Specifically, he seemed to become angry, to the point that we became concerned about the possibility of his becoming assaultive. During debriefing after each of these sessions, he claimed that the description of his crime upset him because it reminded him of the reason he was in jail, and he resented having been incarcerated for so long for an offense which he judged to be of a minor nature. We also felt that presentation of the noxious stimulus in the aversion procedure enhanced his anger.

As described earlier in this chapter, anger has been shown to disrupt inhibition of arousal to rape cues in nonrapists, and it was possible that this rapist's deviant arousal could be affected by the emotional state he was experiencing. To investigate this possibility, the following experiment was conducted. In a single session, three verbal descriptions were presented three times each, in a random order. The three descriptions were the two most severe rape descriptions and the description of the nonsexual assault from Barbaree *et al.* (1979). In each of the three repetitions of each episode, we asked the subject to imagine that he was raping or assaulting one of three women whom he had known previously. We chose three women from his history toward whom he held distinctly different feelings of hostility. Victim (a) was a woman whom he felt had been very cruel to him. They had a romantic relationship for 2 years, but it had been a rocky one. It ended badly, with the woman betraying him with another man. He had always spoken of her with great hostility, and to some extent he blamed her for what had happened to him since. Victim (c) was at the other end of the spectrum. She was his current girlfriend, and he had strong feelings of affection toward her. Victim (b) was his wife during his current offense. He had strong feelings of love and affection for her at the onset of his sentence, but she had since left him for another man. While he did not blame her for not waiting for him, he still was angry at her for her disloyalty. The subject estimated that his anger toward victim (b) was not as great as toward victim (a). Therefore, stimulus presentations during this session were part of a factorial design, with three levels of severity of sexual assault, combined with three victims differentiated by degree of felt hostility. During each description, we asked that the subject imagine committing the offense described against the woman specified before each description.

Figure 6 presents the polygraph outputs for each response in the study. The effect which we had seen in his earlier responses was evident again, namely, that the more severe rape and the nonsexual assault produced the strongest erectile response. However, as can be seen clearly in the figure, the subject's hostility toward the victim influenced the strength of his arousal. When he imagined assaulting the victim toward whom he held the greatest hostility, he

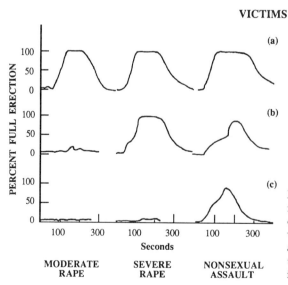

FIGURE 6. Polygraph output of erectile responding in a single subject to verbal descriptions of a "moderate" and a "severe" rape and a nonsexual assault against three victims differentiated by the degree of hostility the subject exhibited toward them.

shows a full erection to all three descriptions. On the other hand, when imagining assaulting the woman toward which he held affection, he shows no erectile response to the two rapes and only a brief longer latency response to the nonsexual assault. Therefore, even when studying men who show a preferential rape pattern of stimulus control, more prosocial attitudes toward the victim are associated with inhibition of rape arousal.

This subject's pattern of stimulus control of arousal was not just distinguished from normative arousal by his responses to deviant cues but also by his weak responses to consenting cues. Not only did he show very weak arousal to consenting stimuli, but he also showed what appeared to be weaker arousal to the consenting stimulus in which the woman was most aroused, the most initiating of sexual behaviors, and the most enthusiastic as a partner. On numerous occasions, one of the clinical staff sat next to him in the isolation room during presentation of sexual episodes. His behavior during the consenting episodes would often indicate emotional distress, including signs of sympathetic nervous system activity: he would become flushed, tremulous, and would appear generally to be nervous. It occurred to us that this subject might be experiencing a similar reaction to consenting episodes as we had postulated to be present in nonoffenders during violent rape episodes. If so, this emotional reaction could cause an inhibition of arousal to the consenting episodes.

We have only indirect evidence of this inhibition from assessments of his erectile responses. As part of an effort on our part to develop a procedure to detect faking of the erectile response, we had written verbal descriptions of sexual and nonsexual interactions which switched abruptly from one kind of episode to another. Figure 7 presents the polygraph output from the subject responding to these episodes which switched abruptly. In the top panel, a

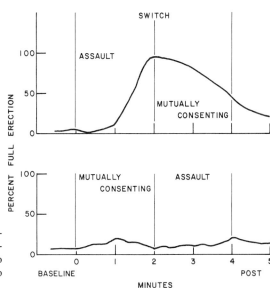

Figure 7. Polygraph output of erectile responding in a single subject to verbal descriptions which switched from assault to consenting and from consenting to assault.

nonsexual assault switched to a mutually consenting episode, and as can be seen, he responded strongly to the nonsexual assault. His erectile response reached near maximal response just before the switch. Upon the switch to mutually consenting interactions, his erectile response detumesces rapidly. This of course need not imply any inhibitory mechanism, since an offset of the excitatory assault cues would be sufficient to explain the detumescence. However, in the lower panel, presentation of the assault stimulus failed to elicit arousal when it was presented immediately after the consenting stimulus. This was the only time this man failed to respond to a presentation of a nonsexual assault in our laboratory. One plausible explanation of this failure was that the inhibitory effect of the consenting episode has continuing or residual effects after its offset and inhibited his response to the assault.

These assessment results are not presented here as necessarily convincing or definitive. Instead, they are presented to suggest how future investigations might increase our understanding of the preferential rape pattern beyond the simple application of the sexual preference hypothesis. This pattern of arousal may be better understood as a combination of excitatory and inhibitory effects of various stimulus elements.

SUMMARY

This chapter has argued that stimulus control of sexual arousal is an important aspect of sexual assault and is best studied in an experimental situation where a single stimulus element is varied among various stimulus presentations. For child molesters, the pattern of stimulus control engendered by the key element of target age has been found to differentiate offenders from nonoffenders and various subgroups of offenders. Stimulus control by the key elements of nonconsent, force and violence, and victim distress indicates that these cues act to inhibit sexual arousal in rapists as well as nonrapists, but more strongly in nonrapists. The strength of stimulus inhibition of arousal to rape cues is likely inversely related to the tendency in men to aggression toward women. Further, the inhibitory effects may be disrupted by anger, permissive instructions, victim blame, victim sexual arousal, and alcohol intoxication. Data reviewed here seem to indicate that the pattern of stimulus control by various key elements may be highly idiosyncratic and particular to individual men. Understanding each individual offender's pattern of stimulus control of arousal may assist in understanding the motivation for his assaults and also give clues as to the most effective treatment for him.

ACKNOWLEDGMENTS. I wish to thank Bill Marshall and Vern Quinsey for their very helpful comments on earlier drafts of this chapter.

REFERENCES

Abel, G. G., Barlow, D. H., Blanchard, E. B., & Mavissakalian, M. (1975). Measurement of sexual arousal in male homosexuals: The effects of instructions and stimulus modality. *Archives of Sexual Behavior, 4*, 623–629.

Abel, G. G., Barlow, D. H., Blanchard, E. B., & Guild, D. (1977). The components of rapist's sexual arousal. *Archives of General Psychiatry, 34,* 895–903.

Abel, G. G., Blanchard, E. B., Becker, J. V., & Djenderedjian, A. (1978). Differentiating sexual aggressives with penile measures. *Criminal Justice and Behavior, 5,* 315–332.

American Psychiatric Association. (1987). *Diagnostic and statistical manual of mental disorders* (3rd ed., revised). Washington, DC: Author.

American Psychological Association. (1985). *Standards of educational and psychological testing.* Washington, DC: Author.

Barbaree, H. E., & Marshall, W. L. (1988). Deviant sexual arousal, offense history, and demographic variables as predictors of reoffense among child molesters. *Behavioral Sciences and the Law, 6,* 267–280.

Barbaree, H. E., & Mewhort, D. J. K. (1989). The effects of Z-score transformations of erectile responses in studies of stimulus control of sexual arousal. Manuscript submitted for publication.

Barbaree, H. E., & Marshall, W. L. (in press). Treatment of the sex offender. In R. M. Wettstein (Ed.), *Treatment of the mentally disordered offender.* New York: Guilford Press.

Barbaree, H. E., & Marshall, W. L. (1989). Erectile responses amongst heterosexual child molesters, father–daughter incest offenders and matched non-offenders: Five distinct age preference profiles. *Canadian Journal of Behavioral Science, 21,* 70–82.

Barbaree, H. E., Marshall, W. L., & Lanthier, R. D. (1979). Deviant sexual arousal in rapists. *Behavior Research and Therapy, 17,* 215–222.

Barbaree, H. E., Marshall, W. L., Yates, E., & Lightfoot, L. O. (1983). Alcohol intoxication and deviant sexual arousal in male social drinkers. *Behavior Research and Therapy, 21,* 365–373.

Baxter, D. J., Marshall, W. L., Barbaree, H. E., Davidson, P. R., & Malcolm, P. B. (1984). Deviant sexual behavior: Differentiating sex offenders by criminal and personal history, psychometric measures and sexual response. *Criminal Justice and Behavior, 11,* 477–501.

Baxter, D. J., Barbaree, H. E., Marshall, W. L. (1986). Sexual responses to consenting and forced sex in a large sample of rapists and nonrapists. *Behavior Research and Therapy, 24,* 513–520.

Briddell, D. W., Rimm, D. C., Caddy, G. R., Krawitz, G., Sholis, D., & Wunderlin, R. J. (1978). Effects of alcohol and cognitive set on sexual arousal to deviant stimuli. *Journal of Abnormal Psychology, 87,* 418–430.

Brownmiller, S. (1975). *Against our will: Men, women and rape.* New York: Simon & Schuster.

Burt, M. R. (1980). Cultural myths and supports for rape. *Journal of Personality and Social Psychology, 38,* 217–230.

Christie, M. M., Marshall, W. L., & Lanthier, R. D. (1979). *A descriptive study of incarcerated rapists and pedophiles.* Report to the Solicitor General of Canada, Ottawa.

Clark, L., & Lewis, D. (1977). *Rape: The price of coercive sexuality.* Toronto: The Women's Press.

Davidson, P. R., & Malcolm, P. B. (1985). The reliability of the rape index: A rapist sample. *Behavioral Assessment, 7,* 283–292.

Earls, C. M., & Marshall, W. L. (1983). The current state of technology in the laboratory assessment of sexual arousal patterns. In J. G. Geer & I. R. Stuart (Eds.), *Sexual aggression: Current perspectives on treatment* (pp. 336–362). New York: Von Nostrand Reinhold.

Earls, C. M., & Proulx, J. (1987). The differentiation of Francophone rapists and nonrapists using penile circumferential measures. *Criminal Justice and Behavior, 13,* 419–429.

Earls, C. M., Quinsey, V. L., & Castonguay, L. G. (1987). A comparison of scoring methods in the measurement of penile circumference changes. *Archives of Sexual Behavior, 6,* 493–500.

Farkas, G. M. (1979). *Trait and state determinants of male sexual arousal to descriptions of coercive sexuality.* Unpublished doctoral dissertation, University of Hawaii.

Farkas, G. M., Evans, I. M., Sine, L. F., Eifert, G., Wittlieb, E., & Vogelmann-Sine, S. (1979). Reliability and validity of the mercury-in-rubber strain gauge measure of penile circumference. *Behavior Therapy, 10,* 555–561.

Finkelhor, D. (1986). Sexual abuse: Beyond the family systems approach. *Journal of Psychotherapy and the Family, 2,* 53–65.

Freund, K. (1963). A laboratory method of diagnosing predominance of homo- and hetero-erotic interest in the male. *Behavior Research and Therapy, 1,* 85–93.

Freund, K. (1967a). Diagnosing homo- or heterosexuality and erotic age-preference by means of a psychophysiological test. *Behavior Research and Therapy, 5,* 209–228.

Freund, K. (1967b). Erotic preference in pedophilia. *Behavior Research and Therapy*, 5, 339–348.

Freund, K. (1981). Assessment of pedophilia. In M. Cook & K. Howells, (Eds.), *Adult sexual interest in children* (pp. 139–179). London, England: Academic Press.

Freund, K., & Blanchard, R. (1981). Assessment of sexual dysfunction and deviation. In M. Hersen & A. S. Bellack (Eds.), *Behavioral assessment: A practical handbook* (2nd ed.) pp. 427–455). New York: Pergamon Press.

Freund, K., McKnight, C. K., & Langevin, R. (1972). The female child as a surrogate object. *Archives of Sexual Behavior*, 2, 119–133.

Freund, K., Scher, H., Racansky, I. G., Campbell, K., & Heasman, G. (1986). Males disposed to commit rape. *Archives of Sexual Behavior*, 15, 23–35.

Gebhard, P., Gagnon, J., Pomeroy, W., & Christenson, C. (1965). *Sex Offenders*. New York: Harper & Row.

Geer, J. H., & Fuhr, R. (1976). Cognitive factors in sexual arousal: The role of distraction. *Journal of Consulting and Clinical Psychology*, 44, 238–243.

Knight, R. A., Rosenberg, R., & Schneider, B. A. (1985). Classification of sexual offenders: Perspectives, methods and validation. In A. W. Burgess (Ed.), *Rape and Sexual Assault* (pp. 222–293). New York: Garland Publishing.

Knight, L. J., Barbaree, H. E., & Boland, F. J. (1986). Alcohol and the balanced-placebo design: The role of experimenter demands in expectancy. *Journal of Abnormal Psychology*, 95, 335–340.

Langevin, R., Ben-Aron, M. H., Coulthard, R., Heasman, R., Purins, J. E., Handy, L., Hucker, S. J., Russon, A. R., Day, D., Roper, V., Bain, J., Wortzman, G., & Webster, C. D. (1985). Sexual aggression: Constructing a predictive equation; A controlled pilot study. In R. Langevin (Ed.), *Erotic preference, gender identity, and aggression in men: New research studies* (pp. 39–76). Hillsdale, NJ: Lawrence Erlbaum.

Lansky, D., & Wilson, G. T. (1981). Alcohol, expectations, and sexual arousal in males: An information processing analysis. *Journal of Abnormal Psychology*, 90, 35–45.

Laws, D. R., & Holmen, M. L. (1978). Sexual response faking by pedophiles. *Criminal Justice and Behavior*, 5, 343–356.

Laws, D. R., & Osborne, C. A. (1983). How to build and operate a behavioral laboratory to evaluate and treat sexual deviance. In J. G. Geer & I. R. Stuart (Eds.), *Sexual aggression: Current perspectives on treatment* (pp. 293–335). New York: Von Nostrand Reinhold.

Laws, D. R., & Rubin, H. B. (1969). Instructional control of an autonomic response. *Journal of Applied Behavior Analysis*, 2, 93–99.

Malamuth, N. M. (1981a). Rape proclivity among males. *Journal of Social Issues*, 37, 138–156.

Malamuth, N. M. (1981b). Rape fantasies as a function of exposure to violent sexual stimuli. *Archives of Sexual Behavior*, 10, 33–47.

Malamuth, N. M. (1983). Factors associated with rape as predictors of laboratory aggression against women. *Journal of Personality and Social Psychology*, 45, 432–442.

Malamuth, N. M. (1986). Predictors of naturalistic sexual aggression. *Journal of Personality and Social Psychology*, 50, 953–962.

Malamuth, N. M., & Check, J. V. P. (1980). Penile tumescence and perceptual responses to rape as a function of victim's perceived reactions. *Journal of Applied Social Psychology*, 10, 528–547.

Malamuth, N. M., & Check, J. V. P. (1981). The effects of media exposure on acceptance of violence against women: A field experiment. *Journal of Research in Personality*, 15, 436–446.

Malamuth, N. M., & Check, J. V. P. (1983). Sexual arousal to rape depictions: Individual differences. *Journal of Abnormal Psychology*, 92, 55–67.

Malamuth, N. M., & Check, J. V. P. (1985). The effects of aggressive pornography on beliefs in rape myths: Individual differences. *Journal of Research in Personality*, 19, 299–320.

Malamuth, N. M., Haber, S., & Feshbach, S. (1980). Testing hypotheses regarding rape: Exposure to sexual violence, sex differences, and the "normality" of rapists. *Journal of Research in Personality*, 14, 121–137.

Malamuth, N. M., Heim, M., & Feshbach, S. (1980). Sexual responsiveness of college students to rape depictions: Inhibitory and disinhibitory effects. *Journal of Personality and Social Psychology*, 38, 399–408.

Malamuth, N. M., Check, J. V. P., & Briere, J. (1986). Sexual arousal in response to aggression: Ideological, aggressive, and sexual correlates. *Journal of Personality and Social Psychology*, 50, 330–340.

Malcolm, P. B., Davidson, P. R., & Marshall, W. L. (1985). Control of penile tumescence: The effects of arousal level and stimulus content. *Behavior Research and Therapy, 23,* 273–280.

Marshall, W. L., & Barbaree, H. E. (1984). A behavioral view of rape. *International Journal of Law and Psychiatry, 7,* 51–77.

Marshall, W. L., Barbaree, H. E., & Christophe, D. (1986). Sexual preferences for age of victims and type of behaviour. *Canadian Journal of Behavioral Science, 18,* 424–439.

Marshall, W. L., Barbaree, H. E., & Butt, J. (1988). Sexual offenders against male children: Sexual preferences for gender, age of victim and type of behavior. *Behavior Research and Therapy, 26,* 383–391.

Murphy, W. D., & Barbaree, H. E. (1988). *Assessments of sexual offenders by measures of erectile response: An examination of their psychometric properties.* Washington, DC: National Institute of Mental Health, Antisocial and Violent Behavior Program Branch.

Murphy, W. D., Krisak, J., Stalgaitis, S., & Anderson, K. (1984). The use of penile tumescence measures with incarcerated rapists: Further validity issues. *Archives of Sexual Behavior, 13,* 545–554.

Murphy, W. D., Haynes, M. R., Stalgaitis, S. J., & Flanagan, B. (1986). Differential sexual responding among four groups of sexual offenders against children. *Journal of Psychopathology and Behavioral Assessment, 8,* 339–353.

Pavlov, I. P. (1927). *Conditioned reflexes: An investigation of the physiological activity of the cerebral cortex.* London: Oxford University Press.

Quinsey, V. L., & Bergersen, S. G. (1976). Instructional control of penile circumference in assessments of sexual preference. *Behavior Therapy, 7,* 489–493.

Quinsey, V. L., & Chaplin, T. C. (1982). Penile responses to nonsexual violence among rapists. *Criminal Justice and Behavior, 9,* 372–381.

Quinsey, V. L., & Chaplin, T. C. (1984). Stimulus control of rapists' and non-sex offenders' sexual arousal. *Behavioral Assessment, 6,* 169–176.

Quinsey, V. L., & Chaplin, T. C. (1988). Preventing faking in phallometric assessments of sexual preference. In R. Prentky & V. L. Quinsey (Eds.), *Human sexual aggression: Current perspectives* (pp. 49–58). Annals of the New York Academy of Sciences.

Quinsey, V. L., & Harris, G. (1976). A comparison of two methods of scoring the penile circumference response: Magnitude and area. *Behavior Therapy, 7,* 702–704.

Quinsey, V. L., & Marshall, W. L. (1983). Procedures for reducing inappropriate sexual arousal: An evaluative review. In J. G. Greer & I. R. Stuart (Eds.), *The sexual aggressor: Current perspectives on treatment* (pp. 267–289). New York: Von Nostrand Reinhold.

Quinsey, V. L., Steinman, C. M., Bergersen, S. G., & Holmes, T. F. (1975). Penile circumference, skin conductance, and ranking responses of child molesters and "normals" to sexual and nonsexual visual stimuli. *Behavior Therapy, 6,* 213–219.

Quinsey, V. L., Chaplin, T. C., & Carrigan, W. F. (1979). Sexual preferences among incestuous and nonincestuous child molesters. *Behavior Therapy, 10,* 562–565.

Quinsey, V. L., Chaplin, T. C., & Varney, G. (1981). A comparison of rapists' and non-sex offenders' sexual preferences for mutually consenting sex, rape, and physical abuse of women. *Behavioral Assessment, 3,* 127–135.

Quinsey, V. L., Chaplin, T. C., & Upfold, D. (1984). Sexual arousal to nonsexual violence and sadomasochistic themes among rapists and non-sex offenders. *Journal of Consulting and Clinical Psychology, 52,* 651–657.

Russell, D. E. H. (1975). *The politics of rape: The victims perspective.* New York: Stein and Day.

Russell, D. E. H. (1982). The prevalence and incidence of forcible rape and attempted rape of females. *Victimology: An International Journal, 7,*(1–4), 81–93.

Russell, D. E. H. (1983). Incidence and prevalence of intrafamilial and extrafamilial sexual abuse of female children. *Child Abuse and Neglect, 7,* 133–146.

Russell, D. E. H. (1984). *Sexual exploitation.* Beverly Hills, CA: Sage.

Russell, D. E. H. (1988). Pornography and rape: A causal model. *Political Psychology, 9,* 41–73.

Seidman, B. T., Marshall, W. L., & Barbaree, H. E. (1989). *Male sexual arousal to rape depictions following exposure to forced and consenting sexual stimuli.* Manuscript submitted for publication.

Sommers, E. K., & Check, J. V. P. (1987). An empirical investigation of the role of pornography in the verbal and physical abuse of women. *Violence and Victims, 2,* 189–209.

Sundberg, S., Barbaree, H. E., & Marshall, W. L. (1989). *Disinhibition of sexual arousal to rape cues as a function of victim blame.* Manuscript submitted for publication.

Tinbergen, N. (1951). *The study of instinct.* London: Oxford University Press.

Wilson, G. T., & Lawson, D. M. (1976). Expectancies, alcohol and sexual arousal in male social drinkers. *Journal of Abnormal Psychology, 85,* 587–594.

Wydra, A., Marshall, W. L., Earls, C. M., & Barbaree, H. E. (1983). Identification of cues and control of sexual arousal by rapists. *Behavior Research and Therapy, 21,* 469–476.

Yates, E., Barbaree, H. E., & Marshall, W. L. (1984). Anger and deviant sexual arousal. *Behavior Therapy, 15,* 287–294.

Zuckerman, M. (1972). Physiological measures of sexual arousal in the human. In N. S. Greenfield & R. A. Sternbach (Eds.), *Handbook of Psychophysiology* (pp. 709–740). New York: Holt, Rinehart and Winston.

9

Social and Cultural Factors in Sexual Assault

LANA E. STERMAC, ZINDEL V. SEGAL, AND ROY GILLIS

The search for causes of sexual aggression has included the examination of many factors, including intra- and interpersonal as well as social and cultural variables. The role of social processes has received considerable attention in this area due to various hypotheses about the relationship between social interaction and sexual aggression.

This chapter will examine the role of social processes in sexual assault against women and children. This will include discussion of (1) the social acceptability and prevalence of sexual aggression in its various forms, (2) social attitudes toward women and children and their relationship to sexual aggression, and (3) social competence and its relationship to sexual aggression. Studies of both offender and nonoffender groups will be discussed. Although this chapter will include discussion of sexual aggression against both women and children, the focus will be on aggression against adults due to the limited research on social factors in sexual aggression against children.

Sexual aggression against women and children has been a historical phenomenon. It appears that sexual violence has not been unique to any one culture or historical period, although it has varied somewhat depending upon its social definition. It is only during the 1980s that extensive attention has been paid to sexual assault and an attempt has been made to identify and examine its contributing factors.

SOCIOCULTURAL FACTORS

Historical examination of societies in which rape was prevalent has revealed that a number of social factors were prominent in these cultures. Societies char-

LANA E. STERMAC • Forensic Division, Clarke Institute of Psychiatry, University of Toronto, Toronto, Ontario M5T 1R8, Canada. ZINDEL V. SEGAL • Cognitive Behavior Therapies Section, Clarke Institute of Psychiatry, University of Toronto, Toronto, Ontario M5T 1R8, Canada. ROY GILLIS • Metropolitan Toronto Forensic Service, Toronto, Ontario M6J 1H4, Canada.

acterized by patrilocality (the marital residence pattern requiring families to reside with the groom's family) as well as high levels of feuding exhibited high levels of rape (Quinsey, 1986). A number of social variables have been positively correlated with rape frequency in tribal societies (Sanday, 1981). These have included (1) raiding other groups for wives, (2) a degree of interpersonal violence, (3) an ideology of male toughness, (4) an ideology of female inferiority and lack of power, (5) generally negative attitudes toward women, and (6) war. Brownmiller (1975) has pointed out the extent of rape among warring nations.

> When men are men, slugging it out among themselves, conquering new land, subjugating new people, driving on toward victory, unquestionably there shall be some raping. Rape was a weapon of terror as the German Hun marched through Belgium during World War I. Rape was a weapon of revenge as the Russian Army marched to Berlin in World War II. Rape flourishes in warfare irrespective of nationality or geographic location. (p. 32)

As will be discussed in this chapter, a number of the social variables associated with sexual aggression in tribal societies are also found in our society today.

Sexual aggression against women appears in many forms. Although stranger assault has received attention historically, assaults and aggression within the family and against friends and acquaintances has only recently become an area of focus. Various factors have contributed to this changing focus, including pressure from a number of advocacy groups—particularly women's groups—the "desecretization" of sexual abuse, and the framing of sexual assault within a social context.

Researchers and clinicians alike have written about male sexual aggression and its relationship to social processes. Wilson, Faison, and Britton (1983) claim that rape is part of the social process which maintains the system of sexual stratification (p. 241). A number of writers (e.g., Clark & Lewis, 1977) have maintained that sexual assault is a social and not a natural phenomenon, produced only by a certain type of society and not by an external immutable human nature. Indeed, cross-cultural studies of sexual aggression have suggested that certain social variables are associated with differing levels of sexual assault. Most of these variables are related to the relative positions of men and women in the respective societies. Feminists have long maintained that sexual intimidation through assault and other forms of sexual aggression have served a role in maintaining social power relationships. Brownmiller (1975) has argued that sexual assault is simply the ultimate exercise of power by men over women. Support for this hypothesis may be found in studies of sexual aggression in "normal" males and within "normal" relationships. These studies examine tolerance and prevalence of sexual aggression, date or acquaintance rape, sexual harassment, and attitudes toward sexual aggression.

Tolerant attitudes toward sexual assault have often been cited as indicative of society's permissive view of rape. Victim blame and minimization of consequences of sexual assault have been found throughout professional and scientific literature. Psychoanalytic literature (e.g., Deutsch, 1944; Eidelberg, 1961) has long emphasized women's masochistic wishes to be raped. More recent empirical studies, such as those of Amir (1971), also focus on the role of the victim. Amir states that aspects of the victim's behavior, such as her reputation, her consumption of alcohol, and her dating behavior, should all be assessed in attributing responsibility to both the victim and the assaulter. The minimization of harmful consequences to sexual assault victims has recently been highlighted in several Canadian cases reported in the media. One case ("Offender's Background," December, 1987) of sexual assault against a woman in a parking lot, involving a significant amount of substantiated physical injury, intimidation, and violence, resulted in a 90-day intermittent (weekend) sentence. According to the judge, the facts influencing sentencing included the fact that the victim did not suffer any lasting trauma from the attack and that the assailant was of good family background.

Contrary to what has been written about aggression against women, little work has been done in the area of sociocultural factors influencing sexual aggression against children. Historical studies of sexual aggression against children are sparse and concentrate on sexual activity with boys (Jones, 1982). Quinsey (1986) points out that the lack of commentary on adult sexual activities with young girls appears to reflect its acceptance and ubiquity. Indeed, even in our culture today, the promotion of adult sexual activities can be found in a number of areas.

The theme of the seductive child has been portrayed throughout literature. Popular writings, such as *Magpie Magazine*, Casimir Dukahz's *The Asbestos Diary*, and Vladimir Nabokov's *Lolita*, are replete with examples of permissive attitudes toward sexual contact with children. Included within these writings are testimonials of children initiating and enjoying sexual activities with adults, accounts of children viewing these sexual experiences as beneficial and as occurring within a loving context, as well as children being able to consent to these activities. Pedophile support groups and societies advocating relationships between adults and children have also gained some momentum since the 1950s (Plummer, 1980). The aim of these organizations is to provide support for their members as well as to advocate the acceptability of physical relations between adults and children.

Evidence of permissive social attitudes toward adult sexual contact with children can also be found throughout the professional and scientific literature. As in the literature on sexual aggression against women, evidence of victim blame, negative stereotyping, and denial of harmful consequences of sexual involvement to children can also be found. Virkkunen (1981) describes the classical child molester as timid and childish. Victims of this type of offender are described as "provocative" of "participating." Virkkunen reviews the earlier works of Revitch and Weiss (1962), who claim that the child victim is often aggressive and seductive and induces the adult to commit the offense. Mohr, Turner, and Jerry (1964) also describe children as willing participants, if not instigators, of sexual acts with adults. More recently, Righton (1981) concluded that available information about sexual activity between adults and children reveals that cuddling, caressing, and genital fondling are the most characteristic activities, which usually occur with the child's willing compliance and in many cases on the child's initiative. Righton further asserts that there is insufficient evidence to conclude that this sexual activity is harmful, as pedophiles are generally concerned with maintaining the sexual aspects of their relationships within the bounds of what a child can encompass without strain. Plummer (1981) agrees with this view and further states that a number of erroneous myths and stereotypes about pedophilia exist. He attempts to dispute what he considers misguided perceptions, namely, that pedophiles are strangers who force sex on children; that the sex act is damaging and dangerous; and that the child is innocent, uninvolved, and nonparticipating.

STUDIES OF NONOFFENDERS

The Prevalence of Sexual Aggression and Harassment

A number of studies have now indicated that aggression and force are common in sexual interactions among a number of "normal" populations (Stille, Malamuth, & Schallow, 1987). These studies indicate that the incidence of sexual aggression among males not identified as sexual offenders may be significantly higher than the incidence reflected in reported rape cases. Early works (Kanin, 1957; Kirkpatrick & Kanin, 1957) suggested that about 60% of university women surveyed reported encountering some type of sexual aggression in the previous year. Approximately 25% of university males admitted to using force in attempted intercourse, even when they knew it was "disagreeable and offensive to the female" (Kanin, 1969). Later studies (Wilson & Faison, 1979) reported that 10 to 20% of college women had encountered males who used violence or threats of violence in attempts to force sexual intercourse. Kanin (1985) revealed that 13% of males from a variety of university classes reported using force or threats in order to obtain coitus from a female.

In a survey of 3862 men and women on college campuses, Koss and Oros (1980) found that 8% of the women stated that they had been physically coerced to have intercourse, while 3% of the men admitted to having used physical force. Alder's (1985) survey of young men in the state of Oregon who participated in the Marion County Youth Study revealed that 13.5% of respondents stated that they had engaged in sexually aggressive behavior at some time. The alarming results of a survey of 930 adult women carried out by Russell (1984) revealed that 41% stated that they had experienced sexual aggression to the extent of rape or attempted rape at least once in their lives.

All of these results suggest that the incidence of sexual aggression and force is quite high in certain populations, particularly university males.

The extent to which "normal" men may possess a proclivity toward sexual aggression or rape has also been examined. In a series of studies, Malamuth and his colleagues (Malamuth, 1981a, 1981b; Malamuth & Check, 1980a; Malamuth, Haber, & Feshbach, 1980) asked college males to indicate how likely they might be to commit a rape if they were assured of not being caught. A fairly consistent finding of approximately 30–35% of the males across the studies indicated that there was some likelihood they would rape under these conditions.

In addition to the frequency of overt sexual aggression, a number of studies have revealed high frequencies of sexual harassment in various populations. Sexual harassment covers a wide range of behaviors, but it is generally considered to include coercive or physically intrusive behaviors related to sexual contacts, offensive verbalizations, and more flirtatious behavior such as compliments and requests for dates (Brewer, 1982). High rates of sexual harassment of women by men in the work force have been documented (Pryor, 1987). It is reported that the effects of sexual harassment on women are extreme; they include reduced productivity, the need for therapeutic intervention, as well as employment termination.

Rates for sexual harassment have ranged from 5% to 40% of women reporting unwanted and intentional physical contact and 15% for sexual assaults (Brewer, 1982). A study of 90 women enlisted in the U.S. Navy (Reilly, 1980) revealed that 90% of the sample had experienced some form of sexual harassment within their jobs. A survey of 20,000 federal government employees in the United States (U.S. Merit Systems Protection Board, 1981) found that 42% of the women and 15% of the men surveyed reported that they had been sexually harassed. In academic settings, reported sexual harassment rates have varied. McCormack (1985) surveyed 523 women in science programs at 16 universities. Her results revealed that 17% of the surveyed women reported sexual harassment by an instructor.

Tangri, Burt, and Johnson (1982) have proposed a number of models to account for sexual harassment within work settings. They described three explanatory models: (1) the natural–biological model, which asserts that sexual harassment is simply natural sexual attraction between people; (2) the organizational model, which asserts that harassment results from certain opportunity structures; and (3) the sociocultural model, which asserts that sexual harassment reflects society's differential distribution of power and status between the sexes. Although results of their survey failed to clearly support any one model, the researchers did find that women are four times more likely to be victims of sexual harassment then are men and that women view sexual harassment much more negatively than do men.

The prevalence of unreported child molesting has also been of considerable concern. As previously mentioned, adult sexual contact with children appears to occur frequently in our society. A number of recent surveys have documented the extent of childhood sexual experience with adults. Finkelhor (1979) interviewed 530 female and 266 male college students about sexual contacts with adults. He found that 11% of the women and 4% of the men had had sexual contacts with adults prior to the age of 12. For females, 37% of the contacts occurred before the age of 9, and for males, 27% occurred before the age of 10.

A Canadian study based upon a national probability sample of 2,008 persons (Committee on Sexual Offenses, 1984a,b) revealed that 54% of females and 31% of males experienced unwanted sexual advances at some point in their lives. The majority of these occurred when the victims were less than 18 years of age. Female respondents who reported victimization before the age of 13 stated that (1) sexual touching and (2) sexual assault or attempted assault accounted for

30% and 22% of the incidents, respectively. For males, touching and assault or attempted assault accounted for 42% and 15% of these incidents, respectively. This survey also revealed the low rate of reporting sexual offenses. Only 24% of females and 11% of males reported unwanted sexual contacts to any other person. This study, along with others, has documented the extent of sexual assaults against children in our society.

Social Attitudes and Beliefs

Questions as to what could account for these high rates of sexual aggression among "normal" populations have led researchers to examine various attitudinal factors. Social factors such as beliefs about what constitutes sexual violence have greatly influenced the general acceptability of this behavior. Rape tolerance, or the extent to which people minimize the seriousness of sexual assault, has been seen through the denial of trauma to the victim, blaming the victim for provoking or precipitating the incident and questioning her credibility, as well as denying the extent of sexual assault (Hall, Howard, & Boezio, 1986).

Tolerance toward sexual aggression has been associated with a number of factors, including perceptions of women's social roles, general attitudes toward women, acceptance of rape myths, and attitudes toward rape.

Tolerance for rape was examined in a study by Hall, Howard, and Boezio (1986). The Rape Attitude Scale developed by the researchers was administered to several groups of men, including university undergraduates, sexual offenders, non-sexual offenders, and community control subjects. Scale items were developed to include rape myths, rationalizations for aggressive behaviors, and situations stereotypically perceived as justifying forced sex. The results of the survey of rape attitudes revealed that incarcerated rapists and non-sexual offenders showed a higher level of rape tolerance than did the community control group. The highest level of rape tolerance, however, was held by the male university undergraduates. Rape tolerance was further found to be associated with a sexist attitude toward heterosexual relationships. Those who tolerated rape tended to perceive women as sex objects and to condone male dominance of women.

Other studies have also supported a relationship between attitudes toward rape and perceptions of sex roles. Most of this work has focused on the endorsement of rape myths and beliefs. One of the earliest and best known studies in this area is Burt's (1980) random survey of 598 Minnesota adult men and women. The Rape Myth Acceptance Scale was constructed, and it consisted of six subscales: (1) own sex-role satisfaction, (2) sex-role stereotyping, (3) adversarial sexual beliefs, (4) sexual conservatism, (5) acceptance of interpersonal violence, and (6) rape myth acceptance. It was found that the acceptance of rape myths was correlated with sex-role stereotyping, acceptance of interpersonal violence, sexual conservatism, adversarial sexual beliefs, and age. It was also found that over half the sample believed that most rapes resulted from revenge seeking against a man or hiding a pregnancy, and it was believed that in the majority of rape cases the victim was promiscuous or had a bad reputation.

A recent study of rape perceptions (Gilmartin-Zena, 1987) supported the finding of gender differences in the perception of rape among university undergraduates. In the administration of a rape myth questionnaire, Gilmartin-Zena found that males continued to endorse rape myths concerning the women's backgrounds, suggestive dress, and saying "no" when they mean to say "yes," as causes of rape. A number of studies (e.g., Bunting & Reeves, 1983; Costin & Schwartz, 1987) have supported a relationship between belief in rape myths and male sex-role orientation.

Stille, Malamuth, and Schallow (1987) examined the relationship between rape myth attitudes and hostility toward women among college undergraduates. They found that the likelihood of using force in a sexual encounter is motivated by a feeling of hostility toward women and by a belief that women deserve or desire rape. This finding supports a series of studies (Malamuth, 1981a; Malamuth & Check, 1980) indicating a link between attitudes toward women and sexual aggression directed at women.

Rapaport and Burkhart (1984) found that the best predictor of sexually coercive behavior was related to adversarial sexual beliefs. These authors concluded that college males who are sexually coercive may be acting on a set of values which include an underlying hostility toward women. Specific attitudes and hostility toward women have been examined in only a few studies. Graff and Chartier (1986) examined gender role socialization and hostility toward women among 100 college men. They reported significant positive relationships among the attitudinal measures reflecting negative beliefs about women. Specifically, rigid male socialization was associated with negative beliefs about women.

One study which did not exclusively focus on college undergraduates was carried out by Costin (1985). He also examined the hypothesis that sexual assault against women is supported in our society by beliefs that encourage male domination and exploitation. Four groups of subjects participated; male and female undergraduates and employed men and women recruited through service and social clubs. A rape scale and an adapted Attitudes Towards Women Scale (Spence & Helmreich, 1973) were administered. Again, the results support the hypothesis that negative stereotypes or myths about rape are positively related to beliefs that women's social roles and rights should be more restricted than those of men. These results were supported by Mosher and Anderson's (1986) study linking sexual aggression with a macho personality constellation.

In summary, there appears to be a considerable body of literature linking sexual aggression against women to a number of social factors. The perception of women's roles in society and sex-role ideology may be important determinants of the amount of sexual aggression demonstrated against women.

The relationship between social attitudes and sexual aggression toward children has not been examined extensively. Anecdotal information from men who have sexual contact with children, however, has long revealed consistently permissive beliefs about their sexual behavior (Stermac, 1988a). As previously discussed, these permissive attitudes and promotion of adult sexual activities with children can be found in several areas. In addition to the sexualization of children in popular literature, media portrayals of children often depict sexual provocation and enticing positions (Stermac, 1988b). Victim blame and negative attitudes toward children can also be seen among criminal justice officials who question the veracity of children's accusations as well as children's complicity in sexual assault.

An example of negative stereotypes about adult sexual contact with children in the criminal justice system is illustrated by a court hearing in Wisconsin (Finklehor, 1984). In January 1982, a judge in Lancaster sentenced a man to a 90-day work release program on a charge of sexually assaulting his 5-year-old stepdaughter. The judge stated, "I am satisfied we have an unusually sexually promiscuous young lady. And he (the defendant) did not know enough to refuse. No way do I believe he initiated the contact" (p. 108).

A recent study by Stermac and Segal (in press) examined the cognitions and attitudes of several groups of subjects toward adult sexual contact with children. Although the focus of the study was on differences between offenders and community groups, they did find that nonoffenders' ratings of children's complicity, adult responsibility, and any perceived benefits to the child from sexual contact with an adult were affected by both the degree or amount of sexual contact as well as the child's response to the contact. In other words, all nonoffender groups saw children as having some responsibility and deriving some benefit from sexual contact with an adult when the child did not actively resist and when the contact did not involve disrobing.

These findings suggest that attitudes toward sexual activities between adults and children are certainly mixed and possibly more permissive than an initial impression would suggest. Evidence of these attitudes in popular literature and other forms of media raises questions of their prevalence among the general population and their effect upon the treatment of both perpetrators and survivors of sexual assault.

STUDIES OF OFFENDERS

Early psychoanalytic formulations developed to explain sexual assault postulated that rapists were extremely disturbed individuals. Rapists were seen as sexual perverts, degenerates who were inadequate in their sexual roles and who could be clearly differentiated from "normal" men. In contrast, more recent formulations of the etiology of sexual assault by authors such as Brownmiller (1975) and Medea and Thompson (1974) argued that the rapist was not a sexual deviant. Instead, rapists were seen as the product of traditional male sex-role stereotypes that taught hostile attitudes toward women, considered them as possessions to be used as one desired, and simultaneously viewed women as being devoid of sexuality and yet being temptresses who could lead men into sin. In this particular variant of the feminist view, rather than lacking in masculinity, rapists are seen as having an excess of maleness. The expression of their sexuality within an aggressive context is seen as an inevitable consequence of the systematic power differentials derived from sex-role stereotypes (Medea & Thompson, 1974).

Attitudes of Offenders

The research investigating sex-role stereotyping and attitudes toward women among convicted or admitted sexual offenders against women will be examined. Suggestions will be made for future research on rapists' attitudes toward women and possible treatment implications.

The construction of classification systems for rapists, often based upon attitudes toward women, appears frequently in the literature. One of the earliest schemes proposed was that of McCaldon (1967), who divided rapists into an "impulsively sociopathic" group and a group with "specific hostilities toward women." A more elaborate and popular classification was developed by Groth and Birnbaum (1979). They distinguished three types of rapists. These were (1) the anger rapist for whom sexuality becomes a hostile act, (2) the power rapist for whom sexuality becomes an expression of conquest, and (3) the sadistic rapist for whom power and anger become eroticized. Numerous investigators have also found evidence of hostility toward women and sexist attitudes in their clinical work with sexual offenders. Abel, Blanchard, and Becker (1978), reporting on their experience and research with a large-scale sexual offender treatment program, stated that "gender role conflicts or preferences for opposite sex gender behavior were rarely seen" (p. 168). Contrastingly, they have observed "hyperidentification with the masculine role." These "hypermasculine" individuals tended to prefer traditional masculine activities.

Based upon his experience in treating rapists, Rada (1978) has observed that the forced sexual act, emphasizing the rapist's control of the situation, was more important than the violence or pain inflicted. Thus, he concluded:

> Therefore, it is not simply hostility toward women that motivates the rapist. Rape is not just an attempt to mete out revenge for previous real or imagined wrongdoing at the hand of significant female figures. Rather, the rapist lacks or feels he lacks, the ability to establish a satisfying love relationship with a woman. (p. 25)

The majority of research which has assessed the attitudes toward women and the acceptance of rape myths of incarcerated rapists has found that rapists do not differ from other sex offenders or from similar socioeconomic status groups in these attitudes (Segal & Stermac, 1984). Incongruously, some researchers have reported that rapists evidence *more* positive attitudes toward women and *less* endorsement of rape myths than do control groups (Marshall, Bates, & Ruhl, 1984; Sattem, Savells, & Murray, 1984). Langevin *et al.* (1985) did find, however, that sadistic rapists exhibited more hostility toward women on two self-report inventories than did nonsadistic sexual assaulters.

A different approach to examining the endorsement of rape myths among convicted rapists was used by Scully and Marolla (1983). They asked two groups of rapists—admitters and nonadmitters of the offense—to describe the sexual assault for which they were convicted. They found that the group of nonadmitters described the offense with stereotypes which blamed the victim and exonerated themselves. They interpreted these findings as indicating an awareness among rapists of culturally and socially acceptable beliefs about sexual behavior which were based upon erroneous conceptions.

It is clear that the self-reports of rapists may be influenced by socially desirable responding. The majority of the instruments in use are quite transparent, and it requires little effort to pick out the socially acceptable responses. This is particularly true for the Attitudes Towards Women Scale (Spence & Helmreich, 1973) used by Segal and Stermac (1984). Part of the solution to this problem would be to use measures of socially desirable responding, such as the Marlowe–Crowne Social Desirability Scale (Crowne & Marlowe, 1960), or inventories which are more subtle in their content and less susceptible to socially desirable responding. Check's Hostility Towards Women Scale (Check, 1984) is a step in this direction, but results of its use with a sex offender population have not yet been published. Another solution would be to use direct observation in addition to self-report inventories. This approach is commonly used in research on social skills, but it has not been used to assess attitudes toward women.

Despite any assurances of confidentiality, it is unlikely that incarcerated rapists are going to report hostile or negative feelings they may have about women or sexuality. Many clinicians have had the experience of a client eventually divulging some damaging personal revelation which they initially denied. Thus, a degree of trust should be developed between subject and experimenter that would allow for more honest disclosure. Compounding the problem of confidentiality is the fact that a number of the studies have collected data on attitudes as part of a treatment evaluation program. Clearly, the research should be conducted truly anonymously so that subjects will feel freer to respond without fear of recrimination.

Another important consideration is specificity in the attitude being measured. Azjen and Fishbein (1980) have noted that one of the reasons why there is such a poor correlation between attitude and behavior relationships is that the attitude being measured is often global (e.g., attitudes toward women), whereas the behavior to be predicted is usually quite specific (i.e., a proclivity for sexual assault). These authors argue that the more closely the attitude measured relates to the behavior to be predicted, the higher the correlation will be.

In summary, then, clinical case studies and feminist formulations of rape point to negative attitudes toward women as being an etiological factor, but this contention has not been fully supported to date by research with rapists.

The attitudes of offenders against children have not been the focus of systematic investigation. It is unknown whether child molesters endorse rape myths or hold negative attitudes toward women and children. One study by Sattem, Savells, and Murray (1984) did examine sex-role stereotyping and attitudes toward women among sexual offenders against both women and children. They used the Attitudes Towards Women Scale (Spence & Helmreich, 1973), the Bem Sex-Role Inventory (Bem, 1974), and the Macho Scale (Villemez & Touhey, 1977). No significant differences were found between child- and adult-oriented offenders or between offenders and nonoffenders on any measures. Unfortunately, the authors did not provide any information about the subject groups or their offenses.

Using the Cognition Scale (Abel *et al.*, 1984), Stermac and Segal (in press) assessed child molesters' attitudes toward adult sexual contact with children and found that child molesters endorsed more permissive attitudes towards sexual contact with children and more strongly supported beliefs that children were the property of adults than did other groups of both offenders and nonoffenders. Abel, Rouleau, and Cunningham-Rathner (1985) report anecdotal data supportive of child molesters' distorted cognitions and attitudes, such as that children consent to sexual activity with adults, that they want sex with an adult, and that these activities are not harmful to them.

Social Skills of Offenders

Another area which has received considerable attention within the sexual assault literature has been the assessment of social interaction abilities or the social competence of sexually assaultive men. Descriptive studies and anecdotal information (e.g., Clark & Lewis, 1977; Laws & Serber, 1975; Marshall, Christie, & Lanthier, 1979) have suggested that the sexual assaulter lacks the social skills necessary to enable him to form "normal" sexual and social relationships with women. This claim, however, does not necessarily oblige the theorist to say that rape is therefore no more than the pursuit of sexual gratification which cannot be secured by prosocial means. It does, on the other hand, usually persuade the theorist to reconceptualize the rapist's fear, anger, and hostility toward women as arising, at least partly, from resentment over social ineptitude.

A number of studies have directly examined the social competence of convicted sexual assaulters. In order to avoid duplication in discussing studies which are presented in the chapter on cognitive factors (Segal & Stermac, Chapter 10, this volume), only behavioral aspects of social skills will be discussed here.

Early studies of offenders' social skills were plagued with methodological difficulties. Barlow, Abel, Blanchard, Bristow, and Young (1977) developed a heterosocial behavior checklist for sexual offenders. Unfortunately, the grouping of all sexual offenders together and the absence of proper control groups did not identify unique social-skill deficits.

Segal and Marshall (1985) compared rapists, child molesters, non-sexual-offenders, and two socioeconomic groups of community control subjects on social skill measures of videotaped conversations with females. They found that while all incarcerated groups were less socially skilled than the community groups, no unique skill deficits were found among the rapist sample. In comparison to child molesters, however, rapists were found to be generally more adequate and more socially skilled. This was one of the first empirical studies demonstrating a skill deficit in child molesters.

These results were supported in part by Overholser and Beck's (1986) multi-method assessment study with matched subjects. In a questionnaire assessment of assertiveness (Rathus, 1973), a trend ($p < .08$) toward lower assertiveness was found for child molesters in comparison to rapists, non-sex offenders, and community controls. In a behavioral assessment of controlled social interaction, both child molesters and rapists were found to be significantly less skilled than community-based subjects low in socioeconomic status on measures of form of conversation as well as overall levels of social skill.

Stermac and Quinsey (1985) carried out a study comparing incarcerated rapists with non-sexual offenders and community control subjects on audiotaped social interactions and conversations. Again, incarcerated groups were found to be less socially skilled than the community group, but no unique deficits were identified for the rapists. This study did, however, find that rapists were less assertive than were all other subjects in heterosexual situations, as measured by the Callner–Ross Assertiveness Schedule (Callner & Ross, 1976). Other studies, however, have failed to replicate this finding with rapists.

Although a number of controlled studies have examined the social skills and interaction abilities of sexual offenders, a clear pattern of deficits has not emerged for either rapists or child molesters. The interpersonal functioning of sexual assaulters may be affected by a complex interaction of a number of variables, including the accuracy with which these men process social cues and information. Indeed, as Morrison and Bellack (1981) point out, the emphasis on behavioral components of social skill has not been adequate to explain the complexity of interpersonal functioning. Social performance requires not only appropriate response skills but also an "ability to accurately read the social environment" (Morrison & Bellack, 1981, p. 70). It has been hypothesized that sexual assaulters have difficulty in processing social information from women and often misconstrue social messages. In a study investigating this hypothesis, Lipton, McDonel, and McFall (1987) compared rapists, violent nonrapists, and nonviolent nonrapists on measures of heterosocial cue-reading accuracy in first-date and in intimate situations. They found that rapists did have social information-processing deficits that predisposed them to misconstrue women's cues, particularly cues involving negative or bad moods on first-date situations.

Social perception among child molesters has also been an area of investigation recently. Segal and Marshall (1986), with the help of female confederates, assessed sex offenders' social perception in heterosexual situations. They found that child molesters, in comparison to other sexual offenders and community controls, were significantly poorer at predicting and evaluating their own performance.

Two recent studies have examined social perception among child molesters from a differing perspective. Barbaree, Marshall, and Connor (1988) examined the social problem-solving skills of child molesters in social situations involving both adults and children. They found that child molesters were equally as good as nonoffenders in *recognizing* the existence of a problem and at generating alternative solutions, but they *chose* socially unacceptable solutions and failed to recognize likely negative outcomes. They concluded that child molesters may demonstrate deficits in the cognitive processing that precedes social behavior. Stermac and Segal (in press) also found differences in cognitive processing between child molesters and others in child molesters' judgments of children's behaviors. Child molesters saw children's behavior as more seductive and judged children as more responsible for sexual contacts than did other groups (for further discussion of cognitive processing among child molesters, see Segal & Stermac, Chapter 10, this volume).

It is clear from this discussion that further work in the area of social skills and social perception needs to be carried out. Although clear patterns of behavioral deficits have not emerged for either rapists or child molesters, some deficits in decoding and cognitive processing of social information have been noted. This is of particular significance, as it indicates a target area for clinical intervention. Further investigation of social perception and processing focusing on the inhibitory effects of information-processing deficits would be fruitful. The role of anger and hostility, particularly among assaulters against women, needs to be examined. It may be that decoding errors in social perception are related to sexual offenders' fear, anger, and hostility toward women and lead to resentment over social incompetence.

CONCLUSIONS

Social factors contributing to the sexual assault of women and children have been identified and discussed in this chapter. The role of social factors in sexual violence has only recently become a focus in understanding gender relations and violence. Traditionally, studies of sexual assault have tended to emphasize individual psychopathology and victim precipitation as causative factors. It was not long ago that rape was viewed as the provocative act of a female. As Amir (1971) stated,

> the victim is the one who is acting out, initiating the interaction between her and the offender, and by her behavior she generates the potentiality for criminal behavior of the offender. (p. 259)

Prior conceptualizations of sexual assault which have focused on the identification of unique characteristics of sexual offenders, including social-skill deficits, have not been generally fruitful.

The studies reviewed in this chapter have highlighted and emphasized the need to conceptualize sexual aggression within a social context. Support for this notion arises from evidence suggesting that sexual aggression in its various forms of stranger and acquaintance assault, abuse within the family, and sexual harassment is far more prevalent than studies of incarcerated offenders have previously suggested. Negative social attitudes toward women, beliefs in rape myths, and sex-role ideology favoring restricted roles for women have all been linked to sexual aggression in males. Conceptualizations of sexual assault which have focused on power relations and the relative positions of men and women in society have provided compelling hypotheses about etiological factors in sexual aggression. This does not, of course, imply that social and cultural factors are the sole contributing factors in sexual violence. Social factors and processes, however, must be seriously examined in any analysis of sexual aggression. As is evidenced from the research literature, attempts to treat individual sexual offenders has historically met with limited success (Quinsey, 1984). Treatment interventions must consider the context of sexual violence as a socially constructed and socially legitimized phenomenon.

REFERENCES

Abel, G. G., Blanchard, E. B., & Becker, J. V. (1978). An integrated treatment program for rapists. In R. T. Rada (Ed.), *Clinical aspects of the rapist* (pp. 161–214). New York: Grune & Stratton.

Abel, G. G., Becker, J. V., Cunningham-Rathner, J., Rouleau, J. L., Kaplan, M., & Reich, J. (1984). *The treatment of child molesters.* Unpublished treatment manual, Emory University, Atlanta.

Abel, G. G., Rouleau, J. L., & Cunningham-Rathner, J. (1985). Sexually aggressive behavior. In W. J. Curran, A. L. McGarry, & S. A. Shah (Eds.), *Forensic psychiatry and psychology* (pp. 289–313). Philadelphia: F. A. Davis.

Alder, C. (1985). An exploration of self-reported sexually aggressive behavior. *Crime and Delinquency, 31,* 306–331.

Amir, M. (1971). *Patterns of forcible rape.* Chicago: University of Chicago Press.

Azjen, I., & Fishbein, M. (1980). *Understanding attitudes and predicting social behavior.* Englewood Cliffs, NJ: Prentice-Hall.

Barbaree, H. E., Marshall, W. L., & Connor, J. (1988). *The social problem-solving of child molesters.* Unpublished manuscript, Queen's University, Kingston, Ontario, Canada.

Barlow, D. H., Abel, G. G., Blanchard, E. B., Bristow, A. R., & Young, D. L. (1977). A heterosocial skills behavior checklist for males. *Behavior Therapy, 8,* 229–239.

Bem, S. L. (1974). The measurement of psychological androgyny. *Journal of Consulting and Clinical Psychology, 42,* 155–162.

Brewer, B. B. (1982). Further beyond nine to five: An integration and future directions. *Journal of Social Issues, 38,* 149–158.

Brownmiller, S. (1975). *Against our will: Men, women, and rape.* New York: Simon & Schuster.

Bunting, A. B., & Reeves, J. B. (1983). Perceived male sex orientation and beliefs about rape. *Deviant Behavior, 4,* 281–295.

Burt, M. (1980). Cultural myths and supports for rape. *Journal of Personality and Social Psychology, 38,* 217–230.

Callner, D. A., & Ross, S. M. (1976). The reliability and validity of three measures of assertion in a drug addict population. *Behavior Therapy, 7,* 659–667.

Check, J. V. (1984). *The hostility towards women scale.* Unpublished doctoral dissertation, University of Manitoba, Winnipeg.

Clark, L., & Lewis, D. J. (1977). *Rape: The price of coercive sexuality.* Toronto: Canadian Women's Educational Press.

Committee on Sexual Offenses Against Children and Youths (1984a). *Sexual offenses against children* (vol. 1). Ottawa: Supply and Services Canada.

Committee on Sexual Offenses Against Children and Youths (1984b). *Sexual offenses against children* (vol. 2). Ottawa: Supply and Services Canada.

Costin, F. (1985). Beliefs about rape and women's social roles—a four nation study. *Archives of Sexual Behavior, 14,* 319–325.

Costin, F., & Schwarz, N. (1987). Beliefs about rape and women's social roles. *Journal of Interpersonal Violence, 2,* 46–56.

Crowne, D., & Marlowe, D. (1960). A new scale of social desirability independent of psychopathology. *Journal of Consulting Psychology, 24,* 349–354.

Deutsch, H. (1944). *Psychology of women.* New York: Grune & Stratton.

Dukahz, C. (1970). *The asbestos diary.* New York: Holt, Rinehart and Winston.

Edelberg, L. (1961). *The dark urge.* New York: Pyramid Books.

Finkelhor, D. (1979). Psychological, cultural and family factors in incest and family sexual abuse. *Journal of Marriage and Family Counseling, 4,* 41–49.

Finkelhor, D. (1984). *Child sexual abuse.* New York: The Free Press.

Gilmartin-Zena, P. (1987, November). *Perceptions about rape: Sex differences within a student population.* Paper presented at the meeting of the American Society of Criminology, Montreal, Canada.

Graff, L. A., & Chartier, B. (1986, June). *Gender socialization and hostility toward women: Their role in men's responses to sexual stimuli.* Paper presented at the Annual Meeting of the Canadian Psychological Association, Toronto, Canada.

Groth, A. N., & Birnbaum, H. J. (1979). *Men who rape—The psychology of the offender.* New York: Plenum.

Hall, E. R., Howard, J. A., & Boezio, S. L. (1986). Tolerance of rape: A sexist or antisocial attitude? *Psychology of Women Quarterly, 10,* 101–108.

Jones, G. P. (1982). The social study of pederasty: In search of a literature base: An annotated bibliography of sources in English. *Journal of Homosexuality, 8,* 61–95.

Kanin, E. J. (1957). Male aggression in dating–courtship relations. *American Journal of Sociology, 63,* 197–204.

Kanin, E. J. (1969). Selected dyadic aspects of male sex aggression. *Journal of Sex Research, 5,* 12–28.

Kanin, E. J. (1985). Date rapists: Differential sexual socialization and relative deprivation. *Archives of Sexual Behavior, 14,* 219–231.

Kirkpatrick, C., & Kanin, E. (1957). Male sex aggression on a university campus. *American Sociological Review, 22,* 52–58.

Koss, M. P., & Oros, C. J. (1980, May). *Hidden rape: A survey of the incidence of sexual aggression and victimization on a university campus.* Paper presented at the annual meeting of the Midwestern Psychological Association, St. Louis, MO.

Langevin, R., Ben-Aron, M., Coulthard, R., Heasman, G., Purins, J., Handy, L., Hucker, S. J., Russon, A. E., Day, D., Roper, V., Bain, J., Wortzman, G., & Webster, C. A. (1985). Sexual aggression: Constructing a predictive equation. In R. Langevin (Ed.), *Erotic preference, gender identity, and aggression in men* (pp. 39–76). Hillsdale, NJ: Lawrence Erlbaum.

Lipton, D. N., McDonel, E. C., & McFall, R. M. (1987). Heterosocial perception in rapists. *Journal of Consulting and Clinical Psychology, 55* (1), 17–21.

Laws, R. D., & Serber, M. (1975). Measurement and evaluation of assertive training with sexual offenders. In R. E. Hosford & C. S. Moss (Eds.), *The crumbling walls: Treatment and counselling of prisoners* (pp. 165–172). Champaign, IL: University of Illinois Press.

Malamuth, N. M. (1981a). Rape proclivity among males. *Journal of Social Issues, 37,* 138–157.

Malamuth, N. M. (1981b). Rape fantasies as a function of exposure to violent sexual stimuli. *Archives of Sexual Behavior, 10,* 33–47.

Malamuth, N. M., & Check, J. V. P. (1980). Penile tumescence and perceptual responses to rape as a function of victim's perceived reactions. *Journal of Applied Social Psychology, 10,* 528–547.

Malamuth, N. M., Haber, S., & Feshbach, S. (1980). Testing hypotheses regarding rape: Exposure to sexual violence, sex differences and the "normality" of rapists. *Journal of Research in Personality, 14,* 121–137.

Marshall, W. L., Christie, M. M., & Lanthier, R. D. (1979). *Social competence, sexual experience, and attitudes to sex in incarcerated rapists and pedophiles.* Report to Solicitor General of Canada, Ottawa.

Marshall, W. L., Bates, L., & Ruhl, M. (1984). *Hostility in sex offenders.* Unpublished manuscript, Queen's University, Kingston, Ontario.

McCaldon, R. J. (1967). Rape. *Canadian Journal of Corrections, 9,* 37–59.

McCormack, A. (1985). The sexual harassment of students by teachers: The case of students in science. *Sex Roles, 13,* 21–32.

Medea, A., & Thompson, K. (1974). *Against rape: A survival manual for women.* New York: Farrar, Straus & Giroux.

Mohr, J. W., Turner, R. E., & Jerry, M. B. (1964). *Pedophilia and exhibitionism: A handbook.* Toronto: University of Toronto Press.

Morrison, R. L., & Bellack, A. S. (1981). The role of social perception in social skills. *Behavior Therapy, 12,* 69–79.

Mosher, D. L. & Anderson, R. D. (1986). Macho personality, sexual aggression, and reactions to guided imagery of realistic rape. *Journal of Research in Personality, 20,* 77–94.

Nabokov, V. (1966). *Lolita.* New York: Berkley Medallion.

Offender's background results in weekend sentence. (1987, December). *Globe and Mail,* p. 18.

Overholser, C., & Beck, S. (1986). Multimethod assessment of rapists, child molesters, and three control groups on behavioral and psychological measures. *Journal of Consulting and Clinical Psychology, 54,* 682–687.

Plummer, K. J. (1980). Self help groups for sexual minorities: The case of the pedophile. In D. J. West (Ed.), *Sexual offenders in the criminal justice system* (pp. 72–90). Cambridge: University of Cambridge Press.

Plummer, K. (1981). Pedophilia: Constructing a sociological baseline. In M. Cook & K. Howells (Eds.), *Adult sexual interest in children* (pp. 221–250). London: Academic Press.

Pryor, J. B. (1987). Sexual harassment proclivities in men. *Sex Roles, 17,* 269–290.

Quinsey, V. L. (1984). Sexual aggression: Studies of offenders against women. In D. N. Weistub (Ed.), *Law and mental health: International perspectives* (vol. 1; pp. 180–209). New York: Pergamon Press.

Quinsey, V. L. (1986). Men who have sex with children. In D. N. Weistub (Ed.), *Law and mental health: International perspectives* (vol. 2; pp. 140–172). New York: Pergamon Press.

Rada, R. T. (1978). Classification of the rapist. In R. T. Rada (Ed.), *Clinical aspects of the rapist* (pp. 117–132). New York: Grune & Stratton.

Rapaport, K., & Burkhart, B. R. (1984). Personality and attitudinal characteristics of sexually coercive college males. *Journal of Abnormal Psychology, 93*(2), 216–221.

Rathus, S. (1973). A 30-item schedule for assessing assertive behavior. *Behavior Therapy, 9,* 398–406.

Reilly, P. J. (1980). *Sexual harassment in the Navy.* Unpublished master's thesis, Naval Postgraduate School, Monterey, CA.

Revitch, E., & Weiss, R. G. (1962). The pedophilic offender. *Diseases of the Nervous System, 23,* 73–78.

Righton, P. (1981). The adult. In B. Taylor (Ed.), *Perspectives on pedophilia* (pp. 24–40). London: Batsford Academic and Educational Ltd.

Russell, D. (1984). *Sexual exploitation.* Beverly Hills, CA: Sage.

Sanday, P. R. (1981). The socio-cultural context of rape: A cross-cultural study. *Journal of Social Issues, 37,* 5–27.

Sattem, L., Savells, J., & Murray, E. (1984). Sex-role stereotypes and commitment of rape. *Sex Roles, 11,* 849–860.

Scully, D., & Marolla, J. (1983). *Incarcerated rapists: Exploring a sociological model.* National Rape Center, National Institute of Mental Health.

Segal, Z. V., & Marshall, W. L. (1985). Heterosexual social skills in a population of rapists and child molesters. *Journal of Consulting and Clinical Psychology, 53,* 55–63.

Segal, Z. V., & Marshall, W. L. (1986). Discrepancies between self-efficacy predictions and actual performance in a population of rapists and child molesters. *Cognitive Therapy and Research, 10*(3), 363–376.

Segal, Z., & Stermac, L. E. (1984). A measure of rapists' attitudes towards women. *International Journal of Law and Psychiatry, 7,* 437–440.

Spence, J. T., Helmreich, R., & Stapp, J. (1973). A short version of the attitudes towards women scale (ATW). *Bulletin of the Psychonomic Society, 2,* 219–220.

Stermac, L. E. (1988a, February). *Child sexual abuse: Myths and realities.* Paper presented at the annual meeting of the Ontario Psychological Association, Toronto, Canada.

Stermac, L. E. (1988b, February). *Sexual stereotyping: New challenges to old myths.* Paper presented at the annual meeting of the Ontario Psychological Association, Toronto, Canada.

Stermac, L. E., & Quinsey, V. L. (1985). Social competence among rapists. *Behavioral Assessment, 8,* 171–185.

Stermac, L. E., & Segal, Z. (in press). *Adult sexual contact with children: An examination of cognitive factors.* Manuscript submitted for publication.

Stille, R. G., Malamuth, N., & Schallow, J. R. (1987, August). *Prediction of rape proclivity by rape myth attitudes and hostility towards women.* Paper presented to the annual meeting of the American Psychological Association, New York.

Tangri, S. S., Burt, R. M., & Johnson, L. B. (1982). Sexual harassment at work: Three explanatory models. *Journal of Social Issues, 38,* 33–54.

U.S. Merit Systems Protection Board (1981). *Sexual harassment in the federal workplace: Is it a problem?* Washington, DC: U.S. Government Printing Office.

Villemez, W. J., & Touhey, J. C. (1977). A measure of individual differences in sex stereotyping and sex discrimination: The Macho scale. *Psychological Reports, 1*(2), 411–415.

Virkkunen, M. (1981). The child as participating victim. In M. Cook & K. Howells (Eds.), *Adult sexual interest in children* (pp. 121–138). Toronto: Academic Press.

Wilson, K., & Faison, R. (1979). Sexual assault in dating: A profile of the victims. *Sociological Research Symposium, 9*, 320–326.

Wilson, K., Faison, R., & Britton, G. M. (1983). Cultural aspects of male sex aggression. *Deviant Behavior, 4*, 241–255.

10

The Role of Cognition in Sexual Assault

ZINDEL V. SEGAL AND LANA E. STERMAC

As even a casual perusal of the psychological literature on sexual assault reveals, the areas of investigation receiving the widest research attention seem to be those related to the constructs of deviant sexual arousal, heterosexual social skills, or the sexual and drug history of the offender. While it has been noted that cognitive variables may be especially relevant to work in these areas, cognition in sexual assault remains virtually unstudied (Lanyon, 1986; Stermac & Segal, in press). The reasons for this may be manifold, yet one explanation which suggests itself is that psychosocial investigations of sexual assault have yet to experience the "cognitive revolution" which has permeated the study of other problem behaviors (e.g., unipolar depression, Segal & Shaw, 1986; anxiety disorders, Ingram & Kendall, 1987). Alternatively, within the area of sexual assault the dominant theoretical construct of deviant sexual arousal has, up till recently, held sway over competing etiological accounts such that it has contributed to the development of a number of unimodal theories which leave little room for additional explanatory constructs (Abel, Barlow, Blanchard, & Guild, 1977). As the explanatory power of models based solely on the role of deviant sexual arousal becomes increasingly questioned (Baxter, Marshall, Barbaree, Davidson, & Malcolm, 1984), the need for multimodal models, which integrate other factors implicated in the commission of sexual assault, becomes apparent.

In such a context, examining the role of cognition in sexual assault and attempting to fashion a link to the social antecedents from which the specific attitudes, beliefs, or processing styles which sex offenders utilize in their interactions with potential victims may be particularly fruitful. It is also important to try to map out the role of cognition in the maintenance or reinforcement of con-

ZINDEL V. SEGAL • Cognitive Behavior Therapies Section, Clarke Institute of Psychiatry, University of Toronto, Toronto, Ontario M5T 1R8, Canada.   LANA E. STERMAC • Clarke Institute of Psychiatry, University of Toronto, Toronto, Ontario M5T 1R8, Canada.

tinued offending once this behavior is established or, conversely, to provide clues to the process of recidivism, once an individual has been able to refrain from sexual misbehavior (Pithers, Marques, Gibat, & Marlatt, 1983). Given that an increasing number of treatment programs are incorporating cognitive elements, or procedures, it is necessary to have a well-articulated position on the role which cognitive factors play, not only for the effectiveness of these treatment elements to be maximized, but also to be able to specify what meaningful cognitive change following treatment would look like.

This chapter will address itself to some of these questions in reviewing those cognitive studies which have been conducted with these populations, as well as attempt to provide a theoretical framework within which their findings can be best construed. To begin with, however, a brief overview of some operative constructs in the assessment of cognition will be provided.

ISSUES IN COGNITIVE ASSESSMENT

One of the most fundamental issues pervading efforts in the cognitive assessment of sex offenders is that concerning which level of analysis is to be employed. The reasons for this are twofold. One has to do with the fact that cognition can be assessed at a number of different levels of abstraction which proceed from a micro to a more macro level of information processing. A second reason is that while most cognitive assessment efforts are guided by a theory which specifies the putative role of cognitive factors in behavioral performance, such a theoretical framework has yet to be established with respect to the role of cognitive factors in sexual assault. Without such a theoretical framework, those studies which have examined cognitive factors have done so in a relatively unsystematic fashion, and in cases where differences have been documented, these differences have yet to be incorporated into a more synthetic framework.

For the present discussion, we can distinguish cognitive processes operating at a number of different levels of interest, namely, cognitive structures, cognitive propositions, cognitive operations, and cognitive products (Hollon & Kriss, 1984; Ingram & Kendall, 1986). *Cognitive structure* refers to the organization of memory content and the various linkages and associations among stored features of memory. *Cognitive propositions* refers to the type of information which is actually stored or represented in the various cognitive structures. An example here would be a cognitive schema of women or a schema of children. *Cognitive operations* can be viewed as the various processes by which the components of the information-processing system operate. These operations emphasize the active manipulation of information throughout the system and emphasize the use of such processes as attention allocation, encoding, control processes, and spreading activation among related concepts. Finally, *cognitive products* are the actual thoughts or images which come to mind that result from the input of information and the interaction of cognitive structures, propositions, and operations. Examples of these may be things such as self-statements, attributions, or inferences.

Having outlined the general categories of interest with respect to the measurement of cognitive variables in sexual assault, the remainder of the chapter will be devoted to an analysis of those studies which have been conducted in this area, specifically, with rapist and child molester populations. In general, the majority of these investigations have focused on the last category of information processing, which is the level of accessible thoughts or attributions. Fewer studies have examined the level of cognitive operations which looks at active processing styles. Studies of cognitive structure or cognitive propositions with these two populations are virtually nonexistent.

SEXUAL ASSAULTERS OF ADULT FEMALES

Cognitive Factors

As explanations of adult sexual assault have veered away from the identification of unique attributes of sexual assaulters to an examination of multiple variables, which can then be meaningfully combined into a predictive equation, the attention paid to cognitive factors has concurrently increased. More often than not, this attention has been placed in the larger context of investigations of heterosexual social skill and social competence. The common rationale for inclusion of cognitive measures in these studies is that a comprehensive assessment of social skill requires that behavioral, physiological, and cognitive aspects of performance be assessed (Curran, 1977; Erickson, Luxenberg, Walbek, & Seely, 1987). Studies of this sort have typically assessed the cognition of sexual assaulters during an interaction with a female confederate and have relied on questionnaires, thought listings, ratings of self-efficacy, or expectations, to achieve this. Keeping in mind the distinctions between the different types of cognitive processing outlined earlier, most of these studies have focused on cognitive products associated with role-play performances, and few of the studies have examined or gone beyond the level of cognitive operations. At the level of generic attitudes, beliefs, and stereotypes, the construct most often assessed in this population has been the attitudes of rapists toward women.

General attitudes toward women or beliefs regarding the acceptability of sexual aggression represent the most generic and accessible level of cognition regarding sexual assault. While clinical and anecdotal evidence suggests that rapists are extremely conservative and stereotyped in their thinking about women and the role of women in society, little systematic research exists exploring the relationship between the way in which men view women in this society and the extent to which they find sexual aggression toward women acceptable (Quinsey, 1984). The hypothesis being advanced here is that certain beliefs, such as (1) sex must be coerced from a woman, (2) men have the right to request sex from a woman, (3) if women were more protected and sheltered they would be less vulnerable to rape, or (4) women who are assaulted are somehow partly to blame, serve to disinhibit individuals, thereby making it more likely that they would act on assaultive impulses under certain circumstances.

Feild (1978) examined this issue by collecting data from a large sample of male and female citizens, police officers, rape counselors and rapists and compared their scores on a measure of attitudes toward women's role in society. His results indicated that negative attitudes toward women were related to perceptions of rape and that subjects who viewed women in more traditional roles were more likely to see rape as being the woman's fault. Liberal or profeminist scores on this measure were correlated with antirape attitudes. Interestingly though, when only the rapists' scores were considered, there were no significant correlations between rape attitudes and scores on the attitudes toward women measure. Segal and Stermac (1984) reported a similar lack of specificity among rapists' attitudes toward women and their attitudes toward rape in an investigation which employed the same measure used in the Feild study. Their data suggest that rapists as a group are not exclusively conservative or negative in their attitudes toward women but hold a value orientation similar to that of non-sex-offender inmates as well as community-based males of similar socioeconomic status.

While these types of attitudinal variables may still prove to be important descriptors of the belief systems which rapists hold, as well as of more socially sanctioned ways of looking at rape, it is probable that investigations utilizing these measures will need to reformulate the way in which their questions are asked. One suggestion would be to include measures of perceptions of rape as a related construct in those studies examining attitudes toward women. The important question seems to be whether specific attitudes concerning rape are related to sexual assault, and if this seems to hold, only then does it make sense to enquire whether more general attitudes toward women's role in society are related to specific attitudes concerning rape. As well, the consideration of respondent groups such as low-socioeconomic controls or other non-sex-offender inmates will be important contrast groups in the attempt to identify belief systems which may be unique to sexual assaulters. One study which has examined both attitudes toward sex and rape myth acceptance was reported by Overholser and Beck (1986). Samples of rapists, non-sex-offender inmates, low-socioeconomic volunteers, and minimal-dater college students were administered a questionnaire examining attitudes toward sexuality as well as rape myth acceptance. No significant effect was found on the rape myth acceptance scale between the groups. Once again, this tends to suggest that rapists' attitudes toward sexuality or sexual aggression may not differ significantly from other institutional or social class controls.

Studies of Cognitive Products

The majority of studies reported in this section were conducted in the context of assessing social competence of rapists. One aspect of this assessment involved the measurement of the cognitive component of heterosexual interaction and as such provides us with the largest literature on cognitive factors in these individuals to date. While different cognitive contents have been assessed, the most common methods have involved either *in vivo* cognitive assessment, following a live interaction with a female, or a questionnaire-based assessment.

In one such assessment study, Overholser and Beck (1986) administered the Fear of Negative Evaluation Scale (FNE) and the Social Anxiety and Distress Scale (SADS) to a number of groups. They reported no differences between rapists and institutional or community controls in the level of fear of being evaluated negatively or feeling distressed in social situations. This lack of cognitive findings stands in contrast to some of the performance deficiencies which were observed between sex-offender subjects and controls. Alexander and Johnson (1980) tried to establish the reliability of heterosocial skill measures in a population of sex offenders, but unfortunately they did not break their sample (composed of rapists, pedophiles, and exhibitionists) into specific groups. No differences in SADS scores between the sex offenders and matched controls were reported. There was, however, a significant association between SADS scores and a measure of social desirability, which points to the potentially confounding role which this factor can play in assessments with this population.

A study by Stermac and Quinsey (1986) also utilized the FNE and SADS and reported no significant difference between rapists and other subjects. They did, however, find skill differences on the behavioral measures of social competence which were the main focus of their study.

The study of assertive behavior in this population is of interest to this discussion since it represents an identifiable performance factor which is thought to be cognitively mediated (Heimberg & Becker, 1981). Differences between rapists and controls have been reported on a number of assertion measures (typically these have been self-report questionnaires), but they have not been replicated in live assertion role plays. Stermac and Quinsey (1986), for example, found that based on their responses to an inventory, rapists were less assertive than community controls and were generally poor in situations involving heterosexual assertion. Segal and Marshall (1985a) administered the same measure to a group of rapists and controls (Callner–Ross Assertion Scale; CRAS), yet they did not find significant differences between these groups on either the heterosexual assertion subscale or the total score on this measure. High-socioeconomic controls were found to be the most assertive group in these comparisons. Assessment of heterosexual assertion in a role play also failed to discern differences between rapists and low-socioeconomic controls, both in their responses during the role play itself as well as on a related questionnaire measuring knowledge of what the appropriate response to the situation would be. Overholser and Beck (1986), using the Rathus Assertiveness Inventory (RAI), also failed to find differences between rapists and their control groups on this measure.

Finally, Segal and Marshall (1985b) utilized the Social Interaction Self Statement Test (SISST) to examine self-statements or automatic thinking following an interaction with a female confederate. An additional cognitive assessment format employed in this study was that of an unstructured thought listing, which essentially asked subjects to record the thoughts they had while they were engaged in conversation with the female confederate. The SISST is composed of 15 positive and 15 negative self-statements and provides scores for each valence type. A group main effect was obtained for negative thoughts on the SISST only. High socioeconomic controls reported fewer negative thoughts than did all other groups. As well, community-based subjects, whether of high- or low-socioeconomic status, endorsed fewer negative thoughts than did inmates. No differential finding was reported between rapists and non-sex-offender inmates or child molesters. The thoughts which subjects recorded during the unstructured thought listing were categorized into dimensions of whether the thought reflected a judgment about who the subject was (self-evaluation) or whether the thought reflected instructions about the performance required (task orientation). These were further subdivided into whether they were positive or negative in tone. Once again, high-socioeconomic controls had more positive thoughts on both of these dimensions than did other subjects. Inmates' thoughts were considerably more negative than thoughts reported by community-based subjects, and this held for both the self-evaluative and task-referent dimensions. Once again, no findings unique to rapists were reported in these two cognitive assessments.

Studies of Cognitive Operation Variables

The studies reported in this section attempt to examine variables which influence the processing of information in a more automatic fashion, meaning that individuals may not intentionally choose to attend to or think about certain information but find that they do so nevertheless. An example of this would be recalling aspects of a picture which one had not intentionally memorized or made an effort to notice. This can be contrasted to processing of a more controlled fashion in which the person actively chooses to focus on specific aspects of the stimulus array and to exclude others (Ingram & Kendall, 1986; Schiffrin & Schneider, 1977). In one especially novel application, McFall's (1982) information-processing model of social competence was used to examine the hypothesis that rapists are selectively deficient in their ability to process interpersonal cues in heterosexual interactions. The automatic processes identified in his model include decoding skills, which center around the perception of incoming sensory information; decision skills, which involve generating response alternatives; and execution skills, which concern the smooth performance of a behavioral response.

The specific hypothesis examined in this study (Lipton, McDonel, & McFall, 1987) was that rapists would misconstrue negative cues received from women and interpret them as positive. This could then lead to responses which would be considered inappropriate sexual advances and which women would regard as sexually intrusive. The study concerned itself with the first stage of McFall's model, namely, that rapists would be deficient in their decoding of women's negative cues, and the measure of decoding utilized was specifically designed to assess the heterosocial cue-reading accuracy of young adults. The measure consisted of seventy-two 30-second videotape vignettes of heterosexual couples interacting, and subjects were instructed to guess which one of five affective cues were being portrayed in each interaction. The specific cues ranged from romantic, positive, neutral, negative, or bad mood. Accuracy scores were computed and served as the dependent measure. Results indicated that rapists were significantly less accurate than either of two inmate control groups (violent nonrapists or nonviolent nonrapists) in interpreting cues in simulated first-date interactions. Rapists were found to be especially deficient in reading women's, as opposed to men's, cues, and errors associated with negative cues accounted for the largest proportion of variance in these findings.

This study suggests that a social cognition approach to the analysis of sexual assault may have some merit, and it serves as a possible model for future investigations with respect to the specificity of its hypotheses. It is possible that the lack of findings in previous cognitive studies of these individuals was due to their global notion of what cognitive factors may be operative in sexual assault and the inability to move beyond questionnaire-based measures in assessing them. The Lipton *et al.* (1987) study avails itself of a theoretical model of social information processing and specifies precise hypotheses as to where deficiencies in rapists' processing may occur. This type of specificity can only aid in evaluating the ultimate utility of cognitive factors in sexual assault.

A study by Segal and Marshall (1986) utilized Bandura's (1977) notion of self-efficacy to analyze the cognitive aspects of heterosexual interaction between rapists and a female confederate. Subjects were asked to indicate their ability and confidence in performing a number of task-relevant behaviors such as introducing themselves, starting the conversation, asking questions, and answering questions. Ratings were made before the role-played interaction as well as after subjects had finished the role play. Discrepancy scores were then calculated by subtracting subjects' pre-role-play predictions from their post-role-play evaluations. Higher discrepancies were significantly related to lower ratings of skill in the interaction as well as higher ratings of anxiety. This effect was stable for anxiety and skill ratings provided not only by the subject but also by the confederate and two independent judges. Males of high-socioeconomic class showed the least discrepancy in their predictions, while rapists as a group did not differ from other males of low-socioeconomic class whether in or out of prison.

While the construct of self-efficacy is not generally considered to be as automatic a process as decoding or selective attention, nevertheless, it does present a uniquely cognitive variable which has been shown to have predictive power in the analysis of avoidance and fear behavior (Williams, 1987) and is an important candidate as a cognitive mediator of behavioral performance related to heterosexual social competence. Once again, this approach is noteworthy for its specificity both in examining discrete behavioral components associated with carrying on a conversation as well as in adapting Bandura's (1977) model to an analysis of this problem. While no unique finding with respect to rapists' self-efficacy discrepancies emerged, this was not true of child molesters. In fact, child molesters seem to be a group whose responding shows more clearly defined comparative differences from controls. It is to a consideration of cognitive factors in sexual assaulters of children that we now turn.

SEXUAL ASSAULTERS AGAINST CHILDREN

Much of what is known about cognitive factors in adult sexual contact with children comes from studies in which samples of child molesters and rapists have been assessed on a number of social competence measures and then compared to various control groups both within and without the institution.

Recognizing the multidimensional nature of the social competence construct (Curran, 1977), and in an attempt to avoid any overlap with the chapter on social processes (Stermac, Segal, & Gillis, Chapter 9, this volume), only the work on cognitive aspects of social skill will be reviewed. One exception to this is a study by Howells (1978), who, rather than assessing social skill, utilized the repertory grid technique to investigate the personal construing of adult females, adult males, and children in a sample of heterosexual pedophiles and matched controls. The results of this study point to differences between the two groups' perceptions of children. What emerged was that pedophiles used constructs related to the dimension of dominance in their descriptions of both children and adults, with children appearing at the nondominant pole of this dimension, whereas adults were seen as overbearing and more threatening, possibly due to their greater potential for dominating pedophiles. In contrast, children were viewed as nonthreatening and easier to relate to, perhaps because of their submissive status. Another finding which emerged from this research was that the cognitions of pedophiles about children are not exclusively sexual in nature but may have to do with other positive or even idealized attributes which they see children as possessing. In this way the attraction of pedophiles to children as sexual partners may be related to the pedophile's search for a context in which he can enjoy nonsexual mastery or dominance over another individual, the idealization of specific aspects of childhood (such as the child's innocence, capacity for unconditional loving, the simplicity of life seen through a child's eyes, etc.), or the enjoyment of a relationship which is free from the problems associated with anxiety-laden adult heterosexuality (Lanyon, 1986; Quinsey, 1986).

Another interesting study in this vein was conducted by Frisbie, Vanasek, and Dingman (1967), who utilized the semantic differential to obtain ratings from groups of institutionalized and community-based child molesters on their actual and ideal views of themselves. This test instrument consists of pairs of bipolar variables which reflect aspects of an individual's physical characteristics, personality traits, and value orientations. Subjects were asked to locate themselves on these bipolar dimensions under two different rating conditions, the first condition being "me, as I am" and the second being "me, as I ought to be." The category of descriptors which showed the largest discrepancies between these two rating stances was composed of adjectives related to interactions with others. Given that this study was originally designed as a methodological examination of differences between individuals in the community and those in hospital, it does not tell us much about the absolute differences in the self-view of child molesters and controls. Yet, it is noteworthy for its approach of attempting to elucidate the personal meanings which these individuals attach to their self-representations.

Studies of social competence of child molesters have also frequently utilized questionnaire assessment methods. In the study by Overholser and Beck (1986), child molesters displayed significantly more fear of being negatively evaluated, as measured by their scores on the FNE, in contrast to rapists and other controls.

Similarly, Segal and Marshall (1985b) reported that the scores of child molesters on the SADS were significantly higher than rapists' scores. While the analysis of self-efficacy discrepancy scores reported by Segal and Marshall (1986) showed rapists to be no different from other low-socioeconomic males in the accuracy of their performance predictions, child molesters had the largest discrepancy scores and showed particular difficulty in gauging their ability to answer the confederate's questions. Similarly, Segal and Marshall (1985a) reported that child molesters scored significantly lower than rapists and other controls on the positive feedback, negative feedback, and general assertion subscales of the CRAS. Findings of this sort suggest that there may be a differential perception of social cues by these two groups of sex offenders.

At this point no systematic research exists which has examined cognitive operations of the sort reported by the McFall group in their work with rapists. This may in part be due to the lack of a specific theory which would predict where child molesters may be deficient in their social information processing. Some of the constructs discussed previously would be logical starting points and include issues related to dominance/submissiveness, the feature of control in relationships with children, and sexual relations free of the anxiety markers attributed to adult sexuality. One important avenue for theory building would be to develop an assessment of child molesters' cognitions with respect to children. This could be the first step in determining whether their perceptions of sexual contact do indeed differ in the ways which previous clinical and anecdotal accounts have led us to believe.

A study which was initiated on this premise was conducted by Stermac and Segal (in press) and employed a number of clinical vignettes depicting various degrees of sexual contact between an adult and a child and different levels of the child's response to such contact. The questions to which subjects were asked to respond after reading each vignette were related to the primary dimensions often identified as being salient in child molesters' descriptions or accounts of their contacts with children. These dimensions included responsibility for the act, the child's complicity in its performance, the extent to which the child may have benefited or learned something from taking part in such contact, and the degree to which performance of this behavior should be punished. Pedophiles were compared to a number of institutional and socioeconomic controls as well as community groups who would have some experience with either prosecuting individuals accused of having had sex with children or treating the offenders or victims of such contact.

The results of the study indicated that child molesters differed from other respondent groups in perceiving more benefit to the child as a result of sexual contact, greater complicity on the child's part in such behavior, less responsibility on the adult's part for the initiation of this behavior, and less need for punishment of the adult. Subject's reactions to the vignettes were moderated in part by the child's response to the contact depicted, such that when the child's response was clearly negative (e.g., the child cries), all groups displayed a concordant pattern of responding. In those situations where the child's response was essentially ambiguous (e.g., just staring at the adult), the child molesters' responding diverged the greatest from the other respondent groups. This may reflect the fact that in the ambiguous situation the prevalent attitudes which child molesters hold were able to surface. No significant correlations with a measure of social desirability were obtained between the groups, and this pattern of endorsement, reflecting greater acceptance of adult sexual contact with children, received convergent support from a questionnaire measuring pedophilotypic cognitions.

Studies of this sort merely represent the tip of the iceberg with respect to the type of work needed, not only to further elucidate child molesters' cognitions about sexual contact with children and their views of children, but also to examine the way in which these dimensions interact with the commission of the offense. For example, do notions of the seductive child or the belief that the child can benefit from such contact make it easier for offenders to contemplate engaging in such acts? Does anger regarding what they deem to be the arbitrary nature of the age limit for lawful intercourse with a minor make it easier to flaunt these laws? This type of analysis will be important in allowing us to decide whether cognitive factors can be meaningfully integrated into multifaceted models which attempt to account for adult sexual contact with children by reference to a number of risk variables (Marshall, Earls, Segal, & Darke, 1983).

FUTURE DIRECTIONS

The general picture which emerges from this overview of cognitive factors in sexual assault is one which contains few reliable findings and many more in need of empirical clarification. Rapists do not seem to differ from other low-socioeconomic controls, whether in or out of prison, on such cognitive measures as attitudes concerning women's role in society, fear of negative evaluations in social situations, or the types of self-statements they emit during a conversation with a female confederate. When we move away from a molar level of analysis to more specific deficiencies in the stream of information processing, we find that rapists have more difficulty in decoding women's negative cues during social interactions. Child molesters stand out as more inadequate on the self-report measures of social competence than rapists, yet both groups do not always differ significantly from institutional controls. While these findings may confirm child molesters' general anxiety in relating to adult females, their perceptions of interactions with children seem to diverge in a consistent fashion from the reactions of a number of control groups. Specifically, child molesters construe sexual contact with children in more accepting terms, believe that the child can benefit from such interactions, and may play a role in initiating this behavior. While these findings may confirm previous clinical and anecdotal accounts of child molesters' explanations for their actions, much remains unknown about the way in which these explanations interact with other factors to facilitate the commission of the offense (Quinsey, 1986).

One variable which has not been considered so far in this research is that of different offender typologies. A potential interaction here is that if individuals assault women or children for consistently different reasons, some of these reasons may reflect greater cognitive mediation than others. For example, the typology proposed to classify child molesters into preference molesters versus situational molesters deserves closer scrutiny (Groth & Birnbaum, 1978; Howells, 1981). Preference molesters often choose male victims and feel that their behavior with children is not inappropriate but that they are being unfairly harassed by a punitive society. In these offenders, their sexual interactions with children are often premeditated and constitute an important part of the individual's life (Lanyon, 1986). Situational molesters, in contrast, tend to have a more typical history of heterosexual development and interactions, yet choose child partners during times of life stress or opportunity. The important point here is that the primary sexual identification of situational molesters is toward adult partners, and their urges toward children are viewed as problematic. While cognitive factors may exist in both categories of offenders, they may play a more facilitative role for the situational molester who begins to ruminate and tries to fight off urges for contact with children. This, in combination with the arousal associated with these urges and beliefs that these acts may help redress difficulties in other areas of the offender's life, could provide a pathway for acting out. Alternatively, the preference offender may have an ingrained belief system regarding the desirability of sexual contact with children and a child's desire for such contact, which makes performance of these acts less of an obstacle. This type of construal pattern is similar to that reported in the Stermac and Segal (in press) vignette study.

In the realm of treatment considerations, cognitive factors may be important targets for modification—assuming that evidence accumulates in favor of their role as mediators—as well as important determinants of risk for recidivism. In fact, the relapse prevention model for the treatment of sexually aggressive individuals (Pithers et al., 1983) places specific emphasis on the analysis of the patient's cognitions in order to understand the way in which they construe their ability to deal with situations which place them at risk to reoffend. This model emphasizes the role of self-efficacy and mastery in the maintenance of successful abstinence from sexual assault. It also teaches coping or adaptive responses to potential lapses, such as engaging in fantasy regarding inappropriate sexual contact with children or adult females. An analysis of the patient's cognitions is important, not only in terms of identifying potential high-risk situations, but also in anticipating the types of responses which would reduce the probability of the final completion of these acts. In this sense treatment is bolstered by an assessment of cognitive risk variables, and the program offers a valuable adjunct for surviving in the community once the patient is no longer in an active program.

It goes without saying that the continued focus on relapse prevention also necessitates a greater understanding of the types of stresses which discharged patients may encounter in their natural environments (Nagayama Hall & Proctor, 1987). Over and above the more typically identified risk factors such as drug use, boredom, and pornography usage, we need a better understanding of what types of interpersonal stress or social environment the individual is likely to return to. This is not meant to substitute for the skills-training aspect of many treatment programs but merely to emphasize that these skills will go unused if the individual returns to an environment which may not elicit this new repertoire of behavioral responses.

CONCLUSIONS

Cognitive factors in sexual assault have been reviewed, and those studies which have examined these variables point to an intriguing area of development which is certainly deserving of future research scrutiny. While this chapter concerned itself exclusively with adult male offenders, there is a need to consider its conclusions with respect to other target groups, such as adolescent (Davis & Leitenberg, 1987) and female (O'Connor, 1987) sex offenders. At this point most of the cognitive factors identified have been the products of accessible and fairly surface-level functions. Without further evidence that these variables may be important in the building of multifaceted theories of sexual assault, or that they possess some explanatory power in predicting future offending, it seems imprudent to suggest the development of methodologies which examine more automatic and less intentional forms of information processing. The field in general could benefit from a greater degree of specificity in the types of predictions which are made regarding the particular cognitive deficits of these individuals.

The use of a theoretical model of social cognition is also valuable in that it can guide future research toward more specific analyses and away from global cognitive constructs which do not seem to discriminate between sexual assaulters and controls. Although one could argue that the lack of sophistication in the types of cognitive measures used accounts for the absence of differential findings among the groups, it seems that this sophistication will only come after research has decided what types of constructs are worth pursuing and which types have not held up well under empirical scrutiny. At this point we have a number of candidates, including attitudes, belief systems, decoding skills, and possibly even representations of the self. All these factors will continue to vie for research attention and, if the requisite explanatory power of cognitive variables in this area is borne out, will guarantee that this domain has an exciting and potentially fruitful future.

REFERENCES

Abel, G. G., Barlow, D. H., Blanchard, E. B., & Guild, D. (1977). The components of rapists' sexual arousal. *Archives of General Psychiatry, 34,* 895–903.

Alexander, B. B., & Johnson, S. B. (1980). Reliability of heterosocial skills measurement with sex offenders. *Journal of Behavioral Assessment, 2,* 225–237.

Bandura, A. (1977). Self-efficacy: Toward a unifying theory of behavioral change. *Psychological Review, 84,* 191–215.

Baxter, D. J., Marshall, W. L., Barbaree, H. E., Davidson, P. R., & Malcolm, P. B. (1984). Differentiating sex offenders by criminal and personal history, psychometric measures, and sexual response. *Criminal Justice and Behavior, 11,* 477–501.

Curran, J. P. (1977). Skills training as an approach to the treatment of heterosexual-social anxiety: A review. *Psychological Bulletin, 84,* 140–157.

Davis, G. E., & Leitenberg, H. (1987). Adolescent sex offenders. *Journal of Consulting and Clinical Psychology, 55,* 417–427.

Erickson, W. D., Luxenburg, M. G., Walbek, N. H., & Seely, R. K. (1987). Frequency of MMPI two-point code types among sex offenders. *Journal of Consulting and Clinical Psychology, 55,* 566–570.

Feild, H. S. (1978). Attitudes toward rape: A comparative analysis of police, rapists, crisis counselors, and citizens. *Journal of Personality and Social Psychology, 36,* 156–179.

Frisbie, L. V., Vanasek, F. J., & Dingman, H. F. (1967). The self and the ideal self: Methodological study of pedophiles. *Psychological Reports, 20,* 599–706.

Groth, A. N., & Birnbaum, H. J. (1978). Adult sexual orientation and attraction to under age persons. *Archives of Sexual Behavior, 7,* 175–181.

Heimberg, R. G., & Becker, R. E. (1981). Cognitive and behavioral models of assertive behavior: Review, analysis, and integration. *Clinical Psychology Review, 1,* 353–373.

Hollon, S. D., & Kriss, M. R. (1984). Cognitive factors in clinical research and practice. *Clinical Psychology Review, 4,* 35–76.

Howells, K. (1978). Some meanings of children for pedophiles. In M. Cook & G. Wilson (Eds.), *Love and attraction* (pp. 57–82). London: Pergamon Press.

Howells, K. (1981). Adult sexual interest in children: Considerations relevant to theories of aetiology. In M. Cook & K. Howells (Eds.), *Adult sexual interest in children* (pp. 55–94). New York: Academic Press.

Ingram, R. E., & Kendall, P. C. (1986). Cognitive clinical psychology: Implications of an information processing perspective. In R. E. Ingram (Ed.), *Information processing approaches to clinical psychology* (pp. 3–22). New York: Academic Press.

Ingram, R. E., & Kendall, P. C. (1987). The cognitive side of anxiety. *Cognitive Therapy and Research, 11,* 523–536.

Lanyon, R. I. (1986). Theory and treatment in child molestation. *Journal of Consulting and Clinical Psychology, 54,* 176–182.

Lipton, D. N., McDonel, E. C., & McFall, R. M. (1987). Heterosocial perception in rapists. *Journal of Consulting and Clinical Psychology, 55,* 17–21.

Marshall, W. L., Earls, C. M., Segal, Z., & Darke, J. L. (1983). A behavioral program for the assessment and treatment of sexual aggressors. In K. D. Craig & R. J. McMahon (Eds.), *Advances in clinical behavior therapy* (pp. 148–174). New York: Brunner/Mazel.

McFall, R. M. (1982). A review and reformulation of the concept of social skills. *Behavioral Assessment, 4,* 1–33.

Nagayama Hall, G. C., & Proctor, W. C. (1987). Criminological predictors of recidivism in a sexual offender population. *Journal of Consulting and Clinical Psychology, 55,* 111–112.

O'Connor, A. A. (1987). Female sex offenders. *British Journal of Psychiatry, 150,* 615–620.

Overholser, J. C., & Beck, S. (1986). Multimethod assessment of rapists, child molesters, and three control groups on behavioral and psychological measures. *Journal of Consulting and Clinical Psychology, 54,* 682–687.

Pithers, P. D., Marques, J. K., Gibat, C. C., & Marlatt, G. A. (1983). Relapse prevention with sexual aggressives: A self-control model of treatment and maintenance of change. In J. G. Greer & I. R. Stuart (Eds.), *The sexual aggressor* (pp. 214–239). New York: Van Nostrand Reinhold.

Quinsey, V. L. (1984). Sexual aggression: Studies of offenders against women. In D. N. Weisstub (Ed.), *Law & mental health: International perspectives* (vol. 1., pp. 84–121). New York: Pergamon Press.

Quinsey, V. L. (1986). Men who have sex with children. In D. N. Weisstub (Ed.), *Law & mental health: International perspectives* (vol. 2., pp. 140–172). New York: Pergamon Press.

Segal, Z. V., & Marshall, W. L. (1985a). Self-report and behavioral assertion in two groups of sexual offenders. *Journal of Behavior Therapy and Experimental Psychiatry, 16,* 223–229.

Segal, Z. V., & Marshall, W. L. (1985b). Heterosexual social skills in a population of rapists and child molesters. *Journal of Consulting and Clinical Psychology, 53,* 55–63.

Segal, Z. V., & Marshall, W. L. (1986). Discrepancies between self-efficacy predictions and actual performance in a population of rapists and child molesters. *Cognitive Therapy and Research, 10,* 363–375.

Segal, Z. V., & Shaw, B. F. (1986). Cognition in depression: A reappraisal of Coyne and Gotlib's critique. *Cognitive Therapy and Research, 10,* 671–694.

Segal, Z. V., & Stermac, L. E. (1984). A measure of rapists' attitudes towards women. *International Journal of Law and Psychiatry, 7,* 219–222.

Shiffrin, R. M., & Schneider, W. (1977). Controlled and automatic human information processing: II. Perceptual learning, automatic attending, and a general theory. *Psychological Review, 84,* 127–190.

Stermac, L. E., & Quinsey, V. L. (1986). Social competence among rapists. *Behavioral Assessment, 8,* 171–185.

Stermac, L. E., & Segal, Z. V. (in press). Adult sexual contact with children: An examination of cognitive factors. *Behavioral Therapy.*

Williams, S. L. (1987). On anxiety and phobia. *Journal of Anxiety Disorders, 1,* 161–180.

III
Theories of Sexual Assault

11

Sex Offenders

A Feminist Perspective

JUDITH LEWIS HERMAN

A FEMINIST SOCIAL ANALYSIS OF SEXUAL VIOLENCE

In the past decade, feminist consciousness-raising and political action have transformed public awareness of sexual violence. The testimony of victims, first in consciousness-raising groups, then in public speakouts, and finally in formal survey research, has documented the high prevalence of all forms of sexual assault. The best currently available data indicate that for women, the risk of being raped is approximately one in four, and that for girls, the risk of sexual abuse by an adult is greater than one in three (Russell, 1984). Boys appear to be at lower, but still substantial, risk for sexual assault by older boys or men (Finkelhor, 1979). The findings that most victims are female and that the vast majority of offenders are male have been reproduced in every major study. They are not artifacts of reporting, which in any case is extremely low; probably less than 10% of all sexual assaults are reported to police, and less than 1% result in arrest, conviction, and imprisonment of the offender (Russell, 1984).

In bringing sexual assault to public attention, feminist thinkers have offered not only documentation but also a social analysis of the problem. In a feminist analysis, sexual assault is understood to be intrinsic to a system of male supremacy. In support of this contention, feminist theorists have called attention to the social legitimacy of many forms of sexual assault and to the glorification of even extreme sexual violence in the dominant culture. If, as many feminists argue, the social definition of sexuality involves the erotization of male dominance and female submission, then the use of coercive means to achieve sexual conquest may represent a crude exaggeration of prevailing norms, but not a

JUDITH LEWIS HERMAN • Department of Psychiatry, Harvard Medical School, Cambridge, Massachusetts 02139; and Women's Mental Health Collective, Somerville, Massachusetts 02143. An expanded version of this chapter has been published in *Signs: Journal of Women in Culture and Society*, 13(4) (Summer, 1988): 695–724.

departure from them (Bart, 1983; Bart & O'Brien, 1985; Connell & Wilson, 1974; Herman, 1981; MacKinnon, 1983). Moreover, feminist theorists suggest that sexual assault serves a political function in preserving the system of male dominance through terror, thus benefiting all men whether or not they personally commit assaults (Brownmiller, 1975; Griffin, 1971). The unanswered question posed by feminists is not why some men rape, but why most men do not.

The feminist analysis of sexual assault challenges conventional beliefs which are widely held both by the general public and by mental health professionals. Traditionally, sexual assault has been understood as deviant and unusual rather than normative and common behavior. Attempts at explanation have focused upon the psychopathology of the individual offender, his victim, or his family. It is a commonplace notion that men who commit sex crimes must be "sick." Feminists contend, rather, that these men are all too normal.

The weight of evidence supporting a feminist analysis of sexual assault is overwhelming. In the first place, there is the matter of epidemiology. Not only are sex offenders almost exclusively male, but there is increasing evidence that a significant proportion of the normal male population has committed sexual offenses. When one-third of the female population has been sexually victimized, common sense would suggest that some comparable percentage of the male population has been doing the victimizing. Data from surveys of normal populations indeed indicate that this is the case. In a national probability survey of adolescents, Ageton (1983) found that 1% of the boys acknowledged an attempted or completed rape in the previous year. Extrapolating to the number of years at risk would yield a rough estimate that between 1 and 7% of boys attempt to complete a sexual assault while still in their teens. In a national survey of male college students (average age 21) Koss, Gidycz, and Wisniewski (1987) found that 4.4% acknowledged having committed rape in a dating situation, and another 3.3% acknowledged attempted rape. Koss et al. further demonstrated a spectrum of sexual behaviors, ranging from unaggressive to highly aggressive. While the majority of young men (74.8%) acknowledged only consensual sexual relations, one in four (25.1%) acknowledged using some form of coercion to achieve sexual relations with an unwilling partner. Similar results have been obtained in two other studies (Briere, Corne, Runtz, & Malamuth, 1984; Rapaport & Burkhart, 1984). Most recently, Finkelhor and Lewis (1987), in a nationwide random-sample survey, found that between 4 and 17% of the male population acknowledge having molested a child.

In cross-cultural studies, high rape prevalence has been shown to be associated with male dominance. Rape is common in cultures where only a male creative deity (rather than a couple or female deity) is worshipped, where warfare is glorified, where women hold little political or economic power, where the sexes are highly segregated, and where care of the children is an inferior occupation (Sanday, 1981). In our own culture, where all of these conditions obtain, rape-supportive attitudes and beliefs are widely held. The most articulate expression of such attitudes may be found in literature that enjoys a predominantly male mass audience—that is, in pornography (Dworkin, 1981)—and in the works of lionized literary figures (Millett, 1970).

The popularity of such literature offers indirect evidence of rape-supportive attitudes; direct evidence is provided by attitudinal survey research (Burt, 1980). A number of large-scale surveys conducted primarily with high school and college students indicates that a majority of students consider the use of force acceptable to achieve sexual relations in certain circumstances (e.g., if a woman is "getting a man sexually excited"). Though students of both sexes endorse these attitudes, males embrace them more heartily than females (Goodchilds & Zellman, 1984). Moreover, a considerable minority of male students (35%) admit to some hypothetical likelihood of committing rape if guaranteed immunity from detection or punishment (Malamuth, 1981).

A significant proportion of the male population not only endorse rape-supportive attitudes and find the fantasy of rape agreeable but also become sexually aroused by depictions of rape. The most widely appealing scenario appears to be one in which a female victim, after being subdued, becomes sexually excited by the rape. In one study, a majority of college males found this scenario as arousing as a portrayal of nonviolent, consensual intercourse, while a significant minority found the coercion scenario *more* arousing. Arousal to depictions of sexual violence appears to be highly correlated with both rape-supportive attitudes and self-reported likelihood of committing rape (Malamuth, 1984).

It is possible that the attitudes and patterns of sexual arousal documented in these studies are characteristic only of adolescents, and that a mature male population might exhibit less hostility to women in general and less enthusiasm for rape in particular. However, at the very least, these findings suggest that the adolescent male subculture provides a powerful indoctrination in sexual violence. If the effects of this socialization were limited to attitudes and masturbatory fantasies, it might be possible to await the supposed maturation process with equanimity. However, there is strong reason to believe that adolescence is a critical period in the development of sexually assaultive behavior. Clinical studies of habitual sex offenders consistently document the occurrence of the first sexual assault in adolescence (Groth, Longo, & McFadin, 1982). Studies of reported rape consistently indicate that about 25% of rapists are under 18 years of age (U.S. Department of Justice, 1981).

Both the adolescent and college student studies demonstrate a strong association between social attitudes and sexually aggressive behavior. In Ageton's (1983) study, boys who committed sexual assaults were more likely to belong to a peer group that accepted all forms of interpersonal violence. Almost half of the young offenders told their peers about their exploits, and most of their friends approved of their behavior. Very few (14%) expressed any feelings of guilt. By contrast, 40% of the *victims* felt guilty. In Koss *et al.'s* (1987) study, the young men who acknowledged an attempted or completed rape were those most likely to endorse rape-supportive attitudes. Briere *et al.* (1984) further demonstrated that young men who had committed sexual assaults differed markedly from their peers on a "rape arousal inventory," a self-report measure of arousal to a fantasized rape scenario. While measures of attitudes and arousal proved to be strongly correlated with actual assaultive behavior, standard psychological measures proved useless as predictors. No significant differences between the sexually assaultive men and their peers could be demonstrated on standard projective-test and screening measures of psychopathology. The young rapists in the college student surveys were demonstrably sexist, but not demonstrably "sick."

PSYCHOLOGICAL STUDIES OF SEX OFFENDERS

Direct psychological studies of sex offenders have been greatly hampered by difficulties in identifying a representative population. Most clinical studies to date have been restricted to sex offenders whose crimes have been reported to police, a group probably comprising less than 10% of all offenders; many are restricted to incarcerated offenders, a group representing perhaps 1% of the total. The processes of reporting, criminal prosecution, conviction, and sentencing are by no means random. The group of sex offenders who become ensnared in the criminal justice system must be considered a highly skewed population, in which minority group men, those who attack strangers, those who use extreme force, and those who lack the social skills to avoid detection are overrepresented. Thus, convicted offenders are far more likely to look abnormal than undetected offenders in the general population.

In spite of this bias in clinical studies, the predictions of feminist theory are generally confirmed: sex offenders look surprisingly ordinary. The great majority of convicted offenders do not suffer from psychiatric conditions that might be invoked to diminish criminal responsibility, that is, from psychotic disorders or mental retardation (Gebhard, Gagnon, Pomeroy, & Christenson, 1965; Groth, 1979; Henn, 1978; Knight, Rosenberg, & Schneider, 1985). Though the majority of convicted sex offenders do not suffer from major psychiatric disorders, many do meet the diagnostic criteria for the so-called personality disorders. Sociopathic, schizoid, paranoid, and narcissistic personality disorders are all frequently described in criminally identified offenders (Henn, 1978; Knight *et al.*, 1985). All of these disorders involve a relative failure of human attachments and social relations—a preoccupation with one's own fantasies, wishes, and needs, a lack of empathy for others, and a desire to control and dominate others rather than to engage in mutual relationships. It is not clear, however, whether such disorders are any more common in convicted sex offenders than in other prisoners; the one adequately controlled study in the literature indicates that they are not (Karacon, Williams, Guerraro, Salis, Thornby, & Hursch, 1974). Moreover, there is no evidence whatsoever that these personality disorders are more common in an *undetected* offender population than they are in the male population at large.

The most striking characteristic of sex offenders, from a diagnostic standpoint, is their apparent normality. Most do not qualify for any psychiatric diagnosis (Abel, Rouleau, & Cunningham-Rathner, 1985). One psychiatrist who has extensive experience in treating undetected offenders in the community describes them as follows:

> These paraphiliacs are not strange people. They are people who have one slice of
> their behavior that is very disruptive to them and to others; behavior they cannot

control. But the other aspects of their lives can be pretty stable. We have executives, computer operators, insurance salesmen, college students, and people in a variety of occupations in our program. They are just like everyone else, except they cannot control one aspect of their behavior. (Abel, quoted in Knopp, 1984, p. 9)

Failing to find any readily apparent mental disorder that characterizes sex offenders, psychological investigators have increasingly focused on aspects of their developmental histories that might offer clues to understanding their behavior. The hypothesis most frequently entertained is that sex offenders were themselves sexually victimized in childhood or adolescence. The sexual offense is then understood as a reenactment of the trauma or as an attempt to overcome it through the mechanism of "identification with the aggressor." Proponents of this theory often invoke the concept of a "cycle of abuse," or of "generational transmission," whereby the sexually victimized children of one generation become the victimizers of the next.

The cycle of abuse has proved to be an extremely popular concept both among mental health professionals and in the mass media, where it is often promoted as an established doctrine. It has been invoked to explain most crimes of violence occurring in the private sphere, such as wife-beating and child abuse. A thorough and well-documented feminist critique of this concept as applied to wife-beating and child abuse may be found elsewhere and will not be repeated here (Kaufman & Zigler, 1987; Pagelow, 1984). Applied to sexual assault, the most glaring weakness of the cycle of abuse concept is its inability to explain the virtual male monpoloy on this type of behavior. Since girls are sexually victimized at least two or three times more commonly than boys, this theory would predict a female rather than a male majority of sex offenders. Unable to account for this contradiction, proponents of the cycle of abuse theory are sometimes reduced to denying reality: it is among adherents of this theory that one still encounters assertions that large undetected reserves of female offenders are yet to be discovered (Groth, 1979; Justice & Justice, 1979).

The best available evidence documenting a connection between childhood abuse and sexually assaultive behavior comes from retrospective studies of identified sex offenders. Not only are these studies unrepresentative of the general (undetected) offender population, but most also lack appropriate comparison groups, and many are quite vague in their definition of childhood sexual abuse. Groth (1979), for example, in a widely quoted study, defines sexual abuse as "any sexual activity witnessed and/or experienced that is emotionally upsetting or disturbing (p. 98)." Few people (certainly few women) are fortunate enough to reach adulthood without being upset by a sexual experience. Thus, the validity of the findings in such studies seems highly questionable. Moreover, the largest available studies indicate that while many offenders (somewhere between 25 and 40% of a clinical population) do appear to have an abuse history, the majority do not (Groth, 1979; Abel, Becker, & Skinner, 1983).

Histories of abuse do seem to be unusually common in pedophiles who prefer boy victims. This particular group has a number of characteristics that distinguish them from other sex offenders. Their behavior is truly deviant; it is not socially condoned or excused. Their sexual interest in young boys often has an early onset, they may lack any significant interest in consenting sexual relations with adults. Their behavior is often extremely compulsive and resistant to treatment. Becker (1985), for example, reports that pedophiles who prefer boy victims are one of the most treatment-resistant groups in her program. This group also has an early onset of compulsive behavior (72% of Becker's subjects have offended by age 19) and has a very high average number of victims per offender. This is the group that Groth, Hobson, and Gary (1982) describe as "fixated" offenders. Impressionistic reports from treatment programs indicate that sexual abuse histories are particularly common in this group, possibly ranging from 40 to 60% (Seghorn, Boucher, & Cohen, 1983). In one outpatient treatment program described by Knopp (1984), the staff estimated that 55% of the child molesters had been victimized, most commonly by male babysitters. They further observed that young men who raped women did *not* appear to have striking abuse histories, but that young men who raped men were almost uniformly victims of sexual abuse.

Taken together, these data suggest the possibility that childhood sexual trauma in boys may be a particularly significant risk factor for the development of sexually abusive behavior *toward other males*. In this area, where feminist theories are relatively weak, the cycle of abuse theory may turn out to be relatively strong. In other words, while traumatic childhood sexual experiences may play an important part in directing male sexual aggression against other males, no such trauma is necessary to direct sexual aggression against females. Normal male socialization is sufficient.

A feminist analysis of sexual assault contends that men engage in sexual assault not only because it is condoned or permitted but also because it is rewarding. Sexual assault asserts male dominance and intimidates women; it also provides the aggressor with sexual pleasure. In early feminist consciousness-raising, an attempt was made to define rape as an aggressive rather than a sexual act. This was necessary in order to challenge the widespread belief that victims derived pleasure from being assaulted. However, the fact that victims loathe being assaulted should not obscure the fact that offenders enjoy assaulting them.

In many psychological formulations of the motives of sex offenders, the sexual offense virtually disappears. Most psychodynamic explanations tend to minimize the sexual component of the offender's behavior and to reinterpret the assault as an ineffectual attempt to meet ordinary human needs. This renders the behavior more comprehensible (and, presumably, more accessible to psychotherapy) and allows the offender to be viewed more sympathetically. The victimizer is seen as a victim, no longer an object of fear but of pity. Groth (1979), for example, describes a type of "power rapist" who commits his crimes "in an effort to combat deep-seated feelings of insecurity and vulnerability" (p. 31). The offense is described as an expression of the offender's wishes for "virility, mastery, and dominance." Groth and Hobson (1983) describe the rapist as a man who "does not have his life under control and experiences adult life demands and responsibilities as overwhelming" (p. 165), and who "finds adult sexuality threatening for it confronts him with his unadmitted doubts about his masculine adequacy" (p. 166). Elsewhere, Groth, Hobson, and Gary (1982) describe the child molester in similar terms:

an immature individual whose pedophilic behavior serves to compensate for his relative helplessness in meeting adult bio-psycho-social life demands . . . through sexual
involvement with a child, the offender attempts to fulfill his psychological needs for
recognition, acceptance, validation, affiliation, mastery, and control. (p. 137)

Emphasizing these "needs" for power and dominance, Groth minimizes the
sexual motivation for the offenses, sometimes calling them "pseudo-sexual
acts." The compulsive, repetitive quality of the sexual assaults is attributed not
to the fact that they are pleasurable but to the fact that they are emotionally
disappointing, in spite of considerable testimony from rapists and other offenders that the sexual assault often produces an intense "high" (Scully & Marolla,
1985; Smithyman, 1978).

The effect of this euphemistic reformulation of the offender's behavior is to
detoxify it, to make it more acceptable. The offender's craving for sexual domination is reinterpreted as a longing for human intimacy. His wish to control
others is reinterpreted as an ordinary masculine need for "mastery." Since
normative concepts of manhood do to some extent include the domination of
women and children, the offender's desire to share in adult male prerogatives is
validated; only his choice of means is considered unfortunate. Since the gratification obtained from the sexual assault itself is minimized, this sort of explanation offers the promise that the assaultive behavior will be readily given up if the
offender can learn other, more socially acceptable ways of achieving "masculine
adequacy."

Such psychodynamic formulations do make it possible to empathize with
the offender, a prerequisite for any rehabilitative effort, and they do offer the
hope that psychological treatment may be effective. The danger in these formulations, however, is inextricable from their advantages. In attempting to
establish an empathic connection with the offender, the would-be therapist runs
the risk of credulously accepting the offender's rationalizations for his crimes (as
well as supplying him with new ones).

Moreover, such formulations allow attention to be diverted from the troub-
ling sexual offense to other problems more amenable to ordinary psychotherapy.

Treatment models based on these psychodynamic concepts tend to focus on
the offender's general social attitudes and relationships or on his own experiences as a victim, but not on the concrete details of his sexual fantasies and
behavior. For example, a prison-based program described by Groth has prolifer-
ated into 10 discussion group components including such topics as sex education, relationships to women, management of anger, stress reduction, and communication skills, but it has no method for monitoring the offender's continued
arousal to fantasies of sexual assault (Groth, Longo, & McFadin, 1982). Another
outpatient treatment program for incest offenders developed by a nationally
famous sex therapist includes social skills training, stress management, couple
therapy, sex therapy, and family therapy, but again, no particular focus on the
offender's sexual desire for children. The patient is required to sign a contract
stating that he will not reoffend while in treatment; but it is not clear how
compliance with this "contract" is monitored or enforced, other than asking the
offender to report on himself (Schwartz & Masters, 1985).

The validity of psychodynamic formulations of sexual assault, and the treatment models generated from them, is not merely a matter of academic interest. The risks inherent in overconfident expectations of the efficacy of treatment are very serious. Since there are very few long-term follow-up studies of treatment outcome, and since the difficulties in carrying out such studies are great, most treatment programs rely on subjective impressions of their own effectiveness. The greater the effort invested in offender treatment, the greater the motivation of the treating professionals to believe in the success of treatment and to overlook evidence to the contrary. When a treatment program minimizes the importance of the actual sexual behavior and does not provide any concrete method for monitoring it, failures are likely to go unrecognized, sometimes with disastrous consequences. In one extreme documented case, a young man mandated to psychiatric treatment after committing a rape at age 14 subsequently committed six additional rapes and five rape-murders *while in treatment*. His psychiatrist was entirely unaware of these crimes and could apparently detect no clues to their occurrence in the material offered by the patient in his treatment sessions (Ressler, Burgess, & Douglas, 1983).

Such dramatic treatment failures may, in fact, be unusual, but few are required to discredit any attempt at treating sex offenders. Disasters of this kind serve as reminders that our current understanding of the psychology of sex offenders is very crude, any treatment must be considered entirely experimental, and claims for therapeutic success should be offered with great caution and received with healthy skepticism.

A MODEL OF ADDICTION

Any behavior that causes intense excitement and pleasure can become compulsive. A social climate which encourages or condones sexual assault will produce a spectrum of behaviors, from opportunistic to highly addictive. Men who rape once may rape again. Behavioral as well as subjective descriptions of sex offenders are often similar to descriptions of alcoholics or other addicts. The compulsive offender behaves as though his primary attachment is to the mood-altering addictive activity. All other relationships are sacrificed or manipulated in the service of this activity. An elaborate defensive structure develops, the purpose of which is the protection and preservation of the addiction (Carnes, 1983). Denial is the primary defensive mode employed, but in addition, an extensive body of paranoid defenses and rationalizations may be developed. If he acknowledges his behavior at all, he generally blames other people for it. An unhappy childhood, stormy marriage, or frustrating job provides the justification and the excuse for the addiction. The rapist's cry and the alcoholic's are one and the same: "She drove me to it!"

Sexually compulsive behavior is often attributed to another more familiar compulsive behavior, namely, drinking. Alcoholism is frequently cited as a contributing factor in sex offenses, not least by offenders themselves who, if they admit their behavior, often attribute it to alcohol intoxication (Scully & Marolla,

1984). In several studies, a significant proportion of convicted sex offenders have been observed to be alcohol abusers: estimates range from 25 to 50% (Knight *et al.*, 1985; Rada, Kellner, Laws, & Winslow, 1978). However, since these studies generally lack appropriate comparison groups, it is not clear whether this extent of alcohol abuse is characteristic of sex offenders specifically, of a general prison population, or of a demographically similar population of men who have not committed crimes. In this regard, it is instructive to note that between 11 and 60% of a large group of working-class men could be described as alcohol abusers, depending upon the definition employed (Vaillant, 1983). The role of alcohol can probably best be understood as a facilitating one: intoxication may serve as an aid to overcoming inhibitions in those already predisposed to commit sexual assaults, while those who have no desire will not do so—drunk or sober.

The concept of sexual assault as a potentially addictive behavior has major implications for treatment and social rehabilitation of detected offenders. The first implication is that at present, the commission of one sexual assault cannot be dismissed as "adolescent curiosity" or any other benign, self-correcting problem. In the absence of well-documented criteria for distinguishing situational offenders from early addicts, it would seem prudent to consider all offenders potential addicts.

The second implication is that when dealing with a sex offender, one can not assume that he has any reliable internal motivation for change. The offender may have lost effective control of his behavior, though he has not lost moral or legal responsibility for it. External motivation for change must therefore be provided. In the case of sex offenders, legal sanctions and careful, sustained supervision (e.g., intensive probation or parole and, in some cases, incarceration) are the most appropriate sources of external motivation. Professionals who attempt treatment must ally and cooperate with law-enforcement authorities and obtain a waiver of confidentiality from the patient. Though such measures are traditionally considered punitive and antitherapeutic, this view fails to distinguish between social control and punishment. The general public and the mental health professions recognize that coercive measures are both therapeutic and necessary when a patient represents a clear danger to himself or others. Sex offenders are dangerous. They cannot be treated or rehabilitated unless their behavior is effectively controlled.

The third implication is that the primary focus of any therapeutic effort must be on changing the addictive behavior itself. For alcoholics, this means that the central focus of treatment is on drinking. For sex offenders, this means that treatment must focus in concrete detail on the unacceptable sexual behavior. The offender's patterns of sexual fantasy and arousal, his modus operandi for securing access to his victims and evading detection, his preferred sexual activities, and his system of excuses and rationalizations must be painstakingly documented, and changes must be closely monitored. The offending sexual behaviors cannot be wished away by describing them as attempts to meet nonsexual "needs" for mastery, nurturance, or anything else; they have a life of their own. Some experienced therapists require that a victim impact statement, describing the offender's crime, be made available in the case record before any form of treatment is attempted, and recommend frequent review of this document in order to counteract the tendencies toward denial and minimization of the offense which both patient and therapist may share.

The minimum components of a potentially successful therapeutic program for sex offenders would include a behavior-modification component directly focused upon the unacceptable sexual activities, a reliable method of monitoring the offender's continuing interest in sexual assault independent of his own self-report, and a supervision structure that reliably and swiftly provides sanctions for repeated offenses. Various operant-conditioning methods have been shown to be at least transiently effective in changing patterns of sexual arousal (Becker & Abel, 1984; Knopp, 1984; Quinsey & Marshall, 1983), and the penile strain gauge, used for measuring arousal to sexual stimuli, has shown promise as a monitoring device (Earls & Marshall, 1983).

Psychopharmacologic methods have also been used in an attempt to change the addict's behavior and motivation. For example, some alcoholism programs rely heavily on daily administration of disulfiram, a medication which changes the patient's metabolism so that ingestion of alcohol produces extremely unpleasant symptoms. In the treatment of sex offenders, antiandrogenic hormones have been used experimentally to decrease sexual arousal. The particular object of the offender's desire is unchanged, but the intensity of the desire is reportedly weakened (Berlin, 1983). Of course, the patient's motivation to comply with treatment cannot be taken for granted. Alcoholics who relapse frequently discontinue their daily dose of disulfiram; similarly, recidivist sex offenders may discontinue their medroxyprogesterone. An effective pharmacological agent alone does not constitute a treatment program.

The treatment of addiction begins with a focus on the negative consequences of the behavior, but it does not end there. An addicted person is not likely to give up the central gratification of his life in response to negative sanctions only. Strong positive inducements must be offered as well. Studying the recovery process in alcoholics and heroin addicts, Vaillant (1983) identified four factors associated with achievement of stable abstinence. The first is a constant reminder of the negative consequences of the addiction. The remaining three are substitute addiction, a new source of hope and self-esteem, and social support.

Highly structured group treatment and self-help programs appear to be the most successful modality for the social rehabilitation of addicts, including sex offenders. A group of peers who are reliably available on demand and who are committed to the goal of recovery through abstinence fulfills all four of these criteria. A constant reminder of the negative consequences of addiction is found in the testimony of group members; a substitute addiction and social support are available in the activities of the group itself; a new source of hope is provided by the testimony of group members who have changed their lives, and a new source of self-esteem is provided by the structure of a program which requires acknowledgment of the harm done but offers an opportunity for restitution and service to others. Some form of structured group process has evolved in almost every existing treatment program for sex offenders (Knopp, 1984). Most programs also explicitly or implicitly define stages of recovery analogous to the 12 steps of Alcoholics Anonymous (Carnes, 1983).

Relinquishing an addiction represents a profound psychological change, analogous to religious conversion. When the addiction has resulted in the commission of crimes, the destruction of social bonds is so extensive that sometimes a religious framework may offer the only hope of redemption. This is not to say that religious conversion guarantees recovery (a sex offender who announces that he has been "born again" is not thereby "cured") but, rather, that something analogous may be an important part of the recovery process. That such conversions are rare and difficult to predict should be a further reminder that any claims for therapeutic success with sex offenders should be offered with great modesty.

A final implication of the addiction model for treatment of sex offenders involves the prognosis for rehabilitation. Significant recovery from any addiction requires a considerable period of time. Addiction interferes with normal maturation and destroys social relationships. These problems remain even after the compulsive behavior is given up. Indeed, it is only after reliable limits have been placed on the addictive behavior that the addict faces the degree to which his abilities and his relationships with others have deteriorated. In recovery from alcoholism, for example, full rehabilitation (i.e., achievement of a level of functioning equal to the best level attained prior to the onset of the addiction) has been shown to require at least 3 years of sustained abstinence (Vaillant, 1983). A similar time course should be anticipated for recovery even with cooperative, well-motivated sex offenders. Current claims of successful treatment outcome after 12 weeks (Schwartz & Masters, 1985) or 6 months (Giarretto, 1982) are unlikely to be borne out with careful follow-up. Even after the achievement of full recovery, some ongoing maintenance activity may be required indefinitely to prevent relapse (Pithers, Marques, Gibat, & Marlatt, 1983). Once an addiction has become established, it must be considered a lifelong process. An addict may achieve abstinence; he does not achieve cure. In the words of one experienced therapist:

> We only talk about *controlling* sexual deviancies, about *reducing* them to minimal levels. Our long-range goal is to eliminate them, but we don't expect realistically to meet that goal. . . . The closest parallel—it is a good, but not a 100 percent analogy—is alcoholism. You don't talk about "ex-alcoholics," because if someone describes himself as an ex-alcoholic you are going to worry about him. And we do not talk about ex-sex offenders. We talk about alcoholics who don't drink any more—sober alcoholics. And we talk about sex offenders who do not offend any more. The conditioning patterns are ingrained in adult clients. We try to educate them to be aware of that, that it is really going to be a lifelong process. If someone in our program tells us "I'll never do it again," we say, "Hey, you are not ready to leave this program." (Roger Wolfe, quoted in Knopp, 1984, p. 19)

Viewing sexual assault as a potentially addicting behavior means coming to terms with the fact that the problem is complex and tenacious and that promises of rapid solution are not likely to be fulfilled. Treatment and rehabilitation of offenders is an ambitious undertaking, requiring constancy of purpose and sustained mobilization of social resources on a large scale. The required degree of cooperation between the criminal justice and mental health systems has rarely been achieved, even for short periods of time. Yet nothing less is likely to be at all effective.

IMPLICATIONS FOR PREVENTION

If the implications for treatment are somewhat discouraging, the addiction concept offers considerable hope for the efficacy of preventive measures. Because patterns of addiction are so highly sensitive to social risk factors, preventive intervention aimed at decreasing known risk factors or at protecting populations known to be at high risk should result in a significant lowering of the rate of sexual assault.

In practical terms, this means that sex education for all children remains a valuable aspect of primary prevention. However, the existing sex education establishment, which generally advocates a male-oriented, libertarian position, cannot be counted upon to implement an acceptable program. Ideally, educational efforts must combine full presentation of accurate information, respect for individual privacy and choice, and an articulated vision of socially responsible conduct. Issues of power and exploitation must be addressed explicitly. Boys and young men might be considered a priority for preventive work. In particular, organized male groups which foster traditional sexist attitudes should be considered high risk, since such misogynist attitudes have been shown to be associated with sexually exploitative behavior. Target populations for preventive intervention might include, for example, athletic teams, college fraternities, and the military. Primary prevention work with groups at high risk for victimization or for offending behavior also predictably results in early disclosure of sexual assaults that have already occurred, increasing the possibility for early intervention and treatment of both victim and offender.

Vigorous enforcement of existing criminal laws prohibiting sexual assault might also be expected to have some preventive effect, since both compulsive and opportunistic offenders are keenly sensitive to external controls. The reforms in rape legislation and the beginning integration of women into the criminal justice system (feminist gains during the 1980s) should result in a greater capability to hold offenders publicly accountable for their crimes. Prosecution is of particular importance in cases where traditional cultural standards legitimate and condone sexual assault (for example, in marital or date rape or the rape of prostitutes). In these cases, prosecution serves an educational function, exposing and challenging traditional rape-supportive attitudes.

Further research is required to identify those factors which seem to protect high-risk boys and men from becoming offenders and, further, to distinguish one-time offenders from those who go on to develop a habitual pattern of sexual assault. The role of pornography in consolidating violent sexual fantasy and behavior remains to be elucidated. Feminist theorists recognize pornography as a definitive ideological expression of male supremacy. But in addition to its ideological function, pornography also plays a role in conditioning masturbatory fantasy and sexual response. Thus a feminist analysis would predict a link between violent pornography and sexual violence. Documentation of such linkage is now emerging (Bart, 1985; Diamond, 1980; Malamuth & Donnerstein, 1984). Recent research indicates that repeated exposure to violent pornography amplifies sexist and rape-supportive attitudes in men (not in women). Of great concern is the finding that the most pronounced effects of violent pornography are seen in men who already have highly adversarial and callous attitudes toward women and admit to a high likelihood of committing rape (Malamuth, 1984).

The effect of the outcome of the first assault on further assaults also merits attention. Becker (1985), for example, believes that an addictive pattern is powerfully reinforced when the first assault meets with no adverse consequences. Early victim resistance and public exposure of the attacker may prove to be an important deterrent to the commission of repeated crimes. The goal of such research should be the identification of a group of "early warning signals" and "early intervention strategies" for use in widespread public prevention campaigns.

A final implication of the addiction model concerns the existence of an organized structure for supplying addicts with the objects of their desire. Heroin addicts have their pushers; sexual addicts have their pornographers, pimps, and sex rings. The existence of a national and international traffic in women and children as sexual objects has been well documented by feminist writers both in the past and in the present (Barry, Bunch, & Castley, 1984; Burgess, Groth, & McCausland, 1981; Rush, 1980). At present, the industry of sexual exploitation has both a nominally criminalized component (prostitution, child sex rings, child and hard-core pornography) and a "legitimate" component (soft-core pornography, men's magazines). Both the legal and supposedly illegal components of the industry operate with little social restriction and increasing audacity. The pornography industry, in particular, has significantly increased its portrayal of explicitly violent sexual assault in the past decade (Malamuth & Donnerstein, 1982). Such depictions are also increasingly common in the general mass media and advertising.

An effective strategy for controlling sexual violence thus must include not only a strategy for early identification, control, and treatment of offenders, not only a strategy for preventive education, but also a strategy for engagement with the organized sex industry. The experience of the temperance movement would suggest that abolition of the industry in its entirety is a goal that must await completion of a feminist revolution. In a culture where individual liberty is valued far more than social responsibility, some form of the sex and pornography industry is likely to be tolerated (even by puritanical conservatives, and even by liberal feminists), just as other addiction industries which injure the public health are tolerated (tobacco subsidized as well as legalized, alcohol legalized, and narcotics largely under prohibition).

Within the scope of short-term reform strategy, the greatest hope for development of a public regulatory consensus may be found on the issue of sexual violence. The recent attempt legally to redefine pornography as the subordination of women and to seek civil rather than criminal remedies represents an important conceptual advance (MacKinnon & Dworkin, 1984). Direct action and boycott strategies, reminiscent of the "women's crusade" against saloons a century ago, have also proved effective against pornographers and advertisers when their materials include blatant sexual violence (Lederer, 1980; Penrod & Linz, 1984).

To a considerable degree, during the 1980s the feminist movement has succeeded in changing the public view of victims of sexual violence and in mobilizing public support in favor of more active prosecution of sex offenders. The final step in this stage of consciousness-raising involves the development of a new consensus in favor of stricter and more effective regulation of the organized sex industry, with particular focus on curtailing the most extreme and outrageous incitements to sexual violence.

A more long-range goal requires effecting a profound change in the general climate of sexual attitudes and socialization, so that no form of sexually exploitative behavior is excused or tolerated. The feminist movement, which in the last two decades has brought the issue of sexual violence into public consciousness, remains the only social force committed to and capable of bringing about such change. It is possible to envision a society whose practices in this regard are exactly the opposite of our own: one which freely permits children to learn safely about sex but which firmly and consistently proscribes any form of sexually exploitative behavior. Such a society should produce few customers for those who traffic in human flesh, few sexual addicts, and few sex offenders.

ACKNOWLEDGMENTS. For critical review of an early draft of this manuscript, thanks to Pauline Bart, Jerry Berndt, Sandra Butler, Phyllis Chesler, Joseph Doherty, David Finkelhor, Jeffrey Masson, Diana Russell, and Maria Sauzier. For sharing of unpublished work, thanks to Judith Becker, John Briere, Jean Goodwin, Mary Koss, and Elizabeth Pleck.

REFERENCES

Abel, G., Becker, J. V., & Skinner, L. (1983). Behavioral approaches to treatment of the violent sex offender. In L. Roth (Ed.), *Clinical treatment of the violent person*. Washington, DC: NIMH Monograph Series.

Abel, G., Rouleau, J., & Cunningham-Rathner, J. (1985). Sexually aggressive behavior. In W. Curran, A. L. McGarry, & S. A. Shah (Eds.), *Forensic psychiatry and psychology: Perspectives and standards for interdisciplinary practice* (pp. 289–313). Philadelphia: F. A. Davis.

Ageton, S. (1983). *Sexual assault among adolescents*. Lexington, MA: Lexington Books.

Barry, K., Bunch, C., & Castley, S. (1984). *International feminism: Networking against female sexual slavery*. New York: International Women's Tribune Centre.

Bart, P. (1983). Why men rape. *Western Sociological Review, 14*, 46–57.

Bart, P. (1985). Pornography: Institutionalizing women-hating and eroticizing dominance and submission for fun and profit. *Justice Quarterly*.

Bart, P., & O'Brien, P. (1985). *Stopping rape: Successful survival strategies*. New York: Pergamon Press.

Becker, J. V. (1985, June). *Behavioral treatment of sex offenders*. Workshop presented at Massachusetts

Department of Mental Health, Conference on Child Sexual Abuse: Comprehensive Approaches to Treatment, Boston, MA.

Becker, J., & Abel, G. (1984). *Methodological and ethical issues in evaluating and treating adolescent sex offenders.* Washington, DC: NIMH Monograph.

Berlin, G. (1983). Sex offenders: A biomedical perspective and a status report on biomedical treatment. In J. G. Greer & I. R. Stuart (Eds.), *The sexual aggressor* (pp. 83–123). New York: Van Nostrand Reinhold.

Briere, J., Corne, S., Runtz, M., & Malamuth, N. (1984, August). *The Rape Arousal Inventory: Predicting actual and potential sexual aggression in a university population.* Paper presented at the 99th Annual Meeting of the American Psychological Association.

Brownmiller, S. (1975). *Against our will: Men, women, and rape.* New York: Simon & Schuster.

Burgess, A., Groth, A. N., & McCausland, M. (1981). Child sex initiation rings. *American Journal of Orthopsychiatry, 51,* 110–119.

Burt, M. (1980). Cultural myths and support for rape. *Journal of Personality and Social Psychology, 38,* 217–230.

Carnes, P. (1983). *The sexual addiction.* Minneapolis, MN: CompCare.

Connell, N., & Wilson, C. (1974). *Rape: The first sourcebook for women.* New York: New American Library.

Diamond, I. (1980). Pornography and repression: A reconsideration. In C. Stimson & E. Person (Eds.), *Women: Sex and Sexuality* (pp. 129–144). Chicago: University of Chicago Press.

Dworkin, A. (1981). *Pornography: Men possessing women.* New York: Perigee.

Earls, C. M., & Marshall, W. (1983). The current state of technology in the laboratory assessment of sexual arousal patterns. In J. G. Greer & I. R. Stuart (Eds.), *The sexual aggressor: Current perspectives on treatment* (pp. 336–362). New York: Van Nostrand Reinhold.

Finkelhor, D. (1979). *Sexually victimized children.* New York: Free Press.

Finkelhor, D., & Lewis, I. A. (1987, January). *An epidemiologic approach to the study of child molestation.* Paper presented to the New York Academy of Sciences Meeting on Human Sexual Aggression, New York.

Gebhard, P., Gagnon, J., Pomeroy, W., & Christenson, C. (1965). *Sex offenders: An analysis of types.* New York: Harper & Row.

Giarretto, H. (1982). *Integrated treatment of child sexual abuse.* Palo Alto, CA: Science and Behavior Books.

Goodchilds, J., & Zellman, G. (1984). Sexual signaling and sexual aggression in adolescent relationships. In N. Malamuth & E. Donnerstein (Eds.), *Pornography and sexual aggression* (pp. 233–243). New York: Academic Press.

Griffin, S. (1971). Rape, the all-American crime. *Ramparts, 10,* 26–35.

Groth, A. N. (1979). *Men who rape.* New York: Plenum.

Groth, A. N., & Hobson, W. F. (1983). The dynamics of sexual assault. In L. B. Schlesinger & E. Revitch (Eds.), *Sexual dynamics of anti-social behavior* (pp. 160–172). Springfield, IL: Charles C. Thomas.

Groth, A. N., Hobson, W. F., & Gary, T. S. (1982). The child molester: Clinical observations. In J. Conte & D. Shore (Eds.), *Social work and child sexual abuse* (pp. 129–142). New York: Haworth.

Groth, A. N., Longo, R. E., & McFadin, J. D. (1982). Undetected recidivism among rapists and child molesters. *Crime and Delinquency,* 102–106.

Henn, F. A. (1978). The aggressive sexual offender. In I. L. Kutash, S. B. Kutash, & L. B. Schlesinger (Eds.), *Violence: Perspectives on murder and aggression.* San Francisco: Jossey-Bass.

Herman, J. L. (1981). *Father–daughter incest.* Cambridge, MA: Harvard University Press.

Justice, B., & Justice, R. (1979). *The broken taboo.* New York: Human Sciences Press.

Karacon, I., Williams, R. L., Guerraro, M. W., Salis, P. J., Thornby, J. I., & Hursch, C. J. (1974). Nocturnal penile tumescence and sleep of convicted rapists and other prisoners. *Archives of Sexual Behavior, 31,* 19–26.

Kaufman, J., & Zigler, E. (1987). Do abused children become abusive parents? *American Journal of Orthopsychiatry, 57,* 186–192.

Knight, R., Rosenberg, R., & Schneider, B. (1985). Classification of sex offenders: Perspectives, methods, and validation. In A. W. Burgess (Ed.), *Rape and sexual assault: A research handbook* (pp. 223–293). New York: Garland.

Knopp, F. H. (1984). *Retraining adult sex offenders: Methods and models.* Syracuse, NY: Safer Society Press.

Koss, M., Gidycz, C., & Wisniewski, N. (1987). The scope of rape: Incidence and prevalence of sexual aggression in a national sample of higher education students. *Journal of Consulting and Clinical Psychology, 55,* 162–170.

Lederer, L. (1980). *Take back the night: Women on pornography.* New York: Morrow.

MacKinnon, C. (1983). Feminism, marxism, method, and the state: Toward feminist jurisprudence. *Signs: Journal of Women in Culture and Society, 8,* 635–658.

MacKinnon, C., & Dworkin, A. (1984). City Council General Ordinance #35, Indianapolis, Indiana.

Malamuth, N. (1981). Rape proclivity among males. *Journal of Social Issues, 37,* 138–157.

Malamuth, N. (1984). Aggression against women: Cultural and individual causes. In N. Malamuth & E. Donnerstein (Eds.), *Pornography and sexual aggression* (pp. 19–52). New York: Academic Press.

Malamuth, N., & Donnerstein, E. (1982). The effects of aggressive-pornographic mass media stimuli. In L. Berkowitz (Ed.), *Advances in experimental social psychology* (vol. 15). New York: Academic Press.

Malamuth, N., & Donnerstein, E. (1984). *Pornography and sexual aggression.* New York: Academic Press.

Millett, K. (1970). *Sexual politics.* New York: Doubleday.

Pagelow, M. (1984). *Family violence.* New York: Praeger.

Penrod, S., & Linz, D. (1984). Using psychological research on violent pornography to inform legal change. In N. Malamuth & E. Donnerstein (Eds.), *Pornography and sexual aggression* (pp. 247–275). New York: Academic Press.

Pithers, W., Marques, J., Gibat, C., & Marlatt, G. A. (1983). Relapse prevention with sexual aggressives: A self-control model of treatment and maintenance of change. In J. G. Greer & I. R. Stuart (Eds.), *The sexual aggressor: Current perspectives on treatment* (pp. 214–239). New York: Van Nostrand Reinhold.

Quinsey, V., & Marshall, W. (1983). Procedures for reducing inappropriate sexual arousal: An evaluation review. In J. G. Greer & I. R. Stuart (Eds.), *The sexual aggressor: Current perspectives on treatment* (pp. 267–289). New York: Van Nostrand Reinhold.

Rada, R., Kellner, R., Laws, D. R., & Winslow, W. (1978). Drinking, alcoholism, and the mentally disordered sex offender. *Bulletin of the American Academy of Psychiatry and Law, 6,* 296–300.

Rapaport, K. & Burkhart, B. R. (1984). Personality and attitudinal characteristics of sexually coercive college males. *Journal of Abnormal Psychology, 93,* 216–221.

Ressler, R., Burgess, A., & Douglas, J. (1983). Rape and rape-murder: One offender and twelve victims. *American Journal of Psychiatry, 140,* 36–40.

Rush, R. (1980). *The best-kept secret: Sexual abuse of children.* Englewood Cliffs, NJ: Prentice-Hall.

Russell, D. E. H. (1984). *Sexual exploitation: Rape, child sexual abuse, and sexual harassment.* Beverly Hills, CA: Sage.

Sanday, P. (1981). *Female power and male dominance: On the origins of sexual inequality.* London: Cambridge University Press.

Schwartz, M., & Masters, W. (1985). Treatment of paraphiliacs, pedophiles, and incest families. In A. W. Burgess (Ed.), *Rape and sexual assault: A research handbook* (pp. 350–364). New York: Garland.

Scully, D., & Marolla, J. (1984). Convicted rapists' vocabulary of motive. *Social Problems, 31,* 530–544.

Scully, D., & Marolla, J. (1985). *Riding the bull at Gilley's: Convicted rapists describe the pleasures of raping.* Unpublished manuscript, Dept. of Sociology/Anthropology, Virginia Commonwealth University, Richmond, VA.

Seghorn, T., Boucher, R., & Cohen, M. (1983, September). *Sexual abuse in the life histories of sexual offenders: A retrospective longitudinal analysis.* Paper presented at the 6th World Congress for Sexology, Washington, DC.

Smithyman, S. D. (1978). *The undetected rapist.* Unpublished doctoral dissertation, Claremont Graduate School.

U. S. Department of Justice, Federal Bureau of Investigation. (1981). *Uniform crime reports (1977–1980)*. Washington, DC: U.S. Government Printing Office.

Vaillant, G. (1983). *The natural history of alcoholism: Causes, patterns, and paths to recovery*. Cambridge, MA: Harvard University Press.

12

Courtship Disorder

KURT FREUND

INTRODUCTION

The courtship disorder hypothesis holds that various anomalous erotic preferences can be seen as expressions of a common "underlying" disorder. In other
words, that in the network of causes of these anomalous preferences there exists
a specific part which they have in common. In calling the hypothesized underlying disturbance a *courtship disorder*, the present writer adopted the terminology
of students of the behavior of birds, who use this term for all precopulatory
reproductive activities (Morris, 1970). But the idea of a disturbance in the realm
of courtship behavior was already put forward by Ellis (1933/1978), when he
called exhibitionism a "symbolic act based on a perversion of courtship" (p.
190). The main putative expressions of a courtship disorder are voyeurism,
exhibitionism, toucheurism or frotteurism, and the preferential rape pattern. For
each of these anomalous erotic preferences a typical behavior pattern exists. In
an earlier paper (Freund & Kolarsky, 1965), a simple reference system was
proposed for the description of human erotic or sexual interaction, which differentiates between roughly four phases: (1) location and first appraisal of a suitable partner, (2) pretactile interaction, consisting mainly in looking, smiling,
posturing, and talking to a prospective partner, (3) tactile interaction, and (4)
effecting genital union (in the following the terms *erotic* or *sexual* will be used as
synonyms). This is only a rough scheme; in real sexual interaction there is often
a reversal of phases. For instance, pretactile interaction is usually reintroduced
after tactile interaction or intercourse; sometimes weeks or months can pass
between the various phases, and more often than not interaction stops before
reaching genital union.

In the anomalous patterns in question, one or another of the four phases of
this progression is extremely intensified and distorted and may therefore be

KURT FREUND • Department of Psychiatry, University of Toronto, and Department of Behavioral
Sexology, Clarke Institute of Psychiatry, Toronto, Ontario, M5T 1R8, Canada.

seen as a caricature of the normal, whereas the remaining phases are either entirely omitted or are retained only in a vestigial way. The anomalous pattern appears to be a rigidified and stylized (Morris, 1957, 1966) pathological shortcut of the richer, more flexible normal pattern. From this point of view (1) voyeurism can be seen as an exaggeration and distortion of the first phase of normal sexual interaction—the phase of location and first appraisal of a potential erotic partner; (2) exhibitionism, as a distortion of normal pretactile interaction; (3) toucheurism–frotteurism, as a distortion of the phase of normal tactile interaction; and (4) the preferential rape pattern, stripped of almost all precopulatory activity, as a distortion of normal genital union (see Table 1). All these putative expressions of a courtship disorder are characterized by a concomitant preference for strangers as the target persons toward whom these activities are directed.

Under the supposition that virtually everybody has a hierarchy of erotic preferences, voyeurism can be defined as an unusually high ranking of the act of observing a person in an erotic context. Based on patients' self-reports, it can also be defined as an overwhelming desire to observe a person of the preferred gender and age in some stage of undress, having intercourse, in the act of excretion, or in similar intimate or very private situations. An auditory analogue of voyeurism also exists. We may call it obscene telephone listening: telephone numbers are available which allow the caller to hear, for a fee, a woman's voice on a tape telling the customer that she is masturbating and describing her feelings during masturbation and intercourse. Some teenagers use this service for masturbation, as a surrogate to intercourse, but some voyeurs obviously prefer obscene listening to normal intercourse. The present writer saw a patient who began having difficulties with his wife because their telephone bills became too high as a result of the frequency with which he used these services.

At this point two related erotic anomalies have to be mentioned which differ from voyeurism proper in that the target person is not a stranger but is the patient's wife or ladyfriend. We cannot as yet even guess whether these anomalies are an expression of or are connected with a courtship disorder. The first of these anomalies, which is usually called troilism or Candaulism (the latter after a figure in ancient Greek history afflicted with this anomaly), is characterized by a man's erotic preference for witnessing, either by viewing or by listening, his partner having intercourse with another man. The second anomaly is characterized by a man's desire to have his erotic partner disrobe partially or fully

TABLE 1. Normal versus Distorted Phases
of Sexual Interaction

Normal phase	Distorted phase
Partner location	Voyeurism
Pretactile interaction	Exhibitionism
Tactile interaction	Toucheurism, frotteurism
Effecting genital union	Preferential rape pattern

where other males could see her. In troilism the target person appears to be still performing for the patient only, whereas in this "partner-showing," she is performing for males at large.

The woman is usually quite distressed by her partner making such demands. Whether this distress is part of the patient's reward situation, that is, whether these patients are (mildly) sadistic, is not clear as yet. In these anomalies the patient's partner appears to be the target person, and the male participants play only an instrumental role. Homosexual motivation (Smith, 1976) does not appear to be involved. These patients get very jealous if a relationship develops between their partner and such a male "pseudopartner," or if she really turns out to be promiscuous (the present writer observed this in a few such cases). According to Yalom (1960), "clear-cut female or homosexual voyeurs . . . are not seen."

Exhibitionism is characterized by an overwhelming desire to expose one's genitals or, less frequently, other parts of the body from a distance to a member of the preferred gender, and, according to Mohr, Turner, and Jerry (1964), taking the onlooker by surprise. Theophrastus described the pattern of exhibitionism as early as the fourth century B.C. (Stevenson & Jones, 1972), and it was first recognized by Lasègue (1877) as a symptom of a pathological condition. According to this writer's clinical experience, androphilic males—that is, males who erotically prefer physically mature male partners—relatively often expose their penis to strangers in washrooms or parks, as an invitation to sexual interaction. These are mostly men who want to remain anonymous—they live as heterosexuals and are often married. It seems, however, that there are few, if any, cases of exhibitionism proper among androphilic males. In homosexual males who prefer minors as sexual partners, on the other hand, true exhibitionism appears to be less rare. It is, however, difficult to differentiate solely on the basis of a clinical interview and a sexual history between homosexual males who expose mainly to initiate other sexual interaction and those for whom exposing itself has an abnormally high erotic value.

Women who expose to men as male exhibitionists expose to women are so rare that every case which comes to an expert's attention is published. A number of such cases have been described of psychotic, mentally retarded, or mentally borderline women. The majority of these case reports are quoted in Cabanis (1972), who described a case of exhibitionism in a mentally retarded girl. Only three cases have been reported in which exhibitionism occurred in a woman who was neither psychotic nor mentally defective. According to Gayford (1981), one such case was described by Herman and Schroeder (1935), but even in this case the anomaly was associated "with a long history of delinquency including theft and fire raising." To this writer's knowledge there are only two published cases of exhibitionism in women who do not seem to have suffered from general mental disorganization to a greater extent than the majority of male exhibitionists.

One of these two cases was reported by Hollender, Brown, and Roback (1977). This patient, "wearing only a raincoat, would stand in a doorway near the club where she worked, and 'flash' (i.e., exhibit her breasts and genitals)

before men she had seen or met previously" (p. 437). The other case was reported by Grob (1985). This woman drove, mostly at night, alongside trucks,
disrobing from an easily removable garment, "experiencing tremendous arousal
and excitement." (A third case of exposing by a woman who was neither psychotic nor mentally handicapped was reported by Zavitzianos [1971].) According to the author there were no witnesses, the alleged exposing occurred only
once—after one of her many psychoanalytic sessions—and according to Zavitzianos, she was a pathological liar.)

Toucheurism and frotteurism are characterized by a subject's unusually
strong desire to touch an unknown woman intimately or to press his penis
against her body. A female counterpart which would consist of the same pattern
has not as yet been described.

Rape can be defined as penile penetration of a nonconsenting victim's vagina, anus, or mouth, with no or almost no preceding erotic interaction, or an
erotic preference for having a nonconsenting person perform fellatio. Numerous
typologies of persons who commit rape exist. The most recent comprehensive
discussions and reviews of research in this area are by Prentky, Cohen, and
Seghorn (1985) and Quinsey (1984). In the present context rape-proneness is of
interest only if it is an expression of an erotic preference for raping as opposed to
intercourse with a consenting partner. Persons for whom raping is less preferred
than intercourse with mutual consent, that is, for whom raping is only a surrogate, are of little interest for the present discussion.

To date only two types of rape-proneness are known in which rape is
preferred to normal intercourse: sadistic rape-proneness and the preferential
rape pattern. In cases of sadistic rape, the act of raping by itself often appears to
be only a by-product of causing fear or pain or of harming the victim. In the
present context, mainly the preferential rape pattern is of interest. While it
implies the use of force or threat like any other type of rape, these features
appear to be only accessory and most probably purely instrumental.

The following two vignettes should illustrate the preferential rape pattern:
(1) A young man who had an attractive wife, after having had intercourse with
her in the evening, got up at night from their bed, dressed, went out of the
apartment building where they lived, and raped an old woman in a parking lot;
(2) a well-educated, well-built, and good-looking businessman used to go out at
night and rape female strangers, whom he dragged into the lanes between
houses. When one of his victims said she would gladly have intercourse with
him if he would accompany her to her apartment, he said no, it must be here
and now, and then he raped her.

The preferential rapist virtually always chooses a woman who is a stranger
or almost a stranger as his victim. Snare (1984) quotes a Swedish study which
differentiates between two polar extremes, a stranger pattern and a partner
pattern. Not all those who demonstrate the stranger pattern are preferential
rapists. There are sadists among them as well, although, on the other hand,
there are sadists who harm or batter their spouses in connection with intercourse. Men who rape in the course of a burglary are relatively often afflicted
with the preferential rape pattern and are less often sadistic rapists, but it seems

unlikely that all burglars who rape after breaking in are afflicted with an anomalous erotic preference.

There may be a female counterpart to this pattern; however, it may not be
exactly analogous to the erotic anomaly occurring in males. The same may apply
to courtship disorders in general. Such a disturbance may manifest itself as a
preference for sexual interaction with unknown males, but this problem should
be better left to research by female sexologists.

Co-Occurrence of the Different Expressions of Courtship Disorder

The association of some of the putative expressions of a courtship disorder
was noted long ago. Freud (1905/1925) proposed that there is a connection
between exhibitionism and voyeurism. He did so in the context of his hypothesis that exhibitionists expect the target person to show her genital region in
return. Yalom (1960) described cases of co-occurrence of voyeurism, exhibitionism, and rape. Cabanis (1966) and Rooth (1973) reported the co-occurrence
of exhibitionism, toucheurism, and frotteurism. Gebhard, Pomeroy, Gagnon,
and Christenson (1965) reported an association of voyeurism and exhibitionism
and estimated that approximately 10% of exhibitionists may commit rape.
Grassberger (1964) found that 12% of men convicted for exhibitionism later
committed rape. It has also been noted that a relatively large proportion of
exhibitionists had been voyeuristically active earlier, often much earlier, than the
time exposing started (Freund, 1969; Rooth, 1973; Smukler & Schiebel, 1975).
Lang, Checkley, Langevin, and Pugh (1987; Langevin & Lang, 1987) suggest,
however, that exposing and voyeuristic activity are common among sexually
anomalous patients in general.

The present writer investigated the co-occurrence of the various putative
expressions of a courtship disorder in a group of 440 patients (*M* age = 28.1
years, *SD* = 8.1 years, mode of education > 8 grades but < 12) seen at the
sexology department of a psychiatric teaching hospital for having demonstrated
one of these expressions. The anomalous behaviors in question, however, do
not have an equal likelihood of coming to the attention of the public. It is likely,
for instance, that many more exhibitionists than voyeurs are caught and that the
diagnosis of voyeurism had to be based more often only on the patient's admission. This probably distorted the relative proportions in Table 2 by diminishing
the respective co-occurrence rate, and thereby introduced a bias against the
proposed hypothesis.

The criterion for classifying a patient as a voyeur, exhibitionist, toucheur,
frotteur, or as rape-prone was an admission to, an accusation of, or a charge for,
such an act. These classifications were not mutually exclusive. While inclusion of
the patient's own admission in the diagnosis increased available information, we
have to be aware of the fact that sex offenders usually try to conceal their
anomalous activities and fantasies because they are afraid of punishment, harsh

treatment, or ostracism. We have to expect that, in particular, harshly punishable activities or propensities to carry out such activities will be underreported. Many patients who freely admit to exhibitionism are nonetheless reluctant to admit to having raped.

The preferential rape pattern did not figure in this classification on its own because it is often particularly difficult to differentiate this pattern from other types of rape-proneness on the basis of a patient's self-report and the usually available bits of information from other sources. Instead all patients seen at the above-mentioned sexology department within the specified period who had raped or had attempted rape were included in the investigated group. On the other hand, the present writer did not adhere to the diagnostic criterion of DSM-III-R (American Psychiatric Association, 1987) that for making a diagnosis of an anomalous erotic preference the subject must have indicated that recurrent sexual urges of this kind or sexual fantasies about these anomalous activities had been present over a period of at least 6 months. This condition would have excluded all those who claimed that their anomalous activities occurred for the first time when they were caught, without their having any fantasies or urges of this kind before or after. It is most likely that these patients were just lying and would be the last to admit to any accompanying anomalous activity (which would further decrease the apparent rates of co-occurrence). However, they were not excluded, because it was felt that selection criteria should be kept to a minimum in order to avoid some uncontrolled artificial selection from being introduced.

There are exhibitionists who expose only to children, or to children and early adolescents, but not to physically mature females. They were not included in the following comparisons. They may be afflicted with two disturbances, exhibitionism and pedophilia, or they may just be pedophiles for whom exposing is a way of initiating further erotic interaction with the child and is not a substitute. The latter appears to be mostly the case, because quite often they have the child touch their penis or sometimes even perform fellatio.

The results of the assessment of co-occurrence of the different putative expressions of a courtship disorder with each other and with two other erotic anomalies in the subject group described above are presented in Table 2.

The first 4 columns of this table show the degree of co-occurrence of the putative expressions of a courtship disorder. The percentages are the proportions of the patients afflicted with the anomaly indicated by the row heading who are also afflicted with the anomaly indicated by the column heading. The numbers below the percentages indicate the actual number of such patients. The fifth column of Table 2 shows the proportion of patients with the putative expression of a courtship disorder indicated by the row heading who were also afflicted with any other of the putative expressions of a courtship disorder, rapists included.

The sixth and seventh columns show analogous comparisons of the different expressions of a courtship disorder with transvestism and sadism. The definitions of these erotic anomalies as well as the reason for including them in the comparison will be given below.

TABLE 2. Mutual Co-Occurrence of Expressions of Courtship Disorder

	V	E	T/F	R	O	TV	S
V (N=94)							
%	—	81.9	38.3	19.1	90.4	9.6	4.3
No.	—	77	36	18	85	9	4
E (N=241)							
%	32.0	—	30.3	15.4	56.4	6.6	5.8
No.	77	—	73	37	136	16	14
T/F (N=119)							
%	30.2	61.3	—	21.8	76.5	10.9	9.2
No.	36	73	—	26	91	13	11
R (N=195)							
%	9.2	19.0	13.3	—	27.7	3.1	15.9
No.	18	37	26	—	6	6	31

Note. V, voyeurism; E, exhibitionism; T/F, toucheurism/frotteurism; R, rape; O, any other putative expression of a courtship disorder; TV, transvestism; S, sadism; N = total number per row; No., number per cell.

Table 2 shows close relationships between the different putative expressions of a courtship disorder, with the exception of the connection with rape. This, however, was to be expected for two reasons: (1) as already mentioned, it is highly probable that only a relatively low proportion of rape cases are due to the preferential rape pattern and (2) under the (earlier described) demand situation obviously prevailing in the present study, rape or attempted rape is probably the last thing a courtship disorder patient would admit to, if not directly caught for it or identified as the perpetrator. Comparable assessments, carried out in the USA, under a different demand situation for the patients, appear to confirm this second reason. They will be reported below. First, however, the overall pattern of the results of this comparable study will be discussed.

In 1986 Abel and coworkers (Abel, Becker, Cunningham-Rathner, Mittelman, & Rouleau, 1988) presented a paper on the co-occurrence of anomalous erotic preferences in general. While these authors' selection criteria as well as the situation in which the patients were interviewed differed from those in the present study, a comparison in respect to co-occurrence of the putative expressions of a courtship disorder is still informative.

The diagnostic procedure of Abel and his coworkers diverged from DSM-III-R (American Psychiatric Association, 1987) in a similar way as that used in the present study by not excluding subjects who denied that the anomaly in question had been there for at least 6 months; however, there were still large differences in design between the two studies. In contrast to the present study, (1) the investigation of Abel and his coworkers did not exclude exhibitionists who directed their anomalous activities only toward children; (2) they included only those who admitted to recurrent repetitive urges to carry out the erotically anomalous behavior; (3) target persons of age 12 to 14 were still classified as children and not as early adolescents; and (4) Abel *et al.* had federal government

permission to treat their patients as research subjects by keeping verbal commu-
nications as well as nonverbal test results anonymous (i.e., totally confidential,
which was thoroughly explained to these patients). This was in sharp contrast to
the demand situation for the subjects prevailing in the present study, in which
the patients were aware that the outcome of the clinical interview and the test
results were to be reported to their physicians, who assessed them for the courts
or for their lawyers or who treated them. Table 3 shows the pertinent results of
Abel and coworkers (1987). The categorization is similar to that of Table 2.

While there were the above-mentioned differences between the two studies
in respect to design, both studies show relatively high rates of co-occurrence of
the different putative expressions of a courtship disorder. In general the rates of
co-occurrence in the study by Abel and coworkers were somewhat lower than in
the present study. This may be explained by the differences in subject selection
specified above.

There are, however, two discrepancies between the otherwise similar patterns of outcome of the two studies. One is the difference in respect to co-
occurrence of the putative expressions of a courtship disorder with rape or
attempted rape. For instance, in the present study only 14.9% of exhibitionists
admitted to having raped or attempted rape, whereas of the 142 exhibitionists in
the study by Abel and coworkers, 25% admitted to this anomalous behavior. This
is most likely due to the above-described difference in the demand situation.

The other discrepancy between the two studies is the much lower rate of co-
occurrence of toucheurism–frotteurism with the remaining putative expressions
of a courtship disorder in the study by Abel and coworkers than that in the
present study. For instance, only 16% of the exhibitionists in the study by Abel
and coworkers were also toucheurs, whereas in the present study the proportion
of exhibitionists who were also toucheurs was 30.3%. This discrepancy appears to

TABLE 3. Proportions as Reported by Abel et al. (1988)

	V	E	T/F	R	TV	S
V (N=62)						
%	—	63	23	37	5	11
No.	—	39	14	23	3	7
E (N=142)						
%	28	—	16	25	8	4
No.	39	—	23	35	11	6
T/F (N=62)						
%	23	37	—	23	2	11
No.	14	23	—	14	1	7
R (N=126)						
%	18	28	11	—	5	10
No.	23	35	14	—	6	13

Note. Abbreviations as in Table 1.

be explained by the fact that at the time when the two studies were conducted, the general diagnostic standard was DSM-III (American Psychiatric Association, 1980), in which frotteurism was lumped together with other anomalies under "atypical paraphilias," and toucheuristic activity was not even mentioned. This may in some instances have practically left this anomaly undiagnosed. The present study departed from DSM-III in regard to toucheurism–frotteurism. There is no mention in the study by Abel and coworkers that their diagnostic procedure may also have diverged in this respect from the diagnostic standard.

The putative expressions of a courtship disorder all appear to be characterized by a widening of the age bracket of target persons. Not too rarely, patients who were charged for exposing to adults were also charged for exposing to children or admitted to it. The proportions of patients with the different putative expressions of a courtship disorder whose target persons were adults as well as minors, or only early adolescents, were also assessed (Table 4). The column headings of Table 4 show the level of physical development of target persons: P denotes early adolescents ("pubescents") of ages 12 to 15; P + A denotes pubescents and physically mature females ("adults"); C + A or C + P + A denotes children under 12 and adults or children and pubescents and adults. The row headings show the various putative expressions of a courtship disorder as well as transvestism and sadism. The proportions in the different cells are to be read like those in Tables 2 and 3.

TABLE 4. Age of Target Persons

Offender	P	P+A	C+A or C+P+A	A
V (N=94)				
%	4.3	17.0	25.5	53.2
No.	4	16	24	50
E (N=241)				
%	3.7	12.9	27.0	56.4
No.	9	31	65	136
T/F (N=119)				
%	3.4	15.1	19.3	62.2
No.	4	18	23	74
R (N=195)				
%	6.2	10.8	9.2	73.8
No.	12	21	18	144
TV (N=24)				
%	0	8.3	16.7	75.0
No.	0	2	4	18
S (N=46)				
%	2.2	8.7	2.2	87.0
No.	1	4	1	40

Note. P, pubescent; A, adult; C, child; other abbreviations as in Table 1.

According to Table 4 there is a very small proportion of patients with a putative expression of a courtship disorder whose target persons are only early adolescents (P). One-quarter of courtship disorder patients, however, may have among their target persons early adolescents and children as well as adults. This appears to support the clinical impression that a substantial proportion of patients with a putative expression of a courtship disorder have a wider age range of target persons than is usual for males who do not suffer from such a disorder. (According to the present writer's clinical impression, there is a similar widening of the age bracket of preferred target persons in sadism.)

CO-OCCURRENCE WITH OTHER ANOMALOUS EROTIC PREFERENCES

Transvestism was included in these comparisons because of recent reports (Lang et al., 1987; Langevin & Lang, 1987) according to which its connection with exhibitionism was found to be as close as the connection between exhibitionism and any of the other putative expressions of a courtship disorder. Sadism was included because there are authors who believe that some of the putative expressions of a courtship disorder are sadistically motivated, and because sadism appears to be similar to these anomalies in respect to a preference for strange target persons and a widening of their age range, although the former attribute is not as strongly expressed in sadism as in courtship disorder.

For the purpose of the present study, we broadened the definition of transvestism so that it not subsumes two diagnostic categories of DSM-III-R: adolescent or adult gender identity disorder and transvestic fetishism. This was possible because the study was only about heterosexual males. For sadism we used Krafft-Ebing's (1886/1978) original definition: Sadism is the experience of sexually pleasurable sensations (including orgasm) produced by acts of cruelty or bodily punishment inflicted on one's own person or when witnessed in others, be they animals or human beings. It may also consist of an innate desire to humiliate, hurt, wound, or even destroy others in order to create sexual pleasure in oneself.

It is not easy to assess cases of co-occurrence of voyeurism with transvestism or sadism. In transvestism, "prowling by night" may be motivated by the desire to go out in female attire without being identified, and the patient may even show himself to people in windows. In sadism such prowling and looking into windows may be part of the sadistic patient's search for a victim. Yalom (1960) believes that voyeurism is an expression of sadism. He documented this contention with seven voyeuristic cases. Patient 1 attempted rape. Patient 2 set fire to the homes of eight women where he had either been unsuccessful in his voyeuristic efforts or had entered and, in the patient's words, "chickened out." Patients 3 and 4 became chronic burglars, and patient 4 also exposed. Patient 5, a voyeur and chronic burglar, set two business offices on fire and remained to watch. Patient 6 described his voyeuristic practices as a "safari" and his target persons as "prey" and said that by his peeping, he was punishing women for their carelessness in allowing themselves to be seen. Patient 7 was a 15-year-old voyeur who filled a sock with pebbles and hit a friend's mother over the head, "intending to knock her unconscious so that he could look at and feel her breasts. Four weeks earlier he had reached through an automobile window and grabbed a strange woman's breast" (Yalom, 1960, p. 316).

Nacke, according to Ellis (1933/1978), believed that exposing was an expression of sadism, and that the exhibitionist's goal was to induce terror in the target person. Ellis did not agree. The present writer recently saw a patient who was afflicted with dangerous sadism and also exposed. When this man was in his late teens he murdered a girl whom he had not known before, in a sexual content, by multiple stabbings. He then spent 12 years in penitentiary. After being released on parole he was caught exposing.

According to the proportions of co-occurrence of the putative expressions of a courtship disorder with transvestism and sadism shown in Tables 2 and 3, there may well be a connection of exhibitionism and possibly of courtship disorder in general with these two anomalies, but these connections appear to be much looser than the ones between the putative expressions of a courtship disorder themselves. The problem of hierarchies of anomalous preferences will have to be approached by discriminant analysis. This is planned for the near future. Such an analysis, however, can only support or falsify specific hypotheses regarding hierarchies of connections of anomalies in a particular population. This means that beforehand the validity of these hypotheses has to be thoroughly investigated. The present study is part of this investigation.

CONCLUSIONS

The courtship disorder hypothesis is based on the observation of the same deviation from a schematized pattern of human sexual interaction in a number of anomalous erotic activities. On the basis of this hypothesis, the prediction was made that a substantial amount of within-subject co-occurrence of these anomalies would be found. This prediction was supported in studies reported earlier (Freund & Blanchard, 1986, Freund, Scher, & Hucker, 1983).

This prediction was further supported by the outcome of studies using the measurement of penile volume changes to auditory descriptions of encounters with a target person typical for the anomalous behaviors in question (Freund *et al.*, 1983, 1984). The results showed that patients who suffered from one of the putative expressions of a courtship disorder other than voyeurism, and who denied voyeuristic activity, nonetheless responded more to narratives describing voyeuristic situations than did controls, and that exhibitionists who denied toucheuristic activity responded more to toucheuristic stimuli than did controls.

The prediction in question, however, cannot be qualified as having been completely unexpected prior to the proposed hypothesis. While the present writer cannot remember having noted this co-occurrence prior to his systematic search for mutual associations between the putative expressions of the disorder after having proposed the hypothesis, there were the earlier mentioned authors who had observed some such associations, and the writer himself may have felt, prior to proposing the hypothesis, that there was such an association, without consciously formulating it. The prediction which, if borne out, would render much stronger support for the courtship disorder hypothesis is the conjecture mentioned at the beginning of this chapter, namely, that in the network of causes of anomalous erotic preferences, there is a part, specific to the putative expressions of this disorder, which is shared by them. This prediction could provide direction to a search for the causes of the putative expressions of a courtship disorder.

ACKNOWLEDGMENTS. This study was supported by Grant No. 975-87-89 of the Ontario Mental Health Foundation. Thanks are due to Mrs. Cathy Spegg (Computer Services Department, Clarke Institute of Psychiatry) for her very valuable cooperation, and to Mr. Doug Rienzo for correcting the manuscript in respect to grammar and style.

REFERENCES

Abel, G. G., Becker, J. V., Cunningham-Rathner, J., Mittelman, M., & Rouleau, J.-L. (1988). Multiple paraphilic diagnoses among sex offenders. *Bulletin of the Academy of Psychiatry and the Law, 16,* 153–168.
American Psychiatric Association. (1980). *Diagnostic and statistical manual of mental disorders* (3rd ed.). Washington, DC: Author.
American Psychiatric Association. (1987). *Diagnostic and statistical manual of mental disorders* (3rd ed., revised). Washington, DC: Author.
Cabanis, D. (1966). *Medizinisch-kriminologische Untersuchung Übes Exhibitionismus.* Unpublished habilitationsschrift, University of West Berlin.
Cabanis, D. (1972). Weiblicher exhibismus [Female exhibitionism]. *Z. Rechtsmedizin, 71,* 126–133.
Ellis, H. (1978). *Psychology of sex.* New York/London: Harcourt Brace Jovanovich. (Original work published 1933)
Freud, S. (1925). *Drei abhandlungen zur sexualtheorie* [Three essays on the theory of sexuality]. Leipzig/Wein: Psychoanalytischer Verlag. (Original work published 1905)
Freud, K. (1969). *Homosexualität* [Homosexuality]. Hamburg, Germany: Rowohlt.
Freund, K., & Blanchard, R. (1986). The concept of courtship disorder. *Journal of Sex & Marital Therapy, 12,* 79–92.
Freund, K., & Kolářský, A. (1965). Grundzüge eines einfachen bezugsystems für die analyse sexueller deviationen [Basic features of a reference system for considering anomalous erotic preferences]. *Psychiatrie, neurologie und medizinische Psychologie, 17,* 221–225.
Freund, K., Scher, H., & Hucker, S. (1983). The courtship disorders. *Archives of Sexual Behavior, 12,* 369–379.
Freund, K., Scher, H., & Hucker, S. (1984). The courtship disorders: A further investigation. *Archives of Sexual Behavior, 13,* 133–139.
Gayford, J. J. (1981). Indecent exposure: A review of the literature. *Medicine, Science and the Law, 21,* 233–242.
Gebhard, P. H., Gagnon, J. H., Pomeroy, W. H., & Christenson, C. V. (1965). *Sex offenders.* New York: Harper & Row.
Grassberger, R. (1964). Der exhibitionismus [Exhibitionism]. *Kriminalistik in Österreich, 18,* 557–562.
Grob, C. S. (1985). Single case study: Female exhibitionism. *Journal of Nervous and Mental Disease, 173,* 253–256.
Hermann, K., & Schroder, G. E. (1936). Un cas d'exhibitionisme chez une femme [A case of exhibitionism in a woman]. *Acta Psychiatrica et Neurologica Scandinavica, 10,* 547–564.

Hollender, M. H., Brown, C. W., & Roback, H. B. (1977). Genital exhibitionism in women. *American Journal of Psychiatry, 134,* 436–438.

Krafft-Ebing, R. (1978). *Psychopathia Sexualis: With especial reference to the antipathic sexual instinct: A medico-forensic study.* New York: Stein and Day. (Original work published 1886)

Lang, R. A., Checkley, K. L., Langevin, R., & Pugh, G. (1987). Genital exhibitionism: Courtship disorder or narcissism? *Canadian Journal of Behavioral Science, 19,* 216–232.

Langevin, R., & Lang, R. A. (1987). The courtship disorders. In G. D. Wilson (Ed.), *Variant sexuality: Research and theory* (pp. 222–228). London: Croom Helm.

Lasègue, C. (1877). Les exhibitionistes [The exhibitionists]. *L'Union Medicale, 23,* (series 3), 5.

Mohr, J. W., Turner, R. E., & Jerry, M. B. (1964). *Pedophilia and exhibitionism.* Toronto: University of Toronto Press.

Morris, D. (1970). 'Typical intensity' and its relationship to the problem of ritualization. In D. Morris (Ed.), *Patterns of reproductive behavior: Collected papers by Desmond Morris* (pp. 187–197). London: Jonathan Cape.

Morris, D. (1970). The rigidification of behavior. In D. Morris (Ed.), *Patterns of reproductive behavior: Collected papers by Desmond Morris* (pp. 512–519). London: Jonathan Cape.

Morris, D. (Ed.) (1970). *Patterns of reproductive behavior: Collected papers by Desmond Morris.* London: Jonathan Cape.

Prentky, R., Cohen, M., & Seghorn, T. (1985). Development of a rational taxonomy for the classification of rapists: The Massachusetts Treatment Center system. *Bulletin of the American Academy of Psychiatry and the Law, 13,* 39–70.

Quinsey, V. L. (1984). Sexual aggression: Studies of offenders against women. In D. Weisstub (Ed.), *Law and mental health: International perspectives* (vol. 1, pp. 84–121). New York: Pergamon Press.

Rooth, G. (1973). Exhibitionism, sexual violence and pedophilia. *British Journal of Psychiatry, 122,* 705–710.

Smith, R. S. (1976). Voyeurism: A review of literature. *Archives of Sexual Behavior, 5,* 585–608.

Smukler, A. J., & Schiebel, D. (1975). Personality characteristics of exhibitionists. *Diseases of the Nervous System, 36,* 600–603.

Snare, A. (1984). Sexual violence against women: A Scandinavian perspective. *Victimology, 9,* 195–210.

Stevenson, J., & Jones, I. H. (1972). Behavior therapy technique for exhibitionism: A preliminary report. *Archives of General Psychiatry, 27,* 839–841.

Yalom, I. D. (1960). Aggression and forbiddenness in voyeurism. *Archives of General Psychiatry, 3,* 305–319.

Zavitzianos, G. (1971). Fetishism and exhibitionism in the female and their relationship to psychopathy and kleptomania. *International Journal of Psycho-Analysis, 52,* 297–305.

13

A Conditioning Theory of the Etiology and Maintenance of Deviant Sexual Preference and Behavior

D. R. Laws and W. L. Marshall

Regarding the etiology of sexual deviance, Quinsey and Marshall (1983) have observed,

> With respect to the concept of inappropriate arousal itself, there are no theories of etiology which have other than laboratory demonstrations of plausibility or anecdotal support. We simply do not know how to account for individual differences in sexual arousal patterns. Clearly, developmental studies of the acquisition of sexual preferences should receive high priority. (p. 30)

Influential studies (Kinsey, Pomeroy, & Martin, 1948; Storms, 1981; Van Wyk & Geist, 1984) have stressed the primacy of conditioning and learning influences on the development of sexual behavior. In the area of sexual deviance there are a handful of what Quinsey and Marshall (1983) call "laboratory demonstrations" of the role of classical conditioning (e.g., Beech, Watts, & Poole, 1971; Langevin & Martin, 1975; Rachman, 1966; Rachman & Hodgson, 1968) or operant conditioning (Quinn, Harbison, & McAllister 1970), but all of these can be faulted on issues of methodological rigor (Earls & Marshall, 1983). The influence of various social learning mechanisms (Bandura, 1973, 1977; Gagnon & Simon, 1973; Plummer, 1984) is undoubtedly of great importance, but how these forces operate to produce sexual deviants is not understood. There is, then, a deficiency in understanding how, once acquired, a deviant sexual orientation is main-

D. R. Laws • Department of Law and Mental Health, Florida Mental Health Institute, University of South Florida, Tampa, Florida 33612-3899.   W. L. Marshall • Department of Psychology, Queen's University, Kingston, Ontario K7L 3N6, Canada.

tained, elaborated, and shaped into a fixed behavioral repertoire with high resistance to alteration.

This chapter presents a theoretical model which describes how a person could develop deviant sexual preferences. It adopts the position of Sidman (1960, p. 61) that "maladaptive behavior can result from quantitative and qualitative combinations of processes which are themselves intrinsically orderly, strictly determined, and normal in origin." Thus, this conditioning and social learning model states that deviant sexual preferences and cognitions are acquired by the same mechanisms by which other persons learn more conventionally accepted modes of sexual expression.

The theoretical model is divided into two parts: (1) acquisition processes and (2) maintenance processes. The model is presented as a set of 13 general principles and 14 derived propositions. The general principles were constructed on the basis of broad generalizations about human behavior. They are descriptive of a learning process or some mechanism of elaborating or refining of basic learning. From each principle we then derived a set of propositions which are more specific statements about the learning of human sexual behavior, especially a deviant sexual orientation.

Throughout the discussion that follows we consider the development of deviant sexual preferences (e.g., interests, arousal, attraction, orientation) which are often assumed to drive deviant sexual behavior. Few would disagree that where there are deviant interests, these drive deviant behavior in offenders. However, many would disagree that *all* sex offenders have deviant sexual preferences. Thus, the theory is an account of the development of deviant preferences (orientation, interests) which may lead to deviant behavior. It is *not* an account which can explain the deviant sexual behavior of those offenders who do not have extensive deviant interests.

Acquisition Processes

Basic Conditioning Processes

In this section, 10 fundamental principles underlying the acquisition of deviant sexual behavior are described. It is important to emphasize that there is no assumption here of the equivalence or equipotentiality of stimuli and behaviors, that is, that unconditioned and conditional stimuli and responses and reinforcers can be associated with equal ease. The world of sexual behavior is not one where arbitrary stimuli such as flashing lights become linked to arbitrary behaviors such as bar presses. Rather, it is a world where highly specific stimuli become linked to highly specific behaviors.

Given this understanding it is entirely reasonable to suppose that the repertoire of human sexual behavior develops along a dimension of preparedness (Seligman, 1970) such that individuals are more *likely* to associate some stimuli and events, rather than others, with sexual arousal and behavior. These highly prepared stimuli and events become the ones *most likely* to be incorporated into the individual's developing repertoire. Seligman (1970, 1971) describes the dimension of preparedness as a continuum of conditioning possibilities arising from the organism's evolutionary history. Thus highly prepared stimuli (i.e., those most readily conditionable) will be those whose acquisition as elicitors of behavior has (or had) survival value for the species. Accordingly, we would expect humans to be highly prepared to acquire sexual responses to opposite-sexed partners. At the other end of the preparedness continuum, we would expect humans to be extremely resistant to acquiring sexual responding to, for example, sexually neutral, inanimate objects. Sexual responses to stimuli consensually deemed to be "deviant" may be understood to lie somewhere along the preparedness continuum between the two extremes of highly prepared to contraprepared. The set of deviant stimuli may further be ranked along the continuum, with responses to age-inappropriate partners and to forced sex being reasonably well-prepared responses, since they might both be considered to be reproductively advantageous or to represent points on a generalization gradient not too far removed from the stimuli (adult heterosexual partners) which are the most advantageous. Toward the other end of the continuum, relatively less prepared stimuli represent the more difficult case of learning to respond sexually. Here we find the more bizarre examples of sexual attractions such as fetishism, transvestism, sadism, masochism, or bestiality.

In discussing deviant sexual behavior as a form of prepared learning, it is important to note Seligman's (1971, pp. 314–316) observations that prepared associations, depending upon their degree of preparedness: (1) can be acquired in one or very few trials, (2) are highly selective and specific to the stimulus, (3) are highly resistant to extinction, and (4) are noncognitive (i.e., primitive) and not readily modifiable by information. This account explains why deviant sexual behavior is so resistant to modification.

Pavlovian Conditioning

General Principle 1. Some stimuli (unconditioned stimuli) have the intrinsic capability of eliciting some physiological responses (unconditioned responses) without prior learning taking place. If a neutral stimulus is regularly associated in time with one that is capable of eliciting a given physiological response, that stimulus alone will eventually acquire the power to elicit the physiological response or some component of it. The formerly neutral stimulus is then called a conditional stimulus, and the behavior elicited by it a conditional response (Bolles, 1979; Mackintosh, 1974; Schwartz, 1984).

Proposition 1. Human sexual arousal is initially an unconditioned response which can occur spontaneously or be elicited by direct stimulation of the genitals or other erogenous zones. Sexual arousal can become a conditional response through temporal pairing of a variety of environmental or symbolic stimuli with this physiological state. These conditional stimuli thereby acquire sexually provocative properties and will, accordingly, elicit sexual behavior.

Subproposition 1. Once conditioning has occurred, any sex-related environmental or sexually symbolic stimulus can also acquire sexual properties through association with these originally conditional stimuli. That is, conditional stimuli can serve the same role as unconditioned stimuli, once they become well entrenched as elicitors of sexual arousal. This process is called second-order Pavlovian conditioning.

Consider, for example, a conventional, hetero-socialized teenaged male without previous sexual experience. He has vague and incomplete knowledge of the rudiments of sexual behavior, but his socialization has prepared him to be accepting. In an initial encounter with an age-inappropriate female partner, he permits the very young girl to fondle his penis. The direct, tactile stimulation (unconditioned stimulus) elicits sexual arousal and full erection (unconditioned response). As this occurs, the boy also touches his younger partner's genitals, examines the shape of the girl's small body, while listening to the content of her speech. These elements, then, become associated with the developing pattern of sexual arousal. On subsequent occasions, sight of the younger partner's body, a fantasy of a similar girl, or a verbalization by the young girl, all of which are conditional stimuli, could all elicit some measure of sexual arousal in the boy (conditional response). Here the individual was initially "prepared" to be sexually stimulated and the experience was heterosexual, but it was pedophilic in nature. An unconventional pattern of conditional stimuli was created and thus set the occasion for the development of deviant rather than conventional sexual behavior.

General Principle 1a: General Autoerotic Influences. As a subvariety of Pavlovian conditioning it may be noted that humans can also deliberately arrange contingencies. That is, they may consciously pair a deliberately selected stimulus with one that is capable of eliciting a primary drive condition, in this case, sexual arousal.

Proposition 1a. A previously conditioned sexual fantasy (conditional stimulus, CS1) plus masturbatory stimulation (unconditioned stimulus, UCS) can produce high sexual arousal plus orgasm. Minor variations of the original fantasy (CS2), successively substituted for the original one (perhaps to avoid boredom) and paired with masturbation, can elicit the same response or some variant of it (Marquis, 1970). For example, having acquired sexual responses to adult females (CS1), a male may gradually introduce elements of youthfulness into his imagined partner during masturbation. Over successive occasions he may progress to imagining unacceptably young partners (CS2) while masturbating, and these repeated associations between fantasies of very young partners and sexual arousal will entrench a deviant sexual attraction. This is an example of second-order Pavlovian conditioning. Such elaborated use of sexual fantasy may account in large part for learning to become aroused to a wide variety of sexual stimuli (McGuire, Carlisle, & Young, 1965) which may be seen as lying along a generalization gradient at the center of which lies the original (CS1) conditional stimulus.

Proposition 1a describes an important element in learning to become sexually aroused to deviant stimuli. The process described can obviously be used to broaden and strengthen interest in and responsiveness to either nondeviant or deviant stimuli. If the initial conditioning is to deviant stimuli, the use of successively minor variations on the original CS would readily permit a broad generalization of sexual arousal. Over time, the use of these variations could shift sexual preferences dramatically away from the original CS, that is, become even more deviant.

Operant Conditioning

General Principle 2. If a behavior is followed closely in time by a stimulus, and future instances of that behavior are seen to increase, operant conditioning is said to have occurred (Bolles, 1979; Mackintosh, 1974; Reynolds, 1968; Schwartz, 1984; Skinner, 1938, 1953).

Proposition 2. If instrumental sexual acts or cognitions, accompanied by sexual arousal, are followed by specific stimuli (e.g., genital stimulation, ejaculation, social approval of the partner, or increased responsiveness of the partner) and those instrumental acts or cognitions increase, sexual responsiveness has been operantly conditioned.

It is difficult to separate the processes of Pavlovian and operant conditioning. They do not operate in isolation from each other but rather work in conjunction, elements of each being seen in the other (Kimble, 1961; Schwartz, 1984). An example was given above of the Pavlovian conditioning of sexual arousal in a teenaged male through being masturbated by a very young female. To extend the example, had the boy ejaculated, producing social approval and increased responsiveness in the girl, that aspect of the sequence could serve to operantly condition the boy's arousal to younger females. If ejaculation produced in the boy a satisfying state of affairs, or if the boy was highly pleased by the young girl's response to his orgasm, then on subsequent occasions, that or a similar sequence of behaviors would likely be repeated, further strengthening the chain. However, it is clear that, throughout this process, old Pavlovian associations are being re-paired, and new pairings are being introduced; old operants continue to be reinforced and new ones are created. Thus, the two processes inextricably interact.

Empirical evidence for the influence of basic conditioning in creating deviant sexual behavior is meagre. Rachman (1966), Rachman and Hodgson (1968), Beech *et al.* (1971), and Langevin and Martin (1975) reported demonstrations of the role of Pavlovian conditioning, and Quinn *et al.* (1970) have done the same for operant conditioning. Unfortunately, however, each of these studies has methodological problems which reduces the persuasiveness of their findings. Conversely, Herman, Barlow, and Agras (1974) found it difficult to classically condition arousal to a novel but sexually relevant stimulus, and Marshall (1974) failed to produce conditioning using an extensive S–S classical paradigm.

Not all learning is useful nor will it be retained, and so we must consider extinction processes.

Extinction

General Principle 3. If a Pavlovian conditioned stimulus–response association is not occasionally re-paired with an unconditioned stimulus, or an operantly conditioned response is not occasionally followed by a reinforcing stimulus, each will weaken and disappear (Mackintosh, 1974; Rescorla & Solomon, 1967; Schwartz, 1984; Skinner, 1938, 1953).

Proposition 3. If a conditioned human sexual response is repeatedly performed in the absence of automatically arousing or reinforcing stimuli, it will weaken and eventually disappear.

The proposition states the classical definitions of Pavlovian and operant extinction. Pavlovian-conditioned erotic stimuli must occasionally be re-paired with original eliciting stimuli (UCS or higher-order CS), or these conditional stimuli will lose their erotic value. Similarly, erotic reinforcing stimuli must occasionally follow instrumental sexual acts or cognitions, or the sexual response elicited by these acts or cognitions will weaken and disappear.

As an illustration we may return to the example of the young male made sexually responsive by the younger girl, and again we can see the interaction of Pavlovian and operant processes. Assume that after a time the young girl grows tired of the relationship and no longer stimulates the young man's penis, is no longer physically forthcoming, and no longer speaks sexual phrases to him. The original Pavlovian associations between this girl and the boy's sexual arousal will begin to weaken, and the boy will experience some difficulty in becoming aroused to this particular girl. For a time, other stimuli associated with the girl (e.g., the boy's fantasies of the girl or just the sight of her on the street) may sustain arousal, but, over time, in the absence of direct involvement, arousal to this partner will fade. This is an example of Pavlovian extinction.

We might assume also that when arousal is present, the boy continues to perform the same instrumental acts as before (e.g., approaching and propositioning the girl), but the physical stimulation which produced ejaculation is now absent, and the boy's behaviors no longer produce social approval or increased responsiveness on her part. In the latter case reinforcing stimuli are absent and operant extinction will occur.

Punishment

General Principle 4. Punishment is a consequence of behavior which reduces the future probability of that behavior. If a supposed punishing stimulus is made to accompany or follow a behavior, and future instances of that behavior are seen to decrease, the stimulus is called an aversive stimulus and the process is called punishment (Azrin & Holz, 1966; Mackintosh, 1974; Schwartz, 1984).

Proposition 4. Many human social behaviors intended to gain sexual reinforcers are learned in ordered sequences or chains of behavior. If any of these initial social-sexual sequences are interrupted or followed by punishment, the future likelihood of the whole chain of behaviors will decrease. With repeated punishment, the sequence will disappear from the person's behavioral repertoire.

In the socialization process significant others intervene to shape a developing individual's sexual behavior. A major way in which they do so is in the application of punishment to children for unwanted behaviors such as masturbation, display of the genitals, sexual talk, or inappropriate sexual advances. Since it has been hypothesized that many of these behaviors are being learned in chains, that reinforcement of each link is necessary, and that some terminal reinforcement must occur to chain the links together (Holland & Skinner, 1961), then it is apparent that punishment of any or all of the links will suppress the chain and eventually eliminate the behavior (Azrin & Holz, 1966; Hake & Azrin, 1965).

The implications of punishment of chained sexual behaviors is clear. If initial social-sexual approach behaviors are followed by unconditioned aversive stimuli (e.g., a physical blow) or, more likely, conditional aversive stimuli (e.g., a frown or other expression of displeasure), the future likelihood of such initial social behaviors will decrease. Because some of these initial behaviors are early components of a behavioral chain which could produce conventional sexual interaction, reinforcement for appropriate social-sexual behavior will not occur.

Associated with Pavlovian and operant conditioning is differential reinforcement and differential punishment, which work concurrently with extinction to entrench certain highly specific behavioral tendencies. These differentiating processes can also shape up chains of thoughts and behaviors which culminate in the precise sexually deviant act.

Differential Consequences

General Principle 5a: Differential Reinforcement. Humans learn to respond in the presence of stimuli which signal that reinforcement is available, and they learn to withhold responding in the presence of those which signal the absence of reinforcement (Bandura, 1969; Mackintosh, 1974; Schwartz, 1984). The absence of reinforcement, of course, represents conditions which produce extinction of a learned response, so that in this context these conditions are to be understood as differential extinction. Differential reinforcement and differential extinction are necessarily inextricably linked.

Proposition 5a. Humans learn to respond differentially to stimuli which signal the availability of reinforcement for sexual behavior and avoid responding to those that do not.

The basic principle states that the interaction of reinforcement and extinction can serve to shape human behavior in one direction rather than another. In the simplest case, given two behavioral options, most individuals will choose the one which frequently produces some type of reinforcement over one which rarely does. The more often these contingencies present themselves, the more likely it is that differential responding will become entrenched. One behavior becomes differentially strengthened through reinforcement while the other extinguishes. When learned behavior occurs more frequently in the presence of some stimuli, but not others, as a result of differential reinforcement processes, such responding is said to be under stimulus control.

Given the assumptions about preparedness, it is not difficult to see how human sexual behavior can be shaped through differential reinforcement. Humans learn to respond differentially to stimuli that are discriminative of reinforcement for sexual behavior and avoid responding to those which are not. This is understood to be part of the learning of sexual preferences, and those preferences could be said to be under stimulus control of identifiable complexes of sexual stimuli.

As an example, consider a man who is experiencing sexual dysfunction with his wife because she no longer finds him physically attractive or sexually stimulating. He finds it difficult to become sexually aroused, and often experiences erectile failure. Since she is not attracted to him, she provides no stimuli to arouse him. The man's responsiveness can, therefore, be understood to be on an extinction schedule. Unsatisfied, the man notices that his teenaged daughter has many characteristics which he finds both physically and sexually attractive. He is aroused by her, approaches her sexually, and she reciprocates; he achieves an erection and is stimulated to ejaculation. Subsequently, they have intercourse frequently and, as a result of the differential reinforcement for his sexual approaches, he loses his attraction to his wife (and possibly other adult females) and becomes strongly attracted to his daughter (and possibly other young girls). Here, through the operation of differential reinforcement, a new set of sexual preferences, albeit inappropriate, are learned.

Consider here, also, the interaction of differential reinforcement and generalization. As noted, we might expect the man's sexual interest and arousal to generalize to other young females who bore physical characteristics and behaviors similar to those of his teenaged daughter. These characteristics, all of which have been associated with reinforcement, might include small, firm breasts, a slim, athletic build, or clear, unblemished and unwrinkled skin. However, the differential reinforcement provided by the social and sexual interactions with his daughter would likely keep this generalization gradient fairly steep. In the absence of subsequent direct contact with other young girls, then, we would not expect generalization of interest and arousal to all prepubertal girls. Similarly, the differential extinction provided by his wife would not be expected to suppress interest in other adult females.

General Principle 5b: Differential Punishment. Punishment for social approaches provides information as to which behaviors produce aversive consequences (Holz & Azrin, 1961), encourages avoidance of that situation or person, and promotes the learning of other, incompatible behaviors (Dinsmoor, 1954).

Proposition 5b. If the behaviors which could lead to socially appropriate sexual interactions are met with punishment, and the individual subsequently learns to secure sexual reinforcement through other, unpunished but perhaps socially inappropriate means (e.g., voyeurism, obscene telephone calls, exhibitionism, pedophilia, rape), these inappropriate sexual chains will be reinforced and will become predominant.

We have here an example of differential punishment where one set of behaviors are punished and other possible sexual behaviors are not punished. When one subset of a class of behaviors are punished and another subset are not, the absence of punishment for the latter may be construed as negative reinforcement. Negative reinforcement is said to occur when the organism escapes from or avoids an aversive experience (Schwartz, 1984). Becoming sexually aroused to unpunished deviant acts, either imaginally or secretively, while being punished for appropriate behaviors, will lead to an increased tendency to act deviantly and a reduced tendency to act appropriately. The deviant tendencies created under these circumstances would be expected to be very strong, given the joint operation here of differential punishment and differential reinforcement (i.e., negative reinforcement of escape or avoidance of aversive feedback as well as the positive reinforcement of sexual arousal).

Chaining of Behavior

General Principle 6. As we have seen, early components of new behaviors are shaped by processes of conditioning and differential consequences. Later these components combine into functionally linked sequences of instrumental acts called chains. Chains are usually performed in serial order, each sequence triggering the next, culminating in some reinforcing activity (Holland & Skinner, 1961).

Proposition 6. Many of the human social-sexual behaviors intended to create sexual arousal or procure sexual interaction and reinforcement are learned in ordered sequences, or chains of instrumental acts. These chains are maintained by stimuli produced by performing each component and by stimuli provided by the prospective sexual partner in response to the person's behavior.

Numerous theorists (Holland & Skinner, 1961; Hull, 1952; Logan & Wagner, 1965; Mackintosh, 1974; Schwartz, 1984; Skinner, 1938; Spence, 1956) have emphasized the importance of instrumental behavior chains. They have advanced an explanation of chaining in which conditional stimuli serve both a discriminative and a reinforcing function. In this analysis, stimuli produced by performance of one component both reinforce the performance of that specific link in the chain and increase its future probability (reinforcing function) as well as set the occasion for the performance of the next component (discriminative function). Each component is thus chained to the next, the dual functions of the accompanying stimuli keeping it intact.

While chains are described as serially ordered and functionally linked sequences, it should not be supposed that this is a rigid and inflexible linkage. They may be *most often* run off in the same sequence in a given situation, but chains appropriate to one set of governing circumstances may, with minor modification, be applied to others. Similarly, individual components of one functional chain may be part of others as well. Chained behavior is thus adaptable to a variety of situations and contingencies.

Examples of the chained sequences of behavior involved in deviant sexual acts can be found in Marshall's (1973) use of fantasy sequences in aversive therapy or in Annon and Robinson's (1985) use of covert sensitization to illustrate to the deviant the steps he engages in to secure access to inappropriate partners. Similarly, Freund's (see Chapter 12, this volume) account of courtship disorders casts all human sexual behavior into sequential phases, from the initial searching and locating responses through displays, approach, and contact behaviors.

In human sexual behavior, however, it is important to note that we are frequently concerned with the interaction of two behavioral chains. The performance of each partner's chain produces its own discriminative and reinforcing stimuli. Similarly, interaction is seen in that performance of behaviors by one partner serves as discriminative and reinforcing stimuli for the production of behaviors by the other. Thus, the principle of behavioral chaining is seen as crucial to the enactment of sexual behavior.

Summary of Conditioning Processes: A Case Example

As an illustrative example, which we will continue to use throughout the balance of the chapter, let us consider how, according to these principles and propositions, a man might become a forcible rapist of adult females.

This is an elaboration of a case history from our files. The male in question experienced a conventional childhood until, at the age of 13 years, he viewed a commercial film which contained very strong elements of sex and violence. In this film, the beautiful wife of a young professional is brutally abused and raped. As is typical of these films, it was difficult for the viewer to determine if the wife was actually resisting and fighting her assaulters or whether she was possibly enjoying the abuse. Our subject found the actress portraying the wife to be very sexually attractive, and during the rape scenes he produced a full erection.

The young male thought about the film for some time. Whenever he thought about the wife, he remembered the look on her face as she was being raped, but he could not remember if the expression was one of pain or pleasure. In his fantasy she was provocative, inviting, and welcoming. He fantasized that she could not resist him, he was powerful, he could force himself upon her and, although she might resist, ultimately she gave in to him. As he imagined a variety of sexual activities with this woman, he began to develop strong sexual arousal and attraction to forceful sex with adult females by means of Pavlovian conditioning. He began to masturbate to these fantasies and, through the combination of genital stimulation and ejaculation, the Pavlovian associations were further reinforced by operant conditioning. Eventually, he broadened his masturbatory fantasies to include similar sexual activities with other adult females.

At the age of 14 years he began to date females his own age. Although he was strongly attracted to female peers, he did not have age-appropriate social skills. He wanted all females to be as sexually inviting as the woman in his fantasies and to expect frank sexual overtures, and he was surprised when he was repeatedly rebuffed by these young women. And the more he tried, it seemed, the more he was refused. He returned to masturbating while fantasizing about being powerful in sexual relations with adult women.

At this time the content of his masturbatory fantasies began to increasingly involve elements of sexual violence, first about the rape scenes from the film, then about rape and violence in general, all directed toward adult females. Fantasies about consenting sex with females were arousing, but not as much as those which contained rape. After a time, he no longer thought much about consenting sexual relationships with women.

At age 16 he forcibly raped a 38-year-old woman in the parking garage of an apartment building. He was very excited as he forced himself upon her, and when she fought with him and pleaded with him to stop, he thought momentarily about the actress in the film who, as he remembered it, first struggled, then enthusiastically submitted. After that, he did not think about the film any more.

In this initial example we see most of the acquisition processes at work. The subject had experienced a conventional heterosexually oriented childhood and was "prepared" for sexual relationships with females. Unfortunately, the initial sexually arousing experience in his teenage years was the sex and violence film. This is exactly the sort of stimulus to which Donnerstein, Linz, and Penrod (1987) refer when they assert that it is not the sex or the violence alone that is dangerous in the development of sexual preferences; rather, it is the juxtaposition of sexual images with violence that creates tendencies toward sexual aggression and negative attitudes toward women (see Murrin & Laws, Chapter 5, this volume).

The basic sexual arousal pattern of this client was established through Pavlovian and operant conditioning and further reinforced by masturbatory fantasy. In these fantasies, differential reinforcement, chaining, and generalization came into play as he imagined a variety of sexual behaviors with the woman in the film and other women. Those elements of the fantasies that produced and maintained arousal were incorporated into these imaginary chains, and those that did not were eliminated by differential extinction.

In early adolescence the subject made inappropriate attempts to establish conventional sexual relationships with same-aged females. These behaviors were punished or extinguished through lack of reinforcement. When he returned to his masturbatory activities, the Pavlovian and operant processes (differential reinforcement, chaining, and generalization) were back at work, this time creating a deviant variation as a result of the introduction of elements of sexual violence in the fantasies.

The activities described in this example are not that unusual in the histories of sexual offenders. A single series of events, only slightly off the center of a

dimension of appropriate sexual behavior, over time and almost by happens-
tance, creates all the necessary conditions for a very strong proclivity to engage
in deviant sexual behavior. As Van Wyk and Geist (1984) have shown in their
extensive study of thousands of cases of early sexual experience, it is (in this
case, regrettably) just as simple as that.

Social Learning Processes

Human sexual behavior is a social behavior. While many of its fundamental
components are a result of conditioning processes, much of its ultimate expression is the result of social learning influences. Through social behavior,
through the observation of the relationship of antecedent and consequent events
as they happen to others, people learn to respond to a variety of stimulus
conditions and situations and develop expectations about those relationships
and their ability to function within them. These same social processes also
encourage individuals to develop self-descriptions which may guide or limit
their behavior. In the following section, a further two fundamental principles,
derived from social learning theory, are elaborated.

General Social Learning Influences

General Principle 7. Conditioning processes play a major role in the acquisition of any human behavior, but much of human social behavior is learned from
other people, from observing what they do and what happens to them as a
result (Bandura, 1973, 1977).

Proposition 7. Human sexual behavior is a social behavior, much of which is
learned from other people. Social learning theory (Bandura, 1973, 1977; Bandura
& Walters, 1963) proposes three major processes which are relevant to the learning of sexual behavior: (1) *participant modeling*, a process of direct tuition in which
the learner observes then copies the behavior of a model; (2) *vicarious learning* by
nonparticipant observation of another's behavior, whether that be *in vivo*, in
print, or visual media; and (3) *symbolic modeling*, in which behavior and its
consequences are developed and elaborated in thought or in mental images.
This latter process is vitally important in the development of deviant sexual
fantasies.

At this point in the development model these processes are considered to be
general in nature. They do indeed work to produce finished sexual behaviors,
but these become much more narrow as a result of more specific social learning
influences.

Participant modeling is evident in the childhood sexual victimization of
boys who are later to become sexual deviants. Quite refined sexual abuse skills
may be learned from an adult model, and the subsequent offenses performed by
the formerly victimized person could be seen as a replication of his own victimization (Freeman-Longo, 1986).

Sexual abuse skills can also be acquired through vicarious learning by non-participant observation. A boy may observe an adult (either directly or through some media presentation) sexually abuse another child, and as a result the growing boy may acquire a variety of behaviors vicariously. The boy may be present when a friend is abused, or he may be told in graphic detail later of an instance of the abuse of a friend. Or, as so often happens, the molester may use pornography to influence a child to engage in sexual acts, offering as a justification, "See? Other kids do it, so it must be all right!"

The use of symbolic modeling is clearly evident in masturbation to deviant sexual fantasies. Abel and Blanchard (1974) note the importance of deviant sexual fantasy in the development of sexual deviation. The use of deviant sexual fantasy during masturbation, according to McGuire *et al.* (1964), may be the most influential learning process in becoming sexually aroused to deviant stimuli. Any initial deviant contact, random deviant fantasy, or exposure to textual or visual representations of deviant behavior may supply sufficient material for later elaboration in masturbatory fantasy.

As a result of these social processes, the young boy may not only learn deviant sexual scripts as behavioral possibilities, he may also come to view himself differently from other boys.

Self-Labeling Influences

General Principle 8. Human beings observe their own behaviors and develop a set of self-statements through which they define for themselves what sort of persons they are (Ullmann & Krasner, 1969).

Proposition 8. By observation of their own sexual behavior, people will develop a self-label to define themselves in sexual terms.

Self-labeling, or self-attribution, is an intra-individual social learning influence which has an important guiding role on future behavior. "A great part of a person's stimulus environment is composed of his own behavior. In part this is noticing the results of behavior and in part it is evaluating and labeling situations" (Ullmann & Krasner, 1969, p. 96). People come to know their attitudes and emotions by inferring them from observations of their own behavior and the context in which it occurs. Based on these observations, individuals develop a set of self-statements, or self-attributions, through which they define what sort of persons they are. Similarly, by observation of his own sexual behavior, a male will develop attributions about himself as a sexual person. These self-statements, the observed behavioral and physiological events, and the reactions of others to his behavior will in large measure form the self-definition of the growing boy's sexuality. If the observed outcomes are discordant with self-expectations and the perceived expectations of others, he is likely to define himself as an "abnormal," sexually unconventional person.

Attributions about sexual experience can produce either advantageous or disadvantageous self-labels. For example, a boy who was roughly abused during a sexual offense, or for whom the molestation was otherwise upsetting or not enjoyable, might label himself as a normal person who was victimized. He will more likely make this attribution if he is told quite clearly by others that he was not responsible for the assault. However, another boy, under different circumstances, might tell himself that his victimization "was not harmful to him, that there were pleasurable aspects to it, and in some cases is thought of as sexually arousing" (Freeman-Longo, 1986, p. 412). If this latter boy sees himself as responsible, or as having enjoyed the encounter, then he might label himself as deviant. When molestation continues for an extended period, and the victim continues to enjoy it, the boy will all the more readily label himself a sexual deviant. Labeling himself in this way will make it easier for the boy, and later the man, to act on deviant thoughts which might otherwise be dismissed.

Summary of Social Learning Influences: A Case Example

In the example given above of the young male learning to become a rapist, the influence of basic conditioning and differential consequences was described. Interwoven with these fundamental processes were strong social learning influences.

Learning to rape is rarely taught by participant modeling, although examples are available (e.g., performing a sexual assault to gain membership in a gang, participating in gang rapes). Vicarious and symbolic modeling, however, play a powerful role.

Before our subject performed his first rape, he gained access to pornographic materials in the form of videotapes and magazines which depicted adult women bound, gagged, and being sexually humiliated. Similar to his experience with the violent film, he often could not discriminate whether the expressions on the women's faces were of pain or pleasure. The pornography seemed to reinforce and legitimize rape, and thus it reinforced his masturbatory fantasies as well. He did not question any of this.

Symbolic modeling was evident in his masturbatory fantasies. At first they were confined to relatively conventional fantasies about the woman in the film, which generalized to other females. Later, the content shifted to more violent sexual activities with women, and finally to fantasies of rape.

As for self-labeling, he did not deceive himself after the first rape at age 16. Up to that point he was well aware of his failure with same-aged females, but he dismissed it as part of the price of growing up. When he was fully adult, he felt he would be able to perform with female peers. After the rape, however, when he compared his early social experiences with young females to his current violent masturbatory fantasies, he admitted to himself that sexual violence was far more arousing and satisfying. Although he did not use the word just yet, he believed that he was probably a rapist.

Maintenance Processes

A set of additional principles is necessary to account for the maintenance phase of sexual deviation, once such a tendency is acquired. Here sexual deviance becomes a fixed and stable orientation in the person's repertoire of sociosexual skills, and it is highly resistant to change. The previously described principles obviously do not cease to operate, and new learning occurs according to the same principles, while nonfunctional components of the old learning extinguish or are discarded. The more fundamental components will survive and be even more strongly entrenched as well as becoming more elaborated and refined over time, according to the following principles.

Specific Autoerotic Influences

General Principle 9. Human beings can deliberately condition themselves to be responsive to certain stimuli through deliberate arrangement of the contingencies. The eliciting power of conditional stimuli can be increased by focusing on those aspects of the stimulus complex which produce an increase in intensity and duration of the conditioned response (Marquis, 1970).

Proposition 9. Conditioned masturbatory stimuli can be made more powerful by selective focus on the most erotic features of any fantasy (McGuire et al., 1965).
Specific autoerotic influences refers to the refinement of the eliciting power of existing conditioned erotic stimuli used in masturbation. This is accomplished by selective focus on the most erotic features of any particular cognition.

> [A] particular cue initially given the slightest emphasis becomes more and more dominant because of the positive feedback involved in the conditioning process; the more sexually stimulating it becomes, the more emphasis it is given in a masturbatory fantasy and consequently, by conditioning it becomes still more stimulating. Other stimuli, in the meanwhile, being deconditioned so that sexual interest becomes more and more specific (McGuire et al., 1965, p. 186).

If this higher-order conditioning is successful, the probability that these refined conditional stimuli will be used in the future increases. The probability that other refinements will continue to be made also increases (Marquis, 1970).
During masturbation the pairing of the powerful erotic physical stimulation with sexual fantasy permits many elements of that fantasy, both sexual and nonsexual, to become eroticized and develop into new conditional stimuli. A person with a brief history of pedophilic behavior might, in masturbation, focus on either real or idealized aspects of an actual or potential victim. Initially the focus might be on general features (e.g., the victim's looks, small stature, or overall shape of the body). Selective focus on more specific aspects of the victim with potential erotic features (e.g., size of the penis, shape of the buttocks, absence of pubic hair) could cause these features to become stronger conditional stimuli which are more dominant than the more general features. The greater emphasis given these features, the more stimulating they become.
Although we speak here of high specificity in learning, through the process of generalization, arousal to a wide variety of stimuli can also be conditioned.

Consider a pedophile with a brief history of sexual interaction with a 10-year-old boy. In these encounters, he fondles the boy's body, in particular his penis and buttocks, and fellates him. In his masturbatory fantasies he expands upon these themes, focusing especially on small penises, absence of pubic hair, and small, firm buttocks. Through the processes described, these features become paramount in his interest and arousal pattern, and his preference becomes highly focused. However, most boys between the ages of 10 and 12 possess these features in varying degrees, and thus we would expect his arousal to generalize to this whole class of young males. Because of the differential reinforcement provided by his specific experiences with this victim and the accompanying masturbatory fantasies, we would expect that his arousal would be mostly confined to this age range and this cluster of physical characteristics. We would not expect him to show interest in very young boys or in teenaged boys who resemble adult males. Thus it is not surprising that we find so many pedophiles attracted to certain age groups that bear similar characteristics.

Specific Social Learning Influences

General Principle 10. The social influences of vicarious learning and symbolic modeling shape basic behaviors but are more central to the elaboration and refinement of behaviors already learned (Bandura, 1977).

Proposition 10. Basic sexual skills may be elaborated and refined through vicarious learning provided by print and visual media, and entire scenarios for deviant sexual behavior may be cognitively modeled.

In the maintenance period the focus of vicarious learning will probably narrow, while the scope of symbolic modeling will increase. Basic skills and knowledge have already been sharpened by exposure to textual and visual media. As a preference becomes more defined, the individual may seek out particular forms of media presentations which will further reinforce this process. If, for example, the individual was initially attracted to and aroused by pictures of nude female children, he may now seek pictures, slides, or videotapes which show these subjects posed sexually, masturbating, or having sex with adults. These processes, derived from exposure to media presentations, are examples of vicarious learning.

Initial symbolic modeling, related to masturbatory fantasy, may have centered around varieties of real-life sexual experiences and fantasies of variations on them. Now the individual may begin to articulate entire scenarios for yet to be performed sexual behavior episodes with a wide variety of antecedents and consequences. When the appropriate opportunity arrives, one of these may be selected as a guide for behavior. At this point, the basic processes described go back to work to shape yet another form of deviant sexual behavior.

Intermittent Reinforcement

General Principle 11. Persons whose response patterns have been reinforced only intermittently will persist in their behavior for a long time despite the low frequency of rewards and despite occasional setbacks (Bandura, 1969; Mackintosh, 1974; Schwartz, 1984).

Proposition 11. Sexual interest and arousal does not occur on a continuous schedule of reinforcement. Therefore, intermittently reinforced behaviors, associated with seeking and gratifying sexual needs, will be persistent, of high frequency, and resistant to extinction.

The basic principle is that persistence pays off. It is not necessary to reinforce every occurrence of a behavior to increase or maintain it (Mackintosh, 1974; Reynolds, 1968; Schwartz, 1984). Indeed, behavior that has been intermittently reinforced, particularly with long and variable intervals or ratios, is far more difficult to eliminate than is behavior which is more consistently rewarded. Any reinforcement of the behavior, adventitious or deliberate, will reinstate it, often at a higher level than previously observed (Bandura, 1969). Related to this, intermittent differential reinforcement of a particular behavior serves to entrench that behavior so well that it becomes strongly resistant to change (Bandura, 1969). Behaviors which are engaged in for the pursuit of sexual gratification lead to desired outcomes only on occasion. Given that society disapproves of deviant sexual acts, we would expect behaviors aimed at satisfying deviant desires to be even less frequently successful. Such behaviors are, therefore, reinforced on a intermittent schedule, and, accordingly, we would expect them to be persistent, to occur at a high frequency, and to be resistant to extinction. That is certainly what we see in sexual offenders.

Summary of Maintenance Processes: A Case Example

By the age of 20, our subject had raped several women. He had no girlfriends and formed no close relationships with females. On occasion he had conventional sexual encounters with women he picked up in bars, or with prostitutes. He could initiate sex with these women, but he could only maintain his arousal if he imagined that he was raping them, torturing them, or even killing them. His masturbation fantasies centered around torture and murder, and he became increasingly interested in different varieties of violent pornography. Only during his rapes did he feel powerful and competent and fully engaged with the woman. He drank a lot, took drugs, and was angry most of the time. He thought a lot about raping and developed many plans for assaults he might perform.

Here we can see that the maintenance processes have done their work, firmly entrenching an elaborate behavioral repertoire of rape-oriented sexual preference. We also see the earlier processes acting—new conditioned associations being formed and the selective operation of differential reinforcement at work—as the subject moved almost completely away from conventional sexual intercourse to a distinct preference for forced sex. Sex with any female was no longer possible without accompanying rape-related imagery. The centrality of violent imagery was clearly reflected in his masturbatory fantasies, which shifted over time from relatively simple forced sexual encounters to images of torture, dismemberment, and murder. As he narrowed the focus in these fantasies to more and more violent images, they became more exciting. Vicarious learning was still evident, as he sought increasingly bizarre and violent forms of pornography. Symbolic modeling became more elaborate, as he developed a variety of scenarios for potential future rapes. Both of these activities stimulated even further variations in his masturbatory fantasies.

Finally, the entire complex was fixed in place by intermittent reinforcement. As we indicated above, due to their socially disapproved nature, the overall likelihood of successfully accomplishing deviant sexual activities is relatively low. This low likelihood, however, is modified by the requirements for accomplishment of the particular deviant act. Thus, we would expect the incidence of easily performed deviant behaviors such as exhibitionism or voyeurism to be relatively high, while rape would occur at a relatively low frequency. In the present case, the requirements for successful accomplishment would be quite elaborate, and, hence, the frequency low. Thus, and this is extremely important, our subject's rape proclivity was very strongly reinforced on a highly intermittent schedule of long and variable intervals; this all but guarantees that, in the absence of effective therapeutic intervention, it would be maintained as a permanent disposition.

Treatment Applications

The strength of a conditioning and social learning theory of deviant sexual interests is that it may be stated in operational terms. Two of the proposed learning principles have central influence: the development of deviant sexual arousal through basic conditioning and the elaborated use of deviant fantasy in masturbation. This basic core is further shaped and refined by a variety of differential consequences and the action of social learning influences, then firmly fixed in place by the action of intermittent reinforcement.

These same operations may be used to redirect old behaviors as well as create new ones, and behavioral researchers and clinicians have developed treatments based on conditioning and social learning principles in an effort to redirect the effects of early learning. A variety of deconditioning techniques, such as electric aversive therapy (Abel, Levis, & Clancy, 1970; Marshall, 1973), covert sensitization (Abel et al., 1984), olfactory aversion (Laws, 1986), and verbal (Laws, 1986) or masturbatory satiation (Marshall, 1979), have been used to decrease deviant sexual arousal and fantasy. Masturbatory reconditioning procedures (Laws, 1985; Marquis, 1970; VanDeventer & Laws, 1978) have been shown to both increase nondeviant arousal while decreasing deviant arousal. These basic procedures are often supplemented by social learning interventions such as social skills training, assertive training, or sex education (Abel et al., 1984; Marshall, Earls, Segal, & Darke, 1983). While there are some data available suggesting that these behavior-specific treatments are superior to more traditional psychotherapeutic interventions, definitive conclusions are not possible at this time.

Conclusions

This chapter has described how sexually deviant interests may be learned through the same mechanisms by which conventional sexuality is learned. In accepting this thesis, we must also acknowledge that the influence of these conditioning and social learning variables is so powerful that it is little wonder that the resultant repertoire of behaviors is so resilient and resistant to alteration. Very few people express wonder at the robustness of a conventional heterosexual orientation, and it is our contention that a deviant orientation should be viewed in the same way. We do not speak here of a momentary diversion, an experimentation, or a phase an individual is going through, such as might be true for some cases of sexual offending. Established deviant sexual preferences, which are clearly found in some offenders, represent a way of viewing and evaluating a major portion of that person's world.

As clinicians and researchers, we wish to believe that sexual deviance, like any human behavior, is the result of orderly and understandable processes and is consequently modifiable. To date, the results of controlled and uncontrolled case and group studies suggest that a deviant sexual orientation can be altered. However, whether these changes can be maintained in the very environment that initially evoked, shaped, and controlled them remains an open question. Conducting therapy exclusively in the therapist's office, however, whether or not behavioral procedures are employed, will not likely produce generalized changes in the client's life. While behavior therapists have used procedures which our theory would expect to be effective, they have only recently and tentatively begun to extend the application of these techniques to the very environment which maintains the deviant behavior.

ACKNOWLEDGMENTS. Preparation of this chapter was supported in part by National Institute of Mental Health Grant MH42035 to D. R. Laws and by the Florida Mental Health Institute.

References

Abel, G. G., & Blanchard, E. B. (1974). The role of fantasy in the treatment of sexual deviation. *Archives of General Psychiatry, 30,* 467–475.

Abel, G. G., Levis, D., & Clancy, J. (1970). Aversion therapy applied to taped sequences of deviant behavior in exhibitionism and other sexual deviation: A preliminary report. *Journal of Behavior Therapy and Experimental Psychiatry, 1,* 58–66.

Abel, G. G., Becker, J. V., Cunningham-Rathner, J., Rouleau, J. L., Kaplan, M., & Reich, J. (1984). *The treatment of child molesters.* Unpublished treatment manual, Emory University, Atlanta.

Annon, J. S., & Robinson, C. H. (1985). Sexual deviation. In M. Hersen & A. S. Bellack (Eds.), *Handbook of clinical behavior therapy with adults* (pp. 631–657). New York: Plenum.

Azrin, N. H., & Holz, W. C. (1966). Punishment. In W. K. Honig (Ed.), *Operant behavior: Areas of research and application* (pp. 380–447). New York: Appleton-Century-Crofts.

Bandura, A. (1969). *Principles of behavior modification.* New York: Holt, Rinehart & Winston.

Bandura, A. (1973). *Aggression: A social learning analysis.* Englewood Cliffs, NJ: Prentice-Hall.

Bandura, A. (1977). *Social learning theory.* Englewood Cliffs, NJ: Prentice-Hall.

Bandura, A., & Walters, R. H. (1963). *Social learning and personality development*. New York: Holt, Rinehart & Winston.

Beech, H. R., Watts, F., & Poole, A. P. (1971). Classical conditioning of a sexual deviation: A preliminary note. *Behavior Therapy, 2,* 400–402.

Bolles, R. D. (1979). *Learning theory* (2nd ed.). New York: Holt, Rinehart & Winston.

Dinsmoor, J. A. (1954). Punishment: I. The avoidance hypothesis. *Psychological Review, 61,* 34–46.

Donnerstein, E., Linz, D., & Penrod, S. (1987). *The question of pornography: Research findings and policy implications*. New York: Free Press.

Earls, C. M., & Marshall, W. L. (1983). The current state of technology in the laboratory assessment of sexual arousal patterns. In J. G. Greer & I. R. Stuart (Eds.), *The sexual aggressor: Current perspectives on treatment* (pp. 336–362). New York: Van Nostrand Reinhold.

Freeman-Longo, R. E. (1986). The impact of sexual victimization on males. *Child Abuse and Neglect, 10,* 411–414.

Gagnon, J. H., & Simon, W. (1973). *Sexual conduct: The social sources of human sexuality*. Chicago: Aldine.

Hake, D. F., & Azrin, N. H. (1965). Conditioned punishment. *Journal of the Experimental Analysis of Behavior, 8,* 279–293.

Herman, S. H., Barlow, D. H., & Agras, W. S. (1974). An experimental analysis of classical conditioning as a method of increasing heterosexual arousal in homosexuals. *Behavior Therapy, 5,* 33–47.

Holland, J. G., & Skinner, B. F. (1961). *The analysis of behavior*. New York: McGraw-Hill.

Holz, W. C., & Azrin, N. H. (1961). Discriminative properties of punishment. *Journal of the Experimental Analysis of Behavior, 4,* 225–232.

Hull, C. L. (1952). *A behavior system*. New Haven: Yale University Press.

Kimble, G. A. (1961). *Hilgard and Marquis' conditioning and learning*. New York: Appleton-Century-Crofts.

Kinsey, A. C., Pomeroy, W. B., & Martin, C. E. (1948). *Sexual behavior in the human male*. Philadelphia: Saunders.

Langevin, R., & Martin, M. (1975). Can erotic responses be classically conditioned? *Behavior Therapy, 6,* 350–355.

Laws, D. R. (1985). Fantasy alternation: Procedural considerations. *Journal of Behavior Therapy & Experimental Psychiatry, 16,* 39–44.

Laws, D. R. (1986). *Prevention of relapse in sex offenders* (Grant No. MH42035). Rockville, MD: National Institute of Mental Health.

Logan, F. A., & Wagner, A. R. (1965). *Reward and punishment*. Boston: Allyn & Bacon.

Mackintosh, N. J. (1974). *The psychology of animal learning*. London: Academic Press.

Marquis, J. (1970). Orgasmic reconditioning: Changing sexual object choice through controlling masturbation fantasies. *Journal of Behavior Therapy and Experimental Psychiatry, 1,* 263–271.

Marshall, W. L. (1973). The modification of sexual fantasies: A combined treatment approach to the reduction of deviant sexual arousal. *Behaviour Research & Therapy, 11,* 557–564.

Marshall, W. L. (1974). The classical conditioning of sexual attractiveness: A report of four therapeutic failures. *Behavior Therapy, 5,* 298–299.

Marshall, W. L. (1979). Satiation therapy: A procedure for reducing deviant sexual arousal. *Journal of Applied Behavior Analysis, 12,* 377–389.

Marshall, W. L., Earls, C. M., Segal, Z., & Darke, J. (1983). A behavioral program for the assessment and treatment of sexual aggressors. In K. Craig & R. McMahon (Eds.), *Advances in clinical behavior therapy* (pp. 148–174). New York: Brunner/Mazel.

McGuire, R. J., Carlisle, J. M., & Young, B. G. (1965). Sexual deviations as conditioned behaviour: A hypothesis. *Behaviour Research and Therapy, 2,* 185–190.

Plummer, K. (1984). Sexual diversity: A sociological perspective. In K. Howells (Ed.), *The psychology of sexual diversity* (pp. 219–253). Oxford, UK: Blackwell.

Quinn, J. T., Harbison, J., & McAllister, H. (1970). An attempt to shape human penile responses. *Behaviour Research and Therapy, 8,* 27–28.

Quinsey, V. L., & Marshall, W. L. (1983). Procedures for reducing inappropriate sexual arousal: An evaluation review. In J. G. Greer & I. R. Stuart (Eds.), *The sexual aggressor: Current perspectives on treatment* (pp. 267–289). New York: Van Nostrand Reinhold.

Rachman, S. (1966). Sexual fetishism: An experimental analogue. *Psychological Record, 16,* 293–296.

Rachman, S., & Hodgson, R. J. (1968). Experimentally induced "sexual fetishism": Replication and development. *Psychological Record, 18,* 25–27.

Rescorla, R. A. & Solomon, R. L. (1967). Two-process learning theory: Relationships between Pavlovian conditioning and instrumental learning. *Psychological Review, 74,* 437–443.

Reynolds, G. S. (1968). *A primer of operant conditioning.* Glenview IL: Scott, Foresman.

Schwartz, B. (1984). *Psychology of learning and behavior* (2nd ed.). New York: Norton.

Seligman, M. E. P. (1970). On the generality of the laws of learning. *Psychological Review, 77,* 406–418.

Seligman, M. E. P. (1971). Phobias and preparedness. *Behavior Therapy, 2,* 307–320.

Sidman, M. (1960). Normal sources of pathological behavior. *Science, 132,* 61–68.

Skinner, B. F. (1938). *The behavior of organisms.* New York: Appleton-Century-Crofts.

Skinner, B. F. (1953). *Science and human behavior.* New York: The Free Press.

Spence, K. W. (1956). *Behavior theory and conditioning.* New Haven: Yale University Press.

Storms, M. D. (1981). A theory of erotic orientation development. *Psychological Review, 88,* 340–353.

Ullmann, L. P., & Krasner, L. (1969). *A psychological approach to abnormal behavior.* Englewood Cliffs, NJ: Prentice-Hall.

VanDeventer, A. D., & Laws, D. R. (1978). Orgasmic reconditioning to redirect sexual arousal in pedophiles. *Behavior Therapy, 9,* 748–765.

Van Wyk, P. H., & Geist, C. S. (1984). Psychosocial development of heterosexual, bisexual, and homosexual behavior. *Archives of Sexual Behavior, 13,* 505–544.

14

The Characteristics of Incestuous Fathers

A Review of Recent Studies

LINDA MEYER WILLIAMS AND DAVID FINKELHOR

Until very recently there has been a dearth of empirical research on incestuous fathers. Even though the number of cases of intrafamilial sexual abuse coming to professional attention has skyrocketed, reaching close to 100,000 in the United States in 1985, studies of the perpetrators of this abuse have been scarce. Professionals have been forced to rely on several less-than-definitive resources.

One major resource has been clinical reviews about the etiology of intrafamilial sexual abuse and the characteristics of incestuous fathers (Butler, 1978; Cormier, Kennedy, & Sangowicz, 1962; Herman, 1981; Lustig, Dresser, Spellman, & Murray, 1966; Meiselman, 1978; Summit & Kryso, 1978). The ideas contained in these pages have been important and widely disseminated, but few of them, despite and perhaps because of their popularity, have been submitted to more formal empirical evaluation.

There has also been an extensive literature on child molesters in general, some of which has included evaluation of incest offenders. The most comprehensive of these studies, and the one that most systematically differentiated incest offenders from other molesters, was that conducted by Gebhard, Gagnon, Pomeroy, and Christenson (1965). But this work, like most of this literature prior to the late 1970s, was limited to studies of incarcerated offenders. There are many reasons to believe that incarcerated offenders from this era were not representative of the more current group of offenders, few of whom go to prison. Moreover, there has been a growing conviction among both clinicians and researchers that incestuous fathers are a distinct group of child molesters needing specialized study.

LINDA MEYER WILLIAMS AND DAVID FINKELHOR • Family Research Laboratory, University of New Hampshire, Durham, New Hampshire 03824.

Finally, there has recently been a surge of studies of both child and adult victims, many of which contain information on offender characteristics and behavior. One of the most detailed and sophisticated of these studies is by Russell (1986), who collected information from 44 women molested by fathers as part of a larger community survey of mostly undisclosed incest and sexual abuse. However, although this kind of information has been very valuable, there are limits to what can be discovered about offenders without examining or interviewing them directly.

Thus it is encouraging to see that in the mid-1980s, the pace of research specifically on incestuous fathers has started to accelerate. Between 1983 and 1987, at least 20 studies of this population have been completed (16 of them as doctoral dissertations), but few of these have appeared in the professional literature, so that the available reviews are almost entirely restricted to the literature prior to 1980 (Langevin, 1983; Meiselman, 1978). Thus, it seems very important to review and evaluate the conclusions of this recent crop of studies.

THE STUDIES REVIEWED

For purposes of this review, we examined studies of incestuous fathers that had been completed in the 10 years starting in 1978. This is the period during which a large and expanding number of cases of intrafamilial sexual abuse began to come to the attention of the child protection system and that extensive programs for the treatment of such families were being established. We limited ourselves to studies which attempted to quantify characteristics and which used for comparison either a control group or statistical norms from widely used psychological measures. Altogether we identified 29 studies that met these criteria (see Table 1).

The studies varied quite extensively in their quality and methodology. Most of them were of incestuous fathers (both natural and stepfathers) recruited from outpatient treatment programs to which many had been referred by the courts. A few included inpatients from psychiatric hospitals or prisons (e.g., Parker & Parker, 1986). Unfortunately, some of the studies lumped under the rubric of incest offender some nonfathers (e.g., older brothers, grandfathers, or mothers), but this was a serious problem only in Quinsey, Chaplin, and Carrigan's (1979) study, where 7 out of 16 were nonfathers. Although all the incestuous fathers had committed at least one offense against their own child or stepchild, some of the men may well have committed extrafamilial offenses as well (see below in section on sexual arousal). In general, studies did not enquire or report systematically about additional extrafamilial offenses, so it is not clear in how many studies we are dealing with a large group of general child molesters who also happened to molest their own child. Twenty-three of the studies collected data directly from the offenders. The six others collected data about the fathers from wives and daughters, and we only used these studies for evaluating characteristics that wives and daughters could be expected to judge (e.g., whether the father had been physically violent).

TABLE 1. Research Studies of Characteristics of Incest Fathers 1978–1988

Author(s)	Incest fathers (N)	Source[a]	Controls Source and type
Abel, Becker, Murphy, & Flanagan (1981)	6	OPT	1. OPT/Child molesters
Baker (1985)	20	OPT	1. OPT/General
Bennett (1985)	34	OPT	1. COM/Convenience (Matched)
Berkowitz (1983)	20	OPT	1. COM/Convenience
Brandon (1985)	20	OPT	1. PROB/Child molesters 2. COM/Convenience
Cammarata (1984)	7	OPT	1. OPT/General 2. COM/Convenience
Feltman (1985)	31	OPT[b]	1. PROB/Daughters
Fredrickson (1981)	32	OPT	1. OPT/Clinical 2. COM/Church groups
Heath (1985)	28	COM[b]	1. COM/Sex assault victims 2. COM/Convenience
Herman (1981)	40	OPT[b]	1. OPT/Daughters
Kirkland & Bauer (1982)	10	CPS	1. COM/Convenience (Matched)
Langevin, Handy, Day, & Russon (1985)	34	IP	1. IP/Child molesters 2. COM/ Convenience
Langevin, Paitich, Freeman, Mann, & Handy (1978)	27	IP	1. IP/Sex offenders 2. COM/Convenience
Lee (1982)	39	OPT	1. OPT/Physically abusive fathers 2. Norms
Mandel (1986)	18[c]	OPT	1. OPT/General 2. COM/Convenience (Matched)
Marshall, Barbaree, & Christophe (1986)	21	OPT	1. OPT/Child molesters 2. COM/Convenience
Olson (1982)	15	OPT	1. OPT/General (Matched)
Panton (1979)	35	P	1. P/Child molesters 2. Norms
Parker & Parker (1986) and Parker (1984)	56	P/OPT/IP	1. P/Nonincest 2. OPT/General 3. IP/Patients (Matched)
Paveza (1987)	34	OPT	1. COM/Random (Matched)
Pelto (1981)	48	OPT	1. OPT /General 2. COM/Convenience
Quinn (1984)	11	OPT	1. OPT/General 2. COM/Convenience
Quinsey, Chaplin, & Carrigan (1979)	16[c]	IP	1. IP/Child molesters
Saunders, McClure, & Murphy (1986, 1987)	41	OPT	1. Norms
Scott & Stone (1986)	62	OPT	1. COM/Convenience (Matched)
Strand (1986)	21	OPT	1. OPT/General 2. COM/Random
Truesdell, McNeil, & Deschner (1986)	30[c]	OPT[b]	1. Norms
Wickes & Madigan (1985)	21[c]	OPT/COM[b]	1. COM/Convenience
Wieder (1985)	15	OPT[b]	1. OPT/General 2. COM/Convenience (Matched)

[a]OPT, outpatient therapy; IP, inpatient psychiatric setting; CPS, child protective services; P, prison; COM, community sample; PROB, probation.
[b]Data for these studies were obtained through interviews with daughters or wives of the incestuous fathers.
[c]Sample includes from 10–40% other incestuous abuse (e.g., grandfather, uncle, mother).

Most of the studies were rather small—16 had fewer than 30 incestuous fathers and 6 had 15 or fewer. Even the largest study only had 62 subjects, all of which testifies to the difficulty of recruitment among this population.

The comparison–control groups varied quite a bit: other psychotherapy patients, other prisoners, convenience samples of men known to the researcher, men recruited from random phone calls in the same community, extrafamilial child molesters and physically abusive fathers. Some of the better-designed studies used both clinical and community controls. Some tried to match controls on characteristics such as social class, education, age, and having a daughter of the same age.

The Context of Incestuous Abuse

The studies reviewed were primarily small and clinically based. Thus, for certain facts about incestuous fathers and the context of their abuse, particularly matters of demographics, we are better off using studies with larger, more representative data bases. One of the largest data bases is the National Reporting Study of Child Abuse and Neglect, which every year aggregates data on all the reported cases of child abuse and neglect from several dozen American states. The last investigators to select out and specifically analyze the cases involving incestuous fathers from this population were Julian, Mohr, and Lapp (1980), working with data from 1978. These authors looked at the demographic characteristics of 615 incestuous fathers, all of whom were natural fathers. From Table 2, we can see that the median age of these fathers (at time of reporting) was 42.3, with 54% being between ages 36 and 45. The racial composition of incestuous fathers was fairly close to the U.S. population as a whole. However, the fathers, two-thirds of whom had not completed high school, were by quite a substantial margin a less educated group than American men over 25 (two-thirds of whom are high school graduates). This low educational status is in all likelihood an artifact of reporting. Epidemiological studies of unreported cases and surveys of adult victims have consistently failed to find higher rates of sexual abuse among those raised in families of lower socioeconomic status (Finkelhor & Baron, 1986). The lower educational status of fathers in the National Clearinghouse data probably results from a greater likelihood of public disclosure of sexual abuse in such households.

To understand the nature of the molestation that occurs in incestuous abuse, victimization surveys are probably the best data source. Russell's data, based on 44 women abused by their fathers, is particularly valuable because it draws on a representative sample of the general population of one city (San Francisco); findings from her study are shown in Table 3. However, it should be noted that Russell's data lack comparability to most of the studies under review here in that (1) all the victims, being adults at the time they were interviewed, were abused at a different historical epoch and (2) few of the cases came to public attention. It is likely that the cases in Russell's sample have a somewhat

TABLE 2. Demographic Characteristics of
Incestuous Fathers from the National
Reporting Study

Characteristics[a]	% of fathers
Age[b]	
Under 25	9
30–34	15
35–39	27
40–44	27
45–49	11
50	11
Education	
Some high school or less	59
High school	31
Some college or more	10
Race	
White	85
Black	9
Latino	4
Other	1
Age of daughter victim	
<9	12
10–13	38
14–17	36

Note. From Julian, Mohr, & Lapp (1980).
[a]For age, education, and race, $N = 615$; for age of
  daughter victim, $N = 1,599$.
[b]Mean age = 42.3 yrs.

greater representation of short-term, less violative situations that would be, as a result, less likely to be discovered and disclosed.

THE CHARACTERISTICS OF INCESTUOUS FATHERS

The studies of incestuous fathers took a variety of theoretical positions and examined a wide range of hypotheses. Some, for example, looked primarily at sex-role related issues, others looked at family dynamics, while others looked at psychological maladjustment. Rather than present these studies as they were reported, we have decided to reorganize them under a small number of common headings. Table 4 lists the number of studies which looked at some aspect of each characteristic and the number which found it significantly more likely to be present among the incestuous fathers. Trends that were nonsignificant were counted as 0, while the confirmation of only one of two or more aspects studied was counted as a half. In the following sections we examine the findings under each heading. There are a number of studies which focused on the charac-

TABLE 3. Characteristics of Incestuous Abuse from a San Francisco
Community Survey[a]

Characteristics	% of abuse
Natural father	60
Stepfather	40
Frequency	
One time	36
2–10 times	26
11+ times	38
Duration	
One time	36
<1 year	29
1–5 years	21
>5 years	14
Vaginal, oral, anal intercourse, cunnilingus	34
Genital fondling, simulates intercourse, digital penetration	32
Other	34
Force	39
No force	61

Note. From Russell, 1986.
[a]$N = 44$.

teristics of the wives of incestuous fathers (Kegan, 1981; King, 1985; Krieger, 1984; Leroi, 1984) and on comparisons of natural fathers and stepfathers (Gordon, 1988; Groff & Hubble, 1984; Phelan, 1986). We have not included analysis of these studies in this review since our focus is on incestuous fathers' characteristics.

Childhood Experiences

Childhood Abuse

It is practically an article of faith among clinicians that "molesters molest because they themselves were molested as children," yet the connection appears far less universal than this claim would have it. Four out of six studies testing the hypothesis of higher sexual abuse among incestuous fathers have confirmed it, and one of the two remaining studies (Brandon, 1985) did find a nonsignificant trend. However, most interestingly, the absolute percentages of incestuous fathers with a history of being victimized is not very high. In Table 5, we see that the highest percentage of these offenders who were sexually abused as children is 35% (Baker, 1985), and the mean is about 20%. These numbers are closer to estimates of the rate of sexual abuse in the community in general and are a far cry from the numbers that one often hears. They suggest that there is much more to sexual abuse than simply "intergenerational transmission."

Some proponents of the hypothesis believe that many offenders deny or have repressed knowledge of their victimizations. However, it is also true that

TABLE 4. Characteristics of Incestuous Fathers

Factor	Number of Studies	+[a]
Childhood experiences[b]		
Sexually abused	6	4
Physically abused	5	3
Poor relations with parents	7	4
Other family problems	7	4
Psychological characteristics[c]		
Mental illness	4	1.5
Psychopathy/criminality	6	4.5
Passivity/inadequacy/dependence	3	2.5
Low self-esteem	2	1.5
Dominance/authoritarianism/abusiveness	9	4
Paranoia	7	4.5
Anxiety	6	6
Depression/distress	8	7
Cognitive impairments	2	2
Low intelligence	2	1
Sexuality and sex role[d]		
Arousal to children	4	1.5
Problems with adult sexuality	5	4
Sex-role disturbances	3	2
Family and social relationships[e]		
Marital quality	5	3
Family disorganization	4	3
Alcohol/drug usage	6	2.5
Empathy/bonding	8	7
Isolation/lack of social skills	8	7.5

[a] + = number of studies with statistically significant evidence ($p < .05$) of each characteristic of incestuous fathers. Nonsignificant trends are counted as 0, and − = negative findings (see following footnotes).
[b] Sexually abused: Baker (1985) (+), Langevin et al. (1985) (+), Pelto (1981) (+), Strand (1986) (+), Brandon (1985) (0) (+ trend), Mandel (1986) (0).
Physically abused: Mandel (1986) (+), Parker & Parker (1986) (+), Strand (1986) (+), Brandon (1985) (0), Lee (1982) (0).
Poor relations with parents: Baker (1985) (+), Berkowitz (1983) (+), Langevin et al. (1985) (+), Strand (1986) (+), Parker & Parker (1986) (0), Mandel (1986) (0), Brandon (1985) (0).
Other family problems: Baker (1985) (+), Bennett (1985) (+), Brandon (1985) (0) (+ trend), Pelto (1981) (+), Saunders et al. (1986) (+ trend), Parker & Parker (1986) (0).
[c] Mental illness: Kirkland & Bauer (1982) (+), Langevin et al. (1985) (+ and 0), Lee (1982) (0), Scott & Stone (1986) (0).
Psychopathy/criminality: Kirkland and Bauer (1982) (+), Fredrickson (1981) (+), Langevin et al. (1985) (+ and 0), Lee (1982) (+ and 0), Panton (1979) (+ and 0), Scott & Stone (1986) (+).
Passivity/inadequacy/dependence: Kirkland & Bauer (1982) (+), Langevin et al. (1985) (+ and 0), Quinn (1984) (+).
Low self-esteem: Berkowitz (1983) (0 and +), Saunders et al. (1986) (+).
Dominance/authoritarianism/abusiveness: Cammarata (1984) (+ and 0), Fredrickson (1981) (+ and 0), Herman (1981) (+), Paveza (1987) (+), Truesdell et al. (1986) (+), Feltman (1985) (0), Lee (1982) (0), Langevin et al. (1985) (−), Quinn (1984) (−).
Paranoia: Fredrickson (1981) (+), Langevin et al. (1985) (+), Saunders et al. (1986) (+), Scott & Stone (1986) (+), Lee (1982) (0 and +), Berkowitz (1983) (0).
Anxiety: Fredrickson (1981) (+), Kirkland & Bauer (1982) (+), Langevin et al. (1985) (+), Panton (1979) (+), Saunders et al. (1986) (+), Scott & Stone (1986) (+).
Depression/distress: Fredrickson (1981) (+), Kirkland & Bauer (1982) (+), Langevin et al. (1985) (+), Panton (1979) (+), Saunders et al. (1986) (+), Scott & Stone (1986) (+), Strand (1986) (+), Lee (1982) (0).
Cognitive impairments: Bennett (1985) (+), Langevin et al. (1985) (+).
Low intelligence: Langevin et al. (1985) (+ and 0).
[d] Arousal to children: Abel et al. (1981) (+), Langevin et al. (1985) (+ and −), Quinsey et al. (1979) (0 and −), Marshall et al. (1986) (0).
Problems with adult sexuality: Abel et al. (1981) (+), Langevin et al. (1985) (+), Marshall et al. (1986) (+), Saunders et al. (1986) (+), Baker (1985) (0).
Sex-role disturbances: Brandon (1985) (+ and 0), Fredrickson (1981) (+), Strand (1986) (+ and 0).
[e] Marital quality: Olson (1982) (+), Paveza (1987) (+), Saunders et al. (1986) (+), Parker & Parker (1986) (0), Baker (1985) (−).
Family disorganization: Olson (1982) (+), Quinn (1984) (+), Wieder (1985) (+), Feltman (1985) (0).
Alcohol/drug usage: Langevin et al. (1985) (+), Lee (1982) (+ and 0), Strand (1986) (+), Herman (1981) (0), Mandel (1986) (0), Parker & Parker (1986) (0).
Empathy/bonding: Berkowitz (1983) (+), Heath (1985) (+), Olson (1982) (+), Parker & Parker (1986) (+), Quinn (1984) (+), Wickes & Madigan (1985) (+), Wieder (1985) (+), Bennett (1985) (0).
Isolation/lack of social skills: Fredrickson (1981) (+), Langevin et al. (1985) (+), Quinn (1984) (+), Saunders et al. (1986) (+), Scott & Stone (1986) (+), Strand (1986) (+), Panton (1979) (+), Parker (1984) (+ and 0).

Table 5. Incestuous Fathers Abused as Children

Study	%	N	Comments
Sexual Abuse[a]			
Baker (1985)	35[b]	20	
Brandon (1985)	21	20	
Kirkland & Bauer (1982)	10	10	Incestuous abuse only
Langevin et al. (1985)	21	34	Sex with a male 18+
Lee (1982)	0	39	
Strand (March, 1988, personal communication)	28	21	
Physical Abuse[a]			
Brandon (1985)	56	20	Excessive physical punishment
Lee (1982)	36	39	
Mandel (1986)	55	18	
Parker & Parker (1986)	59	56	Parental mistreatment
Strand (March, 1988, personal communication)	28	21	

[a]Undefined unless indicated.
[b]We deleted 2 cases where the "abuse" which was reported involved the subject's sexual aggressions against a *younger* sibling.

given the therapy many of the subjects in these studies have received postdisclosure, they have had much more encouragement, motivation, and opportunity than the control subjects to remember or redefine experiences as victimizations. It seems that although intergenerational transmission may be a factor for some incestuous fathers, it does not come close to being universal.

Five studies found indications of high rates of physical abuse in the backgrounds of incestuous fathers. Three of the five found the incest fathers had been subjected to more physical abuse as children than had the comparison groups. The two studies which failed to find group differences compared incestuous fathers with controls who would be expected to have unusual amounts of physical abuse in their backgrounds: in one case, fathers who physically abused their children (Lee, 1982) and, in another, extrafamilial sex offenders (Brandon, 1985). Interestingly, the rates of physical abuse in the backgrounds of incestuous fathers ran consistently higher than rates of sexual abuse. In three of the studies, the rates were over 50%, although the characteristic being measured was sometimes more global than just physical abuse. From the available evidence we conclude that physical maltreatment is more prevalent than sexual abuse and perhaps of more general etiological significance.

Poor Relationship with Parents

In addition to physical and sexual abuse, a number of studies have looked at other difficulties or disruptions in the relationships between incestuous fathers and their own parents. In general, the quality of these relationships has been found to have been consistently poor, but the evidence on actual separation is weaker.

Berkowitz (1983) assessed a number of themes related to the families of origin of these offenders using projective tests and a scale tapping childhood memories. The incestuous fathers had significantly more themes of abandonment, powerlessness, maternal seduction, and paternal rejection. This last theme of paternal rejection is reiterated in a number of other studies. Baker (1985), using the Conceptual Grid, found rejection by the father, but not the mother. In another study (Parker & Parker, 1986), 50% of incestuous fathers reported mistreatment by father compared to 30% reporting mistreatment by mother. And in Mandel (1986), an object relations measure concerning the father showed near significant disturbances, whereas the mother-oriented measure did not. These studies suggest disturbed parental relationships, particularly with fathers.

The studies are less consistent on the question of whether incestuous fathers were more likely to have been separated from one or the other of their parents. Baker (1985) finds that 65% of them report separation from their own father, while 30% were separated from their mother (both significantly different from controls). But Parker (1984) could only detect a trend concerning mother absence and nothing concerning father absence. From the currently available data, mistreatment, rejection, and abuse by parents seem more important factors than simply parental absence.

Other Family Problems

With the kinds of problems already described, it is not surprising that studies report other pathological conditions in the family backgrounds of incestuous fathers as well. Saunders, McClure, and Murphy (1986) found perpetrators' families scored highly dysfunctional on the Family of Origin Scale, with especially high pathology on such things as respect for others, conflict resolution, trust, autonomy, and intimacy. Baker (1985) found alcohol misuse in 35% of the families of origin, and Parker (1984) reported that 35% of the offenders say their parents had a bad relationship compared to 13% of the nonabusers. Berkowitz (1983) found a nonsignificant trend for more domestic violence as well. And confirming another of the generational transmission hypotheses, three studies (Bennett, 1985; Brandon, 1985; Pelto, 1981) note more frequent reports of previous incest (against some other family member) in the offenders' families of origin. There would appear to be many possible pathologies in offenders' backgrounds which may predispose them to be abusive.

Psychological Characteristics

Psychiatric Disturbances

Most recent literature on incestuous abusers stresses that they do not as a group show signs of serious psychiatric disturbance. A commonly cited estimate from the National Committee for the Prevention of Child Abuse (1978) is that no more than 10% are psychiatrically ill.

Unfortunately, psychiatric disturbance is a vague concept, and contradictory findings among studies only complicate the problem of trying to assess the extent of psychiatric impairment among incestuous fathers. For example, Scott and Stone (1986), evaluating a rather large outpatient sample ($N = 62$) using the MMPI (Minnesota Multiphasic Personality Inventory), found that as a group incestuous fathers did not show any mean scores outside the normal range. However, these findings are inconsistent with other studies. For example, Langevin, Handy, Day, and Russon (1985), in their MMPI evaluations, found that 72% had at least one clinically elevated score, while Kirkland and Bauer (1982) found that 90% had at least *two* clinically elevated MMPI scores. Unfortunately, the latter study involved so few subjects ($N = 10$) that it should be treated with caution. Clearly, the degree of pathology can vary quite a bit from sample to sample.

Other clinical evaluations have attempted to identify the size of the subgroup of incestuous fathers with marked signs of psychological impairment. For example, Langevin, Paitich, Freeman, Mann, and Handy (1978), although noting that incestuous fathers were more stable than other groups of sex offenders, concluded from clinical assessments that between a quarter and a third of the sample showed some disturbance of clinical note. A diagnosis of personality disorder was given to 47% of the sample, but it is important to note that 35% did not qualify for any psychiatric diagnosis, and no one was diagnosed as psychotic. Lee (1982) found that 25% of incestuous fathers had received prior treatment, either inpatient or outpatient, for some other psychological problem.

It is somewhat difficult to reconcile these diverse data concerning general psychological disturbance, because the degree of observed disturbance varies considerably across studies. We would endorse the idea that the majority of incestuous fathers do not manifest severe psychiatric impairment. However, whether or not the majority display some abnormality on a measure like the MMPI or on other measures—including projective techniques which have not been systematically applied to incestuous fathers—is unclear. We can conclude that a substantial proportion of incestuous fathers (one-quarter to one-third) seem quite normal. This seems to be an important conclusion for forensic purposes, since it means that the absence of psychiatric problems as measured in an evaluation is not necessarily evidence that no offense was committed.

Personality Disturbances

Psychopathy. Psychopathy refers to a disregard for the interests and concerns of others and a tendency to violate social norms with minimal feelings of guilt. The findings on psychopathy come from six studies, all using the MMPI measure "Pd." All six studies found that compared to normal controls, the incestuous fathers had elevated Pd scores.

According to Langevin *et al.* (1985), 47% of incestuous fathers had mean T scores greater than 70 on this scale, although they did not differ significantly in this respect from extrafamilial molesters. This was similar to Lee's (1982) finding that while incestuous fathers differed from the norms, they were no more likely to have elevated Pd scores than were fathers who physically abused their daughters. These findings suggest a willingness of incestuous fathers to exploit others and to violate social norms, observations which fit well with our later discussions of impaired empathy. It is interesting, however, that incestuous fathers do not generally have histories of committing other criminal offenses (Langevin *et al.*, 1985), suggesting that their psychopathy is moderate and is acted out in ways that have avoided detection by law enforcement.

Passivity–Inadequacy–Dependence. Both research findings and clinical perceptions strongly suggest that incestuous fathers are passive and dependent. Of three studies which measured such characteristics, each found them to a significantly greater degree among the incestuous fathers. Quinn (1984), using the Interpersonal Behavior Survey, found that dependency was the most important variable of any in discriminating between incestuous fathers and both the clinical and the "normal" control groups. Saunders, McClure, and Murphy (1987) found that fully 51% of the incestuous fathers scored in the pathologically unassertive range of the 16 Personality Factor Questionnaire 16PF. Indeed, Langevin *et al.* (1978, 1985) found that the most common psychiatric diagnosis for the incestuous father was the personality disorder immature–inadequate. Consistent with these findings, two studies also support the idea that fathers who sexually abuse their daughters suffer from low self-esteem (Berkowitz, 1983; Saunders *et al.*, 1987).

Dominance–Aggression–Abusiveness. The clinical literature has portrayed incestuous fathers as passive and dependent, yet at the same time, in what at first seems to be a contradiction, they are also frequently described as dominant and tyrannical. "One of the most significant distinguishing characteristics of the incestuous fathers (is) their tendency to dominate their families by the use of force" (Herman, 1981, p. 73). Some try to resolve these contradictions by suggesting that the fathers possess both aggressive and passive traits, while others have suggested that there may be two different types of abusers (Stern & Meyer, 1980).

The evidence from the studies we reviewed on the dominance and assertiveness of incestuous fathers is contradictory and does not resolve the dilemma. Studies relying on tests which measure personality traits (e.g., Langevin *et al.*, 1978, 1985) suggest that incestuous fathers are the *least* assertive of all sex offenders and significantly less assertive than controls (Quinn 1984). In an observational study of family interaction, Cammarata (1984) found that incestuous fathers were no more dominant than community controls, and Fredrickson (1981) found them to be no more authoritarian than community controls. Thus, based on test measures, incestuous fathers seem to be no more assertive and dominant than others.

On the other hand, there are two studies with findings that incestuous fathers engage in other abusive behaviors. Both Paveza (1987) and Truesdell,

McNeil, and Deschner (1986) found that incestuous fathers were more likely to abuse their wives. For example, Truesdell *et al.* found that 73% of all the mothers of incest victims had been physically abused by their partners. Incestuous fathers' rate of wife abuse is clearly higher than in the community at large, although it is about the same as the rate for fathers who have physically abused their children (Lee, 1982).

Surprisingly, little interest was shown in these studies concerning the possibility that incestuous fathers were also physically abusive to their victims, separate from the sexual abuse. In one study (Feltman, 1985) it was found that 19% of incest daughters had been beaten, threatened with a weapon, or abused with a weapon. Although this was not significantly higher than a control group, the control group was made up of families where the daughter had been referred to juvenile court because of non-incest-related problems. Feltman's rate seems clearly higher than in the community at large.

Unfortunately, all these findings do not ultimately resolve the question of why incestuous fathers are described as both dependent and domineering, passive and abusive. Overall the studies are more consistent and convincing in confirming that these fathers are passive, dependent, and conflict avoidant. The evidence for aggression and abusiveness, although not found in direct observation or testing, does emerge in reports from daughters and wives. The aggressiveness is also consistent with the elevated Pd scores, showing disregard for others. These could be two sides of the same coin, or there could be two distinct types of incestuous abuser, with the aggressive type perhaps not being as frequently studied. It should be a high priority to disentangle this dilemma.

Paranoia. Clinically, incestuous fathers have been seen to rationalize their behavior and to externalize responsibility to others who are viewed as hostile. Although all incestuous fathers may not necessarily possess a paranoid personality, it has been hypothesized that paranoid thinking characterizes incestuous fathers (Bennett, 1985).

Five studies found evidence of paranoid ideation (Langevin *et al.*, 1985; Lee, 1982; Fredrickson, 1981; Saunders *et al.*, 1986; Scott & Stone, 1986), and another (Kirkland & Bauer, 1982) found a trend suggesting that incestuous fathers had higher scores. However, a study designed to specifically examine this hypothesis failed to find any indication that incestuous men were paranoid in their thinking (Bennett, 1985). It is possible that the measure of cognitive style and paranoid thinking which Bennett developed for this research does not truly measure paranoia. Her measure used a projective technique, analyzing the paranoid content of the father's response to questions about his relationship with his wife.

There appears to be quite strong support in the research for the idea that a paranoid style of thinking typifies incestuous fathers. Such a style, however, could well be something that develops or is accentuated after the onset of incest, with its need to be secretive, or even after disclosure, when these fathers are subjects of the investigative efforts of law enforcement, child welfare, employers, and family. Some of the paranoia-sensitive items in the MMPI, like

"Someone has it in for me," seem quite rational in the context of an investigation. But paranoia, because it fits into the general picture of dependency and social isolation could also be an important predisposing factor.

Mood Disturbances

In addition to the above problems, incestuous fathers have also been clinically described as anxious and depressed. Five studies that have directly examined anxiety have all found significantly elevated scores for incestuous fathers (Kirkland & Bauer, 1982; Langevin *et al.*, 1985; Panton, 1979; Saunders *et al.*, 1986; Scott & Stone, 1986). It is not clear, however, whether this anxiety is an enduring feature or simply a response to the stress associated with their identification as an offender. Saunders *et al.* (1986) suggest that these elevated anxiety scores, as indications of current levels of stress, might be positive signs of men who are amenable to treatment soon after the disclosure of abuse (personal communication, April 1988).

In addition to anxiety, incestuous fathers also suffer from depression. All five studies which measured depression found significantly elevated levels in these men. Langevin *et al.* (1985), for example, found that 47% of the incestuous fathers had mean T scores greater than 70 on the MMPI depression scale, while depression was this severe for only 19% of the community sample controls. In addition, two studies examined levels of distress and found incestuous fathers to be under more stress than nonincestuous fathers. Again, it is likely that those observed levels of depression are in response to disclosure (Panton, 1979). No studies have attempted to measure the existence of depression and stress prior to the incest or the disclosure.

Cognitive Disturbances

Two studies examining possible cognitive impairments among incestuous fathers have both found evidence of constricted and simplistic thinking. Using the 16PF, Langevin *et al.* (1985) found incest offenders to be less imaginative, and Bennett (1985) found them to be illogical and simplistic in their thinking. Nonincestuous fathers were able to generate more ideas about how to deal with problems, and they developed more satisfying goals. These findings support clinical impressions that incestuous fathers have an impaired ability to get their needs met and are unable to think of ways to deal with problems. These features may lead them to turn to incest.

Most groups of incestuous fathers have been found to have at least average intelligence (Cavallin, 1966; Maisch, 1972; Meiselman, 1978). Moreover, the proportion of incestuous fathers found to be mentally defective in any one sample has decreased, as larger, outpatient samples have replaced studies of prison populations. But even in current studies, some researchers find low intelligence to be a significant factor. For example, Langevin *et al.* (1985) found incestuous fathers to be less intelligent than both the community controls and nonfamilial child molesters. Moreover, Lee (1982) found that while the average intelligence of incest offenders (97) was not statistically different from fathers who physically abused their daughters, there was one interesting difference: 10% of the incestuous fathers had an IQ of 69 or less, while none of the physically abusive fathers scored this low. While it is necessary to rule out chronic depression, which may have an impact on IQ scores, these findings suggest that although low intelligence is not a precondition for incestuous behavior, it may be relevant to understanding some of these men.

Sexuality

Sexual Arousal to Children

One of the few theories concerning incestuous fathers that has provoked debate is the question of whether they have a sexually deviant preference for children. However, discouragingly few studies have attempted to resolve this issue empirically, in spite of the now fairly widespread dissemination of the technology for measuring sexual preference and arousal. For many years, two studies defined the issue. Abel, Becker, Murphy, and Flanagan (1981) detected inappropriate sexual preferences among a sample of six incestuous fathers, while Quinsey *et al.* (1979), with a sample of 16, found normal sexual proclivities.

More recent studies with larger samples point to the likely conclusion that some incestuous fathers may have pedophilic preferences, while others may not. Using the Clarke Sexual History Questionnaire, which indicates what people find sexually desirable or disgusting, Langevin and his colleagues (Langevin *et al.* 1985; Paitich, Langevin, Freeman, Mann, & Handy, 1977) concluded that between a quarter and a third of a sample of 34 incest offenders had pedophilic erotic preferences. As a group, they scored between heterosexual pedophiles and controls on measures of desire for both prepubertal and pubescent children. This is consistent with Abel, Mittleman, Becker, Cunningham-Rathner and Lucas' (1983) recent findings that among 142 incestuous men, 44% had also molested girls outside the family.

Marshall, Barbaree, and Christophe (1986) evaluated the sexual preferences of 21 incestuous fathers using phallometric technology. As a group incestuous fathers were much closer in erotic preference to normals than they were to extrafamilial child molesters. Although 19% of these fathers might have been classified as having deviant arousal to children according to one proposed cut-off criterion, so would 18% of the normals. Instead, the main way in which incestuous fathers were deviant was in their unusually low levels of arousal to adult females. One of the implications of this was that incestuous fathers did not make as much differentiation between pubescent females and adults as did normals, and in this way they were similar to other child molesters. Of the extrafamilial child molesters, 70% had deviant arousal levels to pubescent females, as did 52% of the incest offenders but only 32% of the normals. Interestingly, among both child molesters and incest offenders, men with low IQs were the ones most likely to display the deviant sexual interests.

Curiously, studies have not systematically examined how age of victim is associated with deviant arousal among offenders. It would seem plausible that those incest offenders exhibiting the most pedophilic type of sexual preference patterns would be those who molested the youngest children. Barbaree and Marshall (in press), however, did not find support for this, and more such studies are needed. Until we have such studies, the current data would suggest that some subset, but probably not a majority of incest offenders, and certainly fewer than in the case of extrafamilial molesters, have deviant patterns of sexual arousal.

Sexual Problems with Adults

A pedophilic-type sexual orientation is characterized not simply by arousal to children but also by disinterest in, disgust at, or conflict over, sexual relations with adults. This characteristic has received a number of confirmations. Marshall et al. (1986), as mentioned previously, found that incestuous fathers were less aroused to adult stimuli than either normals or extrafamilial molesters. In the same vein, Langevin et al. (1985) found more disgust about sex with adult females among incestuous fathers than among either normals or pedophiles. It is not clear whether this aversion to adult stimuli is an aspect of an ongoing problem in sexual orientation or a more transitory conflict generated by the marital problems. For example, Saunders et al. (1986) found that 37% of incest offenders scored in the clinical range on the Index of Sexual Satisfaction, and they noted that virtually all the couples (offenders and their wives) reported substantial sexual relationship dysfunction. Of Baker's (1985) incestuous fathers, 50% said they associated frustration and failure with adult sexual experiences, but interestingly, this was not significantly higher than a comparison group of other men receiving psychotherapy. Clearly, a large number of incestuous abusers have conflicts and dissatisfactions about their adult sexual relationships, which may result in or be the result of an inability to feel aroused by adults. These conflicts, even in the absence of strong affirmative sexual arousal to children, may be an important part of what leads to sexual interactions with children.

Sex Role and Masculinity

Early feminist theory about incest suggested that, because such behavior seemed to involve a sexual objectification of daughters, the treating of children as property, and the abuse of patriarchal authority, incestuous fathers would be men with rigidly traditional masculine outlooks. Three very thoughtful dissertations which set out with this hypothesis, however, failed to confirm it. Using the Extended Personal Attributes Questionnaire (a measure of masculinity and femininity), the Sex Role Behavior Scale (a measure of traditional roles in family life), and the Attitudes Toward Women Scale (AWS; a measure of traditional stereotypes of women), Brandon (1985) did not find on any measure more masculine stereotyped self-identifications among incestuous fathers than among normals or other sex offenders. Strand (1986) and Frederickson (1981), both using the Bem Sex Role Inventory, also failed to find that incest offenders endorsed traditional, stereotyped notions of masculinity or femininity. Using the AWS, Frederickson also did not find conservative attitudes toward women compared to community controls, although she did in comparison to therapy controls.

All studies, however, did find suggestions of other sex-role disturbances. Brandon (1985) found that the incestuous fathers scored low on scales that measured masculine behaviors which are taken to be normative only for males (i.e., aggressiveness, dominance, indifference to other's approval, feelings not easily hurt), in contrast to masculine qualities which are normative in either sex. She hypothesized that this meant "a diminished sense of their core masculine identification" (p. 139). Strand (1986) found incestuous fathers represented disproportionately in the "undifferentiated" rather than masculine range of the Bem measure. This undifferentiated category (which is not the same as the androgynous category) is associated with low levels of adjustment, leadership, and sociality. Finally, Frederickson (1981) found the incestuous fathers to be lowest on the masculinity index.

In short, incestuous fathers seem to be inadequate in their masculine identification rather than being overidentified with stereotypical masculinity. However, it should be noted that these researchers were measuring global sex-role identifications. There may also be specific kinds of patriarchal or hypermasculine attitudes (e.g., a sense of ownership of children) that incestuous fathers would endorse if specifically asked. No one has yet studied such specific attitudes with these men.

Family and Social Relations

Marital Quality

Although three studies do confirm poor quality in the marriages of incest abusers, it is interesting, given the almost universal belief in the etiological importance of this factor, that not all studies agree.

One study with a very clear demonstration of the marital difficulties of incestuous fathers was reported by Saunders *et al.* (1986), who found 44% to be in the pathological range on the Dyadic Adjustment Scale and 37% in the pathological range on the Index of Sexual Satisfaction. However, when a study with matched controls (Parker & Parker, 1986) compared incest offenders against other clinical fathers (in this case matched groups of prisoners and outpatients), few significant differences in marital quality appeared. This suggests that the marriages of these abusers are not any worse than one might find among other men experiencing other social and psychological problems.

Another point to remember, of course, is that the disclosure of abuse puts enormous strains on marital quality, and no study has yet attempted to estimate marital quality prior to disclosure. Baker (1985), in an anomalous finding, actually reports that incestuous fathers felt *closer* to their wives than a comparison group. However, all her offenders were recruited through Parents United, a support group that emphasizes and promotes family reunification. This illustrates again how estimates of marital quality may depend on the context in which they are being measured. Current reports of marital quality may be poor proxies for marital quality prior to the onset of incest or the disclosure.

Family Disorganization

A number of investigators, influenced by family systems theory, have looked for general family dysfunctions in addition to marital problems. All of these studies, with the exception of one, have found considerable and significant family pathology.

In one of the few studies that actually observed and rated laboratory interactions in families, Olson (1982) found that incestuous families were significantly different from controls on the following dimensions: they were in disarray; there was an unusual degree of parent–child coalition, low empathy, and unresolved conflict; and they had a hostile–depressed tone, an incongruent picture of themselves, low efficiency in their negotiations, an inability to accept responsibility, and a tendency to make intrusive remarks and obliterate others' autonomy. Quinn (1984) found incestuous families to be conflict avoidant, low in community involvement, and also low in adaptability and cohesion. Saunders et al. (1986) noted the same adaptability and cohesion problems and, in addition, found differences on the Family Environment Scale, particularly in terms of signs of social isolation and chaotic structure, which the family tried to control with religiosity and similar external controls. Only Feltman (1985) found no differences, although he failed to interview any other family members except the daughters, and he used as controls girls from highly chaotic, if nonincestuous, backgrounds (runaways, drug abusers, truants, and victims of neglect).

The picture of incestuous families painted by these studies is one of isolation, disorganization, conflict, and antagonism. This is not to say that these families are all similar, since different pathologies can all manifest in these kinds of symptoms. Moreover, the extent to which these problems are caused or exacerbated by the incest or its disclosure is difficult to evaluate.

Substance Abuse

Alcohol and drug abuse are related to so many social problems that it obviously belongs among any listing of correlates of incestuous abuse. On the other hand, many believe that its popularity as an explanatory factor stems primarily from the fact that offenders so often invoke it themselves to minimize the opprobrium directed toward their crime. Three studies do confirm higher levels of alcohol and drug abuse (Langevin et al., 1985; Lee, 1982; Strand, 1986) among these offenders, but other studies have failed to find a relationship (Herman, 1981; Mandel, 1986; Parker & Parker, 1986). According to the percentages and based on a variety of definitions of alcohol and drug abuse, perhaps the most interesting and important conclusion is that whether the difference is significant or not, the stereotype of the alcoholic or drug abuser describes only a minority of offenders. Lee (1982) found that only 15% of incestuous fathers could be classified as alcohol abusers and 23% as drug abusers. Only 29% of abusers in Parker's (1984) sample said they used alcohol or drugs very often. So while alcohol and drug abuse may or may not make some contribution to offending in some cases, it is not a factor for the majority of incestuous fathers.

Empathy and Bonding

There is increasingly strong evidence that incestuous fathers are impaired in their capacity for empathy or bonding, particularly toward their children. Seven out of eight studies looking at some aspect of this capacity have confirmed such a deficit. The one dissenting study (Bennett, 1985) only evaluated the empathy shown by the offenders toward their wives, not their daughters.

The strongest evidence on this issue comes from Parker (Parker, 1984; Parker & Parker, 1986), who looked at several dimensions. Incestuous fathers, according to Parker's own assessments, were more likely than controls to avoid child care or nurturing activities (53% vs. 24%), and they had higher levels of reported discomfort about these activities. A much higher percentage of incest fathers (59% vs. 14%) reported being out of the household during all or part of their daughters first 3 years, a possibly critical period for some aspects of bonding. Another study (Berkowitz, 1983) found a generalized lack of empathy in incestuous men, using TAT evaluations. Two other studies (Heath, 1985; Wickes & Madigan, 1985) support the idea of an absence of nurturance or empathy, but they based their observations on reports from the daughter victims, whose view of the father's pre-abuse character may certainly have been colored by the later incest. Also consistent with the conclusions about bonding are studies that confirm that daughters are at greater risk for sexual abuse at the hands of stepfathers than natural fathers (Finkelhor & Baron, 1986; Russell, 1984).

In view of these findings, it is interesting to remember that some writers stereotypically characterize the father–daughter incest relationship as one of "daddy's special girl." The evidence on nurturance and empathy, coming from both the father's and daughter's perspective, appears to contradict this image. A finding from Wickes and Madigan (1985) that may temper this apparent contradiction concerns the fact that incestuous fathers, even while demonstrating little caretaking, score very high on overprotection. What appears as special father–daughter closeness may simply be a combination of overprotection and a manipulative father–daughter alliance that isolates the child from the mother and other family members. The "special relationship" between the father and daughter does not seem to be one that entails much real empathy or nurturance.

Social Isolation and Ineptitude

Social isolation and lack of social skills have been noted and confirmed repeatedly as characteristics of child molesters in general (Araji & Finkelhor, 1986), so it should not be surprising that the evidence for this characteristic among incestuous fathers is also strong. All eight studies that have examined this characteristic have found it to some degree. Parker (1984), for example, reports that 31% of incest offenders said they had almost no close friends compared to only 11% of the controls. Strand (1986) found that the biggest difference from controls on the Health–Sickness Rating Scales was the poor quality of the incestuous fathers' interpersonal relationships. Strand (1986) and Quinn (1984) also found that incestuous fathers have low levels of group activity and participation. These findings are confirmed by four studies (Kirkland & Bauer, 1982; Langevin et al., 1985; Panton, 1979; Scott & Stone, 1986) in which psychological testing revealed high levels of introversion among incest offenders. The only dissenting evidence is from Parker (1984), who, in spite of finding that incestuous fathers had few friends, did not find that they had lower levels of church or social club membership than did controls. However, Parker's controls included many men imprisoned for nonsex offenses, and thus they were likely to have few community ties. Overall, then, the studies consistently point to isolation and social-skills problems as being important features of incestuous fathers.

THEORETICAL IMPLICATIONS

Incestuous fathers, at least those available for study, seem to be different from other men in a number of important ways. How have these data advanced our understanding about what kinds of men abuse and why they do so?

One advance that seems fairly obvious and important is the evidence against a simple single-factor hypothesis. There is no characteristic that appears universal or near universal. For example, the idea that *all* incestuous fathers were themselves molested as children was not supported. Even the characteristics that received the strongest empirical support (e.g., maltreatment by parents or social isolation) were not descriptive of more than half of the offenders.

By the same token, while it is not possible to sketch a single profile of the incestuous father, there are characteristics that seem relatively common. Many incestuous fathers appear to be passive, dependent, isolated, somewhat paranoid, and lacking a core masculine identification. Many have been maltreated in their families of origin and report rejection, particularly by their fathers. Many have poor marriages and a low level of sexual satisfaction and arousal with adults. Many have difficulty feeling empathy, particularly with their children, and they report being uninvolved in child caretaking. However, here again, few of these characteristics apply to a majority of offenders. Moreover, the studies have not indicated whether or how these characteristics tend to coalesce. There are also many offenders who do not have these characteristics.

The wide number of characteristics confirmed by various studies, and the lack of universality suggests multiple causes and multiple pathways. Different men probably come to incestuous acts as a result of different needs, motives, and impairments. And very likely this behavior, even within one individual, is multicausal, requiring a combination of ingredients before a predisposition becomes a real act.

Methodological Suggestions

Overall, the studies we have reviewed here represent a significant advance over previous efforts. They show thoughtful theoretical development; they have examined outpatients rather than just prisoners; they have often used sophisticated control groups; and many have employed sound measurement procedures. All this is even more impressive considering how many were completed as doctoral dissertations, without external funding and within narrow time constraints.

However, there are some fairly widespread shortcomings to the research so far that future studies should make an effort to correct. One is the generally small sample size. The biggest problem with this is that it has prohibited the application of multivariate analyses. Most studies demonstrate a series of differences for the incestuous fathers without being able to assess which differences take priority. The study by Parker and Parker (1986) was an exception to this; they used multiple regression on one of the larger samples (56 incestuous fathers and 54 controls) to show that it was the father's involvement in early child-care activities that was the important differences, not the time he spent in the home or his biological status (i.e., natural father or stepfather). Other studies need to follow this example, which undoubtedly means multiple-site investigations to recruit enough subjects. It may turn out that many of the differences noted in the studies here would not survive when subjected to multivariate analysis.

Another problem has to do with the selection of samples which are biased in a number of ways. Unfortunately, incestuous fathers are a fairly recalcitrant group. They often deny their abuse, refuse treatment, and hire attorneys to try to beat the charge. Since a significant number are successful in these endeavors, it may be that studies based on treatment programs, as so many are, do not truly recruit a representative group of incestuous fathers. Even among those who admit their offense, not all will enter treatment, thus reducing the representativeness even further. The observation that incest offenders are passive, inadequate, and score low in masculinity could be due to the fact that aggressive, assertive, and high-masculinity abusers shun treatment at all costs. Unfortunately, such men may shun participation in research, too, making it difficult to recruit them even if researchers search for participants outside of treatment settings. Nonetheless, studies are needed to evaluate how representative clinical samples are of the population of reported offenders.

A second bias often introduced by clinical samples is the bias toward intact families. Many incest treatment programs and groups like Parents United (where research tends to congregate) are organized around or give priority to the goal of maintaining or restoring family integrity. Fathers who are involved in these programs are often the ones whose families are amenable to such an approach. Fathers whose families have rejected them (or fathers who have rejected their families) will be underrepresented. Here again, the remedy is to have studies cast a wide net to capture the full variety of incestuous abusers.

A third important, but difficult to correct, bias in clinical samples is the complete absence of fathers whose abuse has not been identified. Authorities on the prevalence of sexual abuse believe that the majority of abuse still goes undisclosed (Finkelhor & Lewis, 1988; Russell, 1986). The cases coming to public attention are known to be biased in terms of social class (Finkelhor & Baron, 1986) and may also be biased in terms of their duration, severity, and the degree of pathology in the abuser. More normal-appearing and less disturbed abusers may be more effective at preventing disclosure. All the conclusions demonstrated in all the studies reviewed here might be much weaker if they included undetected abusers. This bias is difficult to remedy, because undetected abusers are typically not available for study. But they can be studied, as Abel *et al.* (1984) have demonstrated, and other techniques, such as anonymous surveys, may be possible (Finkelhor & Lewis, 1988). In the meantime, investigators need to stress that their conclusions apply to reported offenders only.

We also have some recommendations for researchers about the kinds of data they need to be collecting in their studies. One of the deficiencies we are most aware of is the failure of investigators to find out if incestuous fathers have committed other, particularly extrafamilial, offenses. Abel *et al.* (1983) found that 44% of incestuous fathers had committed extrafamilial offenses. There is a strong likelihood that this is a different group from those who have molested only within their own family.

A related recommendation concerns the need for typologically oriented research. Most of the studies reviewed here were trying to confirm the presence or absence of characteristics in incestuous fathers as a group. However, such men are not a homogeneous group. Even a characteristic that is not widespread, like low intelligence, may be the marker for a particular subgroup that is theoretically and clinically important.

Studies also need to find ways to insure that they are not simply measuring problems and characteristics that are an effect of the disclosure rather than characteristics of the perpetrator that pre-date the abuse. Depression, anxiety, and paranoia are among the characteristics that could well be the result of the accusations (Wakefield & Underwager, 1988). One way to accomplish this check is to cross validate self-report measures from fathers with descriptions from wives and daughters about predisclosure characteristics. Another is to ask the fathers about the predisclosure period and find out if they have perceived changes in themselves in the interim.

Finally, we would urge researchers to collect data on the offenders' own perceptions about the meaning, causes, and justification for the abuse as well as attitudinal measures. In the study of rape, for example, attitudinal measures concerning hostility toward women or rape myths have proven very effective in identifying rapists. Preliminary investigations (see Segal & Stermac, Chapter 10, this volume, and also the work of Abel & colleagues, 1984, on cognitive distortions) of child molesters offer promise of similar understanding.

SUMMARY AND CONCLUSIONS

This chapter has reviewed findings from over two dozen recent studies of incestuous fathers. The studies reveal a wide range of problems in these offenders' family backgrounds, psychological makeup, sexuality, and family and social relationships. The following are particularly notable: (1) incestuous fathers are consistently and widely reported to have difficulties in empathy, nurturance, and caretaking; (2) social isolation and lack of social skills is also quite widespread; (3) histories of being sexually abused themselves are given only by a fifth of offenders, fewer than the popular stereotype suggested; (4) a history of physical child abuse is more common than sexual abuse, and other parental maltreatment, particularly rejection by fathers, is quite common; (5) a certain proportion of incestuous fathers, estimated to be between a fifth and a third, show signs of general sexual arousal to children, while a more widespread response is a pattern of low sexual arousal to, or even disgust with, normal adult sexual partners; and (6) studies have failed to find that incestuous abusers are identified with traditional masculine sex roles, but rather, they seem more likely to have weak masculine identification.

Information on incestuous fathers has been slow to emerge, but we are now optimistic that a critical mass is being reached. Researchers are taking on a new interest in the problem, and subjects are becoming increasingly available through clinics and courts. Theories are being refined; technology is being disseminated; instruments are being developed and tested. It is our hope that the next decade will see large-scale sophisticated and definitive studies conducted that will dramatically affect thinking and practice.

In the area of child physical abuse, research on perpetrators (such as the finding that they are socially isolated) has had a major impact on strategies for prevention and intervention. Comparable research is needed on sexual abusers before we begin to see plans that win broad support from professionals and policymakers and begin to make major inroads on this distressing problem.

ACKNOWLEDGMENTS. Preparation of this chapter has been made possible by funds from the North Star Foundation, the National Institute of Mental Health, and the National Center on Child Abuse and Neglect. The authors would like to express special appreciation to Frances Lear and Lydia Bronte for encouraging our research; to Donna Wilson for help in preparing the manuscript; and to Lesley Buchanan, Michelle Cutting, and Melissa Rector for research assistance. Valuable comments, criticisms, and editorial revisions were made to an earlier version by Lucy Berliner, David Jones, William Marshall, Linda Sanford, Benjamin Saunders, and Judith Herman.

REFERENCES

Abel, G., Becker, J., Murphy, W., & Flanagan, B. (1981). Identifying dangerous child molesters. In Stuart (Ed.), *Violent behavior: Social learning approaches to prediction, management and treatment* (pp. 116–137). New York: Brunner/Mazel.

Abel, G., Mittelman, M., Becker, J., Cunningham-Rathner, J., & Lucas, L. (1983, December). *The characteristics of men who molest young children.* Paper presented at the World Congress of Behavior Therapy, Washington, DC.

Abel, G., Becker, J. V., Cunningham-Rathner, J., Rouleau, J., Kaplan, M., & Reid, J. (1984). *The treatment of child molesters.* Available from SBC-TM, 722 West 168th Street, Box 17, New York, NY 10032.

Araji, S., & Finkelhor, D. (1986). Abusers: A review of the research. In D. Finkelhor and Associates (Eds.), *A sourcebook on child sexual abuse* (pp. 89–118). Newbury Park, CA: Sage Publications.

Baker, D. (1985). Father–daughter incest: A study of the father (Doctoral dissertation, California School of Professional Psychology, San Diego). *Dissertation Abstracts International, 46*(03), 951B.

Barbaree, H., E., & Marshall, W. L. (in press). Erectile responses amongst heterosexual child molesters, father–daughter incest offenders and matched non offenders: Five distinct age preference profiles. *Canadian Journal of Behavioral Sciences,*

Bennett, S. R. (1985). Cognitive style of incestuous fathers (Doctoral dissertation, Texas Tech University). *Dissertation Abstracts International, 42*(2), 778B.

Berkowitz, A. R. (1983). *Incest as related to feelings of inadequacy, impaired empathy, and early childhood memories.* Unpublished doctoral dissertation, University of Southern California, Los Angeles.

Brandon, C. (1985). Sex role identification in incest: An empirical analysis of the feminist theories (Doctoral dissertation, California School of Professional Psychology, Fresno). *Dissertation Abstracts International, 47*(7), 3099B.

Butler, S. (1978). *Conspiracy of silence: The trauma of incest.* San Francisco: New Glide.

Cammarata, L. (1984). Dominance, power and coalition process in father–daughter incest families (Doctoral dissertation, California School of Professional Psychology, Fresno). *Dissertation Abstracts International 46*(3), 449B.

Cavallin, H. (1966). Incestuous fathers: A clinical report. *American Journal of Psychiatry, 122,* 1132–1138.

Cormier, B., Kennedy, M., & Sangowicz, J. (1962). Psychodynamics of father–daughter incest. *Canadian Psychiatric Association Journal, 7,* 207–217.

Feltman, R. I. (1985). A controlled, correlational study of the psychological functioning of paternal incest victims (Doctoral dissertation, University of Missouri, St. Louis). *Dissertation Abstracts International, 46*(10), 359B.

Finkelhor, D., & Baron, L. (1986). High-risk children. In D. Finkelhor and Associates (Eds.), *A sourcebook on child sexual abuse* (pp. 60–88). Newbury Park, CA: Sage Publications.

Finkelhor, D., & Lewis, I. (1988). An epidemiologic approach to the study of child molestation. *The Annals of the New York Academy of Sciences, 528,* 64–77.

Fredrickson, R. M. (1981). Incest: Family sexual abuse and its relationship to pathology, sex role orientation, attitudes toward women, and authoritarianism (Doctoral dissertation, University of Minnesota). Order No. 8114994. Ann Arbor: University Microfilms.

Gebhard, P., Gagnon, J., Pomeroy, W., & Christenson, C. (1965) *Sex offenders: An analysis of types.* New York: Harper & Row.

Gordon, M. (1988). *The family environment of sexual abuse: A comparison of natal and stepfather abuse.* Paper presented at the American Sociological Association meetings, Atlanta, GA.

Groff, M. G., & Hubble, L. M. (1984). A comparison of father–daughter and stepfather–daughter incest. *Criminal Justice & Behavior, 11,* 461–475.

Heath, R. S. (1985). Perceived parental nurturance, parent identification and sex-role orientation for female victims of sexual abuse (Doctoral dissertation, North Texas State University). *Dissertation Abstracts International, 46*(11), 4015B.

Herman, J. (1981). *Father–daughter incest.* Cambridge, MA: Harvard University Press.

Julian, V., Mohr, C., & Lapp, L. (1980). Father–daughter incest. In W. Holder (Ed.), *Sexual abuse of children: Implications for treatment* (pp. 17–35). Englewood, CO: American Humane Association.

Kegan, K. A. (1981). Attachment and family sexual abuse: An investigation of the families of origin and social histories of mothers from present incest families (Doctoral dissertation, University of Minnesota). Order No. 8206370. Ann Arbor: University Microfilms.

King, H. W. (1985). A study of mothers in families where father–daughter incest has occurred (Doctoral dissertation, California School of Professional Psychology). *Dissertation Abstracts International, 47*(3), 1276B.

Kirkland, K., & Bauer, C. (1982). MMPI traits of incestuous fathers. *Journal of Criminal Psychology, 38,* 645–649.

Krieger, D. S. (1984). Multigenerational patterns in incest (Doctoral dissertation, University of Nevada, Reno). *Dissertation Abstracts International, 45*(12), 3946B.

Langevin, R. (1983). *Sexual strands: Understanding and treating sexual anomalies in men.* Hillsdale, NJ: Erlbaum.

Langevin, R., Paitich, D., Freeman, R., Mann, K., & Handy, L. (1978). Personality characteristics and sexual anomolies in males. *Canadian Journal of Behavioural Science, 10,* 222–238.

Langevin, R., Handy, L., Day, D., & Russon, A. (1985). Are incestuous fathers pedophillic, aggressive and alcoholic? In R. Langevin (Ed.), *Erotic preference, gender identity and aggression* (pp. 161–180). Hillsdale, NJ: Erlbaum.

Lee, R. N. (1982). Analysis of the characteristics of incestuous fathers (Doctoral dissertation, University of Texas at Austin). *Dissertation Abstracts International, 43,* 2343B.

Leroi, D. (1984). The silent partner: An investigation of the familial background, personality structure, sexual behavior and relationships of the mothers of incestuous families (Doctoral dissertation, California School of Professional Psychology, Berkeley). *Dissertation Abstracts International, 45*(11), 3623B.

Lustig, N., Dresser, J., Spellman, S., & Murray, T. (1966). Incest: A family group survival pattern. *Archives of General Psychiatry, 14,* 31–39.

Maisch, H. (1972). *Incest.* New York: Stein and Day.

Mandel, M. D. (1986). An object relation study of sexually abusive fathers (Doctoral dissertation, California School of Professional Psychology, San Diego). *Dissertation Abstracts International, 47* (5), 2173B.

Marshall, W. L., Barbaree, H. E., & Christophe, D. (1986). Sexual offenders against female children: Sexual preferences for age of victims and type of behaviour. *Canadian Journal of Behavioural Science, 18,* 424–439.

Meiselman, K. C. (1978). *Incest: A psychological study of causes and effects with treatment recommendations.* San Francisco, CA: Jossey-Bass.

National Committee for the Prevention of Child Abuse. (1978). *Basic facts about sexual child abuse.* Chicago: Author.

Olson, V. A. (1982). An exploratory study of incest family interaction (Doctoral dissertation, California School of Professional Psychology, Los Angeles). *Dissertation Abstracts International, 43,* 1995B–1996B.

Paitich, D., Langevin, R., Freeman, R., Mann, K., & Handy, L. (1977). The Clarke SHQ: A clinical sex history questionnaire for males. *Archives of Sexual Behavior, 6,* 421–435.

Panton, J. H. (1979). MMPI profile configurations associated with incestuous and non-incestuous child molesting. *Psychological Reports, 45,* 335–338.

Parker, H. (1984). Intrafamilial sexual child abuse: A study of the abusive father (Doctoral dissertation, University of Utah). *Dissertation Abstracts International, 45*(12), 3757A.

Parker, H., & Parker, S. (1986). Father–daughter sexual abuse: An emerging perspective. (American Journal of Orthopsychiatry, 56, 531–549.

Paveza, G. (1987, July). *Risk factors in father–daughter child sexual abuse: Findings from a case-control study.* Paper presented at the Third National Family Violence Research Conference, Family Research Laboratory, Durham, NH.

Pelto, V. L. (1981). Male incest offenders and non offenders: A comparison of early sexual history (Doctoral dissertation, U.S. International University). Order No. 8118142. Ann Arbor: University Microfilms.

Peters, S., Wyatt, G., & Finkelhor, D. (1986). Prevalence. In D. Finkelhor and Associates (Eds.), *A sourcebook on child sexual abuse* (pp. 15–59). Newbury Park, CA: Sage Publications.

Phelan, P. (1986). The process of incest: Biologic father and stepfather families. *Child Abuse and Neglect, 10,* 531–539.

Quinn, T. M. (1984). Father–daughter incest: An ecological model (Doctoral dissertation, California School of Professional Psychology, Fresno). *Dissertation Abstracts International, 45*(12), 3957B.

Quinsey, V. L., Chaplin, T. C., & Carrigan, W. F. (1979). Sexual preferences among incestuous and non incestuous child molesters. *Behavior Therapy, 10,* 562–565.

Russell, D. E. H. (1984). The prevalence and seriousness of incestuous abuse: Stepfathers vs. biological fathers. *Child Abuse & Neglect, 8,* 15–22.

Russell, D. E. H. (1986). *The secret trauma: Incest in the lives of girls and women.* New York: Basic Books.

Saunders, B., McClure, S., & Murphy, S. (1986). *Final report: Profile of incest perpetrators indicating treatability—Part I.* Charleston, SC: Crime Victims Research and Treatment Center.

Saunders, B., McClure, S., & Murphy, S. (1987, July). *Structure, function, and symptoms in father–daughter sexual abuse families: A multilevel–multirespondent empirical assessment.* Paper presented at the Third National Family Violence Research Conference, Family Research Laboratory, Durham, NH.

Scott, R. L, & Stone, D. (1986). MMPI profile consellation in incest families. *Journal of Consulting and Clinical Psychology, 54,* 364–368.

Stern, M. J., & Meyer, L. (1980). Family and couple interactional patterns in cases of father–daughter incest. In B. Jones, L. Jenstrom's and K. MacFarlene (Eds.), *Sexual abuse of children: Selected readings* (pp. 83–86). Washington, DC: National Center on Child Abuse and Neglect.

Strand, V. (1986). Parents in incest families: A study in differences (Doctoral dissertation, Columbia University). *Dissertation Abstracts International, 47*(8), 3191A.

Summit, R., & Kryso, J. (1978). Sexual abuse of children: A clinical spectrum. *American Journal of Orthopsychiatry, 48,* 237–251.

Truesdell, D. L., McNeil, J. S., & Deschner, J. (1986). The incidence of wife abuse in incestuous families. *Social Work,* March–April, 138–140.

Wakefield, H., & Underwager, R. (1988, March). *Scale 6 elevations in MMPIs of persons accused of child sexual abuse.* Paper presented at the 23rd Annual Symposium on Recent Developments in the Use of the MMPI, St. Petersburg Beach, FL.

Wickes, B. R., & Madigan, R. (1985, August). *Paternal bonding, self-esteem and sexual abuse: A retrospective study.* Paper presented at the American Psychological Association, Los Angeles, CA.

Wieder, F. E. (1985). Mother–daughter relationships in incest families: Self/other differentiation within a family system. (Doctoral dissertation, California School of Professional Psychology, San Diego). *Dissertation Abstracts International, 46*(6), 2083-B.

15

An Integrated Theory of the Etiology of Sexual Offending

W. L. MARSHALL AND H. E. BARBAREE

This chapter represents an attempt to integrate a widely disparate literature concerning factors which play a role in the etiology of sex offending and lead to its persistence. In particular we are concerned that most researchers seem to take a rather narrow perspective of this behavior, stressing their own preferred processes (i.e., psychological, biological, or sociological) to the virtual exclusion of others. We have previously emphasized the role of learning experiences (Marshall & Barbaree, 1984a), sociocultural factors (Marshall, 1984a), and biological processes (Marshall 1984b) in the etiology of rape, but this represents our first attempt at integration and the first time we have extended our theorizing to account for other sex offenses. We believe that a proper understanding of sex offending can only be attained when these diverse processes are seen as functionally interdependent.

In order to achieve our goal we will attempt to employ throughout our discussion a unifying thread which we hope will integrate these various influences on behavior. As we see it, the task for human males is to acquire inhibitory controls over a biologically endowed propensity for self-interest associated with a tendency to fuse sex and aggression. The notion of inhibitory controls over biologically endowed aggressive tendencies is not new and will be familiar to students of animal behavior. Indeed, our notion that the development of these controls arises from a socialization process derives directly from animal research (Baenninger, 1974; Karli, Vergnes, Eclander, & Penot, 1977; Moyer, 1976). Moyer (1976) notes that environmental conditions and learning exert powerful controlling influences on behavior, but these influences are understood to operate on innately endowed dispositions. Karli *et al.* (1977) provide evidence indicating that inhibitory constraints are developed through socialization processes and that these inhibitions not only act on biologically endowed tendencies but

W. L. MARSHALL AND H. E. BARBAREE • Department of Psychology, Queen's University, Kingston, Ontario K7L 3N6, Canada.

they are themselves mediated by brain centers, since interference with these (most particularly the amygdala and the septum) eliminates the socially acquired inhibitions over aggression. Thus, nature and nurture are understood to interact in determining behavior. The very factors which interfere with, or make difficult, the development of inhibitory controls, are just those which may, under certain conditions, further facilitate the fusion of sex and aggression.

BIOLOGICAL INFLUENCES

No one doubts that there is an inherited propensity to engage in sexual behavior in all mammalian species; if there was no such biologically entrenched disposition, these species would rapidly have become extinct. It is the direction or manner of expression of that endowed proclivity which has caused disagreement between those who espouse a strictly genetic view and those who argue for the exclusive control of behavior by environmental factors. Our concern here is with whether or not aggressive sexual tendencies have some biological bases.

Although there are some who wish to deny a genetic basis for aggression (Tobach, Gianutos, Topoff, & Gross, 1974), the evidence seems to clearly indicate such a propensity. Species-specific aggressive behavior is consistently displayed by all members of a species under the appropriate conditions, whether or not they have been exposed to environmental conditions which could be expected to "train" them to produce the behavior (Eibl-Eibesfeldt, 1977). Animals reared in isolation from conspecifics, or reared in the company of other members of their own species, display aggression when presented with known species-specific eliciting stimuli (Cullen, 1960; Lack, 1943; Noble & Bradley, 1933).

Evolutionary history has provided human males with various behavioral possibilities which may be employed as ways of obtaining sexual goals (Symons, 1979). We could elaborate on the evidence supporting this claim, but hardly anyone is likely to oppose the view that human males are capable of using aggression, threats, or coercion in a sexual context. Obviously, however, not all men do so, despite evidence that the enactment of violence or engaging in threatening behavior is pleasurable and rewarding (Leon, 1969; Storr, 1972). Some men molest children, and clearly all men are physically capable of such acts; fortunately, most do not engage in these behaviors.

At this point we wish to make it clearly understood that an argument for a biological capacity to enact certain behaviors does not mean that the display of these behaviors should be accepted as inevitable, nor does such an argument in any way excuse someone for engaging in particular behaviors. Those who oppose a biological understanding of aggressive behavior appear to do so because they take such a position to mean that aggression is, therefore, unavoidable and to be excused. While some advocates of a biological perspective do, indeed, seem to take such a stance, or at least do not make their opposition to this position clear (e.g., Eibl-Eibesfeldt, 1973; Lorenz, 1963; Wilson, 1975), we consider biological endowment to simply set the stage for learning, providing limits and possibilities rather than determining outcomes. Indeed, in the case of sexual offending we believe that the contribution of biological factors is minimal once learning has established patterns of behavior. The impact of innate propensities is most strong in initially establishing the learning task and possibly also at pubescence, when hormonal changes are dramatic (Sizonenko, 1978).

If aggression and sex were readily differentiable responses, both physiologically and subjectively, then the task of learning to disentangle these propensities might be rather easy. Unfortunately, however, they are not so clearly and easily differentiable. Aggression and sex appear to be mediated by the same neural substrates (Adams, 1968; MacLean, 1962), which predominately involve midbrain structures such as the hypothalamus, septum, hippocampus, amygdala, and preoptic area (Hamburg & Trudeau, 1981). In addition, the neural networks within these areas appear to be remarkably similar for sex and aggression (Valzelli, 1981). Perhaps more importantly, however, is the fact that the same endocrines, namely the sex steroids, activate both sex and aggression (Moyer, 1976).

The endocrine system basic to these behaviors is quite complex and involves a number of biochemical mediators. Unfortunately, the focus of research in this area has all too frequently been limited to an examination of the relationship between testosterone and overt acts, whereas the various other sex steroids also appear to be important in mediating behavior (Moss & Foreman, 1976; Pfaff, 1973; Vale, Rivier, & Brown, 1977). Similarly, transitory fluctuations in testosterone may be more accurate predictors of behavior than are average levels sampled over several time periods (Kraemer et al., 1976).

The sex steroids have two major functions in both sexual and aggressive behavior: organizational and activational (Bronson & Desjardin, 1969; Money, 1965). For our present purposes it is the activating effects of the sex steroids which are of crucial interest. These activating effects appear to be minimal prior to puberty, but once this begins, hormonal levels increase fourfold within the first 10 months, reaching adult levels after a mere 2 years (Sizonenko, 1978). This is also the time when dramatic increases occur in both sexual (DeLora & Warren, 1977) and aggressive behaviors (Hays, 1981). Puberty and the ensuing early years of adolescence are, therefore, likely to be important times for learning to express and channel sex and aggression. Bateson (1978) has shown that among birds, and at least some mammals, there are critical periods for acquiring behaviors which express sexual needs, and these critical periods occur immediately subsequent to the dramatic changes in hormonal levels which are evident at puberty. Perhaps humans are similarly more powerfully influenced by sociosexual cues at puberty. This readiness to learn sexual behaviors and preferences declines thereafter, although organisms remain somewhat malleable throughout their lives.

Puberty, therefore, appears to be a crucial period for the development of enduring sexual propensities and, given that the same biochemical activators underly aggression, we may reasonably assume that the same is true of aggressive behavior. In this context, Hays (1981) suggests that developmental and environmental factors are the major determinants of these behaviors, with the endocrines playing a facilitating or contributory role. However, the biological factors mediating sex and aggression may vary across individuals, and having unusually high levels of sex steroids (either chronically or persistently intermittently) may make the task of acquiring constraints against sexual aggression all the more difficult.

The possible direct role of abnormally high levels of sex steroids in activating sexual aggression has been investigated in several studies, but most of these have been somewhat incomplete in their assays of hormonal levels, or they have employed strategies inadequate to the task of properly describing the relationship between endocrine levels and sexual behavior. However, there are two studies which report interesting findings. Rada, Laws, and Kellner (1976) found no group differences in plasma testosterone levels between rapists and nonrapists, but when they examined the rapists in more detail, they found elevated testosterone in those who were markedly aggressive in their sexual assaults. Similarly, Langevin et al. (1984) compared sadistic and nonsadistic rapists and found normal levels of various endocrines in the latter group, but elevated dehydroepiandrosterone in the sadists and higher than average levels of luteinizing hormone and follicle-stimulating hormone in one of these men. Among rapists, then, there may be a limited few who are driven by chronically high hormonal levels, but the majority simply appear not to have acquired sufficiently strong inhibitory controls over sex and aggression. There do not appear to be comparable studies of exhibitionists or child molesters.

In our view, then, biological factors present the growing male with the task of learning to appropriately separate sex and aggression and to inhibit aggression in a sexual context. Human males must learn not to use force or threats in the pursuit of their sexual interests; they must learn not to engage in sexual behaviors which are frightening or humiliating to their partner; and they must learn to constantly change the age of their preferred sexual partner as they grow older. Our biological heritage makes these tasks difficult, and fluctuating or abnormally high levels of sex steroids may increase the difficulty. However, developmental and other environmental factors appear to play the most important role in shaping the expression of sexual needs and in bringing aggression under control.

In considering the environmental factors relevant to an understanding of sexual offending, we propose that the acquisition of attitudes and behaviors during childhood set the stage for the developing male to respond to the sudden onset of strong desires characteristic of pubescence with a prosocial or an antisocial mental set. These mental sets will also be strongly influenced at this time by the sociocultural attitudes expressed by the society at large, and these influences may remain as cogent factors throughout the individual's life. Similarly, certain circumstances can disinhibit even rather well-entrenched social controls, such that sexually offensive tendencies can be released in otherwise prosocial males. In the following sections we will consider the influences of these three environmental factors: childhood experiences, the sociocultural context, and transitory situational factors.

Childhood Experiences

It is our contention that the early developmental experiences of boys who are later to become sex offenders inadequately prepares them for the dramatic changes in bodily functioning which occur at puberty and which initiate a strong desire to engage in sex and aggression. Poor socialization, particularly a violent parenting style, will both facilitate the use of aggression as well as cut the youth off from access to more appropriate sociosexual interactions. Exposure to these unfortunate influences is also expected to instill a serious lack of confidence in the growing boy as well as strong feelings of resentment and hostility. These feelings and ineptitudes will certainly not help the pubescent male acquire appropriate inhibitory controls over sex and aggression; indeed, they may serve to entrench quite the opposite dispositions.

Rada (1978) has provided a thorough description of the family background of rapists and the parental training practices to which they are typically exposed as children. Within a general context of violence and sexual abuse, which is typical of the family home, these boys who are to become adult rapists are punished frequently and severely in a manner which is inconsistent and rarely functionally related to their behavior. Langevin *et al.* (1984) found that both the mothers and fathers of rapists were poor parents with whom the children did not identify. The fathers were aggressive, drunken, and in trouble with the law, and their sons reproduced these behaviors as they grew up. In addition, Knight, Prentky, Schneider, and Rosenberg (1983) provide evidence that childhood anti-social behavior, which all too typically arises in the context of a hostile home environment (Robins, 1966), leads to a greater likelihood that the adult will commit rape. Similarly data are available for exhibitionists (Cox & Daitzman, 1980) and child molesters (Finkelhor, 1979, 1984). However, it is important to note that the negative impact of an aggressive, unloving parent can be readily offset by the provision of love and support by the other parent (McCord & McCord, 1964).

From this background it is not a surprise that these children become insensitive adults who are concerned only with their own interests and needs. We would also expect them to be aggressive, due to modeling the behavior of their parents, and to take whatever they want without regard for the rights of others. Similarly, we would not expect them to acquire constraints against sexual aggression, and, indeed, they should learn to use aggression as a way to solve problems and to secure what they want. These are just the sort of personality characteristics and behavioral dispositions commonly found in sex offenders (Langevin, 1983).

As we have noted, the period surrounding pubescence and early adolescence is almost certainly a critical period for the development of sexuality, and it is also an important time for acquiring social competence. If the young boy has been prepared by a loving family environment for the hormonal changes of puberty, and if he is given continued and consistent encouragement for prosocial behavior, then he should be able to make the transition to adult functioning with both the social constraints against aggression in place and the skills necessary to develop effective relationships with appropriate peer-aged partners. However, if the child comes from the kind of disruptive background described above, then the pubertal release of hormones will serve to fuse sex and aggression, enhance his already acquired aggressive proclivities, and lead to a failure to develop sufficiently strong constraints on the expression of sex and aggression.

In this respect perhaps two of the most important outcomes of appropriate parenting are to instill in the young boy a sense of self-confidence and a strong emotional attachment to others. Since appropriate adult sexual interactions usually occur within the context of an intimate, loving relationship, then the growing child needs to develop skills essential to attaining such an intimate bond. We do not mean to imply here that sexual interactions should only take place in the context of a love relationship; we have no doubt that somewhat less intimate sexual interchanges are consistent with a prosocial and production life. The degree of interpersonal involvement in sex no doubt lies along a continuum, and those males who can only express sexual desires within a context where this is absent are clearly more likely to sexually offend than are those men who find impersonal sex to be repugnant. Self-confidence is seen by many theoreticians to be an essential prerequisite for love or intimacy (Fromm, 1963; Maslow, 1970), and the desire for intimacy appears to arise from the development of attachment bonds during childhood (Weiss, 1982).

Since self-esteem appears to be largely determined in males, and particularly in young males, by their sense of their sexual ability (Schimel, 1974), the young boy who cannot develop a relationship with a female may turn to aggressive sex or sex with children as a way of proving to himself that he is masculine. He may do this imaginally during masturbatory fantasies or he may actually enact the behavior. Groth (1979) claims that for many rapists their offenses serve as a means of compensating for underlying feelings of inadequacy. Revitch (1965) has also found that rapists have marked feelings of sexual inferiority, and the insecurities generated by these factors are said to result in the adoption of exaggerated and stereotypical masculine behaviors culminating in rape, as a way of confirming their sense of manliness. Exhibitionists (Rhoads, 1980) and child molesters (Marshall, Christie, & Lantheir, 1979) have also been found to markedly lack self-esteem.

From our understanding of the childhood environment of most sex offenders, the possibility of developing strong and positive attachment bonds seems markedly limited. The absence of a capacity for intimacy as an adult serves to alienate the individual and cause him to experience emotional loneliness (Weiss, 1973). Loneliness has been shown to be highly related to hostility and aggression (Check, Perlman, & Malamuth, 1985; Loucks, 1980), so that ultimately the failure to develop the capacity for intimacy may be expected to result in aggressive behavior, and this should be apparent within a sexual context.

Obviously, of course, to secure an intimate relationship, the growing boy needs the interpersonal skills necessary to interact effectively with females of his own age. A failure to effectively interact with others during adolescence, particularly within a sociosexual context, will lead to anxiety about such interactions, feelings of masculine inadequacy, and possibly anger toward those (particularly females) who are seen as the source of these problems. Social inadequacy, therefore, will not only increase stress and anxiety, which, as we will see, tend to disinhibit sexual aggression, it will also produce attitudes (hostility toward females and feelings of inadequacy) which facilitate sexual offending. Consistent with this expectation, Knight *et al.* (1983) found that childhood social incompetence not only predicted adult social incompetence, it also predicted adult sexual pathology, including a proclivity to rape.

Given the similarity of the family backgrounds of sex offenders and psychopaths generally (Marshall & Barbaree, 1984a, b), we would expect sex offenders to be just as emotionally unresponsive to others as are psychopaths. In the case of psychopaths, this indifference to others appears to be a result of their parents failing to provide affectional models and of their own learned unresponsiveness to discipline due to their experience of severe and noncontingent punishment. Presumably, people who are themselves emotionally indifferent to events which would be distressing to others (e.g., punishers) will be unable to develop empathy, since the response of others to these events will be foreign to the experience of these men. If a man is indifferent to the feelings of others, he will be able to ignore their rights and abuse them however he wishes. He will not only fail to develop inhibitory controls over aggression toward others, he will, in fact, become attracted to the use of violence, since that will more easily secure his goals. As we will see later, processes which dehumanize others (i.e., make us unable to identify with them or feel empathy toward them) increase the likelihood that we will employ cruel and vicious behavior toward them (Bandura, Underwood, & Fromson, 1975).

Actually, it is not so much emotional indifference but oppositional behavior which severe and inconsistent punishment produces (Schmauk, 1970). Wahler (1969) has shown that inconsistent and harsh punishment produces oppositional behavior in children, and that such behavior in children is predictive of a criminal and self-centered orientation in adulthood. This oppositional behavior of adult psychopaths is understood to be expressed not only in unfeeling and criminal behavior but also in a readiness to respond with anger and aggression toward others (Schmauk, 1970). Having a father (or father substitute) who is himself aggressive toward his children and their mother can provide the growing boy with a model to emulate (Bandura, 1973). Not only would we expect these boys to be aggressive, we would also expect them to model their father's attitudes toward women, which are typically quite negative. Negative attitudes toward women characterize rapists (Clark & Lewis, 1977; Gager & Schurr, 1976) as well as those nonrapists who say they would rape if they were sure of escaping detection (Malamuth, 1981; Tieger, 1981).

Exposures to the experiences typical of a sex offender's childhood, then, can be expected to make them relatively unable to develop intimacy and to feel empathy, and it leaves them socially inept, lacking in confidence, self-centered, hostile, aggressive, and negatively disposed toward women. Each of these characteristics will make the changes of pubescence, and the rapid adjustments from childhood to adolescence to adulthood, all the more difficult.

One of the experiences of pubescence and early adolescence, which has been emphasized by those who see sex offending as primarily a sexual behavior (Abel, Blanchard, & Becker, 1978; Freund, 1976; Freund, Scher, & Hucker, 1983), is the imagery used during masturbation. McGuire, Carlisle, and Young (1965) claimed that stimuli were endowed with sexual valence by virtue of being imagined while the person masturbated. It is certainly true that some rapists are sexually excited by the prospect of forcing sex on women, but most are not (Baxter, Barbaree, & Marshall, 1986; Baxter, Marshall, Barbaree, Davidson, & Malcolm, 1984). Similarly, we have found that very few exhibitionists are aroused by the prospect of exposing themselves (Marshall & Barbaree, 1988) and that a limited although significant number of child molesters have developed conditioned arousal to children (Marshall, Barbaree, & Butt, 1988; Marshall, Barbaree, & Christophe, 1986). It appears, then, that far from all sex offenders display deviant sexual interests, but, nevertheless, we need to account for those who are aroused by sexually offensive acts, since this proclivity would serve to disinhibit control over their overt behavior.

It seems obvious that males use, during masturbatory activity, those fantasies which are arousing to them. Since sex serves a variety of purposes additional to physical gratification, it would be no surprise to find that some young boys, who feel cut off from female company, develop fantasies which satisfy their need to see themselves as masculine. In the messages of our society's media, "maleness" is all too often identified with power, control, and either an indifference to or a contempt for women. Within such a society, disadvantaged young boys may entertain sexual fantasies which put them in a position of power and which display an indifference to or contempt for their partner's rights and wishes. Such fantasies may involve rape or exhibitionism or sex with younger, more vulnerable persons. The mechanisms by which sexual fantasies of these kinds become entrenched are suggested in the chapter by Laws and Marshall in the present volume (see Chapter 13).

SOCIOCULTURAL CONTEXT

Acquiring the necessary behavioral inhibitions over sex and aggression seems complex enough for well-adjusted children that it is a wonder more men do not become sex offenders, given the often misleading messages which our society conveys to youths.

While the influence of parents may be primary during childhood, factors outside the family become progressively more important as the young boy grows up. Adolescents are bombarded through various media by all manner of sociocultural messages at a time when many of them are looking outside the home for guidance in living. Those who by their family upbringing have been left poorly prepared to function effectively will seize on those messages which serve their needs. For boys whose self-esteem is low, those attitudes and behaviors which confer on them a sense of power will be more readily accepted than messages conveying egalitarian perspectives. Similarly, parenting behaviors are also shaped by prevailing social mores. Inadequate parents may more readily accept traditional notions of a patriarchal societal structure, and they will no doubt pass on these attitudes to their children. As we will see, these attitudes may facilitate sexual offending.

We cannot cover all the social influences which may enter into the development of a sex offender, and, indeed, we are certainly not aware of what all of these may be. What we will do is identify those factors for which there is suggestive evidence of an influence.

General Cultural Features

Anthropologists have identified three general features of societies which appear to affect the frequency of rape: interpersonal violence, male dominance, and negative attitudes toward females. There are, of course, problems with such studies. In the first place, they involve markedly underdeveloped, even quite primitive, societies, and it is not clear that we can extrapolate directly from the experiences of these societies to our own. Second, the rates of rape in these societies are typically derived by the researcher from the identification by each society's members of the occurrences of such offenses, and it is clear that the definition of rape varies across cultures (Chappell, 1976). However, these problems notwithstanding, it does appear that rape frequencies vary quite markedly in different underdeveloped societies (Quinsey, 1984), and this is just as true for the more industrialized countries (Gibbens & Ahrenfeldt, 1966; Schiff, 1971).

The most consistent feature of societies having high rates of rape is the acceptance of interpersonal violence as a way of dealing with problems. Otterbein (1979) examined 135 nonliterate cultures and found that feuding was one of the main variables associated with higher frequencies of sexual assault. In a similar study of 156 tribal societies, Sanday (1981) found raids on other groups, wars, a high degree of within-tribe violence, and an ideology of male toughness to characterize those tribes who were "rape prone." On the other hand, in those societies where rape is remarkably rare, violence is all but absent (Sanday, 1981).

In North America, Burt (1980) found that among men, the acceptance of interpersonal violence against women was importantly related to their acceptance of rape myths, and Tieger (1981) found that nonoffender males who indicated a high likelihood of raping also thought that nonsexual aggression against females was normal and desirable. Violence in many forms has characterized American society both historically (Hofstadter & Wallace, 1971) and in the present day (Daigon, 1975), and this is particularly true of violence against women (Gelles, 1972; Martin, 1976). Perhaps even worse than this is the portrayal of rewarded violence in the media. Geen (1983) reviewed evidence which suggested there were higher amounts of violence in popular television shows in the United States than in other Western societies. Geen also provided convincing data indicating that television violence increases in the viewer both overt aggression and an acceptance of aggression. It has also been observed that the rate of rape is higher in the United States than in other Western societies (Chappell, 1976; Scanlon, 1982; Schiff, 1971, 1974).

The two other cultural features shown to be associated with high rates of sexual assault concern the social acceptance of male dominance and prevailing negative attitudes toward women. In the rape-prone Yanomamo, males exert all the political power, and women essentially function as the profits of fights and wars, and their sexual desires and interests are all but ignored (Chagnon, 1977). Indeed, when Yanomamo women attempt to ignore male dictates, they are often killed for their recalcitrance. Similarly, in the two studies already mentioned which considered a large range of nonliterate societies (Otterbein, 1979; Sanday, 1981) the ideology of male dominance and correspondingly negative views of women were significantly related to higher frequencies of rape. In contrast, Ashanti society is characterized by sexual equality and a respect for the value of women, and Rattray (1923) could find no evidence of rape among these people.

It has been shown in studies of Western societies that the acceptance by men of male dominance is associated with negative attitudes toward women, an acceptance of rape myths, and either having raped or an admission by the man that he would rape if he could be sure of escaping detection (Burt, 1980; Malamuth, 1981). Also, males who have a strong need for dominance are more accepting of rape and tend to downplay the aggressive elements of sexual assault (Stewart & Sokol, 1977). Many feminists writers (e.g., Brownmiller, 1975; Medea & Thompson, 1974; Russell, 1975), not surprisingly, see rape as a way of perpetuating male dominance. As we noted earlier, Groth (1979) considered most rapes to be motivated by a desire for power over the victim, which is otherwise absent in the lives of these men. While similar research has not yet been conducted with exhibitionists, we believe that similar factors will emerge as relevant to an understanding of varying rates in these offenses. Of course, some societies have apparently tolerated sex between adults and children (Quinsey, 1986), and in these societies we would not expect the same factors to be present.

Availability of Pornography

The United States Commission on Obscenity and Pornography (1970) proclaimed there to be no evidence to indicate that pornography is harmful. Despite numerous subsequent criticisms (Cline, 1974; Court, 1976; Eysenck & Nias, 1978), these conclusions have not only endured, but the findings of the Commission have been taken by some to mean that freely available pornography might have beneficial effects (Ward & Woods, 1972). As Eysenck and Nias (1978) point out, however, we cannot remain consistent and claim that pornographic images exert no influence while claiming that advertising images do. The problem, it seems, is to determine just what sort of influence pornography has, and on whom, rather than simply evaluating whether or not it has any influence.

Check and Malamuth (1986) have considered the possible effects of exposure to pornography from a social learning perspective. They point out that pornography can be expected to modify attitudes and behavior by processes having to do with antecedent and consequent effects. Antecedent factors induce expectancies in the observer that he will enjoy rape because forcefulness in sex is associated in pornography with sexually arousing stimuli, such as a naked female and sexual activities (called "symbolic expectancy learning"), and because the male is depicted as enjoying the rape ("vicarious expectancy learning"). Consequent effects result from the functional value of the observed behavior and serve to disinhibit the man's arousal to rape. These effects arise when the rapist is reinforced for his sexual attack (and the viewer is thereby vicariously reinforced) both by his failure to get caught or otherwise be punished and by the women becoming aroused and enjoying the rape. Both these consequences are typical features of pornographic displays of forced sex. Precisely the same analyses can be applied to pornography involving children.

If pornography does foster the changes suggested above, then it serves to strengthen in the consumer those general sociocultural attitudes and beliefs which, as we have seen, are related to higher frequencies of rape. Malamuth and Check (1981) found that exposure to pornography made interpersonal violence against women more acceptable to normal males and also increased their acceptance of rape myths. They also demonstrated that such exposure increased the strength of violent attitudes toward women. More specifically, Donnerstein (1980) has shown that viewing violent pornography increases the subsequent aggression male display toward females, and Gray (1982) has summarized evidence clearly demonstrating that exposure to hard-core pornography enhances aggression in already-angered males.

Brody (1977) has presented evidence indicating that viewers become desensitized to violence after repeated exposures, and the British Committee on Obscenity and Film Censorship (1979) concluded in their report that similar desensitizing effects of exposure to pornography were evident. Worse than this simple acquired tolerance of violence, however, is the very real threat that exposure to dehumanized violence toward women will lead to the enactment by the viewer of cruelty toward females. As we noted earlier, Bandara *et al.* (1975) demonstrated that dehumanizing others disinhibits the expression of cruelty toward them, and analyses of pornography reveal that women are typically portrayed in a dehumanized way (Brownmiller, 1975; Clark & Lewis, 1977).

Finally, as indicative of the deleterious attitudinal effects of pornography, it was reported by over 40% of rapists, that in their view the widespread availability of pornography contradicted society's response to their crime (Marshall, 1983). These rapists suggested that pornographic depictions of rape, being readily available as entertainment, had led them to conclude that most people did not really think forced sex was wrong but simply took a public stance that it was. Rapists use various means by which to justify their crimes, but this legitimization of rape inherent in violent and degrading pornography is apparent in other ways. For example, Malamuth and Check (1980) found that exposure to the usual depictions of rape in pornography, where the female is portrayed as initially resisting only to be finally and reluctantly aroused to orgasm, had the effect of making male viewers more callous toward the victim and more forgiving of the offender.

The specific effects of pornography concern its possible direct influence on the frequency of sexual crimes; that is, are men more likely to commit sexual offenses or more likely to want to enact deviant sexual behavior after viewing pornography? First, it is important to point out that no one expects all men who view pornography to subsequently rape a woman or molest a child. It has been found, for example, that men with a restricted sexual socialization are more behaviorally affected by exposure to pornography than are males who have had a more normal upbringing (Fisher & Byrne, 1978).

There have been some studies devoted to an attempt to understand the effects of exposure to pornographic material on sexual offenders, but most of these studies have serious methodological problems (Marshall, 1989). Nevertheless, the data which are interpretable suggest, at least, an effect in some sex offenders. Rapists and child molesters characteristically use pornography more frequently than do normal males, and one-third of the offenders report being incited to offend by viewing pornography (Marshall, 1988). Similarly, early exposure to pornography (viewer aged 6 to 10 years) appears to predict high rates of later sexual deviance, particularly sex offending (Davis & Braucht, 1973).

Sociocultural influences of various kinds, then, may facilitate sexual offending, with some males being more vulnerable to these influences than are other males. Even in those males whose childhood experiences have built in a resistance to the corruption of certain sociocultural factors, strong situational features of powerful internal states may overpower these inhibitory controls and release sexual aggression. It is to these transitory situational factors that we now turn.

TRANSITORY SITUATIONAL FACTORS

Valzelli (1967) has observed that testosterone facilitates fighting behavior but notes that this facilitation only occurs within the context of relevant environmental cues. In similar fashion, we believe that certain environmental factors interact with particular states of the individual to facilitate sexual aggression and abuse. Conversely, other factors and internal states curtail the expression of aggression within a sexual context.

Our view of these factors does not mean that we expect all disinhibited males to necessarily sexually offend, but it does suggest that those factors which are found no disinhibit normal males in the laboratory will very likely play a role in the real world in removing whatever controls sex offenders have toward enacting such behaviors. Obviously, sex offenders are able to control themselves, since they typically restrain their tendencies until the opportunity arises for them to enact their desires within a context where the possibility of being caught is limited. Clearly these men recognize, and are responsive to, the social rules which constrain other citizens. Something about the circumstances where they commit their offense(s), or their own state at the time, produces disinhibition of control. No doubt many of the circumstances disinhibitory of sexual offending are deliberately created by the offender himself, but some are externally induced. How vulnerable any one individual is to these influences depends on his history. Some males (those with histories similar to the ones we have outlined above) will be more vulnerable to transitory disinhibitors than others, although the influence of several disinhibitors acting at once, particularly over an extended period, may overcome the constraints of even the most prosocial man. To date, only a few of the possible inhibitors or disinhibitors of sexual aggression have been examined.

Sexual offenders commonly report excessive use of alcohol as a contributory factor in their offenses (Apfelberg, Sugar, & Pfeffer, 1944; Leppman, 1941; Swanson, 1968), although it is often pointed out that these men may exaggerate their alcohol abuse as an excuse (Pacht, Halleck, & Ehrmann, 1962). However, Christie, Marshall, and Lanthier (1979) were able to demonstrate that police and victim reports confirmed intoxication in 70% of the rapes studied. In the laboratory, normal males are sexually disinhibited by alcohol (Wilson & Lawson, 1976), and it has been found that males, who are normally inhibited by aggressive cues in the context of a sexual encounter, fail to be inhibited to the same degree by these cues when they are intoxicated (Barbaree, Marshall, Yates, & Lightfoot, 1983; Briddell et al., 1978).

Many rapists report being angry at the time of a sexual assault; particularly, they report feeling hostile toward females (Rada, 1978). Consistent with these reports, Rada, Laws, and Kellner (1976) found that rapists scored higher on the Buss–Durkee Hostility Inventory than did either other sex offenders or normal controls. We have recently extended these findings by demonstrating that laboratory-induced anger disinhibits arousal to forced sex among normal males (Yates, Barbaree, & Marshall, 1984). We tested normal males under the usual conditions of assessment and found that they were significantly inhibited by the addition of force cues to an ongoing sexual interaction. When we made these same men angry by having a female insult them, however, they showed arousal to forced sex which was equivalent to, or greater than, their arousal to consenting sex.

Malamuth, Haber, and Feshbach (1980) demonstrated that the experience of sexual arousal prior to exposure to particular types of sexual stimuli also disinhibited the responses of normal males to forced sex. However, this study relied on the subjects' self-reports. We have recently replicated certain aspects of this study (Seidman, Marshall, & Barbaree, 1988), using erectile measures of arousal, and obtained quite similar results. We found that prior arousal enhanced responding to all subsequent sexual stimuli, but more importantly, prior arousal induced by forced sex stimuli enhanced arousal to the rape cues presented later on, while prior arousal provoked by a nonexplicit scene of consenting sex markedly increased subsequent responding to the consenting sex scenes. A significant number of our patients have, over the years, told us that they were feeling sexually excitable for an extended period of time before their offensive act(s).

Quinsey, Chaplin, and Varney (1981) told half their subjects that arousal to rape was normal (permissive instructions), while the other half was given neutral instructions. Those normal subjects given the permissive instructions displayed arousal to rape which was equivalent to that shown by rapists and significantly greater than that shown by normals who were given neutral instructions. Instructions which indicate that sexual offending is an acceptable behavior, then, appears to disinhibit the usual constraints which control the expression of arousal to such stimuli. It is important to note that pornography which depicts sexual offending both induces arousal and suggests that such behavior is acceptable. These two conditions may explain why exposure to such pornography disinhibits arousal to later scenes of sex offending, and why such pornography serves to incite abuse in some sex offenders.

Additional transitory influences have been suggested to operate to disinhibit socially entrenched taboos against sexual offending, but these factors have not been subjected to experimental test as yet. In discussing the conditions which occur during warfare, Dietz (1978) declared that "it (is) abundantly clear that these social conditions reduce or eliminate many of the barriers that prevent men from rape in times of relative peace and equality" (p. 102). Anonymity and the markedly reduced possibility of detection and retribution, all of which occur during wartime, also facilitate rape, since as many as 35% of nonrapists indicate some likelihood that they would force a woman to have sex if they were sure of escaping detection (Malamuth, 1981). The anonymity of large cities, as much as their inherent stressors, may be importantly related to the higher rates of rape typically found in crowded urban cities (Federal Bureau of Investigation, 1980). However, while there are numerous experimental demonstrations that anonymity enhanced physical aggression (Prentice-Dunn & Rogers, 1983), there are no comparable studies examining its direct influence on arousal to sexual aggression.

Of course, the anonymity in large cities or in foreign lands is accompanied by an alienation from others, such that most women in these circumstances are strangers. We have already noted Bandura et al.'s (1975) observation that dehumanizing people (making them seem strange and different from us) increases our tendency to behave cruelly toward them, and even amongst infrahuman species this is true. When unfamiliar animals (even conspecifics who are strangers) are placed in a group of animals who are familiar with each other, the latter will attack the strangers (Cairns & Nakelski, 1971; Southwick, 1967). Familiarity, on the other hand, even between animals which typically stand in a predator–prey relationship, will powerfully inhibit aggression (Baenninger, 1974).

Finally, stress and anxiety appear to function as disinhibitors of sexual activity generally, and many sex offenders report being under considerable stress at the time of their offense. Langevin et al. (1984) found both rapists and assaultive non-sex-offenders to be more tense and anxious than matched controls, and they were also more inclined to worry about things. In fact, Groth (1979) states that his book about rapists is primarily about those men who are overwhelmed by the stress of everyday life and who use sex as a way of overcoming their distress. Rosen and Fracher (1983) provide evidence indicating not only that sex offenders are anxious but that tension-reduction techniques eliminate the offensive behaviors of some of these men. In a more general sense, Dohrenwend and Dohrenwend (1974) have clearly made the case that stressful events precipitate a wide variety of deviant and dysfunctional behaviors.

SUMMARY

Biological inheritance confers upon males a ready capacity to sexually aggress which must be overcome by appropriate training to instill social inhibitions toward such behavior. Variations in hormonal functioning may make this task more or less difficult. Poor parenting, particularly the use of inconsistent and harsh discipline in the absence of love, typically fails to instill these constraints and may even serve to facilitate the fusion of sex and aggression rather than separate these two tendencies. Sociocultural attitudes may negatively interact with poor parenting to enhance the likelihood of sexual offending, if these cultural beliefs express traditional patriarchal views. The young male whose childhood experiences have ill-prepared him for a prosocial life may readily accept these views to bolster his sense of masculinity. If such a male gets intoxicated or angry or feels stressed, and he finds himself in circumstances where he is not known or thinks he can get away with offending, then such a male is likely to sexually offend depending upon whether he is aroused at the time or not. All of these factors must be taken into account when planning treatment of these men.

REFERENCES

Abel, G. G., Blanchard, E. B., & Becker, J. V. (1978). An integrated treatment program for rapists. In R. T. Rada (Ed.), *Clinical aspects of the rapist* (pp. 161–214). New York: Grune & Stratton.

Adams, D. B. (1968). Cells related to fighting behavior recorded from midbrain central gray neuropil of cat. *Science, 159*, 894–896.

Apfelberg, B., Sugar, C., & Pfeffer, A. Z. (1944). A psychiatric study of 250 sex offenders. *American Journal of Psychiatry, 100*, 762–770.

Baenninger, R. (1974). Some consequences of aggressive behavior: A selective review of the literature on other animals. *Aggressive Behavior, 1*, 17–37.

Bandura, A. (1973). *Aggression: A social learning analysis*. Englewood Cliffs, NJ: Prentice-Hall.

Bandura, A., Underwood, B., & Fromson, M. E. (1975). Disinhibition of aggression through diffusion of responsibility and dehumanization of victims. *Journal of Research in Personality, 9*, 253–269.

Barbaree, H. E., Marshall, W. L., Yates, E., & Lightfoot, L. (1983). Alcohol intoxication and deviant sexual arousal in male social drinkers. *Behaviour Research and Therapy, 21*, 365–373.

Bateson, P. P. G. (1978). Early experience and sexual preferences. In J. B. Hutchison (Ed.), *Biological determinants of sexual behaviour* (pp. 29–53). New York: John Wiley.

Baxter, D. J., Barbaree, H. E., & Marshall, W. L. (1986). Sexual responses to consenting and forced sex in a large sample of rapists and nonrapists. *Behaviour Research and Therapy, 24*, 513–520.

Baxter, D. J., Marshall, W. L., Barbaree, H. E., Davidson, P. R., & Malcolm, P. B. (1984). Deviant sexual behavior: Differentiating sex offenders by criminal and personal history, psychometric measures, and sexual response. *Criminal Justice and Behavior, 11*, 477–501.

Briddell, D. W., Rimm, D. C., Caddy, G. R., Kravitz, G., Sholis, D., & Wunderlin, R. J. (1978). Effects of alcohol and cognitive set on sexual arousal to deviant stimuli. *Journal of Abnormal Psychology, 87*, 418–430.

British Committee on Obscenity and Film Censorship. (1979). *Report*. London: Her Majesty's Stationery Office.

Brody, S. (1977). *Screen violence and film censorship*. Home Office Research Study No. 40. London: Her Majesty's Stationery Office.

Bronson, F. H., & Desjardin, C. (1969). Aggressive behavior and seminal vesicle function in mice: Differential sensitivity to androgen given neonatally. *Endocrinology, 15*, 971–974.

Brownmiller, S. (1975). *Against our will: Men, women, and rape*. New York: Simon & Schuster.

Burt, M. R. (1980). Cultural myths and support for rape. *Journal of Personality and Social Psychology, 38*, 217–230.

Cairns, R. B., & Nakelski, J. S. (1971). On fighting in mice: Ontogenetic and experiential determinants. *Journal of Comparative and Physiological Psychology, 71*, 354–364.

Chagnon, N. A. (1977). *Yanomamo: The fierce people* (2nd ed.). Toronto: Holt, Rinehart & Winston.
Chappell, D. (1976). Cross-cultural research on forcible rape. *International Journal of Criminology and Penology, 4,* 295–304.
Check, J. V. P., & Malamuth, N. M. (1986). Pornography and sexual aggression: A social learning theory analysis. In M. L. McLaughlin (Ed.), *Communication Yearbook 9* (pp. 181–213). Beverly Hills, CA: Sage.
Check, J. V. P., Perlman, D., & Malamuth, N. M. (1985). Loneliness and aggressive behavior. *Journal of Social and Personal Relationships, 2,* 243–252.
Christie, M. M., Marshall, W. L., & Lanthier, R. D. (1979). *A descriptive study of incarcerated rapists and pedophiles.* Report to the Solicitor General of Canada, Ottawa.
Clark, L., & Lewis, D. (1977). *Rape: The price of coercive sexuality.* Toronto: The Women's Press.
Cline, V. B. (1974). *Where do you draw the line? An exploration into media violence.* Provo, UT: Brigham Young University Press.
Court, J. H. (1976). Pornography and sex-crimes: A re-evaluation in the light of recent trends around the world. *International Journal of Criminology & Penology, 5,* 129–157.
Cox, D. J., & Daitzman, R. J. (1980). *Exhibitionism: Description, assessment and treatment.* New York: Garland STPM Press.
Cullen, E. (1960). Experiments on the effects of social isolation on reproductive behavior in the three-spined stickleback. *Animal Behavior, 8,* 235.
Daigon, A. (1975). *Violence U.S.A.* New York: Bantam Books.
Davis, K. E., & Braucht, G. N. (1973). Exposure to pornography, character, and sexual deviance: A retrospective survey. *Journal of Social Issues, 29,* 183–196.
DeLora, J. S., & Warren, C. A. B. (1977). *Understanding sexual interaction.* Boston: Houghton Mifflin.
Dietz, P. E. (1978). Social factors in rapist behavior. In R. T. Rada (Ed.), *Clinical aspects of the rapist* (pp. 59–115). New York: Grune & Statton.
Dohrenwend, B. S., & Dohrenwend, B. D. (1974). *Stressful life events: Their nature and effects.* New York: Wiley.
Donnerstein, E. (1980). Pornography and violence against women: Experimental studies. *Annals of the New York Academy of Science, 347,* 277–278.
Eibl-Eibesfeldt, I. (1973). *The preprogrammed man.* New York: Viking Press.
Eibl-Eibesfeldt, I. (1977). Evolution of destructive aggression. *Aggressive Behavior, 3,* 127–144.
Eysenck, H. J., & Nias, D. K. B. (1978). *Sex, violence and the media.* London: Maurice Temple Smith.
Federal Bureau of Investigation (1980). *Uniform crime reports,* 1980. Washington, DC: U.S. Government Printing Office.
Finkelhor, D. (1979). *Sexually victimized children.* New York: Free Press.
Finkelhor, D. (1984). *Child sexual abuse: New theory and research.* New York: Free Press.
Fisher, W. A., & Byrne, D. (1978). Individual differences in affective and behavioral responses to an erotic film. *Journal of Applied Social Psychology, 8,* 355–365.
Freund, K. (1976). Diagnosis and treatment of forensically significant anomalous erotic preferences. *Canadian Journal of Criminology and Corrections, 18,* 181–189.
Freund, K., Scher, H., & Hucker, S. (1983). The courtship disorders. *Archives of Sexual Behavior, 12,* 369–379.
Fromm, E. (1963). *The art of loving.* New York: Bantam Books.
Gager, N., & Schurr, C. (1976). *Sexual assault: Confronting rape in America.* New York: Grosset & Dunlap.
Geen, R. G. (1983). Aggression and television violence. In R. G. Geen & E. I. Donnerstein (Eds.), *Aggression: Theoretical and empirical reviews* (vol. 2, pp. 103–125). New York: Academic Press.
Gelles, R. J. (1972). *The violent home: A study of physical aggression between husbands and wives.* Beverly Hills, CA: Sage.
Gibbens, T. C. N., & Ahrenfeldt, R. H. (1966). *Cultural factors in delinquency.* London: Tavistock Press.
Gray, S. H. (1982). Exposure to pornography and aggression toward women: The case of the angry male. *Social Problems, 29,* 387–398.
Groth, A. N. (1979). *Men who rape: The psychology of the offender.* New York: Plenum.
Hamburg, D. A., & Trudeau, M. B. (1981). *Biobehavioral aspects of aggression.* New York: A. R. Liss.

Hays, S. E. (1981). The psychoendrocrinology of puberty and adolescent aggression. In D. A. Hamburg & M. B. Trudeau (Eds.), *Biobehavioral aspects of aggression* (pp. 107–119). New York: A. R. Liss.

Hofstadter, R., & Wallace, M. (1971). *American violence: A documentary history*. New York: Vintage Books.

Karli, P., Vergnes, M., Eclander, F., & Penot, C. (1977). Involvement of the amygdala in inhibitory control over aggression in the rat: A synopsis. *Aggressive Behavior, 3*, 157–162.

Knight, R., Prentky, R., Schneider, B., & Rosenberg, R. (1983). Linear causal modeling of adaptation and criminal history in sex offenders. In K. Van Dusen & S. Mednick (Eds.), *Prospective studies of crime and delinquency*. (pp. 303–341). Boston: Kluwer–Nijhoff.

Kraemar, H. C., Becker, H. B., Brodie, H. K. H., Doering, C. H., Moos, R. H., & Hamburg, D. A. (1976). Orgasmic frequency and plasma testosterone levels in normal males. *Archives of Sexual Behavior, 5*, 125–132.

Lack, D. (1943). *The life of the robin*. Cambridge, UK: Cambridge University Press.

Langevin, R. (1983). *Sexual strands: Understanding and treating sexual anomalies in men*. Hillsdale, NJ: Lawrence Erlbaum.

Langevin, R., Bain, J., Ben-Aron, M., Coulthard, R., Day, D., Handy, L., Heasman, G., Hucker, S., Purdins, J., Roper, V., Russon, A., Webster, C., & Wortzman, G. (1984). Sexual aggression: Constructing a predictive equation. A controlled pilot study. In R. Langevin (Ed.), *Erotic preference, gender identity, and aggression in men: New research studies* (pp. 39–76). Hillsdale, NJ: Lawrence Erlbaum.

Leon, C. (1969). Unusual patterns of crime during La Violencia in Columbia. *American Journal of Psychiatry, 125*, 1564–1575.

Leppman, F. (1941). Essential differences between sex offenders. *Journal of Criminal Law and Criminology, 32*, 366.

Lorenz, K. (1963). *On aggression*. New York: Harcourt Brace.

Loucks, S. (1980). Loneliness, affect, and self-concept: Construct validity of the Bradley Loneliness Scale. *Journal of Personality Assessment, 44*, 142–147.

MacLean, P. D. (1962). New findings relevant to the evolution of psychosexual functions of the brain. *Journal of Nervous and Mental Disease, 135*, 289–301.

Malamuth, N. M. (1981). Rape proclivity among males. *Journal of Social Issues, 37*, 138–157.

Malamuth, N. M., & Check, J. V. P. (1980). Penile tumescence and perceptual responses to rape as a function of victim's perceived responses. *Journal of Applied Social Psychology, 10*, 528–547.

Malamuth, N. M., & Check, J. V. P. (1981). The effects of mass media exposure on acceptance of violence against women: A field experiment. *Journal of Research in Personality, 15*, 436–446.

Malamuth, N., Haber, S., & Feshbach, S. (1980). Testing hypotheses regarding rape: Exposure to sexual violence, sex differences and the "normality" of rape. *Journal of Research in Personality, 14*, 121–137.

Marshall, W. L. (1983). *The use of pornography by rapists and child molesters*. Report to the Policy, Planning and Development Branch of the Canadian Department of Justice, Ottawa.

Marshall, W. L. (1984a). *Rape as a socio-cultural phenomenon*. The J. P. S. Robertson Lecture, Trent University, Peterborough, Ontario.

Marshall, W. L. (1984b). L'avenir de la therapie behaviorale: le behaviorisme bio-social (illustre a partir d'une theorie sur le viol). *Revue de modification du comportement, 14*, 136–149.

Marshall, W. L. (1988). The use of explicit sexual stimuli by rapists, child molesters and nonoffender males. *Journal of Sex Research, 25*, 267–288.

Marshall, W. L. (1989). Pornography and sex offenders. In D. Zillman & J. Bryant (Eds.), *Pornography: recent research, interpretations, and policy considerations* (pp. 185–214). Hillsdale, NJ: Lawrence Erlbaum.

Marshall, W. L., & Barbaree, H. E. (1984a). A behavioral perspective of rape. *International Journal of Law and Psychiatry, 7*, 51–77(a).

Marshall, W. L., & Barbaree, H. E. (1984b). Disorders of personality, impulse, and adjustment. In S. M. Turner & M. Hersen (Eds.), *Adult psychopathology and diagnosis* (pp. 406–449). New York: Wiley.

Marshall, W. L., & Barbaree, H. E. (1988). *Erectile responses of exhibitionists to the act of exposing.* Unpublished manuscript, Queen's University, Kingston, Ontario.

Marshall, W. L., Christie, M. M., & Lanthier, R. D. (1979). *Social competence, sexual experience and attitudes to sex in incarcerated rapists and pedophiles.* Report to Solicitor General of Canada, Ottawa.

Marshall, W. L., Barbaree, H. E., & Christophe, D. (1986). Sexual offenders against female children: Sexual preferences for age of victims and type of behavior. *Canadian Journal of Behavioral Science, 18,* 424–439.

Marshall, W. L., Barbaree, H. E., & Butt, J. (1988). Sexual offenders against male children: Sexual preferences. *Behaviour Research and Therapy, 26,* 383–391.

Martin, D. (1976). *Battered wives.* San Francisco: Glide Foundation.

Maslow, A. H. (1970). *Motivation and personality* (2nd ed.). New York: Harper & Row.

McCord, W., & McCord, J. (1964). *The psychopath: An essay on the criminal mind.* Princeton, NJ: Van Nostrand.

McGuire, R. J., Carlisle, J. M., & Young, B. G. (1965). Sexual deviations as conditioned behavior. *Behaviour Research and Therapy, 2,* 185–190.

Medea, A., & Thompson, K. (1974). *Against rape.* New York: Farrar, Straus & Giroux.

Money, J. (1965). *Sex research: New developments.* New York: Holt, Rinehart & Winston.

Moss, R. L., & Foreman, M. M. (1976). Potentiation of lordosis behavior by intrahypothalamic infusion of synthetic luteinizing hormone-releasing hormone. *Neuroendocrinology, 20,* 176–181.

Moyer, K. E. (1976). *The psychobiology of aggression.* New York: Harper & Row.

Noble, H. K., & Bradley, H. T. (1933). The mating behavior of lizards. *Natural History, 34,* 1–15.

Otterbein, K. F. (1979). A cross-cultural study of rape. *Aggressive Behavior, 5,* 425–435.

Pacht, A. R., Halleck, S. L., & Ehrmann, J. C. (1962). Diagnosis and treatment of the sexual offender: A nine-year study. *American Journal of Psychiatry, 118,* 802–808.

Pfaff, D. W. (1973). Luteinizing hormone-releasing factor potentiates lordosis behavior in hypophysectomized ovariectomized female rats. *Science, 182,* 1148–1149.

Prentice-Dunn, S., & Rogers, R. W. (1983). Deindividuation in aggression. In R. G. Geen & E. I. Donnerstein (Eds.), *Aggression: Theoretical and empirical reviews* (vol. 2, pp. 155–171). New York: Academic Press.

Quinsey, V. L. (1984). Sexual aggression: Studies of offenders against women. In D. Weisstub (Ed.), *Law and mental health: International perspectives* (vol. 1, pp. 84–121). New York: Pergamon Press.

Quinsey, V. L. (1986). Men who have sex with children. In D. Weisstub (Ed.), *Law and mental health: International perspectives* (vol. 2, pp. 140–172). New York: Pergamon Press.

Quinsey, V. L., Chaplin, T. C., & Varney, G. (1981). A comparison of rapists' and sexual offenders' sexual preferences for mutually consenting sex, rape and physical abuse of women. *Behavioral Assessment, 3,* 127–135.

Rada, R. T. (1978). *Clinical aspects of the rapist.* New York: Grune & Stratton.

Rada, R. T., Laws, D. R., & Kellner, R. (1976). Plasma testosterone levels in the rapist. *Psychosomatic Medicine, 38,* 257–268.

Rattray, R. S. (1923). *Ashanti.* Oxford, UK: Claredon Press.

Revitch, E. (1965). Sex murder and the potential sex murderer. *Diseases of the Nervous System, 26,* 640–646.

Rhoads, J. M. (1980). Theoretical and therapeutic integration. In D. J. Cox & R. J. Daitzman (Eds.), *Exhibitionism: Description, assessment, and treatment* (pp. 295–309). New York: Garland STPM Press.

Robins, L. N. (1966). *Deviant children grown up.* Baltimore: Williams & Wilkins.

Rosen, R. C., & Fracher, J. C. (1983). Tension-reduction training in the treatment of compulsive sex offenders. In J. G. Greer & I. R. Stuart (Eds.), *The sexual aggressor: Current perspectives on treatment* (pp. 144–159). New York: Van Nostrand Reinhold.

Russell, D. E. H. (1975). *the politics of rape.* New York: Stein & Day.

Sanday, P. R. (1981). The socio-cultural context of rape: A cross-cultural study. *The Journal of Social Issues, 37,* 5–27.

Scanlon, R. L. (1982). Canadian crime rates: Sources and trends. *Impact, 1,* 1–10.

Schiff, A. F. (1971). Rape in other countries. *Medicine, Science and the Law, 11,* 139–143.

Schiff, A. F. (1974). Rape in foreign countries. *Medical Trial Techniques Quarterly, 20,* 66–74.

Schimel, J. L. (1974). Self-esteem and sex. In L. Gross (Ed.), *Sexual behavior: Current issues* (pp. 249–259). New York: Spectrum.

Schmauk, F. J. (1970). Punishment, arousal, and avoidance learning in sociopaths. *Journal of Abnormal Psychology, 76,* 325–335.

Seidman, B., Marshall, W. L., & Barbaree, H. E. (1988). *The effects of pretest exposures on erectile responses to rape stimuli.* Unpublished manuscript, Queen's University, Department of Psychology, Kingston, Ontario.

Sizonenko, P. C. (1978). Endocrinology in preadolescents and adolescents. *American Journal of Diseases of Children, 132,* 704–712.

Southwick, C. H. (1967). An experimental study of intra-group agonistic behavior in rhesus monkeys (Macaca mulatta). *Behaviour, 28,* 182–209.

Stewart, A. J., & Sokol, M. (1977, September). *Male and female conceptions of rape.* Paper presented at the Meeting of the Eastern Psychological Association, Boston.

Storr, A. (1972). *Human destructiveness.* New York: Morrow.

Swanson, D. W. (1968). Adult sexual abuse of children. *Diseases of the Nervous System, 29,* 677–683.

Symons, D. (1979). *The evolution of human sexuality.* New York: Oxford University Press.

Tieger, T. (1981). Self-reported likelihood of raping and the social perception of rape. *Journal of Research in Personality, 15,* 147–158.

Tobach, E., Gianutos, J., Topoff, H. R., & Gross, C. G. (1974). *The four horsemen: Racism, sexism, militarism and social Darwinism.* New York: Behavioral Publications.

United States Commission on Obscenity and Pornography (1970). *The report of the US Commission on Obscenity and Pornography.* New York: Random House.

Vale, W., Rivier, C., & Brown, M. (1977). Regulatory peptides of the hypothalamus. *Annual Review of Physiology, 39,* 473–527.

Valzelli, L. (1967). Drugs and aggression. *Advances in Pharmacology, 5,* 79–108.

Valzelli, L. (1981). *Psychobiology of aggression and violence.* New York: Raven.

Wahler, R. G. (1969). Oppositional children: A quest for parental reinforcement control. *Journal of Applied Behavior Analysis, 2,* 159–170.

Ward, P., & Woods, G. (1972). *Law and order in Australia.* Sydney: Angus & Robertson.

Weiss, R. S. (1973). *Loneliness: The experience of emotional and social isolation.* Cambridge, MA: MIT Press.

Weiss, R. S. (1982). Attachment in adult life. In C. M. Parkes & J. Stevenson-Hinde (Eds.), *The place of attachment in human behavior* (pp. 43–58). New York: Basic Books.

Wilson, E. O. (1975). *Sociobiology: The new synthesis.* Cambridge, MA: Belknap Press.

Wilson, G. T., & Lawson, D. M. (1976). Expectancies, alcohol and sexual arousal in male social drinkers. *Journal of Abnormal Psychology, 85,* 587–594.

Yates, E., Barbaree, H. E., & Marshall, W. L. (1984). Anger and deviant sexual arousal. *Behavior Therapy, 15,* 287–294.

IV

Treatment of the Offender

16

The Modification of Sexual Preferences

Vernon L. Quinsey and Christopher M. Earls

The modification of inappropriate sexual preferences is of central concern in many treatment programs for sex offenders (Abel, Becker, Cunningham-Rathner, Rouleau, Kaplan, & Reich, 1984; Borzecki, & Wormith, 1987; Griffiths, Quinsey, & Hingsburger, 1989; Marshall, Earls, Segal, & Darke, 1983; Quinsey, Chaplin, Maguire, & Upfold, 1987). This focus on inappropriate sexual interest follows from repeated observations that sex offenders, such as child molesters, rapists, and sadists, frequently report ruminating over sexual fantasies involving the types of behaviors in which they engage; moreover, the relative amount of sexual arousal elicited by deviant and nondeviant cues in phallometric assessment more consistently differentiates sex offenders from other males than any other measure yet tried (see Earls & Quinsey, 1985; Quinsey, 1984a, 1986, for reviews). The clinical importance of inappropriate sexual preferences is reflected in the definition of sexual deviations or paraphilias in DSM-III-R as disorders characterized by intense sexual urges or sexually arousing fantasies involving inappropriate objects or coercive sexual activities (American Psychiatric Association, 1987).

Because of the importance of modifying inappropriate patterns of sexual arousal, there are many recent detailed descriptions of the various methods of accomplishing this. In addition to the program descriptions already cited, a detailed description of how to operate a phallometric laboratory for the assessment and treatment of sexual deviance can be found in Laws & Osborn (1983). Similarly, extensive reviews of the literature on modifying inappropriate sexual preferences are readily available (e.g., Kelly, 1982; Quinsey & Marshall, 1983). Our purpose in writing this chapter, therefore, is not to recapitulate, except in a cursory manner, work done in greater detail elsewhere by ourselves and others

Vernon L. Quinsey • Department of Psychology, Queen's University, Kingston, Ontario K7L 3N6, Canada.   Christopher M. Earls • Department of Psychology, University of Montreal, Montreal, Quebec H3C 3J7, Canada.

but rather to discuss interpretive and theoretical issues pertaining to the modification of inappropriate sexual preferences.

MEASUREMENT OF SEXUAL PREFERENCES

Sexual preferences among males can be measured in a variety of ways. The most common is via some form of client verbal report. The client can be asked to rate or rank exemplars of sexual behavior categories or exemplars of age–gender categories in terms of their sexual interest or attractiveness or, more simply, to report the types of sexual behaviors or partners that he prefers. Although self-report is very helpful, client dissimulation is a commonly encountered problem. Clients may simply deny that they have inappropriate sexual preferences, for a variety of perfectly clear and compelling reasons (e.g., to avoid punishment). Of course, clients may deny paraphilic interests because they do not in fact have any. The latter possibility is less likely for offenders with particular types of histories; for example, among extrafamilial child molesters, those who have had many child victims, chosen male children, recidivated after incarceration, collected child pornography, and so on.

Partly because of the problems with self-report, such as inarticulateness and dissimulation, most investigators have chosen to employ more objective measures of sexual arousal. To date, the results of work comparing patterns of sexual arousal between sex offenders and nonoffenders have been encouraging in that penile tumescence changes occasioned by deviant and nondeviant cues are usually in accord with the offenders' histories (Earls & Quinsey, 1985). It is also encouraging that patterns of deviant sexual interests are often found even when the offender's verbal report indicates otherwise (e.g., Freund, 1981; Marshall & Christie, 1981; Quinsey, Steinman, Bergersen, & Holmes, 1975). There are, however, problems of dissimulation in phallometric examinations as well. For example, it has been repeatedly demonstrated that there are some men who are able to exert considerable instructional control of their erectile response in the laboratory (Quinsey & Chaplin, 1988). The degree to which penile response faking is a problem varies with a variety of instructional sets and other variables. These will be discussed in more detail below. However, before presenting the various methods which can be employed in the modification of sexual preferences and the interpretation of these changes, it would be worthwhile to consider the manner in which data resulting from the evaluation of sexual preferences should be viewed and the various decisions which can be made with respect to the need for treatment.

Interpretation of Deviant Sexual Arousal

Obviously, both the interpretation of data and the decisions regarding treatment will be based on the results of the initial assessment (see H. E. Barbaree, Chapter 8, this volume). Although inappropriate sexual preferences are an important focus of intervention in many, particularly behaviorally oriented, treatment programs, it is important to consider the role of this intervention in a broader clinical context. One of the ways in which this can be done is to construct a list of variables that we either know or believe to be related to the probability with which an individual will commit some paraphilic behavior.

Such a list is shown in Table 1 for extrafamilial child molestation. The leftmost column lists the psychological constructs that are indexed by the variables to its right. The variables are divided into those measured by self-report and those measured by observation or others' reports because of the not uncommon disagreements between these sources of information among sex-offender

TABLE 1. Variables Related to Extrafamilial Child Molesting

Construct	Self-report	Other
Relative sexual preference for children	1. Number previous child sex offenses 2. Ranking of sexual attractiveness of pictures of persons varying in age and sex 3. Description of sexual fantasies involving children 4. Selection of male child victims	1. Number of charges for previous child sex offenses 2. Phallometric examination with slide stimuli 3. Phallometric examination with audio stimuli 4. Collection of child pornography
Salience of sex	1. Masturbatory frequency 2. Rated importance 3. Other paraphilias	1. Police report of other paraphilic behaviors 2. Phallometric examination for other paraphilias 3. Youthfulness 4. Testosterone level (?)
Lack of alternative partners	1. Social-skill self-descriptions 2. Assertion questionnarires 3. Self-perceived homeliness 4. Dating history, marital status 5. Score on Bentler Scale of heterosexual experience 6. Heterosocial anxiety	1. Social-skill ratings 2. Assertion ratings 3. Rated homeliness 4. Low IQ
Pro-sex with children	1. Sex with children desirable 2. Injury to children unlikely 3. Sex with children normative	1. Belong to organization advocating sex with children
Disinhibition	1. Alcohol abuse 2. Drug abuse	1. Alcohol abuse (e.g., arrests, treatment) 2. Drug abuse (e.g., arrests, treatment)
Opportunity	1. Unemployment 2. Idleness, boredom	1. Record of unemployment
Lack of restraint	1. Procriminal statements 2. Criminal associates 3. Property offenses	1. Hare's Psychopathy Scale 2. Police reports of property offenses

populations. This list can function as an informal and low-level theory to guide clinical intervention and alert the clinician to areas that should be addressed in initial intervention, generalization training, and maintenance of treatment gains.

The most obvious implication of Table 1 is that there may be more targets for intervention in a single individual than inappropriate sexual interests. A second implication is that for changes in direction of sexual interest to be maintained in the natural environment by, for example, the reinforcement of appropriate sexual behaviors, issues such as lack of alternative partners (particularly for those for whom sex is highly salient) must be addressed; thus, social-skill training or systematic desensitization to reduce heterosocial anxiety may be required. Finally, as will be discussed in more detail later in this chapter, the kinds of variables depicted in the table can be used to establish expected recidivism base rates which, in turn, affect posttreatment clinical decisions.

With respect to inappropriate sexual interest, the first problem in this decision process is to make some determination as to what to treat; that is, we need some definition of "deviant" sexual arousal. There are two generally accepted methods which are useful in describing patterns of sexual arousal: (1) levels of responding to a particular stimulus can be expressed in a form which is independent of responses to other stimuli, such as percentage of full erection or millimeters of penile circumference change, or (2) levels of responding can be described as relative to responding to other stimuli, for example, a deviancy quotient such as a rape index (see Abel, Blanchard, Becker, & Djenderedjian, 1978; Marshall, Barbaree, & Christophe, 1986) or Z scores (Earls, Quinsey, & Castonguay, 1987). We recommend scoring phallometric data in both ways.

To illustrate the use of expressing data in its "absolute" form, consider a client who is maximally aroused (100% of a full erection) to audiotaped descriptions of a sexual interaction between two consenting adults and manifests no reaction to a stimulus describing sex between an adult male and a female child. Intuitively, such a pattern of responding appears "normal" and suggests no sexual attraction or preference for female children. Similarly, a pattern of maximal responding to stimuli depicting female children accompanied by an absence of arousal to adults would suggest inappropriate sexual arousal. However, the definition of normal versus abnormal becomes less clear for those individuals who respond to deviant cues somewhere between minimal and maximal levels. For example, how do we interpret a response of 50% full erection to children? The interpretation of the erectile response to children is further complicated by the fact that the interpretation of this arousal might have different implications depending upon whether it is accompanied by a high or low level of responding to adults. In order to take into account the relationship between deviant and nondeviant arousal, the data can be expressed in some difference score or ratio form.

In addition to a measure of relative sexual interest, it is also necessary to have some basis of comparison with normative groups to arrive at a treatment decision. The definition of normal versus deviant depends upon how males in general respond to various descriptions of sexual behavior; for example, normal males with no history of child molestation show sizeable erectile responses to slides of pubescent females. While considerable progress has been made in the comparison of arousal levels between subgroups of sexual offenders and non-sexual offenders (Earls & Quinsey, 1985) the relationship between different patterns of sexual arousal and the need for treatment is not completely clear. For example, in experiments comparing penile responding in rapists and non-rapists, the rape index correlates with previous rape history; however, mean levels of absolute responding to different classes of stimuli and the cutoff ratio for discrimination between these two groups vary considerably over studies (Earls, 1988).

Obviously, there is no empirically supported formula for deciding that a particular class of stimuli should be targeted. Rather, such decisions require a consideration of both the client's relative and absolute levels of responding together with existing normative data. In many cases such decisions can also be influenced by economic or methodological considerations; while lacking em-pirical justification, high absolute levels of responding to deviant cues are gener-ally thought to be associated with increased risk of recidivism, thus requiring some form of intervention; low absolute response rates to sexually deviant themes are less often targetted, at least partly because floor effects are likely to obscure treatment success.

Further discussion may clarify these issues. In a phallometric assessment, one can view the essential problem as determining the stimulus category or categories that a client prefers. It can be assumed, *ceteris paribus*, that a client acts in accord with his preferences. In the real world, a person's sexual behaviors are constrained by moral scruples, opportunity, economic and social resources, and so on. A client, therefore, may choose a nonpreferred sexual partner or activity as a surrogate because of a variety of circumstances. In circumstances where a preferred partner or activity was not available, one would expect a client to shift to the next most preferred category when possible; for most heterosexual males, for example, the shift would be from adult to pubescent females (Freund, McKnight, Langevin, & Cibiri, 1972).

What are the implications of this line of reasoning for the selection of treat-ment targets? Firstly, when an inappropriate stimulus category is preferred in a phallometric assessment or where there is very poor discrimination between appropriate and inappropriate stimulus categories, the inappropriate sexual in-terest should be targetted for intervention. Where a client prefers appropriate stimuli but shows more than zero interest in inappropriate sexual stimuli, the decision as to whether sexual arousal to these stimuli should be targetted has to be based on a theory about why a particular client has offended sexually. Such a theory is influenced by the resemblance of the client's phallometrically derived preference structure to that of nonparaphilic males and by an evaluation of the contribution to the offense history of the types of variables shown in Table 1. For example, a young psychopathic individual might rape his pubescent foster daughter when drunk but show normal sexual age and activity preferences in phallometric assessment (i.e., show high levels of sexual arousal to descriptions of consenting sex with adult females and some sexual arousal to both rape scenarios and pubescent females). In this case, it may not be cost effective to attempt to eliminate sexual arousal to rape or pubescent female stimulus categories. However, if the theory identifies inappropriate sexual interest as contributing to the offense history, even if it is not considered to be the most important factor, it should be targetted; this would occur, for example, if the individual described above showed slightly higher than normal sexual arousal to pubescent female stimuli or had committed previous coercive sexual offenses. Once inappropriate interests are targetted, however, we believe (without empirical justification) that the goal of treatment should not be their normalization (i.e., the goal of treatment is not to make the preference profile look normal, although this result would be welcome), but rather their elimination. We prefer to err on the side of caution.

In the following sections, methods of modifying sexual interest in a particular class of stimuli or behaviors will be reviewed. However, it is worth noting that while the major objective in this form of treatment is to reduce deviant sexual arousal in the laboratory (as well as subsequent deviant sexual behavior), it is often necessary to attend to either the development or maintenance of nondeviant sexual arousal. Early investigators assumed that sexual arousal could be likened to a hydraulic system in which any decrease in deviant sexual arousal would be accompanied by increase in nondeviant arousal, whether the nondeviant component was treated or not (Bond & Evans, 1967). This does not appear to be the case. It is sometimes necessary to employ methods aimed at decreasing deviant sexual arousal and to either precede or follow such treatment with an intervention designed to increase nondeviant arousal.

METHODS OF REDUCING INAPPROPRIATE SEXUAL INTEREST

In this section, the methods of reducing sexual interest in a particular class of stimuli or behaviors will be reviewed. Reducing sexual interest in general through hormonal treatment will not be covered here; although, as shown in Table 1, hormonal intervention can be appropriate.

Some form of aversion therapy is most commonly used to reduce inappropriate sexual interest; for example, Kelly (1982) found that 78% of 26 individual and 6 group child molester treatment studies that he located involved aversion therapy. There are a variety of forms of aversion therapy; most of these associate an aversive event with a paraphilic stimulus or with sexual arousal in the presence of a paraphilic stimulus. Nonparaphilic cues are typically presented in these procedures but are unconsequated. For example, a mild shock to the arm can be associated with the presentation of a slide of a nude female child (a classical conditioning paradigm), or a shock to the arm can be delivered when a client exceeds some criterion of penile tumescence increase during an audiotaped description of a violent rape, but not delivered when sexual arousal is occasioned by descriptions of consenting sex (a signaled punishment paradigm).

There are variations in the effectiveness of these methods of changing erectile patterns but, because very few comparative studies have been performed, the reasons for this variability are at present unclear. In one of the few investigations which permit a between methods used in different studies comparison, Quinsey, Chaplin, and Carrigan (1980) found that a signaled punishment plus biofeedback procedure was much more effective than a classical conditioning aversion therapy procedure (Quinsey, Bergersen, & Steinman, 1976). Although the methods used to effect change in electrical aversion are those of classical and/or instrumental conditioning, it does not appear at present that the changes in erectile measures produced by these methods are due to conditioning (Quinsey & Marshall, 1983). A discussion of what mechanism is involved is presented later in this chapter.

One of the disturbing aspects of the literature on electrical aversion is that the literature itself appears to have dried up. Since 1983, we have found no controlled studies in the literature which have investigated the effectiveness of any electrical aversion method in the reduction of inappropriate sexual arousal. For whatever reason (certainly not on empirical grounds), electrical aversion, or at least its evaluation, appears to have gone out of fashion.

Covert sensitization, in which an imagined aversive event is associated with a paraphilic stimulus, has become more popular over the years. The evidence for the efficacy of this technique is not overwhelming (Quinsey & Marshall, 1983), but it can be combined with other techniques to advantage. Maletzky (1980), for example, combined covert sensitization with olfactory aversion in the treatment of 38 homosexual pedophiles and 62 exhibitionists. The treatment consisted of having the client relax and imagine one in a series of paraphilic scenes arranged in increasing order of sexual arousal. When sexual arousal to the scene occurred, the client was presented with an aversive imaginal event and the odor of rotting tissue. Three scenes were presented in each session and tape recordings were made for home practice. Sessions occurred once per week for 24 weeks, followed by quarterly booster sessions for 3 years. Follow-up assessments occurred at 6, 12, 18, 24, and 36 months. A variety of adjunctive techniques were also used during the active treatment phase, including masturbatory fantasy change.

Measures included self-reported frequencies of paraphilic fantasies or acts, penile circumference responses to paraphilic stimuli, reports of progress by a significant other, and legal records of charges or convictions. Dramatic reductions in self-reported urges and acts and in penile responses to paraphilic stimuli were produced by these procedures and maintained over the 36-month follow-up. Of the 100 patients, only 8 reoffended, incurring 11 charges in total during the follow-up period. Four of the 11 charges were against the child molesters. This study is described here at length because of the very low recidivism rate obtained with clients whose offense histories of homosexual child molestation or exhibitionism would lead one to expect very high recidivism rates; particularly inasmuch as there were no dropouts (Maletzky, personal communication, January, 1988). One is left to speculate about the specific determinants of this extremely favorable outcome: Most importantly, is continued community treatment a necessary condition?

Another technique that has been used to reduce inappropriate sexual interest is satiation (Marshall, 1979; Marshall & Lippens, 1977). In this method, a client masturbates to orgasm while fantasizing aloud about sexually appropriate themes and then continues masturbating after switching to a very detailed description of his paraphilic fantasies. The elaboration of deviant fantasy is continued for an hour each session and is designed to produce boredom. This method has been found to reduce deviant sexual interest, as measured phallometrically, in a small number of patients. One advantage of this procedure is that it can be carried out in the client's home, and client compliance can be checked by the therapist spot checking the content of the audiotapes that the client brings in (Abel *et al.*, 1984).

In summary, there is quite a variety of techniques, mostly involving aversion therapy of one form or another, that have been shown to reduce inappropriate sexual interest as measured phallometrically. Although there are differences in the effectiveness of these techniques over various studies, it is not yet known which methods are most efficacious or what procedural details are the most important.

METHODS OF INCREASING NONDEVIANT SEXUAL AROUSAL

Because of the empirical links between deviant sexual arousal and deviant sexual behavior, the majority of treatment efforts have been devoted to the development of intervention strategies to reduce inappropriate sexual arousal. There is comparatively little recent work concerning methods to increase nondeviant sexual arousal. As we have noted elsewhere (Earls & Quinsey, 1985), early treatment efforts concerning sexual "deviations" focused almost exclusively on the reorientation of homosexual behavior. Since, by definition, homosexuals are less aroused to heterosexual stimuli, assessment and treatment programs in the late 1960s and early 1970s attempted to combine treatments designed to increase heterosexual arousal and decrease homosexual arousal (for more complete reviews of this early literature see Barlow, 1974; Brownell & Barlow, 1980). Indeed, one of the best predictors of successful response to aversion therapy designed to reorient homosexuals was found to be whether a client reported that he had had at least some earlier heterosexual sexual arousal (MacCulloch & Feldman, 1967). However, with the changes instituted by the Nomenclature Committee of the American Psychiatric Association in 1973, homosexuality was removed from the list of sexual deviations. The adoption of these changes resulted in an almost complete elimination of work concerning methods to increase appropriate sexual arousal.

Nevertheless, based on these earlier studies, procedures such as systematic desensitization appear to hold some promise in terms of the reduction of anxiety or avoidance of nondeviant heterosexual contact (Barlow, 1974; Marshall, 1971). It has been shown that simple exposure to an explicit heterosexual film may facilitate the development of heterosexual arousal (Herman, Barlow, & Agras, 1974). In addition, the gradual superimposition of a heterosexual stimulus on a homosexual stimulus, while gradually fading out the homosexual cue, appears to result in increases in heterosexual arousal (Barlow & Agras, 1973). However, with one possible exception, to be discussed below, the use of procedures to increase nondeviant sexual arousal does not appear to guarantee decreases in deviant sexual arousal (Barlow, 1973).

In keeping with a conditioning model of sexual behavior, a number of investigators have attempted to "recondition" sexual preferences by pairing the reinforcing effects of genital stimulation and orgasm with sexual fantasies involving sex between two consenting adults (Marquis, 1970; McGuire, Carlisle, & Young, 1965). Briefly, the client is asked to become aroused and masturbate to a deviant sexual fantasy. At the moment of ejaculatory inevitability, the deviant fantasy is switched to an appropriate theme; and gradually, throughout therapy, the moment of switching fantasies is moved backward in time until the patient is able to masturbate and achieve orgasm using the appropriate sexual fantasy. Numerous authors have reported successful treatment outcome using either orgasmic reconditioning alone or in conjunction with other treatments (see Earls & Marshall, 1983). However, among better-controlled studies employing penile tumescence measures the results are mixed. Using a single-case experimental design with four subjects, Conrad and Wincze (1976) found no changes in sexual arousal which could be attributed to the treatment procedures. In contrast, Laws and O'Neil (1981) used a variation of orgasmic reconditioning in which clients were required to alternate inappropriate and appropriate sexual fantasies in weekly blocks of sessions. The results at posttest indicated not only a reduction in deviant sexual arousal but also an increase in nondeviant arousal (see also VanDeventer & Laws, 1978).

In summary, the limitations of the experimental evidence concerning methods of decreasing inappropriate sexual arousal, such as small sample size and the absence of studies comparatively evaluating different methods, apply equally well to studies which have attempted to increase nondeviant sexual arousal. In addition, a combination of historical events, and perhaps a lesser concern among experimenters/clinicians (an absence of appropriate arousal tends to elicit less alarm than the presence of inappropriate arousal), has resulted in considerably less work in this area.

INTERPRETATION OF CHANGES IN SEXUAL PREFERENCE

Specificity of Changes

Given the variety of available treatment procedures for the modification of sexual arousal patterns and the fact that most appear to be at least somewhat effective, it is reasonable to inquire as to whether nonspecific factors common to all these procedures are the active ingredients. The strongest form of this question pertains to whether specialized techniques to bring about changes in sexual preference are necessary. Must deviant sexual arousal be specifically targetted in treatment, or can these changes be mediated by other forms of treatment, for example, reeducation with emphasis on accountability, responsibility training, development of empathy, cognitive restructuring, social skills, anger control, support groups, and so on (Knopp, 1984)?

The answer to the question of identifying the effective aspect of interventions targetting deviant arousal is complex and, as noted earlier, will require considerably more comparative research. It is, however, easier to provide an answer to the specificity of intervention question. Many authors have emphasized the necessity to consider sexual deviations as a multifaceted problem requiring varied and specialized treatment approaches (Barlow, 1974; Marshall, *et al.*, 1983; Quinsey *et al.*, 1987) and, therefore, rarely administer treatment in a manner which allows the relative contribution of each component to be measured. The issue of interest here is not whether these varieties of intervention reduce recidivism but whether some interventions change sexual arousal patterns without specifically targetting them. Some evidence bearing on this issue was provided by Earls and Castonguay (1989), who conducted two standardized evaluations of sexual arousal patterns in a bisexual pedophile. These evaluations were separated by a 6-month period during which the client participated in a variety of treatments on his home ward, none of which were specifically designed to modify sexual preferences. The results of the two assessments indicated an identical pattern of responding: maximal levels of arousal to all stimuli describing sexual interactions with children. It appeared that deviant sexual arousal in this individual was not influenced by changes in other aspects of his behavior.

Further evidence for the specificity of treatments designed to modify sexual arousal comes from studies employing single-case multiple baseline designs. A number of such investigations have found that arousal elicited by different sexually deviant themes varies independently. For example, Earls and Castonguay (1989) initially paired an aversive odor (ammonia) with arousal to homosexual themes involving children. Although they continued to monitor arousal to descriptions of heterosexual behavior with children, this arousal was not immediately treated. Arousal to the homosexual stimuli gradually decreased over a 4-week period, but arousal to the heterosexual pedophilic themes remained unaffected until directly targetted in treatment (see also Brownell, Hayes, & Barlow, 1977; Laws, 1980; Marks & Gelder, 1967). These results are important for two reasons. First, they suggest that treatment for one class of deviation may not necessarily generalize to other classes; second, they lend support to the idea that a specific treatment variable is, in fact, responsible for the observed changes in sexual arousal patterns. If changes in sexual preference associated with treatment in general (or treatment directed toward deviant sexual arousal in particular) depend upon some nonspecific factors which affect sexual preferences, it is difficult to explain the independent modification of sexual arousal elicited by different classes of sexually deviant stimuli.

Process of Change

Changes in sexual preferences, no matter how measured, are best interpreted very conservatively for a variety of substantive and strategic reasons. If a client, for example, has shown statistically significant reductions in inappropriate sexual interests and increases in appropriate sexual interests in a posttreatment phallometric assessment, we have strong evidence that he can at least control his sexual arousal in an artificial situation. This, of course, is real progress but should be viewed as the beginning of the next phase of treatment, not the end of the intervention. Unfortunately, clinicians have tended to view positive changes in phallometrically measured sexual preference as either real (in some conditioned involuntary sense) or faked (in some sneaky sense). In our view, this is the wrong way to think about the changes, and after treatment has begun is certainly the wrong time to start worrying about interpretation.

Although the procedures used in aversion therapy are often those of Pavlovian conditioning, and changes in sexual preference have been asserted to occur because inappropriate sexual stimuli become Pavlovian-conditioned suppressors (Rachman & Teasdale, 1969), there has been little evidence that Pavlovian conditioning occurs in electrical aversion therapy (Hallam, Rachman, & Falkowski, 1972). There is also good reason to believe that the parameters used in electric aversion therapy will not support conditioned suppression in human subjects (Sachs & Keller, 1972), and there is evidence that, if conditioning does occur, it is insufficient to modify clients' preferences (Quinsey & Varney, 1976). These observations, however, only apply to electrical aversion and may very well not hold for other methods, such as olfactory aversion. Recently, for example, it has been found that alcoholics given emetic alcohol-aversion therapy exhibited a number of signs to alcohol stimuli posttreatment which would be expected as a result of conditioning, and that posttreatment alcohol-induced tachycardia was positively correlated with number of days to first drink (Cannon, Baker, Gino, & Nathan, 1986). These observations raise the question of whether an aversive stimulus could be found that would be uniquely suited to the modification of sexual arousal patterns in the same sense that substances producing nausea appear suited to modifying eating or drinking patterns.

Pavlovian conditioning processes aside, however, the finding that classical conditioning operations, operant conditioning operations, biofeedback, satiation, and even simply having the client alternate masturbation to deviant and nondeviant themes (Foote & Laws, 1981) can all, with varying degrees of success, modify paraphilic sexual interests must give one considerable pause when attempting to theorize about a mechanism, much less an involuntary or uncontrollable one.

It has long been known that some sex offenders can fake phallometric measurements of sexual preference (Freund, Chan, & Coulthard, 1979; Laws & Holmen, 1978; Wydra, Marshall, Earls, & Barbaree, 1983). Instructional control of penile tumescence has also repeatedly been demonstrated among non-sex-offenders (see Quinsey & Chaplin, 1988, for a review). A number of methods have been tried to eliminate faking among paraphiliacs and/or abolish instructional control among normal subjects, but none have been exceptionally successful. Recently, however, Quinsey and Chaplin (1988) successfully eliminated instructional control among a group of normal men instructed to fake preference for audiotaped rape and nonsexual violence as opposed to consenting sex scenarios, by the simple method of requiring subjects to track sex and violence themes independently by pressing neither, either, or both of two buttons. This promising technique has not yet been evaluated with sex offenders; it is also difficult to adapt for use with visual stimuli or in age preference assessments.

As an aside, it is important to remember (the material on faking notwithstanding) that phallometric assessments frequently indicate inappropriate sexual preferences in line with offenders' histories and in disagreement with their descriptions of their preferences (e.g., Quinsey et al., 1975) and that the phallometrically measured inappropriate sexual preferences of some sex offenders are not altered by even strenuous and repeated intervention. For example, a sadistic homosexual pedophile at the Oak Ridge maximum security psychiatric institution received first biofeedback, then signaled punishment, and finally satiation over an extended period of time in a completely futile attempt to alter his sexual preferences. Another patient at Oak Ridge consistently exhibited sexual arousal to paraphilic images over a 10-year period after being exposed to antiandrogens, olfactory aversion, social-skills training, and confrontative group therapy.

The question naturally arises as to how faking is related to therapeutic change. If a client exhibits normal preferences during an initial phallometric examination, laboratory intervention to alter sexual preferences would not ordinarily be offered. An error would thus occur if the client had concealed his inappropriate sexual interests during the assessment. This sort of error is very serious because it results in the failure to identify an important treatment target. The elimination of faking in an initial assessment is, therefore, well worth pursuing. Issues surrounding faking therapeutic change, however, are much more complicated.

From a practical (if not a purely sexological) perspective, the interpretation of phallometrically measured change does not depend on how the changes are produced by (or in) the client but rather whether they will predict recidivism, that is, whether the changes demonstrated in a laboratory setting are likely to generalize to the client's everyday life.

From a behavioral point of view, the client should be encouraged and taught to use strategies for modifying sexual arousal in the laboratory that can be used in everyday contexts. From this viewpoint, mechanically interfering with the strain gauge is not a good strategy, but attending to the relatively attractive aspects of an appropriate stimulus and dwelling on the consequences of apprehension during the presentation of a paraphilic stimulus are good strategies. In a similar vein, imagining sexual interactions with children in order to fake sexual arousal to adult stimuli in phallometric assessment is a very bad strategy for the generalization of treatment effects. From a cognitive-behavioral perspective, it is critical in treatment that a client believe he has learned something (a mastery experience) rather than concluding he has fooled a gullible clinician. If the changes are to be interpreted in a behavioral sense, therefore, the client should be encouraged from the beginning of treatment to exhibit self-control. The strategies to be encouraged would be those expected to generalize to real situations, for example, by using naturalistic aversive events in covert sensitization. "Naturalistic" in this context refers to aversive events that can very well occur in reality as a consequence of the paraphilic acts in which the client has engaged. If the client requires external assistance (e.g., signaled punishment or olfactory aversion), he would be encouraged to recall these aversive events in other contexts in order to reduce inappropriate sexual arousal. Unfortunately, to the extent that the results of a posttreatment assessment have important consequences for the client (for example, possible release from an institution), the more difficult it is for the therapist to become the client's ally in developing appropriate self-control strategies.

If, on the other hand, one tries to determine whether a client has been "cured" by using phallometric assessment, one has to be very concerned with faking but need not worry about generalization, because a "cure" is usually conceptualized as being situationally independent. In point of fact, many programs that attempt to alter sexual preferences do not systematically attempt to produce generalization of changes produced in the laboratory. These programs thus implicitly and, in our view, mistakenly endorse a "cure" model.

A behavioral interpretation of these issues leads to some straightforward recommendations. The goal of intervention should be thought of as self-control of inappropriate sexual interest. The method of treatment should be chosen according to its efficiency in producing the desired changes in phallometric data and the likelihood that the method of intervention and the strategies used by the client will promote generalization. Clients should be taught to use a variety of strategies they can use on their own in different contexts. Treatment should extend into the community and be coupled with appropriate supervision. Obviously, where self-control cannot be demonstrated in the laboratory, supervision and/or antiandrogens are likely indicated. These recommendations fit nicely with the relapse prevention model described by Pithers, Marques, Gibatt, and Marlatt (1983).

Decisions Based on Sexual Preference Changes

A clinician cannot escape making at least implicit decisions when a client has exhibited acquisition of control of his sexual preferences. These decisions take the form of release recommendations in an institutional context or in fading out supervision or clinical contact in a community context, and they inevitably involve the prediction of subsequent antisocial behavior with all of the ambiguity and methodological pitfalls that this entails (Monahan, 1981; Quinsey, 1980, 1984b; Quinsey & Maguire, 1986). The very best description of how to interpret and report phallometric data in clinical situations is given in Laws and Osborne (1983).

There are two sorts of predictive variables that must be considered in making a prediction: those that cannot change (e.g., offense history) and those that can be modified by treatment (e.g., social skillfulness and relative sexual preference) or policy (e.g., long sentences affecting age). If there were an available treatment that was completely effective almost all of the time (e.g., brain transplantation), a clinician would not have to consider the client's characteristics or measures of therapeutic change in making a prediction but only whether the client had received the treatment. Unfortunately, because there is no feasible treatment possessing this degree of effectiveness, client characteristics and response to intervention must be evaluated (e.g., Quinsey, 1973). As in the selection of targets for intervention, a predictive decision is guided by an examination of the kinds of variables shown in Table 1 for extrafamilial child molestation. Of course, the literature is simply not advanced enough to permit a clinician to make numerical estimates of the likelihood with which a sex offender of given characteristics will commit a new sex offense under particular circumstances (reviews of the available literature can be found in Quinsey, 1984a and 1986, for rapists and child molesters respectively).

The variables that influence the probability of a new offense such as those shown in Table 1 establish the expected recidivism base rate that intervention is expected to drive downward. For example, child molesters who have exclusively victimized their daughters have lower recidivism rates than those who have selected extrafamilial female victims, who, in turn, have lower rates than offenders who have victimized (Quinsey, 1986). It is highly likely, therefore, that success rates for a given amount and kind of treatment will be affected by these base rates. As would be expected from these considerations, Abel, Rouleau, and Cunningham-Rathner (1986) found that homosexual child molesters had lower post-behavioral treatment success rates than heterosexual child molesters. Similarly, sex offenders are more likely to reoffend the greater the number of previous sex offenses they have committed; the confidence one has in the relation of positive changes produced by treatment to positive outcome must, therefore, decrease with the number of previous offenses an offender has committed. It is ironic that a high base rate of reoffending for a given class of sex offender both helps program evaluation (no floor effects and the possibility of employing short follow-ups in comparative treatment outcome studies) and simultaneously makes clinicians less optimistic about the outcome of treatment for individual members of that class.

Of course, clinical decisions are not only related to probabilities of reoffending but also to the severity of the behaviors of concern (Quinsey, 1977). A very small probability of a sadistic sexual murder, for example, leads to greater caution than a very high probability of indecent exposure. In some cases, such as those involving serial sexual murderers, no conceivable treatment outcome should give a clinician sufficient confidence to recommend a relaxation of supervision.

The relevance of this discussion in the present context is that treatment-related shifts in sexual preference must be interpreted in the context of other variables that are known or believed to be related to the probability and the type of sexual recidivism (see Table 1). Some of these variables can be altered (e.g., substance abuse, social skillfulness), while others (e.g., IQ) cannot. What is so badly needed are long-term follow-up studies that indicate how much treatment-induced changes alter recidivism base rates, that is, the increment in success rates for various client populations associated with different treatments and with different amounts and measures of change occasioned by those treatments. In a very small follow-up study of 30 released child molesters, Quinsey et al. (1980) found that posttreatment penile response data (in the form of ratios of response to adult stimuli divided by response to child stimuli) were related in the expected manner to recidivism over a 29-month period. Obviously, a very great deal more research is required before clinicians will be able to substitute empirically based actuarial tables for an intuitive combination of treatment response and client characteristic variables in making predictions.

ACKNOWLEDGMENTS. We wish to thank G. Harris and M. Rice for their comments on an earlier version of this chapter.

REFERENCES

Abel, G. G., Blanchard, E. B., Becker, J. V., & Djenderedjian, A. (1978). Differentiating sexual aggressiveness with penile measures. *Criminal Justice and Behavior, 5*, 315–332.

Abel, G. G., Becker, J. V., Cunningham-Rathner, J., Rouleau, J. L., Kaplan, M., & Reich, J. (1984). *The treatment of child molesters.* Unpublished manual, Behavioral Medicine Laboratory, Box AF, Emory University, Atlanta, Georgia.

Abel, G. G., Rouleau, J. L., & Cunningham-Rathner, J. (1986). Sexually aggressive behavior. In W. J. Curran, A. L. McGarry, & S. A. Shah (Eds.), *Forensic psychiatry and psychology: Perspectives and standards for interdisciplinary practice* (pp. 289–313). Philadelphia: Davis.

American Psychiatric Association (1987). *Diagnostic and statistical manual of mental disorders.* (3rd ed., revised). Washington, DC: Author.

Barlow, D. H. (1973). Increasing heterosexual responsiveness in the treatment of sexual deviation. *Behavior Therapy, 4*, 655–671.

Barlow, D. H. (1974). The treatment of sexual deviation: Towards a comprehensive behavioral approach. In K. S. Calhoun, H. E. Adams, & K. M. Mitchell (Eds.), *Handbook of behavioral assessment* (pp. 121–147). New York: Wiley.

Barlow, D. H., & Agras, W. S. (1973). Fading to increase heterosexual responsiveness in homosexuals. *Journal of Applied Behavior Analysis, 6*, 355–366.

Bond, I. K., & Evans, D. R. (1967). avoidance therapy: Its use in two cases of underwear fetishism. *Canadian Medical Association Journal, 96*, 1160–1162.

Borzecki, M., & Wormith, J. S. (1987). A survey of treatment programs for sex offenders in North America. *Canadian Psychology, 28*, 30–44.

Brownell, K. D., & Barlow, D. H. (1980). The behavioral treatment of sexual deviation. In A. Goldstein & E. B. Foa (Eds.), *Handbook of behavioral interventions* (pp. 604–672). New York: Wiley.

Brownell, K. D., Hayes, S. C., & Barlow, D. H. (1977). Patterns of appropriate and deviant sexual arousal: The behavioral treatment of multiple sexual deviations. *Journal of Consulting and Clinical Psychology, 45*, 1144–1155.

Cannon, D. S., Baker, J. B., Gino, A., & Nathan, P. E. (1986). Alcohol-aversion therapy: Relation between strength of aversion and abstinence. *Journal of Consulting and Clinical Psychology, 54*, 825–830.

Conrad, S. R., & Wincze, J. P. (1976). Orgasmic reconditioning: A controlled study of its effects upon the sexual arousal and behavior of adult male homosexuals. *Behavior Therapy, 7*, 155–166.

Earls, C. M. (1988). Deviant sexual arousal in sexual offenders. In R. Prentky and V. L. Quinsey (Eds.), *Human sexual aggression: Current perspectives* (pp. 41–48). Annals of the New York Academy of Sciences, Vol. 528.

Earls, C. M., & Castonguay, L. G. (1989). The treatment of a bisexual pedophile using olfactory aversion: A single case experimental design with a multiple baseline across behaviors. *Behavior Therapy, 20*, 137–146.

Earls, C. M., & Marshall, W. L. (1983). The current state of technology in the laboratory assessment of sexual arousal patterns. In J. G. Greer & I. R. Stuart (Eds.), *Sexual aggression: Current perspectives on treatment* (pp. 336–362). New York: Van Nostrand Reinhold.

Earls, C. M., & Quinsey, V. L. (1985). What is to be done? Future research on the assessment and behavioral treatment of sex offenders. *Behavioral Sciences and the Law, 3,* 377–390.

Earls, C. M., Quinsey, V. L., & Castonguay, L. G. (1987). A comparison of scoring methods in the measurement of penile circumference changes. *Archives of Sexual Behavior, 6,* 493–500.

Foote, W. E., & Laws, D. R. (1981). A daily alternation procedure for orgasmic reconditioning with a pedophile. *Journal of Behavior Therapy and Experimental Psychiatry, 12,* 267–273.

Freund, K. (1981). Assessment of pedophilia. In M. Cook & K. Howells (Eds.), *Adult sexual interest in children* (pp. 139–179). Toronto: Academic Press.

Freund, K., McKnight, C. K., Langevin, R., & Cibiri, S. (1972). The female child as a surrogate object. *Archives of Sexual Behavior, 2,* 119–133.

Freund, K., Chan, S., & Coulthard, R. (1979). Phallometric diagnosis with "non-admitters." *Behaviour Research and Therapy, 17,* 451–457.

Griffiths, D., Quinsey, V. L., & Hingsburger, D. (1989). *Community-based treatment of developmentally handicapped individuals displaying inappropriate sexual behaviors.* Boston: Brooke.

Hallam, R., Rachman, S., & Falkowski, W. (1972). Subjective, attitudinal and physiological effects of electrical aversion therapy. *Behaviour Research and Therapy, 10,* 1–13.

Hayes, S. C., Brownell, K. D., & Barlow, D. H. (1983). Heterosocial-skills training and covert sensitization. Effects on social skills and sexual arousal in sexual deviants. *Behaviour Research and Therapy, 21,* 383–392.

Herman, S. H., Barlow, D. H., & Agras, W. S. (1974). An experimental analysis of classical conditioning as a method of increasing heterosexual arousal in homosexuals. *Behavior Therapy, 5,* 33–47.

Kelly, R. J. (1982). Behavioral reorientation of pedophiliacs: Can it be done? *Clinical Psychology Review, 2,* 387–408.

Knopp, F. H. (1984). *Retraining adult sex offenders: Methods and models.* New York: Safer Society Press.

Laws, D. R. (1980). Treatment of bisexual pedophilia by a biofeedback-assisted self-control procedure. *Behaviour Research and Therapy, 18,* 207–211.

Laws, D. R., & Holmen, M. L. (1978). Sexual response faking by pedophiles. *Criminal Justice and Behavior, 5,* 343–356.

Laws, D. R., & O'Neil, J. A. (1981). Variations on masturbatory conditioning. *Behavioural Psychotherapy, 9,* 111–136.

Laws, D. R., & Osborn, C. A. (1983). How to build and operate a behavioral laboratory to evaluate and treat sexual deviance. In J. G. Greer & I. R. Stuart (Eds.), *The sexual aggressor: Current perspectives on treatment* (pp. 293–335). Toronto: Van Nostrand Reinhold.

MacCulloch, M. J., & Feldman, M. P. (1967). Aversion therapy in management of 43 homosexuals. *British Medical Journal, 2,* 594–597.

Maletzky, B. M. (1980). Self-referred versus court-referred sexually deviant patients: Success with assisted covert sensitization. *Behavior Therapy, 11,* 306–314.

Marks, I. M., & Gelder, J. L. (1967). Transvestism and fetishism: clinical and psychological changes during faradic aversion. *British Journal of Psychiatry, 113,* 711–729.

Marquis, J. N. (1970). Orgasmic reconditioning: Changing sexual object choice through controlling masturbation fantasies. *Journal of Behavior Therapy and Experimental Psychiatry, 1,* 263–271.

Marshall, W. L. (1971). A combined treatment method for certain sexual deviations. *Behaviour Research and Therapy, 9,* 293–294.

Marshall, W. L. (1979). Satiation therapy: A procedure for reducing deviant sexual arousal. *Journal of Applied Behavior Analysis, 12,* 10–22.

Marshall, W. L., & Christie, M. M. (1981). Pedophilia and aggression. *Criminal Justice and Behavior, 8,* 145–158.

Marshall, W. L., & Lippens, K. (1977). The clinical value of boredom: A procedure for reducing inappropriate sexual interests. *Journal of Nervous and Mental Disease, 165,* 283–287.

Marshall, W. L., Barbaree, H. E., & Christophe, D. (1986). Sexual offenders against female children: Sexual preferences for age of victims and type of behavior. *Canadian Journal of Behavioural Science, 18,* 424–439.

Marshall, W. L., Earls, C. M., Segal, Z., & Darke, J. (1983). A behavioral program for the assessment and treatment of sexual aggressors. In K. D. Craig & R. J. McMahon (Eds.), *Advances in Clinical Behavior Therapy* (pp. 148–174). New York: Brunner Mazel.

McGuire, R. J., Carlisle, J. M., & Young, B. G. (1965). Sexual deviations as conditioned behavior: A hypothesis. *Behaviour Research and Therapy, 2,* 185–190.

Monahan, J. (1981). *Predicting violent behavior: An assessment of clinical techniques.* Beverly Hills, CA: Sage.

Pithers, W. D., Marques, J. K., Gibatt, C. C., & Marlatt, A. (1983). Relapse prevention with sexual aggressives: A self-control model of treatment and maintenance of change. In J. G. Greer & I. R. Stuart (Eds.), *The sexual aggressor: Current perspectives on treatment* (pp. 214–239). New York: Van Nostrand Reinhold.

Quinsey, V. L. (1973). Methodological issues in evaluating the effectiveness of aversion therapies for institutional child molesters. *Canadian Psychologist, 14,* 350–361.

Quinsey, V. L. (1977). The assessment and treatment of child molesters: a review. *Canadian Psychological Review, 18,* 204–220.

Quinsey, V. L. (1980). The baserate problem and the prediction of dangerousness: A reappraisal. *Journal of Psychiatry and Law, 8,* 329–340.

Quinsey, V. L. (1984a). Sexual aggression: Studies of offenders against women. In D. Weisstub (Ed.), *Law and mental health: International perspectives* (Vol. 1; pp. 84–121). New York: Pergamon Press.

Quinsey, V. L. (1984b). Institutional release policy and the identification of dangerous men: A review of the literature. *Criminologie, 17,* 53–78.

Quinsey, V. L. (1986). Men who have sex with children. In D. N. Weisstub (Ed.), *Law and mental health: International perspectives* (Vol. 2; pp. 140–172). New York: Pergamon Press.

Quinsey, V. L., & Chaplin, T. C. (1988). Preventing faking in phallometric assessments of sexual preference. In R. Prentky & V. L. Quinsey (Eds.), *Human sexual aggression: Contemporary perspectives* (pp. 49–58). Annals of the New York Academy of Sciences, Vol. 528.

Quinsey, V. L., & Maguire, A. M. (1986). Maximum security psychiatric patients: Actuarial and clinical prediction of dangerousness. *Journal of Interpersonal Violence, 1,* 143–171.

Quinsey, V. L., & Marshall, W. L. (1983). Procedures for reducing inappropriate sexual arousal: An evaluation review. In J. G. Greer & I. R. Stuart (Eds.), *The sexual aggressor: Current perspectives on treatment* (pp. 267–289). New York: Van Nostrand Reinhold.

Quinsey, V. L., & Varney, G. W. (1976). Modification of preference in a concurrent schedule by aversive conditioning: An analog study. *Bulletin of the Psychonomic Society, 7,* 211–213.

Quinsey, V. L., Steinman, C. M., Bergersen, S. G., & Holmes, J. (1975). Penile circumference, skin conductance, and ranking responses of child molesters and "normals" to sexual and nonsexual visual stimuli. *Behavior Therapy, 6,* 213–219.

Quinsey, V. L., Bergersen, S. G., & Steinman, C. M. (1976). Changes in physiological and verbal responses of child molesters during aversion therapy. *Canadian Journal of Behavioral Science, 8,* 202–212.

Quinsey, V. L., Chaplin, T. C., & Carrigan, W. F. (1980). Biofeedback and signaled punishment in the modification of inappropriate sexual age preferences. *Behavior Therapy, 11,* 567–576.

Quinsey, V. L., Chaplin, T. C., Maguire, A. M., & Upfold, D. (1987). The behavioral treatment of rapists and child molesters. In E. K. Morris & C. J. Braukmann (Eds.), *Behavioral approaches to crime and delinquency: Application, research, and theory* (pp. 363–382). New York: Plenum.

Rachman, S., & Teasdale, J. (1969). *Aversion therapy and behavioral disorders: An analysis.* Coral Cables, Florida: University of Miami Press.

Sachs, D. A., & Keller, J. (1972). Intensity and temporal characteristics of the CER paradigm with humans. *Journal of General Psychology, 86,* 181–188.

VanDeventer, A. D., & Laws, D. R. (1978). Orgasmic reconditioning to redirect sexual arousal in pedophiles. *Behavior Therapy, 9,* 748–765.

Wydra, A., Marshall, W. L., Earls, C. M., & Barbaree, H. E. (1983). Identification of cues and control of sexual arousal by rapists. *Behaviour Research and Therapy, 21,* 469–476.

17

The Antiandrogen and Hormonal Treatment of Sex Offenders

J. M. W. Bradford

Introduction

The treatment of sexual offenders using hormonal agents and antiandrogens is an increasingly important approach to a difficult clinical problem. As the public becomes more focused on the problem of sexual offenders and particularly child molesters, the demand for longer terms of incarceration as a solution to the problem has escalated, whereas the rehabilitation and treatment component has been deemphasized. It is in this climate that the need for effective treatment approaches supported by outcome studies is essential. At least part of the problem is that the term *sexual offender* can mean anything from a violent sadistic predatory rapist to an inhibited exhibitionist.

The hormonal and antiandrogen approach to treatment has been used in all types of sexual offenders. It is one of the organic treatments of sexual offenders, the other two approaches being surgical castration and stereotaxic neurosurgery.

Organic treatments for the male sexual offender (Bradford, 1985) have traditionally been used to reduce the sexual drive of sexually aggressive men. They have also been used in the treatment of the other paraphilias, where offenders' inability to control their behavior leads to a high rate of victimization and recidivism. Surgical castration is important because its effect on sexual behavior is through the reduction of testosterone and, therefore, has a comparative mechanism of action to the antiandrogen treatments. In addition, the post-castration follow-up studies (Bremer, 1959; Heim & Hursch, 1979; Le Maire, 1956; Ortmann, 1980; Stürup, 1968, 1972) provide the most comprehensive recidivism data in existence. These studies have reported substantial reductions in the rate

J. M. W. Bradford • The Royal Ottawa Hospital and the University of Ottawa, Ottawa, Ontario K1Z 7K4, Canada.

of reoffense, varying from 1.6 to 10.8%. The follow-up periods were up to 20 years, and large numbers of offenders were involved. Further, the offenders were a preselected group of sexual offender recidivists. Ortmann (1980, 1984a, 1984b) studied the recidivism rates of castrated sexual offenders in Denmark and found that castration was used mostly in rapists and homosexual pedophiles.

HORMONAL CONTROLS OVER SEXUAL BEHAVIOR

Testosterone is the principal androgen produced by the testes of most animal species. Along with the other androgens, it forms part of the hypothalamic–pituitary axis with its feedback loops. The androgens are essential biomessengers from fetal life to adulthood. The tissues and end organs regulated by androgens differ widely. Testosterone is a hormone with multiple effects. These include the fusion of the labioscrotal folds in the male embryo in utero, the concomitant male differentiation of the urogenital tract, promotion of spermatogenesis, support of the growth of body and beard hair, muscle development, red blood cell production, hyperplasia of the sebaceous glands, development of male baldness, hyperplasia of the prostate in older males, secretion of the ejaculate, the androgenization of the brain, and the maintenance of sexual behavior in males and some effects on the sexual behavior in females (Wilson & Foster, 1983). Although it was at first thought that this diversity of functions was through different mechanisms of action, it is now known that a single mechanism of action is responsible, namely, the binding of the hormone to a high-affinity intracellular cytoplasmic receptor protein. The receptor–hormone complex is then transported into the nucleus of the target tissue cells, where it binds to DNA and stimulates the synthesis of messenger RNA (Liang, Tymoczko, Chan, Hung, & Liao, 1977). It is the various target tissues that are programmed through gene expression to respond in different ways to the hormone–receptor complex that results in the diverse actions (Liang *et al.*, 1977).

Testosterone is active at the androgen receptors by binding directly to them; otherwise, it is metabolized to other steroids (Lipsett, 1977). Testosterone is converted to dihydrotestosterone, which then binds to the androgen receptors. This conversion occurs mainly in the skin and the reproductive tract. The Leydig cells of the testes are the main production site for testosterone. These steroid-synthesizing cells have receptors for luteinizing hormone (LH), which is the tropic hormone for testosterone production (Mainwaring, 1977). Testosterone may also be converted to estrogens in the brain and may then act through the estrogen receptors (Naftolin, Ryan, & Petro, 1972). It is this process that is critical during fetal brain development. The brain and other organs have bipotential, meaning that they could develop into either male or female organs. In the male, through the process of fetal androgenization, testosterone is responsible for the brain switching to a male pathway as well as for the differentiation of the external genitalia (Dorner, 1977). As a result of this process, feedback control in men and women is different. In both sexes gonadotropin production is under the influence of the dominant steroid, which is testosterone in males and estradiol and progesterone in females.

Testosterone is the most important of the sex hormones influencing sexual behavior in human males. A comprehensive understanding of the relationship between steroid receptors and hormone binding to these receptors and how this influences hormone action is essential to the understanding of the antiandrogen and hormonal treatments. Most steroid hormones have a saturable biological response, and the receptors have a high affinity for their respective hormones. It is the binding of the hormone to the receptor that results in the biological response. Binding to receptor sites can be inhibited by competitive and noncompetitive mechanisms. Competitive inhibitors act by combining with the receptor so that the steroid molecule cannot be bound. Noncompetitive inhibition decreases the number of receptor sites. Both testosterone and dihydrotestosterone have an effect at the androgen receptors. The sensitivity of the androgen receptors in the central nervous system (provided there is sufficient testosterone above a specific individually determined threshold) determines male sexual behavioral patterns.

The androgen receptors are found in the various androgen-sensitive target organs. Androgen receptors are present in the prostate, seminal vesicles, and epididymis, where dihydrotestosterone is the preferentially received hormone (Liang et al., 1977). Androgen receptors in the limbic system, specifically the anterior hypothalamus, respond to testosterone (Liang et al., 1977).

In summary, the effect of castration is to make less androgen available at the receptors without affecting the sensitivity of the receptors or causing a receptor blockade. This is in distinct contrast to the mechanism of action of the antiandrogens (such as cyproterone acetate, CPA) but is similar to the hormonal agents (such as medroxyprogesterone acetate, MPA, and estradiol). The mechanisms of action of these agents are complex, however, and this is an oversimplification.

Steroid hormones are synthesized from the parent molecule cholesterol. The rate of release of the hormone is a product of its rate of synthesis. The majority of the tropic hormones exert control through the rate of hormone synthesis (Wilson & Foster, 1983).

The steroid hormones and particularly testosterone are transported in the plasma on specific transport proteins. In the case of testosterone it is testosterone-binding globulin. This globulin resembles receptor binding protein, as it has a high affinity for testosterone and also specific receptor sites (Wilson & Foster, 1983). A dynamic equilibrium exists between the bound and unbound forms of testosterone, and it is the latter which is the metabolically active portion. The clearance rate of the various hormones is affected by the degree of binding to the transport protein. Females, for instance, have high levels of testosterone-binding globulin and half the clearance of testosterone and dihydrotestosterone as males (Wilson & Foster, 1983).

The behavioral effects of testosterone are the result of its action on the brain, which is principally responsible for the preservation of male sexual behavior and the regulation of LH secretion. This is supported by animal research with lesions and testosterone propionate implants in the medial preoptic region of the hypothalamus (Davidson, Smith, & Damassa, 1977). Although there is still some debate, it appears that the site of action of androgens is initially at the hypothalamic level, where it suppresses luteinizing hormone releasing hormone (LHRH) (Davidson *et al.*, 1977).

In humans the major behavioral manifestation that needs to be identified and controlled is sexual aggression. Various approaches have been used to identify the violent sexual offender (Abel, Barlow, Blanchard, & Guild, 1977; Abel, Blanchard, Becker, & Djenderedjian, 1978; Barbaree, Marshall, & Lanthier, 1979; Davidson & Malcolm, 1985; Groth, 1979; Groth, Burgess, & Holmstrom, 1977; Malamuth, Check, & Briere, 1986; Rada, 1978). The relationship of testosterone to the manifestation of aggressive sexual behavior in man has also been extensively researched, and a number of studies (Bradford & Bourget, 1987; Bradford & McLean, 1984; Brown & Davis, 1975; Ehrenkranz, Bliss, & Sheard, 1974; Kreuz & Rose, 1972; Meyer-Bahlburg, Nat, Boon, Sharma, & Edwards, 1974; Monti, Brown, & Corriveau, 1977; Olweus, Mattsson, Schalling, & Low, 1980; Persky, Smith, & Basu, 1971; Rada, Laws, & Kellner, 1976; Scaramella & Brown, 1978) have shown a relationship between plasma testosterone levels and sexually aggressive behavior. It is these findings that also provide support for the treatment of sexual offenders with antiandrogens.

HORMONES AND OTHER AGENTS IN TREATMENT

Starting initially with estrogens, hormonal agents have also been used for sexual drive reduction (Foote, 1944; Golla & Hodge, 1949; Symmers, 1968; Whittaker, 1959). There are cytosol estrogen receptors similar to the androgen receptors already described. These receptors have been extensively studied, and the information gained in this research has been used to further the understanding of steroid receptor action. This research has shown that the actual number of cytosol receptors can be influenced by exogenous and endogenous steroids, including estrogens (Hsueh, Peck, & Clark, 1976; Lan & Katzenellenbogen, 1976). This is critical in the ultimate understanding of the mechanism of action of the antiandrogens. Estrogen and progesterone receptors are found in the hypothalamus and in the pituitary, and these receptors mainly affect female reproductive and sexual behavior. They can also, theoretically, influence male behavior. Testosterone is converted to estrogens in the brain. These estrogens function through the estrogen receptors and suppress gonadotropin secretion, which in turn causes a decrease in available testosterone. Both progesterone and androgen are physiological antagonists of estrogen. It was from this body of evidence that the use of estrogens to suppress sexual drive in sexual offenders was derived. Although it proved to be a successful treatment, the side effects, such as nausea, vomiting, and feminization, have limited its use (Symmers, 1968).

A number of different phenothiazines have been reported to reduce sexual drive and also sexually deviant behavior. Benperidol, a butyrophenone, has been described as having a specific effect (Field, 1973; Sterkmans & Geerts, 1966). A study by Tennent, Bancroft, and Cass (1974) compared benperidol, chlorpromazine, and a placebo and found that benperidol was significantly more effective in reducing sexual interest than either of the other two agents. In a follow-up study, cyproterone acetate (CPA) and ethinyl estradiol (EE) were compared on a number of parameters of sexual behavior (Bancroft, Tennent, Loucas, & Cass, 1974). These included self-rated frequency of sexual thoughts or interest, a sexual activity score, a sexual attitudes score, and sexual arousal responses to sexual fantasy, slides, and an erotic film. The effects of EE and CPA were very similar, with CPA having the greatest effect on erectile responses. The dyskinetic side effects of benperidol were significant, but no side effects were seen with CPA and EE. One fascinating finding was the drug effect on sexual fantasy and interest outside the experimental situation. In the face of strong erotic stimuli (i.e., the erotic film as opposed to slides), erectile responses continued to be seen despite the action CPA and EE.

Medroxyprogesterone Acetate

The hormonal agent that has received the most attention in the treatment of sexual offenders in North America is medroxyprogesterone acetate (MPA). The first study (Heller, Laidlaw, Harvey, & Nelson, 1958) of MPA reducing the sexual drive in males was reported in 1958. This involved normal males treated with a progestagenic female contraceptive. Sexual drive and ejaculate were reduced. Money (1968) described the first case of MPA being used to treat sexual deviancy. Following this a number of studies were conducted using MPA for the treatment of sexually deviant men (Berlin & Meinecke, 1981; Gagne, 1981; Langevin et al., 1979; Meyer, Walker, Emory, & Smith, 1985; Money, 1970; Money, Wiedeking, Walker, & Gain, 1976; Walker & Meyer, 1981; Wiedeking, Money, & Walker, 1979).

MPA has a mechanism of action principally through the induction of testosterone-A reductase in the liver, thereby accelerating the metabolism of testosterone. This progestational agent affects the plasma levels and production rate of testosterone through an increased clearance rate from the plasma (Southren, Gordon, Vittek, & Altman, 1977). In addition, it has an antigonadotropic effect. It is questionable if it has any effect in competing with the androgens at the androgen receptors (Southren et al., 1977). There is also some effect on the binding to the transport protein in the plasma testosterone-binding globulin.

There are some potential side effects of MPA treatment that have to be considered. Walker and Meyer (1981) reviewed published and unpublished data on MPA and reported a number of potential physiological effects. Although they found no evidence of blood pressure changes or alterations in routine serum biochemistry, they did report weight gain in somewhat less than 50% of subjects. Sperm production decreased initially on treatment but returned to normal levels usually after 6 months of treatment. Basal insulin levels were found to be normal, although there was a hyperinsulinenemic response to a glucose load, and there were some questions raised about gall bladder function and gastrointestinal functioning. There was also reported to be a reversal of any testicular atrophy which might have occurred. Some patients reported a worsening of headaches, and there was a single case of diabetes mellitus. Gagne (1981) reported fatigue, weight gain, hot and cold flushes, phlebitis, nausea and vomiting, headaches, and disturbances of sleep. Berlin and Meinecke (1981) also reported nightmares, hyperglycemia, and cramps of the legs. However, desirable effects on sexual functioning were observed, including reduced sexual drive, decreases in erotic fantasy, reductions in sexual activity, and possibly less aggressiveness (Blumer & Migeon, 1975). Money et al. (1975) reported that the effect on aggressive behavior appeared to be a placebolike response.

Clinical Studies of MPA Treatment

It is valuable to review some of the clinical studies of MPA that have been reported. Not all the studies will be reviewed but rather those studies most often cited in the literature.

John Money (1968, 1970, 1972) provided the first clinical report of the use of MPA in which he described the treatment of nine paraphiliacs. The dosage employed was 300–400 mg per week administered intramuscularly. The effects on sexual behavior were decreased frequency of erections, reductions in sexual drive, and reduced orgasm rates. Subsequently, Money et al. (1976) reported that beneficial effects were still observed 8 years later in 23 patients. Blumer and Migeon (1975) described the treatment of 22 cases with similar results, with the additional observation that MPA reduced aggression.

Wiedeking et al. (1979) treated 11 XYY males who were impulsive and sexually deviant. There was a 1-year follow-up, and behavioral ratings were made in each of five categories, including assault, destructive behavior against property, threatening, stealing, and self-harm. On the behavioral ratings, at the very best a modest treatment outcome was observed. At dosage levels between 100 and 400 mg of MPA per week, only one patient reported a reduction of sexual activity. This same patient reported a reduction of pedophilic fantasies. Two paraphiliac patients who were engaging in inappropriate sexual acts prior to treatment reported a cessation of this activity at the time of follow-up. An exhibitionist continued his offensive behavior despite MPA.

In a study of the treatment of exhibitionists, Langevin et al. (1979) compared MPA to assertiveness training. The use of MPA for 15 weeks unfortunately resulted in a high dropout rate, making interpretation of the results somewhat difficult. In an ancillary study, eight exhibitionists were evaluated in a placebo and active treatment phase using penile tumescence techniques. Unfortunately, the length of the study was only 1 week, which did not allow the occurrence of the full effect of MPA on the sexual arousal responses. There were no differences between placebo and active drug on the penile measures.

Twenty chronic paraphiliac males were treated with MPA by Berlin and Meinecke (1981). Three of the patients relapsed while on MPA, and 10 of the 11 patients who discontinued MPA against medical advice also relapsed. These results raise interesting possibilities. Could the potential relapses have been predicted by penile tumescence testing conducted while they were receiving MPA? Are there differences between those who relapse following the cessation of treatment compared with those who do not? Does the length of treatment have anything to do with the risk of relapse? On the positive side, it is clear that MPA is an effective treatment, provided the patients comply with treatment.

Gagne (1981) combined MPA with milieu therapy for a period of 12 months. He reported on the outcome with 48 patients, the largest group of which were homosexual pedophiles. The treatment regime was aimed at keeping plasma testosterone at less than 250 ng/100 ml. The patients received 200 mg of MPA intramuscularly, three times per week in the first 2 weeks, 200 mg once or twice per week for the next 4 weeks, and then either 100 mg per week or 200 mg every 2 weeks as maintenance treatment. While antisocial personality disorder was associated with a poor prognosis, nevertheless, 40 patients improved substantially, and this was maintained throughout the follow-up period, although the length of follow-up is not given.

In a recent single-case study, MPA was used over a 500-day period to treat a hypersexual pedophile (Cordoba & Chapel, 1983). This 25-year-old man had strong urges to fondle prepubertal girls. He also had other behavioral manifestations of hypersexuality. Treatment with MPA was commenced at 300-mg intramuscular injections at 10-day intervals in order to bring plasma testosterone to prepubertal levels, and subsequently the dosage was titrated to maintain it at these levels. All aspects of this man's sexual behavior were decreased. He reported a drop in the frequency of masturbation, erections, and ejaculations as well as the frequency of his sexual thoughts. There was also a decrease in irritability and verbal aggressiveness. However, plasma testosterone levels did not prove to be a strong indicator of sexual drive, and later in treatment the dosage was adjusted according to the self-report of behavior.

Wincze, Bansal, and Malamud (1986) used MPA in the treatment of three pedophiles with a history of repeated offending. This study used a single-case experimental design with a double-blind procedure in place for the administration of the medication. The results showed that self-reported arousal outside the laboratory setting was unreliable when taken as a desired drug effect. Within the laboratory setting there was a significant reduction in arousal to erotic stimuli, with some overall reduction in penile tumescence. In the placebo phase, these effects were reversed in one subject. Nocturnal penile tumescence was significantly reduced in all cases.

Cyproterone Acetate

Cyproterone acetate (CPA) has antiandrogenic, antigonadotropic, and progestational effects. Its principal mode of action is on the androgen receptors, and as such it is regarded as a true antiandrogen. The response of the androgen receptor is disrupted by CPA, which blocks the intracellular testosterone uptake and the intracellular metabolism of the androgens as well as preventing receptor binding (Bradford, 1983).

CPA has largely dose-dependent effects. The effects on sexual behavior arise as a result of a reduction of plasma testosterone. Erections, ejaculate, and spermatogenesis are all decreased, as are sexual fantasies, which in a large number of cases are completely eliminated.

There are some theoretical risks to CPA treatment, but these are highly unlikely to occur at the dosage levels used to treat the paraphilias. There is the possibility of liver dysfunction and adrenal suppression (Cremonocini, Viginati, & Libroia, 1976; Neumann, 1977), and feminization is a possibility, manifesting with temporary or protracted gynecomastia.

Many patients treated with CPA report a feeling of calm as a result of the treatment. This appears to be specifically related to a reduction of anxiety and irritability (Bradford & Pawlak, in press). This reduction in irritability appears to be part of a general reduction in psychopathological symptoms found during treatment with CPA.

Clinical Studies of CPA Treatment

The first clinical studies of CPA were reported from Germany. Laschet and Laschet (1971) examined the clinical treatment of over 100 men of whom 50% were sexual offenders. The majority of these offenders were exhibitionists, but some of the patients were pedophiles and some were sexual sadists. Treatment duration varied from a minimum of 6 months to over 4 years. In about 5% of cases, there was a complete elimination of all deviant behavior, even after treatment with CPA was terminated. Some of the undesirable side effects reported above were also seen.

Other studies (Cooper, 1981; Cooper, Ismail, Phanjoo, & Love, 1972; Davies, 1974; Mothes, Lehnert, Samimi, & Ufer, 1971; Ott & Hoffet, 1968) have similarly demonstrated the effectiveness of CPA in reducing deviant sexual behaviors. In addition to our own treatment studies, two further reports of the use of CPA deserve mention. In a thorough study of a limited number of patients, Bancroft et al. (1974) compared CPA with ethinyl estradiol (EE) in a double-blind study of 12 patients and found that CPA reduced plasma testosterone, LH, and follicle-stimulating hormone (FSH), whereas EE caused a rise in both plasma testosterone and LH (Murray, Bancroft, Anderson, Tennent, & Carr, 1975). Various measures of sexual activity, as well as erectile responses to a variety of erotic stimuli, were obtained. There were no significant effects of either of the two drugs on the erectile measures, with deviant preferences remaining essentially intact after treatment. When compared to the baseline phase, both drugs significantly lowered self-reported sexual activity. Positive changes were evident in self-rated arousal during the penile tumescence testing as a result of treatment by CPA, but not by EE. CPA had a similar but weaker effect on the erectile responses.

The largest group of sexual deviates ($N = 547$) treated by CPA are reported on jointly by Mothes *et al.* (1971) and Laschet and Laschet (1975). The latter authors provide a more detailed examination of 100 of these patients, plus an additional 200, all of whom were treated with CPA over periods ranging from 2 months to 8 years. Dosages ranged from 50 to 200 mg per day for oral administration, while depo CPA was given at either weekly or two-week intervals, in dosages ranging from 300 to 600 mg per injection. Unwanted side effects observed in the first 2 months included fatigue, hypersomnia, depression, negative nitrogen balance, and weight gain. By 3 months the nitrogen balance had returned to normal as had calcium and phosphate metabolism. At approximately 8 months, in up to 20% of cases, there were some signs of feminization, evidenced by gynecomastia and a reduction of body hair associated with an increase in scalp hair. Positive changes were shown by reductions in ejaculate, erections, sexual fantasies, and sexual drive, which were related to reduced levels of plasma testosterone. These inhibitions of sexuality occurred in 80% of the cases treated with only 100 mg per day via the oral route. Perhaps most importantly for the present purposes, of the 25 patients who were followed for up to 5 years, none recidivated after treatment was discontinued. On the other hand, Laschet and Laschet reported that cases of organic brain damage in association with sexual deviation only partially responded to treatment, while aggressive behavior independent of sexual deviation did not respond at all to CPA.

CPA has been used in the treatment of a variety of paraphilias at the Sexual Behaviors Clinic of the Royal Ottawa Hospital and the University of Ottawa. A double-blind placebo crossover study of 37 patients has been completed, and the results of the first 19 cases in the study have been reported as positive (Bradford & Pawlak, in press). In addition, a single-case study (Bradford & Pawlak, 1987a) with repeated measures showed that CPA produced a significant reduction in sadistic and aggressive arousal responses in a sadistic, homosexual pedophile. This particular case had failed to respond to prior behavioral treatment. Furthermore, the single case demonstrated for the first time a differential effect on sexual arousal responses as a result of treatment with CPA. CPA reduced the arousal responses to pedophilic stimuli, including coercive, noncoercive, and sadistic stimuli. The ability to suppress arousal responses to these stimuli under instruction also substantially improved. The arousal to mutually consenting adult heterosexual intercourse was not affected to the same extent, resulting in a net increase in the overall index of "normal" sexual arousal.

The double-blind placebo crossover study includes 12 sexual offenders with high pretreatment rates of offending (Mean $= 2.5$ previous convictions per offender). During the active treatment phase, CPA significantly reduced testosterone, LH, and FSH levels when compared to placebo and baseline phases. Sexual arousal was measured by standard penile tumescence techniques, using visual stimuli preselected by each subject for their erotic potential as well as a 2-minute period of covert sexual fantasies. Active drug treatment reduced responses to both the slides and the fantasies when compared to placebo administration. Significant reductions were also evident in psychopathology and in self-reported sexual interests and activities. A more detailed study of each individual's reports of sexual activity showed that the active drug reduced sexual tension, sexual fantasies, libido, sexual potency, nocturnal pollution, spontaneous erections in the morning, and masturbation. These changes differed statistically significantly when compared to baseline and placebo. Irritability and aggressiveness were somewhat reduced, but these changes did not reach acceptable levels of statistical significance (Bradford & Pawlak, in press).

In the second phase of this study, the effects of CPA on the sexual arousal patterns of child molesters was examined (Bradford & Pawlak, 1987b). Twenty subjects were classified as belonging to either a high-testosterone group or a low-testosterone group. Analysis of the results confirmed the effects of CPA on the plasma testosterone levels, with the effect being greater on the high-testosterone group. A differential effect on sexual arousal responses was seen, with significant reductions in arousal to pedophilic and coercive sexual stimuli regardless of testosterone grouping. Just as importantly there were no signs of reduced arousal to adult mutually consenting sex scenes. CPA appears to affect the sexual arousal responses of sex offenders in a differential manner, with the degree and nature of the effect moderated by the type of stimulus presented, whether or not plasma testosterone levels are within the normal range or high prior to treatment.

It is clear that CPA can play an important role in the treatment of sexual offenders. It is well documented that it can substantially reduce recidivism rates of sexual offenders, and these beneficial effects continue even when treatment is terminated.

MANAGEMENT STRATEGIES OF ANTIANDROGEN TREATMENT

The treatment of sex offenders with antiandrogens is clearly successful in reducing recidivism rates. There are questions as to how to most effectively use this treatment modality and how to select patients most likely to benefit, with a minimum of unwanted side effects. These questions are the subject of debate at this time, but some guidelines can be formulated. There is clearly a group of medical contraindications that have to be respected at all times. Further, freely given, informed consent is an absolute prerequisite. This latter issue, in my opinion, implies that CPA should have limited use in a correctional facility, where it is not certain that freely given informed consent can be obtained. In these settings, CPA is too likely to become part of a subtle coercion process involving the offer of parole contingent on accepting treatment, without a truly independent psychiatric consultation prior to its use. Furthermore, it is debatable whether it is needed in this setting, where the physical environment is strictly controlled. It is much more likely to be useful once the sex offender is to be paroled and to reenter society, where he will be subject to various temptations. At this point he could be referred to clinics outside of the correctional system for treatment.

The need for indefinite continuation of the treatment is another consideration. From the studies of CPA outlined above, and from my own clinical experience, the need for indefinite and prolonged treatment in all individuals is not essential. After a treatment period of 6 to 12 months, CPA can be gradually tapered off in a significant number of individuals, without causing relapses. This does not seem to be true for MPA. Some individuals are at risk to relapse, and at this time it is not possible to identify them in advance. When treatment with CPA is discontinued it is useful to follow up with a formal behavioral treatment program. Also, it is imperative, especially in pedophiles, to correct cognitive distortions by way of individual and group psychotherapy. Finally, some individuals, such as sadistic sexual offenders, because of the very nature of the deviation, are candidates for long-term treatment on the basis of risk reduction alone.

FUTURE RESEARCH

Future research is needed on the hypothalamic–pituitary axis and its role in the etiology of sexual deviation. At least part of this research can be approached through the use of antiandrogen medication and the careful evaluation of its effects on the system, particularly on the androgen receptors. Clinical trials of treatment of sex offenders, using a variety of antiandrogens, are also important. The various antiandrogens and hormonal agents have different mechanisms of action, as already outlined. More recently there has been the development of both LHRH agonists and antagonists, with differing hormonal effects. The development of the nonsteroidal antiandrogen flutamide offers another opportunity to study antiandrogens in the treatment of the paraphilias.

The selection of patients most suitable for antiandrogen treatment, and those clinical characteristics which would allow for the discontinuation of treatment without risk of relapse after 12 months, needs to be carefully documented. Investigations of the effects of antiandrogens on the intracerebral androgen receptors may provide some of the answer, and they could also provide some further information concerning sexual orientation, if the differential effects of CPA on sexual arousal patterns holds up under further research.

REFERENCES

Abel, G. G., Barlow, D. H., Blanchard, E., & Guild, D. (1977). The components of rapists' sexual arousal. *Archives of General Psychiatry, 43,* 895–903.
Abel, G. G., Blanchard, E., Becker, J., & Djenderedjian, A. (1978). Differentiating sexual aggressives with penile measures. *Criminal Justice and Behavior, 5,* 315–332.
Bancroft, J., Tennent, G., Loucas, K., & Cass, J. (1974). The control of deviant sexual behaviour by drugs: I. Behavioural changes following oestrogens and antiandrogens. *British Journal of Psychiatry, 125,* 310–315.
Barbaree, H. E., Marshall, W. L., & Lanthier, R. D. (1979). Deviant sexual arousal in rapists. *Behaviour Research and Therapy, 17,* 215–222.
Berlin, F. S., & Meinecke, C. F. (1981). Treatment of sex offenders with antiandrogenic medication: Conceptualization, review of treatment modalities and preliminary findings. *American Journal of Psychiatry, 138,* 601–607.

Blumer, D., & Migeon, C. (1975). Hormone and hormonal agents in the treatment of aggression. *Journal of Nervous and Mental Disorders, 160*, 127–137.

Bradford, J. M. W., (1983). Research in sex offenders. In R. L. Sadoff (Ed.), *The psychiatric clinics of North America* (pp. 715–733). Philadelphia: W. B. Saunders.

Bradford, J. M. W. (1985). Organic treatments for the male sexual offender. *Behaviour Sciences & the Law, 3*, 355–375.

Bradford, J. M. W., & Bourget, D. (1987). Sexually aggressive men. *Psychiatric Journal of the University of Ottawa XII(3)*, 169–175.

Bradford, J. M. W., & McLean, D. (1984). Sexual offenders, violence and testosterone: A clinical study. *Canadian Journal of Psychiatry, 29*, 335–343.

Bradford, J. M. W., & Pawlak, A. (1987a). Sadistic homosexual pedophilia: Treatment with cyproterone acetate. A single case study. *Canadian Journal of Psychiatry, 32*, 22–31.

Bradford, J. M. W., & Pawlak, A. (1987b). *The effects of cyproterone acetate on the sexual arousal patterns of pedophiles*. Manuscript submitted for publication.

Bradford, J. M. W., & Pawlak, A. (in press). Double-blind placebo crossover study of cyproterone acetate in the treatment of sexual deviation—Phase 1. *Canadian Journal of Psychiatry*.

Bremer, J. (1959). *Asexualization—A followup study of 244 cases*. New York: MacMillan.

Brown, W. A., & Davis, G. H. (1957). Serum testosterone and irritability in man. *Psychosomatic Medicine, 37*, 87.

Cooper, A. J. (1981). A placebo controlled study of the antiandrogen cyproterone acetate in deviant hypersexuality. *Comprehensive Psychiatry, 22*, 458–464.

Cooper, A. J., Ismail, A. A., Phanjoo, A. L., & Love, D. L. (1972). Antiandrogen (cyproterone acetate) therapy in deviant hypersexuality. *British Journal of Psychiatry, 120*, 59–63.

Cordoba, O. A., & Chapel, J. L. (1983). Medroxyprogesterone acetate antiandrogen treatment of hypersexuality in a paedophiliac sex offender. *American Journal of Psychiatry, 140*, 1036–1039.

Cremonocini, C., Viginati, E., & Libroia, A. (1976). Treatment of hirsutism and acne in women with two combinations of cyproterone acetate and ethinyloestradiol. *Acta European Fertility, 7*, 299–314.

Davidson, J. M., Smith, E. R., & Damassa, D. A. (1977). Comparative analysis of the roles of androgen in the feedback mechanisms and sexual behavior. In L. Martini & M. Motta (Eds.), *Androgens and antiandrogens* (pp. 137–149) New York: Raven Press.

Davidson, P. R., & Malcolm, P. B. (1985). The reliability of the rape index: a rapist sample. *Behavioural Assessment, 7*, 283–292.

Davies, T. D. (1974). Cyproterone acetate for male hypersexuality. *Journal of International Medical Research, 2*, 159–163.

Dorner, G. (1977). Sex-hormone-dependent brain differentiation and reproduction. In J. Money & H. Musaph (Eds.). *Handbook of sexology II. Genetics, hormones and behaviour* (pp. 227–245). New York: Elsevier.

Ehrenkranz, J., Bliss, E., & Sheard, M. H. (1974). Plasma testosterone: Correlation with aggressive behavior and social dominance in man. *Psychosomatic Medicine, 36*, 469–475.

Field, L. H. (1973). Benperidol in the treatment of sex offenders. *Medicine Science & the Law, 13*, 195–196.

Foote, R. M. (1944). Diethystilbestrol in the management of psychopathological states in males. *Journal of Nervous and Mental Disease, 99*, 928–935.

Gagne, P. (1981). Treatment of sex offenders with medroxyprogesterone acetate. *American Journal of Psychiatry, 138*, 644–646.

Golla, F. L., & Hodge, S. R. (1949). Hormone treatment of sexual offenders. *Lancet, 1*, 1006–1007.

Groth, A. N. (1979). *Men who rape: The psychology of the offender*, New York: Plenum.

Groth, A. N., Burgess, A. W., & Holmstrom, L. L. (1977). Rape: Power, anger and sexuality. *American Journal of Psychiatry, 134*, 1239–1243.

Heim, N., & Hursch, C. J. (1979). Castration for sexual offenders: Treatment or punishment? A review and critique of recent European literature. *Archives of Sexual Behavior, 8*, 281–304.

Heller, C. G., Laidlaw, W. M., Harvey, H. I. T., & Nelson, W. O. (1958). Effects of progestational compounds on the reproductive processes of the human male. *Annals of the New York Academy of Science, 71*, 649–655.

Hsueh, A. J., Peck, E. J., & Clark, J. H. (1976). Control of uterine receptor levels by progesterone. *Endocrinology, 98,* 438–444.

Kreuz, L. E., & Rose, R. M. (1972). Assessment of aggressive behaviour and plasma testosterone in a young criminal population. *Psychosomatic Medicine, 34,* 321–332.

Lan, N. C., & Katzenellenbogen, B. S. (1976). Temporal relationships between hormone receptor binding and biological responses in the uterus: Studies with short and long acting derivatives of estradiol. *Endocrinology, 98,* 220–227.

Langevin, R., Paitich, D., Hucker, S., Newman, S., Ramsay, G., Pope, S., Geller, G., & Anderson, C. (1979). The effect of assertiveness training, provera and sex of therapist in the treatment of genital exhibitionism. *Journal of Behavior Therapy & Experimental Psychiatry, 10,* 275–282.

Laschet, U., & Laschet, L. (1971). Psychopharmacotherapy of sex offenders with cyproterone acetate. *Pharmakopsychiatrie Neuropsychopharmakologic, 4,* 99–104.

Laschet, U., & Laschet, L. (1975). Antiandrogens in the treatment of sexual deviations of men. *Journal of Steroid Biochemistry, 6,* 821–826.

Le Maire, L. (1956). Danish experiences regarding the castration of sexual offenders. *Journal of Criminal Law, Criminology and Police Science, 47,* 295–310.

Liang, T., Tymoczko, J. L., Chan, K. M. B., Hung, H. C. & Liao, S. (1977). Androgen action: Receptors and rapid responses. In L. Martini & M. Motta (Eds.). *Androgens and antiandrogens* (pp. 77–89). New York: Raven Press.

Lipsett, M. B., (1977). Regulation of androgen secretion. In L. Martini & M. Motta (Eds)., *Androgens and antiandrogens* (pp. 11–19). New York: Raven Press.

Mainwaring, I. P. (1977). Modes of action of antiandrogens: A survey. In L. Martini & M. Motta (Eds.), *Androgens and antiandrogens* (pp. 151–161). New York: Raven Press.

Malamuth, N. M., Check, J. V. P., & Briere, J. (1986). Sexual arousal in response to aggression: Ideological, aggressive and sexual correlates. *Journal of Personal and Social Psychology, 50,* 330–340.

Meyer, W. J., Walker, P. J., Emory, L. E., & Smith, E. R. (1985). Physical, metabolic and hormonal effects on men of long-term therapy with medroxyprogesterone acetate. *Fertility and Sterility, 43,* 102–109.

Meyer-Bahlburg, H. F. L., Nat, R., Boon, D. A., Sharma, M., & Edwards, J. A. (1974). Aggressiveness and testosterone measures in man. *Psychosomatic Medicine, 36,* 269–274.

Money, J. (1968). Discussion of the hormonal inhibition of libido in male sex offenders. In R. Michael (Ed.), *Endocrinology and human behaviour* (p. 169). London: Oxford University Press.

Money, J. (1970). Use of androgen depleting hormone in the treatment of male sex offenders. *Journal of Sex Research, 6,* 165–172.

Money, J. (1972). The therapeutic use of androgen-depleting hormone. *International Psychiatry Clinics, 8,* 165–174.

Money, J., Wiedeking, C., Walker, P., Migeon, C., Meyer, W., & Borgaonkar, D. (1975). 47, XYY and 46, XY males with antisocial and/or sex-offending behaviour: Antiandrogen therapy plus counselling. *Psychoneuroendocrinology, 1,* 165–178.

Money, J. M., Wiedeking, C., Walker, P. A., & Gain, D. (1976). Combined antiandrogen and counselling program for treatment of 46, XY and 47, XYY sex offenders. In E. Sachar (Ed.), *Hormones, behaviour and psychopathology* (pp. 105–120). New York: Raven Press.

Monti, P. M., Brown, W. A., & Corriveau, D. D. (1977). Testosterone and components of aggressive and sexual behavior in man. *American Journal of Psychiatry, 134,* 692–694.

Mothes, C., Lehnert, J., Samimi, F., & Ufer, J. (1971). Schering symposium uber sexual deviationen und ihre medikamentose Behandlung. *Life Sciences Monograph, 2,* 65.

Murray, M. A. F., Bancroft, J. H. H., Anderson, D. C., Tennent, T. G., & Carr, P. J. (1975). Endocrine changes in male sexual deviants after treatment with antiandrogens, oestrogens or tranquilizers. *Journal of Endocrinology, 67,* 179–188.

Naftolin, F., Ryan, K. J., & Petro, Z. (1972). Aromatization of androstenediol in the anterior hypothalamus of adult male and female rats. *Endocrinology, 90,* 295–298.

Neumann, F. (1977). Pharmacology and potential use of cyproterone acetate. *Hormone and metabolic research, 9,* 1–13.

Olweus, D., Mattsson, A., Schalling, D., & Low, H. (1980). Testosterone, aggression, physical and personality dimensions in normal adolescent males. *Psychosomatic Medicine, 42,* 253–269.

Ortmann, J. (1980). The treatment of sexual offenders, castration and antihormone therapy. *International Journal of Law and Psychiatry, 3,* 443–451.

Ortmann, J. (1984a). *How castration influences on relapsing into sexual criminality among Danish males.* Unpublished manuscript.

Ortmann, J. (1984b). *How antihormone treatment with cyproterone acetate influences on relapsing into sexual criminality in male sexual offenders.* Unpublished manuscript.

Ott, F. & Hoffet, H. (1968). The Influence of Antiandrogens on Libido, Potency, and Testicular Function. *Schweizerische Medizinische Wochenschrift, 98,* 1812–1815.

Persky, H., Smith, K. D., & Basu, G. K. (1971). Relation of psychologic measures of aggression and hostility to testosterone production in man. *Psychosomatic Medicine, 40,* 265–277.

Rada, R. T. (1978). Classification of the rapist. In R. T. Rada (Ed.), *Clinical aspects of the rapist* (pp. 117–132). New York: Grune & Stratton.

Rada, R. T., Laws, D. R., & Kellner, R. (1976). Plasma testosterone levels in the rapist. *Psychosomatic Medicine, 38,* 257–268.

Scaramella, T. J., & Brown, W. A. (1978). Serum testosterone and aggressiveness in hockey players. *Psychosomatic Medicine, 40,* 262–265.

Southren, A. L., Gordon, G. G., Vittek, J., & Altman, K. (1977). Effect of progestagens on androgen metabolism. In L. Martini & M. Motta (Eds.), *Androgens and antiandrogens* (pp. 263–279). New York: Raven Press.

Sterkmans, P., & Geerts, F. (1966). Is benperidol (RF 504) the specific drug for the treatment of excessive and disinhibited sexual behaviour? *Acta Neurologica Psychiatrica (Belgique), 66,* 1030–1040.

Stürup, G. K. (1968). Treatment of sexual offenders in Herstedvester, Denmark: The rapists. *Acta Psychiatrica Scandinavica* (Suppl. 204), 5–61.

Stürup, G. K. (1972). Castration: The total treatment. In H. L. P. Resnik & M. E. Wolfgang (Eds.), *Sexual behaviors: Social, clinical and legal aspects* (pp. 361–382). Massachusetts: Little, Brown.

Symmers, W. S. C. (1968). Carcinoma of the breast in transsexual individuals after surgical and hormonal interference with primary and secondary sex characteristics. *British Medical Journal, 2,* 3–85.

Tennent, G., Bancroft, J., & Cass, J. (1974). The control of deviant sexual behavior by drugs: A double-blind controlled study of benperidol, chlorpromazine and placebo. *Archives of Sexual Behavior, 3,* 261–271.

Walker, P. A., & Meyer, W. J. (1981). Medroxyprogesterone acetate treatment for paraphiliac sex offenders. In J. R. Hays, T. K. Roberts, & K. S. Solway (Eds.), *Violence and the violent individual* (pp. 353–373). New York: S.P. Medical and Scientific Books.

Whittaker, L. H. (1959). Oestrogens and psychosexual disorders. *Medical Journal of Australia, 2,* 547–549.

Wiedeking, C., Money, J., & Walker, P. A. (1979). Follow up of 11 XYY males with impulsive and/or sex-offending behavior. *Psychological Medicine, 9,* 287–292.

Wilson, J. D. & Foster, D. W. (1983). Introduction. In J. D. Wilson & D. W. Foster (Eds.), *Textbook of endocrinology* (pp 1–7). New York: Saunders.

Wincze, W. P., Bansal, S., & Malamud, M. (1986). Effects of medroxyprogesterone acetate on subjective arousal, arousal to erotic stimulation and nocturnal penile tumescence in male sex offenders. *Archives of Sexual Behavior, 15,* 293–305.

18

The Enhancement of Social Skills
An Information-Processing Analysis

RICHARD M. MCFALL

Social-skills training is one of the more commonly prescribed treatments for rapists, pedophiles, and other sex offenders (Abel, Blanchard, & Becker, 1976, 1978; Barlow, Abel, Blanchard, Bristow, & Young, 1977; Becker, Abel, Blanchard, Murphy, & Coleman, 1978; Cohen, Seghorn, & Calmas, 1969; Crawford & Allen, 1979; Marshall & McKnight, 1975; Whitman & Quinsey, 1981). Nevertheless, recent reviews of the literature (Earls & Quinsey, 1985; Hollon & Trower, 1986; Stermac, Segal, & Gillis, Chapter 9, this volume) have concluded that social-skills training is not based on a solid foundation of coherent theory; that it does not consist of explicit and replicable techniques; that it is plagued by serious conceptual, methodological, and measurement problems; and that it is not yet supported by compelling evidence of treatment efficacy. It is not even clear that sex offenders are any less socially skilled than control subjects (Stermac & Quinsey, 1986). In short, the popular use of social-skills training with sex offenders seems to be based largely on the intuitive appeal of the idea and on the implicit faith of the proponents. At best, social-skills training must be considered an approach that has not yet fulfilled its promise.

Given the general lack of positive evidence, we have at least two options. On the one hand, we might conclude that sex offenders do not have special social-skills deficits and that social-skills training is ineffective both in the short run and in the long run. The problem with this option, however, is that it is logically impossible to affirm the null hypothesis simply on the basis of a lack of positive evidence. We never can rule out the possibility that future studies employing different concepts and methods might turn up positive evidence.

On the other hand, we might conclude that the research to date was deficient on conceptual and methodological grounds and, thus, that it simply did not provide an adequate test of the hypothesized roles of social-skills deficits

RICHARD M. MCFALL • Department of Psychology, Indiana University, Bloomington, Indiana 47405.

and social-skills training in the etiology and treatment of sexual deviance. This option is especially appealing if we can specify the inadequacies in the previous research and recommend improved conceptual and methodological alternatives for future research.

The conceptual and methodological weaknesses of past research on social skills and sexual deviance have been discussed thoroughly elsewhere in this book (Stermac *et al.*, Chapter 9, this volume); therefore, they need not be repeated in detail here. Instead, the present chapter outlines a new direction for future research on social-skills training with sex offenders, a direction aimed at overcoming many of the conceptual and methodological problems that have plagued previous research. The first section will introduce a conceptual model of social competence and social skills that I consider a promising new framework for research and treatment. The second section will explore the model's implications for a social-skills analysis of sexual deviance and will summarize the results of recent research based on the model. The final section will sketch some of the model's implications for the future treatment of sex offenders.

AN INFORMATION-PROCESSING MODEL OF SOCIAL SKILLS

Elsewhere (McFall, 1982; McFall & Dodge, 1982) I have proposed a social information-processing model of social skills and social competence. The model was intended both as a framework for the integration of available evidence and as a blueprint for a new research program. Although the model has theoretical implications for a wide range of psychopathological conditions, it was developed with the particular intent of illuminating the determinants of competent and incompetent heterosexual behavior.

This is a two-tiered model in which the constructs of social competence and social skills are hierarchically related, rather than being equivalent or interchangeable. *Competence* is the superordinate construct. It refers to the relativistic social-judgment process by which an individual's performance of a particular task, in a particular setting, at a particular time, is evaluated either by that individual or by significant others to be adequate, relative to the judge's implicit and explicit standards and values. Competence is not an attribute of the person, therefore, but is an attribute of the person's task performance—as perceived by some judge. Competence is not global, but is task specific; a person is judged to be competent at a particular task. Competence is not absolute; different judges may evaluate the same task performance differently because they apply different criteria or because their judgments are shaped by different heuristics and biases (Kahneman, Slovic, & Tversky, 1982).

The subordinate construct of *social skills* refers to the underlying component processes that enable an individual to perform a task in a manner that has been (or will be) judged to be competent. Thus, an analysis of social skills makes sense only within the framework of a given definition of social competence. If the criteria for competent task performance change, then the analysis of the component skills underlying the competence also must change accordingly.

These component processes are organized into a sequential, three-stage system by which the individual transforms incoming stimulus information—or situational task demands—into the observable behaviors that get evaluated as competent or incompetent. Each step in this sequence must be carried out skillfully if the final performance is to satisfy the criteria for competence. The three stages of social-information processing in this model are as follows:

Decoding Skills. These are the afferent processes involved in the accurate reception, perception, and interpretation of incoming sensory information. To illustrate, if a man never receives a woman's social cues, his social behavior toward the woman is more likely to be inappropriate and to be judged incompetent. Similarly, if the man receives the woman's cues, but misperceives or misinterprets them, his behavior will be tailored to the wrong situation and, as a result, is likely to be judged incompetent.

Decision Skills. These are the central processes by which the situation, as defined in the decoding stage, is transformed into the behavioral program to be carried out in the next stage. The specific steps in this stage are: generating response options, matching these to task demands, selecting the best option, searching for that option in the behavioral repertoire, and evaluating the subjective utility of that option's likely outcomes relative to the likely outcomes of other options. If the person encounters a problem at any step, the decision process is recycled until it generates a behavioral program that the person considers appropriate, available, and acceptable. Thus, a man who has decoded a woman's social cues accurately still may perform incompetently as a result of inept decision making. Perhaps he does not know what response is best for a given situation. Even if he knows what to do, perhaps he does not have the preferred response in his repertoire. And even if he knows what to do and how to do it, he still might decide against taking the preferred action if he considers it too risky or costly. Alternatively, a man might decide on an action that others consider incompetent (e.g., coercing a woman sexually), even though he correctly reads the situation (e.g., he knows she rejects his sexual advances), because he believes that this action will get him what he wants and because he considers the potential gains to be worth the risks. Transitory factors, such as alcohol ingestion, anger, social contagion, or sexual arousal, may exert important influences on this decision process, particularly on the appraisal of risk.

Enactment Skills. These are the efferent processes involved in carrying out the behavioral program selected in the preceding stage. The person must execute the program smoothly, monitor its impact on the environment, and make whatever mid-course adjustments are necessary to achieve the intended impact. Thus, even if a man has decoded a woman's social cues accurately and has selected an optimal course of action, he still may be judged incompetent if he either fails to execute the program well or fails to adjust his behavior to environmental feedback.

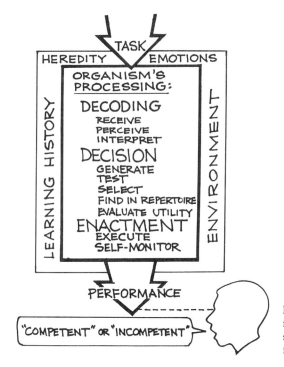

FIGURE 1. Schematic outline of a social information-processing model of social skills and social competence. (Adapted from McFall, 1982.)

Figure 1 graphically summarizes the proposed model. At the top we see the sensory input, or task demands. At the bottom is the behavioral output, or task performance, which is being evaluated for its competence. In the middle, in the black-bordered box between the input and output arrows, is the hypothesized sequence of information-processing stages, or input–output transformations. Surrounding the black box are important contextual variables—constitutional, environmental, emotional, physical, historical—that influence the information-processing sequence and its output.

Most of the time, this social information-processing system operates with incredible speed and efficiency, outside of awareness or conscious control. This is because we typically are performing routine and well-rehearsed tasks that require little attention or active problem solving. Whenever we are faced by novel or challenging tasks, however, the processing system slows down and comes under conscious control. This difference between background and foreground processing corresponds to the distinction some cognitive psychologists make between automatic and controlled processing (Shiffrin & Schneider, 1977).

Several assumptions and implications of this model require amplification. First, the model assumes that skillful processing at each stage is a necessary, but not sufficient, condition for the production of competent task performance. One implication of this assumption is that the model's predictions are asymmetrical. That is, negative information, or evidence of skills deficits, is more predictive than positive information. In a given task, if we know that a person manages one of the information-processing steps skillfully, we cannot predict from this fact alone that the person's task performance will be competent; the person still may be deficient in one or more of the remaining requisite skills. However, if we know that a person is deficient in one of the component skills, we can predict from this fact alone that the person's task performance is likely to be judged incompetent.

Second, the model's assumption that skills are task- and situation-specific has important implications for assessment and prediction. Rather than attempting to assess skills at a global level, with all-purpose measures, we should focus more narrowly on assessing an individual's profile of skills across a limited number of well-defined tasks. We should expect each category of skill to be fairly independent. Furthermore, we should expect variability within categories as a function of specific conditions. For example, a man's ability to decode social cues from women might not be predictive of his ability to decode similar cues from men. Rather, his cue-reading accuracy is likely to vary as a function of the source of cues, type of cues, cue valence, communication setting, relationship between communicators, antecedent events, signal and noise levels, the receiver's cue sensitivity, and the receiver's transient physical and emotional state. No doubt, research will uncover numerous other factors that affect subjects' decoding, decision, and enactment skills. Our long-term goal should be to illuminate these basic processes by identifying lawful if–then relationships that allow us to predict the competence of an individual's performance of a given task under specified conditions.

Third, the model's assumption that social skills and social competence are hierarchically related, rather than synonymous, has additional implications for assessment and prediction. On the basis of an isolated assessment of a given skill, we may predict that a person with a deficit will perform a given task incompetently; however, we would not necessarily be able to predict the exact form of the individual's incompetent behavior. For instance, a man who has trouble reading women's heterosexual cues accurately is likely to be incompetent in heterosexual interactions; however, that man's incompetence might take any number of forms—from aggressive to withdrawn behavior, from too much to too little talking, from acts of self-indulgence to self-denial, and so forth. The specific topography of the man's incompetent behavior will be a function of complex interactions among all the multiple factors depicted in Figure 1—interpersonal, intrapersonal, and contextual.

The complexity of this assessment and prediction problem can be illustrated by an analogy. In chemistry, a single element, say oxygen, assumes different forms depending on the other elements with which it is combined, the relative proportions of the combined elements, and the conditions, such as temperature or pressure, impinging on the elements. Thus, a compound consisting of one part oxygen and two parts hydrogen (water) assessed at 70 degrees Fahrenheit and at sea level will be a liquid. It will be a solid, however, at less than 32 degrees Fahrenheit and a gas at more than 212 degrees Fahrenheit. The picture is complicated further by the fact that the effects of temperature differ slightly at different altitudes. If the chemical composition is altered—say, if two parts oxygen are mixed with one part carbon—the physical properties manifested by the oxygen will change again. Thus, in chemistry, knowing only that a chemical compound contains oxygen does not allow us to predict the compound's physical properties. Similarly, in the proposed competence model, knowing only that a person has a deficit, say, in decoding skills, does not allow us to predict the topography of the person's incompetent behavior. To predict the topography, we first must identify lawful if–then relationships among the complex patterns of information processing, the relevant contextual factors, and the specific behavioral outputs.

Fourth, the hierarchical relationship between this model's two key constructs calls for the development of a new class of theory-based social-skills measures. These measures must be distinct and independent from the criterion measures of social competence. The model specifies what pattern of relationships should occur among the measures. In the past, when the relationship between skill and competence was obscure, social-skills research tended to be little more than a fishing expedition. Investigators tested subjects on a number of loosely related measures (e.g., social skills, competence, anxiety, assertion, inhibition, dating, shyness, etc.) and then sifted through the resulting correlation matrices to see what significant relationships, if any, turned up. In the absence of explicit theory, the pattern of positive and negative associations among measures was essentially unintelligible. Almost no outcome was capable of dampening the enthusiasm—or falsifying the notions—of the social-skills advocates. With the proposed model, however, social-skills research at last can advance beyond a simple search for significant effects. Now it can assess whether the observed relationships among the newly developed measures of social skills, on the one hand, and the criterion measures of social competence, on the other hand, are consistent or inconsistent with the assumptions and predictions of the underlying model.

Our new methods of assessing specific social skills should conform to the guidelines outlined by McClelland (1973): they should employ a criterion-sampling approach; should be designed to reflect changes in functioning, rather than static qualities; should focus on functions relevant to important life outcomes (e.g., communication); should emphasize instrumental behavior; should concentrate on behavioral samples that provide maximum generalizability to real-life actions; and should employ items for which the criterion behavior is explicit, public, and impossible to fake. These methodological ideals can be achieved best by sampling optimal performance under standardized conditions representative of lifelike situations.

Fifth, the model focuses on the processes that lead to observable task performance, as opposed to focusing on the classification of persons into static categories. We are more interested in specifying the processes and conditions that lead persons to engage in deviant behaviors, such as rape, than with tagging persons with absolute labels, such as "rapist." Thus, research based on this model looks for basic principles that might account for commonalities in behavior across populations. For example, the sexually coercive behaviors of college men and incarcerated rapists are viewed as falling on the same continuum and as being subsumed by a common explanatory framework. From this perspective, much might be learned by studying deviance in its less extreme forms, or in less extreme populations, where it still is possible to explore hypothesized processes through experimental manipulations under more naturalistic conditions.

Finally, the model's assumption that the information-processing stages are sequential has implications for our choice of optimal research strategies. Because the output at each stage serves as the input at the next, the most logical place to start testing the model is at the beginning, with decoding skills, where the input signal still is more or less equivalent for everyone. To study later skills in the sequence requires control over the outputs from all antecedent stages, which would be difficult to achieve initially, but should become more feasible as more is learned about the earlier stages.

EVALUATION OF THE SOCIAL INFORMATION-PROCESSING MODEL

For any model to be taken seriously, it must pass two important tests: it must accommodate the evidence accumulated in past research, and it must survive the direct assaults of new research aimed at its falsification. In this section, I will begin by considering how well the social information-processing model of social skills accommodates what is known already about sexual deviance. Then I will describe the results of recent research designed to test the model directly.

Previous Research Evidence

Although the social-skills research reviewed elsewhere in this book (Stermac et al., Chapter 9, this volume) has failed to uncover any distinctive social-skills deficits among sexually deviant subjects, other studies guided by other theoretical perspectives have identified at least two characteristics that seem to differentiate between sexually aggressive and nonaggressive men. First, sexually aggressive men have been found to display deviant patterns of sexual arousal. Aggressive and nonaggressive men do not differ in their arousal to depictions of consensual heterosexual intercourse, or in their arousal to rape scenes in which victims experience involuntary pleasure. However, convicted rapists, as well as college men with a self-reported propensity to rape, become more aroused than control subjects by rape scenes in which the victims experience abhorrence and pain (Abel, Barlow, Blanchard, & Guild, 1977; Barbaree, Marshall, & Lanthier, 1979; Malamuth, Heim, & Feshbach, 1980; Quinsey & Chaplin, 1984; Quinsey, Chaplin, & Varney, 1981). Among rapists, an index of deviant arousal (the ratio of penile tumescence to depictions of rape vs. to depictions of consensual intercourse) has been shown to be positively related to the number of rapes committed and to the degree of injury inflicted on victims (Abel, Blanchard, Becker, & Djenderedjian, 1978).

Second, sexually aggressive men tend to have distorted cognitive schemata (see Neisser, 1976, for discussion of schemata) concerning heterosexual relations

(Segal & Stermac, Chapter 10, this volume). Their schemata reflect confusion about the nature of female sexuality, disregard for women's rights and feelings, and insensitivity to the suffering of rape victims (Clark & Lewis, 1977; Gager & Schurr, 1976). These cognitive schemata, which seem to be promoted and reinforced by violent pornographic depictions of heterosexual interactions, predispose men toward sexual aggression by encouraging them to focus on ambiguous social cues from women; to misinterpret such cues as "come ons"; to believe that women will be receptive to coercive sexual advances; and to perceive victims as desiring and deriving gratification from sexual assaults (Abbey, 1982; Amir, 1971; Aronson, Olah, & Koss, 1978; Burt, 1980; Goodchilds & Zellman, 1984; Malamuth & Check, 1980a, 1980b, 1983; Malamuth, Reisin, & Spinner, 1979; Malamuth, Heim, & Feshbach, 1980; Rapaport & Burkhart, 1984; Tieger, 1981). College men with these cognitive schemata have displayed deviant patterns of sexual arousal similar to those of rapists, and on self-report measures they have shown a higher proclivity to rape (Malamuth, Haber, & Feshbach, 1980).

This evidence paints the following portrait of sexually aggressive men. They enter heterosexual relationship holding distorted cognitive schemata that predispose them to sexual misunderstandings and misguided actions. It is as though these men were "primed" by their schemata to read positive sexual connotations into women's neutral or negative messages; to believe that women secretly wish to be victims of sexual coercion; to misinterpret women's refusals of sexual advances merely as coquettish acceptances; to dismiss women's physical resistance as a primeval sexual ritual; to misperceive women's cries of pain as squeals of pleasure; and to redefine any attempted rebuffs as proof that women are "teases" who deserve whatever they get. Cognitive distortions such as these may account, in part, for the failure of sexually aggressive men to discriminate in their pattern of sexual arousal between consensual and coercive sexual interactions.

If this is an accurate portrait, then we are safe in saying that sexually aggressive men have serious problems processing social information from women. Our social information-processing model of social skills and sexual deviance seems to be consistent with these findings from previous research. Although the model does not suggest that all acts of sexual aggression are due to deficits in decoding skills, many of the characteristics associated with sexual aggression seem to be related in one way or another to men's cognitive distortions of women's signals concerning their feelings and interests.

Of course, some men who normally read women's messages quite accurately still might behave in a sexually aggressive manner toward women as the result of deficits in one or more of the remaining skills in the social information-processing model. Some men also might show infrequent and transient increases in sexual aggression when exposed to special conditions that distort cue-reading accuracy, cloud decision-making judgments, and impair the smooth execution of responses. Three examples of transient conditions likely to disrupt otherwise normal decoding, decision making, and enactment are: alcohol ingestion (George & Marlatt, 1986; Wydra, Marshall, Earls, & Barbaree, 1983), anger arousal (Wolchik *et al.*, 1980; Yates, Barbaree, & Marshall, 1984), and sexual arousal (Donnerstein, 1984).

Little previous research sheds direct light on the possible roles of decision skills and enactment skills in sexual deviance. Segal and Marshall (1986) defined accurate social perception as the discrepancy between subjects' predictions of their efficacy in a role-play task and judges' ratings of subjects' actual efficacy in the task; however, within our social-skills model, this discrepancy measure would fall more appropriately under the heading of decision skills, rather than decoding skills, because it focuses on subjects' appraisal of whether they have the appropriate responses in their repertoire.

On closer inspection, it seems that many of the social-skills measures employed in previous studies have focused on various aspects of what our model would call decision skills. For instance, self-report and role-play measures asking subjects to indicate what they consider to be the most effective response in predefined problem situations are tapping subjects' generation, evaluation, and selection of problem solutions—all of which are aspects of decision skills. The same is true of measures asking subjects to indicate what responses they would be most likely to emit in specific problem situations. One of the more commonly used measures, the Survey of Heterosexual Interactions (SHI; Twentyman, Boland, & McFall, 1981), asks male subjects to rate how likely they would be to initiate a social interaction with a woman in each of several predefined situations. From the perspective of the proposed model, measures such as the SHI assess subjects' appraisal of risk—that is, the "utility evaluation" component within the decision-making process. Finally, few previous studies have used role-play measures that require subjects to demonstrate their ability to carry out *prescribed* responses in *predefined* problem situations; nevertheless, if such measures existed, they would assess subjects' enactment skills, as defined in the proposed model.

Sorting the various measures from previous studies into their respective niches within the social information-processing model, in this way, helps us see why different measures of "social skills" have yielded such divergent and inconsistent results in the past (Alexander & Johnson, 1980; Bellack, 1983). In retrospect, we can see that we should not have expected the measures of different component skills to be highly correlated with one another; nor should we have expected them to be predictive of criterion measures that were only vaguely related to them in task content and context. Future research must take much greater care in the development and selection of social-skills measures and criterion measures, and in predicting which skills measures should be associated with which competence measures for which subjects under which conditions.

RESEARCH BASED ON THE INFORMATION-PROCESSING MODEL

Of course, the most stringent test of a model is not its ability to encompass existing evidence post hoc, but its ability to withstand direct experimental tests of its predictions. My colleagues and I have spent the past several years involved in a research program specifically designed to test the proposed information-processing model of social skills. For strategic reasons discussed earlier, our initial focus was on decoding skills; we began at the beginning of the processing sequence. In the absence of appropriate measures, our first task was to develop new methods of assessing heterosexual decoding skills (McDonel, McFall, Schlundt, & Levenson, 1986).

We approached this task as a signal-detection problem (Green & Swets, 1974). One advantage of the signal-detection methodology is that it prevents subjects from "faking good" by assessing optimal performance. First we developed a series of 74 videotaped, dyadic, heterosexual interactions, each lasting about 30 seconds. Forty of these vignettes depicted couples in "first-date" interactions; 34 depicted couples in more established, or "intimate," relationships. The affective cues emitted by the man and woman in each couple were varied systematically. One person (the nontarget) always emitted positive cues toward the partner; the other person (the target) emitted cues from one of five affect categories: romantic, positive, neutral, negative, or bad mood. Subjects' task was to view these videotaped stimuli on a color monitor and guess, by marking a multiple-choice form, which type of cue was being emitted by each person in each vignette. Because the cue properties were predefined (both by design and by normative pretesting) subjects' guesses could be scored for accuracy. Typically, two points were awarded for each "correct" guess, one point for each "second best" guess, and no points for all other guesses. By analyzing the conditional and unconditional probabilities of the guesses, subjects' cue-reading sensitivity, or decoding skills, could be assessed overall, as well as separately for each of the five affective cues, for cues from men versus women, for cues from targets versus nontargets, for cues in first-date interactions versus intimate interactions, and for any of the various combinations of these factors.

We called our new decoding-skills measure the Test of Reading Affective Cues, or TRAC. Following a series of preliminary studies (Johnson, 1983; McDonel et al., 1986) aimed at determining the TRAC's psychometric properties and its associations with independent measures of heterosexual competence in college students, we employed the measure in a study of the relationship between decoding-skills deficits and heterosexual aggression (Lipton, McDonel, & McFall, 1987). Specifically, we used the new decoding measure to test the validity of our social information-processing model's predictions of specific patterns of differential deficits in decoding skills among sexually aggressive men. The TRAC was administered to three groups of incarcerated offenders: convicted rapists, violent non-sex-offenders, and nonviolent non-sex-offenders. Consistent with the model's predictions, rapists were significantly less accurate than subjects in either control group at reading cues from female targets in the first-date vignettes; they showed no such deficit, relative to control subjects, when reading cues from men. Rapists were better at reading women's cues in intimate interactions than in first-date interactions, where cues are more ambiguous. They showed the highest error rate when reading women's negative cues in first-date interactions. Thus, the rapists displayed a selective and differential deficit in heterosexual cue reading. This finding not only represents one of the first demonstrations of a unique skills deficit among sex offenders, but it also attests to the promise of the social information-processing model.

Incarcerated rapists probably are not the best, or most representative, subjects to use in studies aimed at illuminating the determinants of sexual aggression. Most of the men who commit rape never get reported, arrested, convicted, or sent to prison (Koss, Gidycz, & Wisniewski, 1987). On the assumption that the tendency toward sexual aggression is continuously distributed among men, McDonel (1986) used "normal" college men as subjects in a pair of studies examining the relationships among decoding skills, situational factors affecting cue-reading accuracy, heterosexual attitudes and experiences, and sexual aggression. McDonel hypothesized that heterosexual cue-reading accuracy would be associated with sexual aggression; that sexual arousal, resulting from exposure to nonviolent erotic stimuli, would decrease heterosexual cue-reading accuracy; and that any detrimental effects of exposure to erotic stimuli would be greatest in men predisposed toward sexual aggression. In effect, McDonel expected to establish a link between sexual aggression and decoding skills, to identify conditions that increase the probability that normal men will make cue-reading errors of the type found among rapists, and to identify which men are most likely to be impaired by such conditions.

In the first of two sessions, male volunteers from introductory psychology courses were administered the first-date vignettes of the TRAC (TRAC-D) under one of three randomly assigned experimental conditions. Interpolated at four points in the TRAC-D were film clips, each about 100 seconds long, which subjects were asked to view and rate. Subjects in a neutral-control condition saw excerpts from a television documentary about graffiti writers in New York. Subjects in an arousal-control condition saw clips from an industrial woodshop-safety film portraying accidents and severe injuries. Subjects in a sexual-arousal condition viewed nonviolent, erotic selections from two commercial X-rated films. McDonel conducted this study twice, with 83 and 96 Caucasian subjects, respectively; the only major difference between the two studies was the specific points in the TRAC-D at which the experimental films were interpolated. Ten to 14 days later, all subjects returned for a second session in which they anonymously and privately completed several self-report measures, including a measure of dating satisfaction and acceptance of rape myths; the Malamuth measure of rape proclivity (Malamuth *et al.*, 1980); and a newly developed measure, "When does a woman mean 'No'?" (McDonel, 1986), which assesses men's judgments of the extent to which, under various circumstances, a man might be justified in continuing to make sexual advances toward a woman after she has told him to stop.

The results of the two studies were virtually identical. Although overall group differences in cue-reading accuracy for female targets' cues fell short of statistical significance, post hoc comparisons indicated that subjects exposed to the erotic films earned the lowest mean accuracy score, and that this differed significantly ($p < .05$) from the highest mean accuracy score, which was earned by subjects exposed to the woodshop-accident film. Questionnaire data were analyzed separately to explore the associations between cue-reading accuracy and questionnaire responses; only the unconfounded data from subjects in the neutral-control group were used in these analyses. Cue-reading accuracy was positively correlated with dating satisfaction ($r = .46$ and $.52$ in studies 1 and 2, respectively). Accurate cue reading also was positively correlated with sensitivity to the plight of the rape victim, as depicted in the Malamuth measure; that is, better cue readers were less likely to identify with the man's decision to take what he wanted by force ($r = .40$ and $.41$), and were more likely to indicate that the victim should have reported the incident to the police ($r = .42$ and $.44$). Cue-reading scores also were positively associated (e.g., up to $r = .58$) with the likelihood of stating that men are not justified in continuing to make sexual advances when a woman says "No."

Interestingly, cue reading was not related to scores on Malamuth's self-report measure of propensity to commit rape, nor was it related to scores on the measure of rape myths. Both of these measures are quite transparent, however, which makes them susceptible to "faking good." Therefore, such negative findings are difficult to interpret.

In general, these two studies provided evidence consistent with the proposed information-processing model. There was suggestive evidence that arousal in response to stressful stimuli may increase vigilance and cue-reading accuracy, whereas arousal in response to erotic sexual stimuli may have a detrimental effect on cue-reading accuracy, perhaps by priming subjects to make unwarranted and erroneous sexual interpretations of women's cues. More importantly, the studies revealed that among "normal" male subjects there may be a relationship between the tendency to read women's cues inaccurately and the tendency to condone other men's acts of heterosexual aggression.

Subsequently, McDonel (1986) has developed a new decoding measure that focuses more closely on men's interpretation of women's cues concerning receptivity to sexual advances (the TRAC-S). Using this new measure in a study with prisoners, McDonel found that men exposed to erotic stimuli earned lower cue-reading accuracy scores; this was true of rapists and nonrapists alike. Although exposure to erotic material had not had a clear-cut disruptive effect on cue-reading scores in the previous studies with male college students, such inconsistencies in results are difficult to interpret because several factors (including the specific measure of decoding skills) have been allowed to vary across the different studies. Future research will need to tease apart the implications of these patterns of results.

Of course, deficits in decoding skills may not account for all, or even most, instances of sexual aggression. Thus, although most of the research based on the information-processing model to date has focused on decoding skills, several exploratory studies have investigated the roles of decision and enactment skills in heterosexual competence. For example, Goddard (1987) has assessed the relationship between decision skills and heterosexual competence among college women. Two groups of college women (above and below average in heterosexual competence according to sociometric nominations from female peers) were scheduled for individual assessment sessions, where they were administered the Inventory of Decisions, Evaluations, and Actions (IDEA), a role-play measure of women's heterosexual problem-solving competence developed specifically for this research. Following the IDEA, subjects received a social activities questionnaire and a series of paper-and-pencil measures designed to isolate and assess the separate subcomponents of the hypothesized decision-making process. To control for the effects of individual differences in decoding skills, these subcomponent measures always provided subjects with standard descriptions and interpretations of the problem situations; in effect, the experimenter decoded the situations the same way for all subjects.

The *Response Search* component was assessed by asking subjects to generate as many response options as possible for each of 12 heterosexual problem situations. Both the quality and quantity of subjects' responses were scored. The *Response Test* component was assessed by asking subjects to choose which was their "best" solution for each problem situation. The *Response Selection* component was assessed by presenting 12 new problem situations and asking subjects to rank order, from best to worst, four predefined solutions for each situation. The *Repertoire Search* component was assessed by asking subjects to rate their own ability to execute each of two prescribed solutions to each of 12 problem situations. Finally, the *Utility Evaluation* component was assessed by presenting subjects with predefined solutions to eight problem situations and asking them to estimate (1) the likelihood that they would actually carry out each response and (2) the probability that the problem would be solved if they were to carry out each response.

Subjects identified as heterosexually competent by their peers, in contrast to those identified as heterosexually incompetent, earned significantly higher competence scores on the role-play measure of heterosexual problem solving (the IDEA). On the Response Search measure, the high- and low-competence groups generated an equivalent quantity and quality of solutions overall; however, the solutions identified as "best" by the high-competence group were of significantly higher quality than those identified as "best" by the low-competence group. Between-group differences approached significance in the predicted direction on the Response Test and Response Selection measures. No differences were found on the Repertoire Search and Utility Evaluation measures. Interestingly, compared to low-competence subjects, high-competence subjects were rated as significantly more physically attractive, tended to have more dates per month, were more likely to be involved in a steady relationship, and were more likely to have sought membership in a campus sorority. Currently, Wellman (1988) is conducting an altered replication of Goddard's (1987) research, with a special emphasis on improving the methods of assessing the Utility Evaluation subcomponent. Once an appropriate methodology has been developed, it can be used to explore the links between decision-making skills and sexual aggression in men.

Meanwhile, Shapiro (1982) and Beak (1986) have been developing and validating a new role-play measure of enactment skills in heterosexual interactions: the Behavioral Enactment Skills Test (BEST). To study enactment skills in isolation, the influences of antecedent stages in the information-processing sequence must be controlled. Thus, in each of the 25 test situations on the BEST, the situation is carefully described, its meaning is defined, and subjects are told how to respond. In effect, the decoding and decision-making steps are performed for the subjects by the experimenter; thus, subjects' performances can be attributed, through subtractive logic, to their enactment skills.

To provide a plausible rationale for these control measures, subjects are told that they will be expected to play a part in a videotaped drama. Subjects are assured that their partner in the drama is familiar with the script, will arrange the props and staging, and will help guide them through the filming. Prior to each scene, a narrator in the control room defines both the scene and the role the subjects are expected to enact. The subjects are to do their best to execute their prescribed part in each scene. Each subject interacts with a trained confederate of the opposite sex. The subject's execution of the prescribed role in each of 25 situations is recorded on videotape for subsequent rating of enactment skills by "blind" judges.

Prior to the administration of the BEST, subjects are asked to predict how effectively they could execute the prescribed behaviors in the BEST situations. This measure is called the Predicted Rating of Effectiveness (PRE). Following the administration of the BEST, subjects are allowed to watch their own videotape and are asked to rate the effectiveness of each performance. This measure is called the Personal Opinion of Skills Test (POST).

Finally, unobtrusively videotaped samples of subjects' naturalistic interactions with their confederate partner during a 2-minute period immediately prior to the BEST (Interaction 1) and during another 2-minute period immediately following the BEST (Interaction 2) provide criterion measures of subjects' heterosexual competence. The confederate's behavior is constrained to make it as standardized as possible for all subjects. At the end of the experimental session, subjects are informed of the unobtrusive videotaping of their interactions and are asked to sign a release allowing their videotapes to be analyzed as part of the study. Later, a separate set of judges independently rates subjects' heterosexual competence in these natural interactions.

In two separate studies, enactment skills, as assessed by the BEST, have been found to be significantly correlated ($r = .50$ to $.53$) with heterosexual competence, as assessed by independent ratings of competence in naturalistic Interaction 1. The correlations for Interaction 2 have been a bit lower ($r = .30$ to $.50$), perhaps because by the end of the experimental session the subjects have established a relationship with the confederate and thus find Interaction 2 to be less stressful. Interestingly, subjects have not been very accurate in predicting (PRE) or judging (POST) their own effectiveness in the BEST situations. In both studies, PRE self-ratings correlated poorly with BEST scores ($r = -.04$ and $-.10$); POST self-ratings showed less consistent correlations ($r = .06$ and $.48$, respectively). It is worth noting that male and female subjects were included in the first study, and both groups yielded a similar overall pattern of results. In sum, the research thus far supports the predicted relationship between deficits in enactment skills and heterosexual incompetence. Future research must explore the role that enactment skills might play, separately and in interaction with other skills, in the incidence of sexual aggression.

Perhaps the biggest obstacle to research on social skills and social competence has been the lack of a truly satisfactory method of measuring heterosexual competence. On the one hand, subjects sometimes are asked to interact with an opposite-sex confederate whose behavior is entirely predetermined by a script. In such cases, subjects cannot influence the flow of the confederate's behavior to the extent that they might in more natural, unconstrained interactions. Thus, what this method gains in stimulus control, it loses in ecological validity. On the other hand, subjects sometimes are asked to interact with an unprogrammed confederate who behaves in a spontaneous, reflexive manner. In these cases, subjects can control the flow of the interaction, as in natural transactions, but as a result, no two subjects ever are exposed to the same test situation. Because the confederate's behavior is controlled by unknowable and unreplicable factors, the essence of the measure is lost when the confederate leaves at the end of the experimental session. Thus, what this second method gains in ecological validity, it loses in experimental control.

In an effort to solve this criterion measurement problem, my colleagues and I are in the process of developing a computer-based simulation methodology for assessing naturalistic heterosexual transactions in a way that maintains stimulus control while promoting ecological validity (Beak, 1988). Initially, each male subject will interact with a computer-simulated woman, typing messages on a terminal keyboard and receiving messages on a monitor. In later versions, we plan to exploit the technology of computer-controlled compact discs and laser video discs to simulate oral and visual transactions. In the keyboard version, the subject will be led to believe that his female partner is seated in an adjacent experimental room. The task instructions, displayed on the screen, simply will ask the man and woman to get to know one another by interacting via the computer terminals. The simulated woman starts each interaction session; in this way, every male subject receives the same opening message. After reading this, the subject types his reply to the woman. The experimenter, seated in the control room, reads the subject's response on a computer screen, codes the message using a content coding system we are developing, and enters this code into the computer. The computer is programmed to respond to each code by retrieving from memory an appropriate, predetermined, contingent message from the simulated woman. This message is sent to the subject's screen. Thus, as the interaction proceeds, the subject's responses drive the transaction (within the constraints of the particular simulation program), much as a video arcade customer's responses control the flow of action in computerized video games. At the same time, all subjects must interact with the same standardized, branching program of response contingencies.

One potential advantage of this approach to assessing heterosexual competence is that, because the sequential structure of the interaction is retained, it will permit a detailed analysis of subjects' branching performance at specific stimulus nodes in real time. Also, by systematically varying across trials the characteristics of the woman's programmed contingent responses, the same subject's performance can be assessed repeatedly under different conditions. We expect that heterosexually competent and incompetent men will display different response profiles in these simulated transactions. We also expect that profile differences will be indicative of underlying skills deficits, as predicted by the social information-processing model.

IMPLICATIONS FOR THE ENHANCEMENT OF SOCIAL SKILLS

I began this chapter by noting that there is little or no empirical support for the widespread belief that social-skills training is an effective treatment for sex offenders. I suggested that this lack of support may be due to conceptual and methodological inadequacies in previous work, rather than to insolvable problems or endemic flaws in the basic idea. I presented an alternative conceptual model of social competence and social skills, one aimed at overcoming such inadequacies, and summarized the results of recent research based on this model. In this brief final section, I will return to the treatment question: What implications, if any, does the proposed information-processing model have for the effective treatment of sex offenders or for the prevention of sexual aggression?

The proposed model provides a blueprint for the construction of a series of social-skills assessment tools, each focused narrowly on a different part of the complex process by which humans transform incoming sensory information into task-specific behavioral output. The theoretical assumptions and corollaries underlying the social-skills approach cannot be tested adequately unless and until the necessary assessment tools have been developed and validated. We can imagine, for purposes of illustration, what a battery of such tools might look like and what we might be able to do with these tools.

To assess the treatment needs of a particular sex offender, we might begin by administering a measure of heterosexual decoding skills, such as the TRAC. We might wish to measure decoding skills under different conditions that might differentially affect performance (conditions such as heightened sexual arousal, intoxication, or anger) to determine the overall level of resulting impairment, the specific conditions that promote impairment, and the specific areas of greatest deficit.

Next, we might administer several measures in the general domain of decision skills—a separate measure for each subcomponent. These would focus specifically on decision making in critical heterosexual situations. For example: What solutions does the individual generate in response to specific heterosexual problem situations? Are these solutions available in the individual's behavioral repertoire? Is the individual willing to assume the risks associated with choosing these solutions?

Then we might administer measures of enactment skills (measures similar to the BEST) to assess how effectively the individual executes and monitors his heterosexual behaviors. We might ask, for example: How smoothly and effectively can the individual carry out the behavioral programs that represent solutions to problematic heterosexual situations? Does the individual make the necessary subtle adjustments in his execution of these behavioral programs in response to interpersonal feedback?

Finally, we might administer a criterion measure of the individual's competence in heterosexual interactions; perhaps we would use a computer-simulation measure for this. We might address such questions as: What is the profile of the individual's transactional performance across time, given different types of heterosexual partners? At what points in these heterosexual transactions does the individual seem to have the greatest difficulty responding competently?

The results of these multiple measures might be plotted into a profile of each subject's heterosexual skills and competence. The profile would display graphically the subject's strengths and weaknesses across all of the different component skills within the information-processing model. Based on this profile, an individualized skills-training program would be designed to intervene precisely in those specific skill areas in which the person needs the greatest enhancement. For example, one subject might require training in heterosexual cue reading, another in the evaluation of risks and consequences, a third in the execution of selected responses, and a fourth in all of these areas.

Unfortunately, no research to date has evaluated the therapeutic efficacy of an individualized assessment and treatment approach based on the proposed information-processing model of social competence and social skills. Whether such social-skills training can be an effective treatment for sex offenders remains an open question. Certainly, there are good reasons to be skeptical about the utility of treatments based on overly simplistic, poorly conceived, and inadequately tested models of social skills. There also are good reasons to be encouraged about the prospects for success that might come from a more rigorous and systematic search for methods of assessing and enhancing social skills. Although the proposed model may provide a fruitful framework for such work, it simply is too early, at this point, to judge the model's merits. Thus, this chapter must end with the all-too-familiar call for additional research. Perhaps the concepts, methods, and results presented here will serve as a blueprint for a more coherent and coordinated investigation of the roles of social-skills deficits and social-skills training in the etiology and treatment of sexual deviance.

REFERENCES

Abbey, A. (1982). Sex differences in attributions for friendly behavior: Do males misperceive females' friendliness? *Journal of Personality and Social Psychology, 42,* 830–838.

Abel, G. G., Blanchard, E. B., & Becker, J. V. (1976). Psychological treatment of rapists. In M. J. Walker & S. L. Brodsky (Eds.), *Sexual assault: The victim and the rapist* (pp. 99–115). Lexington, MA: Lexington Books.

Abel, G. G., Barlow, D. H., Blanchard, E. B., & Child, D. (1977). The components of rapists' sexual arousal. *Archives of General Psychiatry, 34,* 895–903.

Abel, G. G., Blanchard, E. B., & Becker, J. V. (1978). An integrated treatment program for rapists. In R. T. Rada (Ed.), *Clinical aspects of the rapist* (pp. 161–214). New York: Grune & Stratton.

Abel, G. G., Blanchard, E. B., Becker, J. V., & Djenderedjian, A. (1978). Differentiating sexual aggressiveness with penile measures. *Criminal Justice and Behavior, 5,* 315–332.

Alexander, B. B., & Johnson, S. B. (1980). Reliability of heterosocial skills measurement with sex offenders. *Journal of Behavioral Assessment, 2,* 225–237.

Amir, M. (1971). *Patterns in forcible rape.* Chicago: University of Chicago Press.

Aronson, D., Olah, R. J., & Koss, M. P. (1978, August). *A study of sexual aggression among university males*. Paper presented at the 86th Annual Convention of the American Psychological Association, Montreal, Canada.

Barbaree, H. E., Marshall, W. L., & Lanthier, R. D. (1979). Deviant sexual arousal in rapists. *Behaviour Research and Therapy, 17*, 215–222.

Barlow, D. H., Abel, G. G., Blanchard, E. B., Bristow, A. R., & Young, L. D. (1977). A heterosocial skills behavior checklist for males. *Behavior Therapy, 8*, 229–239.

Beak, S. W. (1986). *The relation between enactment skill and social competence in heterosocial interactions*. Unpublished manuscript, first-year research report, Indiana University, Bloomington, IN.

Beak, S. W. (1988). *Modeling initial heterosocial interactions of college students*. Unpublished manuscript, second-year research paper, Indiana University, Bloomington, IN.

Becker, J. V., Abel, G. G., Blanchard, E. B., Murphy, W. D., & Coleman, E. (1978). Evaluating social skills of sexual aggressives. *Criminal Justice and Behavior, 5*, 357–368.

Bellack, A. S. (1983). Recurrent problems in the behavioral assessment of social skill. *Behaviour Research and Therapy, 21*, 29–41.

Burt, M. R. (1980). Cultural myths and support for rape. *Journal of Personality and Social Psychology, 38*, 217–230.

Clark, L. M. G., & Lewis, D. J. (1977). *Rape: The price of coercive sexuality*. Toronto, Canada: Women's Press.

Cohen, M., Seghorn, T., & Calmas, W. (1969). Sociometric study of the sex offender. *Journal of Abnormal Psychology, 74*, 249–255.

Crawford, D. A., & Allen, J. V. (1979). A social skills training programme with sex offenders. In M. Cook & G. Wilson (Eds.), *Love and attraction* (pp. 527–536). New York: Pergamon Press.

Donnerstein, E. (1984). Pornography: Its effect on violence against women. In N. M. Malamuth & E. Donnerstein (Eds.), *Pornography and sexual aggression* (pp. 233–243). Orlando, FL: Academic Press.

Earls, C. M., & Quinsey, V. L. (1985). What is to be done? Future research on the assessment and behavioral treatment of sex offenders. *Behavioral Sciences & the Law, 3*, 377–390.

Gager, N., & Schurr, C. (1976). *Sexual assault: Confronting rape in America*. New York: Grosset and Dunlop.

George, W. H., & Marlatt, G. A. (1986). The effects of alcohol and anger on interest in violence, erotica, and deviance. *Journal of Abnormal Psychology, 95*, 150–158.

Goddard, P. (1987). *Development, validation, and extension of an inventory for assessing heterosocial decision skills in college women*. Unpublished doctoral dissertation, Indiana University, Bloomington, IN.

Goodchilds, J. D., & Zellman, G. L. (1984). Sexual signaling and sexual aggression in adolescent relationships. In M. M. Malamuth & E. Donnerstein (Eds.), *Pornography and sexual aggression* (pp. 233–243). Orlando, FL: Academic Press.

Green, D. M., & Swets, J. A. (1974). *Signal detection theory and psychophysics* (rev. ed.). Huntington, NY: R. F. Krieger.

Hollon, C. R., & Trower, P. (1986). *Handbook of social skills training* (2 vols.). Oxford: Pergamon Press.

Johnson, T. J. (1983). *Differences in the timing of decisions in the decoding of heterosexual social cues*. Unpublished undergraduate psychology honors thesis, Indiana University, Bloomington, IN.

Kahneman, D., Slovic, P., & Tversky, A. (1982). *Judgment under uncertainty: Heuristics and biases*. Cambridge: Cambridge University Press.

Koss, M. P., Gidycz, C. A., & Wisniewski, N. (1987). The scope of rape: Incidence and prevalence of sexual aggression and victimization in a national sample of higher education students. *Journal of Consulting and Clinical Psychology, 55*, 162–170.

Lipton, D. N., McDonel, E. C., & McFall, R. M. (1987). Heterosocial perception in rapists. *Journal of Consulting and Clinical Psychology, 55*, 17–21.

Malamuth, N. M., & Check, J. V. P. (1980a). Penile tumescence and perceptual responses to rape as a function of victim's perceived reactions. *Journal of Applied Social Psychology, 10*, 528–547.

Malamuth, N. M., & Check, J. V. P. (1980b). Sexual arousal to rape and consenting depictions: The importance of the woman's arousal. *Journal of Abnormal Psychology, 89*, 763–766.

Malamuth, N. M., & Check, J. V. P. (1983). Sexual arousal to rape depictions: Individual differences. *Journal of Abnormal Psychology, 92,* 55–67.

Malamuth, N. M., Reisin, I., & Spinner, B. (1979, August). *Exposure to pornography and reactions to rape.* Paper presented at the 87th Annual Convention of the American Psychological Association, New York City.

Malamuth, N. M., Haber, S., & Feshbach, S. (1980). Testing hypotheses regarding rape: Exposure to sexual violence, sex differences, and the "normality" of rape. *Journal of Research in Personality, 14,* 121–137.

Malamuth, N. M., Heim, M., & Feshbach, S. (1980). Sexual responsiveness of college students to rape depictions: Inhibitory and disinhibitory effects. *Journal of Personality and Social Psychology, 38,* 399–408.

Marshall, W. L., & McKnight, R. D. (1975). An integrated treatment program for sexual offenders. *Canadian Psychiatric Association Journal, 20,* 133–138.

McClelland, D. C. (1973). Testing for competence rather than for "intelligence." *American Psychologist, 28,* 1–14.

McDonel, E. C. (1986). *Sexual aggression and heterosocial perception: The relationship between decoding accuracy and rape correlates.* Unpublished doctoral dissertation, Indiana University, Bloomington, IN.

McDonel, E. C., McFall, R. M., Schlundt, D. G., & Levenson, R. W. (1986). *Heterosocial perception: Development and validation of a performance measure.* Unpublished manuscript, Indiana University, Bloomington, IN.

McFall, R. M. (1982). A review and reformulation of the concept of social skills. *Behavioral Assessment, 4,* 1–33.

McFall, R. M., & Dodge, K. A. (1982). Self-management and interpersonal skills learning. In P. Karoly & F. Kanfer (Eds.), *Self-management and behavior change: From theory to practice* (pp. 353–392). New York: Pergamon Press.

Neisser, U. (1976). *Cognition and reality.* San Francisco: W. H. Freeman.

Quinsey, V. L., & Chaplin, T. C. (1984). Stimulus control of rapists' and non-sex offenders' sexual arousal. *Behavioral Assessment, 6,* 169–176.

Quinsey, V. L., Chaplin, T. C., & Varney, G. (1981). A comparison of rapists' and non-sex offenders' sexual preferences for mutually consenting sex, rape and physical abuse of women. *Behavioral Assessment, 3,* 127–135.

Rapaport, K., & Burkhart, B. R. (1984). Personality and attitudinal characteristics of sexually coercive college males. *Journal of Abnormal Psychology, 93,* 216–221.

Segal, Z. V., & Marshall, W. L. (1986). Discrepancies between self-efficacy predictions and actual performance in a population of rapists and child molesters. *Cognitive Therapy and Research, 10,* 363–376.

Shapiro, C. F. (1982). *Enactment of response in social interaction.* Unpublished manuscript, first-year research paper, Indiana University, Bloomington, IN.

Shiffrin, R. M., & Schneider, W. (1977). Controlled and automatic human information processing: II. Perceptual learning, automatic attending, and a general theory. *Psychological Review, 84,* 127–190.

Stermac, L. E., & Quinsey, V. L. (1986). Social competence among rapists. *Behavioral Assessment, 8,* 171–185.

Tieger, T. (1981). Self-rated likelihood of raping and the social perception of rape. *Journal of Research in Personality, 15,* 147–158.

Twentyman, C. T., Boland, T., & McFall, R. M. (1981). Heterosocial avoidance in college males: Four studies. *Behavior Modification, 5,* 523–552.

Wellman, C. L. (1988). *Utility evaluation in heterosocial decision-making.* Unpublished manuscript, first-year research report, Indiana University, Bloomington, IN.

Whitman, W. P., & Quinsey, V. L. (1981). Heterosocial skill training for institutionalized rapists and child molesters. *Canadian Journal of Behavioral Science, 13,* 105–114.

Wolchik, S. A., Beggs, V. E., Wincze, J. P., Sakheim, D. K., Barlow, D. H., & Mavissakalian, M. (1980). The effects of emotional arousal on subsequent sexual arousal in men. *Journal of Abnormal Psychology, 89,* 595–598.

Wydra, A., Marshall, W. L., Earls, C. M., & Barbaree, H. E. (1983). Identification of cues and control of sexual arousal by rapists. *Behaviour Research and Therapy, 21,* 469–476.
Yates, E., Barbaree, H. E., & Marshall, W. L. (1984). Anger and deviant sexual arousal. *Behavior Therapy, 15,* 287–294.

19

Assessment and Modification of Cognitive Distortions in Sex Offenders

William D. Murphy

Sexual aggression against children and adults is being recognized both by professionals and by the public as a significant problem for society (Badgley, 1984; Koss, Gidycz, & Wisniewski, 1987; Russell, 1982). In an attempt to address the problem, there have been attempts to more fully understand the individuals who perpetuate such abuse and to determine relevant target areas for treatment. This literature has produced numerous descriptive studies, personality assessment studies, and classification systems which have been well-reviewed previously (Knight, Rosenberg, & Schneider, 1985; Levin & Stava, 1987; Murphy & Stalgaitis, 1987; Prentky, Cohen, & Seghorn, 1985; Quinsey, 1984, 1986). All of these approaches provide some understanding of sex offenders, although they do not always clearly translate into specific treatment programs.

A number of investigators and clinicians, operating from a behavioral or social learning approach, have more directly targeted areas or continuums on which sex offenders may need treatment (Abel, Blanchard, & Becker, 1978; Conte, 1985; Murphy, Coleman, & Haynes, 1983; Murphy & Stalgaitis, 1987). These various models have proposed such factors as denial of sex abuse, nondeviant sexual arousal, deviant sexual arousal, general sexual functioning, social skills, and cognitive factors supportive of sexual abuse as being areas in need of treatment. Some of these areas, such as the area of deviant sexual arousal, have received significant research attention (see Murphy & Barbaree, 1987), while other areas have received less attention. The focus of this chapter is on the role of offender cognitions in sexual offenders. Such factors have been proposed by a number of investigators (Conte, 1985; Murphy & Stalgaitis, 1987) as an impor-

WILLIAM D. MURPHY • Department of Psychiatry, University of Tennessee, Memphis, Tennessee 38105.

tant treatment area but one which has received little systematic study in offender populations.

In this chapter, I will briefly outline approaches taken to describe the role of cognitive factors in sexual abuse and approaches for assessing cognitions (for more details, see Segal and Stermac, Chapter 10, this volume). Finally, treatment procedures will be reviewed that have been proposed to impact on cognitive factors. In general, much of the treatment literature is based on clinical observations, and little empirical data are currently available.

MODELS OF COGNITIVE FACTORS

As pointed out in the earlier chapter by Segal and Stermac, there are a variety of terminologies and concepts used to describe the role of cognitions in sexual abuse. Drawn from the cognitive behavioral literature is the concept of cognitive distortions (Abel *et al.*, 1984; Murphy & Stalgaitis, 1987; Stermac & Segal, 1987). These distortions refer to self-statements made by offenders that allow them to deny, minimize, justify, and rationalize their behavior. In this model, the cognitive factors are not seen as direct causes of deviant sexual behavior, but as steps offenders go through to justify their behaviors which serves to maintain their behavior (Abel *et al.*, 1984; Rouleau, Abel, Mittelman, Becker, & Cunningham-Rathner, 1986; Wolf, 1984).

The second approach to cognitive factors is derived from a more feminist perspective toward rape which describes attitudes supportive of rape, such as rape myth acceptance, sex-role stereotyping, adversarial sexual beliefs, and acceptance of interpersonal violence against women (Burt, 1980; Koss & Dinero, 1987; Malamuth, 1986; Murphy, Coleman, & Haynes, 1986; Rapaport & Burkhart, 1984). This body of literature, and investigators associated with this literature, at least implies that these beliefs do have etiological significance and may be one of the causative factors in sexual aggression.

A third approach to cognitive factors is drawn from the criminological literature epitomized by Yochelson and Samenow's (1977) description of thinking errors (see a description of the Oregon State Hospital program [Knopp, 1984] for an application to sex offenders). This model proposes a number of lifelong patterns of distorted thinking by individuals who engage in criminal behavior. It proposes that such errors of thinking tend to be pervasive in the offender's life and not limited to sex offending. Also, Yochelson and Samenow see the correction of thinking errors as being the major aspect of treatment rather than as one component.

The three models developed in different contexts, with slightly different focuses (e.g., specificity versus generalizability, causative of sexual behavior versus secondary to sexual offending, major areas of treatment focus versus one of a number of areas), do share many things in common. They all deal with the way individuals perceive (or misperceive) and attend to environmental cues, as well as the way they process information and the way each individual evaluates or misevaluates the consequences of the behavior. Bandura's (1977) social learning theory provides a model which incorporates aspects of a number of these approaches. Bandura describes three major cognitive processes, and a number of subcategories within each of these major categories, that allow individuals to basically disengage the normal self-evaluative processes that tend to modulate human behavior. These methods are described as: (1) making reprehensible conduct socially and ethically acceptable, (2) misconstruing the consequences of the behavior, and (3) devaluing or attributing blame to the victim. These major categories, along with specific subcategories and statements made by sex offenders that are representative of these categories, are included in Table 1. Except for the category of psychological justification, these cognitive restructuring concepts are drawn directly from Bandura (1977). This model provides a means of summarizing the cognitive processes hypothesized to be relevant to sex offenders and may serve as a means for the clinician to place the self-statements heard from sex offenders within a conceptual framework. The model does not address the degree to which these processes are specific or general for the sex offender or the degree to which they are causative of, or reactions to engaging in, deviant behavior.

CLINICAL ASSESSMENT APPROACHES

Compared to other areas of assessment with sex offenders, such as assessment of sexual arousal patterns, there have been limited studies related to the

TABLE 1. A Social Learning Model of Cognitive Factors in Sex Offenders

General category and specific process	Specific sex-offender statements
Justifying reprehensible conduct	
Moral justification	"It was sex education"
Psychological justification	"My offense occurred as a result of my wife's lack of understanding; my drinking, my drug abuse"
Palliative comparisons	"But I never had intercourse with the child"
Euphemistic labeling	"I was only fooling around," "I was only playing"
Misperceiving consequences	
Minimizing the consequence	"The child didn't suffer"
Ignoring the consequence	"I don't care"
Misattributing the consequence	"If the parents (Child Protective Service, the police, Rape Crisis Center) had been more sensitive, the victim wouldn't have so many problems"
Devaluing and attributing blame to the victim	
Dehumanization	"She was a whore anyway"
Attribution of blame	"Most women want to be raped"

Note. Adapted from Bandura (1977).

assessment of cognitions. However, until psychometrically sound methods for measuring such factors are developed, there will be limits on our ability to understand the development of cognitive distortions and the role they play in sexual offending.

One of the first scales developed to measure distortions in child molesters was the Abel and Becker Cognition Scale (Abel *et al.*, 1984). This is a 29-item scale which subjects rate from 1 (strongly agree) to 5 (strongly disagree). The scale includes such items as: "A child who doesn't resist an adult's sexual advances really wants to have sex with the adult"; "Having sex with a child is a good way for an adult to teach the child about sex." As anyone who has worked with child molesters can tell, these questions appear to have good face validity. However, it is only recently that psychometric data have appeared to at least provide partial support for the use of this scale. A recent dissertation (Gore, 1988) completed in Abel's laboratory (G. G. Abel, personal communication, January, 1988) provides some basic psychometric data on this scale. The test appears to have good test–retest reliability, and subscales developed through factor analysis also have acceptable Cronbach alphas (.59 to .64) and acceptable test–retest reliabilities (.64 to .76). The subscales significantly separate child molesters from normal controls, and two of the subscales separate child molesters from other types of sex offenders. Similar data on this scale have recently been provided by Stermac and Segal (1987), who also demonstrated that the scale separated sex offenders against children from rapists of adult women and from a number of other non-sex-offender control groups.

The major clinical problem with this scale is that items are rather obvious and may be affected significantly by social desirability. Much of the data reported by Abel and his colleagues were based on a sample of voluntary offenders promised confidentiality, and whether this scale will reveal the same distortions among sex offenders under legal pressure to appear normal needs to be further explored.

A second recent standardized approach that is said to tap cognitive factors are two of the subscales of the Multiphasic Sex Inventory (Nichols & Molinder, 1984), specifically, the Justifications subscale and the Cognitive Distortions and Immaturity subscale. Unfortunately, these two potentially relevant scales are considered by the test developers to be experimental, and, although they are apparently reliable, there are little data available related to their validity.

The Justifications subscale most clearly parallels the concept of cognitive distortions described earlier in this chapter, and it includes a large number of items labeled "psychological justifications" (see Table 1), such as "My sexual offense occurred as a result of my wife's lack of understanding of me" and "My sexual offense occurred because of stresses in my life." There also are a number of items related to attribution of blame to the victim, such as "My sex offense would not have occurred if the victim had not been sexually loose." Although this scale covers a narrower range of potential distortions than does the Abel and Becker Cognition Scale, it has the advantage of being applicable to a wider range of sex offenders than child molesters. The impact of social desirability on this scale is unknown, and an inherent limitation of this scale is that to answer the question, one must admit to being a sex offender.

The Cognitive Distortions and Immaturity subscale is more complex, and although some of the items tap what we have described as being cognitive distortions ("My problem is not sexual, it is that I really love children"), other items may be more relevant to the thinking errors approach of Yochelson and Samenow (1977) and include rather general rationalizations, such as "I'm often hurt by the behavior of others" or "I have suffered more hurt in my life than other people." The face validity of some of the items ("I was curious about sex as a child," "I became interested in sex after high school") is less obvious and may relate more to denial of sexual feelings and sexual issues than distortions. This scale has not been subjected to factor analysis, and therefore clinically one must cautiously interpret elevated scores on this scale. It is unclear, without looking at answers to individual items, whether scores on this scale are actually being elevated because of endorsements of specific cognitive distortions related to sexual abuse.

A third set of scales has been developed to measure a variety of attitudes toward women and aggression thought to be supportive of rape. Many of the studies have used scales developed by Burt (1980), and a majority of studies have been with college student populations and apparently involve sexual aggression in dating situations. Sexual aggression or sexual coercion in college populations appears to be an extensive problem in and of itself (Koss *et al.*, in press). However, it is unclear whether data collected with this population are equally representative of rapists in the correctional system or in treatment programs. In general, the assessment scales used in this area have adequate psychometric properties and have some validity, at least in the populations where they have been applied (Malamuth, 1984). A number of studies have found that subjects who report some likelihood of raping if they could be guaranteed they would not be caught, accept more rape myths than subjects who report no likelihood of raping (Malamuth & Check, 1980; Malamuth, Haber, & Feshbach, 1980; Tieger, 1981). It has also been found that subjects high in sex-role stereotyping respond sexually to rape depictions (Check & Malamuth, 1983) and that rape myth acceptance and acceptance of interpersonal violence are predictive of laboratory aggression against women (Malamuth, 1983). A number of these scales have also been found to be related to self-reported coercive behavior measured in a variety of ways (Koss & Dinero, 1987; Koss, Leonard, Beezley, & Oros, 1985; Malamuth, 1986; Murphy *et al.*, 1986; Rapaport & Burkhart, 1984).

In general, the above studies suggest that a number of scales measuring attitudes derived from a feminist perspective correlate with various measures of sexual aggression in nonclinical samples. There is some variability between studies in terms of which of the specific attitudinal variables are significant predictors. This is not surprising, given that the variables which have been predicted have varied across studies, that these scales are not factorially pure (Briere, Malamuth, & Check 1985), and that they are highly correlated with each other.

A final unique approach to assessing cognitive distortions has recently been presented by Stermac and Segal (1987). They have developed actual case vignettes abstracted from clinical files which varied on level of sexual contact and the child's response to such contact (smiling, passive, or crying). Subjects were then asked to rate the vignettes on a number of scales, including perception of harm versus benefit to the child, child complicity, and adult responsibility. Child molesters perceive the sex offense as being more beneficial to the child, perceive the child as being more responsible for the abuse, and perceive the adult as having less responsibility, than do either rapists or a variety of non-sex-offender control groups that were used in the study. This is one of the few studies to clearly document specific cognitive distortions in sex offenders. It offers a unique approach to assessment in this area, and this warrants further investigation.

There is a need for further studies to better refine existing scales and to develop other methods of assessing distortions in offenders. To date, there are only two unpublished studies showing that offenders against children differ from nonoffenders in terms of cognitive distortions. There is a significant amount of data indicating that a variety of attitudinal measures explain some of the variance in coercive sexual behavior in a nonclinical sample, but little data exist on the applicability of these scales to a rapist population. Until we can clearly measure and define the types of cognitive distortions used by various offenders, it will be impossible to determine the impact treatment programs may have on such distortions or even the need for such programs.

APPROACHES TO CHANGING COGNITIONS

The purpose of this section will be to review clinical approaches that have promise for changing cognitions. In general, the procedures to be described are basically "standard" cognitive therapy or cognitive behavioral approaches (Beck, 1976; Ellis & Grieger, 1977; Meichenbaum, 1977) adapted to sex offenders. These are cognitive restructuring techniques that provide: (1) patients with a rationale for the role cognitions have in maintaining sexual abuse, (2) corrective information and education to the patient usually around such issues as victim impact, (3) ways of helping subjects identify their specific distortions, and (4) exercises to assist patients in challenging and exploring their distortions.

One note which reflects my own bias is the way these standard techniques, especially those that are confrontative, are presented to the patient. Although offenders must be confronted with their distortions, I do not believe that the confrontation has to be aggressive. In fact, Fischer (1986) presents some preliminary evidence showing that a confrontational approach with college males led to more acceptance of rape than did an educational approach. Therefore, our approach tends to be more Socratic, as described by Beck (1976), than the more aggressive approach to cognitive therapy as described by Ellis and Grieger (1977).

One of the first steps necessary when attempting to modify cognitive distortions is to provide the patient some rationale for the role distortions play in sexual abuse and the need to change them. Whether the rationale is based on solid empirical evidence is probably less important than that it makes sense to the patient and elicits his cooperation in the treatment program. Early in treatment, when describing the rationale for such factors as reducing deviant arousal or identifying risk factors, we also give the following type of description (adjusted to the patient's intellectual level and socioeconomic background) for why we will be looking at cognitive distortions as part of their treatment.

> In treating sex offenders over the years, there are common problems we have noted. One of these is that sex offenders are not all bad. They know right from wrong, they feel guilty when they do wrong, and at some level they know that molesting a child (or raping a woman or exposing themselves) causes harm. If they stop and think that what they are doing is hurting someone else, they feel uncomfortable or feel emotional pain. However, we also know that human beings in general try to avoid pain, whether it be physical or emotional pain, such as guilt. Therefore, since sex offenders do have feelings toward other people, and at some level they know they are hurting someone else, they have to do something to avoid these uncomfortable feelings. One way they do this is to tell themselves that what they are doing is not bad, or the child (adult) really wanted to do this, or it could have been worse. Different offenders tell themselves different things. After a while, the things you say to yourself become almost automatic and you may not even realize you are saying them. Our job is to help you identify these things and try to show you why many of them are not true. We call these things you say to yourself excuses, justifications, minimizations, and cognitive distortions. I am sure that at the time you were abusing that if you stopped to think about the potential harm you were causing, you would have stopped. I also want to point out to you that this part of your treatment is not going to be comfortable. The more we help you identify the excuses you have been making and help you realize that these aren't true, the more you are going to have to face that you've potentially caused harm. At times, we are going to have to push you to take a look at yourself, and you may become angry at us for doing that. We understand this and we want you to be able to tell us when you are feeling that way. However, we know that there is no easy way to get control over deviant sexual behavior. We also feel that because you are here you really want to do something about your behavior even though it hurts.

This statement is an attempt to orient the patient to the role distortions may play in maintaining sexual abuse, and it also attempts to let the patient know that treatment is not easy and will probably make him uncomfortable. The message is that such discomfort is necessary and expected. We aim to "reframe" this discomfort by making it a sign that the patient really wants to work on the problem. There have been other similar approaches to orienting patients to the role of cognitions in sex offending, to which the interested reader is referred (Abel et al., 1984; Lange, 1986).

As part of a cognitive restructuring process, offenders need accurate information about sexual abuse and the impact of such abuse on victims. Therefore, a number of programs include the use of educational materials such as books and movies, presented from a victim's standpoint, or planned interactions with victim advocates, victim counselors, or victims themselves. A good example of this approach is the empathy-training module described by Northwest Treatment Associates (Knopp, 1984). In this program, victim counselors, and preferably counselors representing the offender's actual victim, attend group sessions and discuss the impact victimization has had on the victim. In addition, offenders are required to read books written by victims of sexual abuse and to discuss these books in group. In our own program, we spend considerable time educating patients about the long-term consequences of abuse on victims, drawing heavily on the victimization literature. We also point out that the current research literature does not support a variety of rape myths and sex-role stereotypes. Patients are many times asked to develop a written list of the impact sexual abuse has had on their victims and the impact abuse could potentially have on other victims.

There has been little literature that actually evaluates the impact of factual information on cognitive distortions in sex offenders. Malamuth and Check (1984) found that a very short debriefing (stressing the horrors of rape, the legal sanctions for rape, and disputing a number of rape myths) given to subjects participating in a study where they were exposed to pornographic rape stimuli decreased the number of rape myths accepted by subjects. Check and Malamuth (1984), in a similar study, also found that a debriefing which stressed the potential negative side effects of aggressive pornography led subjects to view pornography as a cause of rape. Similarly, Fischer (1986) found that subjects in a human sexuality course who received a lecture on the rape laws became less accepting of rape. In general, these interventions were very limited in scope, and they led to significant but small changes in subject populations whose distortions were probably not as well ingrained as the more chronic sex offenders seen in numerous treatment programs. Whether such didactic approaches alone would be effective with more chronic offenders is unknown.

In addition to straight explanations, most programs use more active procedures to help patients recognize their distortions and to assist them in developing strategies to counter them. A number of programs (Abel *et al.*, 1984; Lange, 1986), including our own, use items from scales such as the Abel and Becker Cognition Scale or the scales developed by Burt to assist in this process. This is typically done in groups, where each patient receives feedback from the therapist and other group members about the inaccuracy of his cognitions.

As a clinical example, consider an incest offender who has molested his 10-year-old daughter. He might agree with the statement: "If my daughter had said no I would have stopped." This statement includes a number of distortions, including the notions that a child can consent to have sex with an adult, that if a child does not say no they have agreed to the sexual act, and that it is the child's responsibility to stop sexual abuse. After an offender has made such a statement, we would explore with him a number of issues. First, we would question the patient regarding whether he would allow his 10-year-old daughter to buy toys (clothes or whatever) on credit. In general, most will respond rather emphatically "Of course not." This response would be followed by questions to explore why he would not do this, and typically the offender finally comes to the conclusion that the child would be too young to enter such a legal contract and would not understand the consequences of entering such a contract. The offender would then be confronted by the therapist or other group members with the proposition that children are also too young to negotiate a sexual contract with an adult since they are also too immature and lack sufficient knowledge to understand the consequences of such an involvement. The offender then would be asked what generally happens when his 10-year-old daughter says no when she is asked to clean her room or pick up her toys. Usually the offender responds by saying that the child would be punished in some way. Then it is pointed out that children are punished almost every time they say no to adults, especially adults who are authority figures. Thus it would be extremely hard for a child to say no to her father regarding sexual activity when the child is punished for saying no at other times. We would next examine the possibility that the child had actually said no. Most offenders (at least those offenders who have been in an ongoing relationship with a child) will say that there were times when the child said no, and they might further claim that they (the offenders) responded by stopping the abuse. We would then try to make the offender realize that in fact although they stopped on this occasion, the next day (next week, next month) they approached the child again and really did not listen to what the child said.

As part of this approach, Abel *et al.* (1984) and Lange (1986) have described using role-playing in a group format in order to get other offenders to challenge the distortions. Abel *et al.* have the therapist role-play a child molester who uses various distortions, while an actual offender is asked to play a probation officer, a policeman, or family member whose job it is to confront the distortions. These therapists consider this role reversal to be a very effective means of getting patients to rethink their perceptions.

Another approach we have used, which is also described by Abel *et al.*, is to have patients who have been sexually abused recount their own abuse, including the feelings, thoughts, and reactions they had at the time they were abused. Rather than using this description of their own abuse to help the patient "work through" the emotional trauma associated with abuse, we instead ask them to relate these feelings of being abused to how their victim must have felt. The program at Northwest Treatment Associates takes this one step further (Knopp, 1984) by asking the offender to simulate his actual experience of being sexually abused.

A final approach used in our program to help offenders identify and confront distortions is to have the patient and therapist review the verbal and masturbatory satiation tapes (see Quinsey and Earls, Chapter 16, this volume for a description of these procedures), with the focus of this review being on recognizing distortions. These tapes involve detailed fantasies which include perceived victim reactions, and we have found these to provide a rich source of information regarding the distortions used by offenders. Initially, we listen to the tape with the offender and stop the tape when we hear the offender making various distortions (e.g., the tape would be stopped when the offender said "She really enjoyed it" or "She didn't say no"), and then we go through the specific steps outlined earlier. Attempts are made to point out to the offender why the distortion is false and to challenge and confront him in order to help him generate alternative and more appropriate statements. After a few sessions, the offenders are given responsibility for stopping the satiation tape whenever they hear themselves engaging in distortions. This provides some check on whether they are actually beginning to recognize the distortions. Patients are also asked to keep a list of distortions as we identify them, and we also have patients write out reasons why the distortions are false. The use of the behavioral tapes in this way is somewhat self-limiting, and after 5 to 10 sessions, the offender will either quit using distortions on the tape or will be able to recognize the distortions quite rapidly.

Whatever approaches are taken by the clinician to change distortions, there are number of factors to consider. First, the clinician needs to be relatively well versed in victimization issues and have accurate information regarding the long-term impact of sexual abuse, as well as have knowledge of the literature concerning the relationship of sexist and aggressive attitudes to coercive sexual behavior. Second, the clinician needs to be alert to the full range of possible distortions, since it is easy to overlook apparently offhand remarks, such as "I only fondled her," "It could have been worse," or "I'm glad I didn't do any more than I did." Such statements minimize the abuse in the offender's perception in a way that downplays the potential negative consequences of what he has done. Third, the clinician needs to avoid letting this form of therapy become highly aversive to the patient. Regardless of the approach taken, the offender is being continually confronted by the harm he has caused others. Facing up to the fact that one has caused harm to others is difficult for anybody to accept, and this is no different for offenders. At times, the patient will feel attacked and become hostile toward the therapist. The clinician should be aware of these feelings and expect such reactions.

SUMMARY

It is clear that the majority of the procedures described above are not unique and have been used with various behavioral and psychiatric problems. It should also be clear that a number of additional procedures used in therapy, such as victim empathy training, modules on victimization issues, sex education, and even procedures for reducing arousal, could all potentially modify cognitive distortions. Thus, it is not just the actual cognitive restructuring techniques which may produce the desired changes in attitudes; every aspect of therapy is likely to change typical patterns of thinking. Given this, it is not surprising that Rouleau et al. (1986), in their treatment program for sex offenders, found that a number of procedures seemed to reduce cognitive distortions, and not just cognitive therapy. It is unclear, however, what effect changing cognitive distortions has on the long-term outcome in the treatment of sex offenders, and such studies are needed.

REFERENCES

Abel, G. G., Blanchard, E. B., & Becker, J. V. (1978). An integrated treatment program for rapists. In R. T. Rada (Ed.), *Clinical aspects of the rapist* (pp. 161–214). New York: Grune & Stratton.

Abel, G. G., Becker, J. V., Cunningham-Rathner, J., Rouleau, J. L., Kaplan, M., & Reich, J. (1984). *The treatment of child molesters.* (Available from G. G. Abel, Behavior Medicine Institute, 5791 Kingston Cross, Stone Mountain, GA 30087).

Badgley, R. F. (1984). *Sexual offenses against children: A report of the committee on sexual offenses against children and youth.* Ottawa: Minister of Supply and Services.

Bandura, A. (1977). *Social learning theory.* Englewood Cliffs, NJ: Prentice-Hall.

Beck, A. T. (1976). *Cognitive therapy and the emotional disorders.* New York: International Universities Press.

Briere, J., Malamuth, N., & Check, J. V. P. (1985). Sexuality and rape-supportive beliefs. *International Journal of Women's Studies, 8,* 398–403.

Burt, M. R. (1980). Cultural myths and supports for rape. *Journal of Personality and Social Psychology, 38,* 217–230.

Check, J. V. P., & Malamuth, N. M. (1983). Sex role stereotyping and reactions to depictions of stranger versus acquaintance rape. *Journal of Personality and Social Psychology, 45,* 344–356.

Check, J. V. P., & Malamuth, N. M. (1984). Can there be positive effects of participation in pornographic experiments? *The Journal of Sex Research, 20,* 14–31.

Conte, J. R. (1985). Clinical dimensions of adult sexual abuse of children. *Behavioral Sciences and the Law, 3,* 341–354.

Ellis, A., & Grieger, R. (1977). *Handbook of rational-emotive therapy.* New York: Springer.

Fischer, G. L. (1986). College student attitudes toward forcible date rape: Changes after taking a human sexuality course. *Journal of Sex Education and Therapy, 12,* 42–46.

Gore, D. K. (1988). *Cognitive distortions of child molesters and the cognition scale: Reliability, validity, treatment effects, and prediction of recidivism.* Unpublished doctoral dissertation, Georgia State University, Atlanta.

Knight, R. A., Rosenberg, R., & Schneider, B. A. (1985). Classification of sexual offenders: Perspectives, methods, and validation. In A. W. Burgess (Ed.), *Rape and sexual assault* (pp. 222–293). New York: Garland.

Knopp, F. H. (1984). *Retraining adult sex offenders: Methods and models.* Syracuse, NY: Safer Society Press.

Koss, M. P., & Dinero, T. E. (1987, January). *Predictors of sexual aggression among a national sample of male college students.* Paper presented at the New York Academy of Sciences Conference on Human Sexual Aggression: Current Perspectives, New York.

Koss, M. P., Leonard, K. E., Beezley, D. A., & Oros, C. J. (1985). Nonstranger sexual aggression: A discriminant analysis of the psychological characteristics of undetected offenders. *Sex Roles, 12,* 981–992.

Koss, M. P., Gidycz, C. A., & Wisniewski, N. (1987). The scope of rape: Incidence and prevalence of sexual aggression and victimization in a national sample of students in higher education. *Journal of Consulting and Clinical Psychology.*

Lange, A. (1986). *Rational-emotive therapy: A treatment manual.* Tampa, FL: Florida Mental Health Institute.

Levin, S. M., & Stava, L. (1987). Personality characteristics of sex offenders: A review. *Archives of Sexual Behavior, 16,* 57–79.

Malamuth, N. M. (1983). Factors associated with rape as predictors of laboratory aggression against women. *Journal of Personality and Social Psychology, 45,* 432–442.

Malamuth, N. M. (1984). Aggression against women: Cultural and individual causes. In N. M. Malamuth & E. Donnerstein (Eds.), *Pornography and sexual aggression* (pp. 19–52). Orlando, FL: Academic Press.

Malamuth, N. M. (1986). Predictors of naturalistic sexual aggression. *Journal of Personality and Social Psychology, 50,* 953–962.

Malamuth, N. M., & Check, J. V. P. (1980). Penile tumescence and perceptual responses to rape as a function of victim's perceived reactions. *Journal of Applied Social Psychology, 10,* 428–547.

Malamuth, N. M., & Check, J. V. P. (1984). Debriefing effectiveness following exposure to pornographic rape depictions. *The Journal of Sex Research, 20,* 1–13.

Malamuth, N. M., Haber, S., & Feshbach, S. (1980). Testing hypotheses regarding rape: Exposure to sexual violence, sex differences, and the "normality" of rapists. *Journal of Research in Personality, 14,* 121–137.

Meichenbaum, D. (1977). *Cognitive-behavior modification: An integrative approach.* New York: Plenum.

Murphy, W. D., & Barbaree, H. E. (1987). *Assessments of sexual offenders by measures of erectile response: Psychometric properties and decision making* (Order #86M0506500501D). Rockville, MD: National Institute of Health.

Murphy, W. D., Coleman, E. M., & Haynes, M. R. (1983). Treatment and evaluation issues with the mentally retarded sex offender. In J. G. Greer & I. R. Stuart (Eds.), *The sexual aggressor: Current perspectives on treatment* (pp. 22–41). New York: Van Nostrand Reinhold.

Murphy, W. D., Coleman, E. M., & Haynes, M. R. (1986). Factors related to coercive sexual behavior in a nonclinical sample of males. *Violence and Victims, 1,* 255–278.

Murphy, W. D., & Stalgaitis, S. J. (1987). Assessment and treatment considerations for sexual offenders against children: Behavioral and social learning approaches. In J. R. McNamara & M. A. Appel (Eds.), *Critical issues, developments, and trends in professional psychology* (vol. 3; pp. 177–210). New York: Praeger.

Nichols, H. R., & Molinder, I. (1984). *Multiphasic Sex Inventory Manual.* Tacoma, WA: Authors.

Prentky, R., Cohen, M., & Seghorn, T. (1985). Development of a rational taxonomy for the classification of rapists: The Massachusetts Treatment Center system. *Bulletin of American Academy of Psychiatry and the Law, 13,* 39–70.

Quinsey, V. L. (1984). Sexual aggression: Studies of offenders against women. In D. Weisstub (Ed.), *Law and mental health: International perspectives* (vol. 1; pp. 84–121). New York: Pergamon.

Quinsey, V. L. (1986). Men who have sex with children. In D. Weisstub (Ed.), *Law and mental health: International perspectives* (vol. 2; pp. 140–172). New York: Pergamon.

Rapaport, K., & Burkhart, B. R. (1984). Personality and attitudinal characteristics of sexually coercive college males. *Journal of Abnormal Psychology, 93,* 216–221.

Rouleau, J. L., Abel, G. G., Mittelman, M. S., Becker, J. V., & Cunningham-Rathner, J. (1986, February). *Effectiveness of each component of a treatment program for non-incarcerated pedophiles.* Paper presented at the NIMH-sponsored Conference on Sex Offenders, Tampa, FL.

Russell, D. E. H. (1982). The prevalence and incidence of forcible rape and attempted rape of females. *Victimology: An International Journal, 7,* 81–93.

Stermac, L., & Segal, Z. (1987, November). *Cognitive assessment of child molesters.* Paper presented at the 21st annual convention of the Association for the Advancement of Behavior Therapy, Boston.

Tieger, T. (1981). Self-rated likelihood of raping and the social perception of rape. *Journal of Research in Personality, 15,* 147–158.

Wolf, S. C. (1984, November). *A multi-factor model of deviant sexuality.* Paper presented at the Third National Conference on Victimology, Lisbon, Portugal.

Yochelson, S., & Samenow, S. E. (1977). *The criminal personality. Vol. II: The change process.* New York: Jason Aronson.

20

Relapse Prevention with Sexual Aggressors

A Method for Maintaining Therapeutic Gain and Enhancing External Supervision

WILLIAM D. PITHERS

Throughout history, whenever a socially frightening disorder existed, and its etiology was not widely known, tentative explanations were invoked that sometimes proved erroneous and regrettable. Ancient Romans feared inhaling nighttime air, believing that it bore vapors, emitted from nearby swamps, which were regarded as the cause of a potentially fatal respiratory disease. Today, "swamp vapors" are called bacteria, and the disorder is known as pneumonia. Epileptics in colonial Salem, Massachusetts, were hanged in the mistaken belief that their seizures signified that they were demon-possessed witches. In current society, both disorders are readily treated and create little concern.

In a similar fashion, society does not yet widely accept an explanation for the existence of sexual aggressors. Struggling to ascertain the determinants of sexually abusive acts so that effective treatments may be devised, early theorists proposed a number of speculative accounts.

PAST THEORIES REGARDING ETIOLOGY OF SEXUAL AGGRESSION

Sexual Aggression as an Impulsive Act

Sexual aggression has often been considered an impulsive act. This notion offers, to some extent, comfort to a society which endorses the belief that most

WILLIAM D. PITHERS • Vermont Center for the Prevention and Treatment of Sexual Abuse, Vermont Department of Corrections, Waterbury, Vermont 05676.

human behavior is a product of rational thought. Our safety seems less precarious if we believe sexual abuse is performed by individuals who have taken momentary leave of their faculties. Such a premise also enables us to evade recognition that many men who do not aggress sexually have momentary impulses to do so. Many aggressors, seeking to minimize their responsibility for offenses, would also have us to believe their behaviors are the product of irresistible impulses overwhelming their self-control.

Offenders have numerous incentives to misrepresent their acts as impulsive rather than as the product of active planning and intention. Some try to convince us they had not thought about sexual abuse prior to performing it, since this might permit them to appear less culpable legally or less disordered psychologically. A small measure of self-esteem may be salvaged by convincing others that one is not the type of person who would intentionally harm someone.

Thus, many offenders who will admit performing the abuse claim that they did so only because they were intoxicated, and they assert that their real problem is alcoholism. Others believe that crimes compelled by uncontrollable impulses might gain them a less punitive sentence, possibly a verdict of guilty but insane. An offender, anticipating commitment to a treatment program, may purport that his offense was impulsive, believing that this etiology will lead to a shorter period in therapy than one involving more fundamental personality defects.

Reinterpretation of the Impulsivity Hypothesis

Sexual offenses may appear impulsive upon first inspection. In reality, many offenders carefully plan offenses so that they appear to occur without forethought. An analysis of common precursors to sexual aggression reveals how planned acts can appear unplanned.

In a review of antecedents to sexual assault (Pithers, Kashima, Cumming, Beal, & Buell, 1987, 1988), more than half of the samples of 64 rapists (56%) and 136 pedophiles (51%) appeared emotionally overcontrolled. Some of these men left hostile interactions without expressing any affect, and, as they brooded about the incident over time, their rage grew. Some offenders in this sample had harbored hatred from a single event for a decade. Although they failed to express anger at the appropriate moment, continual augmentation of the emotion eventually led to an explosive assault later in time. Since the sexual abuse was far removed in time from the instigating event, it appeared situationally noncontingent, or "impulsive." In reality, however, the act was not impulsive at all, only delayed. A similar process with anxiety and depression was noted among pedophiles.

Although victims may be selected opportunistically, the act itself has generally been nurtured for a considerable time in the offender's most secret fantasies. The sex offender's deviant fantasies are tantamount to planning sessions for refinement of future behaviors. The compulsivity of the sexual aggressors' deviant fantasies differentiates them from those of nonoffending men, who may experience a deviant fantasy momentarily but quickly reject any thought of acting upon the impulse as a disgusting notion.

Sex Offenders as "Sexual Psychopaths"

At one time, sex offenders were regarded as "sexual psychopaths." In the United States between 1938 and 1966, thirty-one states enacted sexual psychopath statutes. Sexual psychopath legislation was based on the premise that such offenders were affected by psychopathology which predisposed them to abuse. Under these statutes, if a convicted sex offender was found to be "mentally disordered" by court-appointed mental health practitioners, he was civilly committed to a treatment institution for an indeterminate period. An assumption was made that treatment within an institution would create enduring changes in offenders' personalities, thereby ameliorating their danger to others.

Although creation of sexual psychopath statutes and institutional treatment programs was well intended, a recent review of outcome data from these early efforts demonstrates that the enterprise was a failure (Furby, Weinrott, & Blackshaw, 1989). In the initial research investigations following offenders after release from institutional treatment, no difference in recidivism could be demonstrated between treated and untreated sex offenders. Recidivism data from these early institutional programs have been used to argue that the efficacy of sex-offender treatment has not been proved (Brecher, 1978). Citing these data, the Group for the Advancement of Psychiatry (1977) advocated incarceration, rather than treatment, of sexually aggressive individuals.

Flaws of Sexual Psychopath Legislation

The basic assumptions of sexual psychopath legislation were dramatically mistaken. While such statutes proposed that sex offenders suffer from mental disorders, research consistently concluded that the vast majority were not significantly impaired (Adams & Fay, 1981; Bard et al., 1987; Gebhard, Gagnon, Pomeroy, & Christenson, 1965; Groth, 1979; Justice & Justice, 1979; Rada, 1978; Sanford, 1980; Walters, 1975).

Nearly all of the initial programs for sex offenders adopted a central premise of the medical model: treatment enables cure. Within this framework, if a disorder is sufficiently severe, therapeutic intervention might necessitate hospitalization. For many disorders, the medical model functions superbly. Bacteria causing diseases can be annihilated, inflamed appendices removed, weak hearts and lungs replaced. In regard to sex offenders though, treatment programs adhering to the medical model concept of "cure" have generally been removed and replaced, not the disorder they attempted to address. Treatment programs based upon sexual psychopath statutes remain active in only five states.

Within our current state of technology, cures for some disorders do not exist, regardless of the treatment employed or the setting in which it is implemented. Epilepsy cannot be cured, but control is possible through medication.

Without medication, seizures are likely to recur. Therefore, epileptics receive medication to control their disorder.

Sexual aggressors cannot be cured. Providing offenders with the hope of an irreversible elimination of their disorder establishes an expectation that assures failure. Encouraging offenders to pursue the unrealistic goal of behavioral perfection, thereby insuring a sense of personal inadequacy when lapses in self-management are encountered, encourages reoffending. If one accepts that sex offenses are not impulsive acts committed without forethought, then an alternate goal of enhancing self-management skills of sex offenders may be pursued.

RELAPSE PREVENTION

Relapse prevention (RP) was devised as a method of enhancing maintenance of change in substance abusers. As originally described by Marlatt and colleagues (Chaney, O'Leary, & Marlatt, 1978; Marlatt, 1982; Marlatt & Gordon, 1980, 1985), RP was designed to strengthen self-control by providing clients with methods for identifying problematic situations, analyzing decisions that set up situations enabling resumption of substance abuse, and developing strategies to avoid, or cope more effectively with, these situations. Thus, as originally proposed, RP represented a method of enhancing self-management skills. Pithers, Marques, Gibat, and Marlatt (1983) modified the self-management model of RP for application with sex offenders.

The Relapse Process

Relapse prevention proposes that a variety of factors influence whether or not a sexual offender will avoid committing another abusive act. The interaction of these factors affects the probability of relapse.

By entering treatment, a sexual aggressor essentially declares an intent not to reoffend. As he sees himself gaining therapeutically, he becomes more assured about his ability to handle life's future difficulties without undue distress. Occasionally, his attitude reaches an unrealistic superoptimism that encourages inattention to behavioral maintenance. This self-assuredness increases until the offender encounters a high-risk situation (e.g., a rapist who, driving his vehicle to escape an angry interaction with his spouse, spots a female hitchhiker; a pedophile who is asked to babysit a neighbor's children). High-risk situations, or lapses, are defined as circumstances which threaten an offender's sense of self-control and thus increase risk of relapse.

When an offender deals effectively with a high-risk situation, his sense of self-management is reinforced. To the extent that his expectation about successfully handling future high-risk situations remains realistic, the probability of relapse decreases. Offenders who believe that surviving one high-risk situation signifies that they "have passed the test" and now are able to handle all high-risk situations are primed for relapse. Should the offender fail to cope with a high-risk situation (e.g., purchases pornography while in a book store), his perceived self-management decreases, and a tendency to passively give in to the next high-risk situation ensues.

Generally, each time an offender fails to cope with a high-risk situation, he engages in one of the behaviors involved in his relapse process. In a study examining precursors to sexual aggression, Pithers, Cumming, Beal, Young, and Turner (1989) determined that a common sequence of behaviors comprised the relapse process. The first change from clients' typical functioning was affective. They referred to themselves as "lonely" or "confused." Typically, offenders found themselves unable to deal effectively with this emotional state. The second alteration involved fantasies of performing sexual abuse. For example, an angry offender might attempt to deal with that emotion by visualizing himself sexually degrading a person. Fantasies were converted into distorted thoughts in the third step of the relapse process. Offenders frequently devised rationalizations justifying their soon-to-be-committed acts. Distorted cognitions often attributed inaccurate properties to potential victims, objectifying adults or attributing adult characteristics to children. As the relapse process evolved, offenders cognitively refined a plan that would enable their fantasized behavior to be enacted. Often, this passive planning was accomplished during masturbatory fantasies. An essential element of the plan entailed establishing circumstances for the offense that might make the offender appear less culpable for the abuse. The plan was acted out in the final step of the relapse process. In this relapse process, the initial change that reliably differentiates reoffenders from nonoffenders is the predominance of deviant sexual fantasies. Thus, for most sexual offenders, the initial return of deviant sexual fantasy is defined as the earliest identifiable lapse.

Thus far, the relapse process has been depicted from the point at which a person encounters a high-risk situation. However, RP also examines events that precede high-risk situations. Although some sex offenders lapse in situations which would have been difficult to anticipate, the majority set the stage for lapses by putting themselves into high-risk situations. Offenders can covertly set up a lapse by making a series of "apparently irrelevant decisions," each of which represents another step toward a tempting, high-risk situation. Any single apparently irrelevant decision may seem unrelated to reoffending but, in reality, each choice brings the aggressor closer to the high-risk situation where he must make the final decision to reoffend or not to reoffend. For example, a pedophile who decides to go to a national park for a summer vacation, when school-aged children are likely to be present, is making an apparently irrelevant decision that actually leads him closer to offending.

If a sexual offender has not been prepared to deal with lapses precipitated by an apparently irrelevant decision, he may attempt to hide his errors from therapists and parole officers. He may believe that admitting even a momentary deviant fantasy will be considered an indication that he is totally out of control. Any effort to bury a lapse typically leads to additional lapses that are closer still to reoffending.

Several factors, encompassed by the term *abstinence violation effect*, influence whether or not a lapse becomes a relapse. Conflict between an offender's self-image as a "reformed" sex offender and his recent experience of a lapse represents a major component of the abstinence violation effect. This dissonance may be resolved by the offender deciding his treatment failed and that he remains a sexual offender. Attributing lapses to personal weakness heightens the abstinence violation effect. If lapses are considered personal failures, an expectation for continued failure develops, possibly ending in the ultimate defeat: relapse. The abstinence violation effect is also amplified if the offender selectively recalls only the positive aspects of sexually abusing victims in the past, forgetting about the delayed negative consequences. An angry rapist may focus on the satisfaction derived by violently releasing his hostility during past assaults. Insular pedophiles may recall moments of perceived intimacy from prior abuse of children.

If aggressors selectively remember positive outcomes of prior offenses, but neglect the delayed negative consequences (e.g., arrest, incarceration), probability of relapse increases. Due to the strength of this phenomenon, it has received the title Problem of Immediate Gratification, or the PIG phenomenon.

A final factor affecting the abstinence violation effect is the individual's expectation about the likelihood of lapsing. For offenders who believe that treatment should erase all vestiges of their deviant desires, a momentary loss of control may be interpreted as an irreversible trend. In contrast, if an offender views a lapse as an expected event that represents an opportunity to refine self-management skills through analysis of reversible mistakes, lapses can yield productive outcomes. In such cases, an offender acquires enhanced coping skills and maintains greater vigilance for the earliest signs of relapse.

As originally modified for application to sexual aggressors (Pithers *et al.*, 1983), RP remained solely a means of enhancing offenders' self-control. The initial application of RP, in the Vermont Treatment Program for Sexual Aggressors (Pithers, 1982), demonstrated that the model effectively aided self-management. RP accomplished the goals of increasing the client's awareness of the range of choices that regulate his behavior and developing specific coping skills for high-risk situations.

This aspect of the RP model for sex offenders, now referred to as the Internal Self-Management Dimension, is outlined in the immediately following sections; subsequently, an additional revision of RP for sexual aggressors, the External Supervisory Dimension, is presented.

INTERNAL SELF-MANAGEMENT DIMENSION

Relapse prevention begins by dispelling misconceptions that the client may have regarding the outcome of treatment (i.e., that he will be "cured") and describing more realistic goals. It continues with an assessment of the client's high-risk situations, which are the conditions under which relapse has occurred or is likely to occur in the future. The initial assessment also examines the client's coping skills, since situations can be considered high risk only to the extent that the person has difficulty coping with them. After high-risk situations have been identified, interventions are designed to train the client to minimize lapses and to keep lapses from evolving into a full-blown relapse.

When introducing RP to clients, we emphasize development of realistic expectations about therapy and encourage an active, problem-solving approach on the part of the client. We inform clients explicitly that no cure exists for their disorder. They are told that treatment will diminish their attraction to deviant sexual behaviors, but that fantasies about these behaviors are likely to recur at least momentarily in the future. Clients are informed that the return of a deviant fantasy does not signify that they are necessarily going to reoffend, and that a critical part of treatment involves learning what to do when they feel drawn to deviant sexual activity again. We instruct clients that they will discover a variety of situations in which they make apparently irrelevant decisions which either lead them closer to offending again or take them away from that danger. They are told that developing the ability to recognize these situations and enact alternatives will reduce the likelihood of acting out their deviant fantasies.

We initially recommended introducing the client to RP concepts during the first therapy session (Pithers *et al.*, 1983). However, we have discovered that the highly cognitive strategies of RP can heighten an offender's intellectualized defenses against recognizing the harm inflicted upon victims. Empathy for victims represents a critical source of motivation for the offender's treatment and maintenance (Hildebran & Pithers, 1989). In order to avoid RP being viewed by offenders as an interesting intellectual exercise having little relevance to their lives, we introduce it only after victim empathy has developed.

RELAPSE PREVENTION ASSESSMENT PROCEDURES

Since RP is a highly individualized approach to therapy, thorough assessment is necessary to determine issues to focus upon in treatment. Assessment within RP includes three major tasks: (1) specification of the client's high-risk situations (including apparently irrelevant decisions creating those situations), (2) identification of existing skills for coping with identified high-risk situations, and (3) analysis of early antecedents of the client's abusive acts. Several methods are used to identify factors that increase the threat of relapse for a given offender. These include analysis of case records, structured interviews, self-monitoring, direct observation, and self-report measures.

Assessment of High-Risk Situations

Analysis of Case Records

Factors predisposing sexual abuse can be discerned by reviewing case records (e.g., police report, victim's affidavit, offender's statement, computerized criminal record check, psychological assessments, presentence investigations, etc.). Case reviews also enable generation of hypotheses to be investigated during a clinical interview. This procedure sometimes profoundly changes a case formulation. In the case of an incest victim, an emergency room report noted that surgery had been required to remove a tampon thrust into her body by the forcefulness of her father's assault, suggesting that the assault represented more the dynamic of rape than incest. Plethysmographic evaluation confirmed that the offender experienced peak arousal to stimuli depicting rape rather than incest. A search of the offender's records revealed that he had also raped while an adolescent.

Structured Interview

Circumstances associated with the client's offenses can be explored during a structured interview. Factors predisposing abuse, such as cognitive distortions which attribute adult qualities to children or objectify women, lack of empathy for sex abuse victims, deficient social skills, and inability to recognize or modulate emotions, can be assayed. Guidelines for interview content and process are delineated by Groth (1979) and Pithers, Beal, Armstrong, and Petty (1989).

Self-Monitoring

Even most successful clients encounter antecedents to sexual offenses while in treatment. Self-monitoring enables offenders to identify these affective, cognitive, and behavioral patterns (MacDonald & Pithers, 1989). Clients may discover that they deal with powerful emotion by isolating themselves, heighten the feeling by ruminating, and masturbate to violent fantasies in a maladaptive effort to gain temporary relief from the feeling. Clients record the following information every time they have a strong emotion, a sexual fantasy, a deviant urge, or whenever they masturbate: (1) time of day, (2) description of eliciting internal and situational stimuli, (3) antecedents, (4) their consequent mood and, (5) if the precursor was a cognitive distortion, a corrective self-statement.

Behavioral Assessment of Sexual Arousal Pattern

Some offenders experience greater sexual arousal to fantasies of rape or child abuse than to consenting acts. Clearly, such disordered sexual arousal patterns may predispose abuse. Physiological measurement of the client's erectile response to auditory or visual depictions of various sexual scenarios may reveal disordered arousal to be a high-risk factor that the client has not recognized or reported.

Self-Report Measures

The Rape Myth Belief (Burt, 1980) and Cognition (Abel et al., 1989) scales identify attitudes that enable offenders to justify sexual victimization. The Clarke Sexual History Questionnaire (Langevin, 1983) is used with offenders who admit the abuse in order to gain a highly detailed picture of the client's paraphilic history.

By integrating information from a case record review, clinical interview, self-monitoring record, direct observation, and self-reported beliefs and behaviors, the constellation of situations posing a high risk of relapse may be discerned.

Assessment of Coping Skills

Since a given situation represents risk only to the extent that an offender is unprepared to cope with it, assessment also focuses on his coping skills. Behavioral and self-report measures are used to obtain a profile of the client's strengths and weaknesses in coping. These measures include the Situational Competency Test, self-efficacy ratings, and relapse fantasies.

Situational Competency Test

The client is asked to verbalize a coping strategy in response to descriptions of common problem situations. Responses are scored along several dimensions. Problematic situations are considered to exist when the client fails to state a coping response, elaborates elements of the risky situation, articulates a strategy that is unlikely to be successful, or responds only after a prolonged latency.

Self-Efficacy Ratings

The client is presented with a list of high-risk situations and asked to rate each, along a 7-point scale, according to the difficulty he would have enacting a coping response and avoiding a lapse. The assumption is that motivated clients are often the best predictors of their own relapse episodes, a belief supported by studies of substance abusers (Condiotte & Lichtenstein, 1981).

Relapse Fantasies

In this procedure, the client is asked to provide a fantasized account of a possible future relapse. By reviewing these fantasies, absence of adaptive coping responses and use of maladaptive coping strategies can be noted.

Offenders occasionally become agitated due to the heightened guilt and responsibility they feel as apparently irrelevant decisions and high-risk situations preceding their acts are detailed. It is sometimes necessary to indicate that the intent of recursively detailing these factors is to enable enhanced recognition and coping, not to heighten shame or induce helplessness. Exacerbation of guilt usually dissipates as treatment shifts from identifying offense precursors to developing strategies to cope with them.

Assessment of Determinants of Sexual Aggression

Assessment is not complete until the client and therapist have generated hypotheses regarding why the client's response to a stressful situation involved a sex offense instead of some other response.

A variety of tools are available to help the therapist and client assess early determinants of the client's abusive acts. The structured interview, for example, can be used to explore the relative importance of a number of common factors, such as extreme hostility toward women, deficient social or sexual skills, sexual dysfunction, and compulsive masturbation to deviant fantasies. Case records may reveal sexual, physical, or emotional abuse during the client's childhood.

In addition to identifying early determinants, assessment should include exploration of factors in the client's lifestyle which appear to be predisposing influences. Examples of such predispositions include overworking, chronic substance abuse, dependency, lack of recreational skills, unrealistic expectations of others, rigid defensive structures, a sense of worthlessness, and excessive power needs.

Relapse Prevention Treatment Procedures

Relapse prevention is designed to be an individualized, prescriptive treatment program. A variety of interventions are included in a comprehensive RP approach. Distinct treatment components correspond to each of the various relapse precursors. Interventions are divided into two groups: (1) procedures designed to help the client avoid lapses and (2) procedures intended to minimize the possibility of a lapse precipitating a relapse. These treatment procedures are intended to enhance the client's ability to direct his own behaviors, and, therefore, they are referred to as the Internal Self-Management Dimension of RP.

Treatment Procedures for Avoiding Lapses

Identification of Offense Precursors

Although some lapses in self-management are unavoidable, RP proposes that many events predisposing lapses can be anticipated and circumvented. The initial phase of assisting sexual offenders to avoid lapses entails teaching them to accurately recognize offense precursors involved in their relapse processes. Although this task was introduced as an assessment technique, identification of high-risk situations, apparently irrelevant decisions, and offense precursors continues throughout treatment. As therapy progresses, the client will discern behavioral and attitudinal subtleties that previously were not regarded as related to his offenses. Continued self-monitoring and analysis of case examples in group therapy sessions foster the offender's ability to detect offense precursors.

Once the client has fully delineated his relapse process, the offense precursor constituting a lapse (i.e., the first indication of his relapse process) may be identified. For many offenders, a specific emotion constitutes a lapse (e.g., inhibiting anxiety); for others, a lapse may be a distorted thought (e.g., "That little kid is just trying to seduce me with her eyes"), a behavior (e.g., coaching youth basketball), or some combination of these precursors (e.g., masturbating to fantasies of child abuse when lonely).

Identification of lapses is necessary, but not sufficient, to deter relapses. In many treatment programs, offenders learn to identify "warning signals" to alert them that they are getting into trouble. Unfortunately, while many programs encourage offenders to detect their warning signals, clients seldom are prepared to respond adaptively whenever the warning signal is noted. Thus, clients are aware that they are in extreme trouble, yet have no idea how to deal with the danger.

In contrast, RP provides offenders with strategies to minimize the frequency of lapses and prepares them to cope more effectively with momentary breeches in self-management. Clients are instructed to think of lapses not as signs of absolute failure but as opportunities to enhance self-management by learning from mistakes. Once a lapse is reported by an offender, he and the therapist analyze the circumstances that preceded it. By identifying the factors that overwhelmed the offender's self-control, strategies can be developed to decrease the likelihood of lapsing again in similar situations. Thus, the offender will know precisely what must be done to prevent a lapse from becoming another relapse.

Stimulus Control Procedures

If external stimuli elicit lapses, removing these stimuli from an offender's daily environment may enhance his self-control. For example, a rapist, whose barely suppressed anger toward women is released by alcohol use, should refrain from possessing alcohol or residing in a location where it is present. Individuals whose deviant sexual fantasies are evoked by pornography should remove it from their surroundings.

Avoidance Strategies

Similar to stimulus control procedures, offenders can avoid specific circumstances that evoke lapses. A pedophile should not enter a relationship with a woman who has a child of the gender and age he abused. A rapist, who used vehicles to search for hitchhikers, can be restricted by court order to drive only to and from work along a specific route.

Programmed Coping Responses

Whenever specific high-risk situations can be anticipated, programmed coping responses may be devised to enable the most adaptive response. In such cases, the client engages in a standard problem-solving process. Offenders follow a routine sequence of stages in problem solving: describe the problematic situation in detail, brainstorm potential coping responses, evaluate the likely outcome of each suggested coping strategy, and rate one's ability to enact the behavior. The most adaptive response that the client can perform is selected for practice.

Once a coping response has been identified, the client repeatedly practices it and receives feedback. Repeated practice of coping behaviors resembles instructional drills used by piano teachers who seek to have pupils' hands float naturally across a keyboard or athletic coaches who drill players to exhaustion so that they will respond instinctively in an important game. These "natural" and "instinctive" skills result from intensive, repetitive work. By practicing coping behaviors over time, across situations, and in many moods, generalization to critical circumstances may occur.

Escape Strategies

No matter how thorough the preparation, offenders are rarely able to remove or avoid every situation that could precipitate a lapse. Thus, offenders should be prepared to enact escape routines whenever unexpected risk situations arise. Escape routines should be employed at the earliest moment that an offender recognizes he has entered a high-risk situation that he has not been prepared to handle.

The most important aspect of an escape strategy is the speed with which it is executed. Offenders who find themselves in unexpected risk situations may be compared to individuals who discover themselves alone in a room with a ticking time bomb. In both cases, individuals who make a hasty exist survive. Quick responses may not appear elegant but can interrupt a chain of events leading to disaster. Once a survivor reaches safety, he can take time to review the situation, identify the source of danger, and prepare methods to defuse the situation should he encounter it again.

Coping with Urges

Within the offender's experience, sexual abuse generally resulted in immediate gratification. A power rapist may have derived pleasure from his ability to coerce the victim to utter, "I want you." A socially isolated pedophile likely felt comforted by the intimacy found with a child.

In comparison to the immediate gratification, negative consequences of sexual abuse typically are delayed. Only after the satisfaction of feeling powerful during a rape has faded may self-disgust reemerge. The pedophile may later become depressed as he recognizes that his "intimate relationship" must be kept secret from everyone else in the world. Often, realistic fears of arrest, social disapproval, and incarceration occur only after the temporary gratification from the act has evaporated.

Selectively remembering gratifying aspects of offenses, while neglecting the negative aftereffects, increases the probability of relapse. In compulsive behavior disorders, these positive outcome expectancies are experienced as urges to perform a prohibited behavior. Positive expectancies are particularly problematic if they occur when an individual is in a high-risk situation.

In order to deal with the positive outcome expectancies associated with urges, we inform offenders that their responses to sexual abuse are biphasic: initial gratification is followed by a delayed negative effect. Offenders are informed that urges do not control behavior. Rather, giving in to an urge is an active *decision*, an intentional choice for which he is responsible. In addition, offenders are instructed that if they refrain from choosing to submit to an urge, it will grow weaker and pass away with time. Self-statements, such as "Rape is a bad way of trying to feel good" or "Two minutes of power isn't worth twenty years of prison," can be employed to counter urges. Aversive images represent potent methods for dismantling urges. For example, an offender may be encouraged to visualize a favorite relative looking over his shoulder as he contemplates an urge to fellate a boy. Such images deter passive submission to urges, creating sufficient delay to consider the negative consequences of the act.

Skills-Building Interventions

When sexual offenders do not possess adequate abilities in interpersonal relationships, anger management, problem solving, stress tolerance, sexual knowledge, interpersonal empathy, or basic survival skills, comprehensive treatment programs provide opportunities to remediate these deficits. Since these global interventions are described widely, they are not reviewed here (See, e.g., Abel *et al.*, 1984; Hildebran & Pithers, 1989; Lewinsohn, Antonuccio, Steinmetz & Teri, 1984; Meichenbaum, 1977).

Interventions to Prevent Lapses from Becoming Relapses

Regardless of the adequacy of treatment, lapses in self-management will occur. By adopting this belief, offenders are better able to mitigate the negative impact of the abstinence violation effect whenever a lapse is encountered. Simply providing the offender with this expectation lessens the likelihood of a lapse precipitating relapse. In addition, RP employs several specific treatment procedures to enable offenders to pull out of their relapse process before reoffending.

Cognitive Restructuring

In order to counter the self-defeating cognitive and emotional aspects of the abstinence violation effect, offenders are instructed to cognitively restructure their interpretation of lapses. Within the RP model, offenders are prepared to view lapses as mistakes that present opportunities to learn something new about their relapse process and deficiency in coping skills. Lapses also offer a possibility to develop new coping skills, thereby increasing the offender's self-control. Rather than attributing a lapse to invariable, negative personal characteristics (e.g., "What else can you expect from a sex offender like me?"), it can be viewed as a slip in self-management. A lapse may remain a single event, not a predictor of impending doom, as long as one copes with it.

To assist restructuring of lapses, clients summarize this material in the form of a reminder card. Offenders are required to carry this card at all times. Whenever he has lapsed, the offender immediately reviews its contents. The card contains items such as: (1) what a lapse means (a slip in self-management) and does not mean (an irreversible loss of self-control), (2) a description of the abstinence violation effect and the negative self-attributions that accompany it, (3) reassurance that he does not need to give in to deviant urges and that they will weaken with time, (4) instructions to examine precursors to the lapse in an effort to discern what might be learned from the event to enhance his self-control in the future, and (5) a list of coping responses that can be enacted if the offender feels that he needs additional assistance to refrain from relapsing. Some offenders list telephone numbers of therapists, treatment group members, supportive friends, and police departments on this card.

Contracting

A therapeutic contract, signed by the offender upon entry into treatment, specifies the limits to which he may permit himself to lapse. The therapist and offender together identify the "lapse limit," but the therapist must make certain that this limit is not "beyond the point of no return."

The relevant portion of a treatment contract for a rapist, for whom substance use is an offense precursor, might read:

1. On the first occasion I want a drink, I agree to remain in an alcohol-free location for 1 hour. During this hour, I will pause and review events of the day to identify apparently irrelevant decisions and risk situations I have not dealt with.
2. If my urge continues, I agree to pause 30 minutes to consider my urge to drink and the risks it poses to my reoffending. If at the end of this time I want to drink, any decision to do so will reflect conscious choice rather than submission to urges.
3. If I decide to go to a location where alcohol is available, I agree to go to the nearest such location only in the company of someone approved by my therapist or parole officer. I agree to limit my consumption to a single drink and immediately return home.
4. I agree to inform my therapist and probation officer about this lapse at my next meeting with each of them. At that time I will donate a day's wages to the local victim–witness program. I also agree to take Antabuse for the following 3 months.

In this manner, the contract specifies the limit to which lapses will be tolerated, requires the offender to view his behavior as a clear choice, mandates a delay during which the urge may decay, limits the offender's exposure to a stimulus predisposing sexual abuse, and demands that some penalty is paid for the choice to lapse. In addition, the offender must address the lapse during his next treatment group.

Maintenance Manuals

Each offender develops his own maintenance manual to be used as a refresher after intensive treatment has concluded. The manual may contain his reminder cards, the rationale for avoidance and escape strategies, emergency telephone numbers, a list of his apparently irrelevant decisions, high-risk situations, and offense precursors, self-statements, and self-monitoring forms. Maintenance manuals are particularly useful for offenders transitioning from residential to outpatient therapy. In such cases, manuals enhance maintenance of change and assure continuity of treatment. Since new risk factors can develop, periodically updating the maintenance manual sustains an offender's vigilance for changes in his relapse process.

SHORTCOMINGS OF THE INTERNAL SELF-MANAGEMENT DIMENSION

While the Internal Self-Management Dimension of RP often works well, sexual aggressors may neglect to employ their acquired skills at critical moments. Although the importance of acknowledging lapses to therapists and probation officers is repeatedly stressed in the Vermont Treatment Program for Sexual Aggressors, and the mythical goal of attaining behavioral perfection is dismissed frequently, clients leaving inpatient treatment sometimes neglect to inform us of their lapses, apparently still believing that we expect them to maintain self-managerial perfection. Occasionally, lapses are reported to our treatment team by a released offender's spouse, friends, or coworkers, rather than the client himself. Even when offenders recognized that other clients who self-reported lapses were reinforced by receiving therapeutic intervention and maintaining access to the community, while those whose lapses were reported by third parties received punitive consequences, the trend toward secrecy at critical moments remained.

Generally, RP appeared to enhance sex offenders' self-management skills and decrease the frequency of lapses. However, when lapses occurred, offenders often denied them to professionals involved in their treatment and supervision, and possibly to themselves. Although the Internal Self-Management Dimension of RP was beneficial in enhancing self-control, at critical moments determining the difference between lapse and relapse, the Internal Self-Management Dimension of RP sometimes proved inadequate. Therefore, we developed a new dimension of RP for sex offenders.

EXTERNAL SUPERVISORY DIMENSION: A NEW RELAPSE PREVENTION MODEL

Since offenders are, at times, unreliable informants regarding lapses, creating other methods of gaining access to information about their functioning was considered essential. In order to enhance community safety, an External Supervisory Dimension of the RP model was developed (Pithers, Buell, Kashima, Cumming, & Beal, 1987; Pithers, Cumming, Beal, Young, & Turner, 1989). Three functions of the External Supervisory Dimension may be identified: (1)

enhancing efficacy of supervision by monitoring specific, offense precursors, (2) increasing the efficiency of supervision by creating an informed network of collateral contacts which assists the probation officer in monitoring the offender's behaviors, and (3) creating a collaborative relationship with mental health professionals conducting therapy with the offender.

Traditionally, probation supervision of sexual offenders has been a challenging enterprise. Gaining information essential to adequate supervision was considered nearly impossible. Employers generally reported the offenders to be "hard workers." Parole violations noted frequently among many offenders (e.g., new offenses, intoxication, neglect of supervision appointments, failure to pay restitution) were rarely noted among sex offenders. Often, the lack of detailed information about the offender's behaviors produced a feeling of attempting to conduct supervision within a weightless vacuum, a disquieting position to occupy in an age of heightened professional liability.

In contrast, specification of an offender's apparently irrelevant decisions, high-risk situations, and offense precursors provides probation officers with identifiable indicators of impending danger of relapse. Since officers monitor specific risk factors that are related to the client's sexual offenses (rather than attempting to "keep an eye" on all his behaviors, many of which have no bearing on his reoffending), efficiency of the probation officer's functioning is increased. Whenever the officer detects the presence of an offense precursor, he or she has determined that the sexual offender is involved in his relapse process. Since offense precursors appear most commonly in a distinct sequence (i.e., Emotion–Fantasy–Cognitive Distortion–Plan–Action; Pithers, *et al.*, 1983), the type of precursor exhibited provides an indication of the imminence of potential relapse. With this information, the probation officer may determine the type of intervention required by an offender's lapse (e.g., additional condition of probation, consultation with offender's therapist, probation violation).

A second element of the External Supervisory Dimension entails instruction of collateral contacts on the principles of RP. All members of the collateral network (e.g., spouse, employer, co-workers, friends) are informed about apparently irrelevant decisions, high-risk situations, lapses, the abstinence violation effect, and offense precursors. They learn that assisting the offender's identification of factors involved in his relapse process increases the likelihood of the offender avoiding a reoffense. In the offender's presence, network members are encouraged to report lapses to the probation officer or therapist.

In regions where meetings with collateral contacts are impractical (e.g., sparsely populated rural states or densely populated urban areas), information from the collateral network may still be obtained. A checklist containing the offender's risk factors can be completed weekly by collateral contacts and mailed to his therapist or supervisor.

Care must be exercised in evaluating the ability of collateral contacts to serve this function. A fearful spouse, who has been battered into total submissiveness, is unlikely to disclose information about her husband if she fears additional abuse. Similarly, a spouse who is overly dependent on her husband may be reticent to risk any information that could potentially get him into trouble.

Employers who treasure the compulsive work habits of some sexual offenders may be reluctant to mention information that they fear could lead to loss of cheap labor. Certain individuals, who believe they can show their love for others by forgiving them their misdeeds, may do so rather than tell others. Community members who express hatred for the offender may fabricate reports of the offender's misbehaviors in an effort to damage him. Selection of the collateral network demands good judgment.

By eliciting cooperation from the collateral network, and training them in the intricacies of RP, efficacy of probation and parole supervision is enhanced. Rather than attempting to monitor all the offender's behaviors alone, others, who have more contact with the offender, can help. For some cases, this process creates an extended supervisory network.

We require the offender to inform network members about his offense precursors. The probation officer later requests each network member to summarize what he or she was told. By following this procedure, two goals are accomplished. First, the accuracy and completeness of information presented by the offender can be evaluated, enabling the probation officer to estimate how well the offender understands his offense precursors and the importance others have to his behavioral maintenance. Second, informing his extended network about his offense precursors destroys the secrecy necessary for commission of sexual aggression. Behaviors that once may have seemed unimportant to others, but which were centrally involved in the relapse process, can then be recognized as signs for concern.

The final element of the External Supervisory Dimension of RP is the liaison between the probation officer and mental health professional. Regularly scheduled meetings are essential. By reviewing case-specific information, the probation officer and mental health clinician may discern aspects of the offender's behaviors that were previously unknown. Early in outpatient treatment, it is not unusual to discover that the offender has discussed an important issue with only one of the two (or more) professionals involved in his care. In other instances, the offender may depict an event differently to each professional in his treatment and supervision network.

During regular meetings between the probation officer and mental health professional, the extent and consistency of the offender's disclosures may be compared. In addition to insuring that each professional possesses all available information, these meetings also enable detection of the client's efforts to create disharmony ("divide and conquer") within his supervisory team. Since these scheduled meetings allow exchange of routine information, telephone calls and messages between meetings are regarded as indications of critical events to be dealt with immediately, rather than being viewed as needlessly annoying disruptions in an overburdened schedule.

The combined functions of specially trained probation officers, collateral contacts, and the collaborative relationship between probation and mental health professionals are referred to as the External Supervisory Dimension of the RP model. Since offenders are not consistently reliable informants regarding their own relapse processes, establishing these additional resources is vital to adequate treatment and supervision and, therefore, to the safety of potential victims. Taken together, the Internal and External Dimensions of RP offer improvements over traditional treatment approaches to sexual offenders.

CONCLUSION

Relapse prevention represents a structured method of enhancing self-management skills of sexual aggressors and supervision of sex offenders by treatment professionals. Recidivism data from a 5-year follow-up of 167 offenders (20 rapists, 147 pedophiles) treated under this model revealed a 4% relapse rate (Pithers & Cumming, 1989). While this recidivism rate is likely to increase over time, the initial data suggest that relapse prevention represents an effective means of enhancing maintenance of change in sexual aggressors.

REFERENCES

Abel, G. G., Becker, J. V., Cunningham-Rathner, J., Rouleau, J., Kaplan, M., & Reich, J. (1984). *The treatment of child molesters.* (Available from SBC-TM, 722 West 168th Street, Box 17, New York, NY 10032.)

Adams, C., & Fay, J. (1981). *No more secrets: Protecting your child from sexual assault.* San Luis Obispo, CA: Impact Press.

Bard, L., Carter, D., Cerce, D., Knight, R., Rosenberg, R., & Schneider, B. (1987). A descriptive study of rapists and child molesters: Developmental, clinical and criminal characteristics. *Behavioral Science and the Law, 5*(2), 203–220.

Brecher, E. M. (1978). *Treatment programs for sex offenders.* Washington, DC: U.S. Government Printing Office.

Burt, M. R. (1980). Cultural myths and supports for rape. *Journal of Personality and Social Psychology, 38*(2), 217–230.

Chaney, E. F., O'Leary, M. R., & Marlatt, G. A. (1978). Skill training with alcoholics. *Journal of Consulting and Clinical Psychology, 46,* 1092–1104.

Condiotte, M. M., & Lichtenstein, E. (1981). Self-efficacy and relapse in smoking cessation programs. *Journal of Consulting and Clinical Psychology, 49,* 648–658.

Furby, L., Weinrott, M. R., & Blackshaw, L. (1989). Sex offender recidivism: A review. *Psychological Bulletin, 105,* 3–30.

Gebhard, P. H., Gagnon, J. H., Pomeroy, W. B., & Christenson, C. V. (1965). *Sex offenders: An analysis of types.* New York: Harper & Row.

Groth, A. N. (1979). *Men who rape.* New York: Plenum.

Group for the Advancement of Psychiatry. (1977). *Psychiatry and sex psychopath legislation: The 30's to the 80's.* New York: Author.

Hildebran, D., & Pithers, W. D. (1989). Enhancing offender empathy for sexual abuse victims. In D. R. Laws (Ed.), *Relapse prevention with sexual offenders (pp. 236–243).* New York: Guilford Press.

Justice, B., & Justice, R. (1979). *The broken taboo.* New York: Human Sciences.

Langevin, R. (1983). *Sexual strands: Understanding and treating sexual anomalies in men.* Hillsdale, NJ: Lawrence Erlbaum.

Lewinsohn, P. M., Antonuccio, D. O., Steinmetz, J. L., & Teri, L. (1984). *The coping with depression course.* Eugene, OR: Castalia Publishing.

MacDonald, R. K., & Pithers, W. D. (1989). Self-monitoring to identify high-risk situations. In D. R. Laws (Ed.), *Relapse prevention with sexual offenders (pp. 96–104).* New York: Guilford Press.

Marlatt, G. A. (1982). Relapse prevention: A self-control program for the treatment of addictive behaviors. In R. B. Stuart (Ed.), *Adherence, compliance, and generalization in behavioral medicine* (pp. 329–378). New York: Brunner/Mazel.

Marlatt, G. A., & Gordon, J. (1980). Determinants of relapse: Implications for the maintenance of change. In P. O. Davidson & S. M. Davidson (Eds.), *Behavioral medicine: Changing health lifestyles* (pp. 410–452). New York: Brunner/Mazel.

Marlatt, G. A., & Gordon, J. R. (Eds.). (1985). *Relapse prevention.* New York: Guilford Press.

Meichenbaum, D. (1977). *Cognitive-behavior modification: An integrative approach.* New York: Plenum.

Pithers, W. D. (1982, August). *The Vermont Treatment Program for Sexual Aggressors: A program description.* Waterbury, VT: Vermont Department of Corrections.

Pithers, W. D., & Cumming, G. F. (1989). Can relapses be prevented? Initial outcome data from the Vermont Treatment Program for Sexual Aggressors. In D. R. Laws (Ed.), *Relapse prevention with sex offenders.* New York: Guilford Press.

Pithers, W. D., Marques, J. K., Gibat, C. C., & Marlatt, G. A. (1983). Relapse prevention with sexual aggressives: A self-control model of treatment and maintenance of change. In J. G. Greer & I. R. Stuart (Eds.), *The sexual aggressor: Current perspectives on treatment* (pp. 214–239). New York: Van Nostrand Reinhold.

Pithers, W. D., Buell, M. M., Kashima, K., Cumming, G., & Beal, L. (1987). *Precursors to relapse of sexual offenders.* Paper presented at the first meeting of the Association for the Advancement of Behavior Therapy for Sexual Abusers, Newport, OR.

Pithers, W. D., Kashima, K., Cumming, G. F., Beal, L. S., & Buell, M. (1987, January). *Sexual aggression: An addictive process?* Paper presented at the New York Academy of Sciences, New York.

Pithers, W. D., Kashima, K., Cumming, G. F., Beal, L. S., & Buell, M. (1988). Relapse prevention of sexual aggression. In R. Prentky & V. Quinsey (Eds.), *Annals of the New York Academy of Sciences* (pp. 244–260). New York: New York Academy of Sciences.

Pithers, W. D., Beal, L. S., Armstrong, J., & Petty, J. (1989). Identification of risk factors through clinical interviews and analysis of records. In D. R. Laws (Ed.), *Relapse prevention with sexual offenders.* (pp. 77–87). New York: Guilford Press.

Pithers, W. D., Cumming, G. F., Beal, L. S., Young, W., & Turner, R. (1989). Relapse prevention: A method for enhancing behavioral self-management and external supervision of the sexual aggressor. In B. Schwartz (Ed.), *Sex offenders: Issues in treatment* (pp. 292–310). Washington, DC: National Institute of Corrections.

Rada, R. (1978). *Clinical aspects of the rapist.* New York: Grune & Stratton.

Sanford, L. (1980). *The silent children.* New York: Doubleday.

Walters, D. (1975). *Physical and sexual abuse of children.* Bloomington, IN: Indiana University Press.

21

Outcome of Comprehensive Cognitive-Behavioral Treatment Programs

W. L. MARSHALL AND H. E. BARBAREE

A great variety of treatment programs for sex offenders are now available (Brecher, 1978; Hults, 1981; Knopp, 1984). Evaluations of the outcome from nonbehavioral psychotherapy programs (Barbaree & Marshall, in press-a) reveal that methodological problems present difficulties in determining effectiveness. While those programs appear to consistently result in recidivism rates around or below 10% (Furby, Weinrott, & Blackshaw, 1989), this apparent effectiveness is seriously confounded by selection procedures which exclude the most dangerous offenders from treatment (Barbaree & Marshall, in press-a) and by the failure to provide an adequate comparison group of untreated offenders (Furby *et al.*, 1989; Tracy, Donnelly, Morgenbesser, & Macdonald, 1983). The effectiveness of physical treatment procedures has been evaluated by Bradford (1985; and Chapter 17, this volume), who comes to optimistic conclusions contrary to the views expressed by us in our reviews of this literature (Barbaree & Marshall, in press-a; Quinsey & Marshall, 1983).

Behavioral approaches to the treatment of sex offenders began with quite simplistic notions as to the etiology and maintenance of these behaviors and, therefore, quite limited therapeutic strategies were employed (Quinsey & Marshall, 1983). In these early programs, the offensive behavior was understood to be entirely sexual in motivation, and no other factors were thought to encourage or facilitate the expression of this sexual desire. Consequently, procedures were aimed at changing supposedly deviant sexual preferences (Barlow, 1972, 1973), and in many cases treatment simply attempted to reduce deviant arousal (Bond & Evans, 1967). Marshall (1971) was the first behavior therapist to add

---

W. L. MARSHALL AND H. E. BARBAREE • Department of Psychology, Queen's University, Kingston, Ontario K7L 3N6, Canada.

social-skills training to a treatment package which also attempted to decrease deviant interests and increase appropriate sexual desires. Since that time there has been a progressive expansion of the components in behavioral programs, in particular, the inclusion of procedures aimed at modifying distorted cognitions (Abel, Mittelman, & Becker, 1985). Accordingly, such treatment packages are now more commonly described as "cognitive-behavioral" and are understood to be quite comprehensive in terms of the range of problems addressed in treatment (Abel & Rouleau, 1986; Barbaree & Marshall, in press-a).

Despite the ever-growing popularity of these comprehensive cognitive-behavioral programs, until very recently there was little in the way of outcome evaluations. Before we turn to the issue of the effectiveness of these programs, however, we need to describe their nature.

Nature of Comprehensive Cognitive-Behavioral Programs

Content of Programs

Although some of these programs include relapse prevention strategies, programs with that focus will not be included here since Pithers (Chapter 20, this volume) has reviewed these.

There are a number of cognitive-behavioral programs which have not been described in the literature (Knopp, 1984), much less evaluated, so our review will necessarily be limited. Those programs described in the literature will be taken as representative since most follow a quite similar model, at least in terms of content, although not necessarily in terms of time spent in treatment or in terms of the intensity of contact and expected progress in each program. Included in Knopp's (1984) volume, as well as in a recent monograph (Association for the Behavioral Treatment of Sexual Abusers, 1987) are a number of comprehensive cognitive-behavioral programs (e.g., Levendusky & Ball, 1987; Shaw, 1987; Smith, 1984; Wolfe, 1984). In addition, Laws (1986a) described a similar program presently under evaluation, and Quinsey (Quinsey, Chaplin, Maguire, & Upfold, 1987) has outlined his treatment of sex offenders.

Given the evident diversity, it would be surprising to find completely matched programs operating in different countries or states within countries. However, there is agreement on the major treatment targets, which typically include: (1) sexual behaviors and interests, (2) a broad range of social difficulties, and (3) cognitive distortions about the offensive behavior.

Sexual Behaviors

There are usually two components to this aspect of treatment: (1) deviant sexual preferences and (2) other aspects of sexual functioning.

It has been assumed for many years that sex offenders are characterized by sexual preferences which are unusual and which correspond to the partners they choose or to the behaviors in which they engage. Thus, it was supposed that rapists preferred forced nonconsenting sex to sex with a cooperative woman, that child molesters preferred children as sexual partners, and that exhibitionists preferred exposing behaviors to actual sexual contact. As Barbaree's contribution to this volume reveals, as a group rapists do not appear to prefer forced sex, the data on exhibitionists is equivocal, and only a limited number of child molesters reveal deviant preferences at assessment. However, it is also clear from the literature that some sex offenders do have deviant arousal patterns. Where laboratory assessments reveal deviant interests, the offender is given treatment for these problems.

This appears to be straightforward, but the issue is more complex than it seems. First, there may be value in using certain treatment procedures (e.g., covert sensitization, or self-administered punishers) which were originally meant to serve as ways of changing deviant arousal patterns, even when these arousal patterns are normal. Second, there is the problem of deciding what type of arousal patterns require direct treatment. Finally, there is the possibility that it is unnecessary to direct treatment at sexual preferences even when they appear to be deviant.

On this latter point, behavior therapists take it for granted that the development of deviant sexual interests *precede* deviant sexual behavior (Abel, Rouleau, & Cunningham-Rathner, 1986; Laws, 1986b; McGuire, Carlisle, & Young, 1965; Quinsey *et al.*, 1987). Consistent with this idea, these therapists and researchers assume that deviant sexual preferences revealed at laboratory assessment predict future offensive behavior (Earls & Marshall, 1983) and require modification if treatment is to be successful (Quinsey & Marshall, 1983). Indeed, challenges to the latter notion are likely to be met with astonishment from behaviorists, and they seem to have been successful in persuading therapists of other orientations to accept this idea (Knopp, 1984). As we will see in a later section of this chapter dealing with predictions of posttreatment recidivism, there are no data presently available to support this notion. At present there is no obvious experimental framework (short of withholding this component of treatment) for empirically addressing this issue.

Notwithstanding this paucity of data, when arousal to deviant stimuli or acts is grater than responding to appropriate scenes, behaviorists characteristically agree that change procedures are needed. There seems little doubt from examining clinical practice, that behavior therapists also see a need for treatment when arousal to the inappropriate stimuli is equivalent to that evoked by consensually acceptable acts. However, the problem of whether or not to directly intervene arises when arousal to deviant stimuli is less than that to normal sex but is nevertheless quite high. Suppose, for example, that a client shows 50% of a full erection (FE) to children and 90% FE to adults. These values are often converted to a ratio called a "pedophile index" (PI). For example:

$$PI = \frac{\text{Percent FE to children}}{\text{Percent FE to adults}}$$

The resulting ratio reveals that the relative response level to children is PI = .56, which, according to earlier research (Abel, Becker, Blanchard, & Djenderedjian, 1978; Marshall, Barbaree, & Christophe, 1986; Quinsey, Chaplin, & Varney,

1981), is within normal limits. Despite this observation of *relatively* low arousal to deviant cues, it is our opinion that arousal of this *absolute* magnitude to inappropriate stimuli calls for direct intervention, although it would be unnecessary to enhance appropriate arousal. On the other hand, we have had cases where the deviant index was quite high, and yet absolute arousal was low. Suppose a child molester displayed 15% FE to children and 10% FE to adults. This would produce PI = 1.5, suggesting that deviant arousal needs to be reduced while appropriate desires need to be increased, but it is clear from the absolute response to deviant stimuli that treatment can ignore such tendencies. These hypothetical cases reveal a need to establish criteria for deciding when to intervene. At present there are no agreed upon rules, so the clinician is left to rely on his or her clinical judgment in each equivocal case. The approach we take is to consider absolute arousal above 20% FE to deviant stimuli to be in need of reduction, while absolute arousal to appropriate cues below 30% FE is in need of enhancement.

Several procedures have been described which aim at reducing deviant arousal and increasing arousal to appropriate behaviors or partners. Most of the comprehensive cognitive-behavioral programs, however, use various procedures in combination. For example, Marshall & Barbaree (in press) have used electric or olfactory aversion, while at the same time having the patient use smelling salts to inhibit deviant thoughts occurring in his natural environment, as well as having him change his masturbatory fantasies and repeatedly read covert sensitization scenes throughout each day.

Aversive therapy pairs presently attractive but deviant images with an unpleasant event (either a mild electric shock to the calf muscle or some foul or aversive odor). Repeated pairing of these images and events typically leads to the desired changes in laboratory-assessed sexual preferences (Quinsey & Marshall, 1983). In addition, during his everyday life away from the therapist's office, the patient uses smelling salts as a way of countering deviant thoughts or urges. Whenever the sight of a child (or whatever other stimuli elicit deviant arousal) makes the man feel aroused, he is to hold his bottle of smelling salts, with the cap removed, close to his nose and take a rapid and deep inhalation. This reduces deviant thoughts and provides the opportunity to initiate more positive thoughts.

Covert sensitization scripts, which describe in detail the whole sequence of behaviors leading to offending as well as associated negative consequences, are produced with the patient's help, and subsequently written on pocket-sized cards. The patient carries these cards with him and reads each one (typically we produce five or six such scripts) at least three times each day in various situations. This practice and the patient's use of the smelling salts are meant to increase the likelihood of generalization from therapy to the patient's everyday life.

Finally, if the patient typically masturbates regularly, he is advised to replace, in the masturbatory sequence prior to orgasm, his presently deviant thoughts with more appropriate sexual fantasies. Immediately following orgasm, the patient is to generate aloud every variation he can think of on his deviant fantasies. Sometimes this sequence (called "masturbatory retraining") is done in the office under limited supervision for the first one or two sessions, but more often it is conducted as a part of the man's regular masturbatory activities. This combination of procedures is described in detail by Marshall and Barbaree (in press, 1988) and the reader is referred to Chapter 16 by Quinsey and Earls in this volume.

While we noted that only a limited number of sex offenders display deviant sexual preferences at testing, and that these men need treatment to normalize these preferences, nevertheless the procedures we have outlined here have relevance even for those patients whose patterns of sexual arousal are appropriate. For instance, the offensive behavior of an exhibitionist, who displays a preference for normative interactive sex at laboratory assessment, is obviously elicited by features of the environment. This, of course, is true for all exhibitionists, child molesters, and rapists whether their arousal patterns reveal a preference for normative or deviant acts. Thus, the smelling salts procedure is valuable for all offenders. The same is true of covert sensitization. Indeed, Annon and Robinson (1985) use covert sensitization not only as a way of punishing the deviant response, but also to both reveal to the patient the complete behavioral sequence leading to offending (thereby making it easier for him to exercise control at an early stage) and to constantly remind him of the possible negative consequences. Numerous clinicians have observed that, during an offense, most offenders seem to exclude thoughts having to do with negative outcomes; their whole focus is on the desirable and enjoyable aspects of the situation. Repeated covert rehearsals of the response sequence and its unfortunate effects, then, serves to insert thoughts about the possible negative consequences into the typical pattern of thinking which occurs concurrent with offending, and this should increase the likelihood that the man will abort the sequence before he has offended. Similarly, some patients masturbate (at least occasionally) to fantasies involving their offensive behaviors, and yet they do not show deviant responding at assessment (Marshall, 1988). Clearly, for these patients, use of the masturbatory retraining sequence will be essential to secure treatment benefits.

The other aspects of sexual functioning are typically addressed through sex education, treatment of possible sexual dysfunctions (e.g., impotence, premature ejaculation) and the reduction of unsatisfactory features of their present sexual relations with adults. Sex offenders are often prudish and count as acceptable only vaginal intercourse in the "face-to-face, man-above" position (Record, 1977). It is no wonder then, that they and their partner often claim to be unsatisfied with sex. In addition, however, sex serves many needs (Neubeck, 1974), and yet very few offenders are able to identify more than physical gratification as the goal of sex.

Sex education in our program emphasizes the normative nature of a whole range of sexual activities, introducing evidence on the frequency with which such behaviors are practiced and the apparent increase in the enjoyment of sex by those whose breadth of sexual expression is more open. We point out that only those behaviors which require by their definition that a partner be unwilling (or unable by age or other factors to give informed consent) are properly called "deviant" and are accordingly unacceptable. Within this context we attempt to relieve guilt associated with masturbation and reduce prudishness relating to various precoital acts and to various positions during coitus. We attempt to counter myths concerning sexuality, such as the relevance of the size of the male penis, the goal of simultaneous orgasm, and, indeed, the idea that orgasm is the only goal of sexual interaction. The relationship features of sex are emphasized, and the various motives which sex serves are considered. We do not spend time detailing the anatomical or physiological aspects of sexual functioning, since this knowledge seems to us to be quite unnecessary to a full and effective sexual life, and in any case, such education tends to focus on the objective and physical aspects of sex rather than the crucially important interpersonal features.

Social Incompetence

Some programs have a rather restricted view of what needs to be trained in the area of social functioning. For instance, Quinsey et al. (1987) focus exclusively on conversational skills and anxiety with adult females and on other related aspects of dating skills. A more extensive view of social problems is expressed by Abel and Rouleau (1986). They include the heterosocial problems identified by Quinsey et al., but they also deal with daily living skills and the use of leisure time. Maletzky (1987) targets heterosocial skills and empathy, as well as marital and family issues. We have argued (Marshall & Barbaree, 1984; Chapter 15, present volume) that a broad range of social ineffectiveness makes it difficult for offenders to redirect their sexual interests to adults and also produces high levels of stress which in turn increases the likelihood of reoffending. We, therefore, target a more extensive range of social functioning, including social problem solving, conversational skills, social anxiety, assertiveness, conflict resolution, use of leisure time, empathy and intimacy, self-confidence, and the use of intoxicants.

These social difficulties are dealt with by role-playing, with an appropriate confederate, the hypothetical situations which reveal these problems. Within this context the therapist instructs the patient in the appropriate and inappropriate features of behavior and in a general social problem-solving model (D'Zurilla, 1986). The therapist then models appropriate behaviors, and the patient is provided with the opportunity to imitate these responses with the confederate. He is then given feedback as to adequacy of his behavior along with further advice on how to improve his functioning. Reversal of roles allows the patient to better appreciate the perceptions of his conversational partner.

Empathy training involves the evocation of emotional responding in response to perceived distress in others, which is gradually moved toward empathy for offense victims. Intimacy is trained by first considering the diverse motives for sex (Neubeck, 1974) and how these may be more effectively and appropriately secured, followed by discussion with the patient aimed at revealing his motives and identifying ways in which he can maximize achieving his needs within an acceptable context. The nature of intimacy and its reciprocal, emotional loneliness, and their effects upon behavior are described, as are ways of increasing intimacy and decreasing loneliness (Marshall, Barbaree, & Check, 1988). Self-esteem is typically enhanced as a natural consequence of engaging the patient in effective treatment, but there are available specific strategies which increase self-assurance (Marshall & Christie, 1982).

We also explore with patients their characteristic use of leisure time. This often reveals an absence of activities shared with an adult sexual partner, and we advise them of ways to more effectively occupy their spare time. When there is an absence of leisure activities, the patients typically experience boredom, which increases the likelihood of offending. In attempting to control intoxicated behavior, we aim at both some reduction in the use of intoxicants as well as the development of strategies to increase control over behavior when intoxicated. When the use of intoxicants is excessive, we typically refer the patient to local agencies who have the expertise to deal with such problems. Similarly, when the patient is markedly underassertive or has extreme marital difficulties, we refer him to an agency which specializes in changing these behaviors.

Cognitive Distortions

Cognitive-behavioral therapists have identified various attitudes, beliefs, and perceptions which are nonconsensual and distorted, and which appear to maintain the deviant behavior of sex offenders. These distorted thinking patterns are considered to be essential targets in the treatment of these men (Abel & Rouleau, 1986; Marshall & Barbaree, in press; Shaw, 1987; Smith, 1984; Wolfe, 1984).

Negative attitudes toward women have been shown to characterize the belief systems of rapists (Hegeman & Meikle, 1980), while child molesters have been demonstrated to hold a variety of attitudes and beliefs about sex with children which serve to reinforce their offensive behavior (Abel, Becker, & Cunningham-Rathner, 1984; Stermac & Segal, in press). The prudishness of rapists, noted earlier, may be related to their negative views of women. Burt (1980), for example, has shown that sexual conservatism leads to a ready acceptance of myths about rape, which essentially hold the woman to be responsible and which typically attribute to the victim a desire to be raped. Child molesters all too often believe that their sexual interactions with children are educational or in other ways beneficial to the child (e.g., they claim to give physical affection to emotionally deprived children), despite clear evidence to the contrary. In addition, child molesters see children as sexually provocative, and they believe children enjoy sexual encounters with adults. Similarly, exhibitionists frequently consider they are providing education or sexual titillation to their victims.

In addition, we (Marshall & Barbaree, 1989) consider that most sex offenders deny, or minimize, the harmful effects arising from their offensive behavior. These effects concern the impact on the victim but also the damage done to the offender's family and friends. All too often offenders expect their families, after a brief period of adjustment, to accept them back into the fold with fully reinstated trust and a return to the relationship status which was evident prior to the identification of the man as an offender. In our view offenders typically deny or minimize their responsibility for sexual abuse. They attribute responsibility for the offense(s) to other people (e.g., "My wife did not sexually satisfy me"), or to factors outside their control (e.g., "I was molested as a child"), or to the influence of current states (e.g., "I would not have done this had I not been intoxicated or angry"). Other cognitive-behavioral therapists agree with our claim that these denials of harm and responsibility need to be changed if treatment is to be effective (McGovern & Peters, 1987).

These distorted perceptions, misattributions, and false beliefs, are addressed in treatment using procedures developed by cognitive therapists (Beck, 1976; Thase, 1958). Basically the patient's views are challenged, and the consequences of holding such views are elaborated. At the same time, alternative, more prosocial views are offered, and the benefits of accepting such beliefs are enumerated. Patients must recognize the personal benefits of changing their views before we can expect treatment to have any impact. These challenges are made within a supportive context, although at times a somewhat confrontational manner seems useful.

Format of Programs

Most cognitive-behavioral programs combine individual treatment elements with group therapy components. Changes in sexual preferences are usually targeted by a single therapist in interaction with a single patient, and some aspects of social functioning and cognitive modification may also be dealt with in the same format. However, individual therapy is both costly and inefficient in many respects. Much of what is to be learned in treatment is better presented to groups of patients by more than one therapist. Having both a male and a female therapist serves many valuable purposes. For instance, the female's view of sexual offending can often be helpfully expressed. Modeling by the two therapists of egalitarian male–female relationships can also facilitate changes in attitudes which are beneficial. Also, other group members can often provide insights into fellow patients' problems, on the basis of personal experiences which the therapists do not have. In acquiring new modes of thinking and different ways of socially interacting, group processes have considerable advantages over traditional individualized treatment.

Some of these programs are offered on an outpatient basis (Abel, Mittleman, Becker, Rathner, & Rouleau, 1988; Maletzky, 1987; Marshall & Barbaree, in press, 1988; Wolfe, 1984), while others are located within either secure hospitals or jails (Marshall & Williams, 1975; Quinsey et al., in press; Shaw, 1987; Smith, 1984). The duration of treatment also varies very considerably. For example, Abel et al. (1987) and Marshall and Barbaree (in press) provide approximately 4 months of outpatient treatment, with the possibility of additional therapy if necessary. At the other end of the scale, Smith's (1984) patients spend

24–30 months in treatment while in jail, followed by 3 to 6 months in a graduated release program and a further 18 months in intensive outpatient treatment.
Not all outpatient programs are as brief as those of Abel or Marshall and Barbaree. Maletzky, for example, typically sees patients for some 10 months, followed
by booster treatments once every 3 months for a total time involvement of 18
months to 2 years. Similarly, not all institutional programs are as extensive as
Smith's. Marshall and Williams (1975) describe a program based in a Canadian
penitentiary where the modal duration of treatment is 4 months.

Specific treatment programs evolve their own particular combination of
group and individual formats, and the same is true of the content of these
diverse programs. These somewhat idiosyncratic features of therapy from one
treatment setting to another make outcome comparisons difficult.

OUTCOME EVALUATIONS

The main problem in evaluating treatment programs is the requirement that
outcome data for the treated group be compared with some estimate of expected
recidivism for untreated patients. The ideal comparison group would be patients
who were equally eager to enter treatment but who were refused entry on the
basis of random allocation to an untreated control group. Such a control group
would have to be matched with treated subjects on those demographic, personal, and offense history variables demonstrated or thought to be related to subsequent reoffending. For all manner of practical and ethical reasons, such a control
group has not (and should not) be provided. Some compromise is necessary.

Typically, outcome for treated patients has been compared with reported
recidivism among untreated offenders. Rarely, however, are these data derived
from the same population as those in treatment. Usually the data available in the
literature serve as the standard for comparison. This is quite inadequate, as the
populations from center to center differ markedly on all manner of features
relevant to reoffense rates (Glaser, 1978). To illustrate this we need consider only
one such factor, namely, prior offense frequency. Meyer and Romero (1980), for
example, showed that sex offenders with a low prior rate of arrests for sex crimes
(0–0.3 per year) had a far lower subsequent recidivism rate (7.9%) than did
offenders whose prior arrest rate was high (0.31–1.39 per year); 26.2% of the
latter group reoffended.

Reviews of the literature on recidivism among untreated sex offenders have
revealed widely disparate estimates of subsequent reoffending amongst identified offenders (Furby et al., 1989; Tracy et al., 1983). Incest offenders show the
lowest untreated recidivism, with rates ranging from 4–10% (Gibbens, Soothill,
& Way, 1978, 1981; Frisbie & Dondis, 1965), while rapists (7–35%) and nonfamilial child molesters who abused girls (10–29%) or boys (13–40%) had higher
reoffense rates (Furby et al., 1989). Exhibitionists are consistently observed to
reoffend at the highest rates (41–71%) of all sex offenders (Cox, 1980). While
these reported rates reveal that actual recidivism amongst untreated men will
vary according to the type of offender, the setting where research is conducted,

and the prior offense rate, these data at least provide some basis for estimating the value of treatment in the absence of proper control data.

We should also note that our data (Barbaree & Marshall, in press-b; Marshall & Barbaree, 1988) reveal continuously increasing recidivism over the range of our follow-up period. For example, up to 2 years posttreatment at risk, the overall recidivism rate for all treated child molesters was a mere 5.5%; for those patients who had been at risk for 4 years or more, recidivism had risen to 25%. For untreated offenders, the corresponding rates were 12.5% (up to 2 years) and 64.3% (over 4 years). These are not unusual observations (Davidson, 1948; Gibbens et al., 1981; Soothill, Jack, & Gibbens, 1976) and should be kept in mind when appraising outcome data. In fact, these data strongly suggest that follow-up periods less than 2 years are inadequate.

While we remind the reader of the variations across treatment programs which we have noted, only one of these factors (institutional versus outpatient) will be examined. However, we should note that selection processes also vary considerably. Neither Abel et al. (1987) nor Marshall and Barbaree (in press) deny any patients entry to treatment on the basis of their suitability for the programs, except to exclude offenders who are severely brain damaged or psychotic. Maletzky (1987) rejects those patients who are deemed to be at high risk to reoffend. This strategy, while it may have some sense in that it increases the protection of the community because Maletzky refers them to a secure inpatient facility, nevertheless means that the treated patients are likely to have low recidivism rates even without treatment, since that is the basis for accepting them. His outcome data must, therefore, be viewed with this seriously restricting caveat in mind. Since all the treatment programs reviewed here (other than Abel's and Marshall and Barbaree's) have exclusion criteria which are often quite extensive, similar reservations must be expressed about their outcome data.

Institutional Programs

Three treatment programs have described the application of comprehensive cognitive-behavioral treatment to institutionalized sex offenders, all of whom are either rapists or child molesters. The first of these to appear in the literature was applied to sex offenders incarcerated in the Kingston Penitentiary in Canada (Marshall & Williams, 1975).

In a comparative study, they showed that a behavioral program which included some, but not all, of the elements described above was far more effective than a more traditional psychotherapy program in meeting the within-treatment goals. The behavioral program achieved its goals in changing various features of these offenders (rapists and child molesters), whereas psychotherapy did not. Both of these programs were short and intensive, and all patients completed both in a balanced cross-over design. Some years later, Davidson (1984) reported recidivism data, derived from official police records. Although he used a sophisticated method of calculating recidivism, this particular procedure (proportion of those at risk who recidivated) does not allow comparison with the usual data, which describes the percentage of those treated who have reoffended over specified periods of follow-up. However, Davidson's (1979) earlier report indicated an overall recidivism for treated offenders to be 11.5%, which suggests an effective outcome. Davidson (1984) has provided comparative recidivism data from untreated sex offenders who were incarcerated in the same jails as the treated offenders, but whose period of imprisonment was in the 8 years prior to the availability of the treatment program. While this is not an ideal control group, in that we do not know whether or not these men would have entered treatment had they had the opportunity, it is certainly as good an approximation as possible under the circumstances. These data reveal the effectiveness of treatment for child molesters but marginal benefits for rapists.

Quinsey has over the years described various aspects of the treatment program offered at the Oak Ridge Metal Health Centre in Ontario, Canada (Quinsey, Bergersen, & Steinman, 1976; Quinsey, Chaplin, & Carrigan, 1980; Whitman & Quinsey, 1981). This centre is a maximum security hospital serving a population of sex offenders who have either been declared insane, involuntarily certified, or referred by the courts for psychiatric assessment. We would expect such a population to be particularly difficult to treat. Nonetheless, Quinsey's reports have shown that the treatment procedures produced the expected changes in the treated behaviors (i.e., sexual preferences and social competence). However, although he has indicated (Quinsey, 1983) that recidivism data (apparently derived from official records) support the value of this program, the only data presented by him (Quinsey et al., 1980) reveal 20% recidivism amongst child molesters over a 28-month follow-up period; these data are certainly not remarkably encouraging given the expected rates of untreated child molesters.

The sexual offender unit at Oregon State Hospital (Smith, 1984) was evaluated by Freeman-Longo (1984), and the data are somewhat encouraging. Of those limited number of patients who graduated from this long-term program (only 20 patients were released in the period 1979 to 1983), none committed a sexual offense during the unspecified follow-up period, although two were returned to prison for theft. Again, no comparative data are provided.

While the data on institutionally based programs encourage limited optimism with respect to the value of cognitive-behavioral programs, it cannot be said that these data are more than tentative. The Kingston Penitentiary program (Marshall & Williams, 1975) appears to provide the most encouraging data, since it describes long-term evaluations (5 years) of a reasonable number of offenders (101 sex offenders).

Outpatient Programs

In considering the effectiveness of treatment, Foa and Emmelkamp (1983) have described various indices of success or failure. They note that the value of a program is not only revealed by the success of those who complete treatment, but also by the number of patients who refuse to enter the program or who drop out once they have commenced therapy. Obviously there is not much value to a program which, although its rate of success is high for those patients who complete treatment, is unable to secure the full cooperation of most of its potential clients.

The only reports addressing the issue of treatment refusals which we could find are those conducted by ourselves (Barbaree & Marshall, in press-b; Marshall & Barbaree, 1988), and these concern only outpatient child molesters (incestuous or nonincestuous, against males or females). Of the 169 child molesters who presented at our clinic for assessment and possible treatment, 111 admitted to their offenses prior to assessment, while an additional 15 confessed after being presented with our evaluation data. Forty-three maintained their innocence despite, in most cases, either strong circumstantial evidence or clear signs of deviance at assessment. All of the 126 patients who admitted their guilt expressed a desire to enter treatment, but 58 of them were not able to participate. The reasons for their inability to enter treatment were understandable and not related to any features of the program (i.e., it was not because the treatment model or its procedures were unacceptable to them). Some lived too far away for attendance to be feasible, while others were incarcerated after our assessment and either received treatment while in jail which was satisfactory to them, or had changed their minds about the need for treatment by the time of their release. These 58 subjects represent the untreated patients described below as the comparison group for our treated subjects.

For the present purposes, the 43 men who denied the accusation of child molesting are the most interesting group. Many of these men displayed anger at the charges, and particularly toward us if our evaluations supported the allegations. In 19 of these 43 cases, our physiological assessments revealed deviant interests of sufficient magnitude to cause concern; all of these nonadmitters refused the offer of treatment. Long-term follow-up data revealed that these nonadmitters recidivated at a rate that was, if anything, slightly higher than the untreated admitters. Apparently, then, nonadmitters are just as likely as admitters, in the absence of treatment, to recidivate.

None of these treatment refusers rejected treatment because they did not like the program they were offered; they simply refused because they saw no value in any treatment given their declaration of innocence. In terms of their age, intelligence, socioeconomic status, offense histories, and measured deviant sexual preferences, these nonadmitters did not differ from those who entered treatment. Refusal, then, in this analysis, seems to be simply a function of the failure to admit guilt. We have found no other feature which relates to refusal to accept treatment.

As for dropouts amongst those who enter treatment, Abel (Abel et al., 1988) is the only one to describe these patients. It may be that Abel's is the only report on this problem because his clinic is the only one to have rather large numbers of dropouts. Almost 35% of the patients entering his program withdrew. Of these, 13% were terminated by the therapists because their behavior during treatment was too disruptive, or because they became psychotic, or because their alcoholism became too problematic. Of the rest, 10.4% were jailed before treatment was over, 50.7% refused to continue but did not say why, and 23.9% did not return and could not be contacted thereafter. The patients in Abel's program are apparently repeatedly told that they may withdraw from treatment at any time at no cost to them, and they are constantly reassured of the absolute confidentiality of all that happens in treatment. In our program, as in Wolfe's (1984), quite a number of the patients are under judicial or administrative pressure to enter and remain in treatment, and apparently so are many of Maletzky's patients. One might expect these pressures to account for the low rate of dropouts in these programs, but oddly enough, Abel *et al.* (1988) report that the highest rates of withdrawal from their program occurred in those patients who felt the greatest pressure to participate in therapy.

Abel *et al.* were able to discern who was most likely to fail to complete treatment. A combination of factors produced a most powerful prediction of dropouts. Almost 92% of those offenders who had molested both boys and girls, both children and adolescents, and both their own and other people's children, using both "hands on" and "hands off" (exhibitionism, voyeurism, etc.) behaviors, dropped out of treatment. Each of these factors on its own predicted withdrawal, but the combination was most powerful.

In terms of actual treatment benefits (i.e., success or failure amongst those who complete treatment), four outpatient programs, based on cognitive-behavioral procedures, have described outcome data (Abel *et al.*, 1988; Maletzky, 1987; Marshall & Barbaree, 1988; Wolfe, 1984). Our review here will be restricted to an evaluation of these four programs. While the inpatient programs described above deal only with child molesters and rapists, the outpatient clinics include these two groups (with the child molesters typically being subdivided into incestuous versus nonincestuous offenders and the latter group being further subdivided into male versus female victims), plus exhibitionists, who are characteristically men who expose themselves to unwilling adult females.

Perhaps the most serious problem in evaluating outpatient programs is that many of them must charge their clients in order to continue to operate. Wolfe (1984), for instance, charges $40–$70 for each individual session and $13–$23 for each group session. Since the average stay in treatment is 18 months, with attendance required twice weekly for an initial period and then once weekly, the costs to any individual is so high as to necessarily exclude many potential patients. Indeed, Wolfe reports that his clients are predominantly white and middle class, which seems not to be at all representative of the ethnic and social-class features of sex offenders (Abel *et al.*, 1987; Amir, 1971; Apfelberg, Sugar, & Pfeffer, 1944; Fitch, 1962; McNamara, 1968). Maletzky (1987) deals with this fee-for-service problem by allowing clients schedules of long-term flexible payments, while Marshall and Barbaree's (1988) program is exempt from these difficulties, as they do not charge fees.

Wolfe's (1984) explicit selection processes exclude additional patients. Offenders who are physically violent, psychotic, or "grossly inadequate," or who have problems of addiction, an extensive nonsexual criminal history, poor motivational levels, and counterproductive attitudes, are all excluded from treatment. Most experienced clinicians would expect the group of sex offenders who can both afford Wolfe's treatment and meet the strict entry requirements to be at low risk to reoffend even in the absence of treatment. The Sexual Abuse Clinic in Portland, Oregon (Maletzky, 1987), rejects from treatment all those patients who are "determined to be at a high risk to reoffend within the community." These patients are referred to an inpatient unit and are not, apparently, included in Maletzky's outcome data. Again, we would anticipate that such an exclusion criterion would markedly lower the subsequent untreated recidivism rate of those who are accepted into treatment.

Marshall and Barbaree (1988) excluded only those possible patients who were overtly and floridly psychotic or so severely brain damaged as to be unresponsive to all but the most simple and prolonged learning process. This latter criterion, by the way, does not necessarily exclude all low-intelligence offenders; the lower end of the range of IQ for offenders accepted into our treatment program has been 68. As a result, we have excluded from treatment less than 1% of the clients assessed over the past 15 years. However, if after our thorough assessment process, which includes various tactics (some of which are confrontational) aimed at persuading the man to admit his guilt (see Marshall & Barbaree, 1988, for a fuller discussion of these procedures), the client still denies he has a problem, he is not included in our treatment program.

Abel et al. (1988), in many respects, have a population of offenders who appear to represent patients with very high likely recidivism rates. Abel's patients are referred to his clinic from all across the United States, and it may be that referring agencies send Abel only their worst cases. His patients appear to have committed far more offenses, involving greater forcefulness, more intrusiveness, and sadistic elements, and they have a broader range of paraphilias (Abel et al., 1987) than do the patients of most other programs, including those programs operated in prisons, where we would expect the worst offenders to be housed (Christie, Marshall, & Lanthier, 1979). Also, Abel et al. accept into treatment all those patients who are willing to participate, except, of course, severely psychotic or brain-damaged offenders. Given that Abel's patients can be expected to have high rates of recidivism, his report, in that respect, represents a severe test of the efficacy of treatment. The only qualification to this concerns the already noted high dropout rate from this program.

The comparative outcome data from these four programs are presented in Table 1, and the reader's attention is particularly directed to the length of the follow-up evaluations. Our earlier observation that follow-up periods less than 2 years appear to be unsatisfactory is noted. In terms of the source for estimating recidivism, Wolfe's report is the least adequate, but in fairness to him, his analysis appears to have been a quick estimate in response to Knopp's (1984) survey rather than a systematic study. Future data may reveal clearer estimates of outcome from this program.

As to the issue of relative adequacy of the data base for the remaining three programs, our research may be revealing. We (Barbaree & Marshall, in press-b; Marshall & Barbaree, 1988) examined the relative value of three sources of information concerning recidivism: (1) the self-reports of the offenders; (2) official Royal Canadian Mounted Police records, which include the United States Federal Bureau of Investigation's data and cover all charges (not just convictions) for sexual offenses in both countries; and (3) the reports of reoffenses derived from the unofficial files of both the police and children's protective agencies. These unofficial records yield higher rates of recidivism than the offi-

TABLE 1. Recidivism Data for Outpatient Programs

Programs	Group[a]	Percent reoffending		Data source	Length of follow-up	
		Treated	Untreated		Range	Mean
1. Northwest Treatment Clinic Wolfe (1984)	CMg (N = 67)	4.5	—	Probation reports	1–28 months	13.5 months
	CMb (N = 17)	0	—			
	Rapists (N = 3)	0	—			
	Exhibitionists (N = 27)	14.8	—			
2. Portland Sexual Abuse Clinic Maletsky (1987)	CMg (N = 1719)	5.3	—	Official police re- cords	1–14 years	Mode = 3+ years
	CMb (N = 513)	13.6	—			
	Rapists (N = 87)	26.5	—			
	Exhibitionists (N = 462)	6.9	—			
3. Abel's Clinic Abel et al. (1988)	CMg,b (N = 98)	12.2	—	Patient's self- reports	1 year	1 year
4. Kingston Sexual Behavior Clinic Marshall & Barbaree (1988b)	CMg (N = 49)	17.9	42.9	Official police re- cords plus unof- ficial records of police and child protective agen- cies	12–117 months	48 months
	CMb (N = 29)	13.3	42.9		12–109 months	49 months
	Incest (N = 48)	8.0	21.7		12–93 months	34 months
	Exhibitionists (N = 44)	47.8	66.7		14–125 months	57 months

[a]CMg, men who molest nonfamilial girls; CMb, men who molest nonfamilial boys; CMs, undifferentiated child molesters.

cial data, since they include cases where the information points to unequivocal reoffending and yet the evidence may not be judicially convincing. For example, until 1987, Canadian law required a judge to instruct a jury that they may not convict an accused on the basis of the uncorroborated evidence of a child under 12 years of age, and yet the details of the alleged offenses provided by many children are often so precise and inconsistent with a history free of sexual abuse as to be relatively incontrovertible. Similarly, many victims of exhibitionists report the matter to the police and provide convincing identifications of the offender, and yet they refuse to proceed further, owing to either embarrassment, fear of the cross-examination process, or reluctance to take time off work.

Despite our vigorous and persistent efforts, we were only able to obtain self-reports from 27 of our 126 child molesters. All of these declared themselves to have been entirely free of problems since discharge, and yet official police records revealed that four of these men had been convicted of a sex offense during the follow-up period, while an additional two were recorded in the unofficial files as having reoffended. Obviously, we were, by our methods, unable to secure veridical reports from our patients. These data suggest that we should be suspect of outcome reports which rely on patient's self-reports. However, while Abel relies on these data, his procedures appear to increase the likelihood that such reports will be closer to the truth than ours. He has developed a stringent procedure which guarantees the confidentiality of these reports, and this puts Abel in a far better position than other researchers, with respect to the value of self-reports. Nevertheless, Abel's data must be viewed with some reservation.

Numerous reviewers have argued that official recidivism data can be expected to be an underestimate of actual reoffending (Furby et al., 1989; Quinsey, 1983; Tracy et al., 1983), since arrests and convictions are a product of factors such as the offender's luck or skill at avoiding being caught, the quality of the case against the man, and the inclinations of the victims to report the matter. In comparing our estimates for the child molesters, we found recidivism rates derived from the unofficial sources to be 2.4 times higher than those derived from the official records. For the exhibitionists, the discrepancies were greater; the unofficial records revealed reoffense rates which were 2.8 times higher than those revealed by the official data. In considering the relative effectiveness of treatment programs, then, these issues must be kept in mind.

Since our data (Kingston Sexual Behavior Clinic) are based on the unofficial records, we may assume that we could multiply the child molesters data from Maletzky's report by a factor of 2.4, since his data are based on official records. If we do this, we find that Maletzky seems to be somewhat more successful with those men who molest female children than we are, but it may be that Maletzky has included incest offenders in this group. If we average over our familial and nonfamilial offenders against female children, our data (when corrected for the source of reoffense information) is approximately the same as Maletzky's (i.e., 12.7% for Maletzky and 14% for our program). With respect to men who molest boys, we seem to be far more effective than Maletzky. Indeed, our data on these offenders is contrary to what we had expected and inconsistent with what many clinicians have told us about their experiences over the years. We held the belief that men who molest boys would be far more difficult to treat than other child molesters. Perhaps these pre-data sentiments caused us to inadvertently put grater effort into treating these men or caused us to evolve a program which was particularly suited to them.

If we accept that Abel *et al.*'s (1988) patients are truthful in their reports, then his program seems to be as effective with child molesters as are the other outpatient programs. However, since recidivism increases progressively from time of discharge (Barbaree & Marshall, in press-b; Gibbens *et al.*, 1981; Marshall & Barbaree, 1988) and Abel *et al.* only followed their patients for 1 year, their data are rather disappointing. This observation becomes even gloomier when we consider that despite having at least 64 incest offenders in their group, Abel *et al.* did not distinguish the familial from the nonfamilial offenders in describing recidivism. As we have noted earlier, incest offenders typically have lower re-offense rates than do nonincestuous child molesters.

The possibility that our program is uniquely suited to child molesters is further supported by our relative lack of success with exhibitionists. Even if we multiply Maletzky's data by our derived factor of 2.8, his program is still re-markably more effective than ours. Maletzky's derived recidivism for treated exhibitionists is 19.3% while ours is 47.8%. Wolfe's program is clearly less effective with exhibitionists than it is with other offenders, and his corrected rates of reoffending (40%) are close to ours. Perhaps it is because for the past 10 years Maletzky has been the foremost researcher in the world in designing interventions for exhibitionists that his program is so effective with these men.

Outpatient treatment of sex offenders by cognitive-behavioral procedures, then, seems to be effective. Since both Abel's program and ours accept all clients into treatment, and the data indicate that these patients include some of the very worst offenders, the recidivism data deny the need to take the excessively cautious approach to outpatient services adopted by Wolfe and Maletzky. It seems that even quite dangerous offenders can be effectively treated on an outpatient basis. However, it is important to note that steps are taken to reduce the risk of reoffending while patients are in treatment. We ensure that the man is removed from ready access to children, and we insist on a detailed accounting of his time, confirmed by someone in his everyday life who is capable of monitoring his whereabouts. Like Abel, we also make an initial concentrated effort to reduce deviant sexual arousal in an attempt to further reduce risks. In addition, Abel has developed an excellent surveillance strategy (Abel & Rouleau, 1986) which extends the acquaintance monitoring used by us. Comprehensive surveillance groups are formed for each patient, and these groups are apprised of the usual chain of events which preceded offending for the particular patient. Each member of the patient's group (five acquaintances) is required to complete a surveillance form twice each month. These forms reveal to the therapist whether or not the patient is engaging in risky behaviors. While such a procedure may decrease the risks of reoffending, it is time-consuming, and no doubt it is difficult to find five acquaintances for each offender who are willing to carry out the tasks. We have found that the very fact of identifying the problem and entering treatment is typically sufficient to reduce risks, although these effects may last only until treatment is over.

Predicting Treatment Outcome

There are three studies which have examined the relationship between pretreatment features of the offenders and subsequent posttreatment recidivism. Before discussing the findings of these studies, however, a caveat is in order. It has been the unfortunate, and we believe quite mistaken, view of many earlier researchers who have searched for factors predicting treatment outcome that their job was to determine who should or should not be offered treatment. Feldman and MacCulloch (1971), for example, discerned that homosexuals entering their program who had previous heterosexual experience all failed to benefit from the program. They recommended that such patients not be offered treatment, when a far more sensible conclusion would have been that treatment must be modified to take care of this deficiency.[1] This attempt to improve treatment effectiveness, by determining what features distinguish those who fail, characterizes the approach taken by present-day cognitive-behavior therapists.

In order to achieve this goal, however, those programs which exclude patients who are considered not to be suitable candidates, for whatever reasons (e.g., insufficient intellectual or verbal skills, too high a risk, etc.), effectively eliminate the possibility of securing meaningful predictions of success. In the first place, such a tactic necessarily reduces the variance in the pretreatment data, thereby reducing, as a simple statistical consequence, the chance of discerning relationships between pretreatment indices and outcome. Second, if these selection procedures do indeed eliminate the most recalcitrant patients, then this will necessarily reduce the variance in outcome (i.e., all patients so selected might succeed), again statistically eliminating the possibility of finding meaningful relationships. Of course, the temptations to do just this are very great in this field in particular. Having very few failures results in good press, praise from colleagues, self-satisfaction, and an almost certain guarantee of continued funding. But such tactics cannot be construed as good science and will not help us treat those patients with whom we presently fail. In this respect, we will not properly fulfill our social responsibility of protecting future victims, although we may give the appearance of so doing.

Abel et al.'s (1988) data, although valuable in other ways, is not particularly helpful on the issue of predicting outcome because of the short follow-up period (1 year). As we noted, the bulk of recidivism appears to occur after the first 2 years posttreatment, so it may be misleading to accept Abel et al.'s data without reservation. However, we will report the results of this study for the sake of completeness and because only time will tell whether or not the factors they have discerned will remain as predictors of outcome.

In a discriminant function analysis, Abel et al. found that in decreasing order of statistical power, the following five pretreatment factors together cor-

[1]We simply offer this report as an illustration. It should definitely not be taken to mean that we approve of treating homosexuals as though they were deviants.

rectly classified as successes or failures 85.7% of all patients: (1) molested both boys and girls as well as children and adolescents, (2) failed to accept increased communication with adults as a treatment goal, (3) committed both "hands on" and "hands off" behaviors, (4) divorced, and (5) molested both familial and nonfamilial victims. The first factor was a powerful predictor on its own, correctly classifying as successes or failures 83.7% of all patients. Having all five of these features was a very poor prognostic sign.

Abel *et al.* also list the factors which did not differentiate successes from failures. They found that neither age, race, educational attainment, nor socioeconomic class made any difference to outcome. Unfortunately, they apparently did not estimate intelligence. The number of prior offenses did not predict outcome nor did the patient's sense of control over his pedophilic tendencies.

In our analysis, we entered similar data, and like Abel *et al.* we found no effect for socioeconomic level or the number of prior offenses. Similarly, the age of victims did not predict treatment outcome, nor did intelligence level, although when we looked at the untreated men (Barbaree & Marshall, in press-b), we found that low-intelligence offenders were more likely to reoffend. The failure of both intelligence and education level to predict benefits from treatment is surprising but comforting, and it denies any supposed need for high intellectual skills in order to profit from cognitive-behavioral programs.

We found only two factors which predicted recidivism in the treated patients, and these were not consistent across offense categories. Being over age 40 was a powerful predictor of success in the two groups of nonfamilial child molesters, but it did not differentiate successful from unsuccessful incest offenders. If the offender had genital–genital (or genital–anal) contact with his victim(s), and he had molested female children (his own daughters or the daughters of others), then he was far more likely than other patients to reoffend after discharge from treatment.

Perhaps the most surprising result of our evaluation was that indices of deviant sexual interests did not predict outcome. In order to examine the influence of this factor, we computed Pedophile Indices as described above. Neither pre- or posttreatment quotients nor changes in these quotients predicted outcome. Quinsey (1983) similarly reported that posttreatment deviant quotients do not predict subsequent recidivism, although he found that pretreatment indices did. In an unpublished examination of some early data, Marshall (1975) found that relative changes in arousal to deviant and appropriate stimuli distinguished patients who were either successful or unsuccessful in terms of follow-up behavior. Those patients who showed significant changes with treatment (i.e., reduced deviant arousal and increased appropriate responding) did not reoffend, whereas those who failed to display such changes committed further deviant acts. These data were, however, limited to few patients ($N = 17$), and they were a mixed group with only 58% being offenders. Nevertheless, these data, and those provided by Quinsey, disagree with our current research findings.

Just why these discrepancies exist in the power of deviant quotients to predict treatment outcome is not clear, but at least some of the problem arises from the inherent results of effective treatment. In our program, changing deviant sexual interests is a high priority, and we are successful in attaining this within-treatment goal in almost all patients. Again, this so far reduces the variance in these indices as to preclude the possibility that they can predict outcome. We may simply have to accept this as an insurmountable problem to determining the value of changing sexual interests. Quinsey (1983) claims that when treated offenders recidivate, it is because their sexual interests have returned to pretreatment levels, and he offers two cases as illustrations of this (Quinsey & Marshall, 1983). The same faith in these indices, and the same conviction that deviant sexual interests, as manifest in the laboratory, are basic to sexual offending is to be found in Rosen and Kopel's (1978) discussion of their failed transvestite–exhibitionist. If behaviorists are to maintain this exaggerated faith in erectile measurements, they must solve the experimental riddle of demonstrating the relevance of changing such indices to the maintenance of offensive behavior and, particularly, to the issue of treatment benefits.

Summary

This review of comprehensive cognitive-behavioral programs for the treatment of sex offenders offers encouragement for the continued application and development of such programs. However, there are some inconsistencies in observed outcome across studies. For instance, some programs are very effective in treating exhibitionists (e.g., Maletzky, 1987), while others are not (Marshall & Barbaree, 1988; Wolfe, 1984). Similarly, some programs (Marshall & Barbaree, 1988; Wolfe, 1984) seem to be relatively more effective with men who molest boys than with men who molest girls, while the reverse seems to be true for Maletzky's (1987) patients. Apparently each of these therapists could benefit from more closely examining the other available programs. It is worth noting here that what limited evidence there is (Davidson, 1979, 1984; Maletzky, 1987) indicates that rapists are the least responsive to cognitive-behavioral interventions, and further development of programs for those men is warranted.

Perhaps the most pressing problem facing clinicians in this field is the need to develop indices of treatment effectiveness. As a first step in this process, future treatment evaluations need to go beyond a simple appraisal of outcome, by providing information on changes produced by treatment on the detailed features of sexual preferences, social competence, and cognitive distortions. This information may allow predictions to be made about the likelihood of recidivism in individual cases after treatment. In addition, such data should assist in identifying why it is that different programs fail with particular types of sex offenders.

In any case, the future of cognitive-behavioral approaches to the treatment of sex offenders appears to be positive, although there is much work still to be done.

References

Abel, G. G., & Rouleau, J. L. (1986). Sexual disorders. In G. Winokur & P. Clayton (Eds.), *The medical basis of psychiatry* (pp. 246–267). Philadelphia: W. B. Saunders.

Abel, G. G., Becker, J. V., Blanchard, E. G., & Djenderedjian, A. (1978). Differentiating sexual aggressives with penile measures. *Criminal Justice and Behavior, 5,* 315–332.

Abel, G. G., Becker, J. V., & Cunningham-Rathner, J. (1984). Complications, consent and cognitions in sex between children and adults. *International Journal of Law and Psychiatry, 7,* 89–103.

Abel, G. G., Mittelman, M. S., & Becker, J. V. (1958). Sex offenders: Results of assessment and recommendations for treatment. In M. H. Ben-Aron, S. J. Hucker, & C. D. Webster (Eds.), *Clinical criminology: the assessment and treatment of criminal behavior* (pp. 191–205). Toronto: M. & M. Graphics.

Abel, G. G., Becker, J. V., Mittelman, M., Cunningham-Rathner, J., Rouleau, J. L., & Murphy, W. D. (1987, May). *Self-reported sex crimes of non-incarcerated paraphiliacs.* Paper presented at the 1st Annual Conference on the Assessment and Treatment of Sexual Abusers, Newport, OR.

Abel, G. G., Mittelman, M. S., Becker, J. V., Rathner, J., & Rouleau, J. L. (1988). Predicting child molesters' response to treatment. *Annals of the New York Academy of Sciences, 528,* 223–234.

Abel, G. G., Rouleau, J. L., & Cunningham-Rathner, J. (1986). Sexually aggressive behavior. In W. Curran, A. L. McGarry & S. A. Shah (Eds.), *Modern legal psychiatry and psychology* (pp. 289–313). Philadelphia: Davis & Co.

Amir, M. (1971). *Patterns in forcible rape.* Chicago: University of Chicago Press.

Annon, J. S., & Robinson, C. H. (1985). Sexual deviation. In M. Hersen & A. S. Bellack (Eds.), *Handbook of clinical behavior therapy with adults* (pp. 631–657). New York: Plenum.

Apfelberg, B., Sugar, C., & Pfeffer, A. Z. (1944). A psychiatric study of 250 sex offenders. *American Journal of Psychiatry, 100,* 762–770.

Association for the Behavioral Treatment of Sexual Abusers (1987). *Monograph.* Portland, OR: Author.

Barbaree, H. E., & Marshall, W. L. (in press-a). Treatment of the sexual offender. In R. M. Wettstein (Ed.), *Treatment of the mentally disordered offender.* New York: Guilford Press.

Barbaree, H. E., & Marshall, W. L. (in press-b). Deviant sexual arousal, demographic features, and offense history variables as predictors of reoffense among untreated child molesters and incest offenders. *Behavioral Sciences and the Law.*

Barlow, D. H. (1972). Aversive procedures. In W. S. Agras (Ed.), *Behavior modification: Principles and clinical applications* (pp. 87–125). Boston: Little, Brown & Co.

Barlow, D. G. (1973). Increasing heterosexual responsiveness in the treatment of sexual deviation: A review of the clinical and experimental evidence. *Behavior Therapy, 4,* 655–671.

Beck, A. T. (1976). *Cognitive therapy and the emotional disorders.* New York: International Universities Press.

Bond, I., & Evans, D. (1967). Avoidance therapy: Its use in two cases of underwear fetishism. *Canadian Medical Association Journal, 96,* 1160–1162.

Bradford, J. M. W. (1985). Organic treatment for the male sexual offender. *Behavioral Sciences and the Law, 3,* 355–375.

Brecher, E. (1978). *Treatment programs for sex offenders.* Washington, DC: U.S. Department of Justice.

Burt, M. R. (1980). Cultural myths and supports for rape. *Journal of Personality and Social Psychology, 38,* 217–230.

Christie, M. M., Marshall, W. L., & Lanthier, R. D. (1979). *A descriptive study of incarcerated rapists and pedophiles.* Report to the Solicitor General of Canada, Ottawa.

Cox, D. J. (1980). Exhibitionism: An overview. In D. J. Cox & R. J. Daitzman (Eds.), *Exhibitionism: Description, assessment, and treatment* (pp. 3–10). New York: Garland STPM Press.

Davidson, P. (1979, May). *Recidivism in sexual aggressors: Who are the bad risks?* Paper presented at the 2nd National Conference on the Evaluation and Treatment of Sexual Aggressors, New York.

Davidson, P. (1984, March). *Outcome data for a penitentiary-based treatment program for sex offenders.* Paper presented at the Conference on the Assessment and Treatment of the Sex Offender, Kingston, Ontario, Canada.

D'Zurilla, T. J. (1986). *Problem-solving therapy: A social competence approach to clinical intervention.* New York: Springer.

Earls, C. M., & Marshall, W. L. (1983). The current state of technology in the laboratory assessment of sexual arousal patterns. In J. G. Greer & I. R. Stuart (Eds.), *The sexual aggressor: Current perspectives on treatment* (pp. 336–362). New York: Van Nostrand Reinhold.

Feldman, M. P., & MacCulloch, M. J. (1971). *Homosexual behavior: Therapy and assessment.* Oxford: Pergamon Press.

Fitch, J. H. (1962). Men convicted of sexual offences against children. *British Journal of Criminology, 3,* 18–31.

Foa, E. B., & Emmelkamp, P. M. G. (1983). *Failures in behavior therapy.* New York: Wiley.

Freeman-Longo, R. (1984). The Oregon State Hospital Sex Offender Unit: Treatment outcome. In F. H. Knopp (Ed.), *Retraining adult sex offenders: Methods and models* (pp. 185–209). Syracuse, NY: Safer Society Press.

Frisbie, L. V., & Dondis, E. H. (1965). *Recidivism among treated sex offenders* (Research monograph #5). Sacramento, CA: California Department of Mental Hygiene.

Furby, L., Weinrott, M. R., & Blackshaw, L. (1989). Sex offender recidivism: A review. *Psychological Bulletin, 105,* 3–30.

Gibbens, T. C. N., Soothill, K. L., & Way, C. K. (1978). Sibling and parent–child incest offenders. *British Journal of Criminology, 18,* 40–52.

Gibbens, T. C. N., Soothill, K. L., & Way, C. K. (1981). Sex offenses against young girls: A long-term record study. *Psychological Medicine, 11,* 351–357.

Glaser, D. (1978). Evaluation of sex offender treatment programs. In E. Brecher (Ed.), *Treatment programs for sex offenders* (pp. 14–26). Washington, DC: National Institute of Law Enforcement and Criminal Justice.

Hegeman, N., & Meikle, S. (1980). Motives and attitudes of rapists. *Canadian Journal of Behavioural Science, 4,* 359–372.

Hults, B. (1981). Data on 62 treatment facilities. *TSA News, 4,* 1–7.

Knopp, F. H. (1984). *Retraining adult sex offenders: Methods and models.* Syracuse, NY: Safer Society Press.

Laws, D. R. (1986a, February). *Prevention of relapse in sex offenders.* Paper presented at the NIMH Conference on the Assessment and Treatment of Sex Offenders, Tampa, FL.

Laws, D. R. (1986b, September) *A theoretical formulation of the etiology of sexual deviance.* Paper presented at the 12th Annual Meeting of the International Academy of Sex Research, Amsterdam.

Levendusky, P. G., & Ball, C. J. (1987, May). *Therapeutic contract program: A goal-directed milieu for the treatment of sex offenders.* Paper presented at the 1st Annual Conference on the Assessment and Treatment of Sexual Abusers, Newport, OR.

Maletzky, B. (1987, May). *Data generated by an outpatient sexual abuse clinic.* Paper presented at the 1st Annual Conference on the Assessment and Treatment of Sexual Abusers, Newport, OR.

Marshall, W. L. (1971). A combined treatment method for certain sexual deviations. *Behavior Research and Therapy, 9,* 293–294.

Marshall, W. L. (1975). *Relapses after treatment of sexual deviants.* Unpublished manuscript. Queen's University, Kingston, Ontario, Canada.

Marshall, W. L. (1988). The use of explicit sexual stimuli by rapists, child molesters and nonoffender males. *Journal of Sex Research, 25,* 267–288.

Marshall, W. L., & Barbaree, H. E. (1984). A behavioral view of rape. *International Journal of Law and Psychiatry, 7,* 51–77.

Marshall, W. L., & Barbaree, H. E. (in press). A manual for the treatment of child molesters. *Social and Behavioral Sciences Documents.*

Marshall, W. L., & Barbaree, H. E. (1988). *The long-term evaluation of a cognitive-behavioral treatment program for child molesters.* Manuscript submitted for publication.

Marshall, W. L., & Barbaree, H. E. (1989). Sexual violence. In K. Howells, & C. Hollin (Eds.), *Clinical approaches to aggression and violence* (pp. 205–246). New York: Wiley.

Marshall, W. L., & Christie, M. M. (1982). The enhancement of social self-esteem. *Canadian Counsellor, 16,* 82–89.

Marshall, W. L., & McKnight, R. D. (1975). An integrated treatment program for sexual offenders. *Canadian Psychiatric Association Journal, 20,* 133–138.

Marshall, W. L., & Williams, D. (1975). A behavioral approach to the modification of rape. *Quarterly Bulletin of the British Association for Behavioral Psychotherapy, 4,* 78.

Marshall, W. L., Barbaree, H. E., & Check, J. V. P. (1988). *The relevance of attachment bonds, intimacy and loneliness for the understanding of sexual and nonsexual aggression.* Unpublished manuscript. Queen's University, Kingston, Ontario, Canada.

Marshall, W. L., Barbaree, H. E., & Christophe, D. (1986). Sexual offenders against female children: Sexual preferences for age of victim and type of behavior. *Canadian Journal of Behavioral Science, 18,* 424–439.

McGovern, K., & Peters, J. (1987, May). *Alternatives to sexual abuse.* Paper presented at the 1st Annual Conference on the Assessment and Treatment of Sexual Abusers, Newport, OR.

McGuire, R. J., Carlisle, J. M., & Young, B. G. (1965). Sexual deviations as conditioned behaviour. *Behaviour Research and Therapy, 2,* 185–190.

McNamara, D. E. J. (1968). Sex offenses and sex offenders. *American Academy of Political and Social Sciences Annals, 136,* 148–155.

Meyer, L., & Romero, J. (1980). *A ten-year follow-up of sex offender recidivism.* Philadelphia: Joseph J. Peters Institute.

Neubeck, G. (1974). The myriad motives for sex. In L. Gross (Ed.), *Sexual behavior: Current issues* (pp. 89–100). Flushing, NY: Spectrum.

Quinsey, V. L. (1983). Prediction of recidivism and the evaluation of treatment programs for sex offenders. In S. N. Verdun-Jones & A. A. Keltner (Eds.), *Sexual aggression and the law* (pp. 27–40). Burnaby, BC: Criminology Research Centre Press.

Quinsey, V. L., & Marshall, W. L. (1983). Procedures for reducing inappropriate sexual arousal: An evaluation review. In J. G. Greer & I. R. Stuart (Eds.), *The sexual aggressor: Current perspectives on treatment* (pp. 267–289). New York: Van Nostrand Reinhold.

Quinsey, V. L., Bergersen, S. G., & Steinman, C. M. (1976). Changes in physiological and verbal responses of child molesters during aversion therapy. *Canadian Journal of Behavioral Science, 8,* 202–212.

Quinsey, V. L., Chaplin, T. C., & Carrigan, W. F. (1980). Biofeedback and signalled punishment in the modification of inappropriate age preferences. *Behavior Therapy, 11,* 567–576.

Quinsey, V. L., Chaplin, T. C., & Varney, G. (1981). A comparison of rapists' and non-sex offenders' sexual preferences for mutually consenting sex, rape, and physical abuse of women. *Behavioral Assessment, 3,* 127–135.

Quinsey, V. L., Chaplin, T. C., Maguire, A. M., & Upfold, D. (1987). The behavioral treatment of rapists and child molesters. In E. K. Morris & C. J. Braukman (Eds.), *Behavioral approaches to crime and delinquency: application, research and theory* (pp. 363–382). New York: Plenum.

Record, S. A. (1977). *Personality, sexual attitudes and behavior of sex offenders.* Unpublished doctoral thesis, Queen's University, Kingston, Ontario, Canada.

Rosen, R. C., & Kopel, S. A. (1978). Role of penile tumescence measurement in the behavioral treatment of sexual deviation: Issues of validity. *Journal of Consulting and Clinical Psychology, 46,* 1519–1521.

Shaw, T. (1987). *Treatment program for mentally disordered sex offenders.* Paper presented at the 1st Annual Conference on the Assessment and Treatment of Sexual Abusers, Newport, OR.

Smith, R. (1984). The Oregon State Hospital Sex Offender Unit: Program description. In F. H. Knopp (Ed.), *Retraining adult sex offenders: Methods and models* (pp. 185–209). Syracuse, NY: Safer Society Press.

Soothill, K. L., Jack, A., & Gibbens, T. C. N. (1976). Rape: A 22-year cohort study. *Medical Science and the Law, 16,* 62–69.

Stermac, L. E, & Segal, Z. V. (in press). Adult sexual contact with children: An examination of cognitive factors. *Behavior Therapy.* Manuscript submitted for publication.

Thase, M. E. (1985). Cognitive therapy. In A. S. Bellack & M. Hersen (Eds.), *Dictionary of behavior therapy techniques* (pp. 60–63). New York: Pergamon Press.

Tracy, F., Donnelly, H., Morgenbesser, L., & Macdonald, D. (1983). Program evaluation: Recidivism research involving sex offenders. In J. G. Greer & I. R. Stuart (Eds.), *The sexual aggressor: Current perspectives on treatment* (pp. 198–213). New York: Van Nostrand Reinhold.

Whitman, W. P., & Quinsey, V. L. (1981). Heterosocial skill training for institutionalized rapists and child molesters. *Canadian Journal of Behavioral Science, 13,* 105–114.

Wolfe, R. (1984). Northwest Treatment Associates: A comprehensive, community-based evaluation and treatment program for adult sex offenders. In F. H. Knopp (Ed.), *Retraining adult sex offenders: Methods and models* (pp. 85–101). Syracuse, NY: Safer Society Press.

V
Conclusion

22

Present Status and Future Directions

W. L. Marshall, D. R. Laws, and H. E. Barbaree

This book has provided a nearly exhaustive summary of present thinking and knowledge about sexual offenders. More than anything else, this summary reveals our incomplete knowledge in all aspects of the functioning of these men, and shows greater gaps in our knowledge in specific areas than we had realized. Clearly, continued research is needed, and the chapters of this book encourage confidence that future efforts will continue to give us an increasingly better understanding of both the development and persistence of sexual offending. Theoretical perspectives of the etiology and maintenance of sexual offending are only emerging, and at present the theories that are available represent a diversity of views, although it is clear that common threads are emerging. While it is evident that careful evaluations of treatment are only in their infancy, such appraisals as are at hand indicate that effective treatment programs are available. However, we do need more long-term follow-up studies with larger numbers of subjects than have been involved to date.

Although we believe this book encourages optimism regarding the likely outcome of future efforts to deal with sexual offenders, we feel it necessary to express some concerns with the field. These are primarily areas that could be investigated but are not presently receiving adequate research attention.

THE SELECTIVITY ISSUE

Only a small proportion of sexual offenders needing treatment are offered it, particularly in community settings. Whether in confinement or in the commu-

W. L. Marshall and H. E. Barbaree • Department of Psychology, Queen's University, Kingston, Ontario K7L 3N6, Canada.   D. R. Laws • Department of Law and Mental Health, Florida Mental Health Institute, University of South Florida, Tampa, Florida 33612-3899.

nity, programs are biased toward selecting for treatment the clients thought most likely to succeed in the particular program which is offered. Identifying features of those men who respond most effectively to any particular treatment program should not encourage the establishment of exclusionary criteria but rather encourage treatment researchers to develop additional or alternative programs for those men for whom available treatments presently fail. Scientifically, there are essentially two issues here. Some researchers (e.g., Laws, 1986; Marques, Day, Nelson, & Miner, in press; Pithers, Chapter 20, this volume) argue that the use of entry (rather than exclusionary) criteria permits the isolation of various categories of offenders who are *most likely* to benefit from a particular constellation of treatment modalities. If effective, they argue, this permits wide promulgation of the treatment for those offender categories. Then, the argument goes, it is possible to move on to less amenable populations of offenders. Other researchers (e.g., Marshall & Barbaree, Chapter 15, this volume) argue that this is a highly limited approach, is probably scientifically and statistically unsound, and seriously limits generalizability of any treatment tested under such conditions. These researchers would offer treatment to all candidates, adapt treatment to individual needs, and sort out the groups versus modalities later. Clearly, either process is a lengthy endeavor, and there is at present no empirical support favoring one over the other.

Sometimes the basis for exclusion is simply practical. For instance, offering treatment to incarcerated offenders who have very lengthy sentences is seen by institutional programs as a waste of their resources, at least until there is some hope of imminent release for these inmates. Similarly, many community settings, especially those offering service for a fee, often exclude individuals who also have nonsexual criminal histories or persons with lengthy deviant sexual histories (especially pedophilia or exhibitionism). Such programs also often have restrictions against particular types of offenders such as rapists, violent pedophiles, volatile and dangerous juveniles, or persons with bizarre sexual deviations. The usual reasons given for exclusion are either that these offenders pose too great a risk to the community to be treated on an outpatient basis or that the particular program is "not equipped" to deal with these problems. Unfortunately, all too often, the net effect is that those individuals most in need of self-management and relapse prevention skills do not receive treatment. These programs select for success, where possible choosing low-risk, first-time, nonviolent offenders who, to be sure, make up a large proportion of known sexual criminals. Communities supporting such efforts proudly point to the fact that they are "doing something" about the problem, and their treatment directors can point to low recidivism rates among the treated offenders. However, when it becomes clear that there are violent offenses enacted by some of the untreated men, communities and funding agencies may despair of the value of any attempts at rehabilitating sexual offenders.

SELF-MANAGEMENT AND THE PREVENTION OF RELAPSE

Sexual offending is not a "sickness." We believe that a disease model, which guides far too many treatment programs, is outmoded and based on false assumptions. It is our view that sexual offenders are not suffering from any disease and that their behavior is not out of their control, as such a medical model would imply.

In fact, it is clear from an examination of the behavior of these men that their offending is very well controlled. They typically work assiduously to either set up the circumstances for offending or they knowingly allow those circumstances to unfold. This simply means that these men have in their behavioral repertoire various responses, including sexual assault, and that, prior to treatment at least, they are highly likely to allow the response of sexual assault to occur when the circumstances are seen as maximizing their chances of avoiding apprehension.

As far as treatment is concerned, this view construes intervention as training these men to reduce exposure to risky situations, to alter their views in a prosocial direction, to develop alternative, more acceptable responses to meet their needs, and to provide them with the skills necessary to enact these alternatives. In this respect, treatment is seen as training or education rather than therapy, and it is not counted as a "cure" which will eliminate all future probability of offending. As Laws and Marshall note (Chapter 13, this volume), chronic sexual deviation is a robust disposition, highly resilient and resistant to alteration. It is not a "sickness" that one "gets over." Thus, the offender is seen as continuing to be at some risk after treatment, the aim of treatment being to reduce that risk and make possible subsequent self-management. This approach also dictates that formal treatment (education or training) should be followed by some form of continuing contact with the ex-clients, and there are several long-term options for follow-up, with each of these options requiring development and evaluation.

The procedure adopted by Marshall and Barbaree (1988) is to equip the clients with strategies for dealing with risky situations and with ways of avoiding such situations. Such a strategy is derived from a relapse prevention protocol which is taught to the offenders as part of treatment. This approach does leave the responsibility entirely with the client, and many clinicians think that this is less than satisfactory. However, it is important to note that it remains an empirical question as to whether or not this, or any alternative approach, is satisfactory.

A second approach to the follow-up problem has been to offer "booster" sessions spread over several years after formal treatment has ended. Maletzky (in press) has employed this strategy, and certainly his outcome data are encouraging, although he has not evaluated the effects of these boosters independent of the effects of the prior, formal treatment program.

The final strategy involves direct supervision of the ex-client over an extended posttreatment period. Abel (1987) has described a surveillance procedure which identifies four to five persons who are in regular contact with the ex-client. The members of each client's surveillance group report to the therapist the occurrence of risky situations (e.g., the offender becoming angry, stressed, or bored) or provocative behaviors on the part of the offender (e.g., being in the company of children, near parks or schoolyards, or unable to account for substantial periods of time). Whenever such problems are reported, the therapist takes whatever action is deemed appropriate, which may include booster treatment. A more elaborate version of this approach has been advocated by proponents of relapse prevention, and the outcome from these programs is very encouraging (see Pithers, Chapter 20, this volume). In this variation, probation and parole officers are trained in elaborate relapse prevention strategies, and they in turn train the offenders and monitor their adherence to the program.

Again, there have been no empirical estimates of the value of adding these posttreatment interventions (surveillance groups or relapse prevention supervision) to inpatient or outpatient programs. It may be that some form of supervision is sufficient without prior treatment, or it may be that formal treatment is itself sufficient. Whatever the case, at present there are no data to guide us. If posttreatment programs are found to be valuable additions, we will need to know how long the contact should be continued. All of these issues are open to evaluation, and this appears to be the next required step.

Early Onset of Sexual Offending

There has been a recent intense focus on juvenile sexual offenders (Becker, 1988; Davis & Leitenberg, 1987). The general thesis guiding this effort has been the proposal that if we effectively treat young offenders we will either not have adult offenders or their numbers will be markedly reduced. This view depends upon the demonstration that the majority of sexual offenders commence their deviant careers in their teenage years. Unfortunately, there is only limited evidence in support of this proposition, and the data available can be questioned as to their representativeness.

The only data we are aware of on this issue comes from the research of Abel and his colleagues (e.g., Abel, Rouleau, & Cunningham-Rathner, 1986). Abel's clinic has had a high profile over the years, and it seems likely that, as a result, it may have attracted some of the more extreme cases. Certainly, the evidence presented by Abel and Rouleau (Chapter 2, this volume) on the nature of their population reveals an extent of paraphilias and offense histories which, in contrast to the evidence from other settings, suggests that Abel's clients include a disproportionate number of the most eccentric, dangerous, and persistent offenders. Accordingly, we might expect a high proportion of these clients to have commenced their deviant careers as youngsters. Abel reports (Abel et al., 1986), for example, that over 50% of his sexual offenders had developed their deviant arousal prior to age 18 years, although, importantly, he does *not* claim that they all acted upon this arousal. This latter observation suggests that these men may not have been identified when they were youngsters by their behavior (rather than by their private desires) as sexual offenders, meaning that they would not have been available for treatment until they were adults.

In contrast to Abel's data, Marshall and Barbaree (1988) have extracted information from their clinical files which indicates a far lower rate of early onset both for deviant arousal and for deviant acts. Similarly, Marshall and Barbaree's patients do not show anything like the high rates of offending and the extensive multiple paraphilias which are revealed in the histories of Abel's patients. Finally, K. D. Jenkins-Hall (November 28, 1988, personal communication) determined that approximately 50% of the outpatients seen in Laws' (1986) program experienced early onset of deviant arousal and deviant behavior. Apparently contradictory data exist, and the resolution and clarification of these contrasting observations is urgently needed if we are to adjust the thrust of our treatment programs in order to most effectively reduce future offending.

Certainly, juvenile sexual offenders present a problem, quite irrespective of the early onset issue. Even if the data from Marshall and Barbaree's files turn out to be typical of the client population of most clinics, this should not be construed as meaning that juveniles should not be treated. Clearly, any person who sexually offends, whatever their age, needs to be assessed and treated if the evaluation reveals such a need. And, of course, among juvenile offenders there will certainly be some (although we do not know how many) who, if left untreated, will go on to commit more offenses, some of which may be particularly severe. Becker's (1988) work clearly indicates that juveniles can be effectively assessed and treated, using methods quite similar to those reported for adults in this book.

It appears that one of the major problems in dealing with juvenile sexual offenders is persuading those in charge of them (e.g., parents, teachers, child and family workers, social workers) that intervention is necessary. Claims are often heard that "They're just boys!" or "It's just a phase they're going through!" or "They're just experimenting!" Unfortunately, in that "phase" they are going through they are "experimenting" with rape, exhibitionism, pedophilia, and the like. This experimentation, if not halted, may develop into a well-established repertoire of deviant behaviors. On the other hand, it is possible that a single instance of exposing by a young male or sexual touching of a younger child by a juvenile may reflect a transitory impulse, or it may be that the early identification of the behavior is sufficient to terminate any propensity to continually offend. Clinicians need to be careful not to overreact for fear that their behavior may contribute to a self-labeling process in the immature person which may be harmful (see Laws & Marshall, Chapter 13, this volume).

MISUSE OF MEASUREMENT TECHNOLOGY

We mentioned in the introduction that scientists working in this area have become quite enamored of the technology of penile plethysmography, often to the neglect of other, possibly more important issues. Unquestionably, there has been an overly confident expansion of the application of this technology for assessing sexual preferences. Barbaree (Chapter 8, this volume) states that there are clear limits to the value of erectile assessments in the description of sexual offenders.

Certainly an assessment of sexual preferences *alone* is not a basis for determining the guilt or innocence of an accused. Indeed, many of the most experienced and respected workers in this field would oppose any attempts by clinicians to contribute to a determination of guilt or innocence. While the issue of guilt or innocence is a particularly thorny one, clinicians are consistently asked to make such evaluations, and more particularly they are further asked to indicate the risk an adjudicated offender represents to society. Erectile assessments to determine sexual preferences should contribute to these judgments (if the clinician chooses to comply with such a request), but such assessments can only *contribute* and *not* exclusively determine the answer to these questions. Furthermore, only an experienced examiner can properly interpret these data and fit them into the context of a wealth of other information on the offender.

Neither should these data *alone* provide the basis for deciding whether or not an offender needs treatment, although they can contribute to such a decision. If a man has persistently raped women, molested children, or exposed himself, whether or not he displays deviant sexual arousal in a laboratory evaluation, he clearly needs some form of treatment.

Again, research is needed to investigate the value of a battery of procedures to illuminate these issues. Since we have hardly begun to give attention to this, caution should be exercised if the clinician decides to make these evaluations.

WHAT IS "SEXUAL AROUSAL"?

As we have noted repeatedly, sexual arousal measurement has been one of the hallmarks of work with sexual offenders, primarily because we have had the technology to measure it. But what are we measuring? When the authors in this book speak of sexual arousal, what they mean is some degree of penile erection in the presence of a stimulus presented by an assessor. An act of faith was made long ago which declared that if a subject produced a penile erection to a stimulus deemed "socially inappropriate," that was "deviant arousal," and the producer thereof a "sexual deviant." This is, at very least, a marked overstatement of the available evidence.

In the first place, little is known about what constitutes "normal" (i.e., nondeviant) sexual arousal. Second, the very concept of sexual arousal embodied in this act of faith was naive. In fact, this naive assumption was made at a time when our knowledge of sexual functioning was limited, and it was simply meant to serve as the *raison d'etre* for employing erectile measures in order to begin the process of understanding deviant sexuality. The investigations following from this assumption have, over the years, led to a far greater understanding, not just of sexual deviants but also of sexual functioning itself. For example, Rosen and Beck's (1988) comprehensive appraisal of this literature reveals that sexual arousal is a multiply determined response, with peripheral (erectile) responses being only one manifestation. Future work in this area must treat sexual arousal as a complex, patterned response, and researchers must devote immediate attention to unraveling the relationships between cognitive processes and the physiological expression of these in the sexual response.

CONCLUSION

We hope this book serves to alert readers to the serious problem of sexual offending and to encourage in them an optimism in the continuing unfolding research processes. We believe this book reveals much of the significant progress made to date in understanding and dealing with the offender, although clearly much is left to learn. However, given that systematic research of this topic is a relatively recent phenomenon, we are encouraged by the findings to date, and we feel confident that future research will continue to expand our knowledge.

Presently, there are available effective means for managing and treating these offenders, and if governments and funding agencies can be persuaded to offer greater support for treatment and research efforts, we are convinced that the numbers of innocent women and children who suffer at the hands of these men will be reduced. In the long term, however, treatment of offenders is not the solution to this problem, although it will remain part of the solution. The knowledge that has been gained in work with offenders must be added to that derived from associated research to develop prevention strategies. Some of the steps toward the prevention of these crimes may require courage to implement (e.g., social change which empowers women and children), but since there are so many victims of these assaults, timidity must be set aside if we are to be taken seriously as a truly responsible society.

REFERENCES

Abel, G. G. (1987, May). *Surveillance groups*. Paper presented at the meeting of the Association for the Behavioral Treatment of Sexual Abusers, Newport, OR.

Abel, G. G., Rouleau, J. L., & Cunningham-Rathner, J. (1986). Sexually aggressive behavior. In W. J. Curran, A. L. McGarry, & S. A. Shah (Eds.), *Forensic psychiatry and psychology: Perspectives and standards for interdisciplinary practice* (pp. 289–313). Philadelphia: Davis.

Becker, J. V. (1988). Adolescent sex offenders. *The Behavior Therapist, 11*, 185–187.

Davis, G. E., & Leitenberg, H. (1987). Adolescent sex offenders. *Psychological Bulletin, 101*, 417–427.

Laws, D. R. (1986). *Prevention of relapse in sex offenders*. Unpublished manuscript, Florida Mental Health Institute, Tampa, FL.

Maletzky, B. M. (in press). *The treatment of sex offenders*. New York: Grune & Stratton.

Marques, J. K., Day, D. M., Nelson, C., & Miner, M. H. (in press). The Sex Offender Treatment and Evaluation Project: California's relapse prevention program. In D. R. Laws (Eds.), *Relapse prevention with sex offenders*. New York: Guilford.

Marshall, W. L., & Barbaree, H. E. (1988). [Onset and extent of sexual offending]. Unpublished raw data.

Marshall, W. L., & Barbaree, H. E. (1988). The long-term evaluation of a behavioral treatment program for child molesters. *Behaviour Research and Therapy, 26*, 499–511.

Rosen, R. C. & Beck, J. G. (1988). *Patterns of sexual arousal*. New York: Guilford.

Index

Abel and Becker Cognition Scale, 338
Abstinence violation effect, 347-348
Acquisition processes, 210-222
ACTH, see Adrenocorticotropic hormone
Addiction model, 184-188, 189
Adrenals, 94, 100
Adrenocortical hormones, 94, see also specific
   types
Adrenocorticotropic hormone (ACTH), 93, 94,
   100
Age
   exposure to pornography and, 83, 85, 88
   of incest offenders, 13, 234, 235
   of incest victims, 235
   at onset of deviant sexual interest, 13-14
   at onset of sexual offending, 392-393
   of pedophiles, 13
   of rapists, 179
   of sexual assaulter offenders, 12
   of sexual assault victims, 14-15, 16
   of voyeurs, 13
Aggression, 241-242
   childhood experiences and, 261-262
   genetic basis for, 258-260
   hormonal treatment and, 302
   hormones and, 97-100, 259-260, 261-262, 268
Alcohol, 56, see also Alcohol abuse
Alcohol abuse, 184-185, 186, 187, 239, 269, 313,
   353, 374, see also Alcohol
   brain anomalies and, 110-111
   in incest offenders, 247-248
   rape and, 128, 130-131, 138, 269
   as a rationalization, 344
   social skills and, 318
Alcoholics Anonymous, 187
Amygdala, 258, 259
Androgenic hormones, 93-101, 271, see also
   Androgens; specific types
   aggression and, 259-260, 261-262
   antiandrogenic, 186
   basic physiology of, 93-95
   control over sexual behavior, 298-300
   role in sexual behavior, 259-260
   sex drive and, 95-99

Androgen receptors, 101, 298, 299, 300, 301,
   303
Androgens, 94-95, 298, 299, 300, 301, see also
   Androgenic hormones; specific types
Androstenedione, 94, 100
Antecedent effects, 266
Antiandrogens, 97, 186, 290, 299, 300, see also
   specific types
Antiandrogen treatment, 297, 299, 303-307, see
   also Hormonal treatment
   side effects of, 304, 305
Antisocial personality disorder, 303
Anxiety, 243, 251, 270
Anxiety disorders, 161
Ashanti society, 266
Assertiveness training, 302
Attitudes Toward Rape Scale, 81
Attitudes Towards Women Scale (AWS), 81,
   149, 152, 245, 246
Attorney General's Commission on
   Pornography, 76, 77, 87
Attraction to odors, 15, 16
Australia, 74, 75
Autoerotic influences, 223-224
Automatic processing, 314
Aversion therapy, 134-135, 218, 226, 284-285,
   285, 286, 288, 289, 290-291, 366
Aversive stimuli, 214
Avoidance strategies, 353, 357
AWS, see Attitudes Towards Women Scale

Behavioral Enactment Skills Test (BEST),
   323-324, 326
Behavioral treatment, 186, 331, 363-364, 372,
   see also specific treatments
Bem Sex-Role Inventory, 152, 246
Benperidol, 301
BEST, see Behavioral Enactment Skills Test
Bestiality, 15, 16, 211
Biofeedback, 289, 290
Biological influences, 4, 5, 257, 258-260, 270
Bondage, 56
Bonding, 248
Brain, 103-112, 258, 259

397